PAST LIVES OF LEITH
ARCHAEOLOGICAL WORK FOR EDINBURGH TRAMS

PAST LIVES OF LEITH
ARCHAEOLOGICAL WORK FOR EDINBURGH TRAMS

JULIE FRANKLIN   CARMELITA TROY   KATE BRITTON
DONALD WILSON   JOHN A LAWSON

FIELD TEAM
KAROL ANTONCZYK, EDWARD BAILEY, LAURA BAILEY, ALLISON BORDEN, MAGNAR DALLAND, HÅKAN ERICSSON,
GEORGE GEDDES, LINN GLANCY, PETA GLEW, CANDY HATHERLEY, JAMIE HUMBLE, ANDREW JONES, LIZ JONES,
MARIOLA KANIEWSKA, STEPHEN LANCASTER, LAURA MACCALMAN, PAUL MASSER, JOHN MCCARTHY,
ELEANOR MCCULLOCH, JAMES MCMEEKIN, ROBERT MCMORRAN, JENNI MORRISON, CHRIS MUIRHEAD, ROSS MURRAY,
SOPHIE NICOL, KEVIN PATON, ALISTAIR ROBERTSON, STEVEN ROE, MIKAEL SIMONSSON, SORINA SPANOU,
JÜRGEN VAN WESSEL, DEAN WILLIAMS, DONALD WILSON

CITY OF EDINBURGH COUNCIL (TIE) PROJECT MANAGER
JOHN A LAWSON

HEADLAND PROJECT MANAGERS
ANDREA SMITH, MIKE KIMBER, SORINA SPANOU, JULIE FRANKLIN

CONTRIBUTIONS BY
RICHARD FAWCETT, HAYLEY FISHER, SARAH-JANE HASTON, ABBY MYNETT, PENELOPE WALTON ROGERS, SCOTT TIMPANY

ILLUSTRATIONS BY
JULIA BASTEK-MICHALSKA, RAFAEL MAYA TORCELLY

FORENSIC FACIAL RECONSTRUCTIONS BY
HAYLEY FISHER, PALOMA GALZI, HEATHER GOODRUM, SARAH JAWORSKI, EMILY MCCULLOCH, MIRIAM MODENES,
HEW MORRISON, DAGMARA ROGUSKA AND CRYSTAL SYMES; THE CITY OF EDINBURGH ARCHAEOLOGICAL SERVICE AND
UNIVERSITY OF DUNDEE, CENTRE FOR ANATOMY AND HUMAN IDENTIFICATION INTERNSHIPS

EDINBURGH 2019

Cover design by Headland Archaeology (UK) Ltd © Headland Archaeology (UK) Ltd
Published in 2019 by The City of Edinburgh Council

The City of Edinburgh Council
Museums & Galleries Edinburgh (Retail & Publishing Office)
City Art Centre
2 Market Street
Edinburgh EH1 1DE
United Kingdom
E museumsandgalleries@edinburgh.gov.uk
W www.edinburghmuseums.org.uk

·EDINBVRGH·
THE CITY OF EDINBURGH COUNCIL

British Library Cataloguing-in-Publication Data
A catalogue record for this book is available from the British Library
ISBN 978-0-900353-34-5
Copyright © The City of Edinburgh Council, 2019

This publication was supported by Transport Scotland

TRANSPORT SCOTLAND
CÒMHDHAIL ALBA

Design, typesetting and production by Headland Archaeology

HEADLAND ARCHAEOLOGY

Headland Archaeology (UK) Ltd
13 Jane Street
Edinburgh EH6 5HE
T 0131 467 7705
E publications@headlandarchaeology.com
W www.headlandarchaeology.com

Headland Archaeology (UK) Ltd is a registered company SC342945

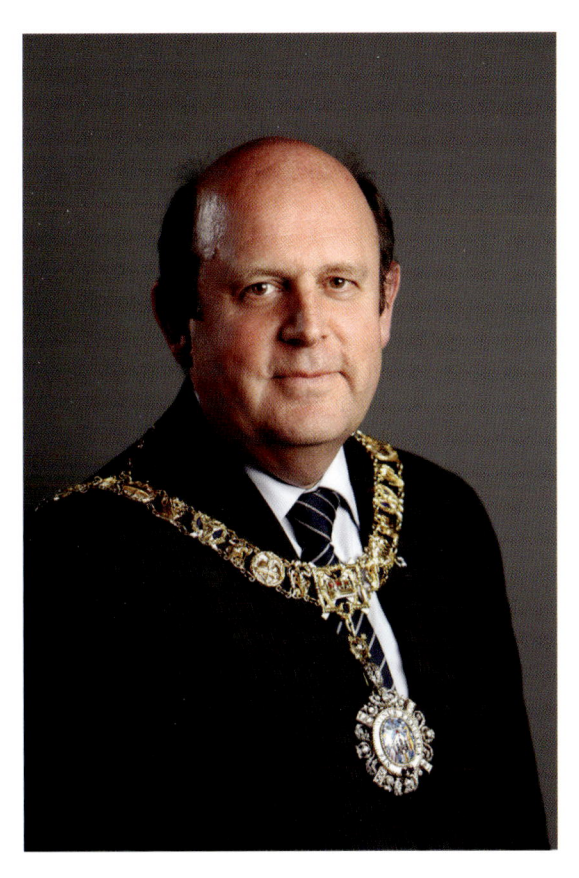

FOREWORD

Think of Edinburgh's heritage and images of the Old and New Towns spring to mind. Winding narrow closes. Wide Georgian avenues. A labyrinth of buildings and prehistoric volcanoes, rising above Princes Street Gardens and watched over by Edinburgh Castle.

Yet, in an ancient city like Scotland's Capital - built on seven hills over many centuries - the secrets to understanding our city's fascinating past are often hidden right underneath our own two feet.

This book is your key to understanding the Edinburgh which lies underground, told through the story of incredible excavations within the historic port and town of Leith. Spanning 10 years of painstaking archaeological fieldwork and scientific analysis, cutting through seven centuries of Scottish life and times, this publication explains how the Edinburgh Trams project altered our understanding of the area's history and its inhabitants.

Archaeologists laboured to excavate these important and high-profile sites and, within these pages, the authors have captured their discoveries in great detail. How they came across an unmarked extension to the graveyard of South Leith's Parish Church and how scientific dating discovered that the site of worship is over 100 years older than we believed. The rediscovery of a 'lost' 15th – 17th century chapel and hospital at Greenside at the top of Leith Walk and new evidence for the 16th century sieges and town defences of Leith.

Their most fascinating discovery of all, however, was that of our ancestors. You will read how the remains of nearly 400 humans were found under Constitution Street, with forensic images which reveal how these medieval residents might have looked some 500 years ago. The result provides a lasting record of the challenges of 21st archaeology in urban areas like Leith but it also tells us about the lives of some of the community's original inhabitants.

The results provide the largest and one of the most important archaeological studies of medieval human remains undertaken in Edinburgh and the authors hope this comprehensive record will inform future developments in field work, in our city and beyond. I certainly hope it provides you with an insight into this important but, until now, little known piece of our people's history: the Past Lives of Leith.

Frank Ross
Rt Hon Lord Provost of the City of Edinburgh
Scotland 2019

LIST OF CONTRIBUTORS

JULIA BASTEK-MICHALSKA	Headland Archaeology	Illustrations, finds photography, cover design, typesetting and layout
KATE BRITTON	University of Aberdeen	Isotope analysis
RICHARD FAWCETT	Emeritus professor, St Andrews University	Architectural fragments
HAYLEY FISHER	The City of Edinburgh Council Forensic Volunteer	Facial reconstructions, 'How the faces of the past were reconstructed'
JULIE FRANKLIN	Headland Archaeology	Principal author, finds, pottery, 'People's Stories'
PALOMA GALZI	The City of Edinburgh Council/University of Dundee intern	Facial reconstructions
HEATHER GOODRUM	The City of Edinburgh Council/University of Dundee intern	Facial reconstructions
SARAH-JANE HASTON	c/o Headland Archaeology	Environmental remains
SARAH JAWORSKI	The City of Edinburgh Council/University of Dundee intern	Facial reconstructions
JOHN A LAWSON	The City of Edinburgh Archaeological Service	Author
EMILY MCCULLOCH	The City of Edinburgh Council/University of Dundee intern	Facial reconstructions
RAFAEL MAYA TORCELLY	Headland Archaeology	Illustrations
MIRIAM MODENES	The City of Edinburgh Council/University of Dundee intern	Facial reconstructions
HEW MORRISON	The City of Edinburgh Council/University of Dundee intern	Facial reconstructions
ABBY MYNETT	c/o Headland Archaeology	Environmental remains
PENELOPE WALTON ROGERS	Anglo-Saxon Laboratory	Textiles
DAGMARA ROGUSKA	The City of Edinburgh Council/University of Dundee intern and volunteer	Facial reconstructions
SUERC	Scottish Universities Environmental Research Centre	C14 dating and isotope data
CRYSTAL SYMES	The City of Edinburgh Council/University of Dundee intern	Facial reconstructions
SCOTT TIMPANY	c/o Headland Archaeology	Environmental remains
CARMELITA TROY	Rubicon Heritage	Human osteology
DONALD WILSON	Headland Archaeology	Author

ACKNOWLEDGEMENTS

The existence of this monograph is due in large part to the efforts of Sorina Spanou and John Lawson, who steered the project towards publication; both had input into the look and content of the finished product. The text was written by Julie Franklin, based on an original draft by Don Wilson and various specialists, most notably Carmelita Troy's osteological work. The rewrite involved further research, reorganisation and several interpretive changes. It was funded by the City of Edinburgh Council and Transport Scotland.

John Lawson would like to thank all those from Parsons Brinkerhoff, Halcrow Group, The City of Edinburgh Council, TIE and Alfred McAlpine who helped make the archaeological project a success, but in particular would like to acknowledge the following individuals for their help and support: from TIE, Sheena Smith, Frank McFadden, Phil Dobbin, Michael Blake, Bob Shaw and Paul Colquhoun; from the Council, Duncan Fraser, Andy Conway, Tom Condie, George Bell, Frank Little, Lynn McMath and Katy Allison.

Julie Franklin would like to thank Don Wilson for answering her many questions over the course of the work and Amy Koonce for tidying the bibliography and compiling the osteological data tables. She would also like to thank: Gordon Cook and Derek Hamilton for help with recalibrating the radiocarbon dates; Alison Stoddart and Vikki Kerr of Edinburgh Libraries and Edinburgh City Archives for their help in tracking down old tram photographs; Philip Brooks of Historic Environment Scotland for his help in locating an old engraving of St Marys Church; Bruce Mann for information on the Aberdeenshire granite industry; and Karen Walker for advice on asthma. She would also like to thank Andy Miller for his patience and Cordelia Miller for her enthusiasm for skeletons.

Kate Britton would like to thank Scott Timpany for initiating her involvement in the isotope study, and to Gordon Cook and Kerry Sayle (SUERC) for sample preparation and isotopic measurements, and also for comments on an earlier version of the isotope report.

The authors would also like to thank Hayley Fisher for help in co-ordinating the facial reconstruction programme and for the support and co-operation of Professor Caroline Wilkinson and Dr Chris Rynn at the University of Dundee, Centre for Anatomy and Human Identification, for suppling internships to The City of Edinburgh Archaeological Service.

Sincere thanks are due to Chris Lowe and Angela Boyle for their very useful comments and corrections to the manuscript and to Alex Smith for copy-editing.

CONTENTS

1 INTRODUCTION — 1
Background to the project — 3
The cemeteries — 3
Other archaeological remains — 4

2 ARCHAEOLOGICAL METHODOLOGY — 7
Excavation of the Constitution Street cemetery — 8
General monitoring of groundworks — 10
Excavations and monitoring at the junction of Leith Walk and London Road — 11
Report structure — 11
Terminology — 11
Radiocarbon dating — 12
Facial reconstructions — 12
Archive — 13

3 HISTORICAL AND ARCHAEOLOGICAL BACKGROUND — 17
Geology and topography — 18
Early Leith from the 11th to 14th centuries — 19
The growth of the town in the 15th century — 20
Fortification, occupation and Reformation in the 16th and 17th centuries — 22
Industry and growth in Leith — 30
Epidemics in Leith — 30
The archaeology of human burial in South Leith — 33
Leith Walk — 36
A chapel, friary and hospital at Greenside — 37
The original tram network — 40
New trams for Edinburgh — 43

4 CONSTITUTION STREET EXCAVATIONS — 49
Constitution Street: archaeological summary — 52
Constitution Street: the early features — 64
    Large cut feature [1153] — 64
    Ditches [0270] and [0084] — 65
Constitution Street: the burials — 67
    Simple burials — 68
    Coffined burials — 68

Double burials	71
Group burials	73
Superimposed burials	76
Charnel and redeposited burials	77
Alignment	77
Body position	79
Dating of the burials	81
Distribution of burial types	83

Constitution Street: the post-medieval ditch and other later features — 88

Cobbled surface (0881)	88
Ditch [0980]	88
Pits [0501], [1096] and [1134]	90

Constitution Street: the human remains — 91

Methodology	91
Preservation and completeness	91
Age at death	92
Sex	92
Stature	93
Non-metric traits	94
Dental health and disease	94
Joint diseases	99
Metabolic diseases	104
Infections	107
Trauma	110
Neoplasms	113
Congenital and developmental defects	116
Osteological discussion	117

Constitution Street: the finds — 122

Textiles	122
Buckles	123
Lace tags	124
Eyelets	124
Pins	124
Summary of evidence for shrouds and clothing	125
Coffin nails	125
Pottery	126

Constitution Street: the environmental evidence — 130

Constitution Street: isotope analysis of bone collagen and tooth enamel — 131

Carbon and nitrogen isotope analysis of bone collagen for dietary reconstruction	131
Strontium and oxygen isotope analysis to investigate origins and population mobility	135

Constitution Street: discussion	140
The burgage plots, ecclesiastical beginnings and the phasing of the cemetery	140
The post-medieval defences and the end of human burial at the site	146
A tentative chronology	149
The lives of the Leithers	150
Death in Leith	151
5 LONDON ROAD EXCAVATIONS	**155**
London Road: the burials	157
The Trench 4 burials	157
The Trench 7 burials	158
Alignment	159
Body position	159
Dating of the burials	159
London Road: the walls	160
London Road: the human remains	160
Age, sex and stature	160
Dental health and disease	160
Joint diseases and conditions	161
Metabolic diseases	161
Infections	162
Trauma	162
Osteological discussion	162
London Road: the finds	162
Eyelets, pin and lace tag	162
Pottery	163
London Road: the environmental evidence	163
London Road: isotope analysis of bone collagen	163
London Road: discussion	164
6 ARCHAEOLOGICAL MONITORING ON CONSTITUTION STREET AND LEITH WALK	**169**
Constitution Street	171
Tower Street to Bernard Street/Baltic Street	171
Bernard Street/Baltic Street to Maritime Lane/Mitchell Street	172
Maritime Lane/Mitchell Street to Queen Charlotte Street	174
Queen Charlotte Street to Coatfield Lane	177
Coatfield Lane to Laurie Street	179
Laurie Street to Great Junction Street/Foot of the Walk/Duke Street	183
Discussion of the Constitution Street monitoring findings	186

Leith Walk	187
Tram cable tunnels	187
Subterranean chambers	189
Other features	194

7   CONCLUSIONS   195

Medieval settlement	196
Late medieval to early post-medieval burial	196
Early post-medieval warfare in Leith	197
Early post-medieval settlement and trade in Leith	197
Later development and infrastructure	198

8   REFERENCES   203

9   APPENDICES   213

Appendix 1 Isotope analyses methodology and results	214
Sample preparation	214
Results	214
Appendix 2 Burial and osteological data	218
Constitution Street burial and osteological data (Table A2.01)	218
London Road burial and osteological data	233
Appendix 3 Recalibrated radiocarbon dates from other sites	234

LIST OF ILLUSTRATIONS

ILLUS 1.01
Location of sites — 2

ILLUS 2.01
Working shot of excavation of Gr0589, against west-facing section of Area 6A, showing tags for skeletons in section — 9

ILLUS 3.01
Petworth Map showing Leith on 7th June 1560, the day it surrendered after the Siege of Leith. It is viewed form the Forth thus north is to the bottom of the map — 23

ILLUS 3.02
Engraving of South Leith Parish Church by J & H.S. Storer, 1819. HES catalogue number SC 1589800 — 24

ILLUS 3.03
Extract from John Adair's 1682 map, showing the defensive walls and the location of St Mary's Church — 25

ILLUS 3.04
Extract from Naish's 1709 plan of Leith showing surviving defences and South Leith Parish Church and graveyard — 26

ILLUS 3.05
Extract from Kirkwood's An Ancient Plan of the City of Edinburgh and its Environs, published in 1817 from a survey by John Fergus and Robert Robinson in 1759, showing surviving defensive banks and the extended South Leith Parish Church graveyard. Constitution Street excavation area overlain — 27

ILLUS 3.06
Extract from John Ainslie's 1804 map, showing South Leith Parish Church and the line of the newly-built Constitution Street with the overlay of the excavation area — 28

ILLUS 3.07
Locations of human remains discovered in South Leith. The location for 19th century finds are approximate, as is the location of St Anthony's preceptory — 34

ILLUS 3.08
Extract from Robert Kirkwood's This plan of the City of Edinburgh and its environs, published in 1817, depicting the proposed new London Road — 38

ILLUS 3.09
Extract from the 1852 OS map, Sheets 25 and 30 marking the presumed location of the Rude Chapel including an overlay of the monitored trench excavations — 39

ILLUS 3.10
A horse drawn tram, Tollcross, 1907 — 40

ILLUS 3.11
This image is labelled 'the first Cable Car at Pilrig 1898 but Hunter (1992) identifies it as a trial run from Shrubhill to St Andrew St, 1st June 1899. The rubble from cable construction work lies all around. The central groove through which the gripper grips the cable can clearly be seen between the tram rails. Most of the passengers appear to be top-hatted dignitaries. The photograph looks down Leith Walk, with the junction of Albert Street on the right and the spire of St Paul's Church, Pilrig visible as a smudge to the left of the tram car — 41

ILLUS 3.12
Shrubhill engine room and cable winding gear, c1900. The men in the centre of the picture show the scale of the machinery. — 42

ILLUS 3.13
Surviving walls of the Shrubhill depot — 43

ILLUS 4.01
Constitution Street site under excavation, looking north-east: opening up the western panel of Area 2. The existing South Leith Parish Church and graveyard are visible in the top right of the picture — 48

ILLUS 4.02
Constitution Street site plan — 50

ILLUS 4.03
Excavating densely packed burials in cramped conditions, Area 5B — 51

ILLUS 4.04
North-west facing section running along Constitution Street, Areas 4–9 — 53

ILLUS 4.05
Constitution Street, Area 2 — 54

ILLUS 4.06
Constitution Street, Area 3 — 55

ILLUS 4.07
Constitution Street, Area 4 — 56

ILLUS 4.08
Constitution Street, Area 5 — 57

ILLUS 4.09
Constitution Street, Area 6 — 58

ILLUS 4.10
Constitution Street, Area 7 — 59

ILLUS 4.11
Constitution Street, Area 8 — 60

ILLUS 4.12
Constitution Street, Area 9 — 61

ILLUS 4.13
Section through pit 1153, Area 5 — 64

ILLUS 4.14
Section through ditch 0270, Area 4 — 65

ILLUS 4.15
Section through ditch 0084, Area 3 — 66

ILLUS 4.16
Row of simple burials in lower levels of Area 7–8 against baulk in centre of road. From top: Sk0704/Gr0710, younger child; Sk0698/Gr0697, younger middle adult female; Sk0713/Gr0714, younger child; Sk0706/Gr0707, older child — 67

ILLUS 4.17
Stepped cut for coffined burial Sk0048/Gr0050, older middle adult female — 68

ILLUS 4.18
Collapsed lid of coffin with skull protruding, Sk0251/Gr0252, adolescent — 69

ILLUS 4.19
Slatted base of coffin for Sk0251/Gr0252, adolescent — 69

ILLUS 4.20
Double burial (mother and child?), Gr0786: Sk0791, younger middle adult woman; Sk0792, younger child — 70

ILLUS 4.21
Double burial, Gr1183: upper, Sk1180, older middle adult man; lower, Sk1181 older adult female — 71

ILLUS 4.22
Group burial Gr0427: Sk0423, adult female; Sk0424, infant; Sk0425, younger adult female; Sk0426, older child. Later cuts for insertion of Sk0420, Sk0428, Sk0429 and Sk0434 — 72

ILLUS 4.23
Group burial Gr0589: Sk0643, younger middle adult female; Sk0637, younger middle adult female; Sk0639, younger middle adult female; Sk0646, older child — 73

ILLUS 4.24
Sk1052/Gr1053, older child, subsiding into darker ditch deposits — 76

ILLUS 4.25
Sk0481/Gr0482, older middle adult female, showing V-shaped grave cut — 77

ILLUS 4.26
Alignment and sex of Constitution Street burials — 80

ILLUS 4.27
Sk1191/Gr1193, older child, possibly prone burial — 81

ILLUS 4.28
Sk0067/Gr0069, younger child, lying on left side within coffin — 81

ILLUS 4.29
Sk0194/Gr0195, adolescent with flexed legs — 82

ILLUS 4.30
Sk0841/Gr0842, younger middle adult male, possibly redeposited semi-articulated — 82

ILLUS 4.31
Constitution Street radiocarbon date ranges, showing relationship to historical dates relating to the Preceptory of St Anthony (1430), St Mary's Church (1483), the Siege of Leith (1560) and the plague (1644) — 85

ILLUS 4.32
Cobbled surface 0881 — 90

ILLUS 4.33
Distribution of age categories (as a percentage of the 232 individuals who could be placed into an age category) — 92

ILLUS 4.34
Sex distribution of adult individuals (188 in situ burials) — 93

ILLUS 4.35
Age at death distribution by sex (shown as percentages of aged adults within each sex category) — 93

ILLUS 4.36
Adult stature — 93

ILLUS 4.37
Calculus, Sk0655/Gr0656, older-middle adult female — 95

ILLUS 4.38
Caries, Sk0378/Gr379, young adult male — 95

ILLUS 4.39
Distribution of caries in the maxillary and mandibular teeth of male and female adults — 97

ILLUS 4.40
Locations of carious cavities in male and female adults — 97

ILLUS 4.41
Periodontal disease, Sk0655/Gr0656, older-middle adult female — 97

ILLUS 4.42
Number and location of permanent teeth with abscesses — 98

ILLUS 4.43
Dental enamel hypoplasia, Sk0796/Gr0797, young adult male — 98

ILLUS 4.44
Osteoarthritic eburnation of left knee, Sk0051/Gr0053, older adult female — 99

ILLUS 4.45
Ankylosis of thoracic vertebrae, Sk0951/Gr0952, younger middle adult male — 102

ILLUS 4.46
Schmorl's nodes on inferior body, Sk1081/Gr1082, younger middle adult male — 103

ILLUS 4.47
Prevalence of Schmorl's nodes by vertebra and sex — 103

ILLUS 4.48
Scoliosis, Sk0566/Gr0568, younger middle adult female — 104

ILLUS 4.49
Tibial bowing, possibly due to childhood rickets, Sk0063/Gr0065, young adult female — 104

ILLUS 4.50
Porotic sphenoid, possibly due to scurvy, Sk0424/Gr0427, infant — 105

ILLUS 4.51
Bilateral porosity in the orbital roofs due to cribra orbitalia, Sk0158/Gr0159, young adult male — 106

ILLUS 4.52
Caries sicca caused by syphilis, Sk0985/Gr0988, adult female? — 107

ILLUS 4.53
Maxillary sinusitis, Sk0643/Gr0589, younger middle adult female — 108

ILLUS 4.54
Sphenoid sinusitis, Sk0512/Pit 0501, adult female? — 109

ILLUS 4.55
Nasal turbinate hypertrophy on right, Sk0718 (disarticulated in cemetery soil), young adult female — 110

ILLUS 4.56
Tibial periostitis, Sk0301/Gr0302, younger middle adult female — 112

ILLUS 4.57
Periostitis and abscess on right mandible, Sk0251/Gr0252, adolescent — 112

ILLUS 4.58
Healed fracture of left femur, Sk0682/Gr0683, older child — 112

ILLUS 4.59
Right tibia and fibula healed fracture, Sk0298/Gr0299, adult male — 113

ILLUS 4.60
Bilateral exostoses of second metatarsals, Sk0207/Gr0189, unsexed adult — 116

ILLUS 4.61
Mental tubercle elongation, Sk1191/Gr1193, older child — 116

ILLUS 4.62
Enlarged mandible, Sk0119/Gr0120, younger middle adult female — 116

ILLUS 4.63
Buckles: A. Copper alloy frame and pin, remains of leather strap in situ, remains of mineralised textile on front of frame, Sk0175/Gr0176, unsexed adult, simple burial, Area 4; B. Iron frame and buckle plate, pin missing, mineralised textile on underside of buckle plate, possibly also leather on top of central bar Sk0910/Gr0911, younger child, coffined burial, Area 8 — 123

ILLUS 4.64
Wire eyelets: A. copper alloy, including one still embedded in edge of textile, Sk0481/Gr0482, older middle adult female; B. Iron, Sk0817/Gr0819, older child — 124

ILLUS 4.65
Beauvais single slip sgraffito dish sherd with bird design, unstratified — 126

ILLUS 4.66
Pottery from midden layers overlying ditch [0084]: A. French chafing dish, deposit (0073); B. Post-medieval oxidised handle jar, deposit (0085) — 127

ILLUS 4.67
Idealised carbon and nitrogen isotope food web, based on the analysis of faunal bone collagen. In light of the systematic variation in food webs, the stable carbon and nitrogen isotope analysis of human bone collagen can be used to infer the source of dietary protein. © Kate Britton — 132

ILLUS 4.68
Carbon and nitrogen isotope values of bone collagen of individuals from Constitution Street and London Road — 133

ILLUS 4.69
Stable carbon isotope data from adult bone collagen at Constitution Street against uncalibrated radiocarbon dates (BP) — 134

ILLUS 4.70
Mean stable carbon and nitrogen isotope values of adult bone collagen from a range of medieval and later medieval sites from Scotland and northern England St Martin's Churchyard at the deserted medieval village of Wharram Percy, Yorkshire (Britton et al 2015); the rural hospital of St. Giles, Yorkshire (Muldner & Richards 2005); the battlefield mass grave at Towton, Yorkshire (Muldner and Richards 2005); the urban friary at Warrington, Yorkshire (Muldner & Richards 2005); the urban site of Fishergate in the City of York (Muldner & Richards 2007); Whithorn Priory, Dumfries and Galloway (Muldner et al 2009); the multi-period site of Newark Bay, Orkney (Richards et al 2006); Constitution Street, Leith and London Road, Edinburgh (this study). — 134

ILLUS 4.71
Strontium and oxygen isotope 'baseline' map of Scotland, previously measured and estimated environmental values can provide a guideline for interpreting human skeletal strontium and oxygen values and inferring mobility (adapted from images/data in Darling & Talbot 2003; Evans et al 2010). © Kate Britton — 136

ILLUS 4.72
Strontium and oxygen isotope values of tooth enamel from individuals from Constitution Street. The dashed-lines enclose the local range of anticipated strontium isotope values and the range of local oxygen isotope values ... 137

ILLUS 4.73
Relative locations of significant features around Constitution Street ... 141

ILLUS 4.74
Putative burgage plot boundaries ... 143

ILLUS 5.01
London Road trenches ... 156

ILLUS 5.02
London Road graves and graveyard wall ... 156

ILLUS 5.03
Graves and graveyard wall [479], Trench 4: A. Sk475 remains and excavated empty graves; B. Sk453; C. Sk466 ... 157

ILLUS 5.04
Double burial (father and child?), Gr461: Sk457, younger middle adult male; Sk462, neonate ... 158

ILLUS 5.05
Double burial, Gr496: left Sk494, younger middle adult female; right Sk495, young adult female ... 158

ILLUS 5.06
London Road radiocarbon date ranges, showing relationship to historical dates relating to the chapel (1456), friary (1520) and leper hospital (1591) ... 159

ILLUS 5.07
Osteophytic lipping on thoracic vertebra, Sk469/Gr470, younger middle adult female ... 161

ILLUS 5.08
Osteoarthritis on vertebra and rib, Sk494/Gr496, younger middle adult female ... 161

ILLUS 5.09
Healed fracture of 12th rib, Sk457/Gr461, younger middle adult male ... 161

ILLUS 5.10
Wire hook, iron, Sk494/Sk495/Gr496 ... 163

ILLUS 6.01
Trenching along Constitution Street ... 170

ILLUS 6.02
Sea wall outside 8 Constitution Street, looking north ... 172

ILLUS 6.03
Cobbled surface (1464), probably 19th century, at junction of Mitchell Street and Constitution Street ... 172

ILLUS 6.04
Clay pipes from midden (1454) at junction of Maritime Lane and Constitution Street: A. 'GC' maker, Tyneside; B. Patrick Crawford, Edinburgh ... 173

ILLUS 6.05
Trenching at junction of Queen Charlotte Street and Constitution Street; section outside Compass bar showing midden layers and cobbles ... 174

ILLUS 6.06
Seville coarseware olive jar rim, midden deposit (271), outside Compass bar ... 175

ILLUS 6.07
Nuremburg jeton, copper alloy, midden deposit (268), outside Compass bar ... 175

ILLUS 6.08
Horseshoe, iron, midden deposit (371), outside Compass bar ... 176

ILLUS 6.09
Unidentified pirlie pig (money box), midden deposit (293), outside police station ... 177

ILLUS 6.10
Round shot from 113–119 Constitution Street: A. stone; B. iron ... 178

ILLUS 6.11
Block with a with a quirked angle roll, buff-yellow sandstone, unstratified from junction of Coatfield Lane and Constitution Street   178

ILLUS 6.12
Buzz-disc, slate, unstratified from Constitution Street, between Queen Charlotte Street and Coatfield Lane   179

ILLUS 6.13
One course of the corner tas-de-charge of a tierceron vault, unstratified outside 133 Constitution Street, opposite graveyard entrance; detail of mason's mark   182

ILLUS 6.14
Trenching at junction of Duke Street and Constitution Street, showing cut of defensive ditch [364/436]; west-facing section through ditch cut at eastern edge of trench   184

ILLUS 6.15
Auguring within defensive ditch [364/436]   185

ILLUS 6.16
Trenching and section through deposits at the Foot of the Walk   185

ILLUS 6.17
Cobbled surface (406) at the Foot of the Walk   186

ILLUS 6.18
Trenching along Leith Walk   188

ILLUS 6.19
Trenching and cable tunnels outside Shrubhill tram depot; section through cable tunnel   190

ILLUS 6.20
Baxter's Place and Greenside Place, Leith Walk, trenching and features   191

ILLUS 6.21
Baxter's Place, chamber supported by props during recording   194

ILLUS 6.22
Stalls within chamber at Baxter's Place   194

LIST OF TABLES

TABLE 3.01
Outbreaks of epidemics in Leith or possibly affecting Leith　32

TABLE 4.01
N-S and S-N burials found in archaeological excavations in Leith　78

TABLE 4.02
Constitution Street radiocarbon dates listed in chronological order　84

TABLE 4.03
Distribution of coffined burials　88

TABLE 4.04
Distribution of double and group burials　88

TABLE 4.05
Osteological age categories with numbers of individuals recovered from Constitution Street　92

TABLE 4.06
Comparison of average statures from various populations　94

TABLE 4.07
Number of teeth lost ante-mortem in adults by tooth position and sex　94

TABLE 4.08
Distribution of individuals with dental pathologies by age　96

TABLE 4.09
Distribution of adult individuals with dental pathologies by sex　96

TABLE 4.10
Prevalence rates of extra-spinal osteoarthritis by sex　99

TABLE 4.11
Distribution of spinal osteoarthritis by sex and age (NB 3 unsexed adults were also assessed and this pathology was not present)　99

TABLE 4.12
Distribution of spinal osteoarthritis by sex and spinal region　99

TABLE 4.13
Distribution of vertebral osteophytosis by sex and age (NB the pathology was also noted in 1 out of 2 unsexed adults)　102

TABLE 4.14
Distribution of vertebral osteophytosis by sex and spinal region (NB 1 unsexed adult of 2 showed this pathology in the thoracic region)　102

TABLE 4.15
Prevalence of porotic hyperostosis and cribra orbitalia by age and sex　106

TABLE 4.16
Adults with both cribra orbitalia and dental enamel hypoplasia　107

TABLE 4.17
Number of individuals with periostitis by specific bone　109

TABLE 4.18
Prevalence of tibial periostitis by age and sex　110

TABLE 4.19
Individuals with trauma and possibly associated conditions　111

TABLE 4.20
Number of skeletons per area broken down by broad age group and sex　118

TABLE 4.21
Proportion of individuals buried within coffins, double burials and group burials by sex — 119

TABLE 4.22
Comparison of prevalence of dental enamel hypoplasia (DEH), cribra orbitalia and porotic hyperostosis between simple and coffined burials — 120

TABLE 4.23
Comparison of average statures between simple and coffined burials — 120

TABLE 4.24
Evidence for shrouds and shroud fittings — 121

TABLE 4.25
Pottery found at Constitution Street (not including modern wares) — 126

TABLE 4.26
Pottery distribution at Constitution Street — 130

TABLE 5.01
London Road radiocarbon dates listed in chronological order — 159

TABLE 5.02
Osteological age categories with numbers of individuals recovered from London Road — 161

TABLE 6.01
Pottery found at Queen Charlotte Street, Compass bar and police station middens — 175

TABLE 6.02
Pottery distribution in Queen Charlotte Street, Compass bar and police station middens — 175

TABLE A1.01
Stable carbon and nitrogen isotope values of bone collagen from 30 individuals from Constitution Street, Leith. Component sampled, collagen yield (%) and C:N ratio are shown, along with the radiocarbon date of each bone collagen sample, and age group, biological sex and notable features of each individual/burial — 215

TABLE A1.02
Stable carbon and nitrogen isotope values of bone collagen from three individuals from London Road, Edinburgh. Component sampled, collagen yield (%) and C:N ratio are shown, along with the radiocarbon date of each bone collagen sample, and age group, biological sex and notable features of each individual/burial — 216

TABLE A1.03
Strontium and oxygen isotope data from tooth enamel of 18 individuals from Constitution Street, Leith, including details of component sampled, original $\delta^{18}O_{V\text{-}PDB}$ value and calculated $\delta^{18}O_{V\text{-}SMOW}$ value (using the conversion equation of Coplen 1988; for age group, see Appendix 2) — 217

TABLE A2.01
Constitution Street burial and osteological data — 218

TABLE A2.02
London Road burial and osteological data — 233

TABLE A3.01
Recalibrated radiocarbon dates from St Andrew Place (van Wessel 2014) and St Mary's Star of the Sea (White & O'Connell 2009) — 234

PEOPLE'S STORIES

How the faces of the past were reconstructed	14
The people's stories – a word of explanation	29
A group of women who died in an epidemic, late 1380s/early 1390s–1420s	44
A boy with bad teeth, 1435–1450	62
A poor man with bad legs, 1435–1456	74
A big bruiser of a man, 1438–1478	86
A man who died with his mother, 1450/1475–1515	100
A woman with allergies, 1480–1502	114
A poor woman who died with her toddler, 1481–1511	128
A man from out of town, 1499–1529	138
A man who lived through interesting times, 1508–1548	152
A young Carmelite friar, 1525–1544	166
A girl with bad lungs, 1538–1554	180
A teenager from out of town, 1590–1604	192
The faces of late medieval and early post-medieval Leith	199

1 | INTRODUCTION

Julie Franklin, John A Lawson and Donald Wilson

The archaeological investigations in Leith and beyond were undertaken as part of a programme of service diversion and advance works in preparation for the construction of the new Edinburgh Tram route to Leith and Newhaven. The archaeological work across the new tram network provided an unprecedented opportunity to find and compare remains over a wide area. This section of the proposed tram route cut a line north to south along the length of Leith Walk and Constitution Street, from the edge of Edinburgh's New Town, through the land between and across the eastern side of medieval and post-medieval Leith, to the point where it met the Firth of Forth.

The most significant discoveries within historic Leith were the remains of a large cemetery on Constitution Street, outside the limits of the current cemetery surrounding the medieval South Leith Parish Church of St Mary's. The dating of some of these burials was earlier than the accepted late 15th-century dating of the establishment of the church and thus have changed the picture of the ecclesiastical history of Leith. Significant remains of the 16th- and 17th-century siege defences were also discovered, along with earlier features providing new evidence for the medieval organisation of the town. Other findings related to the development of post-medieval Leith, including cobbled surfaces and a massive sea wall. Midden deposits of this period provided some colour to local material culture and trade.

The most important discoveries outside of Leith were also human burials, this time connected to the 15th- to 16th-century Chapel and later Carmelite friary and Leper Hospital, which once stood in the vicinity of London Road/Greenside Place. Features relating to the early 20th century Edinburgh cable tram network were also revealed.

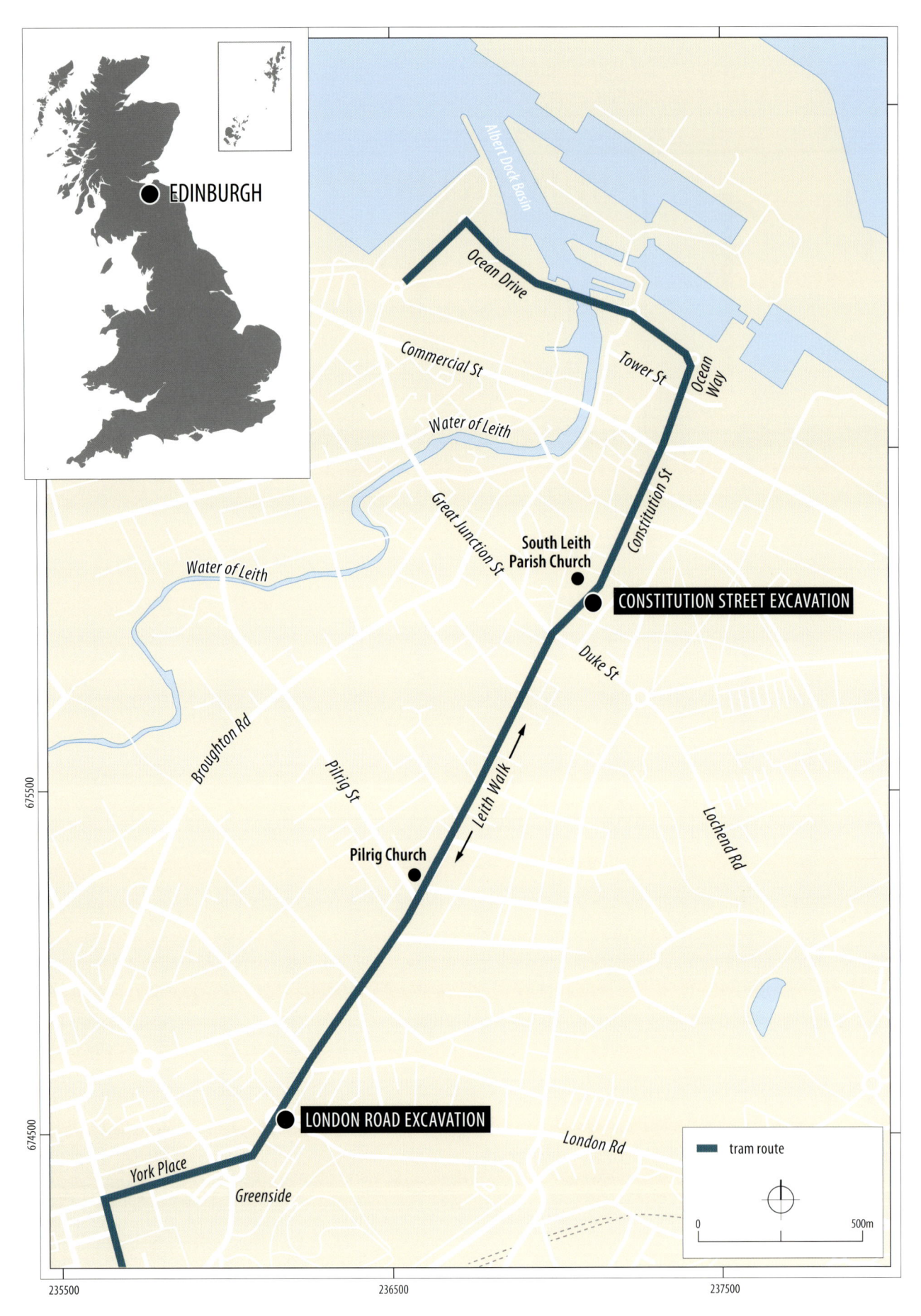

ILLUS 1.01
Location of sites

INTRODUCTION

BACKGROUND TO THE PROJECT

From June 2007 to October 2009 Headland Archaeology (UK) Ltd, with the City of Edinburgh Council's Archaeology Service, undertook a programme of archaeological investigations as part of the advance works and service diversion mitigation. This comprised monitoring, trial trenching and excavation as part of the preliminary groundworks to divert and replace services ahead of construction of a new tram line through Edinburgh. The programme resulted from the series of archaeological mitigation proposals identified within the Parliamentary Act's Environmental Statement, commissioned and prepared by Parsons Brinckerhoff and Halcrow Group on behalf of Transport Initiative Edinburgh (Tie Ltd) and the City of Edinburgh Council (CEC) (Mott Macdonald 2003; Faber Maunsell 2004). A second programme of archaeological works was undertaken by Glasgow University Archaeological Research Division (GUARD), and was completed by GUARD Archaeology Ltd during construction, resulting in two set-piece excavations at Gogar, reported separately (Will & James 2017; Will 2018).

The proposed tram route for which the works were undertaken incorporated an 18.5km line crossing the city from Newhaven to Edinburgh Airport, via the historic heart of Leith and across the Georgian splendour of Princes Street, westwards past Murrayfield, South Gyle, Gogar and terminating at Edinburgh Airport. Subsequently, during construction, due to funding restrictions the initial route had to be shortened to 14km. This led to the abandonment of construction along the 4.5km section to Newhaven and Leith, with the route terminating at the east end of York Place. The initial route would have taken the tram from the quayside at the port of Leith east along Ocean Drive towards the foot of Constitution Street, continuing along the full length of Constitution Street itself (**Illus 1.01**). From there it would have cut across Great Junction Street continuing south along Leith Walk up to Elm Row, at the west end of London Road, before heading to Picardy Place and on to York Place. The now established route from York Place brings the tram on to St Andrews Square and then to the east end of Princes Street and on, westwards, to Edinburgh Airport.

The archaeological works along the length of the tram route and service diversions primarily consisted of monitoring and excavation. By the nature of the fieldwork a number of dispersed sites were recorded on a line snaking across the city. Leith was the area where the greatest archaeological sensitivity was anticipated and where the main archaeological works were undertaken.

THE CEMETERIES

This publication is concerned with the results arising from the unexpected discovery and excavation of two cemeteries. One was at Greenside, at the junction of London Road and Leith Walk, and was linked to the late medieval Rude Chapel, 16th-century Carmelite friary and 16th-17th-century leper hospital, all of which stood on the same site. The other was part of the late medieval to early post-medieval cemetery underlying Constitution Street associated with St Mary's Church (now South Leith Parish Church).

The excavations on Constitution Street were undertaken as the result of the discovery of human remains in 2008 during test-trenching to locate a gas service outside the entrance to the graveyard, and the subsequent recovery of human remains during the monitoring of engineering test-trenching on the opposite side of Constitution Street. In order to avoid delays to the expected construction timetable, it was agreed to bring forward the excavation of this likely cemetery as part of the advanced works (Multi-Utilities Diversion Framework Agreement or MUDFA) package rather than undertake it during the main construction phase (Tram Infrastructure and Maintenance Contract or INFRACO). As a result, the excavations along Constitution Street became one of the main archaeological excavations carried out during this phase of the Edinburgh Tram project.

The Constitution Street excavations revealed the largest archaeological assemblage of human remains from Edinburgh to date (2018). A total of 305 in situ inhumations were recovered plus the remains of a further minimum 73 disarticulated individuals. The burials exhibited a variety of grave types, age and gender, as would be expected in a parish graveyard of this period. Constitution Street itself post-dates the late medieval foundation of the church. The current layout dates to the early 1790s when Constitution Road was extended southwards across South Leith Parish Graveyard to connect with the north end of Leith Walk. This route bypassed the town's original medieval high street, the Kirkgate, to provide better access to and from the growing port of Leith. The route ran along the line of the town's former defences constructed in the mid-16th century and remodelled in the mid-17th century (**Illus 3.04–3.06,** p26–28).

Despite the proximity to a known graveyard, the density and preservation of graves recorded was unexpected. Prior to this work, it had always been assumed that the graveyard did not extend much beyond its current limits, as no finds of human remains had been reported in this area. Indeed, the parish register, recording the sale of the land for the construction of the road in 1790, implied that this area was not used for burials (Robertson & Swan 1925, 94). It became abundantly clear during the excavations at Constitution Street that there had been an apparent widespread contravening of Scots Law of Bona Vacantia regarding the protection and reporting of human remains during the various groundworks previously undertaken in the area.

Although the total number of graves disturbed may never be known, given the scale of development, including the insertion of a large 19th-century sewer and numerous other services over the last two centuries, and given the density of burials apparent from the current excavations, it has been estimated that over 300 skeletons may have been disturbed or removed. The insertion of the road itself c1790 may also have reduced the ground level by approximately 1m and thus may have removed many more.

Pottery spot dates initially indicated a 16th- to 18th-century chronology for the cemetery, in line with historical evidence for the foundation of St Mary's Church (later South Leith Parish Church, Canmore ID 51946) in 1483 and the construction of the road c1790. A subsequent programme of radiocarbon analysis of 30 skeletons, however, has revealed a wider date range, with some of the dated burials predating the establishment of St Mary's. These earlier burials were initially thought to be associated the Preceptory of St Anthony, an early 15th-century hospital founded by Holyrood Abbey and located close to the present church on the opposite, western, side of the Kirkgate (on the site of the present day Newkirkgate shopping centre). However, one of the skeletons returned a date within the 14th century predating even this.

The discovery of human remains at the intersection of London Road and Leith Walk were, similarly, largely unexpected. Although the area was associated with three successive establishments that probably had associated graveyards (a chapel, a friary and a leper hospital) their exact location had been lost following the demolition of the last of these in the mid-17th century. As no modern archaeological evidence had been found for any of these establishments or their graveyards, it had been assumed that later road construction had removed all traces of them. The discovery by workmen diverting water pipes as part of the tram service diversion works in 2008 therefore came as a surprise.

The resultant excavations at London Road were much smaller than at Constitution Street, exposing ten inhumation burials (**Illus 3.09,** p39). The excavations were limited to the width of the trenches and only enlarged to recover fully those remains that were partly disturbed. Radiocarbon dating of three burials established a broad 15th to 17th-century date for the cemetery, and they may therefore relate to any of the three establishments associated with this area: the Rude Chapel, the Carmelite friary and the Greenside Hospital for Lepers. The Rude chapel was founded in 1456 through a grant of land by James II to Holyrood Abbey, before being taken over by the Carmelite Order in 1518. Although dissolved during the Reformation in 1559/60, the empty buildings were turned into a leper hospital in 1591 by Edinburgh merchant John Robertson. The hospital was demolished c1652–7.

OTHER ARCHAEOLOGICAL REMAINS

As well as the cemetery excavations, the results of the MUDFA programme of monitoring of service trench excavations along Leith Walk and Constitution Street are also presented in this volume. These were more extensive along the length of Constitution Street than those undertaken elsewhere along the route of the proposed tram network, primarily due to their location within the area occupied by medieval Leith. The main focus of the tram works in this area comprised a single continuous narrow trench excavated along almost the entire length of Constitution Street. Connected to this were further groundworks carried out in specific areas, including trenches excavated at the junction of Constitution Street and Queen Charlotte Street and at the junction of Constitution Street and Duke Street (**Illus 6.01,** p170). The archaeological monitoring of these works allowed a more detailed picture of the surviving deposits to be recorded. These included, among other features, evidence of Leith's 16th- and 17th-century town defences and post-medieval shore defences.

INTRODUCTION

The archaeological monitoring of groundworks beyond the boundary of medieval Leith saw occasional features being recorded at various points along Leith Walk. All of the monitored trenches on Leith Walk showed a simple soil profile with large tracts of made-ground composed of sands mixed with various amounts of charcoal, building stone and brick, with pottery dating from the mid-18th century or later. In only a few isolated areas was the natural subsoil exposed comprising clean fine orange sand.

Further discoveries were made along other parts of the Tram route but these are not covered by the present publication. Further details are available in unpublished client reports (Murray 2008; Humble & Murray 2008; Bailey et al 2013; Rennie & Will 2013) but they are briefly summarised here.

To the north and north-west of the study area, findings along Ocean Way and Ocean Drive were largely of made ground deposits, associated with 19th- and 20th-century dock construction. Finds within these deposits dated to the 1840s, agreeing with mid-19th-century development of the area. Further west, along Lindsay Road, the remains of a sea wall were found, constructed of large blocks of sandstone and granite and dated by means of cartographic evidence to the mid to late 19th century.

To the south-west of the study area, a number of features were found along Princes Street. Opposite the Royal Scottish Academy three adjoining stone- and brick-built vaulted chambers were found, dating to the Georgian development of the New Town of Edinburgh. Close by were the remains of part of the Crawley Tunnel, a stone-built and rock-cut tunnel built to carry water pipes from the Meadows to the New Town. Part of the original line was found where it crossed Princes Street, as well as a diversion built during the construction of the Royal Scottish Academy at the Mound.

Further monitored works included the recording of air raid shelters at the west end of Princes Street and on West Maitland Street. There was a stone-lined well at the junction of Dalry Road and Haymarket Terrace. Four carved bulls heads were discovered outside Roseberry House on Haymarket Terrace, thought to derive from 19th-century cattle yards located close to the railway line. Throughout central Edinburgh there were also various finds of tram cable tunnels and rails relating to the earlier tram network.

Further west, another well was found at Balgreen. A sub-circular enclosure found at Broomhouse Drive was thought to relate to the designed landscape of Old Saughton House. The findings of the two excavations at Gogar have been published separately. The excavation to the west of Gogar Mains Farm Road uncovered evidence for Neolithic pits, a Bronze Age structure and palisaded enclosure, Iron Age roundhouses and early historic corn-drying kilns (Will & James 2017). Evidence for medieval settlement was found at Gogar Church (Will 2018).

2 | ARCHAEOLOGICAL METHODOLOGY

Julie Franklin, John A Lawson and Donald Wilson

Two major phases of mitigation were undertaken by Headland Archaeology between 2007 and 2009, these comprising an evaluation and subsequent excavation of the tram route section at Constitution Street, Leith, and archaeological monitoring of groundworks along the entire length of the tram route, recording any archaeological deposits and features discovered.

EXCAVATION OF THE CONSTITUTION STREET CEMETERY

Constitution Street was identified from the outset as an area of archaeological significance due to its location within the medieval and post-medieval core of Leith and to its proximity to St Mary's Church and the 16th- and 17th-century town defences. Initial monitoring of groundworks along Constitution Street revealed four articulated skeletons spread between two trenches, one on the west side of Constitution Street, immediately south of the graveyard entrance and the other further south on the east side of the road outside 137 Constitution Street (**Illus 4.02**, p50) (Humble & Murray 2008, 11–12). Those on the west side were 0.4m–1.5m below the road surface, though it was considered that more burials may have lain below the excavation depth limit. Those on the east side of the road were discovered only at the base of the trench at 1.8m below the ground surface. A large number of disarticulated remains were also recovered from the main trench which ran along the eastern side of the street (ibid).

Two trial trenches were then excavated to establish the depth and extent of burials to aid in the development of a strategy for dealing with the archaeological remains (Murray 2008). These were located between and to the south of the previously located remains, outside 143 and 135 Constitution Street, Trenches 1 and 2, respectively (**Illus 4.02**, p50). Part of two graves were found at the western edge of Trench 1. Further graves were found in Trench 2, at the western end at a depth of 0.8m and towards the middle, at a depth of 1.1m below ground surface. The human remains within these graves were left in situ.

The repeated finding of in situ graves gave clear indication that the graveyard had previously extended further east than the modern churchyard wall. The construction of Constitution Street in the early 1790s had plainly cut through the earlier graveyard and defined its modern eastern boundary.

Given the extent and nature of these discoveries, it was decided that the area of Constitution Street adjacent to St Mary's graveyard would be excavated as part of the advanced works (MUDFA) archaeological programme. This would avoid significant delays in the expected construction programme. The excavations were carried out with the specific objective of recording and fully excavating all burials and disarticulated human remains where preservation in situ was not possible.

The site targeted for full excavation was located between the south-eastern corner of the current wall enclosing the churchyard and its entrance gate to the north-east, covering an area of 110m x 10m (0.11ha). The excavation extended beyond the current graveyard boundaries in order to determine the full extent of the earlier cemetery. Traffic management restrictions required that Constitution Street should remain open to traffic throughout and so the full extent was divided into a series of 10m-long areas (termed Areas 1–11; see **Illus 4.02**, p50). Each area was then divided along the middle of the road into two 4m-wide 'panels', the western and eastern halves labelled 'a' and 'b' respectively. The first panels excavated were the western halves, closest to the graveyard wall. These were excavated in small groups from south to north, and then backfilled before the next area was opened. When the whole western strip had been excavated, the same was done along the eastern half of the road, from north to south. As well as minimising disruption to traffic, opening small areas (c10m x 4m) ensured that any articulated burials could be dealt with and removed speedily without leaving them exposed for longer than necessary.

The tarmac and underlying concrete that constituted the current road surface were removed by the main contractor using a concrete breaker and a mechanical excavator down onto the top of the sandy made-ground under direct archaeological supervision. Numerous services, some live, were discovered cut into this made-ground and these had to be exposed in a controlled manner to avoid damaging them. Disused service pipes were removed by the main contractor under archaeological supervision. Following rapid recording of the position of the services, service trenches and the extent of made-ground, excavation proceeded using a mechanical excavator equipped with a flat blade to remove homogeneous deposits of modern made-ground underlying much of Constitution Street. A large amount of disarticulated human bone was recovered within this made-ground deposit and this was removed and stored following standard procedures. The spoil heaps were constantly screened to recover any loose disarticulated human remains. Mechanical excavation ceased at the top of undisturbed soil layers, representing the buried cemetery soil, at which point hand cleaning and excavation of graves began.

The project specification (HA 2009) stated that the required depth of excavation was to be a minimum of 1.2m, the maximum depth to which excavation for the tram tracks was expected to reach. However, where in situ graves were discovered and exposed partly below this depth, the graves were to be fully excavated to avoid possible disturbance during construction and thus the maximum depth reached was 1.4m below the present-day road surface. This allowed for the recovery of all but a few burials towards the northern end of the site, whose grave cuts were seen to be deep enough to avoid being impacted. Burials extending beyond the trench limits at the western edge of the excavation, towards the graveyard, were left in situ. No in situ burials were encountered extending into the eastern excavation limit, due to later truncations (**Illus 4.02**, p50), although burials further east had been encountered during trial

ARCHAEOLOGICAL METHODOLOGY

trenching in what became Area 7 (**Illus 4.02**, p50; Humble & Murray 2008, 11–12).

In several sections over 40 intercutting inhumations were present, along with modern services. Apart from the issue of restricted space, the majority of graves were found along the centre of Constitution Street, and many crossed the boundary from the first panel to the second. Although the preferred method was the excavation of whole graves, this was not always possible in these circumstances. Thus, the required method of excavation necessitated a recovery and recording methodology that allowed accurate correlation between the two panels and facilitated reunification of the skeletons during post-excavation analysis.

The west-facing section along the first series of panels was fully recorded between Areas 4 and 11. Grave cuts and skeletal remains continuing into the eastern panels were marked on the section using paper tags noting their context number, area and grave cut number (**Illus 2.01**). Their levels and position on the section were digitally recorded. Detailed context cards and sketches were drawn indicating the recovered parts of the skeleton and other observed patterns. These were recorded under the area number (eg Area 2A). Care was taken when recovering protruding bones from sections. In most cases, these were tagged under the relevant skeleton number, left in situ and covered with a layer of terram geo-textile prior to the backfilling of each panel with sand and type 1 gravel.

Due to the nature of the above backfilling method, the second series of panels had to be shored using evenly-spaced iron sheeting so as not to damage the unexcavated graves known to continue into the eastern section. On excavation of the second half, the protective layer of terram was carefully and gradually removed to allow recovery of the tags from the previously recorded burials. This was cross-checked using the recorded levels to ensure that the second half of the inhumation could be accurately matched, recorded and stored with the first half.

In many cases, grave cuts were not distinguishable in the surrounding sandy soil matrix. Where coffins were present, the apparent grave cut was often no more than the stain left by the decayed coffin wood. For simple burials with no coffin, there was often no way to distinguish the grave fill from the surrounding soil, the presence of the skeleton being the only available evidence. Where no cut was visible, but the line of the coffin was, then this was used for survey purposes. Where there was no coffin, an arbitrary

ILLUS 2.01
Working shot of excavation of Gr0589, against west-facing section of Area 6A, showing tags for skeletons in section

line was surveyed around the skeleton. Consequently, on site plans, coffined burials tend to appear as rectangular or trapezoidal, while simple burials have more rounded ends, but this does not reflect the edges of the original excavated grave.

No skeletons were hand-drawn in the field. Instead they were all photographed in a manner suitable for subsequent rectification and drawing during post-excavation. This allowed for a more accurate record of the remains to be made and ensured that disruption was kept to a minimum. At least three pairs of survey pins were placed along the body and photographed as vertically as possible. The markers were then surveyed digitally using the skeleton context number. In the case of deep negative features or deep coffins two sets of survey pins were used, one set at the bottom, close to the skeleton and another along the upper cut. Three spot heights were taken on skeletons, at the top of skull, on the sacrum and at the feet. Skeletons, coffins and fills were given unique numbers and the fills were sampled consistently from areas adjacent and below the body, namely in the area of the pelvis, skull, hands and feet, in order to recover small bones.

In addition, excavation exceeded the required depth when it was deemed necessary to further investigate the character of the archaeological remains in sondages, as in the case of ditches. This was agreed with the City of Edinburgh Council Archaeology Service (CECAS) in advance.

Following the excavation of all graves and features within a given panel, a site meeting was held between Headland, CECAS, TIE and the principal contractor, Carillion. Once CECAS had confirmed that an area had been fully excavated, Carillion arranged backfilling and reinstatement of the road surface before opening the next panel. This process was repeated until both halves of all eleven areas had been fully excavated.

GENERAL MONITORING OF GROUNDWORKS

The archaeological monitoring of groundworks for the Edinburgh Trams service diversions project followed both a proactive and reactive approach. The different levels of response were defined in the project specification (HA 2007). Areas that had previously been identified in the Environmental Statement (Mott Macdonald 2003; Faber Maunsell 2004) as having a high archaeological potential were proactively monitored from the outset of ground-breaking. In areas of expected very low potential, an archaeological call-out system was set up to maximise archaeological recovery and minimise the need for continuous archaeological monitoring where the likelihood of finding any significant remains was negligible. The call-out system involved pre-start briefings with the various contractors by CECAS and Headland, noting the most obvious archaeological features likely to be exposed and identified during the course of works (eg walls, wells, human remains).

The work undertaken on Ocean Drive, Constitution Street (except for the area covered by the excavations described above) and the northern part of Leith Walk (north of 269 Leith Walk, the junction with Balfour Street) was undertaken as a proactive response. Archaeological staff were present on site during all ground-breaking works, which comprised linear machine-cut trenches to locate and divert live services. Where archaeological features or deposits were uncovered appropriate excavation and recording were undertaken.

On the southern part of Leith Walk, a system of reactive monitoring was put in place whereby the contractors would contact Headland when unexpected features were encountered during the initial groundworks. This led to archaeologists being called out on numerous occasions to monitor work on service diversions along the route of the tram works. The service diversions generally comprised open cut trenches and small open areas in the roads and pavements. In these areas archaeologists were called to record any features of interest identified by photographic and written record. In some cases, archaeologists then continued to monitor specific groundworks as they progressed in these areas.

EXCAVATIONS AND MONITORING AT THE JUNCTION OF LEITH WALK AND LONDON ROAD

Several skeletons were unexpectedly revealed by contractors during groundworks at the junction of Leith Walk and London Road. Once the initial discovery had been made a methodology was agreed to fully excavate the remains discovered and limit further disturbance of human remains during the remaining works. All soft deposits were excavated by machine in shallow spits down to the top of any surviving archaeology or until the formation levels of the groundwork was reached. All archaeology was excavated by hand. The skeletons revealed during this work were recorded with a combination of hand-drawn plans and rectified digital photography. All further groundworks in this area were continuously monitored by an archaeologist.

REPORT STRUCTURE

After an introductory chapter (Chapter 1), and details of the methodology (Chapter 2), the historical and archaeological background is covered chronologically, pulling out certain themes for more detailed coverage (Chapter 3). The description of the archaeological remains discovered follows and has been divided into three broad sections: the Constitution Street excavations (Chapter 4); the London Road excavations (Chapter 5); the findings from monitoring work in other areas (Chapter 6).

The excavation reports (Chapter 4–5) each follow the same format: the archaeological features are described first; followed by osteological reports on the human remains; the artefactual evidence; the environmental evidence; and then the isotope analysis of the human remains. The discussion of each excavation follows on directly from the description of the findings.

The monitoring works (Chapter 6) provided more piecemeal evidence. These are divided geographically, first broadly, into the findings along Constitution Street and Leith Walk, and within this by individual area. Due to similarities across the monitoring findings along Constitution Street, an overall discussion of this area is included. The Leith Walk findings were more disparate and stand alone. The overall conclusion to this volume (Chapter 7) looks at the findings across all the archaeological works by period. The isotope analysis data and osteological and burial data are presented as appendices (*Appendices 1–2*).

There are also a series of 'People Stories' presented throughout the book relating to facial reconstructions of some of the skulls recovered during the project. These sit outside the main report structure. See *Facial reconstructions* below (p12) for further explanation.

TERMINOLOGY

Context numbers are referred to throughout the text where they allow cross-referencing between different sections of text and illustrations. Skeletons and grave cuts (even where the latter was invisible) were all given context numbers. As the excavations at Constitution Street and the monitoring phase of the works, including the excavations at London Road, were conducted as separate projects, the context numbers for these sections overlap. In an attempt to clarify, the Constitution Street context numbers are all given as four digits (0123, 1234 etc), while the London Road and monitoring context numbers are all three digits (123, 234 etc).

The only exception to this was a short stretch of the monitoring works (Bernard Street/Baltic Street to Maritime Lane/Mitchell Street), where contexts numbers on site were accidentally doubled with the London Road excavations. As these were conducted using the same project code as the monitoring works, they were subsequently changed throughout the archive to avoid later confusion and are now numbered in the 1400s.

The most frequently quoted context numbers are those given to skeletons and graves and these are distinguished by respective prefixes, Sk and Gr. Both skeleton and grave cut numbers are given where relevant to allow the skeletons to be located on the site plans, which are marked with grave numbers only. Other context numbers are shown in brackets with [cuts], [structures], (deposits) and (fills) distinguished by square and round brackets.

The general term cemetery is used to refer to all areas that have been used for articulated human burial. The term graveyard is used more specifically to refer to a cemetery adjacent to an ecclesiastical establishment. Grave orientations are given using cardinal points, the first point given referring to the head end of the grave.

Human remains were given broad osteological age groups (younger child, older middle adult etc) and adults were sexed where possible. The definitions of these age ranges are given in **Table 4.05** (p92) and **Table 5.02** (p161). Age group and sex details are given where skeletons are referred to in the text. More specific age ranges are given in the text only where it is possible to be more precise. The terms adult and subadult are used where more precise ageing was not possible. Where broad age ranges are being discussed in general terms, the words man/men and woman/women and subadult/s are used to refer, respectively, to all adult males and adult females and all juveniles under 18 years.

Statistics are generally given as percentages followed by precise numbers in brackets, for example 79.5% (240/302). Ratios of men and women are given by calculating the number of men for each one woman, eg 0.66M:1F.

RADIOCARBON DATING

AMS radiocarbon dating was undertaken by SUERC on 33 of the skeletons from Constitution Street and London Road. The dates were calibrated using OxCal 4.3 (Bronk Ramsey 2009).

The $\delta^{13}C$ values for these dates indicated a variable but typically high percentage of marine component to the diet of these individuals. The marine reservoir effect would therefore have had a significant effect on these dates, increasing the apparent radiocarbon age making the dates seem earlier than they should be (Arneborg et al 1999). The marine component percentage was calculated on the basis of a $\delta^{13}C$ value of –21.0‰ for a 100% terrestrial diet and –12.5‰ for a 100% marine diet (ibid, 158). The results ranged from 0% to 34% marine component, with an average of 17%. Most were within the range 13% to 20%. The dates were recalibrated in consultation with SUERC, taking into account the $\delta^{13}C$ value of each sample. For these purposes, the IntCal13 atmospheric curve was used (Reimer et al 2013) and the Marine 13 curve (ibid). The marine component was given an error of ±10% and the Delta R value was set at –47±52 (Russell et al 2015).

The results are shown in full in Chapters 4 and 5 (**Tables 4.02** and **5.01**; **Illus 4.31** and **5.06**). They are quoted there and throughout the text at 95.4% probability and have been rounded to the nearest five years. The calibrated date ranges typically cover a range of around 200 years due to a plateau in the calibration curve during the late medieval and early post-medieval period.

FACIAL RECONSTRUCTIONS

A programme of facial reconstruction was carried out as part of a partnership between CECAS and the Centre for Anatomy and Human Identification at the University of Dundee (CAHID), set up in 2013. The reconstructions were undertaken by forensic artist postgraduate interns and graduates volunteering with CECAS. A total of 54 skulls were assessed as suitable for facial reconstruction work. At the time of writing 47 of these have been completed and are included in this publication. Of these, 45 were from Constitution Street and two from London Road. The methodology used is described below (p14–15) and the facial reconstructions are presented at the back of the book (p199–201). A selection of distinctive and interesting stories based on the bones of these individuals is presented throughout the volume (see p29 for how these stories were crafted).

ARCHIVE

The digital and paper archives for the project will be deposited with Historic Environment Scotland, with copies of reports deposited with the City of Edinburgh Council's Archaeology Service HER. The physical archive will be declared to the Treasure Trove Unit in accordance with the Treasure Trove Code of Practice (TTU 2016). At the time of writing the human remains are being curated by the City of Edinburgh Council Archaeology Service as part of their archaeological collections.

HOW THE FACES OF THE PAST WERE RECONSTRUCTED

Hayley Fisher

In collaboration between City of Edinburgh Council Archaeology Service (CECAS) and the University of Dundee, a team of MSc Forensic Art graduates from the Centre for Anatomy and Human Identification have produced a selection of digital facial reconstructions. The reconstructions were selected from a pool of 388 skeletal remains excavated during the archaeological works. The aim was to engage the public with faces from Edinburgh's history by providing a real semblance of individuals from our past. A total of 47 reconstructions were undertaken (45 using skulls from Constitution Street, two from London Road) by Hayley Fisher, Paloma Galzi, Heather Goodrum, Hanna Isaacs, Sarah Jaworski, Emily McCulloch, Miriam Modenes, Hew Morrison, Dagmara Roguska and Crystal Symes.

Forensic art is multimedia in nature, as is any art used within forensic contexts to assist in the identification of the unknown, victims or criminals (Taylor 2001). Within this field, facial reconstruction is used when routine techniques fail to identify the dead and when little or no evidence is available. It can also be used to depict the faces of our ancestors. The technique uses a combination of scientific methods and artistic skill to obtain the image of an individual's face. Regardless of forensic or archaeological context, both involve the same process of layering the soft tissues of the face over the bony tissue of the skull. The images produced by the team are largely two-dimensional, a technique pioneered in the United States, which uses an image of the skull, combined with soft tissue depth estimates, to depict the final face (ibid). The production of these images is fast, requires little material and inflicts no damage upon the remains.

The following gives an insight to the processes of facial reconstruction, using Sk0570 as an example.

Selection and assembly

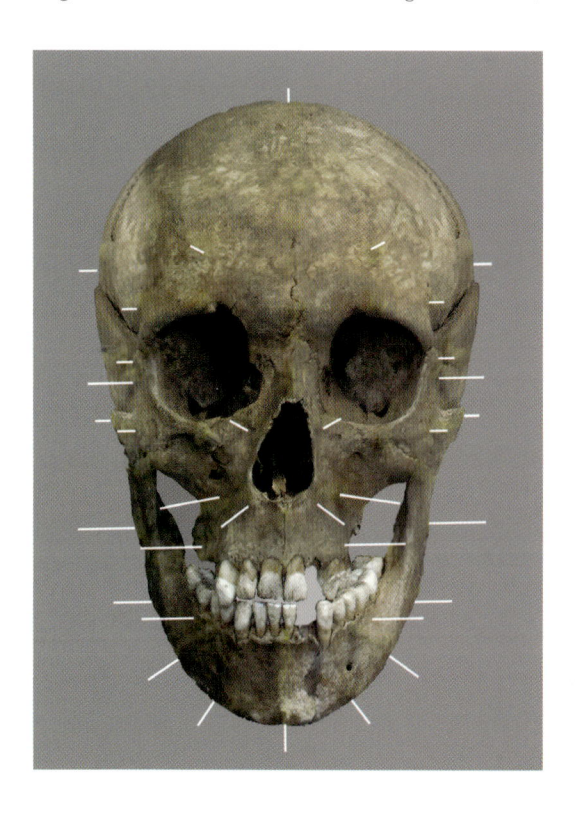

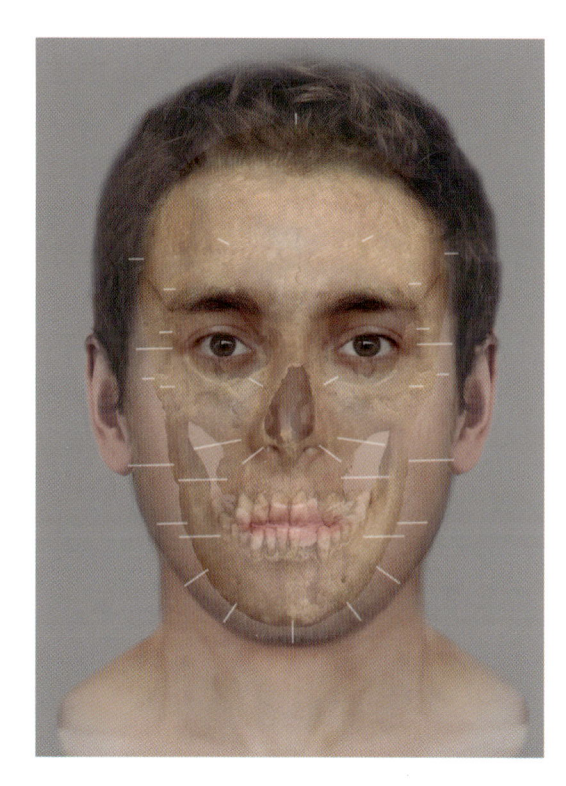

Re-assembly is often required when presented with ancient remains due to post-depositional deterioration and damage. Often areas of bone are completely missing. Individual skulls were selected for this project on the basis of condition and completeness, whilst seeking diversity in age, sex and facial morphology. A sufficient amount of facial bone is required, as these are most influential in the depiction of the face (Prag and Neave 1997). The skull of Sk0570 was relatively complete with minor fragmentation to the zygomatic arches. The arches were modelled later in computer software by mirroring the same area on the other side of the skull (Wilkinson and Neave 2003). Where areas of the facial bone are fragmented, small amounts of dental wax may be used to re-assemble these pieces. This wax causes no damage to the bone and may easily be removed (White and Folkens 2005). Wax may also be used to fix the mandible to the cranium aligning the teeth to their natural position.

Biological and morphological assessment

Once re-assembly is complete, an analysis of the skull is performed to obtain information which will influence the resulting soft tissue face of the individual. Through visual and palpable assessments, a descriptive morphological profile of facial features is derived from the bony details. Similarly, a biological profile is created, estimating the sex, age and ancestry of the individual, which in this case was confirmed with reference to the osteological analysis. Specific craniometrical measurements are carried out upon the hard tissue to approximate soft tissue dimensions for the nose (Rynn 2006) and similarly a correlation can be seen between lip thickness and enamel height for upper and lower teeth and sets of formulae can be utilized for white European populations (Wilkinson et al 2003).

Skull Sk0570 was determined to be of white European ancestry, male, and aged mid-20s to 30s. The shape of the cranial vault and the degree of the gonial angles of the mandible indicated an overall oval face shape with an upright profile (Fedosyutkin and Nainys 1993). The mandible and dentition were notably prominent features, with bony crests on the lower border of the mandible suggesting a well-developed muscle and therefore a large chin. The pronounced upper and lower canines suggested a wide and square lip shape (Gerasimov 1955).

Tissue depth pegs

Tissue depth pegs are then applied to the skull at 34 points on the cranium and mandible (Helmer 1984). These provide average tissue depths at these points in accordance with ancestry groups, sex and age-ranges. There are many datasets available. In the case of Sk0570, the set specific to white European males in the mid-twenties age range was employed. The skull is then orientated in the Frankfurt-horizontal-place, mimicking the natural position of the head in life (Taylor 2001) and high-resolution digital photographs are taken of the skull in both lateral and frontal profiles at a distance of 6ft to reduce perspective distortion.

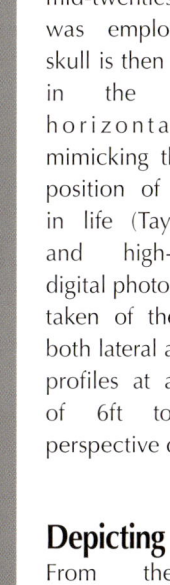

Depicting the face

From there the application of facial features and the final skin layer is done within digital imaging software. Both frontal and lateral views of the skulls are then scaled to the correct life-size and temporary eyeballs placed in the orbits. The approximate measurements for placement and dimensions of facial features are marked out. The skin textures are chosen based on the individual's biological profile. They are applied from high quality images, which can easily be manipulated within the software to fit exactly in accordance to measurements and facial detail derived from skull analysis.

Any notations of trauma or disease effecting the face can now be depicted. Similarly, hair and clothing styles can be applied based on ethnic norms and their historic context.

3 | HISTORICAL AND ARCHAEOLOGICAL BACKGROUND

Julie Franklin, Donald Wilson and John A Lawson

This chapter provides some geographic, archaeological and historical context for the locations and structures revealed during the archaeological investigations in Leith as part of the preparation for the construction of the new tram network.

GEOLOGY AND TOPOGRAPHY

The geology and topography of Leith and the surrounding areas played a significant role in the establishment of the port at Leith and continued to affect the prosperity of the town into the post-medieval and industrial periods. The bedrock geology of this area of coastline mainly comprised sandstone of the Gullane Formation formed in the Carboniferous period. In Leith this is overlain by superficial geology comprising shore-face and beach deposits of sand and gravel formed in the Quaternary period (after 2.6 million years ago). Away from the shoreline the superficial geology alters slightly with raised marine deposits of post-glacial age (after 12,000 years ago) comprising sediments deposited as mud, silt, sand and gravel. Further inland older raised marine deposits relating to the last glacial period (110,000–12,000 years ago) predominate, comprising sand and gravel (BGS 2018). Wind-blown sand is a common feature in archaeological deposits in Leith.

The dominant topographical feature of Leith is the head of the Water of Leith where it flows into the Firth of Forth. This tidal and protected inlet with access to the North Sea and Baltic trading routes helped establish Leith as Edinburgh's port by the start of the 12th century. The water divides the town historically into North Leith (on the north-west bank) and South Leith (on the south-eastern bank). South Leith has traditionally been the larger and more important of the two. The geology also played a role in the increasing industrialisation of the area from the 17th century onwards with, amongst other things, the establishment of a glassworks in 1663 utilising the abundance of local sands.

A change in the bedrock geology along the coastline is seen to the east of Leith around Joppa and Musselburgh. Here the Scottish Middle Coal Measures Formation, formed in the Carboniferous Period, is exposed along the shoreline. These coal measures, although of poor quality anthracite, were a good source of fuel that was heavily exploited from the post-medieval period. This coal was integral to the establishment of the salt pans at Joppa and Musselburgh, the glassworks at Leith and the ceramics industries at Portobello.

The topography of the area around Leith formed a relatively flat and easily accessible area of land, rising gently towards the igneous intrusions of basalt of the Arthur's Seat Volcanic formation. These now form the hills that give Edinburgh its dramatic backdrop, including Arthur's Seat, Calton Hill and Edinburgh Castle Rock. The defensive qualities of Castle Rock were in use from late prehistory onwards and formed the focus of early Edinburgh.

The landscape of Leith has changed significantly since the medieval period. To the north, Commercial Street and Bernard Street follow the line of the late medieval shore line with both Great Junction Street and Constitution Street following the lines of the 16th-century town defences which enclosed the town for the first time and dominated the spatial limits of the port for the next 200 years. Within these parameters the medieval street pattern can still be discerned, with Sandport Street in North Leith following the same alignment for approximately the last 900 years. In South Leith the area close to the shore, including Water's Close, Broad Wynd, Burgess Street and Tolbooth Wynd, still preserve the original layout of the medieval street pattern, though some of the names have changed; respectively, these were once Rotten Row, Broad Wynd, Burgess Close and the High Street. The route of the Kirkgate is preserved by the pedestrian walkway through the Newkirkgate shopping centre and onwards towards Tolbooth Wynd. By the end of the 15th century the Kirkgate formed part of the high street for Leith and acted as the main route to Edinburgh via the road now called Leith Walk. Although the properties in the old town of South Leith are mainly of 18th- and 19th-century origin, the area does include the remains of Lamb's House, on the corner of Burgess Street and Water Street, an early 17th-century merchant's house and one of Leith's oldest standing buildings, as well as South Leith Parish Church, which incorporates the standing remains of the 15th-century St Mary's Church.

To the east of the town is Leith Links, today a substantial public park. Prior to the construction of the town's defences in the mid-16th century it is likely that this area was open farmland running up to the edge of the medieval properties located in the east of the town. The area was crossed by routes leading towards Restalrig and Musselburgh and East Lothian to the east. It was the location of siege works during the Siege of Leith in 1559–60. During the 17th century, parts of it were utilised for a plague quarantine camp and associated cemetery. The name Leith Links derives from its use as a golf course from the 17th century and it is synonymous with the creation of the first rules of golf by John Rattray in the 18th century. The Links were formalised as a public park in 1888 as part of the Leith Improvement Plan.

EARLY LEITH FROM THE 11TH TO 14TH CENTURIES

Since at least the 12th century, Leith has acted as the main harbour and port for Edinburgh and the fortunes of the two have been closely linked. The early medieval shoreline appears to have run approximately parallel and a little to the south of the current day Bernard Street and Commercial Street (Stronach 2002a, 385, Illus 2) with all the land to the north having been reclaimed from the late medieval period onwards (p21). The shoreline along the Forth comprised a wide shallow beach known as Leith Sands, suitable for beaching and offloading cargo. At low tide this probably extended as far as the present Albert Dock, north of Ocean Drive. The Water of Leith was broader where it joined the Firth of Forth and provided a sheltered mooring for boats accessible at high tide.

The first historical reference to Leith was in 1128 when it is mentioned in David I's foundation charter for Holyrood Abbey. In this document David I endowed the abbey with the existing harbour and settlement which occupied both sides of the river mouth. In South Leith the settlement was centred on the shore of the Water of Leith, present-day Coalhill, between Dub Row (now Giles Street/Parliament Street) and the High Street (now Tolbooth Wynd), stretching back from the Water towards the Kirkgate (Mowat 2003, 5). On the north bank, the settlement lined the shore, following present day Sandport Street (ibid). The origins of this settlement remain obscure, but such a useful natural harbour so close to Edinburgh, the site of a settlement since prehistory, is unlikely to have gone unnoticed.

Archaeological evidence for 'pre-charter' settlement was found in North Leith during excavations at Ronaldson's Wharf in 1997, where the remains of early timber buildings were uncovered on the northern side of Sandport Street (Reed & Lawson 1999). These structures predated the formation of burgage plots in the area, which is thought to have occurred soon after the granting of the settlement to Holyrood Abbey. The structures showed evidence of being rebuilt several times and thus it is thought that they may date back to the 10th or 11th centuries. It is possible that a chapel dedicated to St Nicholas was established by the abbey in North Leith in the 12th century (Mowat 2003, 5) to the west of the settlement, in the area between present day Coburg Street, Commercial Street and Dock Street (**Illus 3.01**; Canmore ID 52019; Cowan & Easson 1976, 199). The chapel was certainly in existence by the late 15th century and was demolished in the mid-17th century.

At around the same time as he endowed Holyrood Abbey with a harbour, David I established his own harbour further towards the mouth of the Water of Leith, to the north of Burgess Street, in the area now called the Shore (Mowat 2003, 4). Excavations carried out to the south of Burgess Street and north of Tolbooth Wynd between 1993 and 1995 demonstrated that this area was agricultural land at the start of the 12th century, possibly associated with earlier 'pre-charter' settlement. This 'gap site' was developed during the 12th century, with evidence for domestic occupation and small-scale industry (Collard & Reed 1994; J Lawson 1995).

It is not known if the early 'harbours' involved any construction or modification of the river bank. It is more likely that vessels were beached at high tide or were moored in the river and serviced by smaller boats from the shore. Likewise, there was no bridge across the Water at this time and it was crossed by a ford or ferry. David I was also responsible for granting Edinburgh royal burgh status which marked the beginning of its rise to prominence, though it was not until the reign of James III (1460–88) that Edinburgh was to emerge as Scotland's capital.

This early Leith was essentially a fishing village, exploiting the herring, lythe, pollack, coley, haddock, ling and oyster beds of the Firth of Forth (Marshall 1986, 21; Henderson 2002; Mowat 2003, 4) and there is archaeological evidence for fish-processing in the 13th or 14th centuries (Reed & Lawson 1999; Stronach 2002a, 389). The earliest houses seem to have been timber-built, though it is possible that earlier structures may have been turf-built and left very little archaeological trace. There is evidence that turf was used in construction at both Ronaldson's Wharf and Water Street (Reed & Lawson 1999; Stronach 2002a), in the form of turf banks.

The establishment of the two harbours indicates that trade was in progress from an early date and was probably seasonal, as shown in later records. Wool was exported in late summer and early autumn after shearing and sheepskins in the spring and summer after the slaughter of the lambs. Hides were available in November after the slaughter of cattle before winter, but shipping probably avoided the stormy winter months and they would have been exported in the spring (Mowat 2003, 12). Salt fish and shellfish such as pickled oysters were also big exports (Stronach 2002a, 414; Mowat 2003, 11; 219), fish being in great demand during the medieval period because of ecclesiastical restrictions on the eating of meat on certain days. Archaeological evidence for oyster processing was discovered at Burgess Street, in the form of a clay-lined tank surrounded by a large deposit of oyster shells dating to the 13th or 14th century (Collard & Reed 1994). Imported goods included wine, fine cloth, honey, dried fruit, spices and other luxuries from France and the Low Countries. Timber was probably being imported from the Baltic and this was to go on to become a major commodity for Leith in the 15th and 16th centuries. Grain was probably imported during times of shortage (Mowat 2003, 6). There was also local and regional trade as well as ferries for foot passengers and horses (ibid, 15).

The late 13th and 14th centuries were marked by military upheavals relating to the Wars of Scottish Independence. Leith was in the part of the country under English control from 1298 to 1314 and again from 1332 to 1341 and for a while (1303–8) the Forth marked the border between English-controlled and 'Free Scotland' (Mowat 2003, 11). While Edinburgh Castle was held by the English, Leith was the port by which the garrison was supplied, and records survive of the large volumes of supplies that would have passed through the town for the men and horses at the castle (ibid, 10). Ultimately, Leith was a winner in the aftermath of the Wars of Independence, in that Berwick-upon-Tweed was lost to England. This had been Scotland's busiest port, and, in its absence, Leith took up the mantle. The net effect of all this was a huge increase in the amount of trade passing through Leith, with a 17-fold increase on customs collected there on exports recorded between 1311 and 1326 (ibid, 11), and with trade continuing to rise throughout the rest of the 14th and 15th centuries (ibid, 20–1, 43).

THE GROWTH OF THE TOWN IN THE 15TH CENTURY

How much the people of Leith were able to benefit from the trade passing through it is a point of conjecture revolving around Leith's ambiguous burghal status. It appears Leith was never made an official burgh, and only burghs could engage in trade and hold markets. Tradesmen were required to live and work inside the burgh and had to belong to trade incorporations who set prices, ensured quality and looked after sick members. Only royal burghs, such as Edinburgh, could engage in foreign trade (Marshall 1986, 5; Mowat 2003, 5). Burghs without a suitable harbour were granted ones nearby (Ewan 1990, 7), thus Edinburgh was granted a harbour at Leith. The earliest historical record for this was a charter signed by Robert I in 1329, though it is likely that this was a renewal of existing rights, given the previous two centuries of Edinburgh's burghal status and of the existence of the royal and abbey harbours in Leith (Marshall 1986, 4; Mowat 2003, 1). However, since Leith was not a royal burgh in itself, in theory the goods unloaded at the harbour in Leith had to pass directly through the town and its inhabitants would have had to go to Edinburgh to buy them.

Leith did enjoy some privileges. Marshall (1984, 4), in his colourful account of the history of Leith, speculates that it was made a burgh of barony in 1398, though there is no historical record of the fact. However, incorporations of tailors and cordiners (shoemakers) in Leith date their origins to 1398, which might suggest some kind of official sanction (ibid, 5). The most powerful of the trade organisations in Leith was the Fraternity of Mariners, founded in 1380. The Maltmen, Fleshers, Wrights and Masons also had incorporations in Leith (Marshall 1986, 8), but the burgesses of Edinburgh were not happy about the situation, accusing Leith tradesmen of shoddy workmanship and undercutting Edinburgh prices (ibid, 6). Edinburgh did not recognise the rights of the Leith incorporations and prosecuted Leith tradesmen on a regular basis (ibid, 10). Prosecutions also show that Leithers ignored the ban on foreign trade as far as possible, with Leith merchants boarding foreign vessels and goods being unloaded under cover of darkness (ibid, 17).

Improvements were made to the harbour at the end of the 14th and beginning of the 15th century. In 1398, Sir Robert Logan of Restalrig, Leith's major landowner, granted land and rights to Edinburgh to improve the harbour, presumably in the form of wharves and piers, and to build a bridge (Mowat 2003, 21). The bridge, however, was eventually built by Holyrood Abbey sometime between 1398 and 1439 (ibid, 35–6). It was a little upstream from the current Sandport Place bridge, its southern end being where the river narrows at the west end of Coalhill. Excavations on the north side of the Water identified surviving remnants of part of an early bridge that were dated by reference to historical sources to the late 15th century (Henderson 1999). A bridge was still standing in this location in 1759 (**Illus 3.05**).

Two other important additions to Leith came in the 1430s, the Preceptory of St Anthony and the King's Wark. The Preceptory of St Anthony was founded in 1430 and is widely accepted as the first ecclesiastical establishment in South Leith. It was located on the west side of the Kirkgate, a prime site fronting onto the main road from Edinburgh at the entrance to the port. Its location is remembered on the first edition Ordnance Survey map (Ordnance Survey 1853a) immediately to the south of the present-day St Anthony's Place, though its buildings had long since vanished by this point. The site is now under the Newkirkgate shopping centre. It was believed that the preceptory had been founded by Sir Robert Logan of Restalrig, a wealthy landowner, although it transpires that he only granted the land (Smith 1929, 276). A letter to the bishops of Aquila and Argyll (ibid) indicates that James I founded a church, hospital, cloisters, dormitories, refectories and other divine offices on the site in 1430,

HISTORICAL AND ARCHAEOLOGICAL BACKGROUND

confirmed by Bishop Wardlaw of St Andrews in the same year (Mowat 2003, 31). It is unclear if all the buildings were completed as the letter also stated that the king died (d.1437) before it was finished. The building appears on the 1560 Petworth Map (**Illus 3.01**) as a large apparently cruciform church with associated buildings.

The order of St Anthony was based in Vienne, France, and this was the only house of its kind in Scotland (Rogers 1877, 7). It was populated by about six canons, the earliest inhabitants probably being French. It was endowed with land for a large garden and given revenues from Leith wine imports. St Anthony was particularly associated with pigs and the preceptory's swine roamed the streets of Leith, identified by the bells around their necks (Mowat 2003, 32). The canons ran a song school for local boys for their choir (Marshall 1986, 98), gave absolutions for sins in exchange for contributions to their work (Mowat 2003, 31) and provided care for the sick, aged and poor (Marshall 1986, 7). The skin infection erysipelas, characterised by a red rash with fever and other symptoms, was called St Anthony's Fire and it is possible that the canons specialised in its treatment (Mowat 2003, 31). The Preceptory of St Anthony also provided a local place for Leithers to worship.

Work began on the King's Wark around 1434. James I conceived it as a storehouse for royal cargoes, and an armoury. It also had a royal apartment, though it is not known if it was ever occupied (Mowat 2003, 32–3). It was originally a tower house type structure and was located on a promontory, either natural or artificially enhanced, on the eastern bank of the Water where it met the Firth of Forth. Its location is marked by the present-day public house of the same name at the corner of the Shore and Bernard Street. Subsequent monarchs added to it and it became a substantial complex of buildings. Some of the officials who worked there made their homes in Leith, adding to a growing suburb of wealthy homes of merchant skippers and other local people of influence on the southern side of the town between the old village and St Anthony's and perhaps also spreading onto the eastern side of the Kirkgate (Marshall 1986, 12, illus 3). It was possibly during further work on the King's Wark in 1463 that the adjacent beach area was reclaimed from the sea. Excavations south of Bernard Street discovered up to 1m of soil, sand and domestic refuse deposited on the beach sand to create a flat area above sea level. The finds within the midden deposits dated this activity to the 1460s or 70s (Holmes 1985).

It is generally accepted that St Mary's Church (sometimes called St Mary's Chapel, though the term church has been used throughout this text to avoid confusion with any earlier chapel structure) was built around 1483 (Campbell Irons 1898, vol 1, 77; Marshall 1983, 2; Stevenson et al 1981 give the date as 1438, though this is surely a typographical error as 1483 is the generally accepted date). It was located at the southern edge of town on the eastern side of the Kirkgate across the road from St Anthony's, sharing the same prominent position on the road into Leith from Edinburgh. Part of it still survives and has been reworked into South Leith Parish Church. The foundation was instigated by the Fraternity of Mariners, St Mary being their patron saint (Mary and the infant Jesus aboard a ship at sea appear on the Leith town arms, granted in 1889), with contributions by and chapels for each of the Leith incorporations (Marshall 1986, 7). There are records mentioning various grants and endowments for the church beginning in 1490 (Wilson 1875, 413; Marshall 1986, 8) and of royal gifts to the 'new kyrk of Leith' in 1497 (Dickson 1877).

When finished, St Mary's was a sizeable structure with a cruciform plan, much larger than the current smaller church, which is the result of 16th-century destruction and later reworking. The scale of the original church can possibly be gleaned from the first edition Ordnance Survey map (Ordnance Survey 1853a) which records the 19th-century church as having seats for 1200. Given that this reworked 19th-century building was perhaps about half the size of the original (Marshall 1986, 7), and given that the congregation would originally have been largely standing, it seems that the 15th-century church would have been able to accommodate most of Leith's population, estimated at the time as less than 4000 (ibid, 8). The scale and grandeur of St Mary's Church is a testament to the power and wealth centred in Leith by this time, particularly in view of the existence of St Anthony's and the official parish church at Restalrig.

The larger of the industries undertaken in Leith during the 15th century are evidenced by the incorporations funding the building of St Mary's. As well as the Mariners, there were the Maltmen, Merchants, Hammermen, Cordiners (shoemakers), Fleshers, Wrights and Masons. Brewing had always been a big industry and maltmen could make a good living as beer was needed to supply the town and victual the ships. Brewing was often undertaken by women to supplement their income and was particularly important for widows. Coopers were also much in demand, the barrel being the only available water-tight container in which to store ships' cargoes. Carters, porters, wrights and shipwrights were also needed in the port, as were smiths to supply the thousands of nails needed in shipbuilding. It also seems that more specialist smiths dwelt within the town making arms (Mowat 2003, 33), including battle axes and, later, guns. Skilled gunsmiths were imported from the Low Countries to stock the King's Wark armoury (Mowat 2003, 33). Skinners, weavers and tailors also plied their trade (ibid, 129).

North Leith also received another church during this period. St Ninian's church (or North Leith Church; Canmore ID 159087) was established in 1493 between present day Quayside Street and the Water of Leith and its remains are incorporated into the current Quayside Mills.

FORTIFICATION, OCCUPATION AND REFORMATION IN THE 16TH AND 17TH CENTURIES

By the 16th century, Edinburgh was firmly established as Scotland's capital and was increasing in size and population. The importance of Leith, and the volume of trade passing through it, grew with its neighbour, and so too did its strategic importance as the gateway to Edinburgh. Leith had seen military action in the past, but in the mid-16th century the levels of destruction were far greater.

In 1544, as part of the 'Rough Wooing', an attempt by Henry VIII to force the infant Mary Queen of Scots to marry his son, the future Edward VI, the Earl of Hertford (Edward's uncle) sacked and burnt Leith, Holyrood and Edinburgh and the surrounding countryside. The English plan had originally been to take Leith, fortify it and use it as a supply route to invade Scotland, but the unreliability of this plan meant it was changed to a heavier handed one (Hutchison 1865, 12; Mowat 2003, 107). The Scots were taken by surprise and Leith fell after a short bout of fighting. The pier was destroyed and the ships either taken or burnt. Hertford reported the town was fortified with ditches and ordnance (Mowat 2003, 108) and was surprised by the wealth he was able to loot from the town. It is not clear how total the destruction was, and it is possible that Hertford exaggerated in his report of the incident (ibid, 109). St Mary's was apparently used as a refuge for the homeless. It is likely that the widespread destruction of the surrounding countryside led to famine and hardship, though the spring timing of the attack (compared with autumn) would have limited this to an extent.

In 1547, after the Battle of Pinkie near Musselburgh, Leith was again occupied by English forces under the Earl of Hertford (now Duke of Somerset, Lord Protector of England), and St Mary's was used as a prison for captured Scots (Robertson 1851, 26). The English forces consumed or carried off provisions and the town was again burnt, and ships taken or destroyed.

It is not clear when the defences described by Hertford in 1544 were constructed and where exactly they were. Mowat (2003, 108) speculates they were made by the Earl of Angus in 1543. It might be assumed that later defensive works would have made use of the ditches already excavated but this is not known. The first plan of Leith's defences dates from 1560 (**Illus 3.01**) and this shows the French-built defences ordered by Mary of Guise, acting as regent for her daughter, Queen Mary. From 1548 approximately 6000 troops were brought over by Mary of Guise from her native France and began fortifying the town, the work being completed in 1559. The French fortifications were designed by an Italian engineer, Piero de Strozzi, using the latest Italian designs of low earthen ramparts sloping inwards to deflect cannon fire and was undertaken by 300 Scottish pioneers (military engineers).

The French fortifications enclosed all North and South Leith. At the corners and at intervals along the walls angular bastions were provided as a platform for heavy guns which gave flanking fire along the line of the walls. The harbour was defended by new stone fortifications, including a large bastion called Ramsey's Fort on the foreshore on the seaward side of the King's Wark, in the area now known as the Timberbush. This guarded both the harbour entrance to the west and the King's Wark's sea gate to the east. The western earthwork in North Leith was extended outwards to enclose St Nicholas' Chapel.

These defences are thought to be the first of this kind of bastion defence seen in Britain, with the system not being used again until Berwick-upon-Tweed was fortified ten years later. Recent archaeological excavations have confirmed that the eastern and southern ramparts followed approximately the line of present day Constitution Street and Great Junction Street respectively (Paton & Cook 2016, fig.9).

The French troops were in effect occupying the town and became very unpopular during their 12-year stay (Mowat 2003, 114). By 1559 the Catholic Mary of Guise was becoming ever more unpopular in the increasingly Protestant Scotland and used the fortified Leith as a refuge for herself. While the people of Leith were not necessarily supportive of this move, she won them over by promising to acquire for them the superiority of Leith, freeing them from subservience to Edinburgh (though they were never to receive this). The Protestant rebellion gathered momentum in 1559 and invited English forces to help. Leith was besieged, and the ensuing conflict saw the inevitable food shortages, both within the town and among the besieging armies. Tensions rose within the town between the French forces and the locals, the former presumably keeping more of the supplies for themselves. It also saw constant bombardment, some skirmishes, an assault through a wall breach resulting in the deaths of about 200 soldiers, fire in the Sheriff Brae area on the south-west side of South Leith, and the destruction of the tower of St Anthony's and the tower, transepts and chancel of St Mary's (Wilson 1875, 414). There was significant loss of life on both sides to violence, hunger and disease (Bruce 1840; Wilson 1875, 414; Marshall 1986, 15; Paton and Cook 2016). The siege ended with the death of Mary of Guise on June 11th, 1560, with a ceasefire proclaimed at Leith six days later. Troops were withdrawn on July 13th and the French were ordered to destroy the bastions in the east of the town. This destruction was not total, however, and only rendered the fortifications useless for purposes

HISTORICAL AND ARCHAEOLOGICAL BACKGROUND

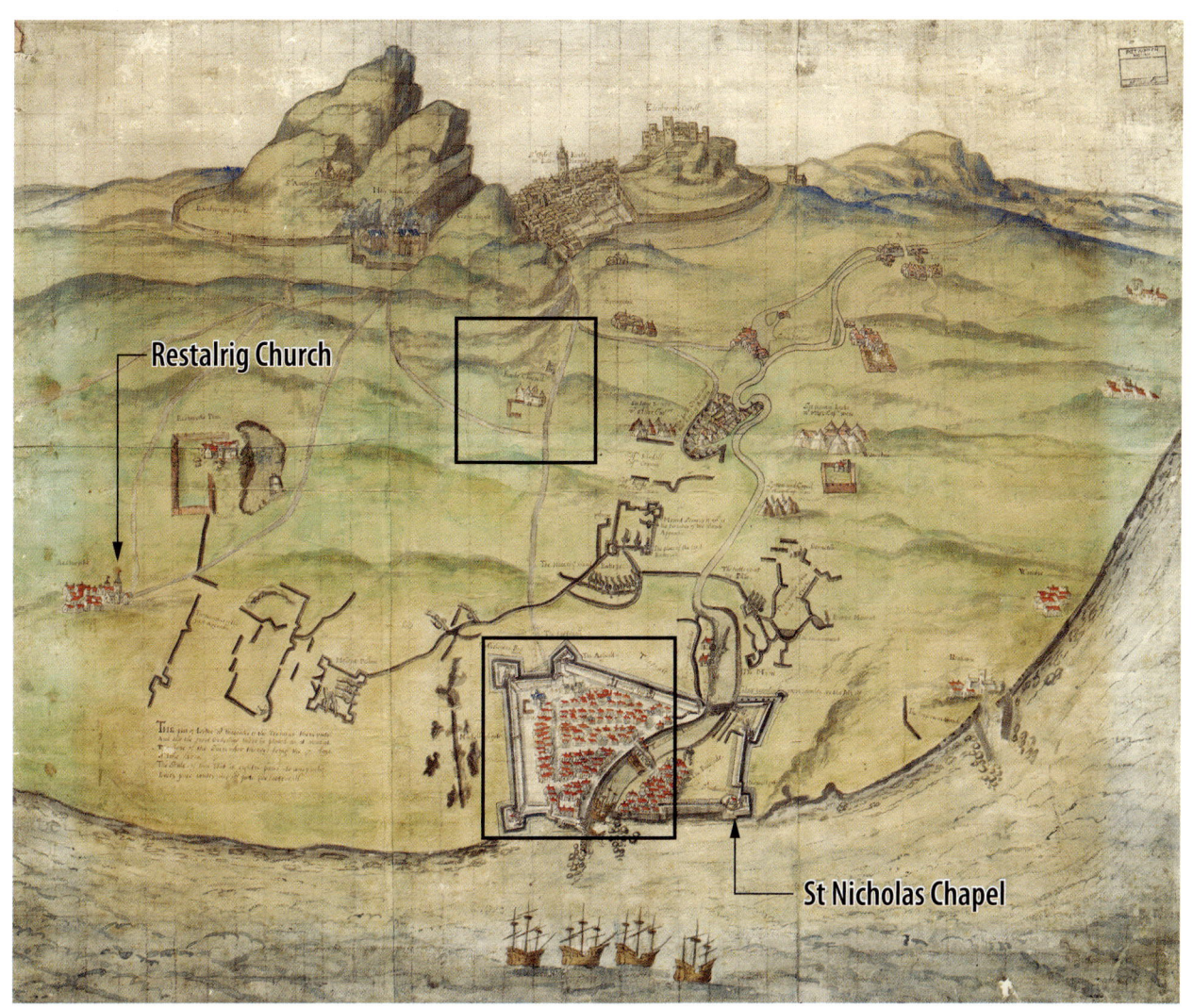

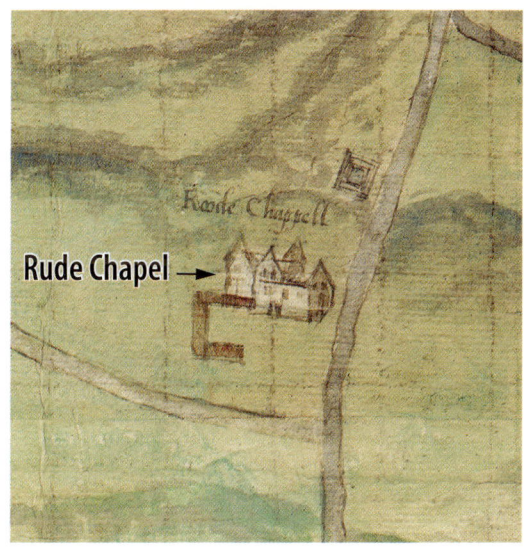

ILLUS 3.01
Petworth Map showing Leith on 7th June 1560, the day it surrendered after the Siege of Leith. It is viewed form the Forth thus north is to the bottom of the map
Reproduced with kind permission of Lord Egremont, Petworth House Archives

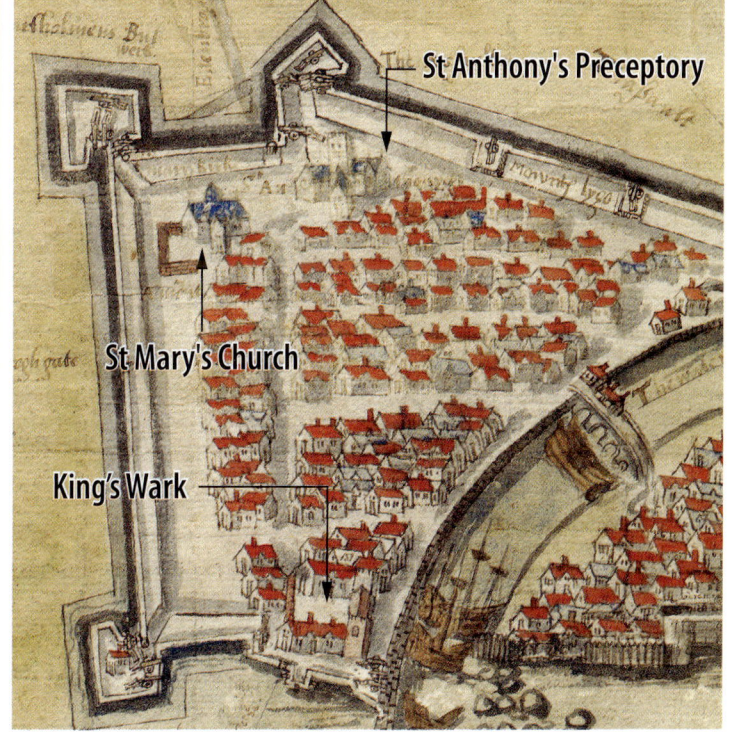

of war, with the remaining earth ramparts probably being allowed to erode naturally.

It is worth pausing at this point to note the evidence provided by the Petworth Map (**Illus 3.01**). It provides not only details of the town defences and siege works but also the first detailed plan of the town of Leith itself. It shows the dense huddle of the old village in the centre with more widely-spaced houses towards the south end of town arranged along streets running west from the Kirkgate. The east side of the Kirkgate was also lined with houses. St Mary's and St Anthony's are shown at the south end of the town, with an apparent churchyard wall enclosing an area to the east of St Mary's. The King's Wark parts of the King's Wark are a pale orange colour but it is not clear what this signifies. It seems the building was never fully repaired after the destruction of the 1540s (Mowat 2003, 126) and the colour perhaps denotes smoke blackening, or possibly stone without lime wash. Holyrood Abbey is depicted in the same colour as is the churchyard wall at St Mary's.

The events of 1560 resulted in Protestantism becoming entrenched in Scotland. The church at Restalrig, with its shrine to St Triduana and opposition to the Reformation, was ordered to be unroofed and parish worship was moved to the damaged St Mary's in Leith (Marshall 1983, 2), though it was not given official parish church status

ILLUS 3.02
Engraving of South Leith Parish Church by J & H.S. Storer, 1819. HES catalogue number SC 1589800
© Courtesy of Historic Environment Scotland

complex of buildings is visible at the northern edge of town on the seafront. The churches are both drawn with white walls and blue roofs, presumably representing stone walls, possibly lime-washed, and slated roofs. Some of the houses also appear to have slated roofs and most have white walls suggesting they are also stone-built. Most of the houses have red roofs and this appears to represent ceramic roof tiles. There is no archaeological evidence for the widespread use of roof tiles in Leith at this period but in terms of fire-proofing they have a clear advantage over thatch or wooden shingles. Both the walls and roofs of until 1609 (ibid, 24–5). The nave was the only functional part of the church left (Wilson 1875, 414) but it was repaired and reworked on a smaller scale (**Illus 3.02**).

Mary Queen of Scots arrived back in Scotland in 1561 to begin her short but eventful personal reign and landed in Leith before progressing up to Edinburgh. A practical benefit to Leith during her reign was the granting of a tolbooth to provide a courtroom and jail. Previously justice had been dispensed from Restalrig Tolbooth but this had been destroyed in Hertford's attack of 1544 and

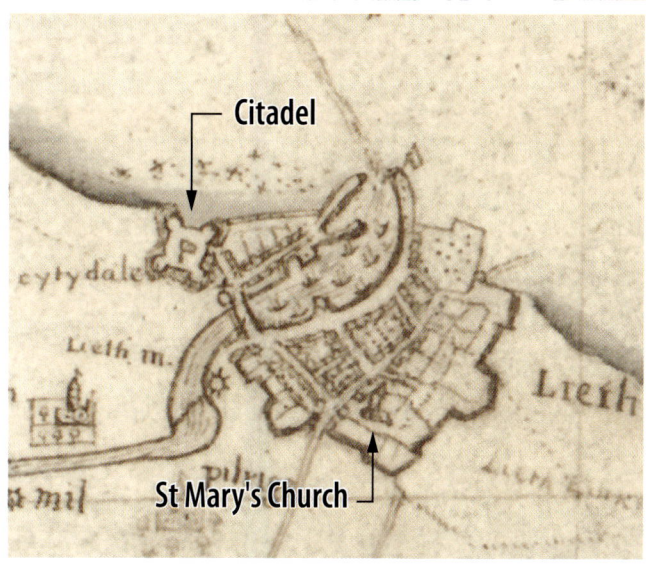

ILLUS 3.03
Extract from John Adair's 1682 map, showing the defensive walls and the location of St Mary's Church
Reproduced by permission of the National Library of Scotland

temporary accommodation had been in use since (Mowat 2003, 127). The building was constructed on the High Street (now Tolbooth Wynd), the site marked on the 1853 Ordnance Survey map (OS1853d) opposite the junction to Shore Place (It is now occupied by a substantial modern housing development). Later, in an effort to raise funds, Mary sold the superiority of Leith to Edinburgh, making Leith entirely bound to Edinburgh for perhaps the first time, and it is likely that this led to a loss of some of Leith's freedoms. Leith's defences were repaired and rebuilt in 1571 by the Earl of Lennox during the civil war between factions for and against Queen Mary, with new trenches being dug on the south and east sides of the town (Mowat 2003, 133; Paton & Cook 2016, 268–9, 276).

St Anthony's limped on after the Reformation, still providing care for the sick and aged, but at the end of the 16th century its wine revenues were transferred to St Mary's on the condition that it carry on St Anthony's good work. As a consequence, the King James Hospital was founded in 1614 in the south-west corner of St Mary's churchyard, across the road from the old St Anthony's (Marshall 1986, 152). Its primary function seems to have been as a home offering bed and board for the elderly and infirm, rather than as a hospital in the modern sense. It opened in about 1620 and initially took in around half a dozen old people, the number of residents rising to 13 in later years (Marshall 1983, 29).

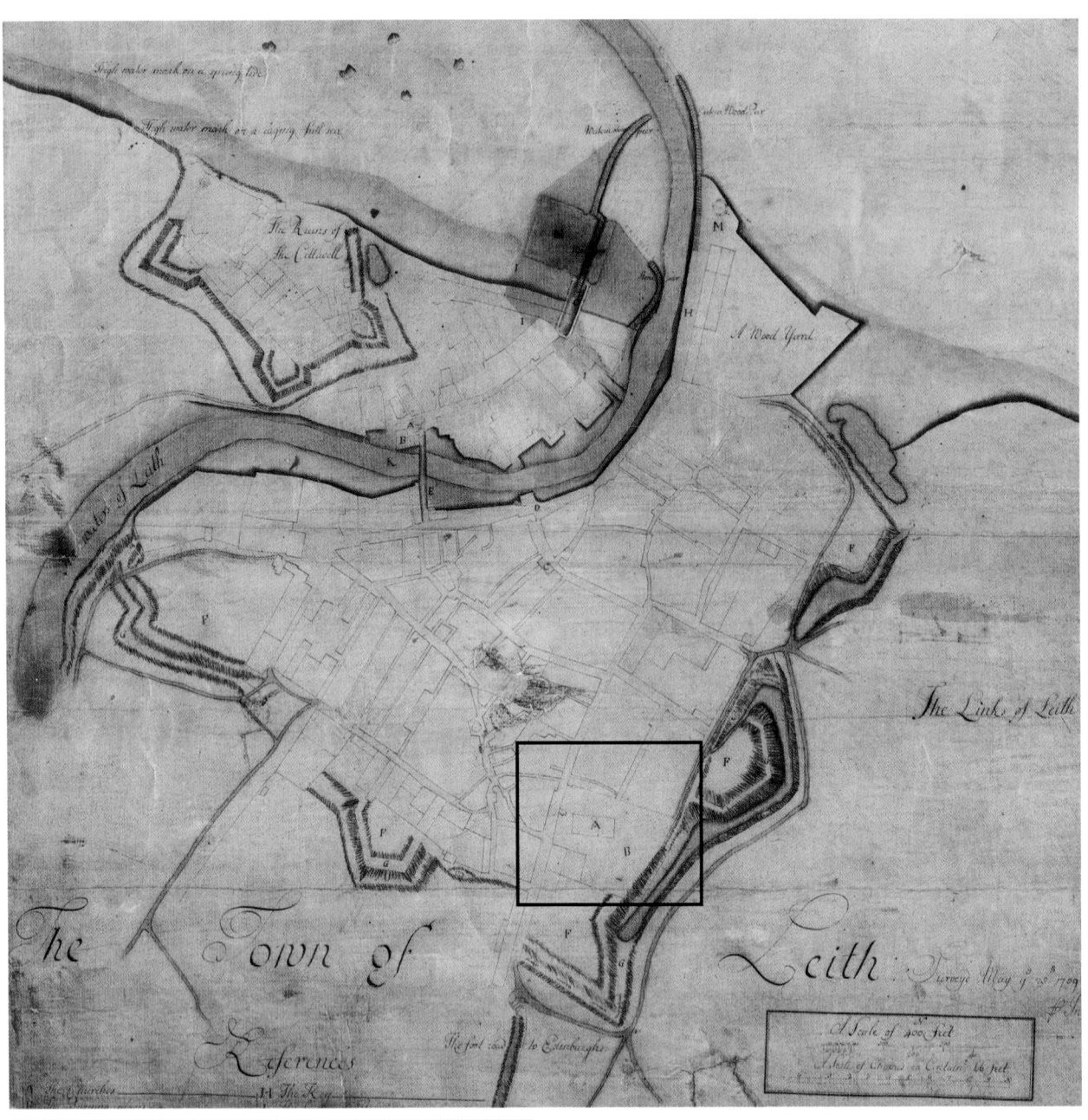

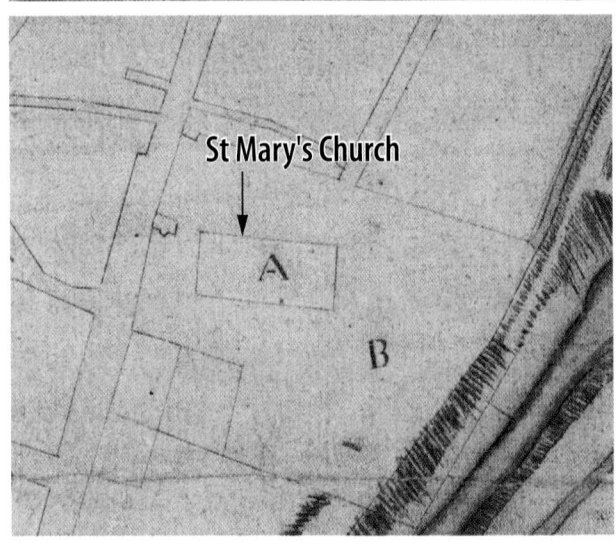

PAST LIVES OF LEITH. ARCHAEOLOGICAL WORK FOR EDINBURGH TRAMS

ILLUS 3.04
Extract from Naish's 1709 plan of Leith showing surviving defences and South Leith Parish Church and graveyard
Reproduced by permission of the National Archives, ref. MPHH1/32

HISTORICAL AND ARCHAEOLOGICAL BACKGROUND

ILLUS 3.05
Extract from Kirkwood's An Ancient Plan of the City of Edinburgh and its Environs, published in 1817 from a survey by John Fergus and Robert Robinson in 1759, showing surviving defensive banks and the extended South Leith Parish Church graveyard. Constitution Street excavation area overlain
Reproduced by permission of the National Library of Scotland

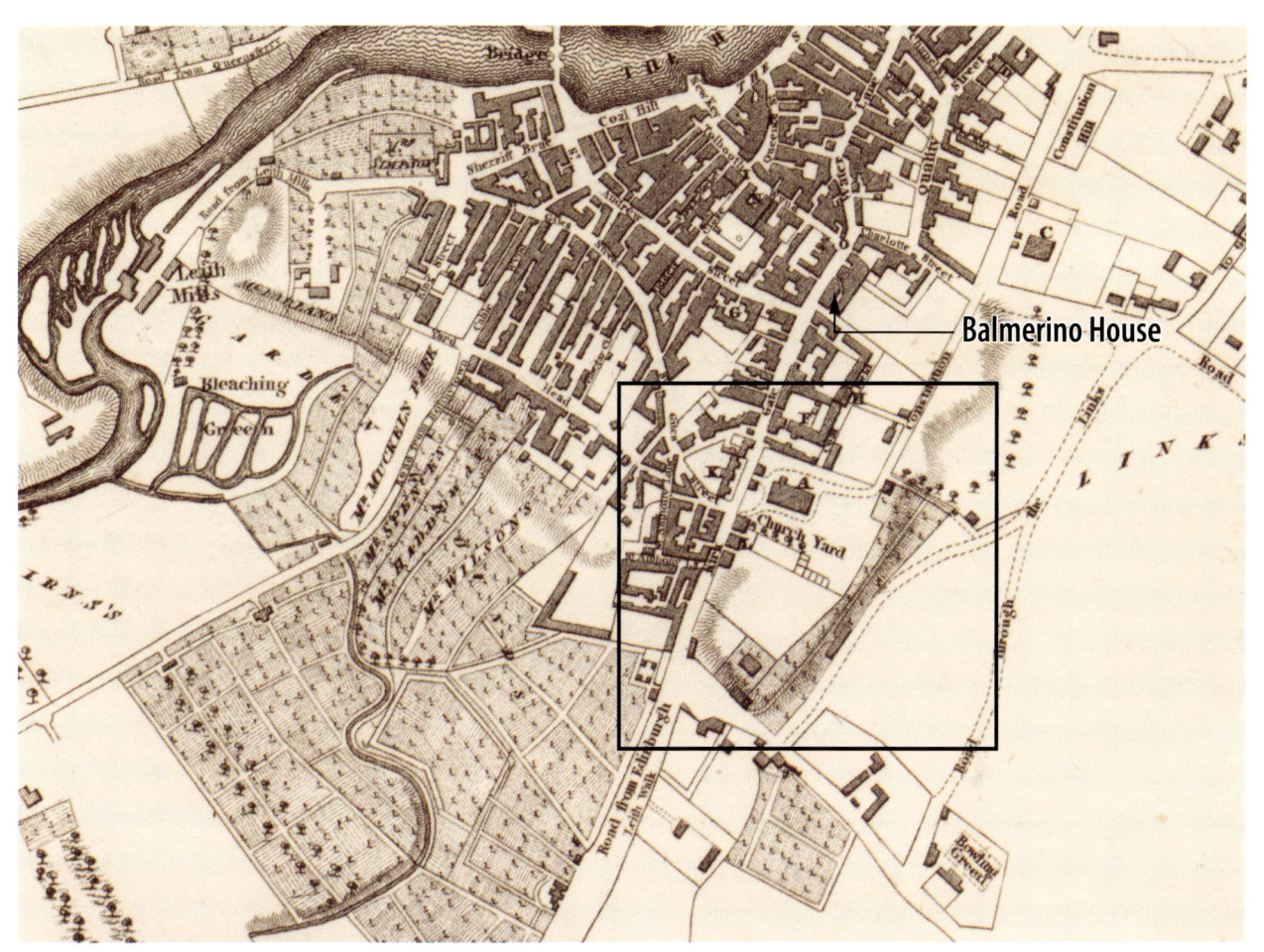

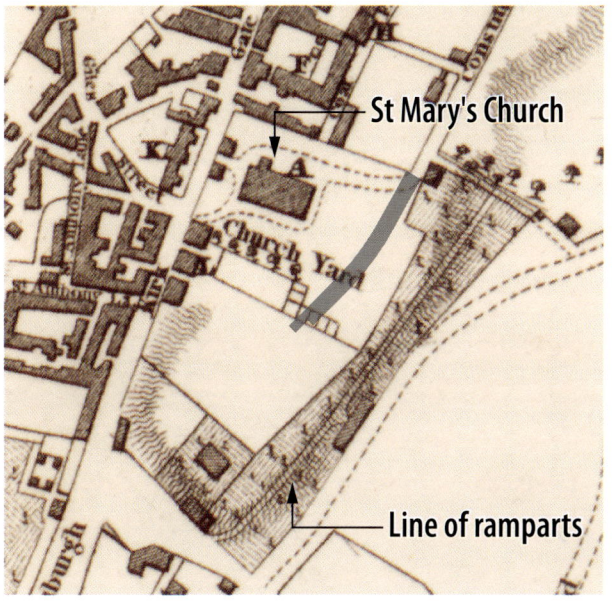

The town of Leith was partially refortified in 1649 in preparation to defend against the Commonwealth army of Oliver Cromwell. The defensive ditches were re-excavated and stone was brought in to aid construction (Mowat 2003, 1834; Paton & Cook 2016). John Adair's map of 1682 (**Illus 3.03**) indicates that the defences followed similar lines to the earlier fortifications. The detail of the eastern side of the defences shows they were enhanced by a bastion half way along the line of the wall.

Charles II had a brief stay in Leith in July 1650 while reviewing troops but was removed to safety when Cromwell's forces drew near. The Scottish force of 40,000 men defended a fortified line along the road between Leith and Edinburgh for nearly three weeks, eventually forcing Cromwell to fall back eastwards. The Scots forces marched after them, leaving a garrison at Leith but were defeated at the Battle of Dunbar in August 1650. Many people fled Leith for fear of the English troops and the

ILLUS 3.06
Extract from John Ainslie's 1804 map, showing South Leith Parish Church and the line of the newly-built Constitution Street with the overlay of the excavation area
Reproduced by permission of the National Library of Scotland

town became Cromwell's Scottish headquarters. His men took over St Mary's Church between 1650 and 1657, using the churchyard for military equipment and stores. They also used the King James Hospital, Trinity House across the road, and the tolbooth (Marshall 1986, 154; Mowat 2003, 182–5). The occupying forces remodelled Leith's defences by constructing a strong pentagonal fortress called the Citadel on the foreshore in North Leith, on or close to the site of a 16th-century bastion, guarding the entrance to the port (also clearly shown on Adair's map; **Illus 3.03**)

The remains of the fortifications were still partially visible until the 18th century. They are clearly marked on Naish's 1709 map of Leith (**Illus 3.04**) and the detail along the future Constitution Street compares well with that on Adair's map. A shaded line on Kirkwood's map, based on a survey undertaken in 1759 (**Illus 3.05**), shows the remains still visible, though somewhat altered. The layout of the fort survives in places in property boundaries and street plans. The layout of Ramsey's fort is reflected today in the arrangement of the Timberbush area (Wilson and Moore 2003). Archaeological traces of the defences and the Citadel in North Leith have been discovered at Dock Street (Stronach 2002b) and Coburg Street/East Cromwell Street (Lawson 1999; Hindmarch 2004), while the remains of the Citadel's gateway still survive as a stone arch in Dock Street.

THE PEOPLE'S STORIES – A WORD OF EXPLANATION

Julie Franklin

These stories do not pretend to be true biographies and mean no disrespect to the real people who lived and died in these bones. They are fictional constructs designed to help understand what life was like for the people of Leith at this time and to illustrate some of the archaeology and history presented in this monograph.

We cannot know these people's names and so cannot trace any details of their true lives. All we know of them are the few bare facts that their bones can tell us through osteological analysis and isotope study, roughly when they lived, and how they were buried. From there, I have filled in the blanks with imagined biographical details, based on what we know of late medieval Leith, in the same way as the hair styles and eye colour have been guessed at based on ethnic norms.

It was very difficult to write about how the people interacted with historical events, without knowing exactly when they were born. The radiocarbon dates gave a broad range for the date of death, but even the tightest of these (at 68.2% probability) covered a span of a generation (21 years) and were often far longer. Age ranges were also inexact, for adults these were typically in ten-year spans. So I assigned each of the people detailed a year of birth based on the mid-point of their age ranges, and on a likely date of death within the radiocarbon range, taking into account site phasing and any historical factors. Those skeletons not radiocarbon dated were given a date of death based on the average dating for burials within that excavation area. In some cases, birth and death dates were adjusted a little to take into account historic events but all are still well within the range of probability. In one case, the death date from some undated remains (p114–15) was pushed back 50 years on the reasoning that the skull was found as charnel within the graveyard soil and thus is likely to have been earlier than the dated articulated burials in that area.

I gave names to three of the individuals only because it was necessary in the narrative to distinguish between them as all were of the same age and sex and referring to them by skeleton number was too de-humanising for present purposes (p44–45). Common Scottish names of the time have been used.

Professions and life experiences were drawn up to match the evidence where possible. Thus, a man with a worn shoulder was assumed to be a joiner (p100–01), a man with broken ribs was assumed to be the victim of inter-personal violence (p86–87), signs of dental enamel hypoplasia (DEH) were taken to be indications of childhood poverty or illness, and familial relationships have been imagined between those in multiple graves. Each of the stories is just one of many possible life stories and scenarios which might have resulted in the archaeological remains recovered.

In some cases, the bones were more informative than others and only the 12 most distinctive cases were chosen for this treatment. Likewise, not all of the interesting stories told in the bones could be illustrated with a facial reconstruction.

All the facial reconstructions are shown at the end of this volume. A snapshot of the faces one might have seen walking through Leith in the 15th century. I live and work in Leith and some of these faces are remarkably similar to these one sees walking through the town in the 21st century.

INDUSTRY AND GROWTH IN LEITH

By the late 17th century, Leith had expanded within the boundaries defined by its defences, though development in North Leith was more limited in scale due to the presence of Cromwell's Citadel. Shipbuilding and outfitting along the Water of Leith continued to dominate. The growth in mercantile trade, in particular trading in Baltic timber, saw the conversion and expansion of Ramsay's Fort into a timber yard and exchange, and it was referred to as the Timberbush from as early as 1578 (Harris 2002, 556).

Traditional Leith industries such as shipbuilding continued to flourish along with all the industries linked to supplying the shipbuilders and outfitting and victualing the ships. A growing number of large-scale industries also began to appear within the town limits. These included a soap works erected by Nathaniel Uddart in 1619 (Russell 1922, 315) and a glassworks opened in 1663 (Turnbull 2001, 116). Other late 17th-century industries included woollen cloth manufacturers and a playing cards manufactory.

Trade in Leith suffered in the first half of the 18th century with the cloth trade particularly hard hit due to increased competition from England. This was one of the many economic issues resulting from the Union of the Parliaments in 1707. The downturn was not to last and by the mid-18th century a marked improvement in trade was taking place. Glass-manufacturing and shipbuilding were greatly increased during this period, with several glass houses in operation by the late 18th century (Russell 1922, 382). By the mid-18th century Leith began to expand beyond its fortifications, and in the early 1790s Constitution Street was formed to provide better access to Bernard Street and the Shore (Harris 2002, 179) (**Illus 3.06**). Great Junction Street was also formed at this time. Both these roads followed the approximate line of the earlier 16th- and 17th-century ramparts.

As the importance of the port increased over the following century, its development allowed for ever increasing trade. With the addition of deep water docks and an expansion westward to Newhaven in the 19th century, the docks became increasingly industrialised. South Leith Parish Church, in its present form, dates from a campaign of rebuilding of the old St Mary's by Thomas Hamilton in 1847–8. Little of the original 15th-century church is now visible, although the west piers of the original crossing can still be seen in the vestibules at the east end of the building.

The town's expansion led to a housing shortage and by the early 20th century there were many people living in slum conditions (Marshall 1986, 184). Slum clearance and town planning in the 1960s saw the building of high-rise flats and the destruction of the Kirkgate, Leith's main thoroughfare and retail street. The Newkirkgate shopping centre was built over its southern end and its route is preserved by the pedestrian path that leads through the shopping centre and continues north to Tolbooth Wynd. A few older buildings along its route still survive, most notably St Mary's/South Leith Parish Church and Trinity House.

EPIDEMICS IN LEITH

Julie Franklin

Epidemics characterised the later medieval and early post-medieval period in Leith as they did in the rest of Britain. In view of the nature of the archaeology discovered at Constitution Street it is worth considering these as major causes of death among the population. Records, however, are patchy, particularly in the earlier years. The severity of epidemics and the resulting death toll are rarely known with any accuracy and identification of the pathogens involved is not an exact science. However, for an epidemic to be recorded historically it must have had a reasonably high death toll and in many ways the exact pathogen involved is irrelevant for present purposes, compared to the death toll and the human reaction to it.

There were other mass causes of death and some of these in turn caused or exacerbated epidemic outbreaks. Famine was a constant threat and in years of poor harvests would have caused many deaths. It also had the effect of weakening the population, making outbreaks of disease more deadly. The later medieval period was characterised by cooler and wetter weather compared to the 13th-century medieval climatic optimum and harvests failed in a number of years (Oram 2014). Some of these famines were followed directly by outbreaks of disease. Warfare also took its toll when invading armies slashed and burned their way across the countryside. The famine of 1338–41 seems to have been due, at least in part, to the destruction wrought by English forces (Mowat 2003, 17). The famine of 1439 appears to have been of natural causes, caused by inclement weather, as does that of 1573–5 (ibid, 139). The English attacks of 1544 and 1547 (p22) also led to hardship. The Siege of Leith itself of 1559–60 led to hundreds of military deaths on both sides and would also have taken its toll on the civilian inhabitants (Campbell Irons 1898, vol 1, 280–6).

The most famous epidemic of all was the Europe-wide pandemic of the Black Death in the mid-14th century. Its effects in Scotland in 1349–51 have been played down in the past as there are relatively few historical records relating to it, but more recent studies have suggested that Scotland was severely affected and it is likely to have been worse in towns and ports with greater populations, more movement of goods and people and more unsanitary living conditions (Jillings 2003; Oram 2014, 234). The Black Death is no longer equated solely with bubonic plague, but debate continues about the exact disease responsible. It may have been a combination of bubonic, pneumonic and septicaemic plague (Jillings 2003, 17–24), or possibly a haemorrhagic fever or another unknown virus (Raoult et al 2000; Duncan and Scott 2004; Prentice et al 2004; Gilchrist and Sloane 2005, 209). It is believed to have killed one third of the Scottish population (Oram 2014, 230). Its effects on Leith were identified archaeologically at Water Street, where the area seems to have been abandoned for a time in the mid-14th century (Stronach 2002a, 419).

There were further outbreaks in 1361–2 and 1380, which were potentially as bad (Oram 2014, 230), and the following centuries were to see more plague outbreaks as well as epidemics of other diseases, including dysentery and possibly influenza and cholera. Other diseases which might have caused epidemics at this time include smallpox, measles, typhus, pneumonia, whooping cough, enteric fevers, tuberculosis, diphtheria, erysipelas (St Anthony's fire, see p21) and poliomyelitis (Shrewsbury 1970, 126–7).

The earliest surviving legislation for epidemic control measures dates to 1456 and includes quarantine of infected people in their homes, burning of infected property and restrictions on the movements of people (Oram 2007, 22). Scotland was ahead of England in this respect, possibly due to its regular contacts with Italy, France and the Low Countries (ibid). Further measures were introduced during subsequent outbreaks. During the 1499 outbreak all external trade and communications were shut down, the markets and schools were closed, and children, dogs and pigs kept off the streets (ibid, 24). Wool, skins, hides and cloth were particularly suspected of carrying plague and cargoes could be impounded and burnt. During the 1490s officials or 'cleansers' were employed to enforce plague restrictions, including burning or fumigating property and burying the dead (ibid, 28). The risk of transporting corpses across the parish and for large gatherings at funerals was understood by the beginning of the 16th century (ibid, 18). Penalties for concealing cases of plague were severe and could include hanging or drowning, but more often branding, banishment and forfeiture of goods (ibid, 26).

Foreign trade could often be blamed for the spread of plague and it is probable that Leith provided the conduit for some of these outbreaks; the 1624 outbreak in Edinburgh, for example, was blamed on the arrival of an infected individual from Gdansk (Oram 2007, 27). Ships could be quarantined and were sunk by drilling boreholes in the hull and then refloated after the sea had cleansed them. There are several examples where plague seems to have spread to Edinburgh from its rural hinterland rather than from foreign climes (ibid, 18). Nevertheless, the people of Edinburgh and the Lothian hinterland had reason to be wary of communication with Leith.

There was an outbreak of a disease in Leith and Edinburgh in 1495 which was identified in 1497 as 'grandgore', a Scots term for syphilis (Mowat 2003, 62). Attempts were made to curb the spread of the disease in Edinburgh and Leith by quarantining the victims on Inchkeith, an island in the Forth (Hamilton 1981, 18; Mowat 2003, 62). However, while syphilis was virulent and spread quickly in 16th-century Europe, it took years to kill sufferers and initial infection does not produce particularly distinctive symptoms. Thus, though the disease was little understood at the time, it is likely to have produced a different reaction to plague. Plague does seem to have followed shortly afterwards, however, with restrictions on movement and trade to limit the spread of the disease being implemented in 1499 (Oram 2007, 24).

The last major plague outbreak to hit Leith was in 1645–6 and is the best recorded. It seems to have been one of the more severe epidemics, though the lack of early records mean that the severity of earlier episodes cannot be fully understood. The death toll was recorded as 2421, which is half the estimated population of 4000–5000 people (Campbell 1827; Campbell Irons 1898, vol 2, 36). The large number of fatalities led to significant social and environmental health problems. At its height, in the summer of 1645, the session clerk of St Mary's noted that people who had died were being left unburied (Robertson 1911, 60). Plague victims were moved to temporary camps in Wester Links (adjacent to St Mary's) and Easter Links (beside Boothacre, Seafield) (ibid, 55). Many of the dead were buried on Leith Links. Archaeological evidence for this was discovered recently at St Mary's Primary School (p34–35), thought to represent some of those who died at the Boothacre camp.

The psychological problems of the survivors from such epidemics must have been significant. However, it is likely that the population bounced back fairly quickly after these outbreaks through a combination of increased

TABLE 3.01
Outbreaks of epidemics in Leith or possibly affecting Leith (Shrewsbury 1970, 188, 209, 260–1, 288; Gordon 1984, 118; Mullay 1996, 272–3; MacLennan 2001; Jillings 2003; Mowat 2003, 62–3, 111, 131, 139, 178, 178–9; Oram 2007; Oram 2014, 230–1; Oram pers comm)

DATE	DISEASE	LOCATION AND SEVERITY
1349–51	'the black Death' – bubonic, pneumonic and septicaemic plague?	Europe-wide pandemic, killed one third of Scots, archaeological evidence of affects in Leith, worse for the poor
1362–3	?plague	Possibly worse in southern Scotland, killed one third of Scots?, worse for rich
1379–80	?plague	Killed one third of Scots?
1401	?plague	Diminishing levels of mortality?
1402	dysentery	In eastern Scotland
1420	'le qwhew' – pulmonary, highly contagious and frequently fatal	In Scotland, worse for rich
1429–30	'flying sickness', 'swiftly spreading pestilence' – possibly influenza	Widespread in Edinburgh and Lothian
1439	'the wame ill' – gastro-enteric, possibly cholera	In Scotland, 'killed as many as any previous pestilence'
1456	?plague	In Edinburgh
1498–1500	?plague	In Edinburgh and surrounding area
1504–5	?plague	In Leith, St Anthony's badly affected
1529–30	?plague	In Edinburgh and Fife
1545	'violent peste' – plague?	In Leith and Edinburgh
1568–9	?plague	In Leith, Edinburgh and Canongate
1574–5	?plague	In Leith, Edinburgh and Forth area; Edinburgh lost 10% of population
1585–6	?plague	In Edinburgh and Fife
1587	?plague	'very grievous in Leith'
1597	?plague	In Leith and Edinburgh
1603–6	?plague	In Leith and Edinburgh
1624	?plague	In Edinburgh and ?Leith
1635	?plague	In Edinburgh and surrounding area
1644–5	plague	Death toll in Leith 2421, estimated as half population

birth-rate and immigration from neighbouring areas, which would also increase fertility (Chamberlain 2006, 172–3). Studies from elsewhere have shown that after an epidemic, population continues to rise until it reaches a level where the death-rate increases due to infectious disease and poor nutrition, and population levels fall again in a 44-year cycle. (Scott & Duncan 1998, 140, 187). In Leith, the continuing plague outbreaks over the course of this period would have considerably confused this model, though it is interesting to note the approximate 44-year gap between the outbreak of 1456 and that of 1498–1500.

A list of periods of epidemic in Leith has been compiled from a number of sources (**Table 3.01**), though this list should not be regarded as definitive or exhaustive, and some of the epidemics may have joined together to form longer outbreaks (eg 1498–1505). The noted locations record whether Leith and Edinburgh were specifically known to have been infected or if we can only assume they were based on infection in the vicinity or wider area, but the locations noted are by no means exclusive. While the effects on Leith were not always specified, the amount of traffic and trade through Leith from Edinburgh, the rural hinterland, other parts of Scotland and Europe mean that it would be difficult to isolate it from any outbreak in the vicinity. The crowded and unsanitary conditions in towns of this period would also have meant the disease spread more quickly there, particularly among the poor.

HISTORICAL AND ARCHAEOLOGICAL BACKGROUND

THE ARCHAEOLOGY OF HUMAN BURIAL IN SOUTH LEITH

It might be assumed that the history of human burial in Leith was closely linked to the ecclesiastical establishments of North Leith and South Leith. However, very few previous finds of human remains can be tied to any of these establishments with any certainty. North Leith grew out of the established settlement granted to Holyrood Abbey in its foundation Charter of 1128. Accordingly, it retained close associations with the abbey through the medieval period, though there is no historic evidence for any church, chapel or graveyard in North Leith until the 15th century. The small North Leith burial ground between Coburg Street and the Water of Leith dates from at least the mid-16th century, but, being close to the both St Ninian's to the east and St Nicholas' to the north, its origins are likely to be earlier with both dating from at least the late 15th century and St Nicholas' having a possible 12th-century origin (p19).

As South Leith was originally part of the parish of Restalrig, it has always been assumed that the people of early South Leith were buried at the parish church there. The church lies about 2km to the south-east (Canmore ID 52103; **Illus 3.01**) and is known to have existed from at least the 12th century. The graveyard of St Anthony's was presumably established with the preceptory in 1430 and is thought to have been to the south of the buildings, south of the now vanished St Anthony's Street and north of the present day Great Junction Street (Ordnance Survey 1853a). It was probably used by its canons, hospital patients, benefactors, and possibly also the wider towns-people. The graveyard of St Mary's is still extant around the present South Leith Parish Church and prior to this project was assumed to date back to the establishment of the church in 1483. It continued in regular use into the 19th century with occasional use up to the early 20th century.

In view of the findings at Constitution Street described in Chapter 4, it is worth reviewing other archaeological finds of human remains and the assumptions made to date, some of which are challenged by the Constitution Street discoveries. A newspaper report from 1834 (Scotsman 1834) records three separate incidents of finding human remains in that year and the few years prior to it. The first was in St Anthony's Street (which then ran west from the Kirkgate, about 80m south-west of St Mary's Church, now underneath the north-western part of the Newkirkgate shopping centre), during the installation of gas pipes (**Illus 3.07A**). Few details were given but they were reported to be in a decayed state and, as one of the skulls was noted to contain a musket ball, they were connected at the time to the Siege of Leith. In retrospect, it seems more likely that they relate to the graveyard of St Anthony's. The second find noted in the same report was while excavating the foundations of a new church on the Links, which must mean St Andrews Church (the only church which fits the details given, built in 1827 at the south-west corner of the Links, now the Edinburgh Hindu Mandir and Cultural Centre on St Andrew Place), about 180m south-east of St Mary's (**Illus 3.07G**). No details of these bones were noted but, given the descriptions of the other remains, this implies this was a deposit of unremarkable charnel.

The third group reported in 1834 was found 'at the head of Wellington Place behind Constitution Street', which would place it on the corner of Wellington Place and Laurie Street, approximately 90m south-east of St Mary's (**Illus 3.07E**). This amounted to 'several human skeletons embedded in a dry sandy mould mixed with submarine deposits' and more intriguingly, 'at a farther depth' nearly 100 skulls. The skulls were well-preserved, and the reporter was surprised to observe 'scarcely a carious tooth to be found among them' and 'sabre wounds' on 'one or two of the skulls'. He also noted 'in the same place' two pieces of large round shot (though does not note if these were stone or cast iron) weighing 6lb and 12lb.

The skulls were again understandably linked at the time to the Siege of Leith. However, if they had died during the siege, then where are the rest of their bodies? There are no historical records of mass beheadings which might have led to such a deposit. Given that the area was directly outside the defences in 1560, it seems unlikely that anyone from either side would have paused there long enough to bury human remains during the siege itself. The presence of the round shot is probably misleading. The shot may well relate to the siege, but only in so far as this area was heavily bombarded in 1560. The sabre wounds would suggest violent death, but these do not necessarily point towards this one specific event. The reporter's level of expertise in pathology (or his opportunity to examine the bones closely) should anyway be questioned due to his observation of a near complete lack of caries among the skulls. It is hard to imagine any population from this time, medieval or post-medieval, high born or low, Scottish, English or French, where caries was not rife. It is possible that they are in fact far older and date back to prehistory when caries levels were lower (Roberts and Cox 2003, 31), but they were recorded as well-preserved suggesting this is unlikely. It seems more likely that the skulls represent charnel disturbed during the cutting of the mid-17th-century defensive ditch (**Illus 4.73**, p141 for approximate relative locations of remains, E, and ramparts). This special treatment of displaced skulls was noted on a smaller scale during the Constitution Street excavations. In this context, it is possible that the reported sabre wounds on the skulls actually represented spade or mattock cuts made by the workmen (either in 1834 or during the original ditch-cutting). The finding of presumably in situ burials in the same location might represent an eastward extension of St Mary's graveyard, though they were probably found too far south to make this likely. It is also possible that they

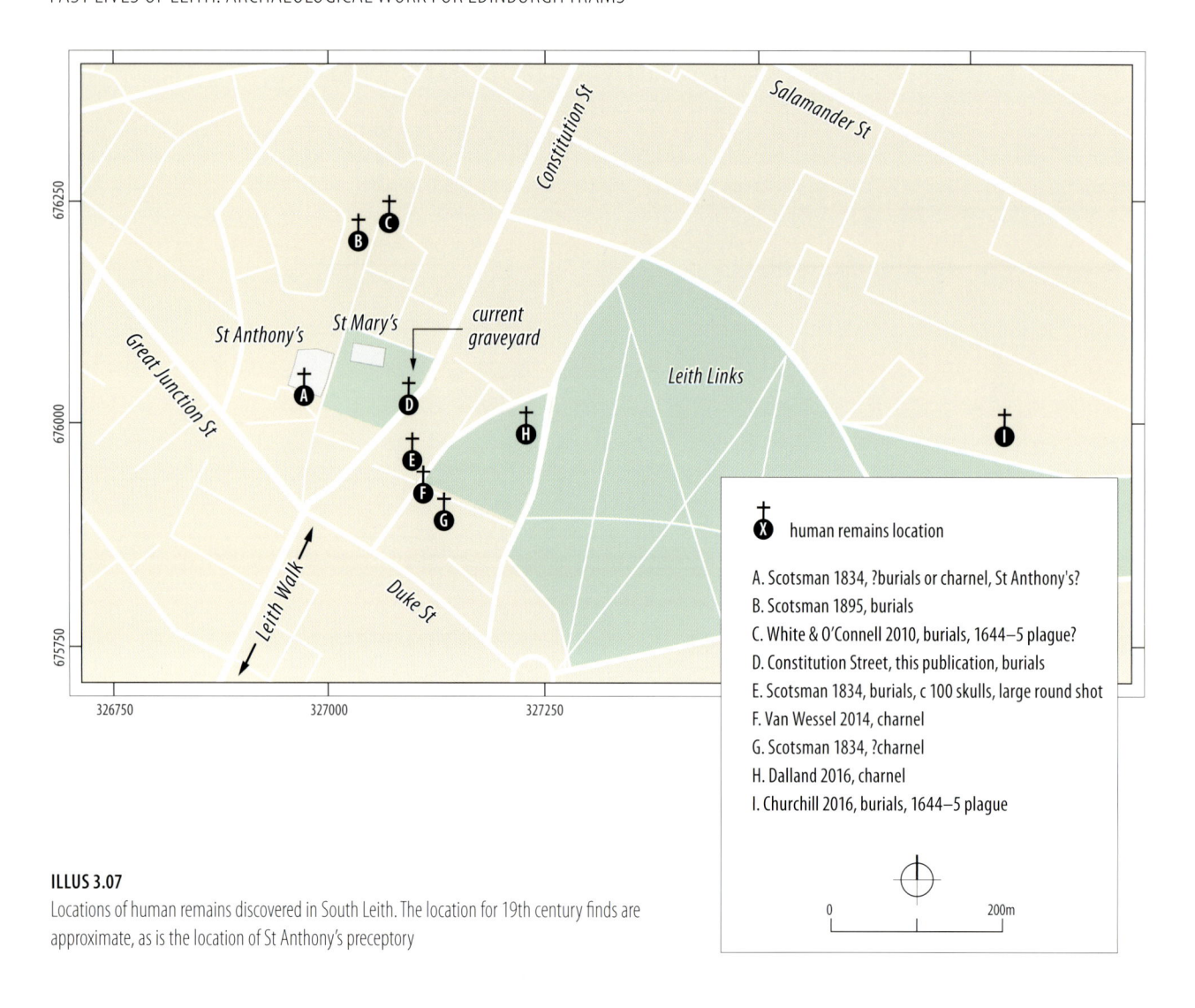

ILLUS 3.07
Locations of human remains discovered in South Leith. The location for 19th century finds are approximate, as is the location of St Anthony's preceptory

Map legend:
- human remains location
- A. Scotsman 1834, ?burials or charnel, St Anthony's?
- B. Scotsman 1895, burials
- C. White & O'Connell 2010, burials, 1644–5 plague?
- D. Constitution Street, this publication, burials
- E. Scotsman 1834, burials, c 100 skulls, large round shot
- F. Van Wessel 2014, charnel
- G. Scotsman 1834, ?charnel
- H. Dalland 2016, charnel
- I. Churchill 2016, burials, 1644–5 plague

represent part of the cemetery attached to the Wester Links plague camp of the 1644–5 plague outbreak (p31).

More recently there have been two other finds of disarticulated human bone in this same area. In 2013, a pit directly to the west of St Andrew's Church on the corner of St Andrew Place and Academy Street, about 140m south-east of St Mary's Church (**Illus 3.07F**), was found to contain human remains with other disarticulated fragments found nearby. These were interpreted as the reinterred remains discovered during the construction of the St Andrew's Church (noted above). Radiocarbon dates were obtained for bones within and outwith the charnel pit and were both contemporary (SUERC-49161, 434±34; SUERC-49162, 445±34). These dates calibrated (to 95% probability) to 1416–1618 and 1411–1615. Based on their location and dating, it was suggested that they may date from one of Leith's plague outbreaks (van Wessel 2014, 3). The original calibration of these dates did not consider the marine reservoir effect. The $\delta^{13}C$ levels indicate the marine component to the diet of these individuals would have been 26% and 12% respectively (p12). A recalibration using the same parameters for dates during this project gives results of 1455–1645 and 1435–1635 (*Appendix 3*, p234).

Several more disarticulated bones were found in a series of charnel pits on the Links just to the north-east of St Andrew's (**Illus 3.07H**) during the excavation of a new service trench in 2015, about 190m east of St Mary's Church. These were not dated but, again, were interpreted as reinterred remains disturbed during construction work in the area, and with a possible connection to plague burials (Dalland 2016, 3).

Evidence for the burial of 81 individuals was discovered in 2016 at St Mary's Primary School, prior to the construction of a new school extension. The site lies on the north-eastern side of the Links about 750m east of St Mary's Church (**Illus 3.07I**). The earliest burials were in pits and some of the later individual graves were aligned N-S and S-N. Most of the latter were buried in coffins. Post-excavation work on this assemblage was at an early stage at the time of writing but numismatic dating from coin purses buried with some of the bodies places these burials squarely in the mid-17th century, contemporary with the 1644–5 plague outbreak (Churchill 2016). This cemetery would seem to be for some of those who died at the Boothacre camp on Easter Links (p31) and provides the first firm archaeological evidence for the burial of the plague dead on the Links.

In 2004, excavations in advance of the construction of a new church hall to the rear of the 19th-century church of St Mary's Star of the Sea found a small cemetery (White and O'Connell 2009). The site was formerly occupied by Balmerino House constructed in 1631 fronting onto the Kirkgate between the current Coatfield Lane and Queen Charlotte Street, about 140m north of St Mary's (**Illus 3.07C**). Four inhumations were discovered, with a few disarticulated remains representing at least two other individuals. The in situ burials were all of well-built adult men apparently buried without coffins and, unusually, all were aligned approximately N-S. One individual displayed signs of trauma with healed fractures to the skull, foot and several ribs. The stratigraphic relationship of the burials to the house was not clear. Two skeletons were radiocarbon dated (SUERC-5369, 315±40; SUERC-5370, 380±40) and were calibrated (to 95% probability) to 1470–1650 and 1440–1640. However, pipe facets in the teeth (hemispherical tooth wear caused by the habitual clenching of a clay tobacco pipe stem between the teeth) of both dated individuals indicated they were very unlikely to date to before c 1590 when the smoking of tobacco in clay pipes began to be practiced in Britain. It was also reasoned that the burials could not post-date c 1630 after which point they would have been 'outside the front door of [Balmerino] house' (White and O'Connell 2009, 29). It was suggested that the burials either formed part of a larger St Mary's graveyard that was later truncated, were soldiers who died during the 1560 Siege of Leith, or were hanging victims, executed at the nearby tolbooth (ibid, 17–18).

There are, however, problems with all these theories. An association with the Siege of Leith is inconsistent, chronologically, with the presence of pipe facets in the teeth. The depiction of the town on the Petworth Map of 1560 (**Illus 3.01**) shows urban development as far south as the church and thus it seems unlikely that the graveyard extended significantly (ie 120m) further north in the late 16th or early 17th century. It also seems unlikely, on this basis, that there was open ground in this area at this time suitable for the burial of executed criminals. The hanged felons theory otherwise has some merit. It would fit chronologically and would be consistent with the unusual orientation of the burials, denying the men true Christian burial. The lack of trauma associated with hanging (ie a fractured hyoid bone) is not inconsistent as this occurs only rarely (White and O'Connell 2009, 18). Arguably, the lack of women in the group might also agree with the theory and while most executed felons were collected by their families and buried conventionally, it is possible that these were the exceptions.

It is interesting to note that once again both dated samples had $\delta^{13}C$ levels consistent with high marine components to their diet (Sk1, 21%; Sk5, 25%). A recalibration of these dates taking this into account (using the same parameters as noted above, see p12) gives significantly later dates for both burials (1490–1955; 1460–1795; see *Appendix 3*, p234). This changes the picture considerably and, assuming both burials are contemporary and date from a period when clay pipe smoking was commonplace, then it is very likely that both are 17th century, with a peak of probability around the mid-17th century. If this is so, then they do indeed post-date the construction Balmerino House and were buried very close to it. There are two periods during the mid-17th century during which circumstances might have necessitated unusual burial practices: the plague of 1644–5 or the military and political events of 1650.

Given the presence of only well-built men and the distinct signs of trauma in one, it is possible that these men were soldiers, though there is no sign that any met a violent death. The house, from 1643, belonged to Lord Balmerino, who was a leading Covenanter. That same year he took up arms against the parliamentary forces in England, accompanying General David Leslie on his march south. Balmerino died in 1649. When Charles II stayed in Leith the following year in July 1650, he lodged at Balmerino House, showing continued links between the family and the royalist cause. Shortly after, the town was under siege for several weeks. After the defeat at the Battle of Dunbar, Leith was occupied by Cromwell's troops (p27–28). Although there is no evidence they took over Balmerino House, given its Royalist connections it seems unlikely that it would have escaped their attention. It certainly seems likely Balmerino's family were elsewhere by this point and the house may have been empty. It is possible to imagine during these dramatic events some sort of incident that might have led to four men being killed in the vicinity of the house. However, it is not clear why that might have led to their being buried in this manner. If the deaths were violent then there is no osteological trace of this. If the deaths were in some way underhand then why were they buried in four separate and relatively neat graves, and if they were not then why were they not buried in the neighbouring St Mary's graveyard? Both areas were within the defences.

The unusual N-S alignment, however, may offer the key. They provide a clear link to the plague of 1644–5 via the burials recently discovered at St Mary's Primary School. As described above, some of the St Mary's Primary School burials were aligned N-S and there was a demonstrable link to the 1645 Easter Links plague camp. It is possible that the Balmerino House burials represent the northern end of the cemetery used by the Wester Links plague camp near St Mary's. It might be imagined that plague burials during this time would have been further east, being as they are, very close to Balmerino House. At the time, the town was probably largely unenclosed to the east. It is likely that little remained of the 16th-century defences and, in 1645, the Cromwellian defences were yet to be built. There were no buildings further east than the house, even as late as 1759 (**Illus 3.05**). It is possible then that there was no barrier and little to demark this burial area from the Links and that it may have been brought into use as part of the Wester Links camp. Equally, the men may represent members of the Balmerino household, or military retainers of Lord Balmerino, who had accompanied their lord into England in 1643. They may have died at the height of the outbreak and been buried as best as could be managed given the restrictions in place at the time. The associated disarticulated remains would seem to be at odds with this being a single use burial site, although disarticulated remains were also found at St Mary's Primary School and they are such frequent finds in this general area of Leith that their presence should not cause any surprise.

Another newspaper report in 1895 (Scotsman 1895) records finds of human remains 'at the premises of Messrs Gibson, fish-traders'. Cross-referencing between Post Office directories and the Ordnance Survey map (Post-Office Directory 1895, 113; Ordnance Survey 1948b) locates this at 124–6 Kirkgate at the south-west corner of the then St Andrew Street and the Kirkgate, about 110m north of St Mary's Church (**Illus 3.07B**). Five skeletons were noted, and were clearly articulated, one being in 'an almost complete state of preservation'. Two of the skulls had 'marks which might have been inflicted by violence'. Though their orientations were not noted they are very close to the burials found outside Balmerino House and it is tempting to suggest they form part of the same cemetery. However, they are located on the opposing side of the Kirkgate to Balmerino House, so this seems unlikely. They are also close to the St Mary's graveyard but, again, on the wrong side of the Kirkgate and the derivation of these remains is therefore unclear.

The Constitution Street excavation revealed the largest archaeological assemblage of human remains in South Leith (**Illus 3.07D**) and indeed in Edinburgh. Their place within this archaeological background, and in view of new research into the archaeology of the Siege of Leith (Paton and Cook 2016), is discussed in Chapter 4 and alternative interpretations for some of the earlier finds of human remains are suggested.

LEITH WALK

Leith Walk forms the main historic access linking the two medieval burghs of Edinburgh and Canongate with their port. The road follows a direct line from the Neitherbow Port at the eastern end of the Old Town via the Calton Gorge (present day Leith Street), linking with Leith's Kirkgate. Given the natural line of the route it is almost certain that Leith Walk predates the first mention of the Kirkgate in 1398 (Harris 2002, 346). The road is clearly depicted on the 1560 Petworth Map (**Illus 3.01**).

The strategic importance of Leith Walk was emphasized in the 17th century when the road was fortified by the cutting of two deep ditches and construction of an embankment along its length under the orders of General Leslie as a defensive measure against the Commonwealth army of Oliver Cromwell in 1650 (Chambers 1967, 360). The ditches were subsequently filled in during 1652, probably using much of the existing bank material (Leith Research Group 1978–9, 3). This would suggest that the raised embankment was not as prominent as initially thought, although enough may have survived to form a reasonable path. The route was described by Daniel Defoe in 1725:

a very handsome Gravel-walk, 20 Feet broad, continued to the Town of Leith, which is kept in good repair at the public charge, and no horse suffered to come upon it (Defoe 1762, 86).

Development along this route was slow at first with a new 'Botanick Garden' established at Shrubhill in 1764 by Professor John Hope being one of the earlier features (Leith Research Group 1978–9, 4). As Edinburgh expanded into the New Town in the 18th century the opening of the North Bridge seemed to be the catalyst for development along Leith Walk. As a result of the increase in wheeled traffic, by 1776 the road was in a serious state of disrepair and Edinburgh Council let a contract for its reconstruction as a metalled surface. The surrounding area gradually developed over the 18th and 19th centuries from farmland and estates with isolated pockets of housing to a more built-up urban character. Ainslie's map of 1804 shows a road edged by market gardens, with housing along about half the street frontage on the west side, less on the east.

By 1852 the Ordnance Survey map shows more housing encroaching from both the Edinburgh and Leith ends, with another area of development along the western side around the church at Pilrig (Ordnance Survey 1853b; 1853c). Pilrig, to this day, marks the traditional boundary

HISTORICAL AND ARCHAEOLOGICAL BACKGROUND

between Edinburgh and Leith. In 1852 the Leith Walk area was still dominated by market gardens but the beginnings of industry were also present, particularly on the eastern side of the road with a chemical works and two foundries, a saw mill and a malt kiln towards the northern end, and a glassworks, engine and machine works, another sawmill and various other workshops towards the southern end. By 1877 housing and industry were beginning to squeeze out the gardens (Ordnance Survey 1876; 1877) and by 1896 (Ordnance Survey 1896a; 1896b) the area was largely recognisable in its modern form with many of the existing tenements already constructed.

A CHAPEL, FRIARY AND HOSPITAL AT GREENSIDE

Greenside is the name given to the area on the lower north-western slopes of Calton Hill, on the east side of the road between Edinburgh and Leith (now Leith Walk). It has been called this since at least the 12th century (Harris 2002, 289), and the name is preserved in the current street names Greenside Place, Greenside Row and Greenside Lane. The earliest structure reputed to have been built at Greenside is that of the Rude Chapel of Greenside (rude or rood being a term for cross). The name probably derived from its association with Holyrood Abbey, which was located less than 1km to the south-east. In 1456 James II granted land belonging to Holyrood Abbey at Greenside on the northern slopes of Calton Hill to Edinburgh to be used for tournaments, outdoor plays and revels (Grant 1883, vol.3, 102). At the same time, it is thought that he established a chapel at the site, though it is possible that one may have existed prior to this. Harris (2002, 289) suggested that the purpose of the chapel was to provide for the dead and wounded of the tournaments.

Part of the lands of Greenside was later given to the Carmelite order in 1518 for the foundation of a friary. The Carmelites were established in Scotland as early as the 13th century and they had an existing house at South Queensferry (now South Queensferry Parish Church). The Provost of Edinburgh, James, Earl of Arran, and the burgesses of Edinburgh gave the charter to John Malcolme, Provincial of the Carmelite Order which included the lands of Greenside with the Chapel of the Holy Cross (Wilson 1875, 411). The chapel therefore clearly already existed at this time though the charter provides the first evidence for it. A chaplain, Sir Thomas Cannye, was appointed in 1520, two years after the grant and the friary is thought to have been completed in 1526 (Canmore ID 52403). It is assumed that the friary complex included the earlier chapel but there is no firm evidence of this and it is therefore possible that the friary was built elsewhere on the lands.

Although short-lived, the friary had an interesting history. Shortly after it was completed there seems to have been some friction between it and Holyrood Abbey in 1529/30. This resulted in the 'downcasting' of the house where the friars lived (Cowan and Easson 1976, 136), though the friary continued in use. In 1534 the friary again gained notoriety when fisherman David Straton and priest Norman Gurley (or Courley) were both burned at the stake outside the chapel at Greenside, having committed separate acts of heresy to established Catholic doctrine and then refusing to recant. The location for the execution was chosen because it was visible as far afield as Fife and might encourage those who saw it not to follow suit (Foxe 1583, 1006). The friary is further mentioned in 1554/5 when money was given to it by the city for repairs (Grant 1883, vol.5, 151).

The only known depiction of the establishment is on the Petworth Map of the Siege of Leith in 1560 (**Illus 3.01**). There it is labelled as 'Roode Chappell' rather than as a friary, and shown as two perpendicular buildings both roofless, implying it was derelict by this time. It is possible that this was a recent occurrence. Both of Edinburgh's other friaries, Dominican and Franciscan (or Blackfriars and Greyfriars, both on the southern side Edinburgh), had been destroyed by Reformers in June 1559, though there is no record of similar destruction at Greenside. Equally, it is possible that it was damaged by Protestant forces during the Siege of Leith itself. It was certainly no longer occupied by 1563 (Cowan and Easson 1976, 136). Interestingly, the title of the Padre Prior di Greenside survived until at least 1845 within the Carmelite Order in Rome.

The derelict chapel or friary site became the Greenside Hospital for Lepers in 1591. The hospital was established by Edinburgh merchant John Robertson 'pursuant to a vow on his receiving a message from God' (Wilson 1875, 411–2). This was the last of many leper hospitals established in Scotland, the first of which was set up in Aniston, Scottish Borders, in 1177 (Hall 2006, 90). It was recorded that on its first day the Greenside hospital took in five male lepers accompanied by two wives of their own volition. It is unclear as to the scale of the general population of the hospital, but records do survive recording its operational regulations and the severity of punishments meted out

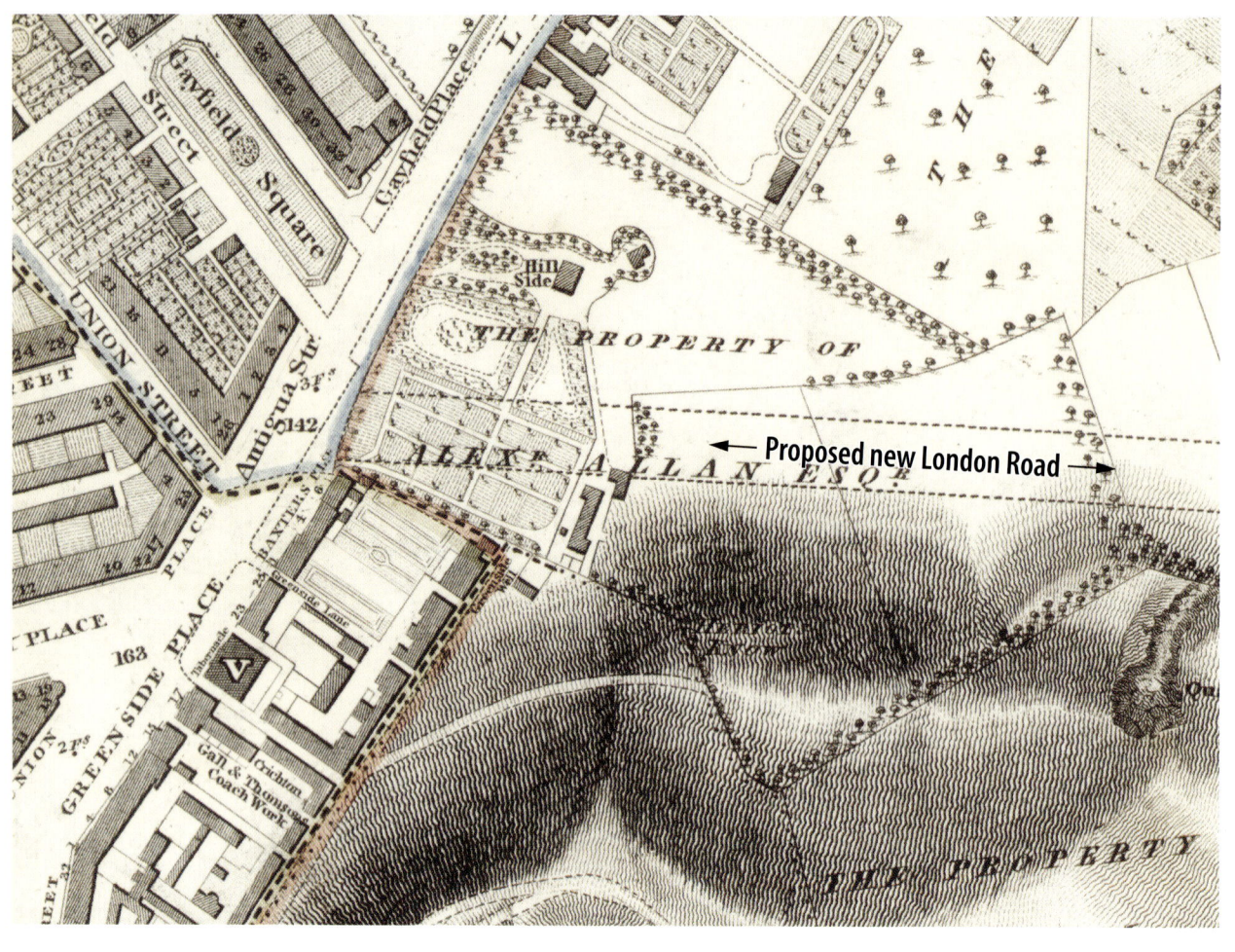

ILLUS 3.08
Extract from Robert Kirkwood's This plan of the City of Edinburgh and its environs, published in 1817, depicting the proposed new London Road
Reproduced by permission of the National Library of Scotland

for transgressions. The gates were opened from sunrise to sunset so that the inmates could beg alms from passers-by, but they had to remain within the walls at all times. The keeper could hang without trial any leper who left or attempted to leave the establishment, on the hospital's own gallows. In 1636 Charles I granted the hospital to Edinburgh Council and it was demolished between about 1652 and 1657 (Arnott 1818, 198, 258; Chalmers 1887, 760; RCAHMS 1951).

Until the London Road excavations, the exact location of the chapel, friary and hospital was unknown. Although clearly marked on the 1560 Petworth Map (**Illus 3.01**) to the north of Calton Hill, subsequent mapping failed to identify the location of any buildings belonging to this site. Kirkwood's and Roy's surveys of the 1750s, for example, both show the area as open farmland (Kirkwood 1817a; Roy 1755). It has been asserted that the chapel was located in the vicinity of the Gallows Lee (Grant 1883, vol.5, 151). These gallows were located halfway between Pilrig and Greenside (presently Shrub Place) as marked on Adair's 1682 map (**Illus 3.03**) and again on Kirkwood's 1759 survey (Kirkwood 1817a). This is problematic as it causes some confusion as to the exact location of the chapel and it seems likely that the author had the Gallows Lee confused with the separate gallows known to have existed at the site of the leper hospital. Grant's belief that hangings were still being carried out at Greenside in 1717 (Grant 1883, vol.3, 182–3) confirms that he had indeed confused the two gallows sites, the hospital having been demolished some 60 years prior to this.

The area around Greenside Place and the top of Leith Walk were soon encroached upon. In 1780 James Craig prepared plans to widen Leith Walk, involving the demolition of a number of buildings. John Ainslie's map of 1804 (Ainslie 1804) is the first to clearly depict a number of buildings and gardens to the east side of Leith Walk, including a house and large planned garden belonging to a Mr Alexander Allan at the location of the junction with the future London Road. It seems little or nothing remained of the chapel, friary or hospital by that time as no ancient ecclesiastical structures were marked on this map.

Kirkwood's 1817 map (**Illus 3.08**) names Mr Allan's house as Hill Side and depicts the proposed route for the soon to be constructed London Road. Designs by the architect William Henry Playfair were used to develop the northern

HISTORICAL AND ARCHAEOLOGICAL BACKGROUND

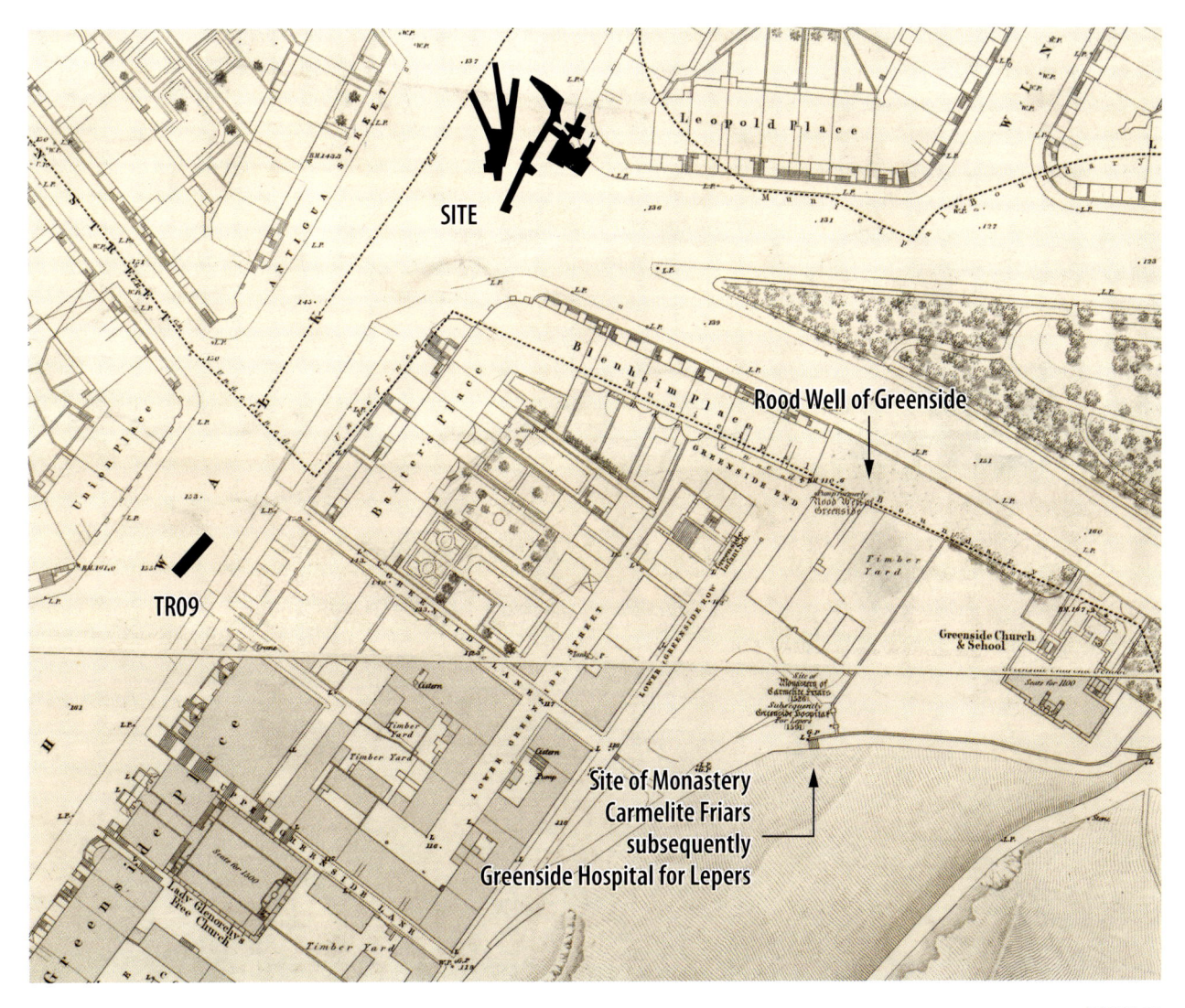

ILLUS 3.09
Extract from the 1852 OS map, Sheets 25 and 30 marking the presumed location of the Rude Chapel including an overlay of the monitored trench excavations
Reproduced by permission of the National Library of Scotland

side of Calton Hill from 1820 onwards. Kirkwood's 1821 plan (Kirkwood 1821) depicts the proposed design for Royal Terrace to the south of London Road, on the northern slopes of the hill, and for the street plan to the north of London Road. Much of this was eventually constructed, though building work continued until the end of the 19th century.

The 1852 Ordnance Survey map (Ordnance Survey 1853c; 1854) (**Illus 3.09**) is the first to mark the site of the friary and hospital on an area of ground at the north-east end of what is now known as Greenside Row, to the south of Blenheim Place on the north side of Calton Hill. This map also records the location to the north of a pump formerly the 'Rood Well of Greenside'. This well is marked on Ainslie's earlier map (Ainslie 1804) in association with a small rectangular building identified as a washing house. This same structure appears to be marked on Kirkwood's 1759 survey (Kirkwood 1817a), the first detailed map of the area, and survives until the 1830s (Wood 1831; Thomson 1832). It is possible that the wash house well was misattributed by the later Ordnance Survey surveyors, but equally possible that an old friary well continued in use long after the destruction of the buildings it originally served.

THE ORIGINAL TRAM NETWORK

DLG Hunter (1992) has written a detailed history of Edinburgh's transport in two volumes and the following is adapted from his account. Prior to the introduction of stage coaches into Scotland in the late 17th century, people generally either walked or rode a horse. The rapid expansion of stage coaches followed quickly behind the improvements in the road surfaces across the country. The first public coaches in Scotland were between Edinburgh and Leith, established by Mr Henry Anderson in 1610 at a cost of 2d per journey. By 1673, 20 hackney coaches were registered in Edinburgh. These were apparently not very successful as only nine coaches were registered in 1778. At this time sedan chairs were still popular with 188 being recorded for hire (Bremner 1869).

Public transport in Edinburgh was spasmodic and small-scale until the early 19th century, with light railways and omnibuses developing from the 1830s. Key events included the opening of the Union Canal in 1822 and the establishment of the Edinburgh to Glasgow railway in 1838. Railways provided the most important means of travel between Edinburgh and its outskirts after the 1840s, but inner-city transport was dominated by horse-pulled buses operated by a number of different proprietors, with John Croall being the most predominant. Steam buses were trialled but found to be unsuited to the roads and unreliable.

Changes in the legal framework allowed the inception of a tram company in Edinburgh from 1871. The system was expected to be more comfortable and reliable, though was still fully reliant and legally bound to horse power (Booth 1988, 3). The inaugural service (Haymarket to Bernard Street) ran on 6 November 1871. The tracks were laid by Sir James Gowans with John Macrae as engineer. These lines complemented and partly replaced the pre-existing horse-drawn carriage from Edinburgh to Leith, the only essential difference being the addition of guide rails. The tram cars were double-decked holding a total of 36 passengers and pulled by two horses (**Illus 3.10**). Shrubhill on Leith Walk was used as the depot for the Edinburgh Street Tramways Company from 1871. Initially the company rented horses from John Croall, but took this over themselves in the ensuing decade. By 1879 trams were being built at the Shrubhill depot with eight trams a year being constructed there. The hills and the heavy

ILLUS 3.10
A horse drawn tram, Tollcross, 1907
Reproduced by kind permission of Edinburgh City Archives, Lothian Regional Transport Collection

HISTORICAL AND ARCHAEOLOGICAL BACKGROUND

ILLUS 3.11
This image is labelled 'the first Cable Car at Pilrig 1898 but Hunter (1992) identifies it as a trial run from Shrubhill to St Andrew St, 1st June 1899. The rubble from cable construction work lies all around. The central groove through which the gripper grips the cable can clearly be seen between the tram rails. Most of the passengers appear to be top-hatted dignitaries. The photograph looks down Leith Walk, with the junction of Albert Street on the right and the spire of St Paul's Church, Pilrig visible as a smudge to the left of the tram car
Reproduced by kind permission of Edinburgh City Archives, Lothian Regional Transport Collection

loads took their toll on the horses and the average life span of a tram horse was just four years.

The horse-pulled tram network did not serve Edinburgh fully, having particular problems with the steep hills in the north part of the town. After some negotiation, a new bill was passed and the Edinburgh Northern Tramways Company was formed in 1884. This was backed by Dick Kerr and Co, a Kilmarnock rolling stock and engineering firm. The first cable-hauled routes in January 1888 were from Trinity and Stockbridge to the centre of town, powered by the two 300hp Dick Kerr engines at the Henderson Row depot. The cable haulage system used a cable housed in a shallow trough between the tram rails and could haul larger tram cars that could hold up to 54 passengers (**Illus 3.11**). However, cable breakages could reduce the entire system to a standstill.

In 1894 Edinburgh and District Tramways took over the running of the trams in Edinburgh but not in Leith or Portobello. Their operations stopped at the boundary between Edinburgh and Leith, half way down Leith Walk at Pilrig. A power station was constructed at the end of the Edinburgh line at Shrubhill, becoming active in 1899. The Shrubhill depot contained a large engine house and boiler house with two pairs of engines, each of 500hp, and three coal-fired boilers (**Illus 3.12**). All the tram company's buildings were of a high standard, but those at Shrubhill were larger than elsewhere and more decorative (**Illus 3.13**).

The separate tram companies caused many problems for commuters, not least of all being the 'Pilrig Muddle'. This was caused by passengers between Edinburgh and Leith having to change trams (from cable-drawn to horse-drawn) at Pilrig on Leith Walk. Petitions were sent to the Board of Trade to end this predicament but between 1889 and 1895 arguments and petty bickering between the different corporations failed to resolve the issue (Campbell Irons 1898, vol 2, 349). The trams in Leith were still horse-drawn until they were taken over by the Leith Corporation who introduced an electric system in 1905, powered by overhead cables, the first to be introduced in Scotland. This did not end the problems at Pilrig, as the Edinburgh trams continued to operate the cable system.

ILLUS 3.12
Shrubhill engine room and cable winding gear, c1900. The men in the centre of the picture show the scale of the machinery.
Reproduced by kind permission of Edinburgh City Archives, Lothian Regional Transport Collection

The Leith Corporation was eventually taken over by the Edinburgh Corporation in 1920 who quickly moved ahead with the electrification of the Edinburgh routes, mainly due to cheaper running costs and less complex engineering, putting an end to the confused exchange of passengers at Pilrig. Henderson Row power station in Stockbridge was shut down first and Tollcross on the western side of Edinburgh transferred to run on oil rather than coal. The Shrubhill engines were shut down in June 1922 and the last power station at Tollcross ran the last cable trams to Shrubhill. The Tollcross cable station was powered down in March 1923.

Edinburgh Corporation introduced its first motor bus in 1914. In 1928, given the increasing importance of buses, the Edinburgh Corporation Tramways Department was renamed the Edinburgh Corporation Transport Department. The tram network of Edinburgh was eventually phased out between 1952 and 1956 with the final tram turning into Shrubhill depot on Friday 16th November 1956 (Booth 1988, 9). The Shrubhill depot now stands derelict. Most of the building has been demolished but the brick elevations of the earlier part of the structure have been preserved along with a tall chimney. The depot at Tollcross was converted into a bus depot but was subsequently demolished in 1967 to make way for a modern fire station. The depot at Henderson Row had been used as a police vehicle pound and a garage prior to being converted into offices. All that remains of its original use are two large pulley wheels set into the wall as a monument to its original use.

HISTORICAL AND ARCHAEOLOGICAL BACKGROUND

ILLUS 3.13
Surviving walls of the Shrubhill depot

NEW TRAMS FOR EDINBURGH

Following public consultation in 2003, plans for a new tram network for Edinburgh were agreed by the Scottish Parliament. After approval and funding, preparation works commenced in 2007. The first tram ran on 31st May 2014, 143 years after the first Edinburgh tram ran and 58 years after the last. Unlike the original double-decker trams the new trams, supplied by Construcciones y Auxiliar de Ferrocarriles of Spain, comprise single-decked multi-carriage rolling stock 43m long, with the capacity to carry up to 250 passengers. The top speed of these trams is 80km/h (50mph). The modern trams, like Edinburgh's last trams, are powered by an overhead electrical supply supported on frequent posts placed along the route. Other tram furniture includes a number of raised platforms with glass shelters, electronic displays and ticketing machines.

The existing line is 14km long from York Place in the New Town to Edinburgh Airport. An earlier proposed route extended the line down Leith Walk and Constitution Street to the Shore and onwards to Ocean Terminal in Newhaven (p3). This is yet to be built, though it is still being discussed and plans may yet come to fruition. Chapters 4 to 7 provide an account and discussion of the archaeological findings along this proposed route to Leith, from the south end of Leith Walk to the north end of Constitution Street.

PEOPLE'S STORIES

A GROUP OF WOMEN WHO DIED IN AN EPIDEMIC, LATE 1380S/EARLY 1390s–1420s

These women, we will call them Mary, Margaret and Janet, were all born within four years of each other. Margaret and Janet were sisters, born in 1388 and 1392, the daughters of an Edinburgh journeyman cordiner, a maker of shoes, wooden pattens and other leather goods. The girls helped their mother with the housework from an early age. Margaret was the older of the two and had to draw the household's water from the well and carry it to the house in wooden stave-built buckets, work that took its toll on her back. Janet suffered frequent periods of ill health as a child and was given easier work, mainly tending the open hearth in the centre of the room and cooking. With no chimney, the room was smoky which left her congested and wheezy and often with a pain in her nose and head. Both girls had to help with the chore of the weekly laundry.

Mary was born in 1390 to a father who was a Leith boat skipper, ferrying people, animals and goods across the Forth to and from Fife. He made a decent living as he and his fellow boatmen conspired to fleece travellers for as much as they could get away with. Their passengers were in no position to argue, the only alternative being facing the equally roguish ferrymen of Queensferry, 10 miles upriver, or a 70-mile detour via Stirling Bridge.

In 1398 Margaret and Janet's father saw an opportunity to better himself. He couldn't afford to join Edinburgh's Incorporation of Cordiners, but he could afford to become a founder member of the Leith Incorporation of Cordiners. The family piled their possessions on a hired cart and walked out of the Netherbow Port and down the track to Leith. They had lodgings on Broad Wynd, a cramped shop front with two rooms behind. Business was good. Leith was beginning to prosper in its new status as Scotland's leading port. A new wooden wharf was being built at the harbour to allow ships to unload cargoes more easily. The constant stream of ships and sailors meant there was far more trade than there should have been for such a small town and the locals were happy to be able to shop without walking up the hill to Edinburgh.

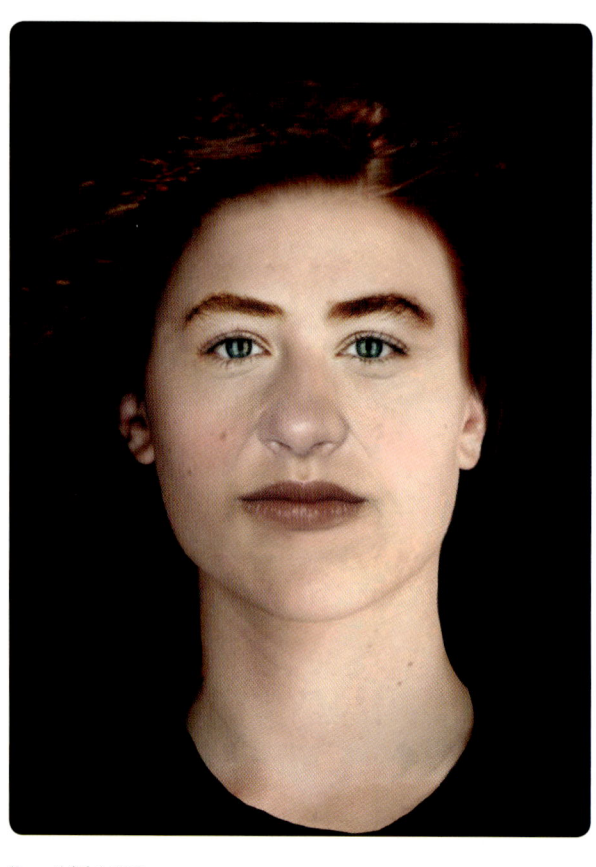

In 1400 the girls and their mother watched from behind curtained windows as the Henry IV of England and his troops landed in Leith and marched through the town to besiege Edinburgh Castle. All were very keen to catch a glimpse of the English king. The shiny armour and colourful banners waving in the wind were an impressive sight, but all agreed the 33-year-old king was disappointingly ordinary looking. He was, though, preferable to the 62-year-old current king of Scotland, Robert III, who they had glimpsed on another occasion. Mary had a closer view of the proceedings as her father had been engaged to row supplies from Henry's ships, there being so many they could not all dock at the new wharf, and she begged him to take her with him.

The following year there was an outbreak of plague. The boatman was one of the first to be afflicted by the pestilence, catching it from an infected passenger from Fife. He passed it to the rest of the family, and he, Mary's mother and two of her brothers died. The cordiner and his family closed shop and stayed indoors and prayed. Both parents had survived

'Janet' (Sk0643)

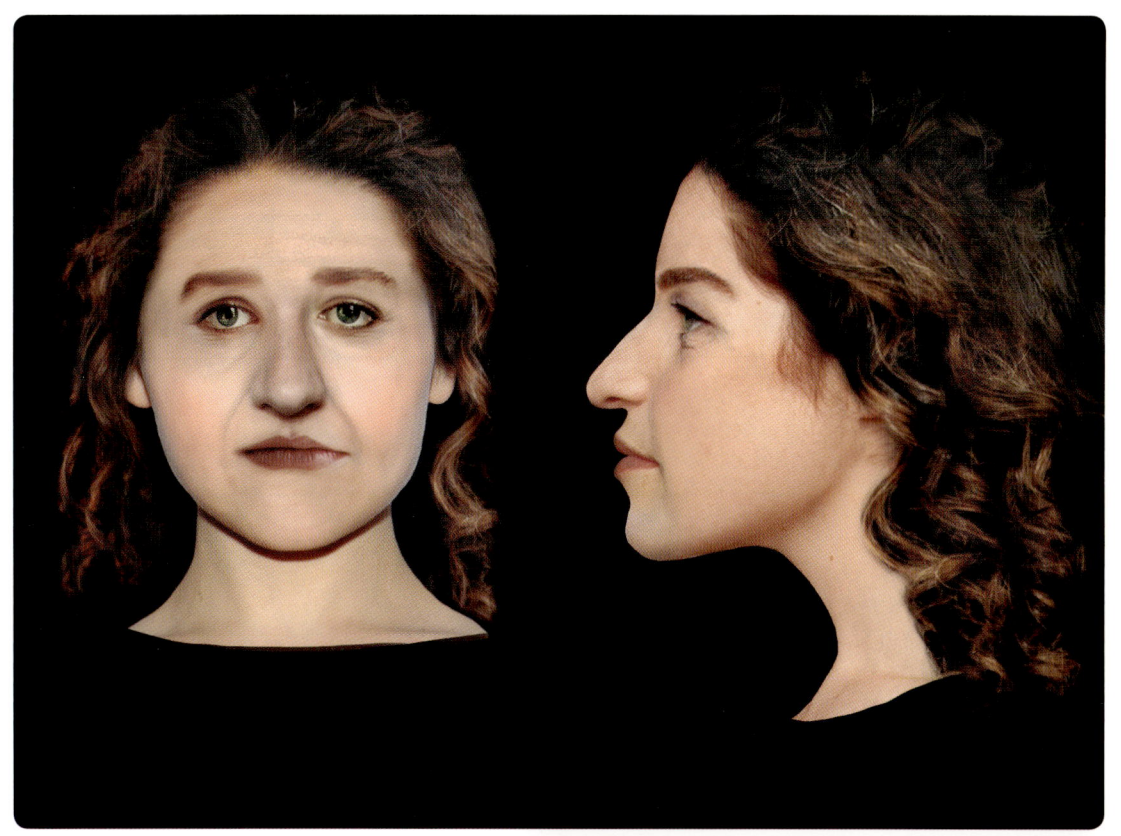

'Margaret' (Sk0639)

the outbreak of 1380 and knew what to expect. They were all spared. But these were the start of hard times for the 11-year-old Mary and her only surviving little brother. They were taken in by a widowed aunt who ran a cookshop, cooking big pots of stew to feed locals who had no cooking facilities. She barely made enough to keep herself and she made the children work hard to earn their keep. They all lived off stale leftovers.

The cordiner and his family meanwhile had settled into their new life and home. He took on an apprentice to help fulfil orders and a scullery maid to help with the housework. He had a flesher for a neighbour now. He complained about the smell of the carcasses rotting in the yard behind his shop, but they made their peace with a deal for a supply of hides from his slaughtered cattle, which they sent to be tanned at a workshop on the edge of town. All was going well for them when, cruelly, the bloody flux struck the town in 1402 and, in the unsanitary conditions in the growing town, it spread quickly and there were many sick on Broad Wynd. The girls' mother died, and the 14-year-old Margaret now became mistress of the house. She cooked, cleaned and jealously guarded the household keys which

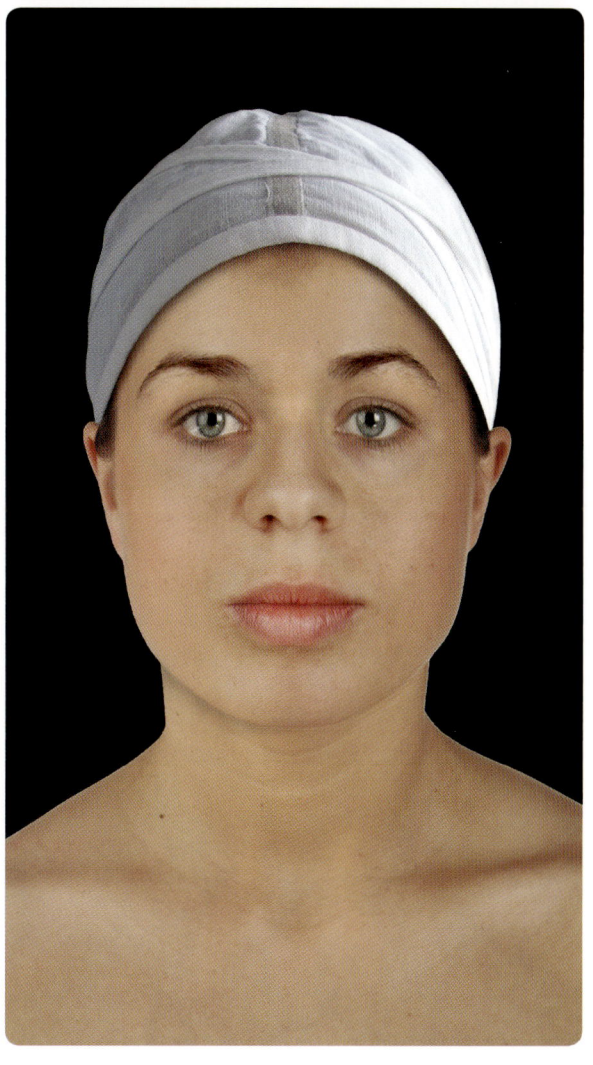

'Mary' (Sk0637)

A GROUP OF WOMEN WHO DIED IN AN EPIDEMIC, LATE 1380S/EARLY 1390s–1420

PEOPLE'S STORIES

Grave 0589, from left to right Sk0643, Sk0637, Sk0639, Sk0646

hung from her belt and were a symbol of her status. She married her father's apprentice and her father was pleased enough, seeing it as a way of keeping the business within the family.

Mary meanwhile had caught the eye of the flesher of Broad Wynd who delivered meat to her aunt. She agreed to be his wife, only too glad to get away from her aunt. She quickly made friends with the cordiner's daughters next door. The next few years, Mary and Margaret shared the joys and sorrows of pregnancy and motherhood together. Between them they suffered stillbirths, miscarriages, and two of their children died before they were a year old, but they ended their first decade of marriage with seven children between them and counted themselves blessed. Janet, meanwhile, helped in the workshop. She was a good seamstress. She had had much time to practice during her childhood years of illness, and she helped with the decorative finishing of their fancier products. She still had regular headaches. She would commiserate with Mary who often suffered from toothache. Mary's teeth were weak due to her childhood privations and they became worse during her first pregnancy, one of them falling out.

Le qwhew (**Table 3.01**) struck the following year. It started with a sore throat before developing into a high fever. Most young children and the elderly seemed to shake it off fairly easily. It was the otherwise healthy adults who were the worst hit. Many of those who caught it quickly developed breathing difficulties and died. The neighbours on Broad Wynd, having lived through pestilence before, thought themselves safe. The cordiner's

Irregularities in the bone of the nasal chamber caused by chronic maxillary sinusitis due to upper respiratory infection, allergies, smoke, environmental pollution or dust. Condition would have caused a number of unpleasant symptoms, including congestion, facial and dental pain, coughing, sore throat, bad breath and wheezing. Sk0643 ('Janet')

SKELETON	0637, 0639, 0643
Grave	0589
Location of grave	Constitution Street, Area 6
Burial details	Three of four bodies buried in group burial, along with older child (6½–8½), Sk0646
Age	All younger middle adults (25–35)
Sex	All female
Stature	Sk0637 ('Mary'), 147cm or 4'10" Sk0639 ('Margaret'), 151cm or 4'11" Sk0643 ('Janet'), 156cm or 5'2"
Radiocarbon date	Associated Sk0646 1400–1440 (68% probability) 1315–1355, 1390–1455 (95% probability) see Table 4.02, Illus 4.31, p84–85
Other dating evidence	Possibly linked to an epidemic outbreak? Found in Phase 1 cemetery, in use from beginning
Finds	–
Pathology	Sk0637 ('Mary'), canine (33) with two roots, AM tooth loss, calculus, caries, DEH, periodontal disease Sk0639 ('Margaret'), spinal and costal DJD, Schmorl's nodes Sk0643 ('Janet'), right maxillary sinusitis, left mild cribra orbitalia, enamel pearl on molar, lingual aspect of root, Schmorl's nodes, Calculus, DEH, periodontal disease
C/N isotope (diet)	–
O/S isotope (origins)	–
See also	Illus 4.09, p58; p73; Illus 4.23, p82; p88; p89; p108; Illus 4.53
Facial reconstruction artist	Paloma Galzi (Sk0639 'Margaret', Sk0643 'Janet'), Hew Morrison (Sk0637 'Mary')

house was worst hit. Mary came around from next door to help nurse the sick but was soon ill herself and dare not return home for fear of passing it to her family. Mary, Janet, Margaret, and her 7-old-son, all perished on the same day. It was the height of the epidemic and all but one of the chapel gravediggers were also sick. Margaret's husband was still weak, and Mary's had just fallen ill himself. They all had the remaining children to care for. The old cordiner took the bodies of his daughters, his grandson and neighbour down to the chapel and he and the one remaining elderly gravedigger dug a large grave for all of them. Together they placed them in, first the child, then Margaret, his mother, next to him, then Mary and finally Janet. The cordiner took some comfort from the fact that his girls would lie next to each other in death and prayed they might be with their mother in heaven.

A GROUP OF WOMEN WHO DIED IN AN EPIDEMIC, LATE 1380S/EARLY 1390s–1420

ILLUS 4.01
Constitution Street site under excavation, looking north-east: opening up the western panel of Area 2. The existing South Leith Parish Church and graveyard are visible in the top right of the picture

4 | CONSTITUTION STREET EXCAVATIONS

Julie Franklin with contributions by Carmelita Troy, Penelope Walton Rogers, Scott Timpany, Sarah-Jane Haston, Kate Britton and John A Lawson

Prior to this project it was thought that the graveyard of St Mary's Church, the current South Leith Parish Church, did not extend eastwards beyond its present boundaries. The first evidence that it did was found when engineering test-pit investigations in April 2008 identified articulated human remains beneath Constitution Street (Humble & Murray 2008). Subsequent evaluation work from September to October 2008 identified further articulated human remains. The cemetery was shown to extend across Constitution Street immediately below the present road surface and both pavements (Humble & Murray 2008; Murray 2008). As a result, and to avoid delays in the expected construction timetable, a set-piece archaeological excavation was undertaken between April and September 2009 to exhume the human remains and investigate associated archaeological deposits that were to be affected by the proposed construction of the tram network (**Illus 4.01**).

The excavation covered an area of 110m x 8m across the existing road surface. Due to traffic management restrictions the full area was divided into a series of 10m areas termed Areas 1 to 11 (p8–10; **Illus 4.02**). The excavations did not include the areas below the pavements.

A total of 305 articulated skeletons and disarticulated skulls representing a minimum of 73 further skeletons were excavated, and there were a further 15 graves with no associated skeletal remains. Many of these burials were packed densely within the excavated area (**Illus 4.03**). The survival of complete skeletons was rare due to truncation by later burials, ditches or modern services. Men, women and children were all represented and there was evidence for a variety of grave types.

Of the 305 in situ inhumation burials excavated 30 were selected for radiocarbon dating (**Table 4.02**, p84). The calibrated dates ranged from 1275–1395 to 1475–1795. Significantly, three of the dates certainly predated the established 1483 date for the foundation of St Mary's Church and the results have thus challenged the accepted ecclesiastical history of South Leith (p82–83).

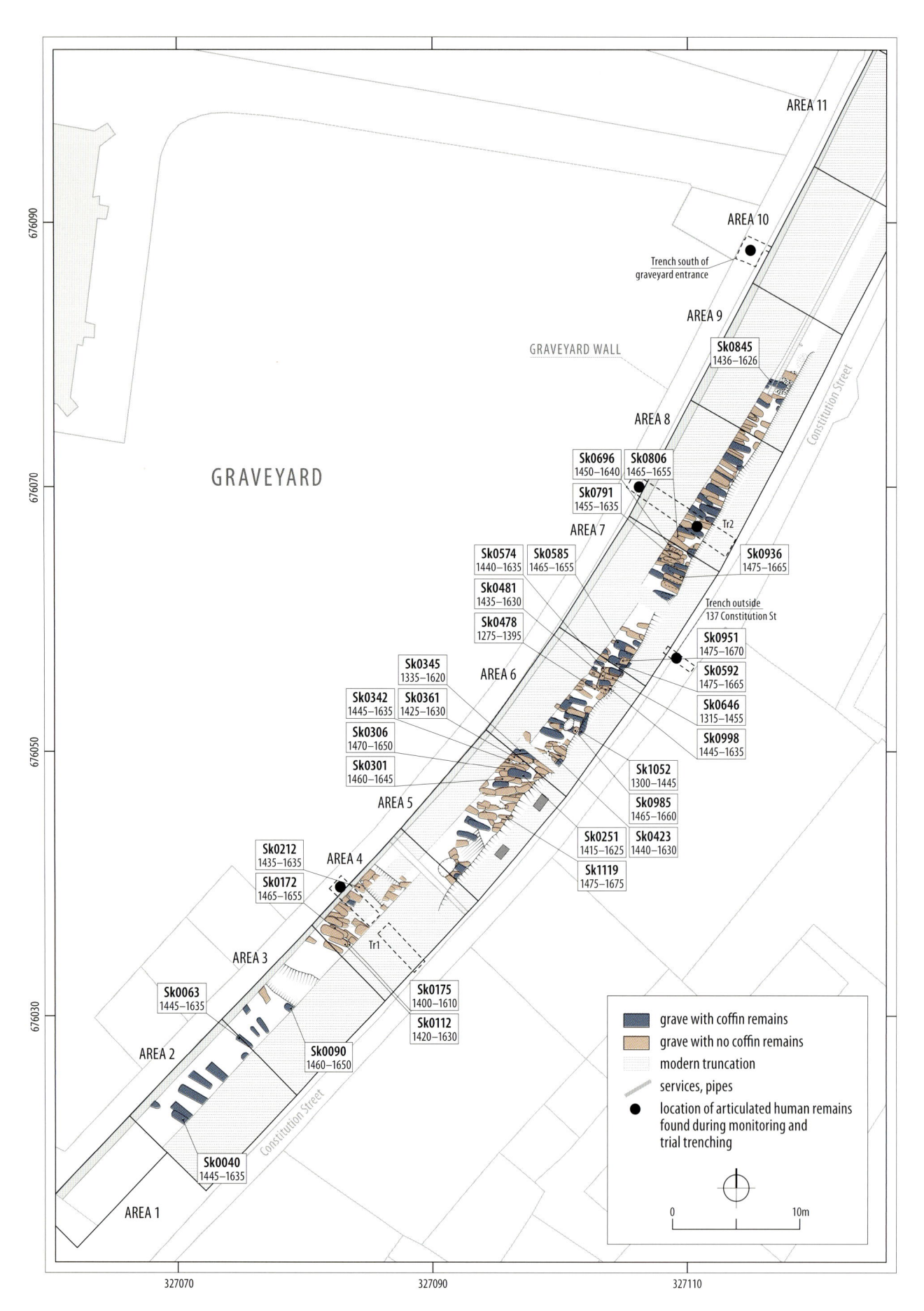

ILLUS 4.02
Constitution Street site plan

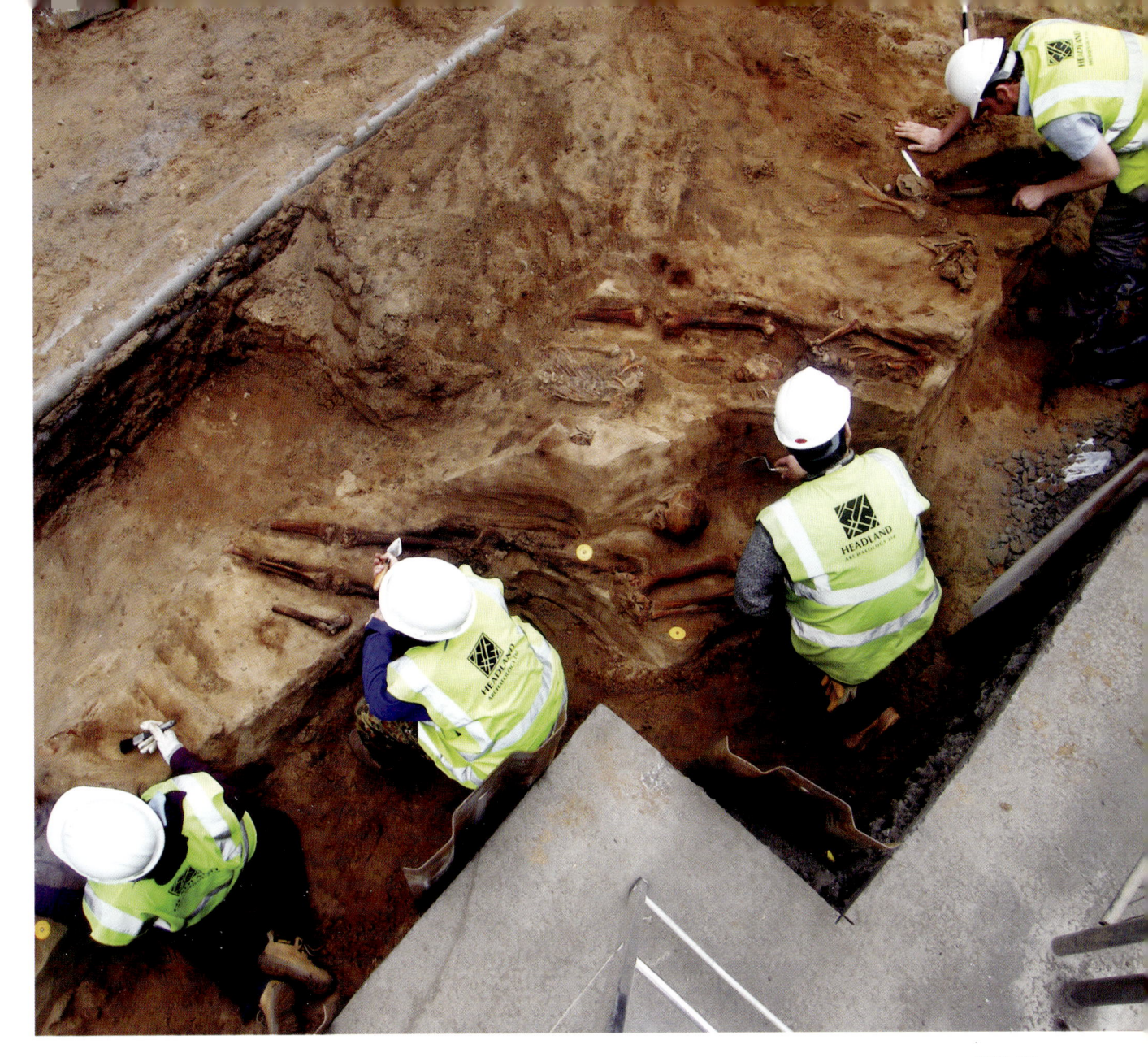

ILLUS 4.03
Excavating densely packed burials in cramped conditions, Area 5B

Osteological analysis has recovered evidence of a population, who undertook physically-demanding work and had a poor diet. Isotope analysis of the bones and teeth suggests that the people had a variable marine and terrestrial diet with evidence of a certain degree of population mobility. Facial reconstructions were undertaken on 45 of the skulls (p12–13).

CONSTITUTION STREET: ARCHAEOLOGICAL SUMMARY

The underlying natural deposits indicate that this area was part of the same system of wind-blown sand dunes which extended eastwards to Leith Links and beyond, along the coast to Portobello and Musselburgh. The surface of the dune sand was pale yellow and was found at depth of c 7.9m AOD, and appeared to be naturally gently undulating though it is possible that it had been affected by later truncation (**Illus 4.04**). Occasional thin layers of darker yellow-brown, mottled sand were encountered at different depths within or capping the dune sand and were interpreted as turf stabilisation layers. These are thought to indicate multiple episodes of levelling or turfing interspersed by episodes of sand-blow.

Deposits beneath the dune sand were only seen within the excavation area when the contractor undertook trial excavations in the vicinity of a manhole to a maximum depth of 2.2m below the present road surface. At 7.5m AOD the deposits changed in appearance to pale sand interleaved with bands of fine gravel and were interpreted as beach deposits. These deposits continued to the base of the sondage at 6.9m AOD.

Overlying the dune sand was a layer of cemetery soil, encountered at a height of 7.5m AOD at the northern end of the site, rising to 8.5m AOD at the southern end, in a layer c 0.2–0.7m thick. The colour and consistency of these deposits varied from light brown sand with few inclusions to more compacted, dark brown-orange sand with inclusions of charcoal. The darker colour was interpreted as staining from a turf horizon. In some cases, a more compacted horizon overlying these deposits indicated trampled surfaces.

Numerous graves were encountered cut into the cemetery soil and the underlying dune sand (**Illus 4.05–4.12**). The heights of the tops of the grave cuts ranged from 8.8m AOD (0.4m below the current road surface) to 6.6m AOD. Even deeper grave cuts were visible, though being below the prescribed excavation depth, they were preserved in situ. In the central and northern parts of the excavation area, graves often cut other graves. As in many burial sites of this nature, graves were filled with the same cemetery soil they had been cut into, thus rendering their cuts, in many cases, indistinguishable. The exact sequence of burials in some areas was therefore unclear.

Three large features cut into the natural dune sand in Areas 3, 4 and 5 appeared to predate the use of the area for burial. There is no independent dating evidence for these features, other than their relationship to the burials. Two of the features were ditches, in Areas 3 and 4, [0084], [0270]. One was cut by later burials. The feature in Area 5, [1153], was large but enigmatic; its full extent and shape could not be determined due to later truncation. It too was cut by a number of burials.

From Areas 4 to 9, ditch [0980] cut the burials on the eastern side of the road. It seems likely that this formed part of the post-medieval defences.

Overlying the graves and cemetery soil was a c 0.2–0.5m thick deposit of made-ground consisting of brown coarse sand containing fragments of sandstone and abundant disarticulated human remains. This deposit was interpreted as levelling material associated with the construction of Constitution Street. Into this deposit numerous services had been cut over the succeeding two centuries. These consisted of cast-iron pipes and modern ceramic and plastic ducts set into trenches between 0.4m and 0.9m wide, and up to 1m deep. These truncated large numbers of graves, and in some cases the basal fills of grave cuts were discovered immediately below the pipes. The majority of services ran parallel to the road and were predominantly located along each side of the road adjacent to the respective pavements. In addition to these, various other modern cuts and disused service pipes were encountered at different locations and alignments.

The two largest areas of modern disturbance were on the entire eastern half of the road in Areas 2–4 and much of the western half of the road from the north end of Area 4 northwards. The eastern edge of the road from Area 5 onwards was also disturbed. These either removed all preceding archaeological evidence down to the excavation limit of 1.2m or they rendered it inaccessible. The services along the eastern side of the road ran along the area already cut by the defensive ditch. Thus, though few burials are likely to have been disturbed by the services, it does limit the archaeological detail gleaned for the ditch itself. Two sondages were cut through this in Area 5 to ascertain whether undisturbed deposits existed. Made-ground was found to continue down to the excavation limit of 1.2m below the present ground surface. Much of the disturbance on the western half of the road was caused by a large and deep cut for a main sewer inserted in the 19th century and running the length of the road. The disturbance to the western side of the road at the southern end was caused by a large linear cut of uncertain function. After the excavation of the western panels (see p8–10 for explanation of the excavation method), the west-facing section showed sharply sloping tipping lines of fine sand and coarser gravelly sand. The archaeology between, around and under these services was excavated where possible.

The construction of Constitution Street itself in the 1790s is also thought to have caused considerable disturbance

CONSTITUTION STREET EXCAVATIONS

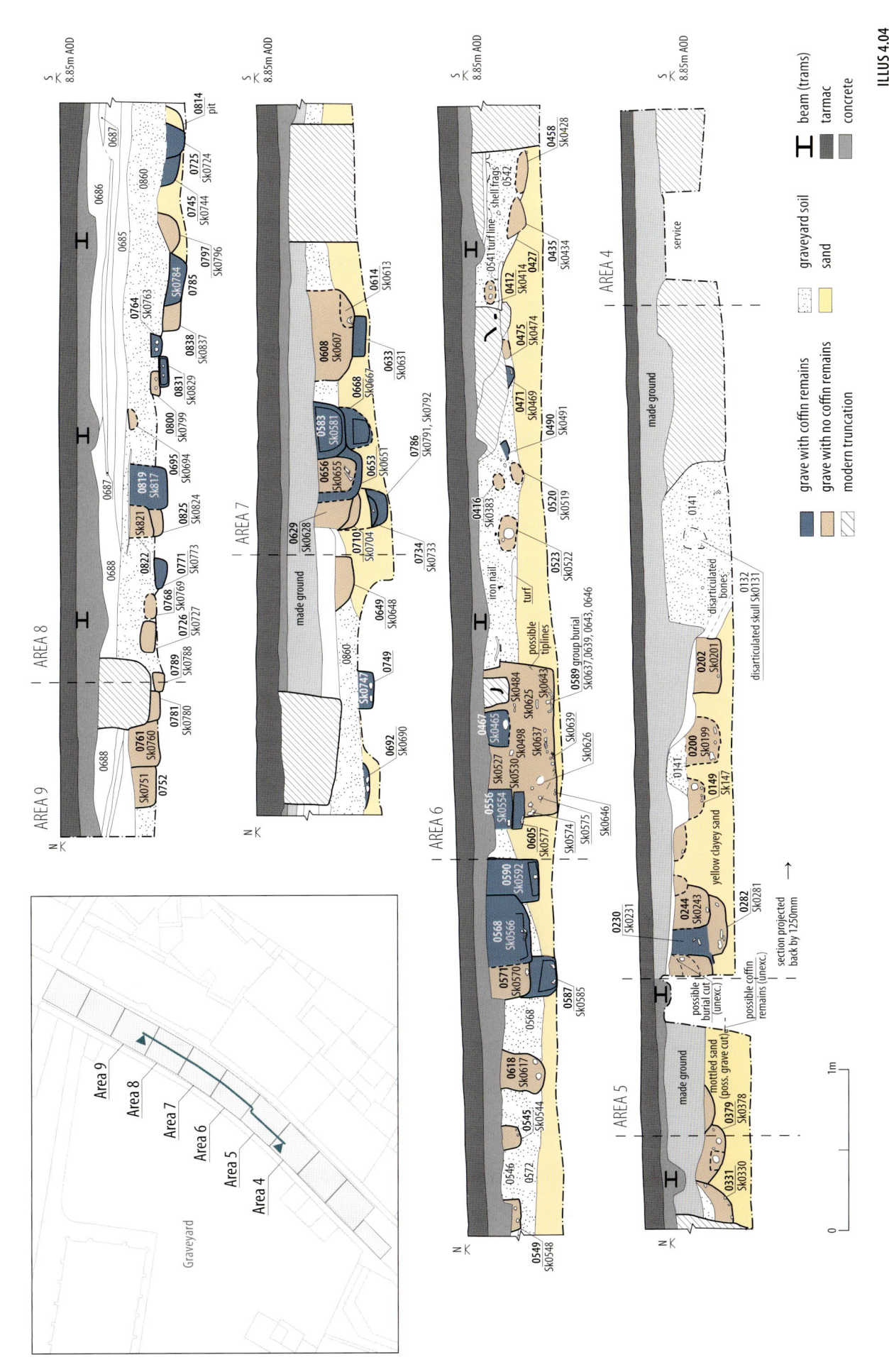

ILLUS 4.04 North-west facing section running along Constitution Street, Areas 4–9

PAST LIVES OF LEITH. ARCHAEOLOGICAL WORK FOR EDINBURGH TRAMS

and truncation. The ground level within the current graveyard is about 1m higher than the level of the road, suggesting that substantial amounts of material were removed at this time. Periodic resurfacing of the road has also caused further disturbance. It is estimated that the various works during and after the construction of Constitution Street had removed over 50% of the earlier archaeology.

ILLUS 4.05
Constitution Street, Area 2

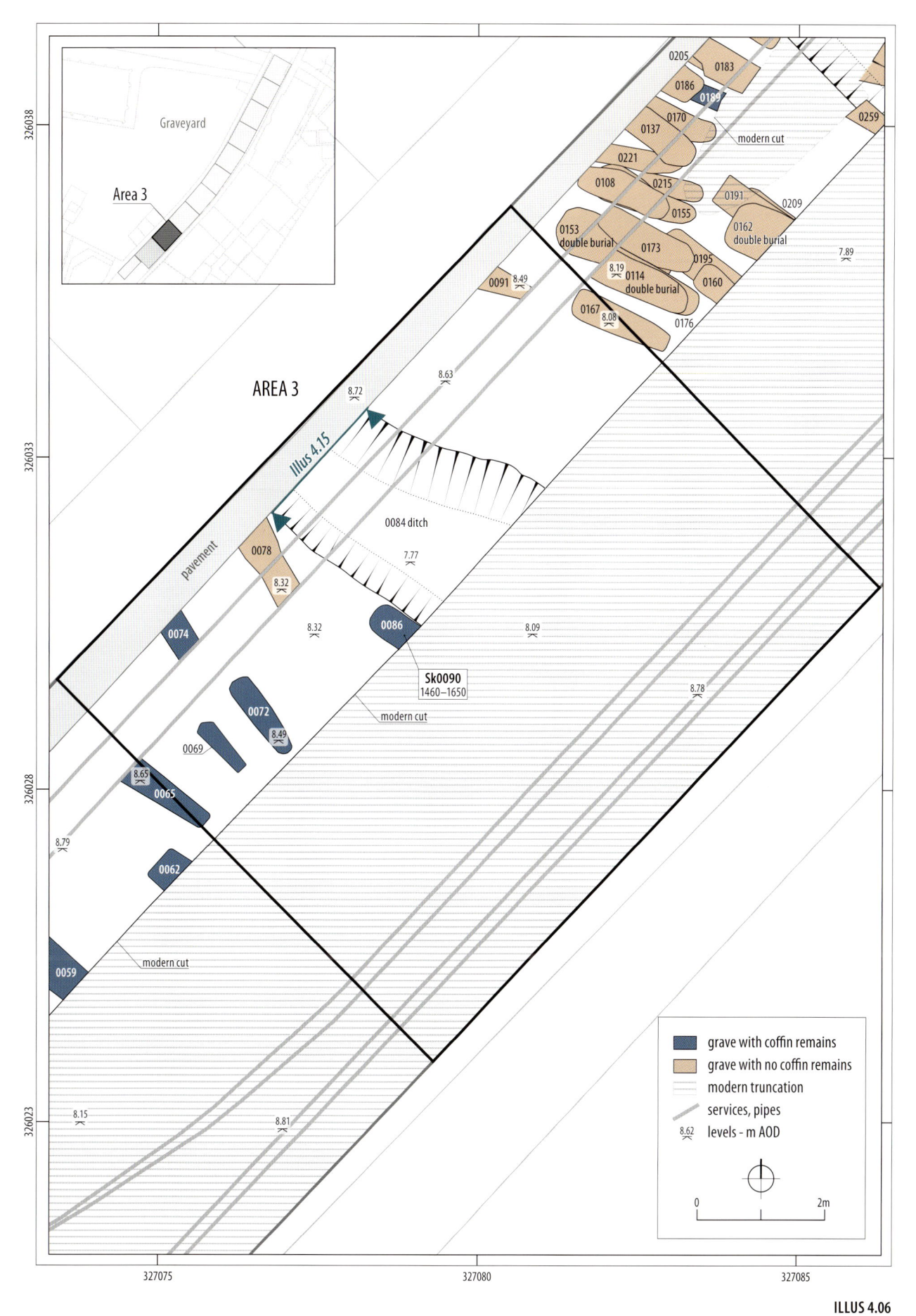

CONSTITUTION STREET EXCAVATIONS

ILLUS 4.06
Constitution Street, Area 3

55

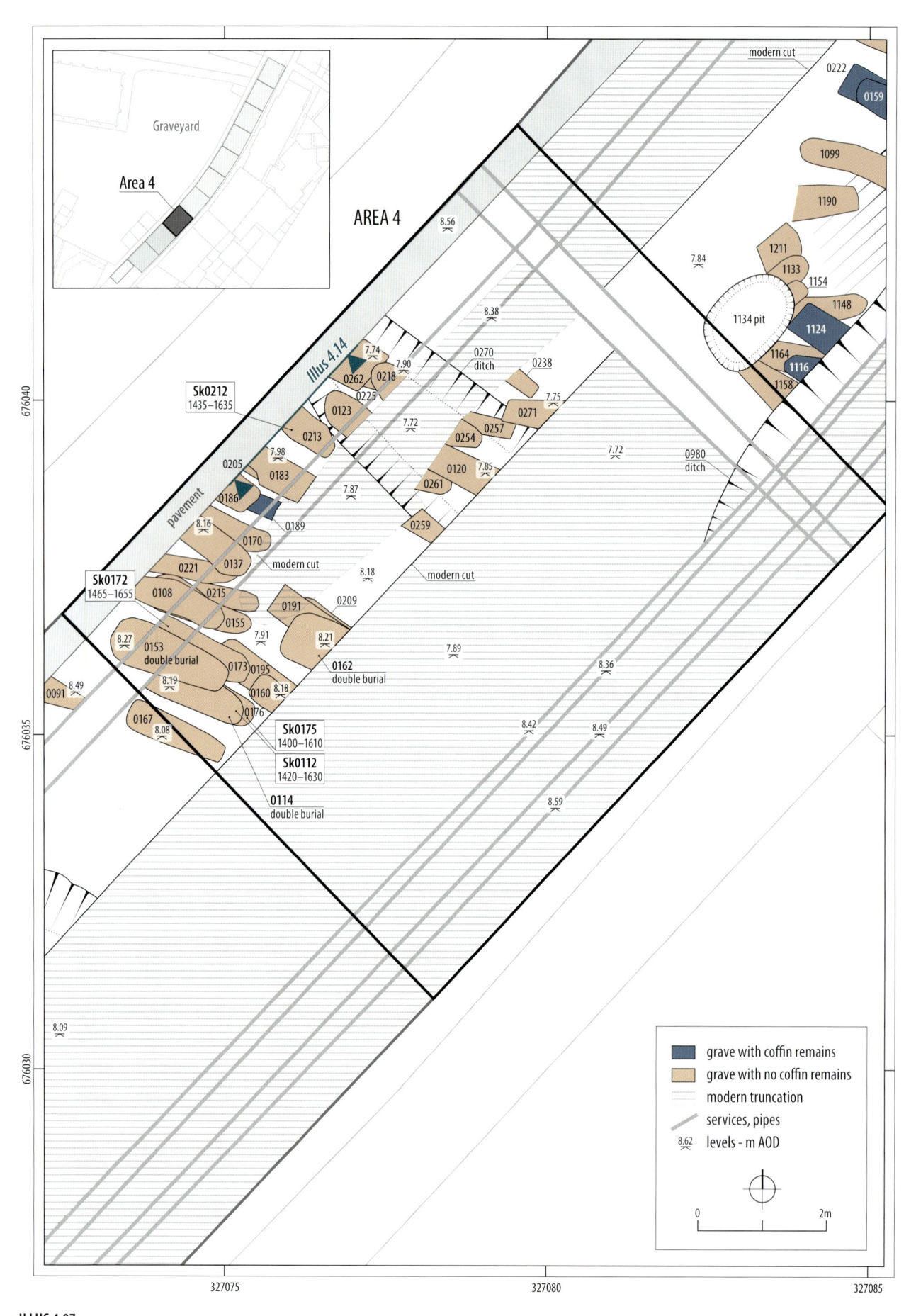

PAST LIVES OF LEITH. ARCHAEOLOGICAL WORK FOR EDINBURGH TRAMS

ILLUS 4.07
Constitution Street, Area 4

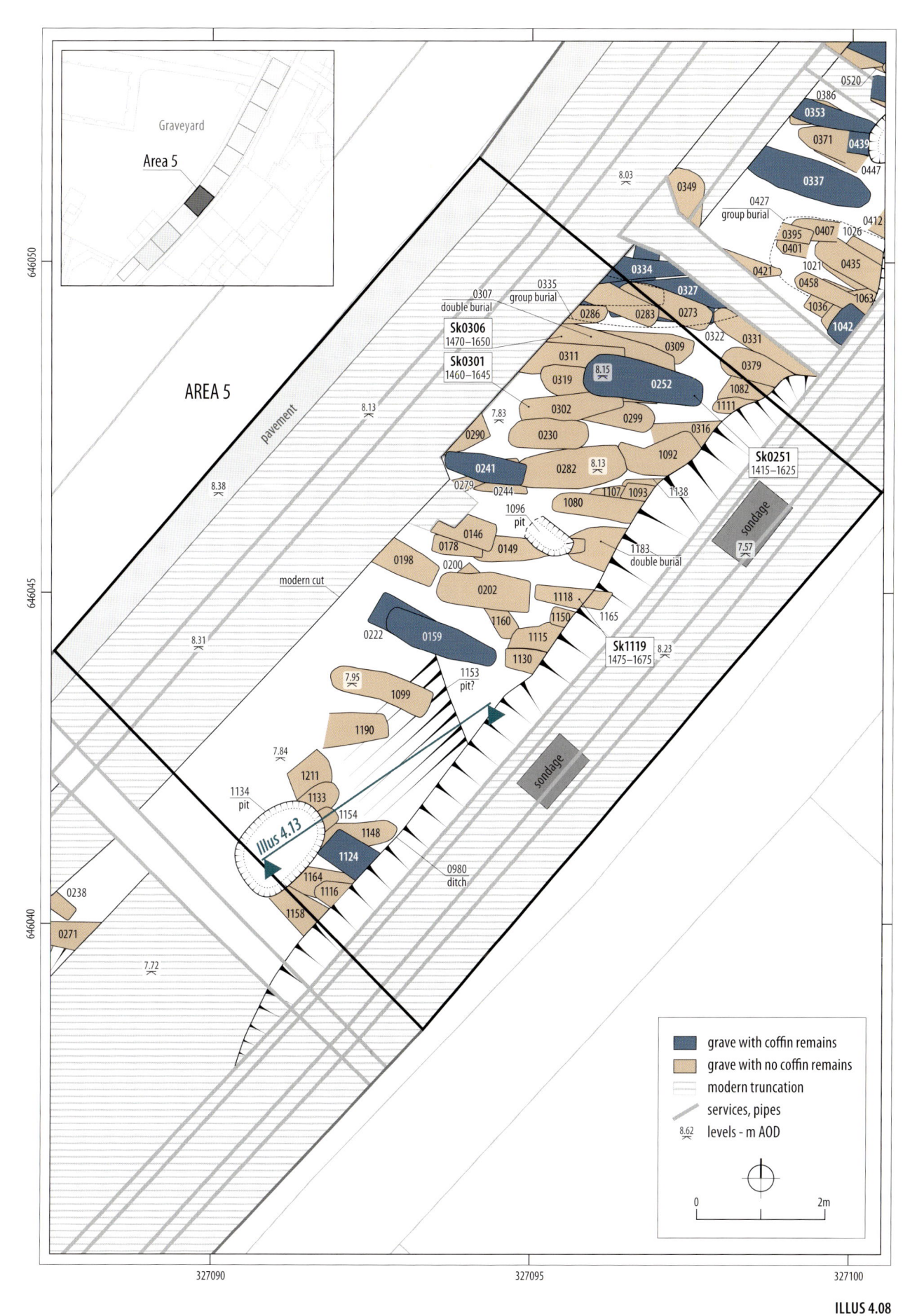

CONSTITUTION STREET EXCAVATIONS

ILLUS 4.08
Constitution Street, Area 5

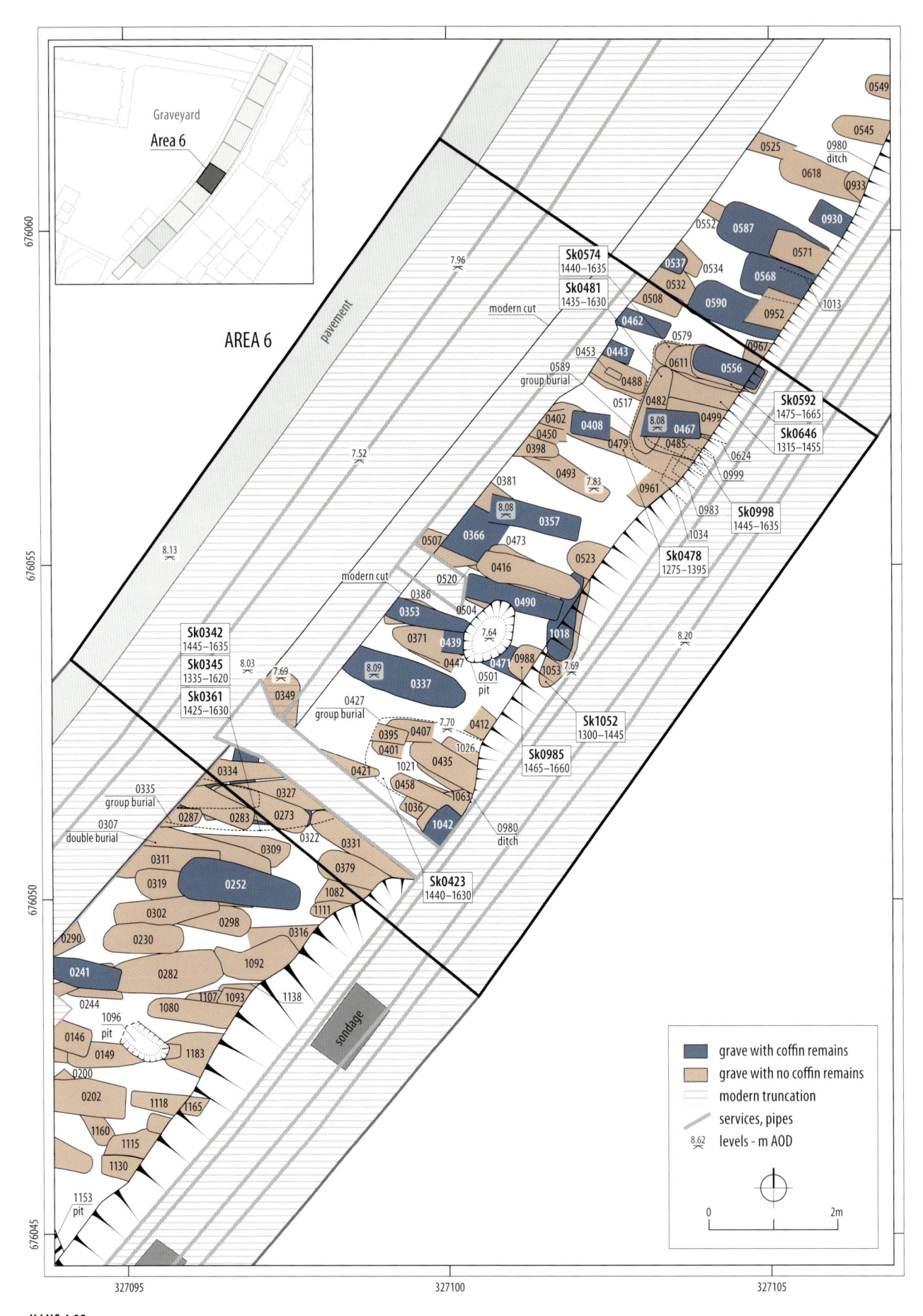

PAST LIVES OF LEITH. ARCHAEOLOGICAL WORK FOR EDINBURGH TRAMS

ILLUS 4.09
Constitution Street, Area 6

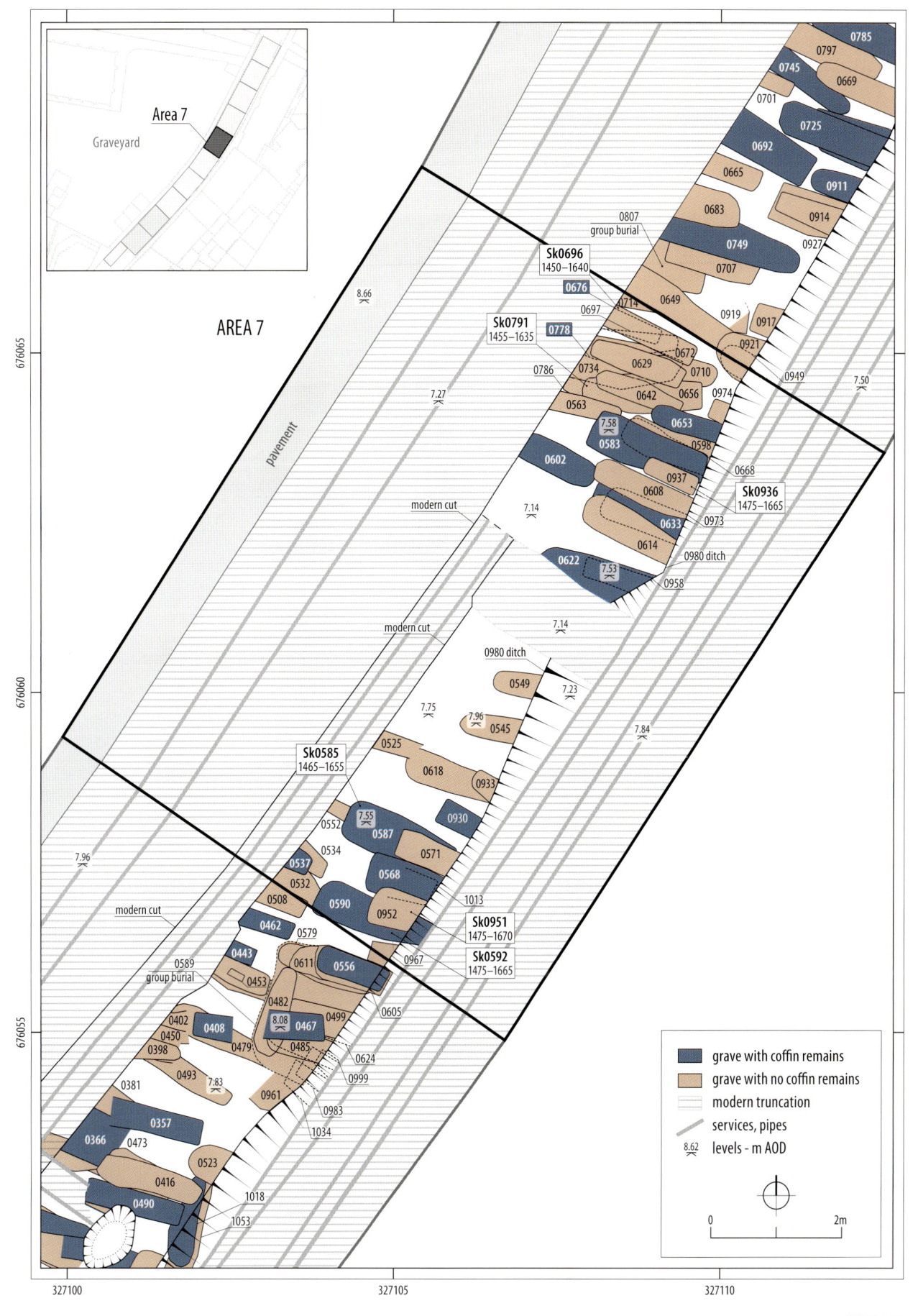

CONSTITUTION STREET EXCAVATIONS

ILLUS 4.10
Constitution Street, Area 7

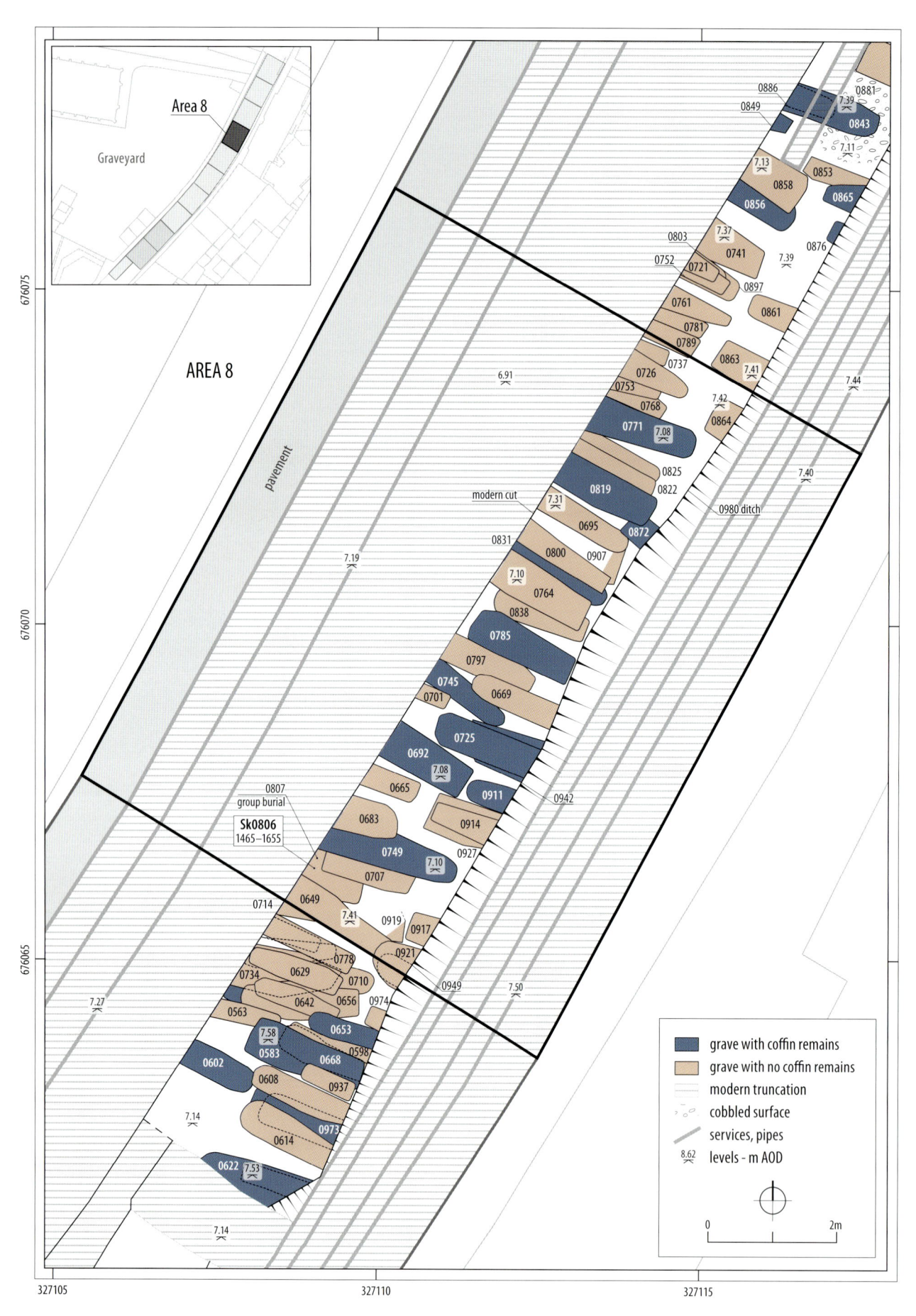

PAST LIVES OF LEITH. ARCHAEOLOGICAL WORK FOR EDINBURGH TRAMS

ILLUS 4.11
Constitution Street, Area 8

CONSTITUTION STREET EXCAVATIONS

ILLUS 4.12
Constitution Street, Area 9

PEOPLE'S STORIES

A BOY WITH BAD TEETH, 1435–1450

This boy was born in 1435 to an armourer. His father had worked his way up from a humble blacksmith's apprentice and now specialised in making swords. His father had recently moved to Leith to practice his craft for the king in the newly finished armoury at the King's Wark, as building work continued around them. He brought with him his new wife, who was already with child at the time, and they took a house along the Kirkgate, close to the new St Anthony's Preceptory and a few minutes' walk to the armoury. For a man who had worked his way up from nothing, it was a considerable step up to be working for the king. His new house was built of stone. It had its own kitchen and bread oven and was well-stocked with iron and bronze pots, pans and pitchers, and they ate off pewter plates. He could never quite forget his humble origins though and was always careful with money. They could afford wheat bread, wine and good meat on days the church allowed it. They could even treat themselves to grapes and figs. However, he mainly did so only when guests were staying. The rest of the time he preferred to eat more simply.

King James visited the armoury on many occasions and was interested in everything that went on there. The boy's father prided himself that the king knew him by name. When the boy was not yet two, on a cold February day, the news reached the King's Wark that the king had been murdered in Perth. The new king was only six years old and the father feared for his position, but arms were always needed, and he continued his work under the regencies of Douglas and Crichton, though they were considerably less interested in chatting with the craftsmen.

The boy was sickly as a child, and his mother was fretful and over-protective of her first born. She tried to feed him up with large steaming bowls of porridge and honey. She kept him indoors when he was four and the *wame ill* (**Table 3.01**, p32) spread through the town. His father determined that his eldest son should follow him into the trade and took him as an apprentice from the age of 12. He thought the work would build him up, but the boy did not take well to it and preferred to spend his time reading.

His teeth had never been strong, and he began to suffer more with them as he reached his teens. Though he did not know it, his fondness of porridge did not help, as the soft mulch coated his teeth and got into the gaps between them. His younger sisters would clean their teeth using the splayed end of a chewed green birch twig. Their mother said it would keep their teeth white and their breath sweet to help them catch a good husband. Their father laughed at such old wives' tales and his sons cared little for what colour their teeth were.

The boy suffered from toothache for months. His mother got him oil of cloves from the canons of St Anthony's which dulled the pain but did not cure it. He tried burning a candle close to the tooth so that the worm which was said to cause the pain by

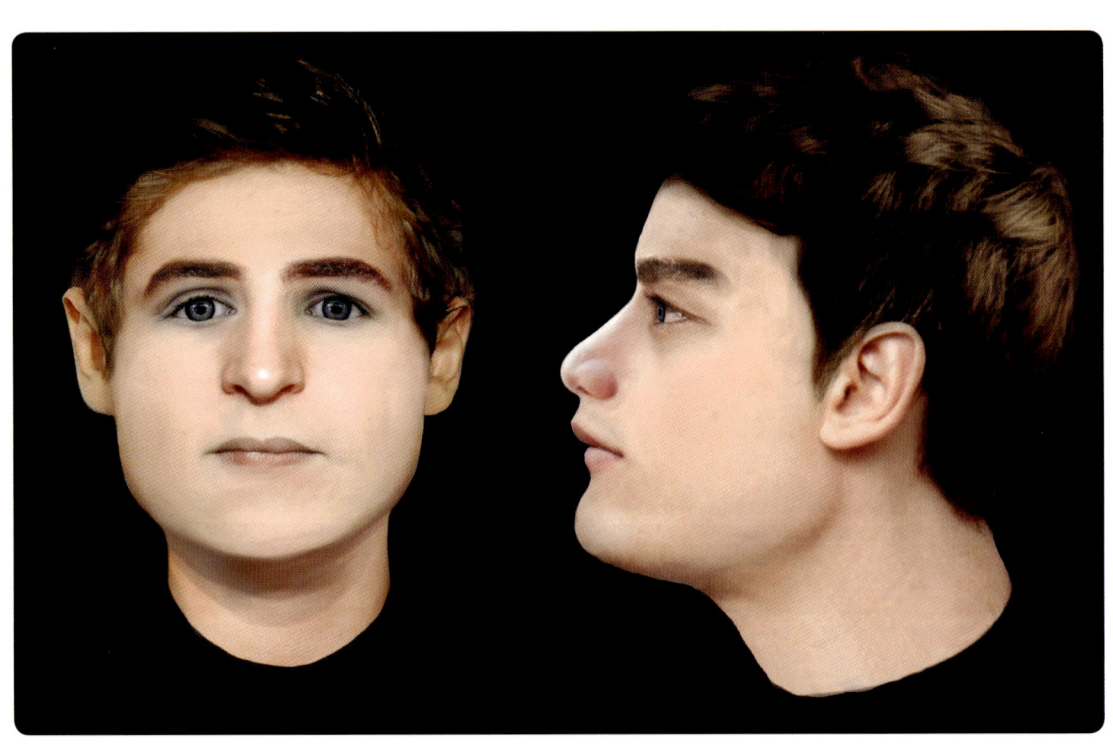

His mother wanted him buried in a coffin to preserve his body from the horrors of the grave. His father wanted to indulge her but balked at the cost. He did not see the point in spending so much on something that was to be buried and no one would see. His poor dead boy would hardly know the difference. He found a local joiner who would make a cheaper coffin. It looked the same but the base was made of cheap reused planks. The base was covered in cloth on both sides and the gaps did not show. The coffin was placed on the bier, wheeled to the local chapel graveyard and was laid to rest there.

SKELETON	0251
Grave	0252
Location of grave	Constitution Street, Area 5
Burial details	Slat-based coffin, overlying lots of simple burials
Age	Adolescent, 12–18
Sex	?
Stature	–
Radiocarbon date	1430–1505 (68% probability) 1415–1535, 1555–1625 (95% probability) see Table 4.02; Illus 4.31, p84–85
Other dating evidence	Found in Phase 1 cemetery in use from c 1380s
Finds	–
Pathology	Severe periostitis at mandible, abscess, caries, calculus, mild bilateral cribra orbitalia, porotic hyperostosis, Schmorl's nodes.
C/N isotope (diet)	Normal (c24% marine) see p132–35; Illus 4.68; Table A1.01, p216–17
O/S isotope (origins)	Local see p136–40; Table A1.03, p218
See also	Illus 4.08, p57; Illus 4.18–19, p69; p70–71; Illus 4.57, p112
Facial reconstruction artist	Paloma Galzi

gnawing at the tooth would fall out but to no avail. He tried to chew on the other side but eating became increasingly difficult, with porridge and beer being the only things he could get down. The pain got worse and his face began to swell up on one side, he became feverish and then began to have trouble breathing and swallowing. The infection spread through his system and he weakened quickly. He was just 15 when he died.

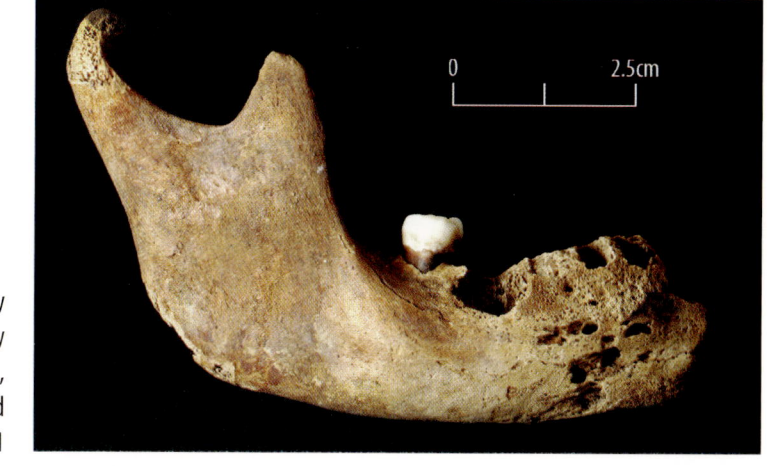

Pitting in mandible, caused by periostitis, probably caused by abscess. Leads to intense pain, difficulty using affected area and fever. Sk0251

A BOY WITH BAD TEETH, 1435–1450

CONSTITUTION STREET: THE EARLY FEATURES

Parts of three large cut features were found. The use of two of these predated the graves, while the third seems to have still been open during the period of use of the cemetery. There was no clear archaeological evidence for when any of these features were dug, but their backfill can be dated, largely by their relationship to the burials. They seem to represent two medieval property boundary ditches and a larger more enigmatic feature.

LARGE CUT FEATURE [1153]

This was a substantial feature though its full dimensions are not known. One edge was exposed running in a straight line NNW-SSE for 1.5m across the eastern half of Area 5 (**Illus 4.08**). A narrow sondage was excavated down to a depth of 1.4m at which point excavation ceased without having reached the bottom of the backfill deposits. Its eastern side was gently sloping although it appeared to become steeper before flattening out towards the base. The south end of the visible edge in plan was cut by ditch [0980], the northern end was cut by burials and the feature was not visible to the north of these leading to the impression on site that the feature did not continue northwards. Modern service cuts 1m north of the burials removed the possibility of picking up any continuation of the feature there. It was best seen in section (**Illus 4.13**) and, assuming a symmetrical profile, extrapolating from the existing section gives a width of at least 5m and a depth of at least 2.5m. This would place its western edge in an area of modern truncation in Area 4.

It was filled with a complex sequence of interleaving fills suggesting periods of silting, sand-blow and rain-wash and other more purposeful backfilling events. Some of the fills were black and organic-rich, including small quantities of burnt oats, animal bone and marine shell, but no finds were recovered to aid dating. The final infill of the feature might even post-date the beginning of use of the area for burial as fragments of human bone were found in the fills. Ten graves were cut into the upper fills. None of these graves were dated but the general dating for graves in this area (**Table 4.02**, p84–85) implies the feature was backfilled by or in the 15th century. The burials over the feature are not as densely packed as those to its east and it is possible that the feature was filled to create more space for burials.

The feature's size, shape and profile are poorly understood from the remains observed. The evidence tentatively suggests the single observable cut edge did not continue to the north suggesting it was not a linear feature but rather a large rectangular, sub-rounded or irregular-shaped feature. Its dating is similarly poorly defined. Its relationship to the burials implies it is 15th century or earlier. The feature certainly predates ditch [0980] which cuts its southern end and is suggested as dating to the 16th or 17th century (p146–48).

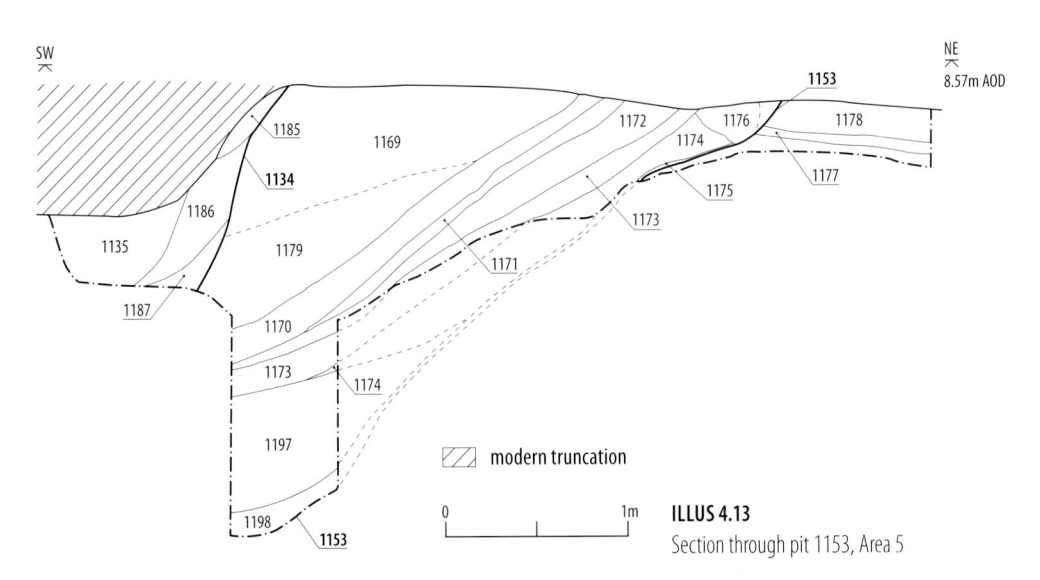

ILLUS 4.13
Section through pit 1153, Area 5

If the feature were a ditch its location and alignment do not readily suit interpretation as either boundary or defensive ditch. It is arguably too large for a property boundary ditch and is unlikely to mark a burgage plot boundary contemporary with ditches [0084] and [0270] (see *Ditches [0270] and [0084]* below). It is over twice as wide, significantly deeper, on a different alignment and too close to [0270]. Its scale is more consistent with a defensive ditch, but again, the location and alignment argue against it. Assuming the one edge observed in plan is part of a linear feature and its alignment is broadly representative of the alignment of the overall feature, then extrapolating it northwards leads into the middle of the old town, to the Coalhill or Shore area. A defensive ditch on this south-east side of town would be more likely to be aligned SW-NE, to enclose the town, as did the 16th-century defences as depicted on the contemporary Petworth Map (**Illus 3.01**, p23). The dating evidence also suggests it is unlikely to represent the earlier defensive scheme observed by the Earl of Hertford in 1544 (p22). It is possible that during the Wars of Independence in the late 13th and early 14th century it may have been necessary to defend Leith on its landward side. However, the 13th- and 14th-century town is not thought to have extended south of Dub Row (in the vicinity of the northern part of the present-day Giles Street) and probably went no further east than the Kirkgate and Rotten Row (part of the route of which is preserved in present day Water Street) (Mowat 2003, 45). A defensive line in this location is therefore too far south-east to fulfil this function efficiently, enclosing a larger area than would have been necessary.

The best fitting theory given the current evidence is that it was not a linear feature at all. Given this, the size of the feature suggests it may have been a large sand quarry pit. Similar large pits have been excavated in Leith at Burgess St and Ronaldson's Wharf/Sandport Street (Collard & Reed 1994; J Lawson 1995; Reed & Lawson 1999). It is thought that the demands for sand during this period stemmed from its use in the production of mortar, which in turn would have been needed for large building projects such as the Preceptory of St Anthony and the King's Wark in the 1430s. The building of St Mary's Church would also have needed mortar, and, as the nearest substantial medieval building it is ostensibly the most likely to be associated with a sand quarry in this location. However, this would have dating implications for the burials cut into the top of the feature which make this unlikely. These are explored in more detail below (p142).

DITCHES [0270] AND [0084]

Two parallel ditches cut across the southern part of the excavation area. Both were aligned approximately NW-SE, perpendicular to Constitution Street. Ditch [0270] ran across Area 4 (**Illus 4.07**). It had been heavily truncated, its line only visible in the west-facing section of the excavation and partially in plan to the north-west in between utility services. The ditch was about 2.1m wide with steeply sloping sides to a depth of 1.55m (c 7.7m AOD). It appeared to flatten out towards the limit of excavation but its base was not reached. Its fill was similar in consistency to the surrounding cemetery soil and layers of wind-blown sand seem to have accumulated between episodes of backfilling. The lowest fill (0233, **Illus 4.14**) contained two sherds of pottery of late whiteware and post-medieval reduced ware which suggest a 15th- or 16th-century date for the ditch backfill but the sherds were few, small and abraded and should not be taken as secure dating evidence. Fragments of burnt animal bone were found within the fill and also a small quantity of flax seed (*Linum usitatissimum*).

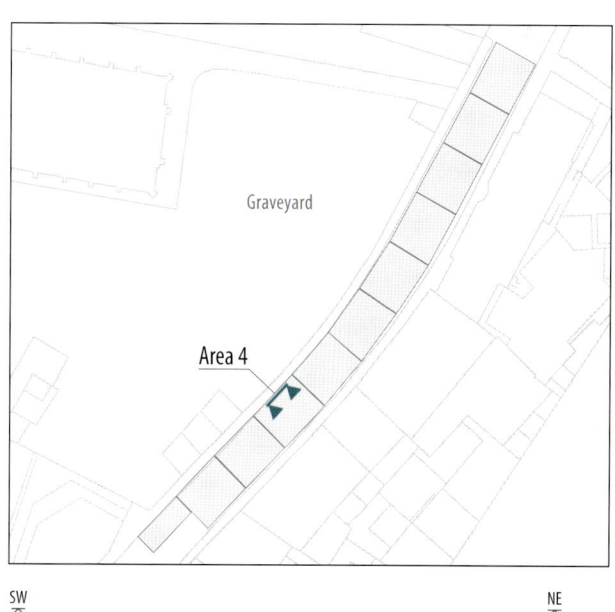

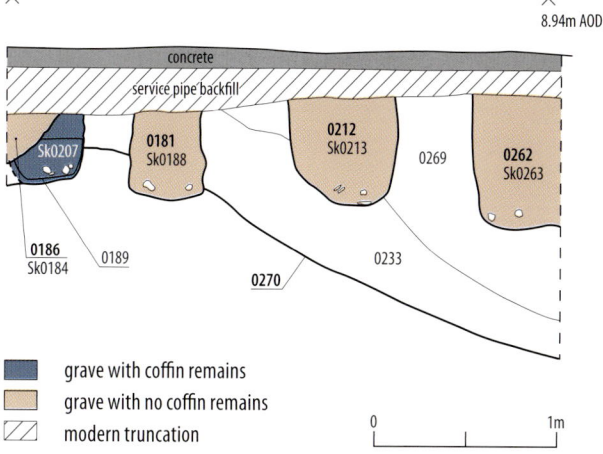

ILLUS 4.14
Section through ditch 0270, Area 4

Ten graves were cut into the top of the ditch at various depths. None was dated, but Sk0212/Gr0213 which sits on the very edge of the ditch, so close it must surely post-date it, was dated (1435–1635; see **Table 4.02**), suggesting that the ditch was backfilled in or around the 15th century.

Ditch [0084] ran across Area 3 (**Illus 4.06**), 8.3m south-east of ditch [0270]. It was recorded at a depth of 8.3m AOD cutting the sandy subsoil. Its full section was exposed (**Illus 4.15**) but it was truncated to the north-west by services and to the south-east by a modern linear cut. The ditch was 2.5m wide and 0.6m deep with regular, gradually sloping sides and a flat base. Its basal fills, (0100) and (0101), were of wind-blown sand deposited soon after it was opened. The main fill (0099) was of a similar material to the surrounding cemetery soil and included fragments of charcoal, bone and burnt plant remains in the form of oat, hulled barley and spelt wheat. Other anthropogenic material included a small fragment of iron and one sherd of 16th-century pottery. The latter is potentially intrusive, from overlying layers, and does not necessarily date the backfilling of the ditch.

Overlying the top of the ditch was a midden deposit (0073/0082/0085) extending further to the south-west and the north-west but which had slumped into the top of the ditch fills where they had settled. It included a mixture of food waste material and other domestic debris. Charred cereal grains included oat, hulled barley, spelt wheat and rye, abundant animal bone, fish bone, marine shell (including oyster and whelk) and cinders. Finds included pottery and iron nails. The pottery provides useful dating evidence suggesting the midden was deposited at the end of the 16th or early 17th century. Distinctive sherds within it included a fragment of a 16th-century French chafing dish (**Illus 4.66A**, p127; Hurst 1974, 233–47; Hurst et al 1986, 78–82), a sherd of Weser slipware dish imported from Germany between c 1590 and c 1620 (deposit 0085; not illus; Hurst et al 1986, 250–9), and a Low Countries redware cooking pot tripod foot (deposit 0073; not illus; Baart 1994). Accompanying local post-medieval reduced and oxidised wares include sherds of handled jars (**Illus 4.66B**) and jugs, typical of 16th-century assemblages (eg Franklin 1997) (p127). The lack of clay pipes suggest deposition was no later than c 1620/30.

No burials cut the ditch, though five graves (Sk0067/Gr0069, Sk0070/Gr0072, Sk0076/Gr0074, Sk0079/Gr0078, Sk0090/Gr0086) cut the midden deposit overlying it and thus must post-date c 1600. One of these burials, Sk0090/Gr0086, was radiocarbon dated to 1460–1650 (**Table 4.02**) and was very close to the ditch's southern edge. The pattern of burial south of the ditch was distinctly different to that to the north and the area seems to have formed a distinct part of the cemetery which came into use later. It is therefore possible that the ditch was still open when burials began to the north and it may have marked the southern boundary of the cemetery for a time (p144). It was clearly backfilled and obscured by the early 17th century.

In terms of their original function, both ditches can be readily identified as medieval property boundaries. They are of similar dimensions (2–2.5m wide) and similar alignment. The alignment places them roughly perpendicular to the Kirkgate and about 85m back from it. The ditches are about 8.3m apart (or 10.5m southern edge to southern edge) and this conforms well to burgage plot widths seen in Edinburgh and other burghs (typically 7m to 9.5m in Edinburgh and Canongate) (Tait 2006; 2008; 2010). Plot lengths vary according to available space but plots longer than 85m are common.

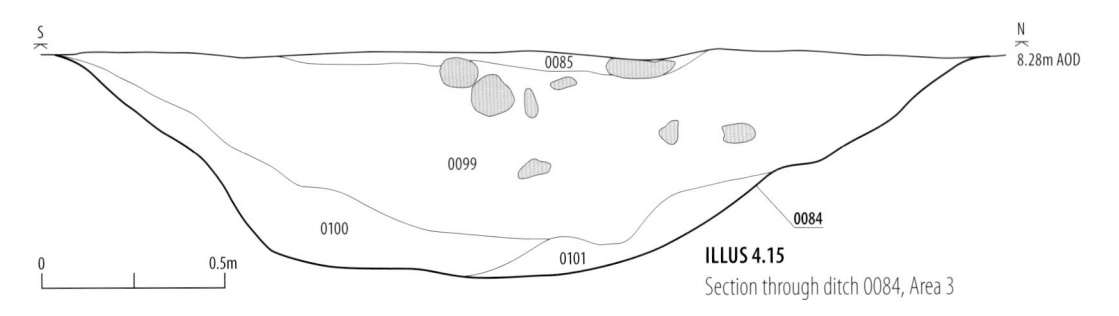

ILLUS 4.15
Section through ditch 0084, Area 3

CONSTITUTION STREET: THE BURIALS

The various modern disturbances already detailed (p52) and the cutting of ditch [0980] had a significant impact on the surviving funerary remains. The burials survived on narrow 'islands' of in situ undisturbed deposits (**Illus 4.05–4.12**). Most of graves were located centrally within Areas 4 to 8, petering out to the south-west in Areas 2 and 3 and to the north-east in Area 9. The amount of truncation meant that skeletal completeness was variable.

Graves were encountered at varying depths depending upon the degree of truncation and local topographical factors. Their stratigraphic associations were often unclear due to indiscernible grave cuts, horizontal truncation and dense intercutting layers of graves. No clear vertical stratigraphy was identified. The upper graves were cut into a dark brown-orange, or grey sandy cemetery soil and truncated parts of earlier burials. The lower graves had been cut into cleaner, paler sand with fewer inclusions, resembling wind-blown dune sand. The latter deposit was most evident in Areas 7–9 where graves were discovered as deep as 1.8m below the present road surface, some of which were preserved in situ.

Less than 20% of all grave cuts survived as complete or near complete features. Their depth varied widely, reflecting, in some instances, an uneven ground surface, based on the underlying dunes, and varying degrees of later truncation. There was also no legislation as regards burial depth so the diligence, or lack thereof, of individual gravediggers must also have been a factor. Wide variation of grave depth has been noted in medieval graves from 1.2 to as much as 2.5m (Gilchrist & Sloane 2005, 131).

A table summarising all the osteological and burial data is given in *Appendix 2* (**Table A2.01**, p219). There were 305 articulated skeletons excavated. A collection of disarticulated skulls represented a further 73 skeletons. The skulls were found either in the general cemetery soil, redeposited in later graves or potentially in situ in graves that were so heavily truncated to the east that only the skull remained.

There were a further 15 graves which were not associated with any skeletal remains. Ten of these were heavily truncated, either vertically or horizontally; some contained no skeletal remains, while others had nothing that could be identified as articulated and in situ or so little it was not worthy of analysis. The remaining five graves (all in Area 8) were not excavated because they were sufficiently below the excavation depth to avoid disturbance by the

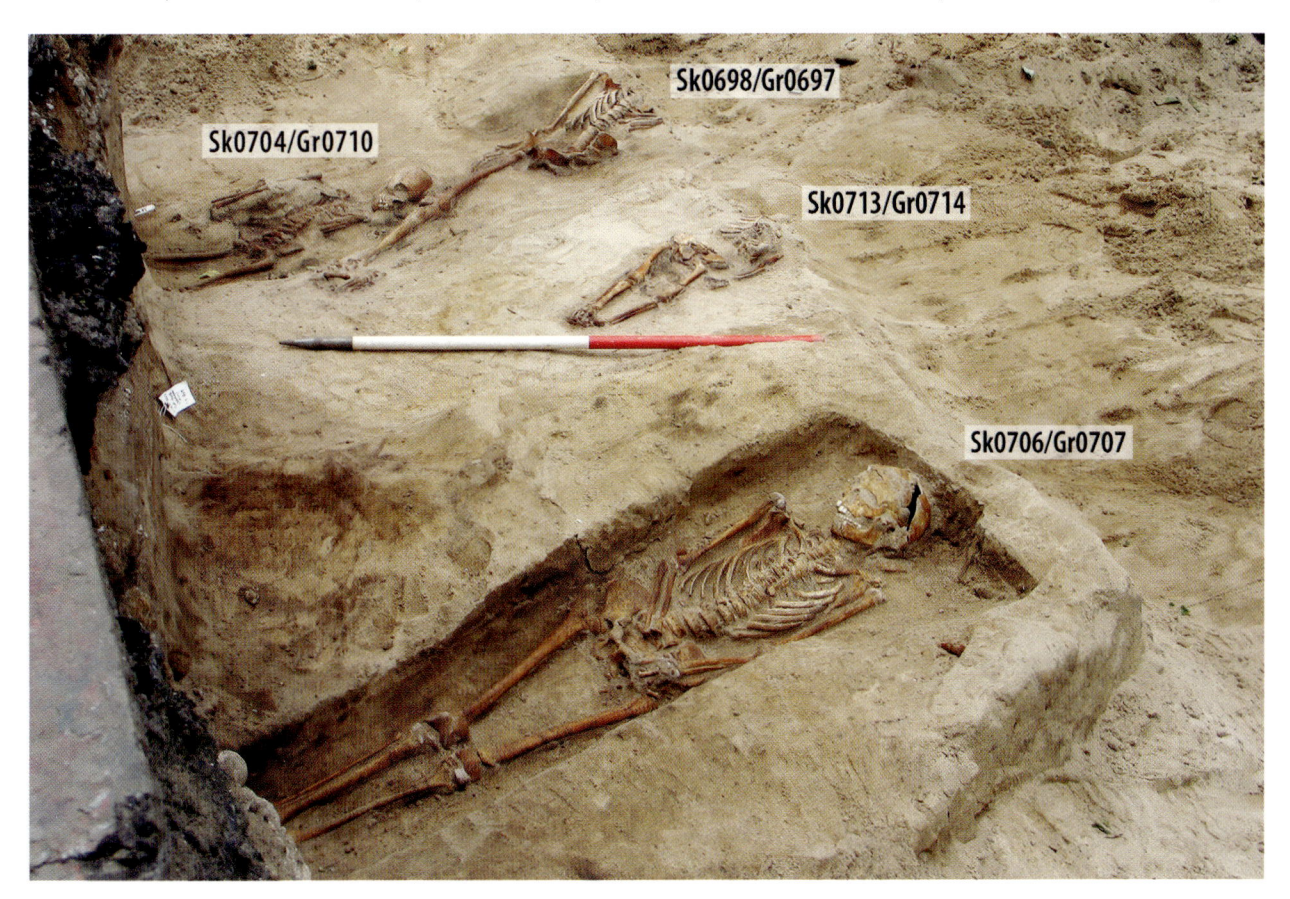

ILLUS 4.16
Row of simple burials in lower levels of Area 7–8 against baulk in centre of road. From top: Sk0704/Gr0710, younger child; Sk0698/Gr0697, younger middle adult female; Sk0713/Gr0714, younger child; Sk0706/Gr0707, older child

construction works and were preserved in situ. These 15 graves are shown on site plans (**Illus 4.05–4.12**) and in the grave summary table (**Table A2.01**) but are not included in any statistics for graves on the basis that they are poorly understood and would yield unreliable data. Six of the 15 showed coffin remains but this is likely to be an over-representation as the difficulty of identifying grave cuts meant that a grave containing neither coffin nor skeleton might easily have been missed.

With no means of clearly chronologically phasing the graves, they were classified by the manner of burial to aid reporting and discussion. The distinction was made between burials within wooden coffins (coffined) and those without coffins (simple). Some graves contained more than one inhumation. In these cases, an attempt was made to distinguish between simultaneous multiple burials (see *Double burials* and *Group burials* below, p71–76) and multiple episodes of reusing the same burial plot (see *Superimposed burials* below, p76–77), though this was not always clear.

SIMPLE BURIALS

These graves contained no evidence for wooden coffins and were by far the most common type of grave encountered. While burial within a wooden coffin was known during the medieval period it generally accounts for only a small minority of burials in regular Christian cemeteries (Gilchrist & Sloane 2005, 111–6). The most common medieval burial rite saw the body wrapped in a shroud and carried to church in a coffin or on a bier and then removed from it and placed into the grave wrapped only in a burial shroud (ibid, 111).

Simple burials accounted for 79% (242/305) of all excavated graves. Where discernible, these grave cuts were either rectangular or sub-rectangular with rounded corners, vertical sides and flat bases (**Illus 4.16**). Following burial, the grave cuts were then backfilled with the same sandy subsoil, and in the absence of a coffin, these ephemeral cuts in many cases were indistinguishable in the surrounding soil matrix. They were generally narrow with a maximum width of 0.50m. The greatest density of simple, superimposed, intercutting graves was observed in Areas 4–6 (**Illus 4.07–4.09**), which was also where the earliest dated graves were located (p82).

COFFINED BURIALS

Coffins were identified based on poorly preserved wooden remains. No further coffins were identified through the presence of coffin nails alone (ie a grave containing no preserved wood but more than five nails), suggesting that this figure is representative of coffin use at the site. At best the coffins survived as a soft, thin layer of degraded wood 5–10mm thick lining the long sides of graves, and in very few cases as better preserved lids with the securing iron nails still in situ. Sometimes all that remained was a dark stain. Most lids were found collapsed inwards with the skulls protruding through the wood (**Illus 4.18**). The base of coffins was rarely observed and, where it was, appeared as degraded dark organic material below the skeleton. Woodworking nails were often seen in situ, spaced at approximate 0.20m intervals along the sides. The coffins were typically trapezoidal, less commonly rectangular, in shape.

The wood was not sufficiently preserved for a detailed post-excavation species analysis and crumbled upon excavation. Field identifications of some in situ remains indicated the presence of pine and also some oak coffins (Scott Timpany pers comm). Both are known to have been used in medieval coffin construction, as were elm, ash and beech (Gilchrist & Sloane 2005, 111–12).

The cuts for these coffined burials were usually better defined, with straight sides, vertical edges and flat bases, though sometimes the perceived 'cut' was in fact the stain left by the coffin walls themselves. In a few cases, a 'stepped' cut was observed comprising an upper, wider cut and a lower, narrower cut to receive the coffin. The cut for Sk0048/Gr0050 in Area 2, for example (**Illus 4.17**), comprised an upper cut 0.77m wide and 0.22m deep and a lower cut 0.40m wide narrowing to 0.25m wide at the foot of coffin and 0.11m deep. It is not clear why this should be and may represent post-depositional processes where the coffin settled into the sandy deposits beneath it.

ILLUS 4.17
Stepped cut for coffined burial Sk0048/Gr0050, older middle adult female

ILLUS 4.18
Collapsed lid of coffin with skull protruding, Sk0251/Gr0252, adolescent

Coffins were found with 21% (63/305) of the total burials. This is well within the range for coffin use in medieval cemeteries (Gilchrist & Sloane 2005, 113–6). It is considerably lower than coffin use within a contemporary phase at St Giles Cathedral, Edinburgh, where 43% (16/37) of the late 14th to 16th-century burials were within coffins (Collard et al 2006, 19–20). These burials were within the cathedral and thus more likely to be of higher status. At the graveyard of the Carmelite friary in Aberdeen (late 13th to 17th century), 30% (15/50) of the burials were coffined (Stones 1989a, 114). At the Dominican friary (or Blackfriars) in Edinburgh, coffin use was considerably less with evidence of coffins in only 5% (4/88) of the graves (Wilson in prep) and at Holyrood Abbey, coffin use was similarly low at 6% (3/51) (Bain 1998, 1054). The distribution of coffin use by area, date and sex is considered in more detail below (see *Distribution of burial types*, p83–88; *Demography*, p117–19).

One coffined burial of a young man, Sk0158/Gr0159, in Area 5 contained faint traces of a white powdered substance below the skeleton and coating patches of the bones. The scant remains were tentatively identified on site as lime, though no chemical analysis was attempted. No coffin remains were seen where this deposit was noted, thus it is not clear whether the deposit was placed inside the grave

ILLUS 4.19
Slatted base of coffin for Sk0251/Gr0252, adolescent

base or inside the coffin itself. The fact that the deposit was found on the upper side of some of the bones suggests the later is the more likely. There is precedent for the use of lime, mortar or plaster as a coffin lining and as a grave lining, though to date it has only been noted in the south of England (Gilchrist & Sloane 2005, 123–4 and 142–3). It is predominantly associated with men and it has been suggested that it is linked to religious men of some type, the white making the grave more visually impressive and possibly emulating a stone lined grave (ibid, 143). The use of quicklime was also prescribed at a later date for the burial of plague victims to prevent the spread of the disease (Harding 1993).

The most distinctive of the coffins were two with slatted bases. The base of the coffin, rather than being formed from solid longitudinal planks, was formed

ILLUS 4.20
Double burial (mother and child?), Gr0786: Sk0791, younger middle adult woman; Sk0792, younger child

from short transverse planks of irregular width, spaced along the length of the base with gaps between. The best-preserved example was with Sk0251/Gr0252 in Area 5 (**Illus 4.18**– **4.19**), an adolescent. The coffin was 1.75m long, of trapezoidal shape, 0.45m at the head end, narrowing to 0.30m at the foot end. The lid was found almost intact although in poor condition having collapsed over the skeleton. Several iron nails were found on the upper edges of the lid. The base consisted of six or seven planks 100–200mm wide, spaced out with gaps of similar width between them and secured with iron nails. The skeleton was radiocarbon dated to 1415–1625 (**Table 4.02**). The slat-based coffin of Sk0696/Gr0676 in Area 7, an older child, was less well-preserved but the skeleton was radiocarbon dated to 1450–1640 (**Table 4.02**).

Similar finds have been revealed at a handful of other medieval sites, though these seem to represent two different phenomena. In most cases the remains have been identified as planks lining the base of a grave. Plank linings were noted at Battle Abbey, Sussex (Hare 1985, 22), and at the priory of St Mary Sandwell, Staffordshire (Hodder 1991). All were intramural graves, within the chapter house or church, and contained adults, mostly men. They contained no other wooden remains and thus represented either a wooden lining at the base of the grave or else the bier used to transport the body to the grave which was then interred with it.

At St Giles Cathedral, Edinburgh, by contrast, plank remains clearly related to portable nailed coffins with slatted bases and wooden sides (Collard et al 2006, 22–3; McCullagh 2006). All five coffins at St Giles which were well enough preserved for analysis had slatted bases. The earliest were of 13th- or 14th-century date and were extramural. The latest dated to between the mid-15th and mid-16th century and were probably within the body of the extended cathedral, thus broadly contemporary with those found in Leith. The coffins were made of Scots pine (*Pinus silvestris*) and spruce (*Picea abies*). The latter would have had to be imported from northern Europe and was only used for the base boards. They all contained adults (two women, two men, one unsexed).

Five finds from the Carmelite friary in Perth were superficially very similar to those from St Giles (Boyd 1989, 117–8; Hall 1989, 99–110). They were made of Scots pine (*Pinus sylvestris*) and oak (*Quercus*). In the best-preserved example, peg holes were clearly visible but as these did not align with corresponding holes in neighbouring boards, and as there were no finds of iron nails or wooden pegs, it was concluded that the boards were reused, the hole relating to their previous function, and that the boards were not fixed to form a portable coffin. They therefore formed a wooden lining to both the base and walls of the grave, presumably to make the grave more visually impressive during the burial. Three of the graves dated to the 13th or 14th century and were found in the friary presbytery. The other two were of probable 17th-century date and were found in the graveyard. Again, all were adults (three women, one man, one unsexed).

Both the Constitution Street slat-based coffins contained numbers of iron nails (Sk0251/Gr0252, 30 nails; Sk0696/Gr0676, 16 nails), thus both would seem to have more in common with the St Giles burials than those from Perth or the English sites. Poor wood preservation would render these types of coffin archaeologically invisible as they cannot be securely identified from patterns of nail use alone. Thus, their distribution is uncertain. However, to date, this type of slat-based, nailed, portable coffin has only been identified (in Britain at least) in Edinburgh and Leith and may thus represent a local tradition. They may be limited to the 14th and 15th centuries, though a longer currency (13th to 17th century) is possible. No such coffins were found during excavations at the Edinburgh Blackfriars site (Wilson in prep) or at Holyrood Abbey (Bain 1998), though wood preservation was poor at these sites.

In Europe, similar coffins have been noted in 12th- to 14th-century Scandinavia (Blomqvist and Martenson 1963, Chapter 3, 5; Long 1975, 16). This connection to northern Europe is also noted in the use of spruce at St Giles, and the phenomenon may therefore relate to Edinburgh and Leith's strong trading links to the Baltic, and in particular to the importation of Baltic timber. It is unlikely that the coffins were imported from the Baltic ready-made; the evidence suggests that coffins during this period were generally made to measure by local craftsmen (Gilchrist & Sloane 2005, 112). Rather, there might have been a local joinery tradition inspired by Baltic connections within the town (p19; 30), or even Baltic craftsmen living and working within the local area.

The fact that these coffins were used with subadults at Constitution Street suggests that this was not a coffin type connected with the top end of the market. It seems likely that the use of fewer, shorter and possibly reused boards for the base made the coffin a cheaper option. It seems likely that the body within the coffin was wrapped in a shroud and the coffin base may also have been covered in cloth, so that there would have been no danger of anything falling or protruding through the gaps in the coffin base during transportation or burial. If the coffin was transported on a bier then the base of the coffin may never have been visible during the funeral.

DOUBLE BURIALS

Double burials are here defined as graves containing two bodies, interred during

ILLUS 4.21
Double burial, Gr1183: upper, Sk1180, older middle adult man; lower, Sk1181 older adult female

the same burial event. The contemporaneity of the burials was judged based on the presence of a single visible cut and on the relative positions of the bodies.

There were eight instances of double burials. The dimensions of the grave cuts generally did not differ appreciably from those for single inhumations. Five of these contained an adult with a child. Four of these adults were women, the other was unsexed. Of the remaining three, one included two children, the others two adults (a man and woman, and a man and unsexed adult). All were simple burials but for one pair buried in Gr0335 who were both in coffins.

In the four woman-child burials, where it was possible to establish age, the women were all between 20 and 35, the children were between 1½ and 10½ years. The relative ages in all cases would be consistent with a mother and child relationship but not with either death being directly related to childbirth. Gr0114 in Area 4 contained a younger child (for definition of age ranges, see **Table 4.05**, p92), Sk0112 (5½–7½ years), in a prone position, above a younger adult woman, Sk0113, who was supine with arms by her sides (see also p79). The child was radiocarbon dated to 1420–1630 (Sk0112; **Table 4.02**, p84). The grave was truncated to the north-west and south-east by modern services and hence more precise details of the body positioning cannot be determined. In Gr0162, Area 4, an older child, Sk0161 (9½ years), was again placed above a younger middle adult woman, Sk0164, this time, both supine. A pair within Gr0335, Area 6, comprised a younger middle adult female, Sk0346, and an older child (9½–10½ years), Sk0345. The child appeared to be lying on its left side facing away from the woman (see also p81), and was radiocarbon dated to 1335–1620 (**Table 4.02**).

In Gr0786, Area 8, a younger child, Sk0792 (1½–2½ years), was placed beside a younger middle adult woman, Sk0791 (**Illus 4.20**). The child was lying on its right side, the woman on her left side, with their heads turned towards each other. The woman's legs were slightly flexed and her left arm was bent with her

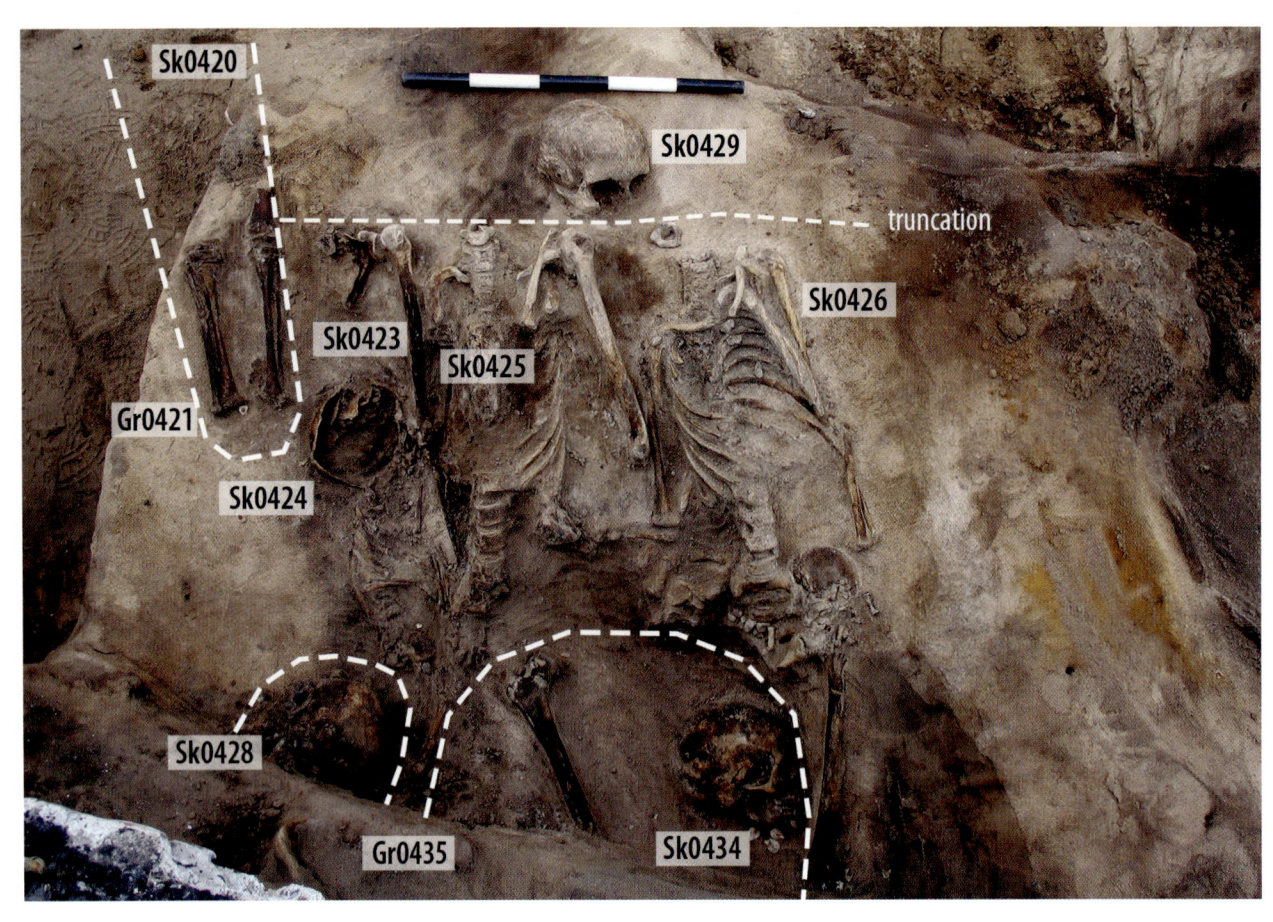

ILLUS 4.22
Group burial Gr0427: Sk0423, adult female; Sk0424, infant; Sk0425, younger adult female; Sk0426, older child. Later cuts for insertion of Sk0420, Sk0428, Sk0429 and Sk0434

elbow pointing towards the child. Interestingly this arm position suggests she was not shrouded when placed into the grave. The position of arm and legs were perhaps intended to stabilise her lying on her side facing the child, though equally this may have been the position in which she died, preserved through the onset of *rigor mortis*, as has been suggested for other flexed burials (Gilchrist & Sloane 2005, 154–5; see also p81). The woman was radiocarbon dated to 1455–1635 (**Table 4.02**).

In other double burials, the bodies seem to have been placed with little care for position, possibly due to limited space within the grave or to over-hasty disposal. In Gr0153, Area 4, younger child (3½–4½ years), Sk0151, and older child (10½–11½ years), Sk0152, were side by side but part overlapping. In Gr0307, Area 5, a younger adult man, Sk0303, and an adult of indeterminate age and sex, Sk0305, both lay supine but placed haphazardly with their legs entangled. In Gr1183, Area 5, an older middle adult man, Sk1180, was lying on top of an older adult woman, Sk1181 (**Illus 4.21**). The positioning in the latter grave might suggest that the upper, male, body was placed in the grave at a later date. However, the proximity of the two burials (the skull of the man rested directly on the rib cage of the woman) combined with lack of damage to the lower burial suggests this was not the case and that they were both interred at the same time.

Another pair of burials, within Gr0335, were the only double burials to have been placed within coffins. Both coffins lay side by side, about 0.2m apart, containing an adult of unknown sex, Sk0361, and a subadult, Sk0363. Only their legs survived, due to later truncation. The adult was radiocarbon dated to 1425–1630 (**Table 4.02**). (Gr0335 is discussed further in *Superimposed burials* below, p76).

Double burials are relatively regular finds in medieval cemeteries and often involved children, both with adults and with other children (eg Coleman 1996, 79–80; Cardy 1997, 551). They may represent family members who died at the same time, possibly of an infectious disease, or a particular rite associated with children (Gilchrist & Sloane 2005, 156–7). Typically, only one or two are noted at any particular site and thus the numbers of these double burials and the inclusion of adult only examples at Constitution Street is unusual.

GROUP BURIALS

Group burials are here defined as grave cuts containing three or more individuals interred during the same burial event. Given the density of burials, poorly defined grave cuts and levels of truncation, and the narrow excavation limits, it was often difficult to distinguish between graves where several people were buried at the same time and grave plots that were reused on different occasions. Contemporaneity seemed reasonably clear where the skeletons touched each other but did not cut each other. In other cases, it was assumed where the grave cut was relatively visible and where the bodies were well aligned and buried in the same manner. Three of these group burials were identified. Discounting any burials which seem to have been cut in later, each grave contained four individuals.

Gr0427 in Area 6 was 0.8m wide and contained four individuals, of various ages: an older child (8½–9 years) Sk0426; two women, Sk0425 and Sk0423; and an infant (6 months–1 year), Sk0424. All were laid out neatly, if rather tightly packed, side by side, except for the infant who was placed on its left side over the lower torso of one of the women, possibly its mother (**Illus 4.22**, see also p81). One of the adults was radiocarbon dated to 1440–1630 (Sk0423; **Table 4.02**). Various other burials were later cut into this grave. A cut along the top of the grave removed the heads of all the adults, a disarticulated skull (Sk0429) from a different (adolescent) individual was found in this location. Sk0420/Gr0421 was cut into the south-west corner of the grave.

Gr0589 in Area 6 appeared to be another group burial, though graves in this area were densely packed and the sequence of burial remains unclear. The four skeletons seemed to lie in a row in the same large rectangular cut, 1.86m wide. The two in the middle, Sk0637 and Sk0639, both younger middle adult females, would appear to have been interred together as the shoulder of one rested over the shoulder of the other (**Illus 4.23**). The others, Sk0643, another younger middle adult woman and Sk0646, an older child (6½–8½ years) were set a little apart but there is no indication that these lay within separate cuts. Radiocarbon dating of the child provided one of the earliest dates from the site of 1315–1455 (**Table 4.02**). It is unclear whether Sk0625/Gr0624, a younger middle adult female, and Sk0626/Gr1218, a younger middle adult male, which overlay the lowest four burials, were placed in at the same time or buried later. Their grave cuts were imperceptible. The picture was considerably confused by a number of other burials of men, women and children overlying the lower burials (Sk0465/Gr0467, Sk0481/Gr0482, Sk0484/Gr0485, Sk0498/Gr0499, Sk0554/Gr0556, Sk0574/Gr0579, Sk0575/Gr0611, Sk0577/Gr0605). The positions of the skeletons and various instances of their cutting the group grave cut and each other suggest these were later insertions. Two were dated and the dates suggest they are indeed later (Sk0481/Gr0482, 1435–1630; Sk0574/Gr0579, 1440–1635; **Table 4.02**).

ILLUS 4.23
Group burial Gr0589: Sk0643, younger middle adult female; Sk0637, younger middle adult female; Sk0639, younger middle adult female; Sk0646, older child

PEOPLE'S STORIES

A POOR MAN WITH BAD LEGS, 1435–1456

Born in 1435, this man was orphaned at the age of four. His mother had died the day after he was born, and his father died in the *wame ill* outbreak (**Table 3.01**, p32). They had nothing and no extended family nearby to take him in. He was left to fend for himself and had to grow up fast, begging for scraps and scavenging in middens. He learnt that dogs were good at sniffing out food and that he could follow them. What they found was barely edible and sometimes made him ill, but it was better than nothing. He befriended one dog in particular and they would share food with each other. The dog also came in useful when he had to defend himself from the rougher elements on the streets.

He knew he could often find a meal and a bed at St Anthony's, though some of the canons were nicer than others. He was put to work there at harvest time to help bring in the crops. When one of the canons heard him singing while he worked, he enrolled him in the song school and made sure he had a decent meal after each choir practice.

The choirmaster eventually found him steady work tending the town's cattle. Many people in the town owned a cow or two to provide the family with milk and each day during the warmer months, they were taken to graze on Leith Links, the large (much larger than today) area of common land to the east of the town. The boy had to stop them wandering off or getting into growing crops and then drive them home at night. He came to know each one by name and in good weather, enjoyed spending his days outside of town, idling in the sun with his dog. It gave him time to practice his singing. His dog would hunt rabbits and when she caught one they would share it. In autumn he could supplement his meagre diet by collecting blackberries from the brambles that grew along the back of the dunes. He was paid in bread, ale and a small amount of coin. He could also make extra money in the alehouses and taverns and in the street by singing ballads about the latest political intrigues.

Even so, he often went hungry and cold, especially in winter. He was painfully thin, and his clothes were thread-bare and patched. He had no shoes, though occasionally he was able to fashion workable footwear from odd broken shoes and scraps of leather and fabric he found during his scavenging trips. He had a keen eye for anything of use by this time. His creations rarely lasted long though and in the summer on the links, it was easier to go barefoot.

He cut his feet several times on sharp stones, and once, while herding the cows past a site where a new house was being built near St Anthony's, a rusty nail had gone through his right foot. He could not abandon his cattle, so he bound it up as best he could and walked on it all day through the muck on the streets. It never really healed properly. Infection crept up both legs, and his right felt particularly sore. He was already feeling weak and feverish when the first cases of plague were noticed in 1456 but he still had to go out and work and scavenge. He fell easy victim to the disease. He found the characteristic painful black swelling or bubo in his groin a few days later and tried to make it to St Anthony's where he hoped his friends might heal him, or at least give him somewhere comfortable to die. He felt dizzy and weak along the way and stopped for a rest in a shed which he knew, from experience, was abandoned. He was found dead there two weeks later by one of the town cleansers, his old dog lying mournfully by his side. His remains were in such a state that they had to be placed in a coffin to move them and were covered in a layer of ash in an attempt to soak up the putrefaction and contain the pestilence. He was taken to the nearest burial ground at the chapel across the road from St Anthony's and given a hasty burial.

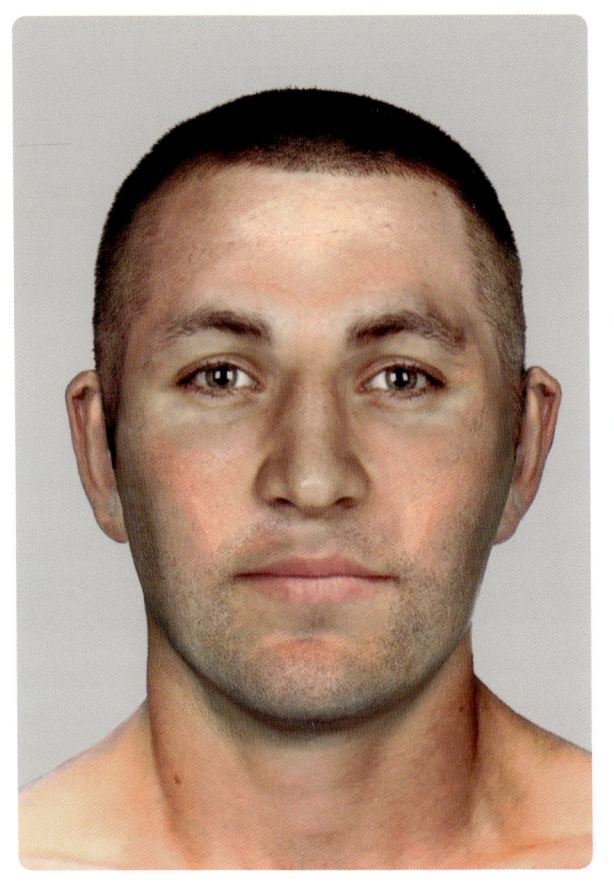

SKELETON	0158
Grave	0159
Location of grave	Constitution Street, Area 5
Burial details	Coffin, possibly with lime deposit within
Age	Young Adult, 18–24
Sex	Male
Stature	170cm or 5'7"
Radiocarbon date	–
Other dating evidence	In phase 2 cemetery, probably only in use after c1430s, overlying possible sand quarry
Finds	–
Pathology	Enamel pearl on tooth (lingual), calculus, periodontal disease, DEH, bilateral periostitis on tibiae and fubulae, and right femur, bilateral severe cribra orbitalia and porotic hyperostosis, Schmorl's nodes
C/N isotope (diet)	–
O/S isotope (origins)	–
See also	Illus 4.08, p57; p69–70; Illus 4.51, p106
Facial reconstruction artist	Emily McCulloch

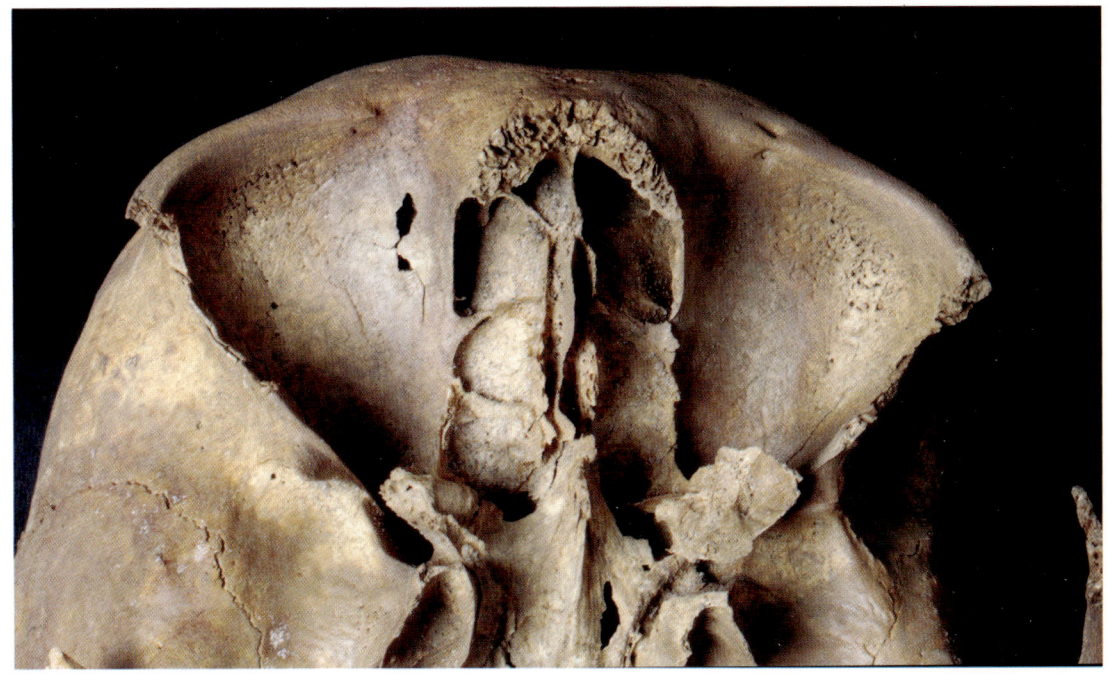

Pitting on the roof of the eye orbit (cribra orbitalia), caused by childhood systemic stress due to nutritional deprivation, disease or parasitic infection. Sk0158

A POOR MAN WITH BAD LEGS, 1435–1456

Gr0807 in Area 8 was truncated to the west, with only the legs surviving. The cut was wider than normal at 0.74m, to accommodate two burials comfortably. Two subadults were placed side by side within it, adolescent Sk0827 and older child Sk0826 (6½–7 years). Above these were two adults, young adult male, Sk0806 and adult female Sk0805. All seem to have been buried at the same time. The man was radiocarbon dated to 1465–1655 (Sk0806; see **Table 4.02**). The truncation and burial pattern in this grave makes its identification as a group burial less certain and it is possible that this grave in fact represents two double burials within a reused plot.

It seems likely that the group burials contained individuals who died at a time of high mortality, such as during famines or epidemics. They may or may not also have had a familial relationship. It is interesting to note that all three of the possible group burials contained almost exclusively women and children. All three group burials account for 12 people in total, six women, one man and five children. This represents a higher proportion of the women buried at the site (6.7%; 6/91) compared with men (1.7%; 1/60) (**Table 4.21**). The only possible man was found in Gr0807, the identification of which as a group burial is more tentative. Gr0807 was also the only one of the three group burials outside of Area 6. Gr0427 and Gr0589 were both within 6m of each other in Area 6, the most densely packed burial area excavated (**Table 4.04**).

SUPERIMPOSED BURIALS

There were many instances where burials overlay other burials and where it seemed the placement might be a deliberate superimposition. In areas as densely packed as Area 6 it is perhaps inevitable that some burials would directly overlie others, by mere coincidence. There were three areas where a sequence of burials was particularly marked and might suggest a deliberate placement.

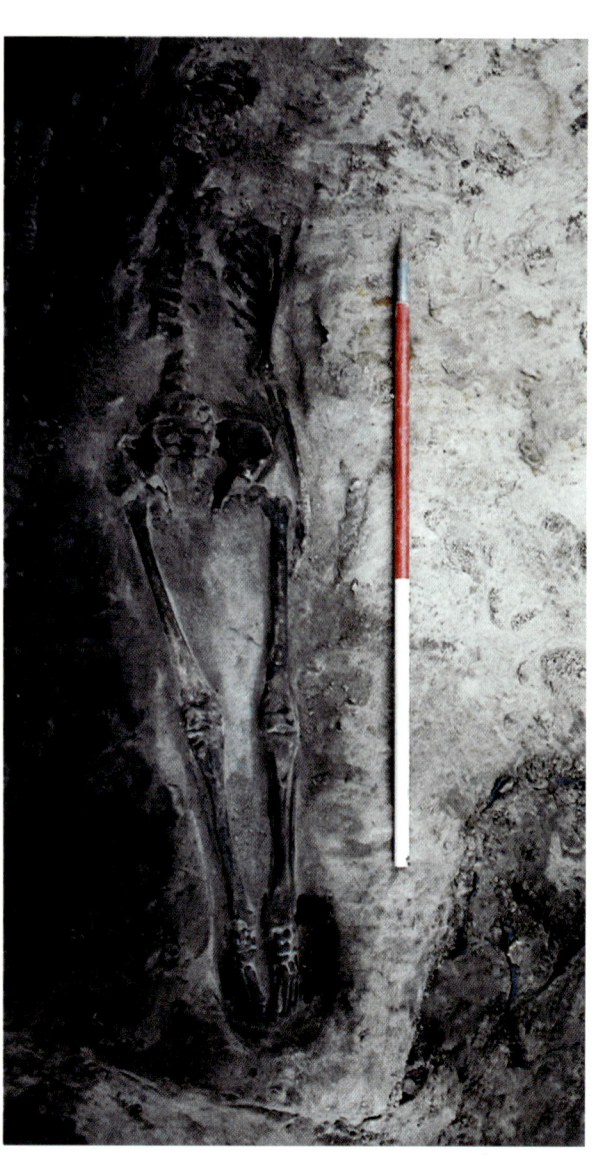

ILLUS 4.24
Sk1052/Gr1053, older child, subsiding into darker ditch deposits

Gr0335, on the border of Areas 5 and 6, was recorded on site as a single cut and might represent another group burial, though is more disorderly than those noted above (see *Group burials*, p73–76). The remains of five people were found within it but differences in the manner and position of the burials suggests the interments were not contemporary. It was severely truncated by a service trench to the north-east and a sewer cut to the north-west but at its southern extent was at least 2m long and 1m wide. Since four of the interments were in two pairs, these burials are also discussed as double burials above (p72). The first burials were placed in side by side, both in coffins, Sk0361 and Sk0363, an adult of unknown sex and a subadult. Truncation to the west meant that only their legs survived. Another pair, Sk0345 and Sk0346, an older child (9½–10½ years) and a younger middle adult woman, were placed on top of these, without coffins, and differently placed so that their heads were level with the waists of the lower bodies. They were in poor condition and were described during excavation as being 'squashed'. Sk0342, an adult female, was above these, again represented only by legs. Three of the burials were dated (**Table 4.02**); in stratigraphic order, from the lowest, these were 1425–1630 (Sk0361), 1335–1620 (Sk0345), 1445–1635 (Sk0342), giving a broad range of early 15th to early 17th century for the all the burials.

Another series of four burials were placed one of top of the other over the top of the cut for group burial Gr0589 in Area 6. They were neatly placed, but with some variation in terms of E-W positioning. The first of them, Sk0574/Sk0579, a younger adult female, was dated to 1440–1635 (**Table 4.02**). Above her was Sk0575/Gr0611, a younger middle adult possible male, then Sk0577/Gr0605, an older middle adult woman, buried in a coffin. Above her was Sk0554/Gr0556, an older child (11½–12 years), also in a coffin.

Another grave, Gr0137 in Area 4, identified as a group burial on site, may also have been a series of superimposed burials. The grave cut was about 1m wide but only the eastern end was visible, the western end being outside the excavation area. Four burials, each represented only by the legs (sometimes only lower legs), were placed one on top of the other, seemingly within the same grave cut. Sk0143, an unsexed adult, was first, followed by Sk0136, a younger middle adult female, then Sk0135, a younger child a little to the side, and lastly Sk0134, a younger adult female, which cut the remains of underlying Sk0136.

Assuming a degree of intention in these sequences, it suggests that these may have been particularly desirable locations for burials, such as in front of a graveyard cross (Gilchrist & Sloane 2005, 52) or another now invisible landmark. The very dense cluster at the north end of Area 6 (around and over Gr0589) might support this. The mix of ages found in all three sequences is consistent with use as a family burial plot. Similar superimposed burials have been noted in other cemeteries, though typically these only involved sequences of two or three burials. Larger 'vaults' are generally only found in intramural settings (Gilchrist & Sloane 2005, 158–9). Nevertheless, it is possible that these sequences or parts of them represented a desire on the part of the individuals concerned to be buried close to loved ones. For this to be possible, the grave would have had to be marked in some way, perhaps with a wooden cross (ibid, 190–4); there is no evidence for the use of stone grave markers at the site.

If these were formally marked family burial plots reused a number of times, then it seems likely that this would have incurred a certain amount of cost in terms of burial fees. It is perhaps of note, therefore, that there was a higher rate of coffin use among these burials (33.3%; 4/12) compared with 21% (63/305) for the cemetery as a whole (p69), though the small sample size and the complexity of factors surrounding the use of coffins for burial (p83) means this figure provides, at best, tentative evidence for social status. As in the group burials described above (p76), a higher proportion of women (5.5%; 5/91 of all adult female burials) and subadults (3.4%; 4/117) were involved in these superimposed burials than men (1.7%; 1/60).

CHARNEL AND REDEPOSITED BURIALS

As in most Christian cemeteries of the period, intercutting of graves was common and disarticulated human bone was widely spread through the cemetery soil. Any remains disturbed during gravedigging seem to have been reinterred within the new grave. There seems to have been a special treatment of skulls in these circumstances. They were often placed in with care between the legs or next to the head of the new body. Other bones may have been simply shovelled in with the rest of the backfill. This treatment of skulls has been noted elsewhere (Gilchrist & Sloane 2005, 180). Only two instances were noted of pits which seem to have been specifically dug to dispose of charnel, pits [0501] and [1096]. These may relate to the cutting of ditch [0980] through the cemetery rather than to gravedigging within it and have been described below (p88–89).

One body (Sk0841/Gr0842; **Illus 4.30**) seems to have been disturbed while in a semi-decomposed state and was reinterred partially articulated and in an unusual position (p81). Again, this was possibly related to the cutting of ditch [0980].

ALIGNMENT

In keeping with all Christian cemeteries, almost all burials at Constitution Street were aligned W-E (the head end of the grave is given first in all descriptions of alignments). The medieval rationale was that on the day of judgement the body would rise up and face Christ in the east (Gilchrist & Sloane 2005, 152). There were no E-W burials at Constitution Street. This rite has been often linked to the burial of priests, so that they might rise up facing their flocks, but there is no evidence this was practiced during the medieval period (ibid, 153). While E-W burials are sometimes found on medieval sites (Lindsay 1989a; Stroud & Kemp 1993, 137; Coleman 1996, 80; Cardy 1997,

ILLUS 4.25
Sk0481/Gr0482, older middle adult female, showing V-shaped grave cut

551), some of these are of women and children and there is no evidence to link any of the men so buried to the priesthood (Gilchrist & Sloane 2005, 153).

Three individuals were aligned S-N, all in Area 6 (**Illus 4.09**). Two were found one on top of the other: Sk1017/Gr1018, a coffined younger middle adult woman, overlying Sk1052/Gr1053, an older child (12½–13 years) simple burial. Both were found along the edge of ditch [0980], both sloping down into the ditch at their southern (head) end (**Illus 4.24**). The lower of these two, Sk1052, was radiocarbon dated to 1300–1445 (**Table 4.02**). Their relationship to the ditch was a little ambiguous. It appeared superficially that they must post-date the ditch backfill. However, the sloping position and the outward curve of the ditch edge in this location suggest that erosion of the sandy deposits of the ditch edge might have caused these bodies to slump into it after it was cut. The 14th or early 15th-century dating of Sk1052 also suggests it predates the ditch (p148).

It was considered that these bodies may have been disturbed during ditch cutting and were then reinterred along the ditch edge. However, since it seems that a minimum of several decades would have passed between the burial and reburial it is very unlikely that either burial, particularly the uncoffined Sk1052, would have been well enough preserved to be buried fully articulated. Over a period of 30 years or more the body would have been, at best nearly and more likely completely, skeletonised (Byers 2010, 118–9). It is far more likely that in such circumstances, the body would have been reburied as a collection of charnel. Thus, given that the two burials predate the ditch, their unusual alignment can have nothing to do with their proximity to it and would appear to be largely coincidental.

The third S-N burial, Sk0481/Gr0482, an older middle adult woman (**Illus 4.25**), lay about 1m to the west of the ditch edge. There was a distinct V-shape to the profile of the skeleton, the pelvis lying lower than the head and feet, and to the east the right side of the body was lower than the left. Thus, it would seem either that the grave cut was poorly excavated or that there was subsequent subsidence. The grave did overly an extremely dense concentration of burials including group burial Gr0589, thus the latter is possible. There was an inward rotation to the shoulders suggesting the body was placed in a narrow grave cut or was tightly wrapped when it was interred. It was radiocarbon dated to 1435–1630 (**Table 4.02**) and thus is possibly contemporary with Sk1052, though is more likely to be later. There were a number of other unusual aspects to this burial, in terms of associated finds, and it seems likely that she was buried wearing clothing (p122; 124; 152).

Burials oriented S-N and N-S are rare finds in medieval and post-medieval cemeteries (Gilchrist & Sloane 2005, 153). Links have been suggested with executed felons (eg Anderson 2009, 17; Stirland 2009), though there does not appear to be any direct proof of this. A man found buried N-S face down in a ditch at Perth Carmelite friary in the late 16th century may have been murdered and dumped rather than formally buried (Hall 1989, 106). There was also a single N-S skeleton found in a mass battle grave at Towton, Yorkshire (Fiorato et al 2000, fig. 4.6), though this could well be incidental, based on the practical need to fit as many bodies as possible into the pit.

Recent excavations, however, have revealed the practice of N-S and S-N burials to be distinctly more common in Leith than is apparent elsewhere. They have been found at all three of the modern archaeological excavations of articulated human remains in Leith, including all four of the burials at St Mary's Star of the Sea (Anderson 2009) and nine of the 71 burials at St Mary's Primary School (Churchill 2016, 17–20). Including the Constitution Street excavations, 4.2% of all the articulated burials excavated and recorded under modern archaeological conditions in Leith have been buried in this alignment (**Table 4.01**). St Mary's Primary School also provides a causative link for the alignment in that there is convincing historical and archaeological evidence to suggest that all the burials there were of victims of the 1644–5 plague outbreak. It seems distinctly possible that the burials at St Mary's Star of the Sea were also victims of the same plague (p35–36).

Gordon notes that this was an occasional practice for plague victims in Scotland (Gordon 1984, 120) though does not suggest why this was the case. The practice may be related to those who suffered a 'bad death', that is dying without the benefit of the last rites (Gilchrist & Sloane 2005, 71–7). This would clearly be more common during times of high plague mortality, though could include other types of death as well, such as sudden violent death, women who died in childbirth and indeed, executed felons. The rite has not been noted among individual burials excavated in plague cemeteries in London, though was observed in mass graves at one site (ibid, 153), where again this was considered to be a purely practical affair.

TABLE 4.01

N-S and S-N burials found in archaeological excavations in Leith

SITE	TOTAL ARTICULATED BURIALS	N-S	S-N	TOTAL N-S/S-N	% OF TOTAL BURIALS
St Mary's Star of the Sea (Anderson 2009)	4	4	–	4	100
St Mary's Primary School (Churchill 2016, 17–20)	71	6	3	9	12.7
Constitution Street (this volume)	305	–	3	3	1.0
TOTAL	380	10	6	16	4.2

Both the Constitution Street and St Mary's Primary School skeletons were demographically similar, representing a mix of ages. The former was made up of two women and a subadult. Osteological work on the latter is in preliminary stages but the remains included six adults, one of which was possibly female, and three subadults. The St Mary's Star of the Sea burials are different in this respect, being all well-built men, though as they are also the only burials apparently outside official cemeteries, there may be specific reasons for this (p35–36). Thus, though there is clearly a plague connection to this form of burial in Leith, it is not clear to what extent it was exclusive to plague victims or if it encompassed other types of bad death as well. Nor is it clear on what criteria this rite was chosen, given that even at St Mary's Primary where it seems likely that all the individuals died of plague, only 13% were so buried. It is also unclear whether there was any distinction made at the time between S-N and N-S burial, though dating may have been a factor, with N-S becoming more common later.

The S-N burials at Constitution Street all seem to predate those at both the other Leith sites. One was radiocarbon dated at least two centuries earlier (Sk1052, 1300–1445; see **Table 4.02**), and one was later but still predating the 1644–5 plague (Sk0481, 1435–1630; see **Table 4.02**). Another, Sk1017, was undated, but considering it directly overlay Sk1052 and both were in identical alignment, it seems likely that they are contemporary. It is possible that these earlier S-N burials at Constitution Street were buried in this way for an entirely different reason, but equally it seems this may have been a very local but long-lived custom for the burial of some plague victims.

Though the graves have been described above as W-E and S-N, there was, in practice, considerable variation in the exact grave alignment with none aligned true to the cardinal points. It has been suggested that variation in grave alignment was seasonal, with each grave aligned to the rising sun, but this does not stand up to scrutiny (Gilchrist & Sloane 2005, 15). Instead, graves generally appear to be aligned to nearby landmarks, to the church itself or often to boundaries and paths (ibid, 49; Boucher et al 2015, 89–92).

The current South Leith Parish Church is aligned between W-E and WNW-ESE, 9° off true W-E, and this presumably matches the alignment of the original St Mary's Church of which it formed part. Few of the burials match this and those that most closely match it are largely limited to Areas 5 and 6 (**Illus 4.26**). Most of the burials were aligned approximately WNW-ESE (22.5° off true W-E), varying from 15° to 32°. These most closely match the alignment of ditch [0084] in Area 3 (which appears, in the excavated portion, to be between about 22° and 35°). This implies that the ditch, or at least the boundary it represented, was still visible during the burial period (see *Ditches [0270] and [0084]* p65–66).

They are also approximately perpendicular to the Kirkgate which, as depicted on the first edition Ordnance Survey map (Ordnance Survey 1853a), was about 17° off true N-S where it ran past St Mary's. A few burials were aligned closer to NW-SE (45°), that is between 35° and 53°; most of these were found in Areas 2–4. They match the orientation of ditch [0270] in Area 4 (38–45°). It is reasonably clear that the ditch was backfilled and obscured during the burial period, so this may be coincidence. The burials in these different alignments may represent burial phases though there was no clear chronological pattern in the alignment of the dated burials.

BODY POSITION

Bodies were subject to a certain amount of movement during decomposition and thus the position in which the skeleton was found does not necessarily reflect the exact position in which it was placed in the grave. As in most Christian cemeteries, the vast majority were laid in the grave or coffin in the extended supine position. Arms were most commonly folded either across the abdomen or pelvic area or were straight by their sides. The preference for one arm position over another might have been entirely practical. At Hereford Cathedral, a correlation was noted between burials with folded arms and shroud burials, while coffined burials were more likely to have arms by their sides. (Boucher et al 2015, 89). When winding in a shroud, placing the arms over the body would have stopped them falling out of position as the body was manoeuvred. No equivalent correlation was noted at Constitution Street. In all, 73 of the burials were well enough preserved to determine arm position, 50 from simple burials and 23 coffined. The arms were folded in 72% (36/50) of the simple burials, though this was also the most common position in the coffined burials (65%, 15/23). The smaller sample size and condition of the burials might have affected these statistics.

Two prone burials were found, both simple burials of children. Sk0112/Gr0114 in Area 4 was a younger child (5½–7½ years) lying directly over an adult woman, Sk0113 (described above, p71). The age of the individuals suggests the pair could have been mother and child. The other prone burial, Sk1191/Gr1193 in Area 5, was an older child (11½ years). It was heavily truncated, represented only by its head and upper torso which were sloping upwards towards the head. It may have moved from its original position after burial (**Illus 4.27**).

It is likely that there were various reasons for prone burials: as punishment, as a penance, for burial of unbaptised infants or simply an accidental positioning during a hurried burial (Gilchrist & Sloane 2005, 154). It seems unlikely that any of these, apart from arguably the latter, apply to the younger child, Sk0112, and its prone position in the double burial may have been a deliberate echoing of the maternal relationship.

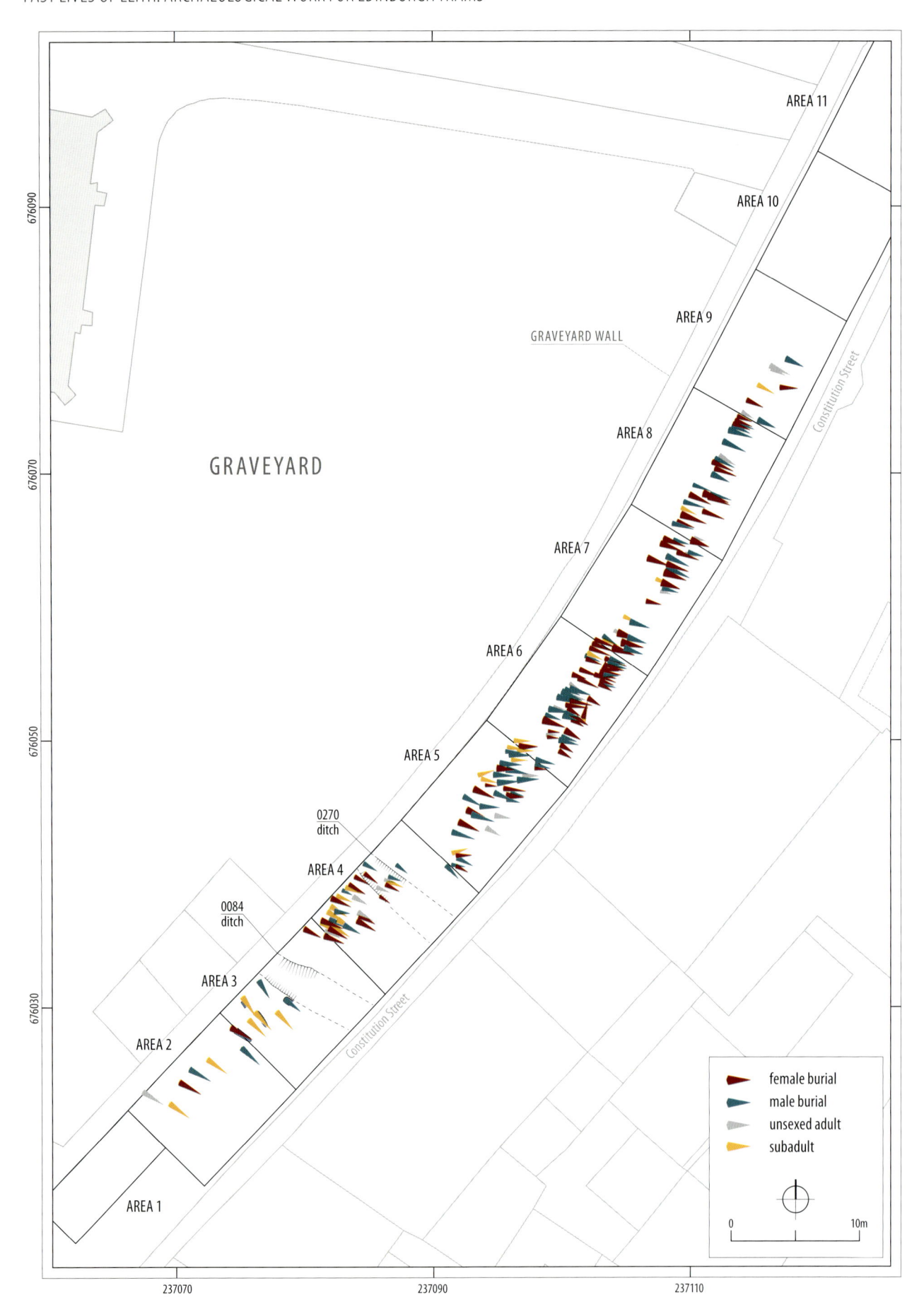

PAST LIVES OF LEITH. ARCHAEOLOGICAL WORK FOR EDINBURGH TRAMS

ILLUS 4.26
Alignment and sex of Constitution Street burials

CONSTITUTION STREET EXCAVATIONS

A more gruesome possibility for older child Sk1191 was suggested in the case of a similarly positioned burial at Perth Dominican friary (Bowler & Hall 1995, 944). A female skeleton was found in a prone position, as if doing press-ups, not dissimilar to the position of Sk1191, though the latter was missing its arms. It was suggested that the Perth woman was buried alive and the position was the result of her trying to push her way out of the grave. Another woman was found in a similar position at Linlithgow Carmelite friary, where it was suggested she died in a fire or was buried during *rigor mortis* (Cross & Bruce 1989, 141).

A few individuals, mostly children, seemed to have been buried on their sides with their legs flexed. This seems to have been a relatively common occurrence generally in the graves of infants and young children and it may be that they were placed in a natural sleeping position (Gilchrist & Sloane 2005, 155–6). Several of these were in multiple graves and are also described above (p71–76). Sk0345/Gr0335 in Area 6 was an older child (9½–10½ years) and was lying on its left side, facing away from the woman with whom it was buried. Sk0424/Gr0427 in Area 6, an infant (6–12 months), was also on its left side but on top of a woman within a group burial (**Illus 4.22**). Sk0067/Gr0069 in Area 3, a younger child (2–3 years), was also lying on its left side, with partly flexed legs, but within a coffin in a single grave (**Illus 4.28**).

Gr0786 in Area 7 was the only grave to feature a child (Sk0792, younger child, 1½–2½ years) lying on its right side and included an unusual case of an adult (Sk0791, younger middle adult female) also on her side (**Illus 4.20**). The pair were buried facing each other and may represent a rather poignant placing of mother and child.

Sk0194/Gr0195 in Area 4, an adolescent, was buried in a simple grave, in a supine position but for flexed legs (**Illus 4.29**). The arms were somewhat casually placed, one by the side, the other crossed over the body. The feet were truncated by modern disturbance. There was otherwise nothing remarkable about this burial. It is possible that this was, once again, a case of burial during *rigor mortis* (Gilchrist & Sloane 2005, 155) or it is possible that the grave was simply found to be too small during the burial.

Sk0841/Gr0842 in Area 9 (**Illus 4.12**), a younger middle adult male, was the most northerly of all the excavated burials. He was found in an almost crouched position with his spine curving forwards (**Illus 4.30**). Most of his arms were missing, but for part of the lower right and some finger bones. His head and legs seem to have been truncated by later cuts. There was no trace of a coffin. It seems that he was rather unceremoniously dumped in this grave, albeit broadly in the correct alignment. The position of the body, the displacement of the pelvis and the absence of some of the arm bones suggests this was redeposition of a partially decomposed body rather than a primary burial. The torso seems to have been articulated enough to stay in one piece, though the arms may not have been. This suggests a period between burial and reburial of 1–30 years (Byers 2010, 118–9). The body overlay cobbled surface (0881). The redeposition might relate to the cutting of nearby ditch [0980] though its relationship to the ditch was unclear (p77).

DATING OF THE BURIALS

The dating of the burials derives chiefly from the programme of radiocarbon dating, but further inferences could be gleaned from the stratigraphic relationship to the

ILLUS 4.27
Sk1191/Gr1193, older child, possibly prone burial

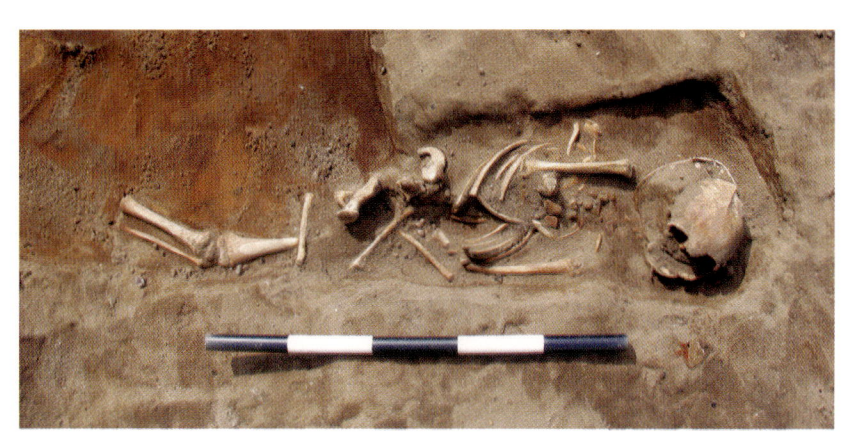

ILLUS 4.28
Sk0067/Gr0069, younger child, lying on left side within coffin

ILLUS 4.29
Sk0194/Gr0195, adolescent with flexed legs

ILLUS 4.30
Sk0841/Gr0842, younger middle adult male, possibly redeposited semi-articulated

various other features, particularly ditch [0980] which cut a number of the graves, and midden (0073/0082/0085), which was cut by several Area 3 graves. It was decided to radiocarbon date 10% of the burials. The resulting 30 dates were chosen to provide a range across the different excavation areas and burial types. One disarticulated skull (Sk0985/Gr0988) was dated on the basis that it presented interesting pathology (p108; 122) and might provide early dating for the presence of syphilis in Leith. The dates have been calibrated taking into account the marine reservoir effect caused by the high marine component of the diet of many of the individuals dated (see p12 for explanation). The results are presented in full in **Table 4.02** and **Illus 4.31** in chronological order.

The results produced a much wider range of dates than had initially been expected, challenging the perceived ecclesiastical history of the area. It had been assumed that the burials would all post-date c1483, the generally cited date for the foundation of St Mary's Church. In practice, however, the dates ranged from 1275–1395 (Sk0478/Gr0479) to 1475–1795 (Sk1119/Gr1118). The spread of dates implies this part of the cemetery was in use from the 14th to the 17th centuries.

Quoted at 95% probability, three of the dates (Sk0478/Gr0479, Sk1052/Gr1053, Sk0646/Gr0589) fall entirely before 1483 and it is possible that a significant number of the other burials also predate 1483. It is conceivable that early use of the cemetery might have been related to the Preceptory of St Anthony, founded in c1430 on the opposite side of the Kirkgate to St Mary's (p20–21). However, the earliest date also appears to predate this by at least several decades and there is no historical evidence that this area was ever used by St Anthony's, whose graveyard seems to have been to the south of the preceptory buildings (p33).

The earliest three dates (1275–1396 to 1315–1455) were all from Area 6 and the earliest 13 dates (1275–1395 to 1445–1635) were all from Areas 4 to 6, suggesting the area initially used for burial was considerably smaller than that brought into use subsequently. Later dates from these central areas, however, shows that their use continued throughout the burial period represented at the site.

The earliest date outside of this nucleus was from Area 2 to the south, 1445–1635 (Sk0040/Gr0042), though the presence of early 17th-century midden deposit (0073/0082/0085) underlying some of the graves in Area 3 suggest this southern part of the cemetery did not come into use until the latter part of the radiocarbon range of the three dated burials there. The earliest date from the northern areas was from Area 7, 1450–1640 (Sk0696/Gr0676), though the presence of graves in this area left in situ and undated below the excavation depth limit might mean that burial actually began earlier there. The dates imply that, at some point after the mid-15th century, the cemetery expanded to the north. The dating also suggests this may have coincided with the traditional c1483 dating for the construction of St Mary's. The expansion to the south in Areas 2 and 3 during the early 17th century may have been around 1609 when St Mary's was given official parish church status, or in 1614 with the foundation of the King James Hospital.

The dating for the cessation of burial within the excavation area is unclear. The radiocarbon dates suggest this was most likely some time during the 16th or first half of the 17th century. However, burial was clearly happening in Areas 2 and 3 in the 17th century. The dating of ditch [0980] is key as it cut a number of the burials along the eastern side of the site between Areas 4 and 9 and there is no convincing evidence of any burials stratigraphically post-dating the cutting or backfilling of the ditch (**Illus 4.02**; **Illus 4.08–4.12**). A few burials do appear to cut into the ditch edge, but these seem to represent the later erosion of the ditch edge and the subsequent subsidence of earlier graves into it (p89). The ditch is likely to relate to the defences of either the mid-16th century or the mid-17th century (see p146–148, for further discussion of this point).

DISTRIBUTION OF BURIAL TYPES

Distribution of the burials by date and area has already been discussed (p81–83) and distribution by age and sex is considered elsewhere (p117–19). This section considers the distribution of coffined/simple burials and of multiple burials and S-N aligned burials, both spatially and temporally.

Coffin use in post-medieval cemeteries was commonplace and appears to have been largely linked to status. Over the course of the 17th century, burial within coffins became more common than without (Harding 2002, 59–60). However, the cost of the coffin and higher burials fees for coffined burials meant that their use was precluded for the poorer elements of society (Gilchrist & Sloane 2005, 116). During the medieval period, however, the link between status and coffin use is not so clear and there is no clear general progression of coffin burial becoming more common over time. Some people eschewed the trappings of wealth for a more humble burial with no coffin (ibid, 24). Increased levels of coffin use have been recorded in plague cemeteries and in regular graveyards during plague years (ibid, 114), possibly for practical reasons if burying bodies that had been lying unburied for some weeks, in an effort to avoid contagion. At some monastic graveyards increased coffin use has been noted in relation to women and children due to the belief that their bodies were more prone to decay (ibid, 222).

There was no such demographic correlation at Constitution Street (p117–19; **Table 4.21**), where coffin use was slightly higher for men. There was, however, a slight correlation observable osteologically between status and coffin use (p119–20; **Table 4.22**, **Table 4.23**). There also appears to be an increase in coffin use over time as demonstrated by the dated burials. Of the earliest 15 dated burials (1275–1395 to 1445–1635), three were buried in coffins. Of the latest 15 burials (1445–1635 to 1475–1795), six were in coffins. Thus, though the use of coffins seems to have increased over time, it was still in the minority.

The greater proportion of coffin use at the north (Areas 7–9) and south (Areas 2–3) ends of the excavation area (**Table 4.03**, **Illus 4.02**, **Illus 4.05–12**) must at least in part be due to lack of early graves in those areas, as they seem to have come into use some time later than Areas 4 to 6. The difference was more marked at the south end of the site. All but one of the 13 graves in Areas 2 and 3, south of ditch [0084], contained a coffin. The burials were also sparser and more widely spaced than in the rest of the site. The lack of intercutting burials would suggest that the graves were marked with wooden crosses or other grave markers, or that the use of the cemetery was relatively short-lived and therefore each grave was naturally marked by a fresh mound of earth.

Again, dating is probably a major factor in this difference. Though the radiocarbon dates of the southern burials fall well within the range of dates for the rest of the site, their stratigraphic relationship to the early 17th-century midden deposit in this area suggests that they may be later, or at least among the latest burials on site. The difference might also be related to the nature of those buried within this area. It is possible it was set aside for wealthier members of the congregation, possibly for use by a specific trade incorporation. One of the primary roles of medieval guilds, incorporations and fraternities was to act as a kind of 'burial club' where members were assured of a funeral and prayers to protect them after death (McRee 1992). Separate burial plots within graveyards have been noted historically at other sites (Gilchrist & Sloane 2005, 64). However, this area contained a high proportion of subadults (p117–19) and the usual (for this site) majority of women among the adult burials. Thus, if it was used by the incorporations, it must have been for their families rather than for the members themselves. It is also possible that, given the connection between plague and high coffin use seen at some English sites (see above), that this was part of an area used during a specific plague outbreak.

PAST LIVES OF LEITH. ARCHAEOLOGICAL WORK FOR EDINBURGH TRAMS

TABLE 4.02
Constitution Street radiocarbon dates listed in chronological order. Note: all the calibrated dates are cal AD; the marine component percentage is calculated from the $\delta^{13}C$ value (p12), *see p142–43, Illus 4.74

AREA	PLOT*	SK	GR	BURIAL DETAILS	RELATIONSHIPS	LAB CODE	UNCALIBRATED BP	$\delta^{13}C‰$	MARINE %	CALIBRATED 95.4% PROBABILITY	CALIBRATED 68.2% PROBABILITY	AGE	SEX
6	F	0478	0479	Simple	–	SUERC–38388	685 ± 30	–20.9	1%	1275–1395	1285–1315, 1360–1385	YA	F
6	E/F	1052	1053	Simple, S-N	Slipping into ditch 0980	SUERC–38408	625 ± 30	–19.3	20%	1300–1445	1320–1355, 1390–1425	OC	U
6	F	0646	0589	Simple, Group	Cut by ditch 0980	SUERC–38396	550 ± 30	–20.6	5%	1315–1355, 1390–1455	1400–1440	OC	U
5/6	E	0345	0335	Simple, Double, Superimposed?	Above Sk0361, below Sk0342	SUERC–38385	530 ± 30	–19.4	19%	1335, 1395–1525 1595–1620	1415–1470	OC	U
4	C	0175	0176	Simple	Below Sk0112/Gr0114	SUERC–38376	505 ± 30	–20.3	8%	1400–1515, 1605–1610	1415–1455	AD	U
5	E	0251	0252	Coffin (slat-based)	–	SUERC–38378	515 ± 30	–19.0	24%	1415–1535, 1555–1625	1430–1505	ADOL	U
4	C	0112	0114	Simple, Double	Above Sk0175/Gr0176	SUERC–38374	470 ± 30	–19.9	13%	1420–1530, 1555–1630	1430–1510	YC	U
5/6	E	0361	0335	Coffin, Double, Superimposed?	Below Sk0345 & Sk0342	SUERC–38386	460 ± 30	–20.1	11%	1425–1530, 1555–1630	1435–1515, 1605–1610	AD	U
6	F	0481	0482	Simple, S-N	–	SUERC–38392	445 ± 30	–19.9	13%	1435–1535, 1540–1630	1445–1520, 1600–1615	OMA	F
4	C	0212	0213	Simple	On edge of ditch 0270	SUERC–38377	450 ± 30	–19.8	14%	1435–1535, 1540–1635	1440–1520, 1600–1615	AD	F
6	E	0423	0427	Simple, Group	–	SUERC–38387	390 ± 30	–21.0	0%	1440–1525, 1560 1570–1630	1445–1495, 1510 1600–1615	AD	F
6	F	0574	0579	Simple, Superimposed?	–	SUERC–38393	420 ± 30	–20.4	7%	1440–1535, 1540–1635	1445–1520, 1590–1620	YA	F
6	F	0998	0999	Simple	Cut by ditch 0980	SUERC–38407	450 ± 30	–19.3	20%	1445–1635	1450–1525, 1575–1620	OC	U
2	A	0040	0042	Coffin	–	SUERC–38368	440 ± 30	–19.3	20%	1445–1635	1455–1525, 1575–1585 1590–1625	ADOL	U
2/3	B	0063	0065	Coffin	–	SUERC–38372	435 ± 30	–19.8	14%	1445–1635	1445–1525, 1590–1620	YA	F
5/6	E	0342	0335	Simple, Superimposed?	Above Sk0361 & Sk0345	SUERC–38384	440 ± 30	–19.3	20%	1445–1635	1455–1525, 1575–1585 1590–1625	AD	F
7	G	0696	0676	Coffin (slat-based)	–	SUERC–38398	425 ± 30	–19.5	18%	1450–1640	1465–1525, 1560–1565 1570–1625	OC	U
7	G	0791	0786	Simple, Double	–	SUERC–38397	405 ± 30	–19.9	13%	1455–1635	1470–1525, 1565–1625	YMA	F
5	E	0301	0302	Simple	–	SUERC–38382	400 ± 30	–19.6	16%	1460–1645	1490–1530, 1550–1630	YMA	F
3	B	0090	0086	Coffin	On edge of ditch 0084	SUERC–38373	410 ± 30	–19.0	24%	1460–1650	1515–1635	ADOL	U
8	G	0806	0807	Simple, Group	–	SUERC–38402	400 ± 30	–19.1	22%	1465–1655	1520–1640	YMA	M?
7	F	0585	0587	Coffin	–	SUERC–38394	390 ± 30	–19.4	19%	1465–1655	1520–1640	YMA	F
4	C	0172	0173	Simple	–	SUERC–38375	385 ± 30	–19.4	19%	1465–1655	1520–1605, 1610–1640	YMA	M?
5	E	0306	0311	Simple	–	SUERC–38383	370 ± 30	–19.5	13%	1470–1650	1520–1600, 1615–1645	YA	U
6	E	0985	0988	Disart skull in grave	Cut by ditch 0980	SUERC–38406	430 ± 30	–18.4	31%	1465–1660	1520–1640	AD	F
9	H	0845	0843	Coffin	Above cobbles 0881	SUERC–38403	400 ± 30	–18.8	26%	1470–1665	1520–1605 1610–1645	AD	U
7	G	0936	0937	Simple	–	SUERC–38404	370 ± 30	–19.9	18%	1475–1665	1515–1600 1610–1640	PE	U
7	F	0592	0590	Coffin	Slipping into ditch 0980	SUERC–38395	375 ± 30	–19.2	21%	1475–1665	1520–1600 1615–1650	OMA	F
7	F	0951	0952	Simple	Cut by ditch 0980	SUERC–38405	350 ± 30	–19.6	16%	1475–1670	1520–1595 1615–1655	YMA	U
5	D/E	1119	1118	Simple	Cut by ditch 0980	SUERC–38412	350 ± 30	–19.5	18%	1475–1675, 1785–1795	1525–1595 1620–1655	OC	M?

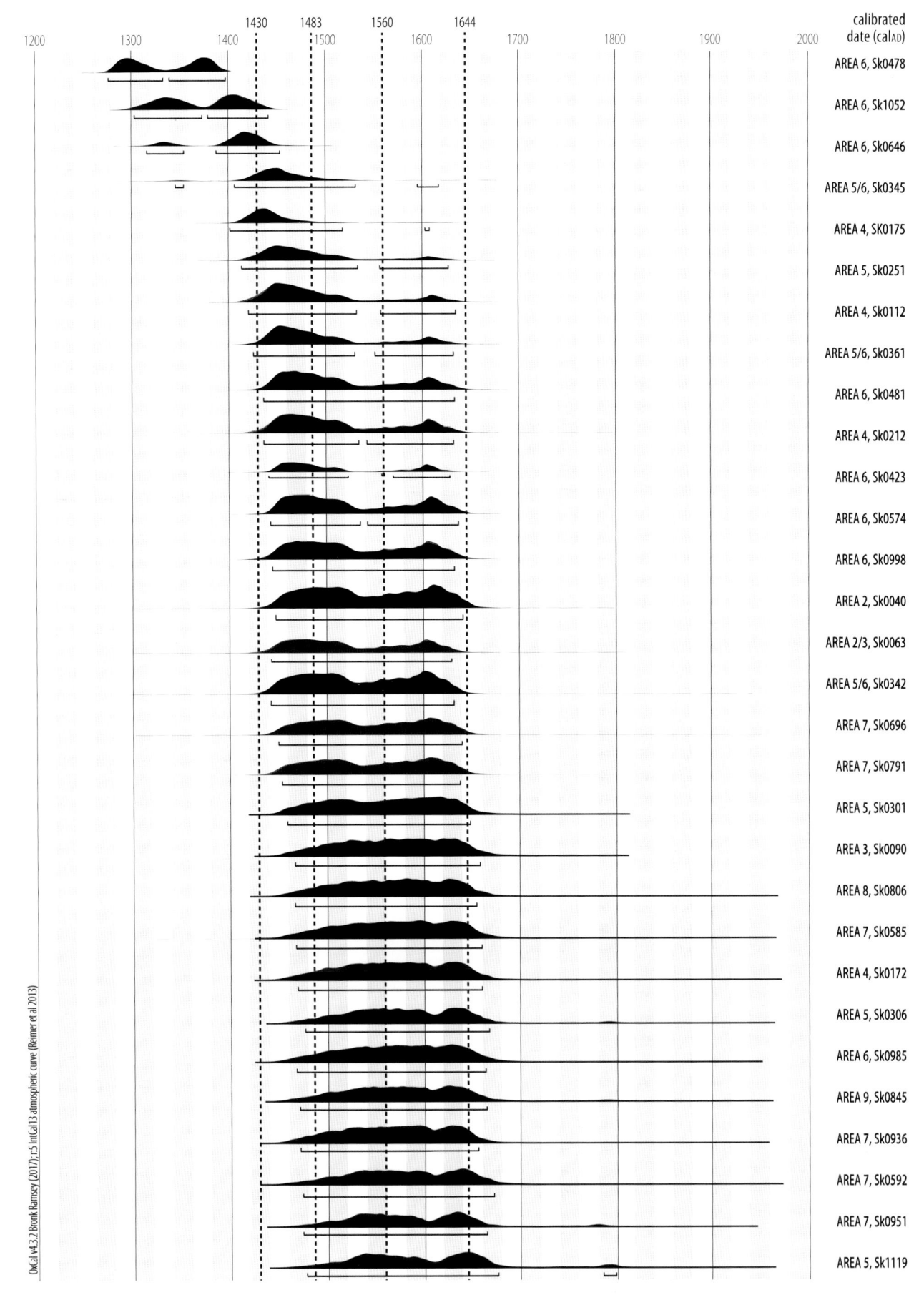

CONSTITUTION STREET EXCAVATIONS

ILLUS 4.31
Constitution Street radiocarbon date ranges, showing relationship to historical dates relating to the Preceptory of St Anthony (1430), St Mary's Church (1483), the Siege of Leith (1560) and the plague (1644)

A BIG BRUISER OF A MAN, 1438–1478

This man was born in 1438, the year after the six-year old James II ascended the throne. It was said that the new king had a red birthmark on his face which was a sure sign of a fiery temper, and the boy showed signs of a similar temperament, even as an infant. The man's family was not rich. His father was a common sailor and was often away. His mother made do as best she could for money during these times. He both looked forward to and dreaded his father's return. He would invariably get drunk and find fault with his wife and would often use his fists against both her and the children. But he also brought tales of the far-flung ports he visited and adventures and privations they had along the way and there was always more food on the table. The boy ate as much as could and grew up tall and strong.

His father did not return from a voyage when the boy was 13 and he had to find work to help keep the rest of the family. He had no wish to go to sea himself, he had heard too many stories of how unpleasant it could be, and he found work instead as a porter at the docks. By the time he was 18 he was 6 feet tall, a full 5 inches above average, and his size and strength meant he was not short of work. The plague that swept through Leith that year left him untouched and the lack of fit healthy men during the pestilence meant he could demand more for his services at the docks.

When he was 25 the town officials put into action a plan to create more space on the north side of the town by dumping tons of rubbish, rubble and dirt on the shore to the east of the King's Wark to raise it above the high tide level and make it stable enough to build on. The man helped shovel and move cartloads and sand and soil and the townsfolk were encouraged to dump anything there they could to raise the ground level. The work took its toll on his large frame and he had the aches and pains to show for it, with bad shoulders, a bad back and bad hips.

He never married and would get his meals from the local cookshop and spend the rest of his wages on beer, cock-fighting and, when he had to, on rent. His size made him a target for other men, especially after beer had been taken, and one altercation over a gambling debt left him with six broken ribs.

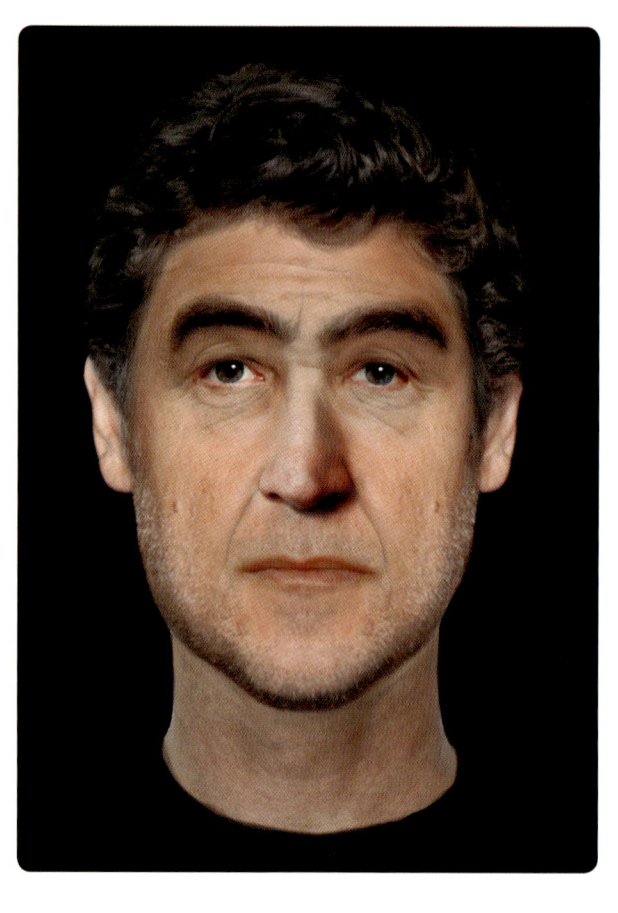

His favourite days of the year were the weapons showings on Leith Links. The king insisted on these days so that the people could be prepared in times of war and King James II in 1457 had even gone as far as banning the new sport of golf as it was distracting men from military training. There were archery contests and opportunities to practice with other deadly weapons. His size meant he generally did well at these contests. It was also an opportunity to wear his favourite green coat. He was only allowed to wear this on festivals and feast days, as opposed to the white and grey that he normally had to wear as a member of the labouring classes.

As well as the wear and tear suffered from his job, he was no stranger to toothache and he also had an annoying ache in his side. Though he was not to know it, he had a small lump on the inside of one of his ribs.

When he was 40, he came down with a fever after a night spent drinking with the crew of a hulk newly arrived from Cadiz. After a few days he found his chest and arms covered in red spots, he was sore all over and became delirious. He died a few days later and was buried simply at the local chapel graveyard. As he was placed in the grave, the diggers

PEOPLE'S STORIES

realised they had cut the grave a little too small for his large frame and there was a comic moment when he would not fit. Some of the man's drinking friends began smirking, and but other mourners began muttering that it was a bad omen, that he didn't want to go and would rise to walk at night as a revenant. The priest was not amused and glared at the gravediggers. They hastily cut a few inches out of one end with a spade and once again lowered the body in. It just about fitted. The priest threw a spadeful of soil over the body, crossed himself and stalked off vowing to discuss their ineptitude with the sexton. The mourners each threw in a spadeful of soil and then drifted away, leaving the gravediggers to backfill the grave.

SKELETON	0617
Grave	0618
Location of grave	Constitution Street, Area 7
Burial details	Simple burial, head at angle in grave, suggests grave cut a little too small
Age	Older Middle Adult, 35–45
Sex	Male
Stature	183cm or 6'0"
Radiocarbon date	–
Other dating evidence	Cut by ditch [0980] so probably predating mid–16th century, in Phase 1 cemetery in use from 1380s onwards
Finds	–
Pathology	Fractured six left ribs (sternal), osteoma on one left rib (visceral, 5.2 x 4.2mm), supernumeral two left ribs, costal & spinal DJD, Schmorl's nodes, bilateral hip DJD, bilateral acromioclavicular DJD, right sternoclavicular DJD, antemortem tooth loss, calculus, caries, DEH, periodontal disease
C/N isotope (diet)	–
O/S isotope (origins)	–
See also	Illus 4.04, p53; p111; Table 4.19; p113; p121
Facial reconstruction artist	Paloma Galzi

A BIG BRUISER OF A MAN, 1438–1478

TABLE 4.03
Distribution of coffined burials

AREA	2	3	4	5	6	7	8	9	TOTAL
Total burials	8	9	40	52	91	49	42	14	305
Coffined burials	8	4	2	5	17	14	9	4	63
%	100	44.4	5.0	9.6	18.7	28.6	21.4	28.6	20.7

TABLE 4.04
Distribution of double and group burials

AREA	2	3	4	5	6	7	8	9	TOTAL
Total burials	8	9	40	52	91	49	42	14	305
Double graves	–	–	3	2	2	1	–	–	8
Group graves	–	–	–	–	2	–	1	–	3
Individuals buried in double and group graves	–	–	6	4	12	2	4	–	28
% of individuals	–	–	15	7.7	13.2	4.1	9.5	–	9.2

Most of the double and group burials were found in Areas 4 to 6 (**Table 4.04**) and it seems that these multiple burials were more common in the earlier part of the cemetery's history. Of the seven dated skeletons found in them (Sk0646, Sk0345, Sk0112, Sk0361, Sk0423, Sk0791, Sk0806), five fall within the earliest eleven dates (1315–1455 to 1440–1630; **Table 4.02**) and all of these early examples were found in Areas 4 to 6. One double burial (Gr0786) was found in Area 7 and was dated slightly later (Sk0791, 1455–1635). Significantly, the only group burial outside of Area 4 to 6, and the latest dated (Sk0806/Gr0807, Area 8, 1465–1655), was heavily truncated and of uncertain identification.

The three burials aligned S-N were all found in Area 6, the densest area of burial and the two dated examples were relatively early, within the earliest nine dates in the sequence (Sk1052, 1300–1445; Sk0481, 1435–1630).

CONSTITUTION STREET: THE POST-MEDIEVAL DITCH AND OTHER LATER FEATURES

COBBLED SURFACE (0881)

An area of cobbling at the northern end of the site appeared to post-date one grave and certainly predated two other burials (**Illus 4.12**, **Illus 4.32**). Sk0885/Gr0886 appeared to have been truncated by the surface, though the relationship was not clear. Sk0845/Gr0843 and Sk0841/Gr0842 overlay the surface. The former was radiocarbon dated to 1470–1665 (Sk0845; **Table 4.02**), the latter appeared to have been redeposited in an unusual position (p81). The surface was cut on its eastern edge by ditch [0980]. It was overlain by cemetery soil and a number of disarticulated bones were found among the stones. Thus, the only secure dating evidence for it is the *terminus ante quem* given by Sk0845 which suggests it does not post-date the mid-17th century.

The surviving surface measured 4.5m N-S and 1.0m W-E. It was made up of sub-angular and sub-rounded stones 100–200mm in size with occasional patches of gravelly sand over and between the larger stones. It was rather crude, and the angularity of the stones suggests this may have been bedding material for another surface, now lost, rather than a surface in itself.

Too little survives to ascertain if this was a path or yard surface. However, its location is roughly aligned with the middle of the eastern façade of the existing church and about 55m from it. The late 15th- and early 16th-century church probably extended further east (the existing church being the remodelled nave of the original; see p22; 30) and the 1560 Petworth Map (**Illus 3.01**, p23) depicts it with an east entrance. It is possible that the surface represents a wide path leading to this entrance. The subsequent use of the area for burial might post-date the partial destruction of the church during the siege of 1560 (p22).

DITCH [0980]

A long linear cut ran along the eastern edge of the excavation area from Areas 4 to 9 (**Illus 4.07**–**4.12**, p56–61), matching the NE-SW orientation of the road. A number of modern services were cut inside it, severely truncating it to the east. Its eastern extent was not identified with any certainty. A lower eastern edge was tentatively identified in one sondage, which implied a relatively narrow (less than 2m) width, though this is far from definitive. The base was flat, possibly a little concave, and was recorded at a depth of c 1.54m from its preserved top edge.

It was initially thought to have been a service cut, when encountered at the north end of the site in the eastern panel of Area 9. However, there were distinctive differences compared with the other service cuts running along and across the road. The sides varied in steepness and from 75° to nearly vertical along its visible length, suggesting it was hand excavated. It was filled with redeposited cemetery soil rather than with the aggregate or pipe-bedding material that were found in the other modern service cuts. There were also no obvious services associated with it, being positioned too far west than was necessary to house the services to its east and not strictly parallel with them. It was identified as a separate feature in Area 6 where its divergence from the modern services was more pronounced. It was then given a cut number which was retrospectively applied to the cut already found further north. Variations in the angle of the ditch edge gave the cut an irregular line and for a short stretch in Area 6 it was too far east to be seen beyond the modern services. In Areas 4 and 9 it also disappeared under the modern services though it is not clear if this represents a turn to the east or another irregularity. Substantial modern truncation in Areas 2 to 4 meant that any further trace of the ditch to the south was lost.

Along most of its length its relationship to the graves was clear. It cut the eastern edges of the graves and clearly post-dated them. A few graves in Areas 5 to 7 appeared superficially to cut into the top of the ditch fills (**Illus 4.08–4.10**, p57–59). However, a closer inspection of these burials shows that most, if not all, had in fact been truncated by the ditch cut and there seemed to have been subsequent post-depositional movement that had caused the burials to slope downwards into the ditch (eg Sk1052/Gr1053, Area 6; see **Illus 4.09**, p58; **4.24**, p76) suggesting a general slumping of deposits along the ditch edge. It is of note that a number of these burials were in places where the edge of the ditch curves outwards a little, suggesting the edge of the ditch eroded westwards, no doubt an on-going issue with such sandy subsoil. There was also a considerable number of disarticulated skulls, including Sk1027–Sk1031, recorded close to the edge of the ditch which seem likely to have been redeposited when the ditch was cut.

Radiocarbon dating confirms these observations. One of the burials which appeared to be overlying the ditch (Sk1052/Gr1053, Area 6; see **Illus 4.09**, p58, **4.24**, p76) returned one of the earliest dates (1300–1445; **Table 4.02**, p84). The two latest dated burials (Sk0951/Gr0952, Area 7, 1475–1670, see **Illus 4.10**, p59; Sk1119/1118, Area 5, 1475–1795, see **Illus 4.08**, p57), however, were both cut by the ditch and thus clearly earlier than it. Since the ditch is unlikely to be both earlier than Sk1052 and later than Sk1119 it seems more probable that the ditch post-dates Sk1052, which was then subject to later subsidence.

Despite its relationship to the burials, the dating of ditch [0980] is problematic. It cut five dated burials (Sk0646/Gr0589, Sk0951/Gr0952, Sk0985/Gr0988, Sk0998/Gr0999, Sk1119/Gr1118), with dates ranging from 1315–1455 to 1475–1795 (**Table 4.02**). This implies the ditch was cut no earlier than the late 15th century, and more likely some time later, but it is not clear how much later it may have been. The ditch also cut Sk0910/Gr0911 in Area 8, which contained a buckle typologically dated to the period 1575–1700 and appeared to be contemporary with the burial (p123). If the date and relationships are to be believed, then this would push the dating of the ditch into the later 16th or 17th century.

Two other features were cut by ditch [0980]: large feature [1153] (**Illus 4.08**; **4.13**) and cobbled surface (0881) (**Illus 4.12**; **4.32**). However, since the only dating for these features are vague *termini ante quem* dates provided by the burials above them, they are of little help in dating the later ditch. The cobbled surface was perhaps associated with the late 15th-century church and feature [1153] is assumed to be of 15th-century date (p142).

The dating of the infilling of the ditch is similarly vague. Subsequent truncation by modern services meant that there was little opportunity to examine the ditch fills in detail. No natural silting deposits were observed suggesting the ditch was not open for long. On the other hand, there was apparent erosion of the ditch edge and subsequent subsidence of several burials into it. This implies the ditch was open for a while, though it is possible some subsidence could have occurred after backfilling, if the fill deposits were loosely packed. Where the fills were observable there was a basal fill, a thick homogeneous brown sandy deposit containing a fragmentary and empty coffin which seems to have collapsed into the ditch, a sherd of window glass, coffin nails, mortar fragments, marine shell and a small fragment of glass waste. It was suggested that this might represent the slumping of material from an associated bank to the west into the ditch. Had this occurred it would seem to be consistent with the slumped burials at the ditch edge. The upper fill (0994) was a similar homogeneous sandy deposit, paler in colour and containing much disarticulated human bone, charcoal fragments and a clay pipe stem which dates to the 17th or early 18th century. The homogeneity of the deposits suggests a rapid backfilling event.

The dating for this infilling rests entirely on the handful of finds recovered from the fill. The clay pipe and glass waste suggest a date no earlier than the mid-17th century (see p187, for dating of glass waste). The scarcity of these finds, however, and the amount of subsequent disturbance in the area, means they cannot be used as secure dating evidence.

ILLUS 4.32
Cobbled surface 0881

The available dating evidence suggests a 16th- or 17th-century date is most likely for the ditch. There is a certain amount of evidence to link this ditch with one of various defensive schemes which surrounded Leith at various times in the 16th and 17th centuries. This is considered in detail below (p146–48).

PITS [0501], [1096] AND [1134]

There were three ovoid pits cut into the top of the burials (**Illus 4.08–4.09**, p57–58). None was in turn cut by any other burials and they may thus post-date the burial period in this area. All were set back less than 1m from the edge of ditch [0980]. The smaller pits, [1096] in Area 5 and [0501] in Area 6, both contained charnel. Pit [1096] contained a skull and long bones, possibly from the same individual. Pit [0501] contained a large amount of disarticulated bone, predominantly long bones and at least four fragmented skulls. Pit [0501] also contained some iron slag and a fragment of pan tile. Pit [1134] in Area 5 was larger at 1.5 by 1.1m and cut though the burials and the underlying feature [1153] (**Illus 4.13**, p64). It contained four fills of mixed sands and gravels but was archaeologically sterile.

The smaller pits were probably dug specifically to rebury charnel. Given their location and stratigraphic relationship to the burials, it seems likely that these represented human remains disturbed either during the cutting of ditch [0980], or during the construction of Constitution Street in the 1790s. Pit [1134] might also relate to this work, though its function is unclear.

CONSTITUTION STREET: THE HUMAN REMAINS

Carmelita Troy

The articulated human bone assemblage from Constitution Street consisted of 305 inhumations (in varying degrees of completeness). There were also 73 disarticulated skulls which were also analysed, though other disarticulated bone was not included in the study. All 378 skeletons were subjected to osteological analysis with the aim of exploring the health and physical attributes of the assemblage and to place the findings in context by reference to comparative assemblages. The analysis aimed to determine age at death, sex and stature and to identify any traces of health issues, diseases, and injuries. The 73 disarticulated skulls have not been included in the statistics for age or sex on the grounds that a redeposited skull may belong to the same individual as an incomplete skeleton in a truncated grave. They have, however, been included in the statistics on dental and cranial pathologies since they are unlikely to affect prevalence rates. A complete catalogue of the skeletal remains is included as an appendix (**Table A2.01**, p218–33).

METHODOLOGY

The adult burials were assessed using a range of morphological and metrical analyses, according to internationally agreed standards. A visual and written inventory was created for all surviving bone (Brickley 2004). Preservation levels were recorded following McKinley (2004). The dentition was recorded using Buikstra and Ubelaker (1994) to record presence/absence, attrition and dental pathology. Cranial and post-cranial metrics were taken at a standard 19 landmarks (where possible) as described by Buikstra and Ubelaker (1994); post-cranial metrics were also employed in the assessment of sex and stature (Trotter & Gleser 1952; 1958; Trotter 1970). Sex was assessed using diagnostic criteria of the cranium and pelvis (Buikstra & Ubelaker 1994). Age at death was assessed using morphological changes in the pelvis (Lovejoy et al 1985; Brooks & Suchey 1990), cranial suture closure (Buikstra and Ubelaker 1994) and dental attrition (Miles 1962; Brothwell 1981). Adult individuals were placed into one of four age categories (**Table 4.05**). Cranial and post-cranial non-metric traits as described by Berry and Berry (1967) and Finnegan (1978) were recorded. Pathology was recorded using guidelines set down by Roberts and Connell (2004). Assessments of joint disease followed Rogers et al (1987).

Analysis of the subadult remains followed different criteria for some categories. As with the adult remains, a full inventory of skeletal and dental material was created for each individual (Brickley 2004; McKinley 2004); dental pathology and skeletal measurements were taken using Buikstra and Ubelaker (1994). It is generally agreed by most authors that the accurate assessment of sex is not possible in subadult remains, as sexual dimorphism of the skeleton only becomes clear after puberty (Scheuer & Black 2000). Assessment of the subadult remains, therefore, concentrated on the accurate assessment of age at death, using the following techniques: diaphysis length (Maresh 1970; Scheuer & Black 2000); regression equations of diaphyseal length (Scheuer et al 1980); epiphyseal fusion and primary ossification centres (Buikstra & Ubelaker 1994; Scheuer & Black 2000); and dental eruption and development (Ubelaker 1978; Moorrees et al 1963a, 1963b). There are several systems used in the categorization of subadult remains. In this case, they were placed into one of eight age categories (**Table 4.05**), as used by skeletal biologists and clinicians (Scheuer & Black 2000).

PRESERVATION AND COMPLETENESS

Levels of preservation were assessed using three categories: poor, moderate and good. Poor preservation is classed as suffering from heavy erosion and fragmentation, severely impacting on the amount of retrievable data. Material classed as moderate maintains its general morphology and allows for a detailed level of analysis, but has suffered some erosion and fragmentation. Good preservation refers to material which maintains a fresh appearance and retains all morphological detail, allowing full analysis to take place. The condition of the assemblage was mixed but nearly half (48.9%) was classed as good. Soil acidity and bone shape and density can contribute to the bone preservation. Subadult bones often do not preserve as well as adult bones as they are more porous and smaller than adult elements (Buckberry 2000). This was evident at Constitution Street where a slightly higher proportion of adults than subadults were classed as good (47.3%, 89/188 adults; 45.3%, 53/117 subadults) and moderate (31.4%, 59/188 adults; 29.9% 35/117 subadults) and a slightly higher proportion of subadults than adults were poorly preserved (21.3%, 40/188 adults; 24.8%, 29/117 subadults).

Each skeleton was assessed and placed into one of the following four categories of completeness: >75%; 75%; 50%; and <25%. Of the in situ burials, nearly half the skeletons (46%, 136/305) were less than 25% complete, indicative of the confines of the excavation area, where skeletons were not chased beyond the excavation limits and also to the amount of disturbance and truncation noted in the cemetery. Only 23% (71/305) of the skeletons were 75% or more complete. This clearly limits the potential for osteological information. The osteological

TABLE 4.05
Osteological age categories with numbers of individuals recovered from Constitution Street

AGE CATEGORY	AGE RANGE	MALE	FEMALE	UNSEXED	TOTAL
Foetus (FO)	3rd foetal month until birth	–	–	–	–
Perinate (PE)	Around the time of birth	–	–	1	1
Neonate (NEO)	Birth - 2 months	–	–	–	–
Infant (INF)	2 months - 1 year	–	–	2	2
Younger child (YC)	1– 6 years	–	–	32	32
Older child (OC)	7– 12 years	–	–	53	53
Adolescent (ADOL)	13– 17 years	–	–	20	20
Subadult (SA)	Under 18 years	–	–	9	9
Total sub-adults		–	–	117	117
Younger adult (YA)	18– 25 years	14	23	1	38
Younger middle adult (YMA)	25– 35 years	24	36	3	63
Older middle adult (OMA)	35– 45 years	8	12	–	20
Older adult (OA)	45 + years	1	2	–	3
Adult (AD)	Over 18 years	13	18	33	64
Total adults		60	91	37	188
TOTAL		60	91	154	305

results are therefore limited and the prevalence rates of pathology and demographics should be treated with caution.

AGE AT DEATH

Of the 305 individuals examined, 76.1% (232/305) of the assemblage could be assigned an age category. The remaining 73 skeletons (64 adults and 9 subadults) could only be determined as 'adult' or 'subadult', using epiphyseal fusion rates. The number of skeletons which could only be placed into these broad age categories was quite high and could affect the interpretation of the results. Adults were placed into one of five age categories, subadults into one of eight categories (**Table 4.05**).

Peak mortality rates occurred during the older child (22.8%, 53/232) and younger middle adult (27.2%, 63/232) stages (**Illus 4.33**). The low number of older adults is notable and suggests few people reached this age, though the 73 skeletons in the broad adult category means this may not be significant. Children were susceptible to infections and nutritional deficiencies. In historic times the highest death rates occurred among those less than ten years of age and children in this age range suffered most from epidemic and endemic diseases (Power 1995, 67). Birth and the early post-natal period was also a dangerous time for the child. Infant mortality rates of 10%–30% are cited for medieval European populations (Scott 1999). The dearth of children under 1 years old in the assemblage is therefore unexpected and may be a factor of bone preservation in that the smaller softer bones were less likely to survive. Alternatively, it may be that a different part of the cemetery was used for the burial of young children (see p118–19, for further discussion of this possibility).

SEX

Sex was determined based on the morphology of the pelvis and skull (Buikstra & Ubelaker 1994). Greater weight is assigned to the pelvis as its features are more sexually dimorphic from an earlier age than those of the skull. The development of features of the skull are highly dependent upon when puberty occurs and may be influenced by genetics, cultural practices and disease, among other factors (Mays & Cox 2000). An individual exhibiting female skull characteristics and male pelvic characteristics is not unusual (Walker 1995). Thus, the lack of complete skeletons found at Constitution Street means there were a significant number of adult skeletons (19.7%, 37/188) which could not be sexed. This number could affect the data if the male/female ratio within this group varied significantly from that observed in the sexed skeletons. For statistical purposes, it is assumed that the sexed skeletons are a representative sample of those buried in the cemetery, though of course, this is by no means certain and the high proportion of unsexed adults means that the statistics should be viewed with a degree of caution.

Of the 188 adult burials within the assemblage, 80.3% (151/188) could be ascribed to a biological sex category. Of all the sex determined adults, 91 showed female characteristics (of which 79 were definitely identified as

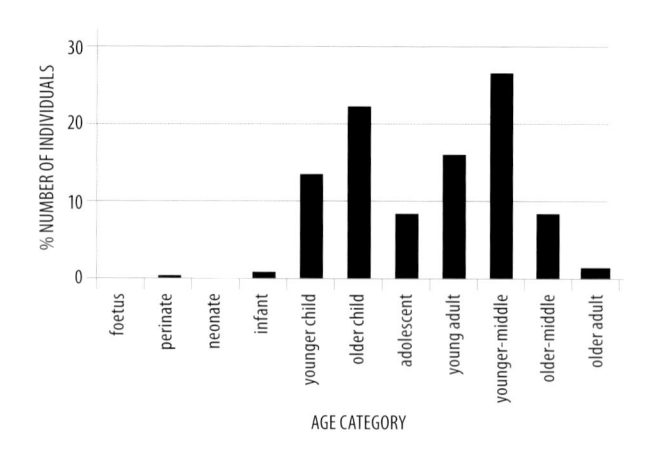

ILLUS 4.33
Distribution of age categories (as a percentage of the 232 individuals who could be placed into an age category)

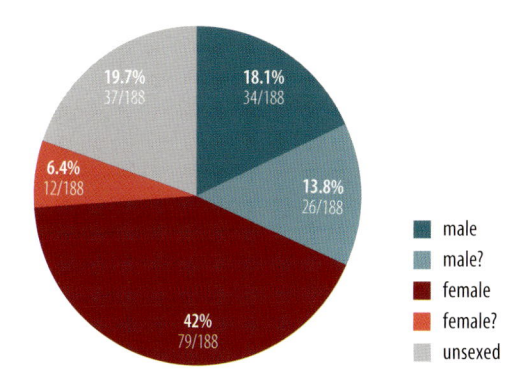

CONSTITUTION STREET EXCAVATIONS

ILLUS 4.34
Sex distribution of adult individuals (188 in situ burials)

female, a further 12 as probably female) and 60 showed male characteristics (34 definite, a further 26 probable) (**Illus 4.34**). Of the sex-determined adults, therefore, 60.3% (91/151) were female, 39.7% (60/151) male, otherwise expressed as a male to female ratio of 0.66M:1F. The significance of this high proportion of women is discussed below (p117–18).

The relationship between sex and age at death was also investigated. A total of 120 adults could be sex determined and attributed a specific age category (ie not just classed as adult). It is possible to detect a peak of male and female mortality between the ages of 25–35 years but distribution of males and females between the age categories were largely comparable. (**Illus 4.35**).

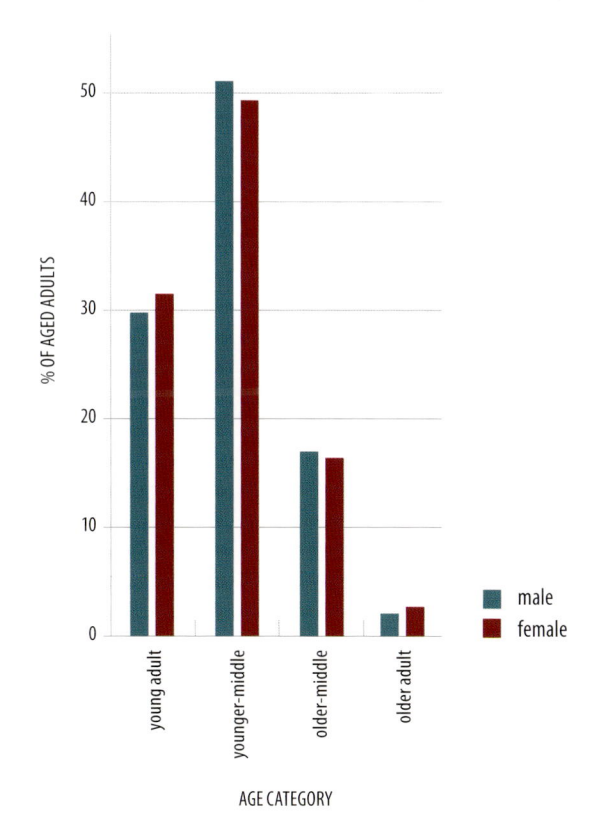

STATURE

Stature was calculated using formulae developed by measurement of long bones of adults of known height (Trotter 1970). The femur is the most useful bone in this respect as it shows the least variation relative to stature, but it is possible to calculate stature from the length of the humerus, radius, ulna or tibia. Again, the lack of complete skeletons at Constitution Street will have affected this data to an extent.

Adult stature is determined by many factors, including genetics and environmental influences such as malnutrition and poor health in childhood, and can be used as an indicator of social status. The analysis of stature was restricted to those individuals for whom sex had been allocated, as overall height is known to vary slightly between males and females in relation to longbone lengths.

It was possible to calculate the statures of 102 adults: 63 females, and 39 males. Female stature in this assemblage ranged from 143.8cm to 167.0cm with an average of 154.9cm (5 feet 1 inch). Male stature ranged from 160.8cm to 182.8cm with an average of 169.7cm (5 feet 7 inches) (**Illus 4.36**). Both male and female statures were below average for late medieval Britain. Male stature was broadly comparable with that from other sites; in fact the men are a little taller on average than the medieval population represented at St Giles Cathedral, Edinburgh and, surprisingly, also taller than the post-medieval population at Spitalfields, London (**Table 4.06**). Female stature, however, is significantly lower than the national

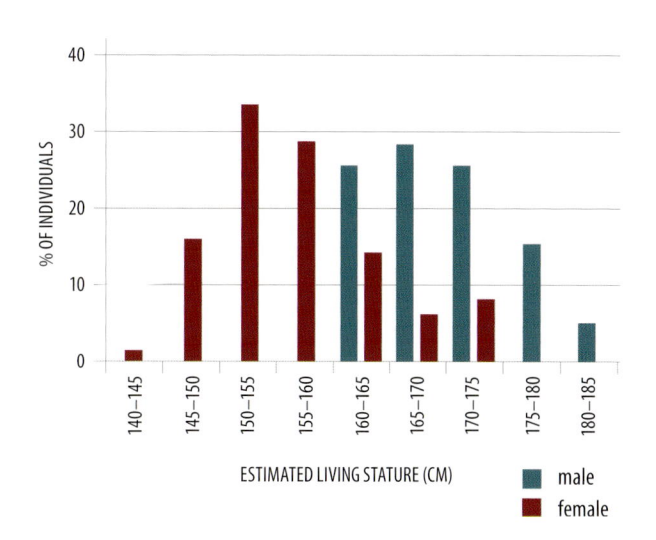

ILLUS 4.35
Age at death distribution by sex (shown as percentages of aged adults within each sex category)

ILLUS 4.36
Adult stature

TABLE 4.06
Comparison of average statures from various populations

SITE/REGION	PERIOD	REFERENCE	FEMALE AVERAGE (CM)	MALE AVERAGE (CM)
Scotland	Modern	Bromley et al 2009	163.5	178.2
Great Britain	Post-medieval	Roberts & Cox 2003, 391	160.0	171.0
Great Britain	Late medieval	Roberts & Cox 2003, 391	159.0	171.0
St Andrews, Fishergate, York	Medieval	Stroud & Kemp 1993	159.0	171.0
Hereford Cathedral	Medieval to post-medieval	Boucher et al 2015, 105	159.3	170.4
St Peters, Barton-upon-Humber, Lincolnshire	Medieval	Waldron 2007	158.0	170.0
Wharram Percy, North Yorkshire	Medieval	Mays 2007a	157.8	168.8
Constitution Street, Leith	Late medieval	this volume	154.9	169.7
Christ Church, Spitalfields, London	Post-medieval	Molleson & Cox 1993	156.0	168.0
St Giles Cathedral, Edinburgh	Medieval	Henderson 2006, 29	155.9	167.7
London Road, Edinburgh	Medieval	this volume	154.8	166.0

TABLE 4.07
Number of teeth lost ante-mortem in adults by tooth position and sex

	I1	I2	C	PM1	PM2	M1	M2	M3	TOTAL
MAXILLA									
Male	3	3	1	–	5	27	18	11	68
Female	3	3	1	4	4	11	10	7	43
Unsexed	–	–	–	–	–	1	1	–	2
Total	6	6	2	4	9	39	29	18	113
MANDIBLE									
Male	–	–	–	2	4	23	7	4	40
Female	2	3	1	3	1	10	5	1	26
Unsexed	–	–	–	–	–	–	–	–	–
Total	2	3	1	5	5	33	12	5	66

late medieval average, by 4.1cm and was amongst the lowest noted among the comparative sites given.

NON-METRIC TRAITS

Non-metric traits is the term used for non-pathological variations in bone morphology. There is some argument in the literature as to the cause and significance of these traits and several studies have used them as markers of bio-distance between populations and within samples (Ossenberg 1976; Bondioli et al 1986). The relationship between trait expression and age is controversial; trait expression is not necessarily an indicator of familial relationships. Many infra-cranial traits may be related to physiological rather than genetic factors (Tyrrell 2000, 296–7).

Cranial

The adult assemblage was assessed for eight non-metric cranial traits. The most frequent cranial trait was the identification of ossicles in the lambdoid suture between the occipital and parietal bone (56.9%, 58/102 adults). These are commonly found in the skull with, typically, nearly 40% of skulls containing sutural bones in the vicinity of the lambdoid suture (Bergman et al 1988). Studies have shown that the presence of sutural bones is associated with other cranial and central nervous system abnormalities (Pryles & Khan 1979; Das et al 2005). It is possible there is a genetic factor to the presence of these bones (El-Najjar & Dawson 1977).

Post-cranial

The adult assemblage was assessed for eleven non-metric post-cranial traits. The most commonly expressed post-cranial trait was the lateral squatting facets on the distal tibia at 67.5% (52/77), affecting a higher rate of women (70.3%, 26/37) compared to men (60.0%, 15/25). Squatting facets are thought to develop as a result of habitual extreme dorsi-flexion of the ankle joint, as occurs during squatting posture. They are common in modern Asian populations, but very rare in present-day Europeans. However, they have been found frequently in medieval populations. The assemblage from Wharram Percy, England (Mays 1998), was found to have a similar incidence of 55% within the adult sample. That from Hereford Cathedral showed a similar higher incidence in women (41% female, 28% male) and it was speculated that women would have performed more tasks closer to the ground such as tending the hearth and cooking (Boucher et al 2015, 113–4).

Another trait that is thought to be activity-related is a *hypotrochanteric fossa*, which is a depression on the back of the thigh bone where the large posterior muscle, gluteus maximus, attaches. This was recorded in 35.6% of adults (26/73), affecting more males (48.0%, 12/25) than females (29.2%, 14/48).

DENTAL HEALTH AND DISEASE

Dental disease is the most immediate form of evidence for diet in the past. The presence of caries (cavities), calculus (tartar) and the level of wear all provide information on the kind of food consumed, as well as levels of hygiene and the overall health of a population. In general, medieval populations tended to have poor oral health, though typically it was better than in the post-medieval period when the increased availability of sugar led to a corresponding rise in caries and other dental problems (Mays 1998, 222).

Some 173 individuals had at least part of their dentition present. A total of 3,114 permanent teeth were recorded. Of the 97 adults with teeth, 44 were male, 49 female and four unsexed. There were also 63 subadults, whose dentition included 406 deciduous teeth. Just 8.7% of all adult teeth had been lost post-mortem, more from the maxilla than mandible, due to the more robust nature of the latter. The most common lost tooth from both jaws were the central incisors, which have a single straight and tapered root and are more easily dislodged.

Ante-mortem tooth loss

Fifty of the 156 observable individuals with surviving full dentition had lost at least one tooth prior to death (32.1%), 3.4% of subadults (2/59) and 49.5% of adults (48/97). A loss of 185 permanent teeth (5.6%, 185/3286) were recorded, 0.6% of subadults (6/982) and 7.8% of adults (179/2304). There was a significant difference between adult male (65.9%, 29/44) and female (36.7%, 18/49) crude rates of loss. This pattern remained when the true prevalence rates were calculated, with 9.9% of male tooth positions (108/1093) and 6.1% of female tooth positions (69/2374) affected (**Table 4.07**). A break-down by tooth position in **Table 4.07** shows that over three quarters of all permanent adult teeth lost during life were molars (76.0%, 136/179).

Two subadults (Sk0429, Sk0966, both adolescents) displayed ante-mortem tooth loss. Sk0429 lost both the right maxillary and mandibular first molar. Sk0966 had four teeth affected, the left and right mandibular first and second molars. All six subadult teeth with recorded tooth loss were molars from the permanent dentition.

In modern dentitions, ante-mortem tooth loss before middle age almost always results from dental caries. This is not necessarily so in late medieval dentitions where a combination of severe attrition, caries and periodontal disease may all be responsible. There is possibly an association between tooth loss and apical abscesses at Constitution Street, but this is difficult to illustrate as the infected tooth may have been lost and the associated socket and lesion totally remodelled well before death. The rate is similar to the British late medieval average of 36.4% by individual but a wide variation is noted during the period and rates of around 70% have been noted at other sites (Roberts & Cox 2003, 262–3).

Calculus

If plaque is not removed from the tooth surface, it can mineralise into calculus (tartar), either sub- or supra-gingival (**Illus 4.37**). Sub-gingival calculus is associated with the development of periodontal disease. Calculus is considered to be extremely common in almost all

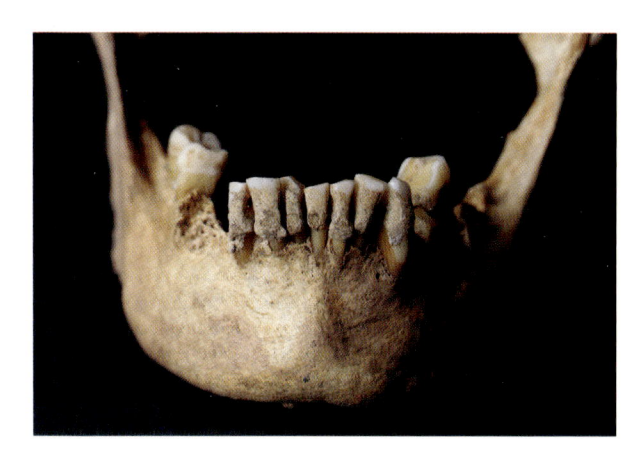

ILLUS 4.37
Calculus, Sk0655/Gr0656, older–middle adult female

archaeological populations (Roberts & Manchester 2010, 72) and its presence in quantity is frequently taken as an indicator of poor oral hygiene.

The pH or acidity of the mouth depends upon the amount and type of carbohydrate in the diet. Plaque grows faster on the surfaces of the teeth when sucrose is added to the diet than when other sugars, such as fructose or glucose, are added. Large quantities of sugars lower the

ILLUS 4.38
Caries, Sk0378/Gr379, young adult male

TABLE 4.08
Distribution of individuals with dental pathologies by age

AGE	CALCULUS		CARIES		PERIODONTAL DISEASE		ABSCESS		DEH	
	NO	%	NO	%	NO	%	NO	%	NO	%
Infant	0/3	–	0/3	–	0/2	–	0/3	–	–	–
Younger child	6/20	30.0	1/20	5.0	0/18	–	0/19	–	7/20	35.0
Older child	18/30	60.0	2/30	6.7	2/29	6.9	0/30	–	22/30	73.3
Adolescent	21/23	91.3	4/23	17.4	9/12	75.0	3/13	23.1	13/13	100
Total subadult	45/76	59.2	7/76	9.2	11/61	18.0	3/65	4.6	42/63	66.7
Younger adult	33/34	97.1	11/34	32.4	26/33	78.8	3/33	9.1	31/34	91.2
Younger–middle adult	41/44	93.2	23/44	52.3	41/44	93.2	9/54	16.7	39/44	88.6
Older–middle adult	13/13	100	9/13	69.2	12/13	92.3	5/13	38.5	10/13	76.9
Older adult	1/1	100	0/1	–	1/1	100	0/1	–	1/1	100
Adult	4/5	80.0	4/5	80.0	4/5	80.0	1/6	16.7	4/5	80.0
Total adult	92/97	94.8	47/97	48.5	84/96	87.5	18/107	16.8	85/97	87.6
TOTAL	137/173	79.2	54/173	31.2	95/157	60.5	21/172	12.2	127/160	79.4

pH levels close to the teeth, decalcifying the enamel and leading to caries, but paradoxically give an unfavourable environment for the calcification of thick, mature and highly complex bacterial plaque and the formation of calculus.

The teeth of 137 individuals show some evidence of the presence of calculus, 79.2% (137/173) of the cemetery population with dentition. These included 59.2% of subadults (45/76) and 94.8% of adults (92/97) (**Table 4.08**). There was little difference in the rate of calculus between males and females (**Table 4.09**). The average rate for calculus in British late medieval populations is 59.2%, ranging from 4.2% to 100% (Roberts & Cox 2003, 261–2).

Caries

Carious lesions are referred to in modern terms as cavities in the enamel of the teeth. The lesions are believed to occur primarily as a result of a high carbohydrate intake. Bacteria contained in plaque can metabolise certain carbohydrates into an acidic waste that can dissolve the enamel of teeth resulting in cavities (Mays 1998, 148). In archaeological populations caries occur in three main areas: between the crowns of adjacent teeth (**Illus 4.38**); in later life, around the neck of the tooth especially after recession of the alveolar margin; and in wear facets in exposed dentine (Hillson 2005, 293).

Of all individuals with dentition, 31.2% (45/173) had one or more carious lesions affecting 7.6% (158/2,071) of all teeth. The percentage of men suffering from caries was greater than women (**Table 4.09**). The number of individual male teeth with carious lesions, 8.7% (81/926), was also greater than that of all female teeth, 5.1% (53/1,047). Unsurprisingly, the problem also appears to have got worse with age (**Table 4.08**). The average prevalence rate for caries in British late medieval populations is 52.6% and the average rate of affected teeth is 5.6% (Roberts and Cox 2003, 259).

Of the permanent teeth, the molars, particularly the first and second, were most commonly affected, followed by the second premolars (**Illus 4.39**). This pattern is almost universal for caries, due mainly to the intricate morphology of the molars and premolars where the teeth do not fit tightly against each other and the crowns contain hollows and fissures where food and bacterial plaque can accumulate. Many of the teeth lost antemortem may have been shed as a result of caries.

The majority of cavities, 23.2% (32/138), occurred at the distal surface of the crown (**Illus 4.40**). In the mature individual,

TABLE 4.09
Distribution of adult individuals with dental pathologies by sex

AGE GROUP	CALCULUS		CARIES		PERIODONTAL DISEASE		ABSCESS		DEH	
	No	%	No	%	No	%	No	%	No	%
Male	41/44	93.2	26/44	59.1	38/43	88.4	12/54	22.2	37/44	84.1
Female	47/49	95.9	19/49	38.8	44/49	89.8	6/49	12.2	45/49	91.8
Unsexed	4/4	100	2/4	50.0	2/4	50.0	0/4	–	3/4	75.0
TOTAL	92/97	94.8	47/97	48.5	84/96	87.5	18/107	16.8	85/97	87.6

CONSTITUTION STREET EXCAVATIONS

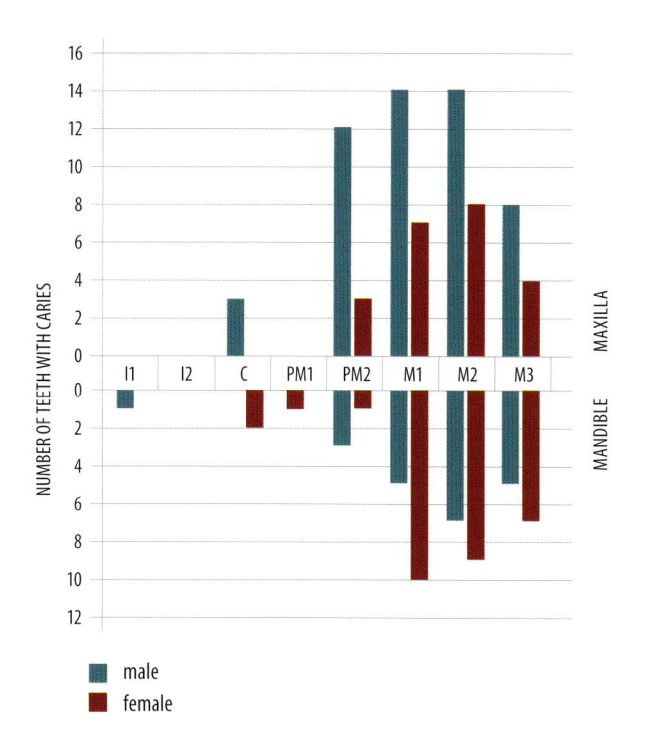

ILLUS 4.39
Distribution of caries in the maxillary and mandibular teeth of male and female adults

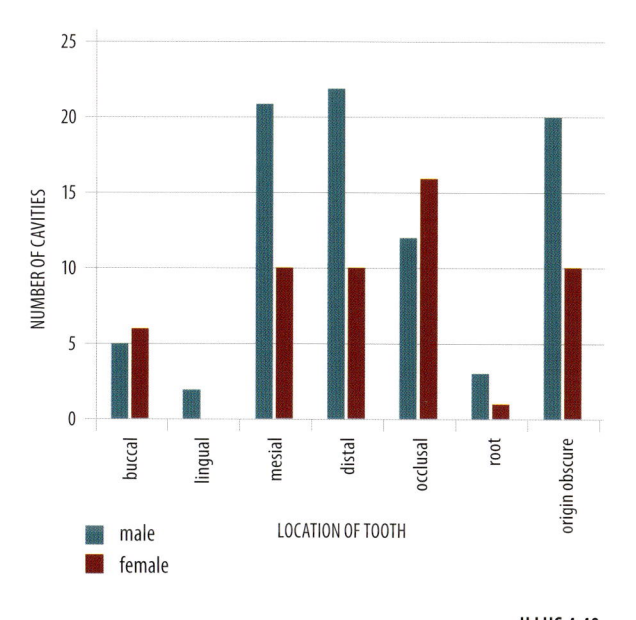

ILLUS 4.40
Locations of carious cavities in male and female adults

attrition caused by abrasive foodstuffs will almost certainly have removed the occlusal pits and fissures, and the large areas of wear-exposed dentine provide new opportunities for occlusal caries to develop (Hillson 2005, 293).

Periodontal disease

Periodontal disease is connected to poor oral hygiene, where a build-up of plaque and subsequently calculus causes inflammation of the gums leading to gingivitis and gradual recession of the alveolar bone (**Illus 4.41**).

ILLUS 4.41
Periodontal disease, Sk0655/Gr0656, older-middle adult female

Eventually this condition leads to tooth loss. Contributing factors are a soft, carbohydrate diet, dental anomalies such as crowding and malocclusion, and nutritional deficiencies such as scurvy, which cause general problems with epithelial tissues (Hillson 2005). It is a common condition and affects most individuals over the age of 35 years (ibid, 306). Only moderate to severe cases were noted in the statistics given here. In all, 95 individuals were affected representing 60.5% of all dentitions (**Table 4.08**). The effects can be noted in younger individuals though, with high levels already apparent in adolescents and very high levels from younger middle adulthood (25–35 years). There is no marked difference in occurrence between males and females (**Table 4.09**). The average rate for periodontal disease in British late medieval populations is 37.5%, ranging from 5.9 to 100% (Roberts & Cox 2003, 260–1).

Abscesses

Dental abscesses occur as a result of the exposure of the pulp cavity of the tooth through attrition, caries, or trauma and the subsequent infection of that cavity by bacteria. The pus resulting from the infection extrudes from the area of the tooth root out through the alveolar bone. The abscess can occur externally on the outside portion of the maxilla and mandible or it may drain inwards, particularly into the maxillary sinuses, and can cause a variety of other physiological problems.

At Constitution Street 12.2% of the dentitions had evidence of at least one abscess (**Table 4.08**). The average rate for abscesses in British late medieval populations is 26.3%, ranging from 0.7% to 53.3% (Roberts & Cox 2003, 259–60). Some 18 adults (12 males and six females) had a total of 28 abscesses in the permanent dentition (**Table 4.09**). The maxillary teeth are almost four times more likely to be involved than the mandibular, which is partly due to the fact that they are easily exposed to observation behind the thin maxillary cortical plate. However, radiographs would probably reveal many undetected lesions in the

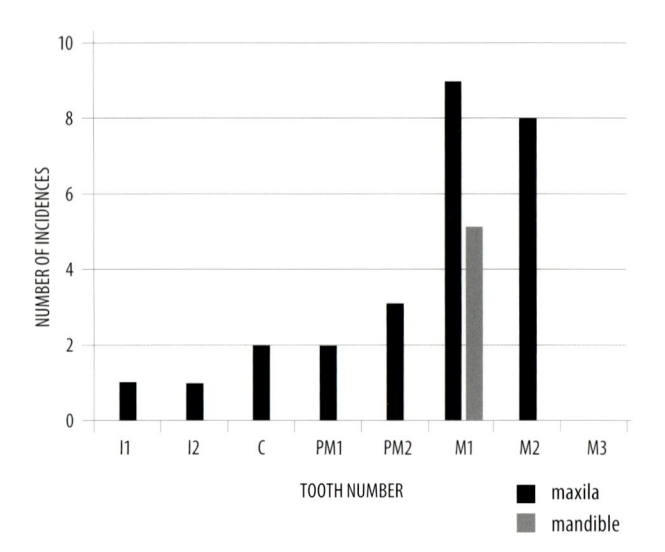

ILLUS 4.42
Number and location of permanent teeth with abscesses

mandibles. The maxillary first molar is the most common tooth to be affected, followed by the maxillary second molar (**Illus 4.42**). As with all the other plaque-related dental pathologies, there is a direct association with the length of time the teeth have been exposed to the oral environment. The first molars erupt at least six years earlier into the mouth than the other molars.

Dental enamel hypoplasia

Dental enamel hypoplastic (DEH) defects can appear as a depressed line or a series of lines or pits on the surface of the enamel (**Illus 4.43**). They occur as a result of disturbance to the growth of the organic matrix, which is later mineralised to form enamel. The disturbance to the growth is consequently reflected in the enamel (Mays 1998; Hillson 2005). The defects can occur as a result of a number of diseases and/or nutritional deficiencies including diarrhoea, parasitic infestations of the gut, scurvy, rickets, allergic reactions, vitamin deficiencies and general malnutrition (Mays 1998). Once the enamel is formed the growth patterns cannot be altered. Teeth calcify in childhood and therefore enamel hypoplastic defects are a relation of stresses suffered by an individual in youth. By measuring the location of a lesion on a particular tooth it is possible to determine approximately the age at which the stress occurred, as teeth form at a known rate. However, it is noted that the range of stresses that may cause these defects are considerable and vary greatly in severity.

In this study, hypoplasia was simply assessed as being present or absent. A total of 127 individuals (79.4% of the dentate population) had some observable enamel hypoplasia in the permanent dentition (**Table 4.08**). This compares to a late medieval average of 35.4% (Roberts & Cox 2003, 264). As would be expected, the most common affected tooth was the canine (19% of affected teeth) as its crown forms for longer than any other tooth (Goodman & Rose 1990) and is therefore at greatest risk of having its growth interrupted by bouts of ill health. Interestingly, this is the only dental pathology that is significantly higher in females than males (**Table 4.09**).

Dental anomalies

A few dental anomalies were noted. Hypodontia is the congenital failure of one or more teeth to develop. At Constitution Street, 33 individuals (15 male, 13 female) had an absence of one or more teeth, 29 of which involved the third molar, which is typically the most commonly affected tooth. Seven individuals had a congenital absent tooth in another position and it is notable that the majority of these are female (four female, one male). One older child (Sk0152/Gr0153, 10½–11½ years) was affected by microdontia; a single upper third molar is considerably smaller than the other dentition. Two individuals had supernumerary teeth: an extra upper right central incisor in young adult male Sk0115 (disarticulated in Gr0160); an extra left mandibular central incisor in older middle adult female Sk0655/Gr0656. Three individuals displayed enamel pearls on a maxillary molar.

Impaction is where a tooth fails to emerge into the dental arch, usually due to either space deficiency or the presence of an entity blocking its path affected. The tooth rarely causes symptoms if it fails to erupt, but partial eruption often leads to infection and pain. Five individuals were affected by impaction, three younger middle adult females, an adolescent and an older child. Four of these cases involved upper canines. Nine individuals were affected by rotation where the teeth are out of alignment.

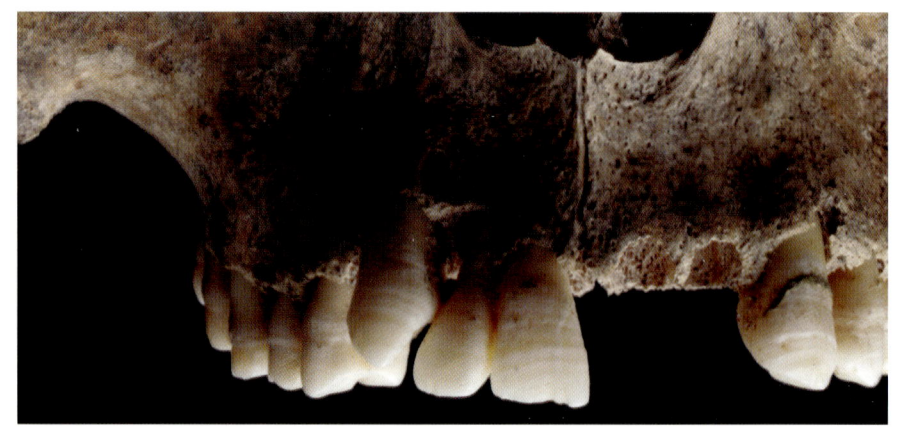

ILLUS 4.43
Dental enamel hypoplasia, Sk0796/Gr0797, young adult male

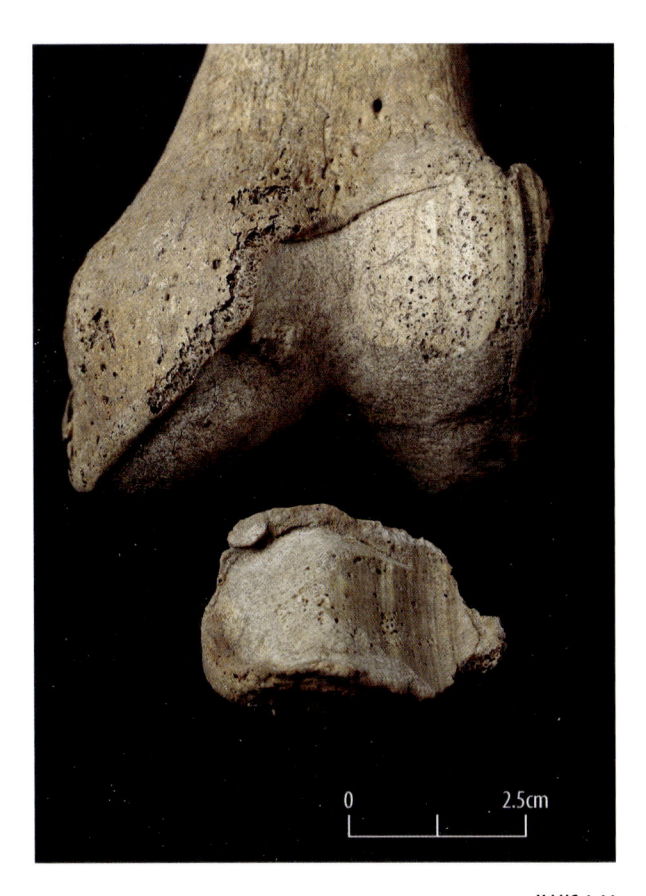

ILLUS 4.44
Osteoarthritic eburnation of left knee, Sk0051/Gr0053, older adult female

this had impacted the permanent canine, while in the other (Sk0585/Gr0587) the permanent tooth and erupted beside it. An older child (Sk1119/Gr1118, 8½–9 years) had a heterotopic canine where it had projected through the palate behind the lateral incisor.

JOINT DISEASES

A process of gradual degeneration begins once growth of the bone and joint is complete. Degenerative joint disease (DJD) is indicated by marginal lipping, although the rate at which this occurs varies greatly between individuals and it appears to result primarily from repeated 'wear and tear' on the joints with degeneration of the articular cartilage (Ortner 2003, 546). The disease can be accelerated by occupational activities and may also be brought on by trauma. Osteoarthritis affects the synovial articulations, which include the major joints between the longbones, the small joints in the hands and feet and the facet joints between the vertebral bodies of the spine (Rogers and Waldron 1995). In cases of osteoarthritis, eburnation or polishing of the bone can occur as the bones of the joint rub off each other. The presence of eburnation is a particular characteristic of osteoarthritis. Where changes to the joints are less severe, for example as indicated by slight degrees of osteophytic lipping (additional bone growths) or porosity, degenerative joint disease is the preferred term.

Extra-spinal osteoarthritis

Osteoarthritis is characterised by destruction of the articular cartilage in a joint and formation of adjacent

Overcrowding of one or more teeth was identified in four individuals. Two younger middle adult females retained deciduous upper canine, in one case (Sk0166/Gr0167)

TABLE 4.10
Prevalence rates of extra-spinal osteoarthritis by sex

JOINT	MALES		FEMALES		TOTAL	
	No	%	No	%	No	%
Temporomandibular joint (jaw)	1/58	1.7	0/56	–	1/114	0.9
Sternoclavicular (chest)	1/33	3.0	2/45	4.4	3/78	3.8
Acromioclavicular (upper shoulder)	4/38	10.5	3/47	6.4	7/85	8.2
Shoulder	2/39	5.1	0/53	–	2/93	2.2
Elbow	1/34	2.9	0/59	–	1/93	1.1
Wrist	1/25	8.0	2/45	4.4	3/70	4.3
Hand	0/25	–	1/48	2.1	1/73	1.4
Hip	3/38	7.9	2/64	3.1	5/102	4.9
Knee	1/34	2.9	2/62	3.2	3/96	3.1
Ankle	2/26	7.7	0/41	–	2/67	3.0
Feet	2/26	7.7	0/44	–	2/70	2.9
TOTAL	12/85	14.1	7/106	6.6	19/191	9.9

TABLE 4.11
Distribution of spinal osteoarthritis by sex and age (NB 3 unsexed adults were also assessed and this pathology was not present)

SEX	YOUNG ADULT		YOUNGER MIDDLE ADULT		OLDER MIDDLE ADULT		OLDER ADULT		TOTAL	
	No	%	No	%	No	%	No	%	No	%
Male	0/9	–	6/17	35.3	5/7	71.4	0/0	–	11/33	32.4
Female	0/10	–	3/22	13.6	4/7	57.1	1/1	100	8/40	20.0
TOTAL	0/19	–	9/39	23.1	9/14	64.3	1/1	100	19/74	25.7

TABLE 4.12
Distribution of spinal osteoarthritis by sex and spinal region

SEX	CERVICAL		THORACIC		LUMBAR	
	N	%	No	%	No	%
Male	6/33	18.2	5/29	17.2	2/22	9.1
Female	4/38	10.5	7/36	19.4	0/33	–
TOTAL	10/71	14.1	12/65	18.5	2/55	3.6

PEOPLE'S STORIES

A MAN WHO DIED WITH HIS MOTHER, 1450/1475–1515

The woman was born around 1450. Pestilence swept through Leith when she was six, and she and her siblings took ill, but all pulled through. Her father was not so lucky, but her mother supported the family as best she could, brewing beer to sell at the quayside to victual the ships. Times were often hard, especially when the harvest failed and bread prices were high, and typically there was not enough to eat. As a child she would help her mother at her business and accompany her on her trips to the quayside and grew used to the constant sound of hammering and shouting from the King's Wark, where there always seemed to be building work going on. At the quayside, she would watch the wool being loaded in summer and the grain in autumn and the barrels of goods coming back from Danzig and Antwerp. The sailors liked to tell her tall tales of their exploits and she dreamed of sailing away and having adventures, but she never left Leith.

She married a joiner who worked for a shipwright and had three surviving children including a son born in 1475 who was born full of energy and appetite. They lived in one room in the crowded old part of town, with an earth floor and had two benches to sit on during the day around the hearth in the centre of the room. At night they moved the benches back against the walls and rolled out straw-filled mattresses to sleep on. She worked hard to feed her family, sometimes going without food so that they might eat. When her mother became infirm, she moved in with them and the two continued the brewing business together, though this mainly involved her mother criticising her work from a chair by the fire.

Her husband found work on the building site of the new St Mary's church. He took his 8-year-old son along to work with him to begin his apprenticeship. The whole family would pass it every Sunday on their way to and from mass at St Anthony's and would always stop look at its progress. The boy was nearly 10 before the nave was complete and they could attend their first mass there. The boy and his father were keen to point out their contributions. Their womenfolk were awed by the scale of it, the largest building they had ever been inside, and by its brightly coloured carvings of saints.

The boy, meanwhile, continued to eat and grow, and was taller than his mother by the time he was 13. When he wasn't working, he often ran wild on the street with his friends and found great sport in chasing the St Anthony's pigs which roamed free about the streets with bells on their necks. That is until the day he was caught at it, chased through the streets and fell, breaking his collar bone. His mother dragged him up to the Preceptory to apologise and ask if they had something to ease his pain. The canons told him the pain was God's punishment and for good measure gave him additional penance in the form of prayers. He left the pigs alone after that.

The building work continued at St Mary's on the aisles, transepts and great central tower. It provided steady employment but took its toll on his back and right shoulder. Pestilence swept through the town again when he was 23 and continued to rumble on for years. His mother seemed immune to it, but his father succumbed in 1504. His two sisters were gone by this time, one had married a journeyman carpenter but had died in childbed, the other had married an Arbroath fisherman and was living away with four children of her own. The son stayed to take care of his widowed mother whose back was becoming increasingly creaky. He could not, anyway, afford lodgings anywhere else.

He had never given much thought to his appearance and had never made any effort to keep his teeth clean. His diet of beer and porridge had eaten into them and he suffered from toothache. On one occasion, after much beer, he persuaded a friend to pull out the worst offending tooth.

One night, a spark from the fire landed on a sack of malt and caught fire. The neighbours raised the alarm and the fire was doused using dozens of people forming a bucket chain from the shore. Luckily, the preceding days had been damp, or else the fire could quickly have become uncontrollable in the dense maze of thatched cottages in the old town. More rain fell as dawn broke and doused the last of the flames. Both the man and his mother were found dead inside their lodgings. The fire had not touched them, but the smoke had smothered them as they slept. There was no family left to dress the bodies or pay for the funeral mass or grave plot. They were buried in the same grave, placed unceremoniously on top of each other without a shroud wrapping. The old woman went in first, her son on top, his head resting on her chest.

SKELETON	1180, 1181
Grave	1183
Location of grave	Constitution Street, Area 5
Burial details	Buried one of top of the other, in double grave. Woman place in first, man on top with head resting on woman's chest
Age	Sk1180, older middle adult, 35–45 Sk1181, older adult, 45+
Sex	Sk1180 male; Sk1181 female
Stature	Sk1180, 178cm or 5'10" Sk1181, 154cm or 5'1"
Radiocarbon date	–
Other dating evidence	Cut by ditch [0980] so probably predating mid–16th century, found within Phase 1/2 cemetery, probably in use from late 14th century
Finds	–
Pathology	Sk1180, spinal DJD, fractured right clavicle (healed childhood injury), right acromioclavicular DJD, antemortem tooth loss, severe calculus, caries, DEH, periodontal disease. Sk1181, calculus, DEH, periodontal disease, bilateral mild cribra orbitalia, spinal and costal DJD
C/N isotope (diet)	–
O/S isotope (origins)	–
See also	Illus 4.08, p57; Illus 4.21, p71; p72; Table 4.19, p111; p119
Facial reconstruction artist	Miriam Modenes

A MAN WHO DIED WITH HIS MOTHER, 1450/1475–1515

TABLE 4.13
Distribution of vertebral osteophytosis by sex and age (NB the pathology was also noted in 1 out of 2 unsexed adults)

SEX	YOUNG ADULT		YOUNGER-MIDDLE ADULT		OLDER-MIDDLE ADULT		OLDER ADULT		TOTAL	
	No	%	No	%	No	%	No	%	No	%
Male	1/9	11.1	7/17	41.2	5/7	71.4	0/0	–	13/33	39.4
Female	0/9	–	7/22	31.8	6/7	85.7	1/1	100	14/39	35.9
TOTAL	1/18	5.6	14/39	35.9	11/14	78.6	1/1	100	27/72	37.5

TABLE 4.14
Distribution of vertebral osteophytosis by sex and spinal region (NB 1 unsexed adult of 2 showed this pathology in the thoracic region)

SEX	CERVICAL		THORACIC		LUMBAR	
	No	%	No	%	No	%
Male	10/33	30.3	11/27	40.7	6/20	30
Female	7/37	18.9	12/32	37.5	3/31	9.7
TOTAL	17/70	24.3	23/59	39.0	9/51	17.6

ILLUS 4.45
Ankylosis of thoracic vertebrae, Sk0951/Gr0952, younger middle adult male

bone, in the form of bony lipping and spur formation (osteophytes) around the edges of the joint (White et al 2012, 441). The causes of this disease are for the most part mechanical, that is wear and tear. The disease occurs most commonly in load-bearing joints, particularly in the spine, the hip and the knees and is an inherent part of the ageing process. A phenomenon often found with osteoarthritis is eburnation (**Illus 4.44**), the result of bone being exposed when cartilage is destroyed and rubbing against other bones in the joint. Bone affected this way takes on a polished, ivory-like appearance (ibid).

A total of 19 individuals suffered from osteoarthritis of one or more of the joints in their appendicular skeleton (limbs, shoulders and hips). It affected 19 individuals and was significantly more common in males than females (**Table 4.10**). The overall 9.9% of the sex-determined population is below the British average for this period, which sees a rate of 14.1% (Roberts & Cox 2003, 282–3).

In general, the lesions of osteoarthritis were mild to moderate in severity. The most commonly diseased joint was the upper shoulder (acromioclavicular), afflicting 10.5% of males. The acromioclavicular joint is not very stable and subject to constant shearing stresses (stress component parallel to a given surface) (DePalma 1983, 239). Moreover, it may show signs of deterioration as early as 35 years of age in modern populations (Boylston and Lee 2008). At Constitution Street it was noticeably more common on the right-hand side than left, afflicting 6.8% (5/73) of right shoulders and 3.8% (3/78) of left.

Spinal osteoarthritis

The joints of the posterior spine were affected by varying degrees of the classic signs of osteoarthritis and scored as mild, moderate or severe. Of all adult spines assessed, 24.7% (19/77), were affected which is slightly below the average rate in British late medieval populations of 27.9%, (Roberts & Cox 2003, 281–2). Males had a higher incidence rate of spinal osteoarthritis than females and there is an obvious increase with age (**Table 4.11**).

The thoracic region was the most frequently affected, slightly more commonly in females (**Table 4.12**). The cervical region was far more commonly affected in males and only males had osteoarthritis of the vertebral facets in the lumbar region.

Vertebral osteophytosis

Vertebral osteophytes are the formation of new bone (exostoses) forming projections from the margins of the vertebral bodies. It is thought to be a response to bone and ligament damage. They vary in severity from slight projections to complete ankylosis or fusion of adjacent vertebral bodies (**Illus 4.45**). Of all adult spines recorded, 37.8% (28/74) had a degree of osteophytosis, compared with 19.2% of the upper class, post-medieval population from St Marylebone Church, London (Miles et al 2008, 134). The prevalence was similar in many ways to that of spinal osteoarthritis, just discussed. It was clearly age-related and was more common in males than females (**Table 4.13**),

CONSTITUTION STREET EXCAVATIONS

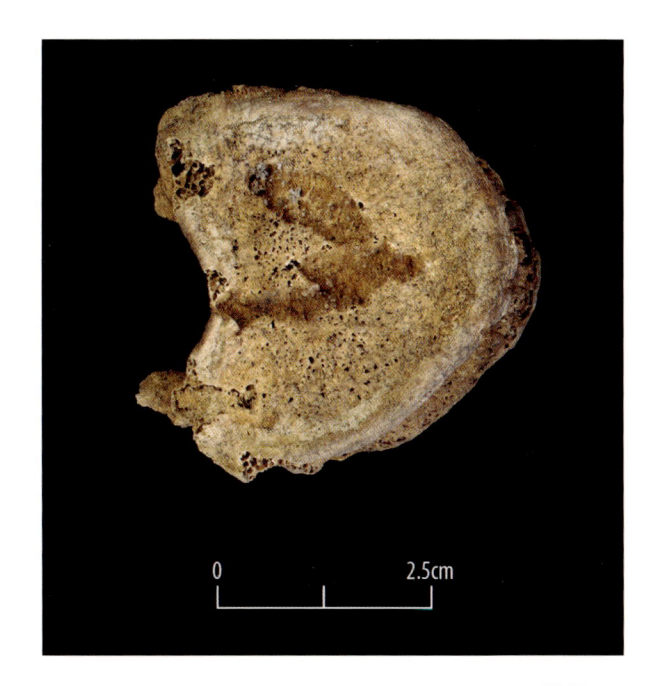

ILLUS 4.46
Schmorl's nodes on inferior body, Sk1081/Gr1082, younger middle adult male

with strenuous activity (Schmorl & Junghanns 1971). A total of 50.0% of adult spines were affected to some degree, identical to the prevalence noted in medieval Hereford (Boucher et al 2015, 111). Again, they were more common in males, with 64.3% (18/28) of males affected on one or more vertebrae compared with 38.2% (13/34) of females. The lower thoracic and upper lumbar vertebrae were particularly affected (**Illus 4.47**). This is an area where increased stress is placed on the intervertebral discs.

Unlike the degenerative spinal conditions, Schmorl's nodes do not increase in frequency with age; in fact, in some cases the prevalence decreases. They often arise during adolescence whilst the intervertebral disc is still gelatinous, and some lesions will remodel in later life. These nodes occurred with a relatively high frequency in the young adults of both sexes, suggesting that these individuals were involved in strenuous labour from a young age. The obligation for adolescents and perhaps older children to undertake severe workloads is not surprising in a society where child labour would be considered an important economic factor, often being employed in urban centres as apprentices and servants (Roberts & Cox 2003, 294).

though the difference was less marked than with spinal osteoarthritis. The prevalence in older middle adults was in fact, higher for females. Again, the thoracic region was the most frequently affected, though the cervical region was also commonly affected in males (**Table 4.14**).

Schmorl's nodes

Schmorl's nodes are pits or depressions on the surface of the vertebral bodies (**Illus 4.46**). They first occur during adolescence and young adulthood and are caused by the protrusion of the herniated disc into the adjacent body. Their incidence rate has been used to demonstrate the degree to which manual labour was carried out in the past, based upon the theory that they are closely associated

Compressed vertebrae

In a compression fracture of the vertebra, the vertebral bone collapses. More than one vertebra may be affected. Direct injury to the spine may cause a bone fracture anywhere along the vertebral column. This condition may be caused by osteoporosis (loss of bone density) which can weaken vertebrae, causing them to fracture or collapse, and is the most common cause (p105). Trauma can also be a cause, as can tumours that started in the bone or spread to the bone from elsewhere (Zieve & Ma 2010). Vertebral compression was noted in eight individuals (four male, three female, one adolescent).

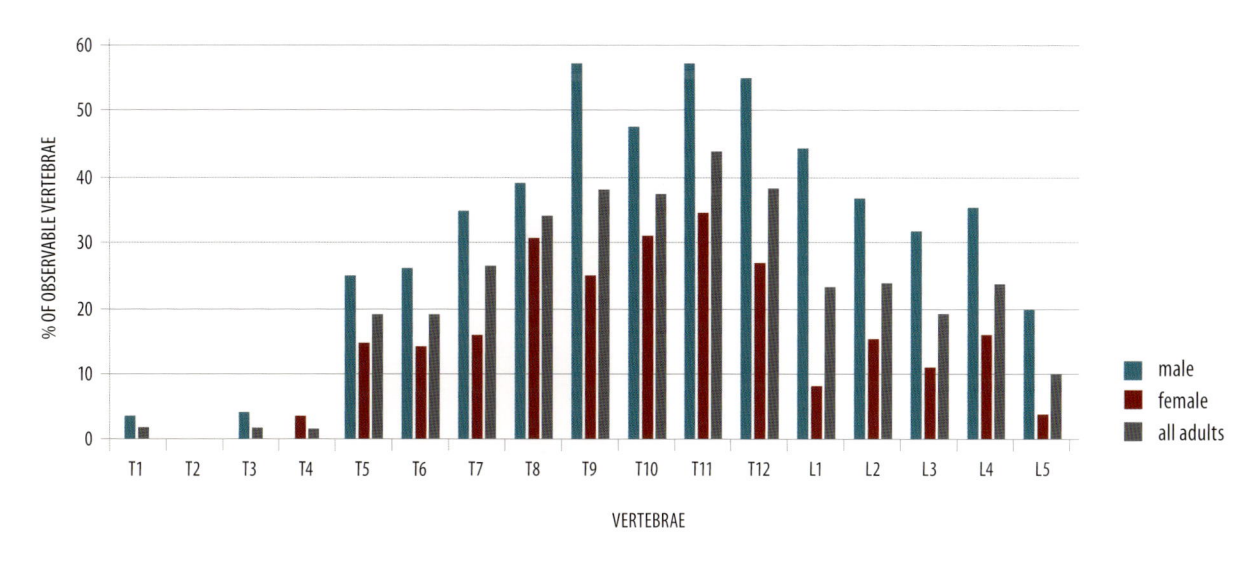

ILLUS 4.47
Prevalence of Schmorl's nodes by vertebra and sex

ILLUS 4.48
Scoliosis, Sk0566/Gr0568, younger middle adult female

T1–4 were compressed on the right side, T5–8 on the left and T9–12 again on the right.

Ankylosis of hands and feet
Ankylosis, a fusing of the bones in the appendicular skeleton, is usually associated with a chronic disease and is a non-specific response of the skeletal system. Therefore, it is often not easy to determine the root cause of the pathology. It can be caused by rheumatoid arthritis, traumatic arthritis, ankylosing spondylitis, Reiter's syndrome, psoriatic arthritis, neurotrophic arthropathy, haeomatological disorders or infections. Two individuals were observed with ankylosis in the hand and/or foot. Adult male Sk0237/Gr0238 had severe osteolytic bone growth at his right ankle, fusing the tibia and fibula together. Older child (11½–12 years) Sk0554/Gr0556 had both left hand and right foot affected, with intermediate and distal phalanges fused on the fifth finger and second toe.

METABOLIC DISEASES
Metabolic diseases result from deficiency and excess of essential vitamins or minerals which produce a reaction in the skeleton, visible as a reduction in bone mass or an increase in bone density.

Spondylolysis
Spondylolysis is a common condition that can result in lower back pain. It is caused by a defect or stress fracture in the vertebrae caused by repeated hyperextension or rotation of the spine. Some people are more genetically susceptible. It most frequently affects the lowest L5 vertebra (Blanda et al 1993; Standaert & Herring 2000). Nine individuals displayed this condition (9/126, 7.1%) which is just above the average of about 5–6% of individuals that showed signs of spondylolysis in European and American populations (Roche & Rowe 1951). All involved the lumbar vertebrae, L4, and most frequently, L5. There was no marked difference between prevalence in males and females.

Scoliosis
Scoliosis is the term used for lateral deviations of the spinal column (Ortner 2003, 466). It often starts in childhood and progresses throughout the growing age and early adult life. The deformity usually shows a double curvature, which permits the position of the head close to normal. Sk0566/Gr0568, a younger middle adult female, had an S-shaped curvature of the spine (**Illus 4.48**), the vertebrae

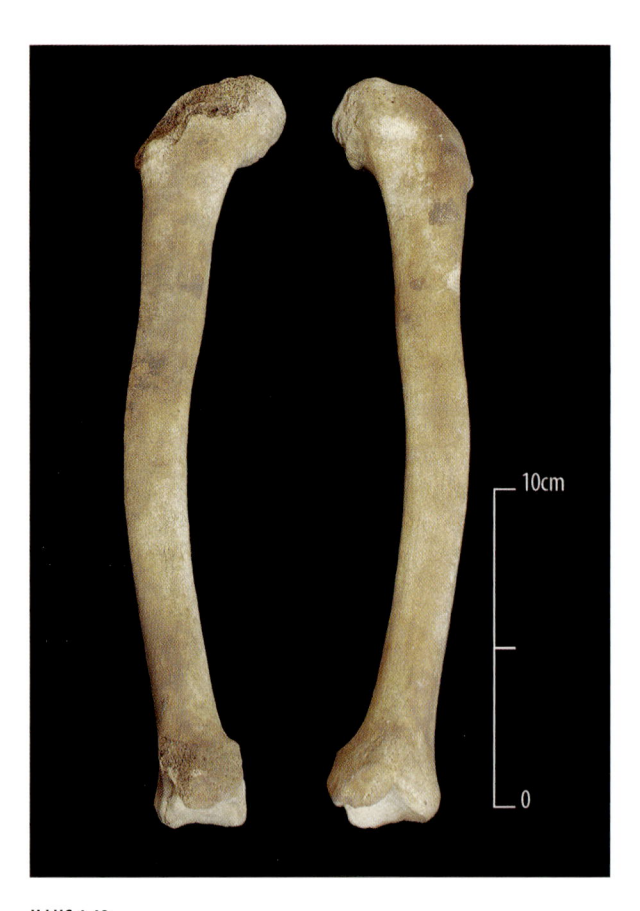

ILLUS 4.49
Tibial bowing, possibly due to childhood rickets, Sk0063/Gr0065, young adult female

Rickets

Rickets is caused by a lack of vitamin D, calcium, or phosphate, which leads to softening and weakening of the bones. Vitamin D is found in fish and can also be synthesized in the body if exposed to sufficient sunlight. Rickets is most likely to occur in children during periods of rapid growth, when the body needs high levels of calcium and phosphate. Rickets may be seen in children, aged 6 months to 2 years. Skeletal changes as a result of rickets include retarded growth and characteristic deformed bones. In active infantile rickets the cranial vault may develop thin and soft areas. Thickening of the cranial vault is also seen. In this process of remodelling, the entire thickness of the cranial vault has a porous appearance (Ortner 2003, 394). In severe rickets, the vertebral bodies may have decreased height due to compression, often combined with a deeper scalloping of the endplate. Long bones can be characterised by brittle thin cortex. Stress fractures are common and lead to bending deformities. In the adult skeleton, change may be totally remodelled or simply visible as bowing and twisting to the long bones (**Illus 4.49**). After healing, these bending deformities remain for the rest of the individual's life, while minor bowing can become insignificant. Four individuals were affected with bowing of the leg bones: Sk0135/Gr0137, younger child (3–4 years); Sk0682/Gr0683, older child (11–11½ years); and Sk0063/Gr0065 and Sk0425/Gr0427, both young adult females.

Scurvy

Scurvy is a disease caused by prolonged insufficient intake of vitamin C (ascorbic acid). It is found in people deprived of fresh vegetables and fruits. As vitamin C is destroyed by high temperatures and by exposure to air, deficiencies are prone to manifest in populations that consume mainly cooked foods. It affects many organs and in severe cases has a high mortality. Deficiency of vitamin C leads to impaired collagen synthesis, causing capillary fragility, poor wound healing, and bony abnormalities in affected adults and children. Infantile scurvy is seldom observed before 4 months of age and reaches its maximum prevalence between 8 and 10 months of age (Ortner 2003, 384). Sk0424/Gr0427, an infant (6 months – 1 year), displayed porosity and reactive bone growth within the skull and ribs (**Illus 4.50**), which, combined with the pathological changes in this individual, suggests the presence of an underlying vitamin C deficiency at time of death (Brickley and Ives 2006).

Osteoporosis

Osteoporosis is a condition characterized by a decrease in the density of bone, decreasing its strength and resulting in fragile bones. It leads to abnormally porous bone that is compressible, like a sponge. This disorder of the skeleton weakens the bone and results in frequent fractures. Bones that are affected by osteoporosis can break as a result

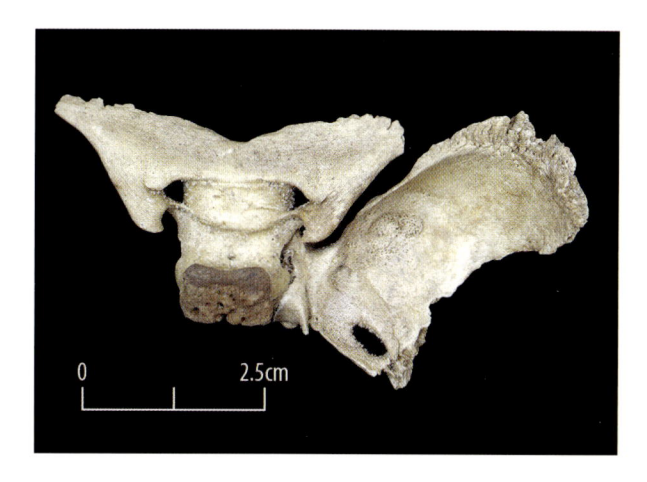

ILLUS 4.50
Porotic sphenoid, possibly due to scurvy, Sk0424/Gr0427, infant

of relatively minor injuries. The fracture can be either in the form of cracking (as in a hip fracture) or collapsing (as in a compression fracture of vertebrae of the spine). Fractures of the spine such as this can cause severe 'band-like' pain that radiates from the back to the sides of the body. Over the years, repeated spinal fractures can lead to chronic lower back pain as well as loss of height or curving of the spine due to collapse of the vertebrae. The collapse gives individuals a hunched-back appearance of the upper back, often called a 'dowager hump' because it commonly is seen in elderly women.

Apart from the spine, the hips, ribs and wrists are common areas where bone fractures occur as a result of osteoporosis, although osteoporosis-related fractures can occur in almost any skeletal bone. Of the longbones, the femoral neck shows the most characteristic changes. Alveolar resorption and thinning of the parietal bones of the skull do occur with increasing age and there is some support for an association between biparietal thinning and osteoporosis (Lodge 1967). Osteoporosis can be present without any symptoms for decades. It usually does not manifest itself before the fifth decade, and is more frequent and more severe in females than males. This is largely due to the sharp decline in oestrogen at menopause, compared to the more gradual decrease of testosterone in ageing males. Osteoporosis is extremely difficult to identify confidently without measurements of bone mineral content (Brickley 2000). It is possible that a number of individuals displaying compressed vertebrae suffered from osteoporosis, particularly older adults Sk0051/Gr0053 and Sk0214/Gr0215 (female and male, respectively).

Porotic hyperostosis and cribra orbitalia

Porotic hyperostosis and cribra orbitalia are both minor metabolic disorders evident by osseous change. They are non-specific indicators of stress and result from the stresses and strains placed on the body during development. They may be due to a variety of causes including nutritional deprivation, disease and parasitic infection. In

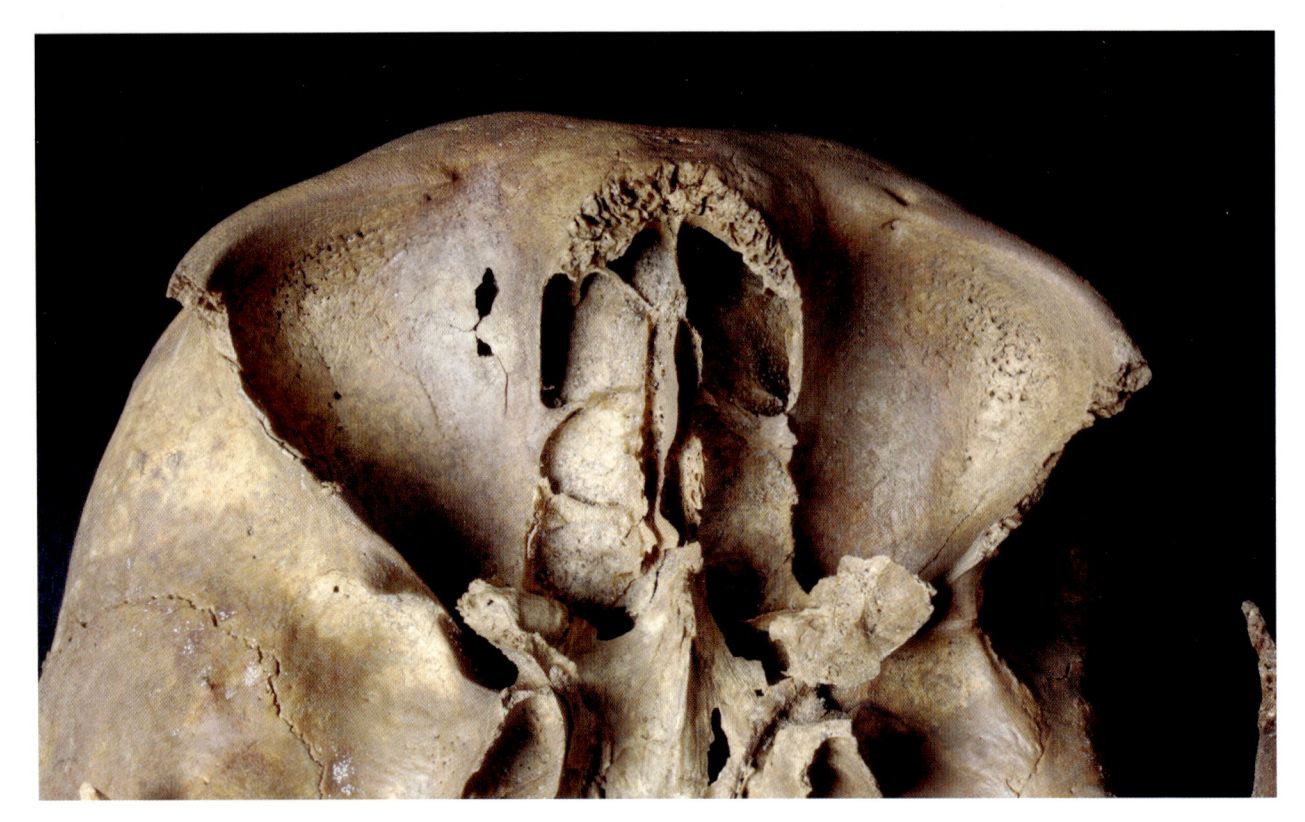

ILLUS 4.51
Bilateral porosity in the orbital roofs due to cribra orbitalia, Sk0158/Gr0159, young adult male

general, these different aetiologies are difficult to identify due to the general nature of the pathological response. Used in isolation, they mean little but, where they occur in collections, they may be used to indicate or highlight the evidence for long-term stress within the community. Dental enamel hypoplasia (DEH) is another non-specific indicator of stress and has already been discussed (p98).

Pitting and porosity on the external surface of the cranial vault (porotic hyperostosis) and orbital roof (cribra orbitalia) (**Illus 4.51**) are among the most frequent pathological lesions seen in archaeological human skeletal assemblages. The conditions are multi-factorial and widely assumed to be related to iron deficiency but also deficiency of other vitamins and minerals, general poor diet, poor living conditions, compromised immunity and poor health (Griffeth et al 1997; Schultz 2001; Brickley and Ives 2006; Walker et al 2009).

The prevalence of cribra orbitalia of 35.8% at Constitution Street (**Table 4.15**) is well above the average rate for late medieval Britain of 10.8% (Roberts & Cox 2003, 235) and few of the given sites show equivalent figures, most that do being small data sets. Prevalence was particularly high among children (55.3%). Prevalence of porotic hyperostosis is lower, and in contrast to cribra orbitalia, is lower in subadults and slightly higher in men than women.

When the prevalence of cribra orbitalia and dental enamel hypoplasia in the same individual is considered, it gives a good indication of those who were the poorest and the most nutritionally deprived in a society. Approximately a quarter of adults are affected by both and figures for males and females are broadly equivalent (**Table 4.16**).

TABLE 4.15
Prevalence of porotic hyperostosis and cribra orbitalia by age and sex

AGE/SEX	POROTIC HYPEROSTOSIS		CRIBRA ORBITALIA	
	NO	%	NO	%
Infant	1/3	33.3	0/3	-
Child (YC/OC)	2/49	4.1	21/38	55.3
Adolescent	5/14	35.7	3/10	30.0
Subadult	0/8	-	2/3	66.7
Total subadult	8/74	10.8	26/54	48.1
Adult male	12/55	21.8	12/43	27.9
Adult female	9/54	16.7	12/45	26.7
Adult unsexed	2/9	22.2	3/6	50.0
Total adult	23/118	19.5	27/94	28.7
TOTAL	31/192	16.1	53/148	35.8

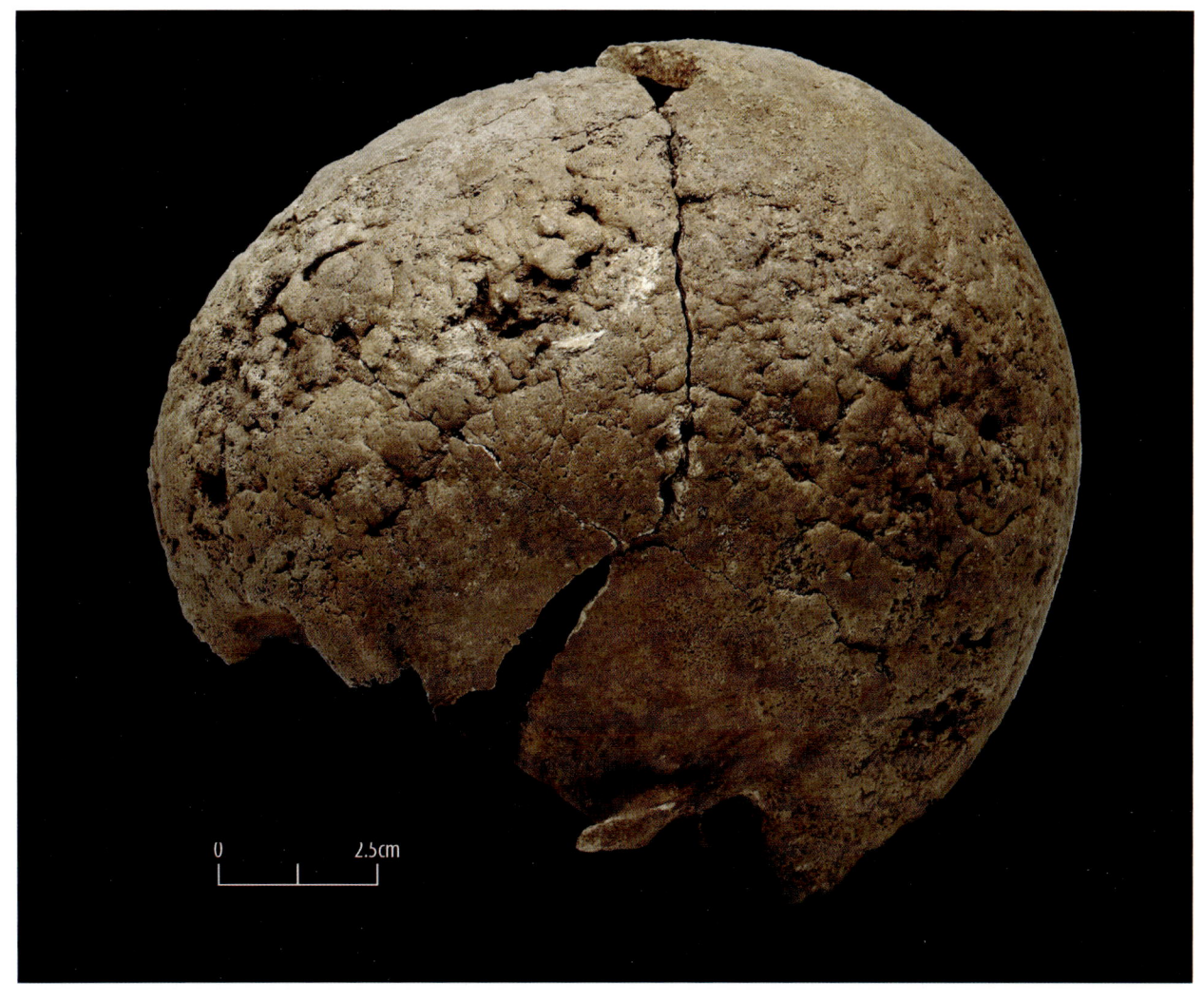

ILLUS 4.52
Caries sicca caused by syphilis, Sk0985/Gr0988, adult female?

INFECTIONS

Evidence of infection can be specific, that is where the exact causative organism is known, such as in cases of leprosy, tuberculosis or syphilis (Roberts & Manchester 2010, 182), or non-specific, that is infection by a bacterium or other pathogen indistinguishable from others (ibid, 168). Skeletal material can show evidence of infection in the form of osteomyelitis, periostitis or sinusitis but with no clear indication of what type of organism was responsible.

TABLE 4.16
Adults with both cribra orbitalia and dental enamel hypoplasia

SEX	NO	%
Male	8/35	22.9
Female	9/39	23.1
Unsexed	2/3	66.7
TOTAL	**19/77**	**24.7**

Syphilis

Syphilis is a chronic infection that is transmitted through sexual contact and is one of a larger group of diseases referred to as the treponematoses, caused by bacteria of the genus *Treponema*. In addition to venereal syphilis, these include pinta, yaws, and endemic syphilis. These four diseases are characterized by primary and secondary lesions, a latent period, and late, destructive lesions (Aufderheide & Rodríguez-Martín 1998). Pinta, yaws, and endemic syphilis are usually diseases of childhood, while venereal syphilis affects adults (Roberts & Manchester 2010, 209). Venereal syphilis can also be passed to the developing foetus of an infected mother; this is termed congenital syphilis (Ortner 2003).

Bone involvement (10–12% of cases) typically occurs during the final or tertiary stage of the disease (Roberts & Manchester 2010, 208); the most characteristic lesions are those involving the cranial vault (caries sicca). The tibia is the most affected skeletal element, but the nasal-palatal region can also manifest severe, destructive lesions (Aufderheide & Rodríguez-Martín 1998). In the tertiary stage of syphilis many organs may be affected. Common symptoms include fever, painful, non-healing skin ulcers, bone pain, liver disease and anaemia. Tertiary syphilis can also affect the nervous system (resulting in the loss of mental functioning) and the aorta (resulting in heart disease) (Kennard 2017).

Sk0985/Gr0988, an adult possible female, displayed caries sicca over the majority of the exterior of the cranium (**Illus 4.52**). Unfortunately, this was a disarticulated skull found redeposited in the grave of Sk0987 and thus there was no opportunity to look for signs of the disease in the rest of the skeleton.

Sinusitis

Inflammation of the air cavities within the passages of the nose (paranasal sinuses) is referred to as sinusitis. It can occur in the upper respiratory area, known as maxillary sinusitis or, less commonly, at the very back part of the nose just beneath the base of the brain, known as sphenoid sinusitis.

Maxillary sinusitis can be caused by upper respiratory infections, but also by allergies, smoke, environmental pollution and dust (Roberts & Manchester 2010, 174). Tending fires for heat and cooking within houses would have exposed individuals to smoky environments (Merrett & Pfeiffer 2000). The prevalence of maxillary sinusitis is significantly higher in those exposed to the high levels of air pollutants in urban environments than those living in rural settings (Lewis et al 1995).

When identifying maxillary sinusitis in skeletal material it is the chronic condition that is recognized in the form of porosity or small irregular patches of new bone in the chamber (Lewis et al 1995). Symptoms include nasal congestion, pus-forming discharge, facial and dental pain, coughing, fluid around the eyes, earache, sore throat, bad breath, wheezing and fever (Evans 1994; Roberts 2007).

Six individuals (older child Sk0929/Gr0930, 12 years, three younger middle adult females, Sk0625/Gr0624, Sk0643/Gr0589, Sk1073/Gr1199, young adult possible male Sk0117/Gr0160 and adult possible male Sk0708/disarticulated skull in cemetery soil) displayed irregular pitting and new bone formation (**Illus 4.53**). Sk0708 also had poor dental health, with infection draining from abscesses of the upper right first and second molars (respective teeth were subsequently lost ante-mortem). Dental infection is responsible for about 10% of maxillary sinusitis due to the close anatomical relationship between the floor of the sinuses and the roots of the teeth (Hickish 1985).

Sphenoid sinusitis may cause a bad, dull, non-descript, vague headache that will not go away but the classic sinus symptoms, such as a runny nose, are often absent. The headache may be made worse by changes in posture, walking, stooping or prolonged standing. It is caused as the mucus membranes that line the cavity become

ILLUS 4.53
Maxillary sinusitis, Sk0643/Gr0589, younger middle adult female

inflamed as the immune system struggles to fight off the infection. This causes the pressure on the surrounding bones that leads to the pain (Hawyes 2011). Sk0512/Pit 0501, an adult possible female, displayed evidence of sphenoid sinusitis in the form of grape-like masses called polyps (**Illus 4.54**).

Nasal turbinate hypertrophy (pneumatised turbinate)

Nasal turbinate hypertrophy is an enlarged nasal concha, which appears to be swollen and rounded (**Illus 4.55**). This causes the bony nasal septum to thicken and warp. During life the combined abnormal septum and enlarged middle turbinates compromise the nasal airways.

Nasal findings in two skulls (young adult possible female Sk0718/disarticulated skull, and younger middle adult female Sk0913/Gr0914) displayed enlarged nasal conchae, and are suspected to be the result of allergic rhinitis. Rhinitis is defined as inflammation of the nasal membranes (Togias 2000) and is characterised by any combination of the following: sneezing, nasal congestion, nasal itching, and runny nose (Druce 1998). The eyes, ears, sinuses and throat can also be involved. Allergies are the most common cause. Allergies affect soft tissue primarily, but prolonged allergy can cause nasal and sinus bone changes but is difficult to diagnose in archaeological remains (Gregg 2000). Allergic rhinitis often co-exists with other disorders, such as asthma, and may be associated with asthma attacks (Nayak 2003).

Periostitis

Periostitis is the inflammation of the periosteum, a dense membrane composed of fibrous connective tissue that surrounds the bone. It is a reaction to inflammation or infection and can be seen as a deposit of new bone on the surface of the skeletal element.

The total prevalence rate of non-specific infections for the Constitution Street population is 11.9% (45/378) (**Table 4.17**). This is a little below the late medieval average of 14.1% (Roberts & Cox 2003, 235).

Infection of the lower limb was particularly common, where 25 individuals had an affected tibia (**Illus 4.56**) and 15 had an affected fibula. This is a very common location for periostitis as the shin bone lies close to the surface and as a consequence is subject to recurrent injury. In 13 individuals both the tibia and fibula exhibited subperiosteal bone reaction and, of these, eight included both legs. The condition is more common in males (**Table 4.18**). In the tarsals of the feet, the bone most frequently affected by periostitis is the calcaneus as it is one of the main pressure points of the foot and therefore more susceptible to injury. In Constitution Street, one young adult female (Sk0383/Gr0416) displayed such a case.

It is also common to find reactive new bone at the tooth sockets (alveolar bone) of the maxilla and mandible where there has been an abscess (**Illus 4.57**) or ante-mortem

TABLE 4.17
Number of individuals with periostitis by specific bone

BONE		ADULT	SUBADULT	TOTAL
Maxilla		2	1	3
Mandible		1	3	4
Rib		2	1	3
Scapula		–	1	1
Sacrum (base of the spine)		–	1	1
Innominate (hip)		1	1	2
Femur		6	2	8
Tibia		17	8	25
Fibula		9	6	15
Tarsal		1	–	1
Foot phalanx		1	–	1
TOTAL	NO	27/238	18/140	45/378
	%	11.3	12.9	11.9

ILLUS 4.54
Sphenoid sinusitis, Sk0512/Pit 0501, adult female?

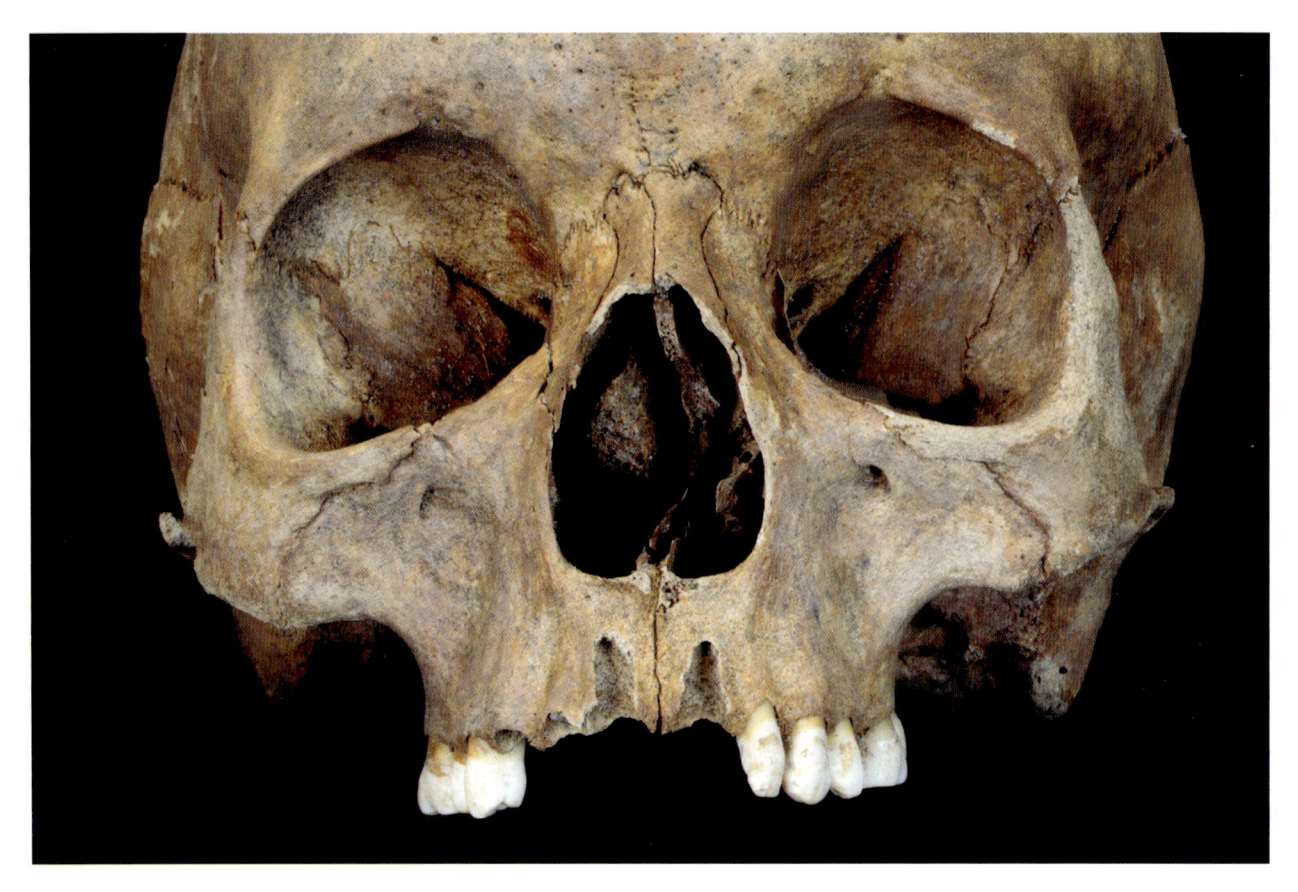

ILLUS 4.55
Nasal turbinate hypertrophy on right, Sk0718 (disarticulated in cemetery soil), young adult female

tooth loss. Six of the seven individuals with periostitis of the maxilla or mandible had it in the alveolae, three of these also had ante-mortem tooth loss and/or abscesses. Other cases probably resulted from localised infection in the facial area.

Three individuals (younger middle adult female Sk0597/Gr0598, adolescent Sk0966/Gr0968 (15–16 years), young adult female Sk0987/Gr0988) had subperiosteal reactive new bone formation on the visceral surface of the ribs. These are thought to result from chronic respiratory infections, the most common being pleurisy, pneumonia, bronchiectasis and tuberculosis.

TABLE 4.18
Prevalence of tibial periostitis by age and sex

AGE/SEX	NO	%
Subadult	8/68	11.8
Adult male	5/30	16.7
Adult female	8/78	10.3
Adult unsexed	4/25	16.0
TOTAL	25/201	12.4

TRAUMA
Trauma refers to injuries caused by accidents, conflict and ill health. Types that can affect the skeleton include fracture, dislocation and post-traumatic deformity. Sometimes severe soft tissue trauma can also leave a mark (Ortner 2003, 119).

Fracture
A fracture can be defined as the result of any traumatic event that leads to a complete or partial break of a bone (Roberts & Manchester 2010, 84). In total 12 individuals suffered from fractures (3.2%, 12/378) 11 adults, seven of which were males, and only one subadult (**Table 4.19**). Males displaying the highest frequency is a phenomenon also observed clinically (Judd 2004). All the fractures were healed and thus none represents a fatal injury.

Sk0718/disarticulated female skull, displayed a possible well-healed depressed cranial fracture on the right frontal cranium. The depression measured 12mm by 9mm. Injuries to the skull are associated with violence, although accidents can also occur. The majority of the examples of cranial trauma do not initially lead to the person's death, as in this example.

Three clavicle injuries occurred among three adults, including two males. All exhibited injuries typical of indirect force (Richards & Corley 1996). A fractured clavicle is the most common of all clinical childhood fractures (Kleinheinz 2017) and it is possible that these traumas occurred during the childhood of the adult individuals affected.

Sk0617/Gr0618 (male) had six broken ribs at the left sternal aspect. Rib fractures are typically the result of blunt force trauma caused by a fall or interpersonal violence (Lovell 1997, 66; Sirmali et al 2003, 136).

Sk1087/Gr1203 (male) had a fractured elbow involving the end of the humerus. His radius and ulna were poorly preserved, but the ulna did also show signs of trauma. The trauma had severely affected the joint, as new bone growth was present. Elbow fractures are not common injuries in adults (Cluett 2017) and are most commonly caused by falls.

Hand injuries can result from a twisting injury, a fall, a crush injury, or direct trauma. Two adults displayed left hand metacarpal fractures, one (Sk0806/Gr0807) also appears to have hurt his left ankle, possibly in the same incident (see also p113).

The femur is one of the largest and strongest bones in the body and because of this it takes a tremendous force to cause a femur to fracture. In patients with normal bone strength, the most common cause is a fall from height. The left femur of an older child (Sk0682/Gr0683, 11–11½ years) displayed a fracture on the shaft which had misaligned during healing and was slightly bowed (**Illus 4.58**). Children's bones are particularly supple and heal quickly so that lesions may not be visible in the archaeological record, unless the injury did not heal very well or occurred close to death. The child also displayed bowing on the right femur (see also p105).

Three lower leg fractures were in evidence (detailed below), two involving the tibia and fibula, one the fibula and metatarsal. These can be caused by falls, direct force trauma or ankle-twisting injuries. Foot bones can be broken by similar means or by hitting the foot against hard objects.

Sk0494/Gr0493 (female) and Sk0298/Gr0299 (male) both displayed fractures to the tibia and fibula (**Illus 4.59**). The latter also had secondary degenerative joint disease at the corresponding ankle joint. These two individuals would have been incapacitated for a period and the injury probably made any weight-bearing activity painful.

Sk0700/Gr0701 (male) had suffered from three fractured bones in the lower leg and feet, probably during two separate incidents. His left leg suffered a fractured distal

TABLE 4.19
Individuals with trauma and possibly associated conditions
AD = adult; OC = older child; OMA = older middle adult; YA = younger adult; YMA = younger middle adult

SK	GR	AGE	SEX	AREA	INJURIES	INTERPRETATION
0298	0299	AD	M	5	Healed fracture of R tibia & fibula (Illus 72). Secondary (traumatic) DJD on distal tibia, fibula & talus.	Broken leg - twist or fall
1114	1115	YMA	?	5	Healed fracture of L clavicle.	Broken collar bone - childhood injury?
1180	1183	OMA	M	5	Healed fracture of R clavicle. R acromioclavicular DJD.	Broken collar bone - childhood injury?
0494	0493	OMA	F	6	Healed fracture of R tibia & fibula.	Broken leg - twist or fall
0592	0590	OMA	F	7	Healed fracture of distal L 2nd metacarpal.	Broken hand - fall or crush
0617	0618	OMA	M	7	Healed fracture of six L sternal ribs	Blow to ribs - violence or fall
1087	1200	YMA	M	7	Healed fracture of R distal humerus and proximal ulna.	Broken elbow - fall?
0648	0649	YMA	F	8	Traumatic bowing deformity of L humerus. Bilateral. Traumatic myositis ossifcans to L distal fibula.	Turned ankle & broken arm? Both on left, same incident?
0682	0683	OC (11–11.5 years)	–	8	Healed fracture of L femur (Illus 71) possibly rickets-related bowing to R femur	Broken leg - fall?
0700	0701	AD	M?	8	Healed fracture of L distal fibula and avulsion fracture of L 5th metatarsal. Healed fracture of distal R 2nd metatarsal	Two turned ankles, different incidents?
0718	0721	YA	F?	8	Possible well healed depressed R frontal cranial fracture	Blow to head – violence or fall
0784	0785	OMA	M	8	Traumatic myositis ossifcans to R distal fibula. Periostitis on R 1st and 2nd proximal foot phalanges.	Turned ankle
0796	0797	YA	M	8	Healed fracture of R clavicle.	Broken collar bone - childhood injury?
0806	0807	YMA	M?	8	Healed fracture on L proximal 1st metacarpal. Traumatic myositis ossifcans to L distal fibula.	Turned ankle & broken hand? Both on left, same incident?

ILLUS 4.56
Tibial periostitis, Sk0301/Gr0302, younger middle adult female

ILLUS 4.57
Periostitis and abscess on right mandible, Sk0251/Gr0252, adolescent

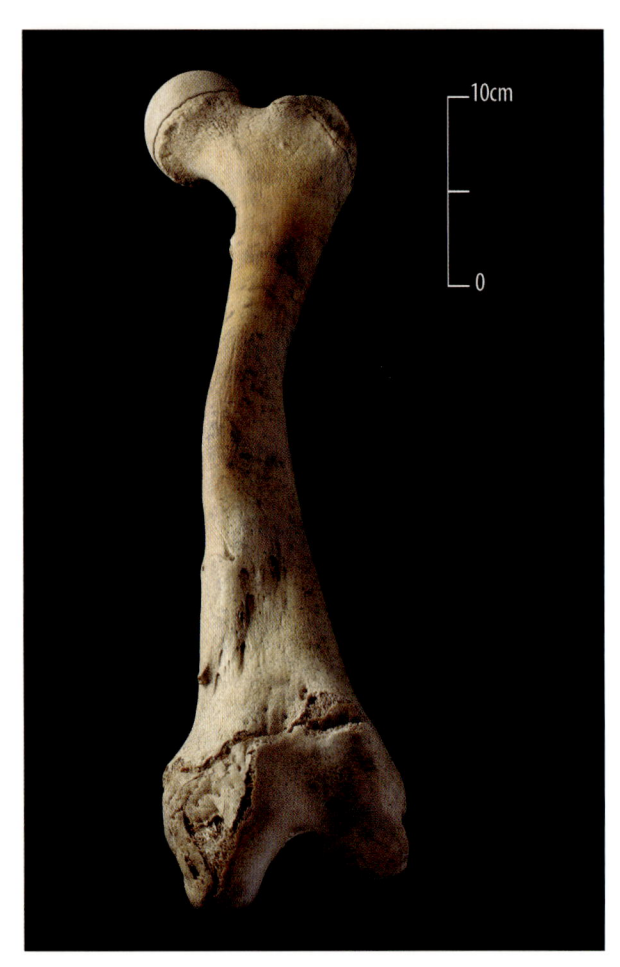

ILLUS 4.58
Healed fracture of left femur, Sk0682/Gr0683, older child

fibula and an avulsion fracture of the fifth metatarsal of the foot. Avulsion fractures are the most common fractures involving the fifth metatarsal. They occur after forced inversion (turning inward) of the foot (Strayer et al 1999) when the tendon pulls off a tiny fragment of bone (Cluett 2017) and they cause a sudden onset of pain. The same incident if severe enough could also have led to the fibula fracture. The slight form of the fibula makes it susceptible to breakage, but as it is not weight-bearing it has little effect on the individual's ability to function, though the leg and foot would have been extremely painful for some time. His right foot also displayed a fractured second metatarsal which had healed slightly misaligned, probably representing a separate incident. Fractures of the foot bones are common and are caused by falls, twisting injuries, or direct impact of the foot against hard objects. Foot fractures cause considerable pain, which are almost always made worse by attempting to walk or put weight on the foot (Roberts 2008).

Traumatic bowing deformity

Sk0648/Gr0649 (younger middle adult female) had marked bowing with rotation of the left humerus (**Table**

4.19). The bowing in the humerus may be the result of a healed fracture of the humeral midshaft that occurred during childhood (Stuart-Macadam et al 1998). In very young children, fractures may be remodelled completely, leaving no indication of the injury, except perhaps the presence of a bowing deformity (Pietrusewsky and Douglas 2002, 109). This same woman also appears to have turned her ankle (see below), possibly in the same incident.

Traumatic myositis ossificans

Evidence for soft-tissue blunt trauma was found on the distal fibula of Sk0648/Gr0649 (younger middle adult female), Sk0784/Gr0785 (older middle adult male) and Sk0806/Gr0807 (younger middle adult male) (**Table 4.19**). There is evidence for new bone growth where a muscle has been pulled away from the bone at the ankle and caused bleeding. As the site of injury was close to the periosteum, the membrane covering the bone, this was stimulated to produce a mass of calcified bone, resulting in the distinctive bone formation. At some time prior to their death, the individuals had probably sustained trauma, probably in the form of a turned ankle crushing part of the membrane which extends between and connects the shafts of the tibia and fibula. Periostitis noted on two proximal foot phalanges of the left foot of Sk0806 might also be related. Two of these individuals also have evidence for trauma to the arm or hand, in both cases on the same side as the ossification, suggesting these happened during the same incident: Sk0648 with traumatic bowing deformity of the humerus; Sk0806 with a fractured metacarpal.

NEOPLASMS

Neoplasms cover diseases associated with the formation of tumours, although generally those seen in the bone are benign 'warty' lesions. A neoplasm, or tumour, is an uncontrolled growth of cells. Benign tumours tend to be slow-growing and remain localised. Malignant tumours are rare in archaeological bones but when they do occur they may be faster-growing and spread to other parts of the body via the bloodstream or lymphatic system. Neoplasms may be bone-forming, bone-destroying or a combination of both (Mays 1998, 127).

Osteomas

Osteomas are relatively common in archaeological specimens. Small button osteomas are asymptomatic and benign and occur primarily on the outer surface and more rarely on the inner table of the skull vault, as well as on the facial bones, near to or within the frontal and ethmoidal sinuses (Ortner 2003, 516; Aufderheide & Rodríguez-Martín 1998, 375) and are more common in older people. They were present on the crania of five individuals, Sk1057/

ILLUS 4.59
Right tibia and fibula healed fracture, Sk0298/Gr0299, adult male

Gr1036, an older middle adult male, having two on the right temporal and parietal (side and roof of the skull).

Also benign are osteoid osteomas, a centre of growing cells surrounded by a hard shell of thickened bone. They tend to be small, less than 1cm, and they may occur in any bone in the body. Their cause is unclear (Ortner 2003, 506; AAOS 2009) and they affect men more than women. One older middle adult male, Sk0617/Gr0618, displayed a 5mm osteoid osteoma on the inside of a left rib. It probably caused him a moderate dull ache.

Osteochondroma

Osteochondroma are one of the most common benign bone tumours and are most commonly found on the

A WOMAN WITH ALLERGIES, 1480–1502

This woman was born in 1480. Her father was a baker, but he made a poor living. He was often drunk and occasionally violent, and customers complained his flour was cut with sawdust. He once hit his young daughter so hard that she fell and fractured her head on the hearthstone and he thought he had killed her. It shocked him enough to reign in his drinking for a while.

They kept a cat to deal with the rats and mice that beset the storeroom at night, but the animal was not a good mouser and preferred to scavenge its food from the middens in the street. It had become infected with tapeworm and had inadvertently passed it to most of the rest of the family. The girl was thin and often poorly, and was fed mainly on stale bread, vegetable broth and offal.

The dust and flour in the air at home made her sneeze and made her eyes itch. When the cat was in the room, she had trouble breathing. In winter the smoke hung thick over the town, which made her chest worse and in summer she had hay fever. She was usually congested and sneezing, and her nose was sore. She suffered several asthma attacks, each worse than the last. She took advice from an aunt who suggested treating it by stuffing mustard and onions up her nose. It made her nose even more sore but otherwise seemed to have little effect.

Despite her red nose, she caught many an eye, but most were put off by her foul-mouthed father glowering at them from the back of the shop. When she was not serving in the shop, she kept house in the room above. She cooked what little they had in a dented iron pot hung over the fire. On special occasions she would make their budget stretch to a little mutton or pork. When she had finished her housekeeping chores in the evening, she would sit by the fire spinning wool with a drop spindle, weighted with her mother's stone spindle whorl. It was marked with three crosses to ward evil spirits away from the home and it was her only treasured possession.

One day a well-healed timber merchant's son spied her sweeping the street outside the bakery and thereafter would detour that way and when she was there, go in to buy bread. It took him weeks to build up the courage to ask her if he might call on her and walk her to church. He wasn't much to look at, but he was kind and he was rich. She could see an escape from home and an end to her privations and she thought that would be enough

PEOPLE'S STORIES

to make her happy. He asked her to marry him a week later and she accepted.

His parents, however, did not approve of the match and sought to put an end to it. They threatened to disinherit the boy unless he broke off the engagement. Her father became enraged that they should consider his daughter as not worthy of their son. He marched around to their house, his daughter running after him, tugging at his sleeve and pleading with him to turn back as he was only going to make it worse. He harangued the boy and his parents and, when he saw that they were not going to change their minds, started claiming that their son had impregnated his daughter, and demanding money in recompense or else they would risk public humiliation when he reported their son to the church authorities. The boy began to waver in his affections, seeing the true colours of his future father-in-law. The girl, seeing her future hopes fading before her eyes, found she could not breathe. However much she tried she could not get enough air into her lungs, her chest tightened, she gasped for breath and everything went white and she passed out on the floor. She died in her young man's arms, her father looking on aghast, his parents in equal parts, sorry, irritated and relieved.

She was buried in a simple grave in a crowded part of the graveyard, her father could afford nothing better, but she was not to rest there for long. Twenty years later, another burial disturbed her grave. The old gravedigger remembered the baker's lass and cradled her skull as he told his friends the sad story of the beautiful maid who died so tragically young. Then they placed her skull carefully back in the ground and covered it with earth again.

SKELETON	0718
Grave	Disarticulated skull found in cemetery soil
Location of grave	Constitution Street, Area 8
Burial details	Unknown, found disarticulated
Age	Young Adult, 17–25
Sex	Female?
Stature	–
Radiocarbon date	–
Other dating evidence	Found in Phase 3 cemetery, probably only in use after 1480s
Finds	–
Pathology	Skull only, right nasal turbinate, possible cranial trauma (right frontal), left cribra orbitalia & porotic hyperostosis, calculus, DEH
C/N isotope (diet)	–
O/S isotope (origins)	–
See also	p108–10; Illus 4.55; Table 4.19, p111; p121
Facial reconstruction artist	Paloma Galzi

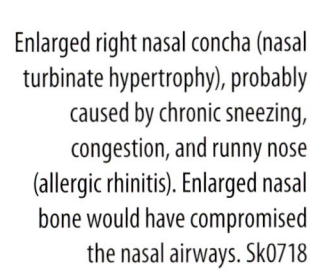

Enlarged right nasal concha (nasal turbinate hypertrophy), probably caused by chronic sneezing, congestion, and runny nose (allergic rhinitis). Enlarged nasal bone would have compromised the nasal airways. Sk0718

A WOMAN WITH ALLERGIES, 1480–1502

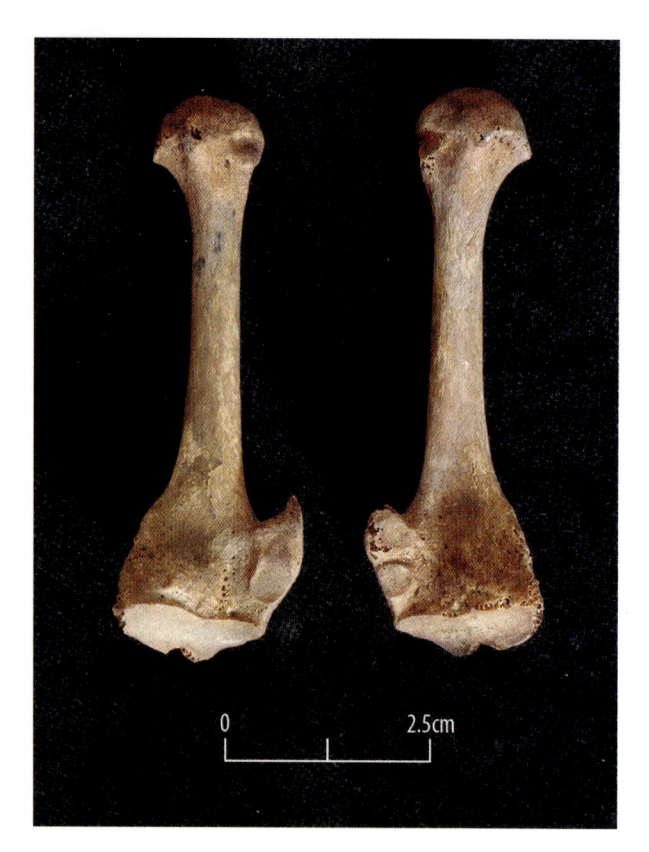

ILLUS 4.60
Bilateral exostoses of second metatarsals, Sk0207/Gr0189, unsexed adult

were recovered but these also displayed another anomaly in the form of an unusually short fourth right metatarsal.

CONGENITAL AND DEVELOPMENTAL DEFECTS

A congenital physical anomaly is an abnormality of the structure of a body part. An anomaly may or may not be perceived as a problem condition. Many, if not most, people have one or more minor physical anomalies if examined carefully. Examples of minor anomalies can include curvature of the fifth finger, tiny indentations of the skin near the ears, shortness of the fourth metacarpal or metatarsal bones, or dimples over the lower spine. Some minor anomalies may be clues to more significant internal abnormalities (Farooq 2007). Anomalies can be inherited through gene transmission or started by

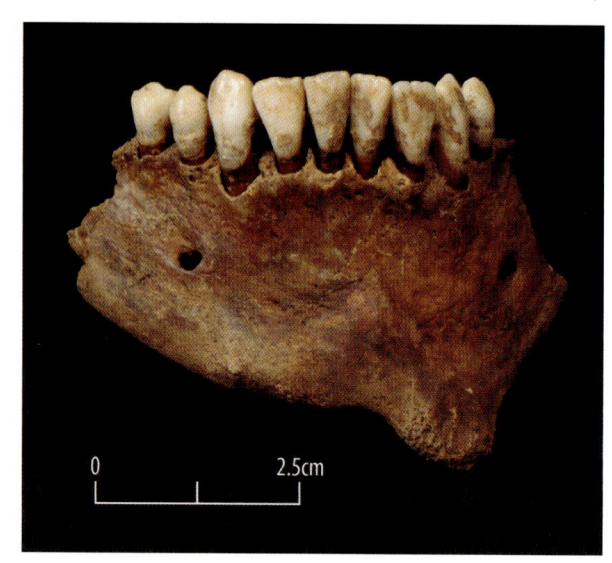

humerus, femur and tibia. They may occur spontaneously, or as a result of injury, such as a pulled muscle (D'Ambrosia & Ferguson 1968; Waldron 2009, 175–6). In life they appear as painless swellings, though irritation of surrounding tendons, muscles or nerves can result in pain (Coenen & Biltjies 1992; Mnif et al 2009) and they can fracture during vigorous physical activity. A single example of this was noted on the right tibia of an old middle adult female, Sk0592/Gr0590, an elongated 8mm long structure pointing down from the knee joint.

Hereditary multiple exostoses

Hereditary multiple exostoses (HME) refers to a group of disorders characterized by multiple cartilaginous tumours (osteochondrosarcomas or exostoses) growing outward from the metaphyses of long bones (Legeai-Mallet 2002). Exostoses may produce pain and other complications by pressing on nearby tissue; they may also limit movement of joints, resulting in short stature or discrepancies of limb length. Both the locations and sizes of exostoses vary. There is also a risk that they may become malignant. The most commonly-affected bones are those of the arms, legs hands and feet. Exostoses on the arm or leg nearly always develop near the joints (elbow, wrist, knee, or ankle) (Polzin 2011). Sk0207/Gr0189 (unsexed adult) displayed bilateral exostoses on both second metatarsal bones (**Illus 4.60**). Unfortunately, only the feet of this individual

ILLUS 4.61
Mental tubercle elongation, Sk1191/Gr1193, older child

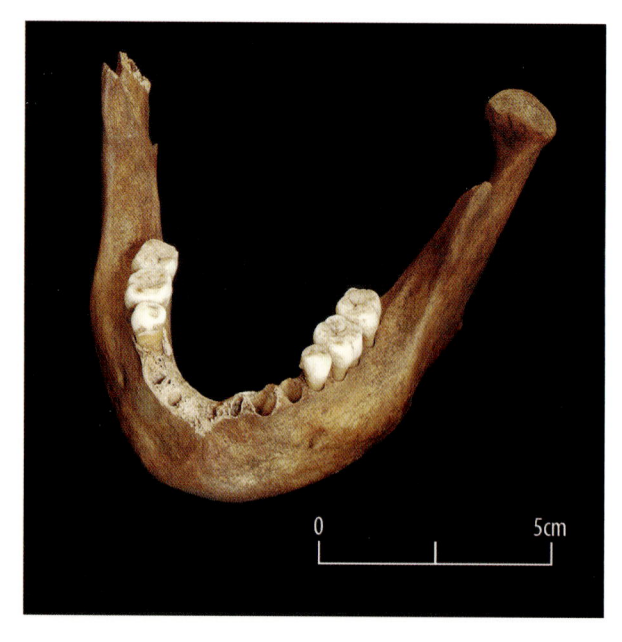

ILLUS 4.62
Enlarged mandible, Sk0119/Gr0120, younger middle adult female

physical, chemical, or microbiological stimulus during the formation and development of the embryo (Moore 1978; Gregg & Gregg 1987). Alteration in formation and development of bone can appear during embryo development or manifest in later life

The cause of 40–60% of congenital birth defects in humans is unknown. For 20–25% of anomalies there seems to be a 'multifactorial' cause, meaning a complex interaction of multiple minor genetic abnormalities with environmental risk factors. Another 10–13% of anomalies have a purely environmental cause (eg infections or illness in the mother). Only 12–25% of anomalies have a purely genetic cause or which the majority are chromosomal abnormalities (Farooq 2007).

Several were noted among the assemblage. Sk0667/Gr0668, an older child (12–12½ years), displayed unilateral glenoid hypoplasia, an incomplete ossification of the narrower part of the scapula (Wirth et al 1993; Currarino et al 1998; Munshi & Davidson 2000). Sk0951/Gr0952, a younger middle adult male, had his first and second right ribs fused. It is unlikely that either condition seriously affected the individuals concerned and they may well have been unaware of them.

More noticeable was a large elongation of the left mental tubercle of older child (11½ years) Sk1191/Gr1193 (**Illus 4.61**), which would have caused a very prominent lump to one side of the chin. While unlikely to have caused any physical problems, as a distinct and unusual facial disfiguration it would have affected the child's life.

Less prominent but also affecting the appearance of the face was the enlarged mandible of Sk0119/Gr0120, a younger middle adult female. The mandible was enlarged in the area of the molar teeth, bilaterally but with the left side more pronounced, which would have given the jawline a lumpy and lopsided appearance (**Illus 4.62**). There are various causes for an enlarged mandible, including the rare and potentially life-threatening acromegaly, which also causes growth to the feet hands and tongue. The primary cause, however, is developmental or congenital (Jainkittivong and Langlais 2000; Bouquot 2011; Hatcher Rice 2011).

OSTEOLOGICAL DISCUSSION
Julie Franklin and Carmelita Troy

The human remains provide a picture of the types of people buried in the excavated part of the cemetery. They also tell us of their general health and well-being, living and working conditions and access to adequate food and water. These are inevitably linked to social status, but also to the individual's exposure to disease, genetic predispositions and contemporary standards of healthcare. There are, nevertheless, limitations on this data. Paradoxically, for pathological lesions to be visible in a skeleton, the individual would have had to be healthy enough to survive the period of stress that caused them (Lewis 2002, 14). In other words, chronic conditions that people lived with are more likely to show up in skeletal remains than acute conditions that killed quickly.

Demography
Demographically, since only a small part of the cemetery was excavated there is no way of knowing to what extent this was representative of the whole cemetery or of the contemporary population. The three most striking factors about the demography of the excavated skeletons is the low ratio of men and the near absence of babies under 1 year old and of adults over 45 years (**Table 4.05**).

As regards the proportion of men to women, even allowing for a certain amount of caution as noted above with regards the number of incomplete skeletons and unsexed adults, (p92) the ratio of men to women is strikingly low at 0.66M:1F. There was some variation across the site. In areas containing more than ten sexed adult burials (Areas 4 to 8), the ratio typically varied from 0.38M:1F to 0.63M:1F. Only in Area 5 were there more men than women, and in this case there were significantly more, with a ratio of 1.89M:1F (**Table 4.20**; **Illus 4.26**).

Sex ratios within parish graveyard excavations vary. The Constitution Street ratio is similar to that at St Helen-on-the-Walls, York of 0.72M:1F (Dawes & Magilton 1980, 11). Others show a higher proportion of men, such as 1.27M:1F at St Nicholas Shambles, London (White 1988, 30), 1.36M:1F at Hereford Cathedral (Boucher et al 2015, 100) and 1.58M:1F at Wharram Percy, Yorkshire (Mays 1998, 71–2).

The high proportion of women in Areas 4, 6 and 8, in particular (0.38M:1F - 0.54M:1F), is similar to that recorded in excavations in nunnery graveyards, such as the ratios of 0.37M:1F and 0.48M:1F found at Elstow, Bedfordshire, and Clementhorpe, York, respectively (Keeping 2000). The high proportion of men in Area 5 is not dissimilar to that found in some friary excavations, though far below that found in monasteries (Gilchrist and Sloane 2005, 204). Similar variations have been noted at other medieval graveyards (eg Cardy 1997, 553; King 2002, 138; Henderson 2006, 29), though rarely is enough of the graveyard excavated to provide a clear picture. At St Helen-on-the-Walls there were more women found in the south corner of the graveyard (0.44M:1F) and south-east of the church (0.59M:1F), compared with north-west of the church (0.93M:1F) (Magilton and Dawes 1980, 33–6). It is interesting to note in this context that the entire excavated portion of the cemetery at Constitution Street is south-east and east of the church. It is possible that the excavated part of the graveyard was more popular in general for the burial of women.

TABLE 4.20
Number of skeletons per area broken down by broad age group and sex (NB male and female groups include possible male and females)

AREA		2	3	4	5	6	7	8	9	TOTAL
Adult female	No	3	1	13	9	33	16	13	3	91
	%	37.5	12.5	32.5	17.3	36.3	33.3	31.7	21.4	29.8
Adult male	No	2	1	5	17	16	10	7	2	60
	%	25.0	12.5	12.5	32.7	17.6	20.8	17.1	14.2	19.7
Adult unsexed	No	1	0	7	9	12	4	1	3	37
	%	12.5	-	17.5	17.3	13.2	8.3	2.4	21.4	12.1
Total adults	No	6	2	25	35	61	30	21	8	188
	%	75.0	22.2	62.5	67.3	67.0	61.2	50.0	57.1	61.6
Subadult	No	2	7	15	17	30	19	21	6	117
	%	25.0	77.8	37.5	32.7	33.0	38.8	50.0	42.9	38.4
TOTAL INDIVIDUALS	NO	8	9	40	52	91	49	42	14	305
	%	100	100	100	100	100	100	100	100	100

Other differences were noted in terms of the manner of burial of men and women. Men were more likely to be buried in coffins, though the distinction is not marked, 25% (15/60) of men compared to 20.9% (19/91) of women were coffined and fewer children (**Table 4.21**). At some monastic graveyards it has been noted that women and children were more likely to be buried in a coffin, and the practice has been linked to the medieval scholarly belief that the bodies of women and children were softer and more prone to decay (Gilchrist & Sloane 2005, 222), but this was clearly not practiced here.

Women were also far more likely at Constitution Street to be buried in multiple burials, these accounting for 12.1% (11/91) of adult females compared to 5% (3/60) of males (**Table 4.21**). In the group burials men were particularly rare, with only one possible man out of 12 individuals (Sk0806/Gr0807, see p76); the remainder consisting of six women and five subadults.

The overall proportion of subadults excavated was 38.4% (117/305; **Table 4.20**), which is within the range seen at other sites. Subadults usually make up 21%–47% of parish graveyards (Gilchrist & Sloane 2005, 209). At Constitution Street, the proportion was largely consistent within the most populous areas (Areas 4–8, 32.7%–38.8%) with a slight peak in Area 8 (50%). There was no marked difference in Area 5 to match the marked difference in adult sex ratio there. There was also a high proportion of subadults in Areas 2 and 3. The area south of ditch [0084], which seems to have come into use later than the rest of the cemetery (p82; 144), contained 13 burials, six of which were subadults, or 46.1% of the total. Again, the low number of burials in these areas mean these figures should not be given undue importance.

Given the high rates of infant mortality during this period, the lack of babies under 1 year old is odd, with only three examples found, a perinate (Sk0936/Gr0937, Area 7), and two infants (Sk0424/Gr0427, Area 7; Sk1151/Gr1150, Area 5), that is 2.6% (3/117) of the in situ subadults. One (Sk0424) was found in a group burial, the others in individual graves. None was buried in a coffin. Bones of young children are smaller, softer and more prone to decay, and it is also possible that they were buried less deeply and were therefore more prone to post-depositional disturbance (Dawes & Magilton 1980, 11). At other graveyards, however, infants were found in higher numbers, though direct comparison of data is hampered by differences in age group definitions. Infants at the sites cited below were defined as under 2 years. Approximately nine of the 32 younger children were identified as being 1–2 years, thus the equivalent figure for Constitution Street would be 10.3% (12/117). This is broadly equivalent to that noted at Whithorn, Galloway, where babies and infants under 2 years made up 12% of the immature population in the late medieval graveyard, though there they were also considered to be under-represented (Cardy 1997, 520). At Aberdeen friary, 23% (10/43) of subadults died before the age of two years (Cross & Bruce 1989, 122, table 10); at Linlithgow friary it was 40% (48/119) (ibid).

Infant burials are often clustered along boundary walls or ditches, or around porches or paths (Gilchrist & Sloane 2005, 223). Given that a relatively small part of the cemetery was excavated at Constitution Street, it seems that the area or areas traditionally used for infant burial was

TABLE 4.21
Proportion of individuals buried within coffins, double burials and group burials by sex

AGE/SEX	TOTAL BURIALS	COFFINS N	COFFINS %	DOUBLE BURIALS N	DOUBLE BURIALS %	GROUP BURIALS N	GROUP BURIALS %
Adult female	91	19	20.9	5	5.5	6	6.7
Adult male	60	15	25.0	2	3.3	1	1.7
Unsexed adult	37	11	29.7	2	5.4	0	–
Subadult	117	18	15.4	7	6.0	5	4.3
TOTAL	305	64	21.0	16	5.2	12	3.9

outwith the excavation area. A similar dearth of infants as found at St Helen-on-the-Walls, York, where a far larger proportion of the graveyard was excavated. There it was speculated that they might have been buried in the city ramparts or in a detached part of the graveyard (Dawes & Magilton 1980, 11). Given this apparent selective absence of very young children, it is probably futile to speculate on mortality rates for children. More older children were found than younger children, but it is not clear if the selection processes apparently at play for infants also extended to younger children.

Peak mortality rates for adults were within the 25–35 age range for both men and women (**Table 4.05**, p92). For women, a similar peak was noted at St Helen-on-the-Walls, though for men it was higher, at 35–45 years (Grauer 1991, 408). It was assumed the distinction relates to the greater risk faced by women during childbirth. The relatively young mortality peak for men at Constitution Street might suggest generally unhealthy living and working conditions. The very low levels of older people, suggest this was the case. There were only three individuals found who were aged over 45, two women (Sk0051/Gr0053, Area 2; Sk1181/Gr1183, Area 5) and one man (Sk0214/Gr0215, Area 4). This represents only 2.4% (3/124) of ageable adults.

Again, it is possible that there were factors of preservation affecting this pattern. A similar lack of older adults at Whithorn (3% of the adult population) was put down to older osteoporotic bones being more susceptible to post-depositional deterioration (Cardy 1997, 520–1). However, older adults are found in far higher numbers in most medieval cemeteries. At St Nicholas Shambles, London, 8–11% of ageable adults fell within this age bracket (White 1988, 30); at Hereford Cathedral it was 21.9% (Boucher et al 2015, 100); at St Giles Cathedral, Edinburgh 21.5% (Henderson 2006, 28); at St Helen-on-the-Walls, York, 22–50% (Lewis 2002, 31); and at Wharram Percy, Yorkshire, 36–43% (Mays 1998, 71). The latter was a rural graveyard and thus it is possible this is a reflection of shorter life expectancy in urban settings. Leith however, though urban, was not a large urban centre like London or York. It is possible that conditions within the town were very poor even by medieval standards, though this is not the picture observed in 1544 where it was noted that the town was 'full of riches' with an 'abundance of wine and victuals' (Marshall 1986, 12), for some of its inhabitants at least. There is no evidence for the zoning of the burials of older adults at other sites (Gilchrist & Sloane 2005, 223) in the same way that women and young children could be zoned. However, it is possible that there was a measure of selection at work and that people who reached a more venerable age were more likely to have been buried elsewhere, possibly at the neighbouring Preceptory of St Anthony or at the parish church at Restalrig. St Anthony's is known to have cared for, among others, the elderly (Marshall 1986, 7), and anyone who died there would doubtless have been buried in its graveyard. Thus, it is possible that burials of the elderly are underrepresented elsewhere in Leith.

Malnutrition

Malnutrition is much in evidence at Constitution Street. Porotic hyperostosis and cribra orbitalia point towards general stress and poor diet. Dental enamel hypoplasia and bones bowed through rickets point towards malnutrition in childhood. A case of possible infantile scurvy was also identified, suggesting a lack of fresh fruit and vegetables in the child's diet.

In general, the most frequently present and therefore best statistical indicators of diet and health are dental enamel hypoplasia (DEH), cribra orbitalia and porotic hyperostosis. The former two are significantly more common than the late medieval averages, with DEH over twice as common and cribra orbitalia over three times as common (statistics not available for average prevalence of porotic hyperostosis). There does not seem to be any great distinction based on sex at Constitution Street. However, given the assumed connection between wealth and coffined burials (p83), it is interesting to compare the prevalence of these conditions between these different burial types, and the coffined burials do indeed appear to have been in better health (**Table 4.22**). The distinction is particularly visible in cribra orbitalia which was 40% more likely to be present in simple burials compared to coffined ones. Adults displaying both cribra orbitalia and DEH were 75% more common in simple burials, though the data set was not large. Nevertheless, prevalence among those who could afford a coffin is still significant and illustrates the fact that coffin use was not solely linked to wealth and status (p83). Furthermore, these conditions were not solely linked to malnutrition and poor health may also be a factor, where chronic disease, parasitic infection or poor dental health might result in poor levels of nutrition.

TABLE 4.22
Comparison of prevalence of dental enamel hypoplasia (DEH), cribra orbitalia and porotic hyperostosis between simple and coffined burials

BURIAL TYPE	DEH No	DEH %	CRIBRA ORBITALIA No	CRIBRA ORBITALIA %	POROTIC HYPEROSTOSIS No	POROTIC HYPEROSTOSIS %	CRIBRA ORBITALIA + DEH (ADULTS ONLY) No	CRIBRA ORBITALIA + DEH (ADULTS ONLY) %
Simple	102/127	80.3	44/115	38.3	26/159	16.4	16/58	27.6
Coffined	25/33	75.8	9/33	27.3	5/33	15.2	3/19	15.8
TOTAL	127/160	79.4	53/148	35.8	31/192	16.1	19/77	24.7
% increase in prevalence in simple burials compared to coffined		5.9		40.3		7.9		74.7

Rickets is specifically related to lack of vitamin D, and might indicate a lack of fish in the diet or lack of exposure to sunlight, although this last was not as big a problem in medieval Britain as it was to become in later and murkier industrial towns (Roberts & Cox 2003, 247). Given the local fishing industry and the relatively small size of Leith at the time, it is possible that rickets may be a result of either general severe malnutrition during childhood, or another childhood disease which kept the individual indoors. The skulls were not present in any of the four rickets victims identified so it was not possible to identify the other common malnutrition indicators, but all died in childhood or early adulthood. The signs of scurvy in one infant were active at the time of death.

Entirely absent on the other hand from the skeletal assemblage are any traces of diffuse idiopathic skeletal hyperostosis (DISH), which is commonly associated with obesity. It causes a fusing of the spine and is generally more common in men (Roberts & Cox 2003, 245–6). The average late medieval prevalence in Britain is low (3.3%), but nevertheless a few individuals might statistically have been expected among the Constitution Street assemblage.

Another crude indicator of health and nutrition is stature. Stature is genetically determined but prolonged periods of childhood malnutrition can prevent people from reaching their full potential height (Mays 1998). Both the average male and female statures from Constitution Street were below the British average for this period, particularly so for females, being over 4cm below average (**Table 4.06,** p94).

Again, a comparison of average statures between the different burial types shows a difference, albeit a small one. It was possible to determine stature in 26 coffined burials and 76 simple burials, and those within coffins were on average slightly taller (**Table 4.23**). The difference was larger in males, the coffined individuals being on average 1.1cm taller (170.4cm to 169.3cm). However, the tallest man measured at the site was in fact buried without a coffin and was over 2cm taller than the next tallest (and coffined) individual (182.8 to 180.5cm). If this outlier is excluded, then the average height for men in simple burials falls to 168.8cm.

Dental hygiene

The overall dental health of the Constitution Street population was relatively good for the period. The prevalence of the more minor conditions of calculus and periodontal disease, which would not have bothered the affected individuals unduly, were significantly above average for the period but the rates for the more painful conditions of caries and abscess were significantly below average. The rate for ante-mortem tooth loss was above average and this fact combined with the prevalence of the other dental pathologies might suggest the presence of efficient local dental 'care'. The high rate of calculus in this population is consistent with a diet of the medieval staples of bread and porridge (Roberts and Cox 2003, 242). The soft carbohydrates in conjunction with poor oral hygiene would encourage the build-up of plaque and in turn lead to the rise of periodontal disease.

The rate of calculus and periodontal disease were largely similar between the two sexes, but caries, abscesses and ante-mortem tooth loss were significantly more common in men. Consumption of more carbohydrates and sugar would lead to poorer dental health and consumption of more meat would improve it, as meat-eaters tend to have less caries than those who have a high vegetable content in their diet (Power 1995). However, consumption of meat and sugar at this period was largely proportionate to wealth rather than sex. Higher levels of DEH would lead to teeth more prone to problems in adulthood but levels of DEH were slightly higher in women. The answer may be that women took better care of their teeth than men, possibly for purely aesthetic reasons. It is also likely that a proportion of the men were seafarers. Though this would probably have involved short trading voyages across the North Sea and Baltic rather than long trans-Atlantic voyages, it still might have involved periods of scurvy during their lives. This could have led to ante-mortem tooth loss and possibly a higher rate of abscess, while being otherwise invisible in skeletal remains.

TABLE 4.23
Comparison of average statures between simple and coffined burials

BURIALS TYPE	FEMALE AVERAGE (CM)	MALE AVERAGE (CM)
Simple burials	154.9	169.3
Coffined burials	155.1	170.4
TOTAL	154.9	169.7

Wear and tear

Wear and tear is evident in terms of osteoarthritis, osteophytosis and Schmorl's nodes. All of these are more common in men than women suggesting that, while some women undertook hard physical work, men's lives were, on average, more physically demanding. Rates of osteoarthritis are in general slightly lower than the late medieval average, but this must largely be due to the relatively low numbers of older people in the assemblage. The prevalence of Schmorl's nodes indicates that men in particular were introduced to heavy work at a young age. Squatting facets on the other hand are generally more prevalent in women in medieval populations. Women would have spent more time tending hearths and other household tasks close to the ground (Boucher et al 2015, 113).

Accidents and violence

The low number of individuals with evidence of trauma indicates that occupations and lifestyles were low risk, though the incompleteness of the majority of skeletons recovered may have skewed the results. The most likely explanation for most of the injuries is a fall or a turned ankle. The best suggestions of inter-personal violence are in the head injury noted in Sk0718/disarticulated skull and the rib fractures in Sk0617/Gr0618. Notably, the latter was on the left ribs, the area where a right-handed assailant would be most likely to attack. All the injuries had healed and while the people involved would have been incapacitated or in some pain for a while, none is likely to have been particularly serious.

It is interesting to note that 11 of the 14 individuals displaying trauma (**Table 4.19**) were found in the relatively sparsely populated Areas 7 and 8, where the burials were typically dated a little later (p82–88; 144). Two were radiocarbon dated, both returning late dates (Sk0592/Gr0590, Sk0806/Gr0807). These included evidence for no less than four turned ankles, several incidences of serious falls, as well as the two possible incidences of violence. It is easy to imagine that as Leith grew in size and importance as a port that it grew more dangerous.

Men were more likely to be injured, but this is a common phenomenon (Judd 2004). Men during this period would have tended to lead more active lives and would have been more likely to suffer occupation-related injuries.

Infectious diseases

Infectious diseases caused by bacterial and viral infections, which were a major cause of death during this period, rarely leave evidence in the bone. Inflammatory lesions present in bone are the result of chronic infections and are often not the immediate cause of death whereas acute infections would have resulted in a quick death and would not have left any evidence on the bone.

TABLE 4.24
Evidence for shrouds and shroud fittings
AD = adult; OC = older child; OMA = older middle adult; YA = young adult; YC = younger child; YMA = younger middle adult

SK	GR	AREA	AGE	SEX	BURIAL TYPE	CLOTHING/SHROUD EVIDENCE	CLOTHING OR SHROUD?	C14
0040	0042	2	AD	?	Coffin	Pin (stamped), Tag	Clothing?	1445–1635
0060	0062	2	YA	M?	Coffin	Tag	Clothing?	–
0175	0176	4	AD	?	Simple	Buckled belt securing inner clothing, coarse wool textile representing outer coat or cloak	Clothing	1400–1610
0481	0482	6	OMA	F	Simple, S–N aligned	8 copper alloy eyelets representing corset, wool flannel textile representing dress	Clothing	1435–1630
0570	0571	7	YMA	M	Simple	Pin (soldered)	Shroud?	–
0585	0587	7	YMA	F	Coffin	Textile	?	1465–1655
0667	0668	7	OC	–	Coffin	Tag	Clothing?	–
0673	0672	7	OC	–	Simple	Pin (soldered)	Shroud?	–
0730	0731	8	OC	–	Simple	Pin (stamped)	Shroud?	–
0784	0785	8	OMA	M	Coffin	iron eyelet	Clothing?	–
0817	0819	8	OC	–	Coffin	iron eyelet	Clothing?	–
0824	0825	8	YMA	M	Simple	Tag	Clothing?	–
0910	0911	8	YC	–	Coffin	Buckled belt and textile	Clothing	–
0926	0921	8	AD	?	Simple	Pin (shaft only)	Shroud?	–
0948	0949	8	YMA	F?	Simple	Pin (stamped)	Shroud?	–

The most distinctive evidence of infectious disease came from Sk0985/Gr0988, an adult possible female who appears to have died from syphilis (p108). Syphilis was once thought to have been introduced to Europe from the New World after Christopher Columbus's expeditions from 1492 onwards. However, there is now a growing body of evidence to suggest it was already present in Britain by this time (Roberts & Cox 2003, 272; Roberts & Manchester 2010, 211–5). Nevertheless, it did spread rapidly and virulently throughout Europe in the late 15th and early 16th centuries. It was not until the 1520s that the fact that it was transmitted sexually was fully understood, though before this it was linked to sexual sin (Roberts & Cox 2003, 340; Gilchrist & Sloane 2005, 206), which led to the inevitable moralising. Treatments mainly involved mercury, which typically did more harm than good (Roberts & Cox 2003, 340). Only her skull was recovered, one of three skulls found as charnel within a simple grave in Area 6 (Gr0988, **Illus 4.09**, p58 which contained the articulated Sk0987). The skull was radiocarbon dated to 1465–1660 (**Table 4.02**, p84).

The only other possible specific diseases identified were three cases of possible pneumonia or tuberculosis, though equally this damage to the ribs might be the result of pleurisy or bronchiectasis. These three individuals were buried in simple graves in Areas 6, 7, and 8 (Sk0597/Gr0589, Sk0966/Gr0968, Sk0987/Gr0988). Sk0597 and Sk0966 showed evidence of malnutrition in the form of DEH and cribra orbitalia, Sk0966 also had porotic hyperostosis. Malnutrition would have weakened their immune systems and made them more susceptible to disease.

CONSTITUTION STREET: THE FINDS

Julie Franklin with contribution by Penelope Walton Rogers

Most of the finds related to the use of the cemetery. These included coffin nails and evidence for shrouds and clothing used to dress the dead in the form of pins, lace ends, wire eyelets and buckles, as well as some fragments of cloth. There were no items placed in the graves deliberately to accompany the dead. There were a few sherds of residual pottery, which broadly agree with the radiocarbon dating but also provide some interest in terms of Leith's foreign connections.

TEXTILES

Penelope Walton Rogers

Remains of textiles were visible in four graves, preserved either due to the relatively dry conditions inherent on such a sandy site (Sk0481/Gr0482, Area 6; Sk0585/Gr0587, Area 7), or by mineralisation, where textile had decayed in contact with metal objects (Sk0175/Gr0176, Area 4; Sk0910/Gr0911, Area 8). In two cases (Sk0481, Sk0175), the remains were well enough preserved to identify the type of fabric. Both appeared to relate to clothing the body was dressed in for burial.

Associated with Sk0481 (dated 1435–1630; see **Table 4.02**, p84), an older middle adult woman in Area 6, were a number of fragments in varying stages of decay recovered from the layer of black organic material under the skeleton. They represent the remains of a medium-weight wool flannel fabric, woven in tabby (plain weave) (with 10/Z x 9/S threads per cm). This could be the remains of a grave liner but more probably is a clothing fabric. Similar textiles have been recorded in a number of urban dumps or middens roughly contemporary with the grave, in the 15th to early 17th centuries (Walton 1981, 194–5; 1983, 220–1; Crowfoot et al 1992, 44–5). They are unusual in graves, since this was the period of linen shrouds (in England at least), but, in view of the presence of eyelets, which are likely to be from a laced garment, this seems to have been a clothed burial and the textile can be interpreted as the remains of a garment, perhaps a wool dress. Its quality suggests no particularly high status for the wearer. The burial was unusual in other respects (p78; 152).

The textile mineralised on a buckle (**Illus 4.63A**, see below) found with Sk0175/Gr0176 in Area 4, an unsexed adult simple burial, was coarser (6/S x 6/S threads per cm), but made from a better-quality wool, lacking the hairy fibres seen on the textile noted above associated with Sk0481. It is a blanket-quality fabric, unusually coarse for clothing or a ready-made shroud. It presumably represents either a coarse piece of outer clothing such as a cloak or coat or, indeed, a blanket. This burial was radiocarbon dated and was relatively early (1400–1610; see **Table 4.02**, p84). This burial is further discussed below, in relation to the buckle.

CONSTITUTION STREET EXCAVATIONS

ILLUS 4.63
Buckles: A. Copper alloy frame and pin, remains of leather strap in situ, remains of mineralised textile on front of frame, Sk0175/Gr0176, unsexed adult, simple burial, Area 4; B. Iron frame and buckle plate, pin missing, mineralised textile on underside of buckle plate, possibly also leather on top of central bar Sk0910/Gr0911, younger child, coffined burial, Area 8

BUCKLES

Two buckles were found in two separate burials. Both had central bars and asymmetric loops, and these are generally dated to the period 1575–1700 (Whitehead 1996, 89–93). A few medieval examples exist of asymmetrical buckles of not dissimilar form (eg Hinton 1990, 512, no.1103; Egan & Pritchard 1991, 94, no.424; Ottaway & Rogers 2002, 2895, no.13270), though no exact medieval analogies could be found. A post-medieval date is more likely for both.

The first (**Illus 4.63A**) was made of copper alloy with a double-looped asymmetrical buckle frame (34x30mm) with an angled profile, a square front end and an expanded rounded back end. It is possible there was originally moulded decoration on the rounded end which would have been visible when worn. The buckle was clearly in use when it was buried. There is a leather strap attached to the central bar by means of four rivets with another length, the free end of the belt, threading through the buckle and held by the pin. The mineralised textile remains (see above) suggest a cloak, coat or blanket, but were attached to the top of the buckle frame, not the underside. If the strap were used to secure an item of clothing this would have led to mineralised cloth on the underside of the buckle frame. Thus, the belt presumably secured an inner lighter garment, the remains of which did not survive, while the preserved textile represents an outer garment.

The buckle was found in the fill of Sk0175/Gr0176 in Area 4, an unsexed adult simple burial, which was radiocarbon dated to 1400–1610 (**Table 4.02**, p84). It was found in the grave fill and no definitive relationship with the skeleton was observed, thus it is possible that the buckle was intrusive. The grave was in a densely packed part of the cemetery with later graves truncating it to the west and a modern service cut running directly to its east (**Illus 4.07**, p56). The in situ belt strap and mineralised textile indicate it was clearly interred in a grave, however, rather than, for example, as a chance loss in the cemetery, and it is unlikely the leather remains would have survived in such good condition had the buckle been subjected to much disturbance. On balance, it is most likely to have derived from the grave in which it was found. The combination of the typological date for the buckle and the radiocarbon dating of the burial imply a date in the early 17th century. The radiocarbon date, however, is more likely to fall in the earlier part of its range (**Illus 4.31**, p85), that is 15th to early 16th century, and the burial directly underlies another dated burial (Sk0112/Gr0114, 1420–1630; **Table 4.02**, **Illus 4.31**), which is similarly more likely to be 15th or early 16th century. It is possible that the typological date of the buckle is misleading.

The second buckle (**Illus 4.63B**) was made of iron and had a double looped frame (31x26mm) with one end D-shaped, the other expanding trapezoidal with a sheet roller on its outer edge. Poorly-preserved mineralised textile adhered to the underside of the buckle plate, with possible leather on top of the central bar and bone fragments corroded onto the underside of the frame. Like the previous example therefore it had clearly been interred in a burial. It was found in the centre of the waist area of a young child (2½–3 years), Sk0910/Gr0911 in Area 8, who was buried in a coffin. The position implies this was part of a waist belt worn by the child. The grave was cut by ditch [0980] and the implications of this as regards the dating of both grave and ditch are discussed in more detail below (p146–49).

Belts are sometimes found in medieval burials, particularly those of men (Gilchrist & Sloane 2005, 84), and occasionally women. The inclusion here of a belt, apparently in situ in the burial of a young child, is surprising and implies it was dressed in adult-style clothing for burial.

LACE TAGS

Lace tags are small rolls of copper alloy sheet used to bind the ends of laces to ease threading and prevent fraying. They were common dress accessories from the 15th to the 17th century, during which time many forms of male and female clothing were secured with laces (Margeson 1993). They are also regular though occasional finds in graves of the period (Stones 1989a, 159; Nicholson 1997, 375; Franklin & Collard 2006). This may imply shrouds were sometimes laced up, though it is possible they represent clothing.

Four examples were found in graves (**Table 4.24**) (Sk0040/Gr0042, Area 2; Sk0060/Gr0062, Area 2; Sk0667/Gr0668, Area 7; Sk0824/Gr0825, Area 8), though once again it is hard to ascertain if these were in situ. The finds were used in pairs but no more than one was found in any one grave. One associated skeleton was dated (Sk0040/Gr0042, 1445–1635; **Table 4.02**, p84). Typically, the tags were about an inch long (24–27mm) and simply made of a small rectangular sheet rolled with an edge-to-edge seam. One smaller (17mm) example (Sk0060/Gr0062) was more finely made, tapering towards one end. There was no apparent pattern to how these were used, in terms of their location relative to the skeleton.

EYELETS

These were small circular loops made of wire with the ends twisted together (**Illus 4.64**). Ten were found within graves at the site (**Table 4.24**), including eight copper alloy examples from the same grave, Sk0481/Gr0482, an older middle adult woman in Area 6. The single examples from graves Sk0784/Gr0785 and Sk0817/Gr0819, both in Area 8, were made of iron. Iron eyelets are relatively unusual finds, but this is probably a matter of the unlikely survival of so small an iron object. Iron may well have been the norm and these finds could have been far more common than the archaeological record suggests. Four eyelets recovered during the London Road excavations were all made of iron (p162–63). The iron loops were typically twice the size of the copper alloy examples (11–13mm for iron, 6–7mm for copper alloy).

These are generally assumed to be dress fittings used as fasteners and are regular finds in 15th- and 16th-century contexts (Woodfield 1981, 98; Margeson 1993, 20; Egan 2005, 62). They are often found in burials of the same period (Lindsay 1989b, fiche 12, G2–3; Nicholson 1997, 384; Franklin & Collard 2006, 52–4) and it has been considered that they were also used to aid in the fastening of shrouds. At Linlithgow friary, most were found in the graveyard soil, with one being attached to a piece of leather, and it was speculated that they might have been used in conjunction with wooden toggles to secure leather shrouds (Stones 1989b, 159). At St Margaret's church, Norwich, they were found positioned along the arms of several skeletons and suggested that these represented sleeve fastenings in the clothed burials of hastily buried plague victims (Margeson 1993, 20).

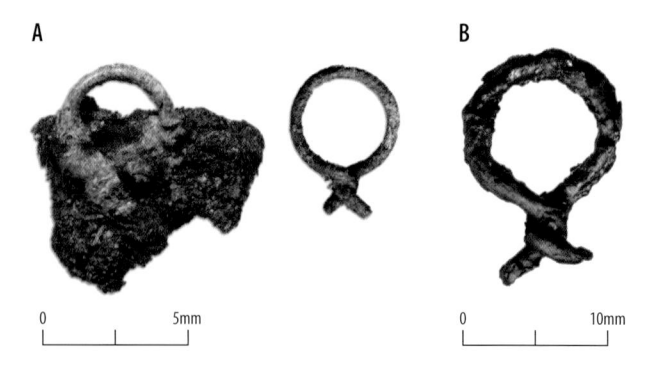

ILLUS 4.64
Wire eyelets: A. copper alloy, including one still embedded in edge of textile, Sk0481/Gr0482, older middle adult female; B. Iron, Sk0817/Gr0819, older child

The only clear evidence from Constitution Street for how the eyelets were used was found with Sk0481, the woman buried with at least eight eyelets. Two of the eyelets were found in close proximity under the left elbow and the remains of three were found between the thighs. Preserved textile remains associated with one eyelet suggests it was sewn into a hemmed or reinforced edge, with the eyelet extending outwards forming a semi-circular loop along the edge of the fabric (**Illus 4.64A**). Two of those found between the thighs seem to have been placed directly side by side in the same piece of fabric. It is possible that, as at Norwich, these were originally sleeve fastenings. Alternatively, they may have been part of the fastenings of a bodice or corset. The skeleton was radiocarbon dated to 1435–1630 (**Table 4.02**, p84) which is in agreement with the typological date of the finds. Whatever their exact function, it seems likely that Sk0481 was buried wearing her regular clothing. The burial was unusual in other respects (p77–78; 122; **Illus 4.25**). Only single examples were found with the two burials in Area 8 and so it is not clear whether these were used in those graves or were residual.

PINS

Six copper alloy wire pins were recovered from grave fills (**Table 4.24**). Pins become increasingly common finds in burials from the late 14th century onwards, reflecting changes in material culture in society at large at the time. The increase in the availability and use of metal in the late medieval period led to its increased use for dress accessories. Wire pins were used both to fix items of costume and in dressmaking. The same types of pin are also found in graves. It is likely that they were used to secure the shroud for stitching and were probably removed after this. Their inclusion in burials would probably therefore have been accidental (Gilchrist and Sloane 2005, 110).

Early wire pins had heads made from a small coil of wire soldered onto the end of the shaft. From the 16th century onwards these coiled heads were stamped in place giving them a spherical shape (Caple 1983). This latter form continued in use through to the 19th century when machine-made pins with integral heads were introduced.

It is generally difficult to ascertain if these pins were in situ. They are small and easily moved and graves were frequently disturbed and intercut. Two of the pins (Sk0570/Gr0571, Area 7; Sk0673/Gr0672, Area 7) had soldered heads and are thus more likely to predate the late 15th century. Another three (Sk0040/Gr0042, Area 2; Sk0730/Gr0731, Area 8; Sk0948/Gr0949, Area 8) had stamped heads suggesting a 16th-century or later date. One of the latter was found in a grave radiocarbon dated to 1445–1635 (Sk0040/Gr0042; see **Table 4.02**). The locations of the pins relative to the skeleton show no clear pattern as regards how these were used; they could be found at the head or foot end or waist.

SUMMARY OF EVIDENCE FOR SHROUDS AND CLOTHING

There is reasonably clear evidence for bodies dressed in regular clothing in three graves (Sk0175, Sk0481 and Sk0910) and suggestions of clothing in a further six (Sk0040, Sk0060, Sk0667, Sk0784, Sk0817, Sk0824) (**Table 4.24**). Thus between 1% and 3% of the 305 bodies excavated had some evidence for being clothed.

Clothed burials are known during the medieval period though they are in the minority. In their wide-ranging study of medieval burials, Gilchrist and Sloane noted a figure of 2.6% for clothed burials. They identify a link between this practice and status, the wealthier members of society wishing to be buried in their finery. There was also a link with plague outbreaks when the burials were probably more hurried and where there may have been no one available or willing to undertake the usual rite washing and enshrouding the body (Gilchrist and Sloane 2005, 80; 83–4).

There was no clear link between status and the clothed burials at Constitution Street. While there appears to be higher coffin use among the possibly clothed burials (67%, 6/9 compared to 21%, 63/305 for the cemetery as a whole) this is more likely to reflect the greater protection afforded by the coffin to aid in the preservation and containment of small or delicate finds of metal and textile. Sk0910/Gr0911 may well be of high status, as it appears to represent the burial of a young child wearing adult-style clothing in a coffin. On the other hand, the woollen dress fabric used by Sk0481 was not of particularly high quality. There was a certain amount of evidence, however, to point towards this woman being a hurriedly buried plague victim (p78–79). Too little remains of Sk0175/Gr0176 to ascertain other details about the manner of burial, except that there was no associated coffin.

The majority of people would have been interred wrapped only in a shroud, probably made of linen (Gilchrist and Sloane 2005, 106–7) and these seem to have decayed leaving no archaeological trace. The only surviving evidence is in the form of the accidental inclusion of pins, though it is difficult to identify any as definitely in situ. Interestingly, it was noted in at least one burial (Sk0791/Gr0786) that the arm position implies they were not wrapped in a shroud (p72). There were no finds of textile or dress accessories found in this grave to point towards how the body was covered.

COFFIN NAILS

In all, 580 iron nails were found within 80 graves, though some of these are clearly residual. It takes at least 12 nails to construct a coffin, though it is possible to construct one using only wooden pegs (Boyd 1989, 118). The number of nails within these graves varies from one to 37, though it is likely that many have been lost to corrosion or post-depositional disturbance. In broadly contemporary burials in St Giles cathedral (Collard et al 2006, 20) between 24 and 60 nails were found with each coffin.

Typically, the nails were small to medium sized wood-working nails with flat round heads between 8mm and 18mm wide. The shafts of the 226 complete nails were measured and ranged from 26mm to 97mm. The largest concentration was between 37mm and 55mm, with 65% falling into this bracket. The most commonly used nail for coffin construction then was about 2" long. This would have been sufficient for the joints around the coffin sides, though smaller nails would have sufficed for fixing the lid.

Few of these coffins were well enough preserved to provide clues to their construction. At least two of the coffins appear to have had slatted bases (p69–71). Only some of the nails survive, but each slat appears to have been secured with two nails at each end, leading to the nails being closely spaced in pairs. In other coffins, where the nail pattern was observable, the nails were more evenly spaced, suggesting a solid base.

The pattern of nail use was observable in only a handful of other coffins, none of which was complete. Two were radiocarbon dated, both relatively late (Sk0585/Gr0587, Area 7, 1465–1655; Sk0592/Gr0590, Area 7, 1475–1665; **Table 4.02**, p84). The exact construction no doubt varied from maker to maker and according to size but, typically, nails are found in rows of three to five across the ends of the lids and base boards, with nails also spaced along the edges, typically about nine, spaced at approximate 200mm intervals. There may also have been nails fixing the corner joints. Constructed thus, each adult coffin would have required 40–52 nails.

There were no finds of other coffin-related fittings. The lack of hinges, handles or corner brackets implies coffins were for the most part very simply made. Handles, if they were present at all, may have been made of rope or other organic material. There was one find of a copper alloy stud. These can be found in large quantities in post-medieval cemeteries, used to attach baize to the coffin exterior, sometimes in decorative patterns. This example was a residual find during trial-trenching, in the location that was to become Area 8. It is likely that it relates to 17th- and 18th-century use of the parish graveyard.

POTTERY

Very few objects were found at the site which could not be tied to the use of the cemetery and the best part of this was the pottery. Other finds included a few fragments of glass waste and ironworking waste, two clay pipe stems and two fragments of iron too small and corroded to identify. They point towards local industry and occupation, mainly in the post-medieval period. The pottery assemblage, on the other hand, though small, was unusually colourful. Of the 42 sherds found, nine (21%) were from imported vessels (**Table 4.25**) no doubt due in the main to the proximity of the site to the port of Leith and to local merchants' houses, and also perhaps to the great, though brief, influx of French inhabitants in the mid-16th century.

Pottery was found in midden deposit (0073/0082/0085) overlying ditch [0084], two of the ditch fills and in the cemetery soils and grave fills (**Table 4.26**). All appear to be the result of secondary deposition. The dating of the sherds supports the general dating of activity in the area from the 14th to 17th centuries. It includes the usual locally-produced types and the imports are, for the most part, typical of North Sea trade at the time.

TABLE 4.25
Pottery found at Constitution Street (not including modern wares)

FABRIC	REFERENCE	SHERDS	WGT (g)	DATING
Scottish white gritty ware	Jones et al 2003	3	11	12th–15th
Scottish late medieval redware	Haggarty et al 2011, 7–132	3	23	13th–15th
Scottish late whiteware	Franklin 2011, 44	5	112	15th–16th
Scottish post–medieval oxidised and reduced	Haggarty et al 2011, 13–21	22	515	16th–18th
Low Countries redware	Baart 1984	2	33	15th–17th
Seigburg stoneware	Gaimster 1997, 163–185	1	2	M15th–M16th
Weser slipware	Hurst et al 1986, 250–9	1	11	1590–1620
Tin-glazed earthenware	Korf 1981	2	8	M16th–17th
Beauvais single slip sgraffito	Hurst et al 1986, 108–14	1	38	E–M16th
French chafing dish	Hurst 1974, 233–47; Hurst et al 1986, 78–82	1	17	16th
Unidentified green–glazed sherd, possibly from Yorkshire or France	–	1	2	Medi?
TOTAL		42	772	

The most unusual of the imports was an unstratified sherd from a Beauvais single slip sgraffito dish, depicting a bird (**Illus 4.65**). The vessel is made of white earthenware, slipped in red and the design scratched through the surface, the whole then being glazed in a pale yellow glaze so that the design appears yellow on a red-brown background. Typically, these vessels date to the first half of the 16th century (Hurst et al 1986, 108; Haggarty 2006, file 26, 3). Though finds of Beauvais white earthenware are relatively regular finds on 16th-century sites in Scotland (Haggarty 2006, file 26, Map F), typically these are either plain glazed or decorated in double slip sgraffito, the decoration appearing red-brown over a pale ground. Zoological motifs are also less common than other types of decoration (ibid, 3). The rarity of this vessel in Scotland suggests it came to Leith in the baggage of a French visitor rather than as part of an import trade.

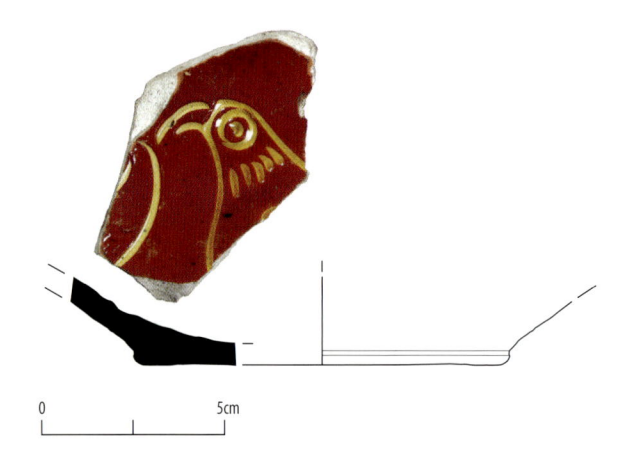

ILLUS 4.65
Beauvais single slip sgraffito dish sherd with bird design, unstratified

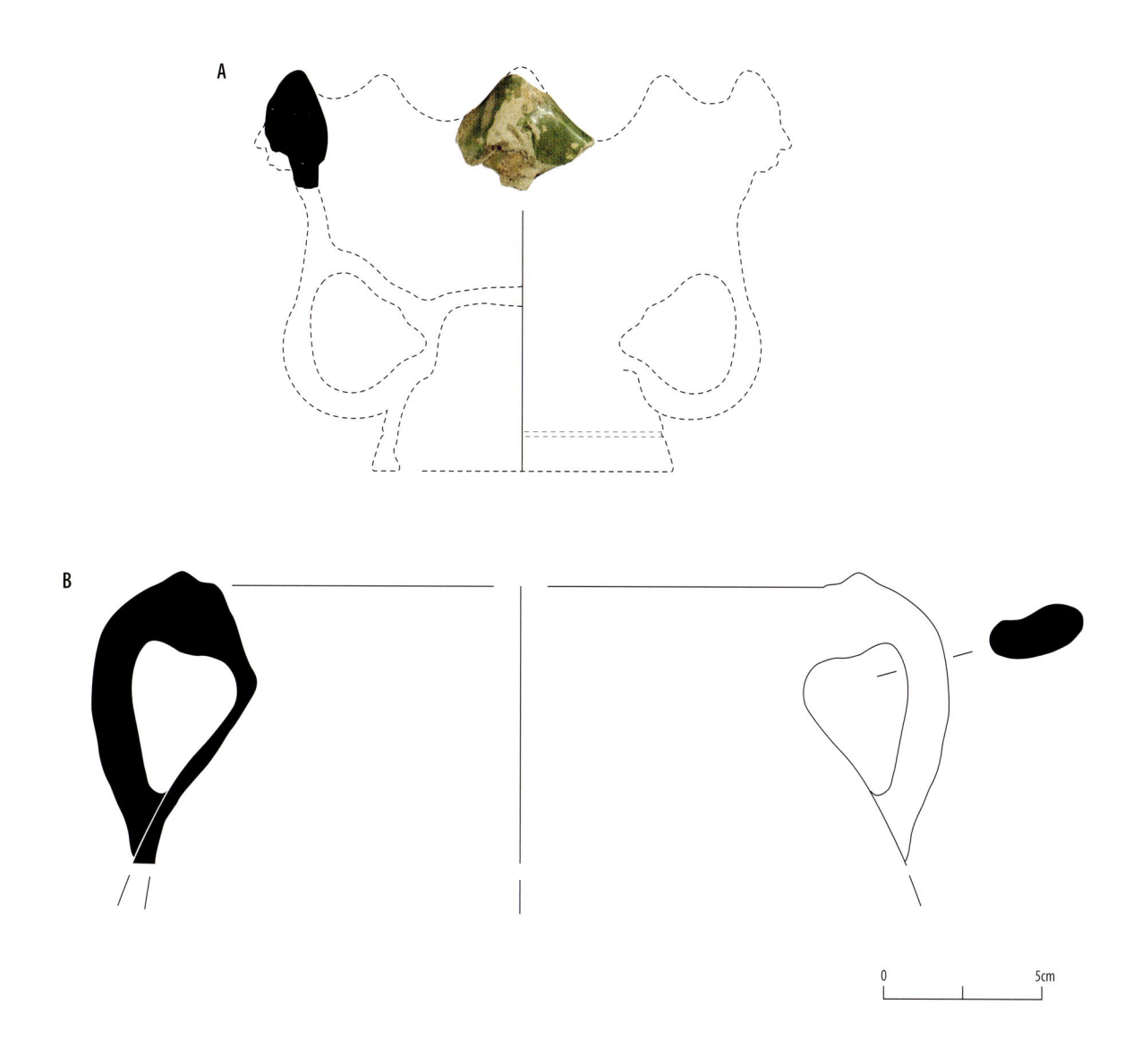

ILLUS 4.66
Pottery from midden layers overlying ditch [0084]: A. French chafing dish, deposit (0073); B. Post-medieval oxidised handle jar, deposit (0085)

Also, of 16th-century French origin was a fragment of a chafing dish (**Illus 4.66A**), found in midden deposit (0073). It was small and abraded but was clearly the remains of a simple pointed knop, from the rim of a chafing dish of Hurst's Type I (Hurst 1974, 233–47; Hurst et al 1986, 78–82) which he dates to the 16th century. It was glazed bright green and, though the moulded face was largely lost, the characteristic straw holes which held the piece together during firing were clearly visible. Chafing dishes were used to keep food warm at the table, the bowl filled with hot coals and a dish placed on top of them. They could also be used for cooking (Haggarty 2006, file 14). Similar vessels were made in the Saintonge and central France. Chafing dishes are regular if not common finds on sites in Scotland (ibid, map D) and Type I are the most common of these. Type I dishes have been found at Leith sites Burgess Street, Ronaldson's Wharf and Quayside Mills (ibid, file 42, 4–8). Sherds from another possible chafing dish were also found further north along Constitution Street (p177).

Other finds from this midden deposit (0073/0082/0085) included a sherd of a Weser slipware dish, imported from Germany between c 1590 and c 1620 (not illus; Hurst et al 1986, 250–9). There was also a tripod foot from a Low Countries redware cooking pot (not illus; Baart 1994), well sooted from use. These vessels had a long history, but the majority found in Scotland were imported in the 16th and 17th centuries (Hurst et al 1986, 130–8; Baart 1994). Accompanying local post-medieval reduced and oxidised wares included sherds of handled jars (**Illus 4.66B**) and jugs, typical of 16th-century assemblages (eg Franklin 1997).

A POOR WOMAN WHO DIED WITH HER TODDLER, 1481–1511

This was a young woman, born around 1481 in a village near East Linton in Haddingtonshire (today part of East Lothian). Her family were poor and bad weather meant poor harvests in the first three years of her life. As a toddler she rarely had enough to eat and as a consequence she was always small for her age, reaching only 4ft 9in when fully grown (4 inches below average).

Her childhood sweetheart who laboured on a nearby farm asked her to marry him when she was 16. She said yes, but her parents asked her to wait until her siblings were grown a little bigger and her mother needed her less at home. They were married at last when they were both 19. The lad was hard-working and ambitious and said there were opportunities to be had in Edinburgh or Leith where plague had recently struck down so many and work was easy to find for those who wanted it. He dreamed of his own little shop with a comfortable room to live in, and children playing at his feet.

Amid many tears, they said goodbye to their families, hoisted their meagre belongings on their backs and walked the 20 miles to Leith. However, fate was not kind to them. Work was harder to find than they hoped. They were looked down upon as country peasants and as they were illiterate were assumed to be stupid, though there were plenty of townsfolk who also couldn't read. Her husband sometimes found work at the docks or labouring at the ongoing building works at the new kirk of St Mary. She took in laundry. At harvest time they could generally find work in the nearby fields. They lived hand to mouth in a small shack built of turf and wood in the backlands behind a fishmonger. They could rarely afford to go to the bakers for bread and made do instead with bannocks and oatcakes which she could cook over the fire. The fishmonger gutted fish behind his shop, outside their door and the close smelt of animal dung and sewage. It was a shock after the relative cleanliness of the country air. In the summer it was over-powering. It was not what he promised her, he said, but it was theirs and it would get better.

Pestilence struck the town yet again in 1504, their third year in the town. It passed by their shack, though it knocked at many other doors. The canons at St Anthony's sold mixtures of herbs said to ward off the pestilence and ministered the last rites to the dying. Their reward was to be called sooner to God. Of the half dozen canons only two survived. The town became eerily quiet with no children, dogs or pigs on the streets and no singing from the song school. The port and the market shut down. The smell of burning heather hung over the town from the fumigating of houses and the cleansers were feared by all. They had little supervision and much power to enforce plague restrictions and they often abused it.

Oddly, it was during this horrible year that they started to feel more at home in Leith. When times were hard, the town pulled together and persevered. They had helped their neighbours and made some friends and were beginning to feel less like outsiders. When the pestilence abated the next year, her husband found work came a little easier to him but their dreams of a better life where they did not have to worry where their next meal or the rent was coming from still seemed a long way off.

Of all the dreams they lost in Leith, that of a brood of happy children was the hardest one to let go. She was so small and slight, her work so hard and her diet so meagre that she struggled to carry a baby to term. She had two miscarriages, had one baby

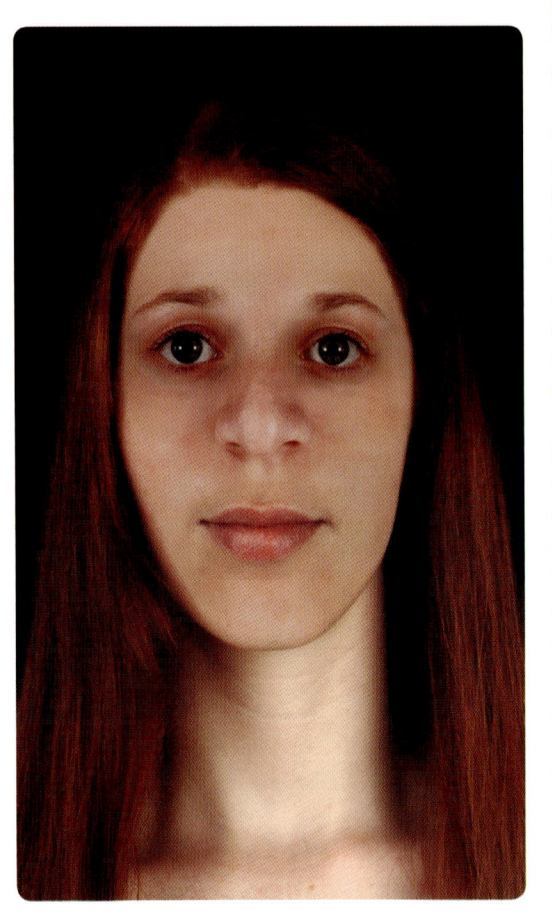

PEOPLE'S STORIES

stillborn and lost a son to a fever at four weeks. Great was their joy when she had a daughter who lived past her first year. But the pregnancies had taken their toll on the mother and the baby was never strong. The extra mouth to feed also put an added strain on their resources.

One morning she awoke feeling tired and hot. Her head and back ached and she was too dizzy to rise from bed. Her daughter did not understand and wanted to play. Her husband had to go to work. He returned in the evening to find his wife's fever raging and his daughter in tears. Two days later red spots appeared on her face, arms and legs and they knew it for the small pox. An old lady two doors down had died from it not a fortnight before. Worse, the bairn had begun to sicken too. The spots grew into weeping sores and the small girl would scream with pain. Her husband was at a loss what to do. He could not afford a physician and tended them both as well as he could. He took comfort when his daughter stopped crying.

His wife and daughter were both cold and stiff before he would believe that they were dead. He still could not bear to leave them, and it was neighbours who called in the priests from St Mary's. The bodies were too stiff to be dressed for burial and none of the local women wanted to help for fear that they would catch the pox. The bodies were taken to the cemetery on the bier, covered with a sheet. They could not be laid out properly in the grave, being still stiff in the position they died in, his wife and daughter facing each other, together in death. He stayed by the graveside until the sexton threw him out at sunset.

SKELETON	0791
Grave	0786
Location of grave	Constitution Street, Area 7
Burial details	Buried in double grave with younger child, Sk0792 (1½–2½), both placed on sides, facing each other, probably not shrouded
Age	Younger Middle Adult, 25–35
Sex	Female
Stature	145cm or 4'9"
Radiocarbon date	1470–1525, 1565–1625 (68% probability) 1455–1635 (95% probability) see Table 4.02, Illus 4.31, p84–85
Other dating evidence	In Phase 3 cemetery, probably only in use after 1480s
Finds	—
Pathology	Bilateral spondylolysis of L5 vertebra, calculus, DEH, periodontal disease, bilateral cribra orbitalia & porotic hyperostosis, costal DJD
C/N isotope (diet)	Normal (c13% marine) see p132–35; Illus 4.68; Table A1.01, p216–17
O/S isotope (origins)	North Berwick, East Linton, Haddington or Glasgow, Lennoxtown, Bearsden? see p136–40; Table A1.03, p218
See also	Illus 4.04, p53; Illus 4.20, p70; p72; p81; p88; p125
Facial reconstruction artist	Hew Morrison

A POOR WOMAN WHO DIED WITH HER TODDLER, 1481–1511

TABLE 4.26
Pottery distribution at Constitution Street

FEATURE		SCOTTISH WHITE GRITTY WARE	SCOTTISH LATE MEDIEVAL REDWARE	SCOTTISH LATE WHITEWARE	SCOTTISH POST–MEDIEVAL OXIDISED AND REDUCED	LOW COUNTRIES REDWARE	SEIGBURG STONEWARE	WESER SLIPWARE	TIN–GLAZED EARTHENWARE	BEAUVAIS SINGLE SLIP SGRAFFITO	FRENCH CHAFING DISH	UNIDENTIFIED GREEN–GLAZED SHERD, POSSIBLY FROM YORKSHIRE OR FRANCE	TOTAL	DATING
Ditch 0270 (primary fill 0233)	Sherds	–	–	1	1	–	–	–	–	–	–	–	2	15th/16th
	Wgt (g)	–	–	8	4	–	–	–	–	–	–	–	12	
Ditch 0084 (main fill 0099)	Sherds	–	–	–	1	–	–	–	–	–	–	–	1	16th?
	Wgt (g)	–	–	–	19	–	–	–	–	–	–	–	19	
Midden (0085 & 0073, 0082), overlying Ditch 0084	Sherds	1	–	–	9	1	–	1	–	–	1	–	13	L16th/E17th
	Wgt (g)	1	–	–	313	31	–	11	–	–	17	–	373	
Graveyard	Sherds	2	3	4	11	1	1	–	2	1	–	1	26	15th–16th
	Wgt (g)	10	23	104	179	2	2	–	8	38	–	2	368	
TOTAL	**SHERDS**	3	3	5	22	2	1	1	2	1	1	1	42	
	WGT (G)	11	23	112	515	33	2	11	8	38	17	2	772	

Two other unstratified sherds were of interest. The first was a rim from a Siegburg stoneware drinking bowl from Area 5 (not illus). It was unglazed but for a patch of orange ash glaze on the exterior. These cups were popular in the 15th and early 16th centuries (Gaimster 1997, 168), with several among the large stoneware assemblage found at Edinburgh's High Street site dating to the first half of the 15th century (Clarke 1976, fig 20:4–6).

The second was a decorative dish sherd of painted tin-glazed earthenware from Area 8 (not illus), probably imported from the Low Countries. The sherd has blue concentric rings and an area of cross-hatching in orange. The two-tone decoration and the lead glaze on the underside of the vessel indicate an early date for this sherd, probably in the first half of the 17th century or possibly as early as the second half of the 16th century (cf Korf 1981, 110, no.227; 112, no.233; 134, no.319).

CONSTITUTION STREET: THE ENVIRONMENTAL EVIDENCE

Scott Timpany and Sarah-Jane Haston

Little environmental evidence of value could be gleaned from the cemetery or the ditches beyond a general background of urban activity. There was a general paucity of charred plant remains, animal bone and other environmental evidence with which to illustrate the nature of the surrounding area and reconstruct local diet and economy. This is clearly related to the nature of the deposits and the lack of environmental evidence reflects the dearth of artefactual evidence and midden deposits in general. The poor stratigraphy in the cemetery also means that it is difficult to date these finds with any accuracy.

Samples were taken from several deposits of surviving ground surface. Field observations suggest this was a turfed-over sandy deposit representing an area that was at one point sand dunes. Fragments of this ground surface between graves and modern truncations were visible in Areas 2, 3, 4, 6, 7 and 8 (contexts (0047), (0066), (0141), (0558), (0572) and (0925) respectively). These deposits were essentially natural, but being located on the edge of the town contained a small amount of urban detritus, including charcoal, cereal grains, mortar, metalworking debris, animal bone and marine shell. The latter may have been deposited naturally or represent the remains of food waste. The grave fills contained similar material but the disturbance caused by the many grave cuts means that the remains are redeposited and cannot be dated with any accuracy. The ditches and pits fills, though better stratified, contained little dating evidence and similarly small quantities of the same kinds of environmental detritus. The only deposit which contained abundant environmental evidence was midden deposit (0073/0082/0085) overlying ditch [0084]. It included four types of cereal, though all in small quantities, abundant charcoal, animal bone, fish bone and marine shell. Artefactual evidence dates this deposit to the 16th or 17th centuries.

Cereal grains were found in seven of the 46 samples, though never in great numbers. These included the usual medieval species of oat (*Avena* sp.), hulled barley (*Hordeum vulgare*) and spelt wheat (*Triticum spelta*). Rye (*Secale cereale*) was only present in midden deposit (0085). These probably represent crops processed within the town for baking or brewing. A small quantity of charred bramble (*Rubus* sp.) seeds were found in one of the grave fills (Sk0481/Gr0482, Area 6) which could relate to the consumption of wild foodstuffs or suggest areas of overgrown bushes in the vicinity. Seeds from a member of the pea family (*Fabaceae* sp.) found within ditch [0084] (fill 0099) probably relate to the presence of weed plants such as vetches rather than food crops. Flax (*Linum usitassimum*) was found in the upper fill (0269) of ditch [0270]. The ditch was probably backfilled in or around the 15th century. Although only a small quantity was found, its presence may be associated with the production of linen in the vicinity and it may have been cultivated nearby. Charcoal fragments were found in a number of samples, though were generally rare with only the midden deposit (0085) containing substantial quantities. The fragments were too small for species identification. Fragments of animal bone were found thinly scattered in a number of samples. Fish bone was mainly limited to midden deposit (0073/0085). Marine shell was widespread and included oyster, mussel and whelks, all common species at this period in the Forth. These may derive from food waste or shellfish processing, but a proportion may also be naturally occurring in the dune sand deposits. They may also derive in part from use in the production of lime mortar for construction work.

CONSTITUTION STREET: ISOTOPE ANALYSIS OF BONE COLLAGEN AND TOOTH ENAMEL

Kate Britton

Carbon and nitrogen isotope analysis of human bone collagen was undertaken on the 30 individuals from Constitution Street that were radiocarbon dated. Three individuals from London Road were also analysed, the results for these detailed with the results for that excavation (p163–64). The aims were primarily to provide insight into the dietary habits of the individuals concerned and to infer population-level trends, particularly with reference to the proportion of marine fish in the diet of these communities. Strontium and oxygen isotope measurements were analysed from the tooth enamel of 18 individuals (most of which were radiocarbon dated). The aim was to identify immigrants into the area in order to explore population movements.

It must be noted that while the isotope data presented in this volume were analysed and interpreted by Kate Britton, all laboratory work including sample pretreatment and isotope ratio determinations were carried out at SUERC.

CARBON AND NITROGEN ISOTOPE ANALYSIS OF BONE COLLAGEN FOR DIETARY RECONSTRUCTION

The use of stable carbon and nitrogen isotope analysis for palaeodietary reconstruction is based on the principle that the isotope composition of food ingested by an individual is reflected in that of their body tissues. Isotopes are atoms of the same element that have the same number of protons but a different number of neutrons, resulting in differences in their atomic mass. The relative abundance of different isotopes (isotope signature or ratios) varies systematically in natural ecosystems, and subsequently between certain different types of food. When consumed, these isotope ratios are reflected (albeit somewhat altered) in the isotopic composition of the consumer's body tissues. Some tissues, such as the protein bone collagen, are preserved in the burial environment and can be analysed in archaeological samples in order to infer sources of dietary protein consumed during life (DeNiro and Epstein 1978; 1981). Bone collagen is most commonly analysed in archaeological isotope studies, not least due to the common preservation of bone at archaeological sites. Bone is renewed constantly and bone collagen reflects a long term $\delta^{13}C$ and $\delta^{15}N$ dietary averages of more than a decade (Ambrose and Norr 1993; Hedges et al 2007), and potentially up to 30 years (Libby et al 1964; Stenhouse and Baxter 1977; 1979). Collagen is primarily synthesised from dietary protein, with its stable isotope composition reflecting the main sources of protein in the diet rather than other dietary macros (eg fats, carbohydrates) or whole diet (Ambrose 1993; Tieszen and Fagre 1993). Consequently, low protein foods can be undetectable in the bone collagen stable isotope signature, which predominantly reflects high protein food sources in the diet, such as meat or dairy products. The consumption of meat or dairy products from the same species cannot be differentiated using stable isotope analysis, as both are different types of protein from the same animal (O'Connell et al 2001).

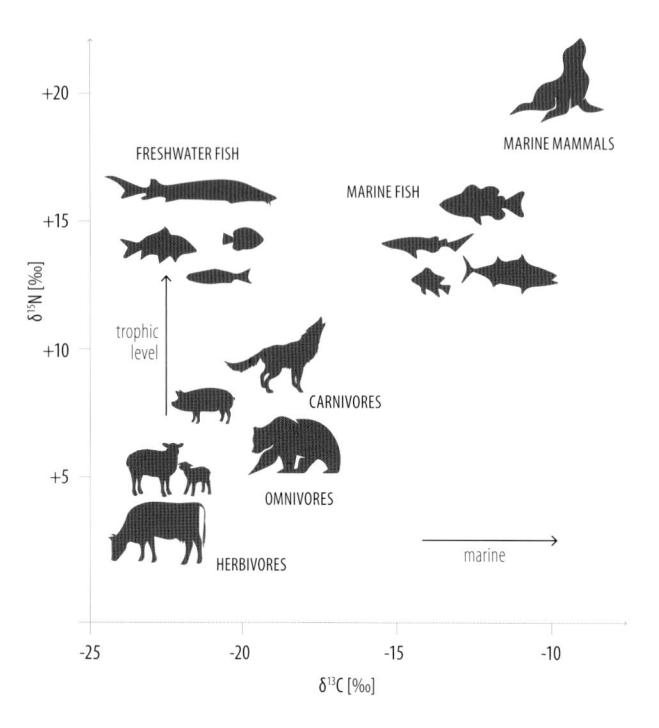

Carbon stable isotope ratios ($\delta^{13}C$) vary characteristically between different biological communities, for example between plants of different photosynthetic pathways (Smith and Epstein 1971; DeNiro and Epstein 1978) or between terrestrial and marine ecosystems (Schoeninger and DeNiro 1984). Terrestrial plants derive their carbon from atmospheric sources, whereas in marine systems, plants gain carbon largely from dissolved inorganic carbon (Farquhar et al 1989), leading marine organisms to exhibit less negative $\delta^{13}C$ values than their terrestrial counterparts (ie more similar to the internal standard used in carbon isotope analysis, a marine carbonate rock) (ibid). Nitrogen stable isotope ratios ($\delta^{15}N$) can be used to determine the trophic level of the protein consumed. In general, $\delta^{15}N$ values increase by 3–5‰ with each step up the food chain, whereas $\delta^{13}C$ values are enriched by ~1‰ (Bocherens and Drucker 2003). $\delta^{15}N$ values can also be used to indicate freshwater or marine dietary inputs (Schoeninger and DeNiro 1984), as aquatic ecosystems tend to have longer food chains (Richards et al 2001), resulting in higher $\delta^{15}N$ values. Therefore, the measurement of $\delta^{13}C$ and $\delta^{15}N$ values of humans and different animal species can allow the reconstruction of trophic relationships within archaeological ecosystems (Schoeninger and DeNiro 1984; Schoeninger et al 1983) and allow the identification of likely sources of human dietary protein, and the relative contribution of marine and terrestrial protein to the diet (**Illus 4.67**). Such studies not only illuminate subsistence practices and patterns of consumption but also allow the exploration of hunting strategies (eg Britton et al 2013); diachronic dietary change (eg Müldner and Richards 2007b); religious dietary habits (eg Müldner et al 2009) and dietary differences with gender/sex and socio-economic status (eg Richards et al 1998; Richards 2003).

In addition to the systematic variation described above, it is also now widely accepted that stable carbon and isotope ratios can vary more subtly temporally, geographically and across different biomes – even in the same organism (van Klinken et al 2000; Richards and Hedges 2003; Britton et al 2008). Variations can also come about due to differences in local environment/climate (Schwarcz et al 1999) and due to differences in land management and agricultural regimes, such as the use of natural fertilizers (Bogaard et al 2007). In order to factor in such 'baseline' variations, stable isotope analysis of animal remains, ideally from the same site and time period, are usually incorporated into human stable isotope dietary studies.

Dietary interpretation of results

Although a lack of 'baseline' stable isotope data from contemporary faunal samples from medieval Edinburgh precludes a detailed dietary assessment, within-study and cross-study comparison (ie with other published Scottish and British sites) allows general dietary features to be inferred. The data are given in diagrammatic form (**Illus**

ILLUS 4.67
Idealised carbon and nitrogen isotope food web, based on the analysis of faunal bone collagen. In light of the systematic variation in food webs, the stable carbon and nitrogen isotope analysis of human bone collagen can be used to infer the source of dietary protein. © Kate Britton

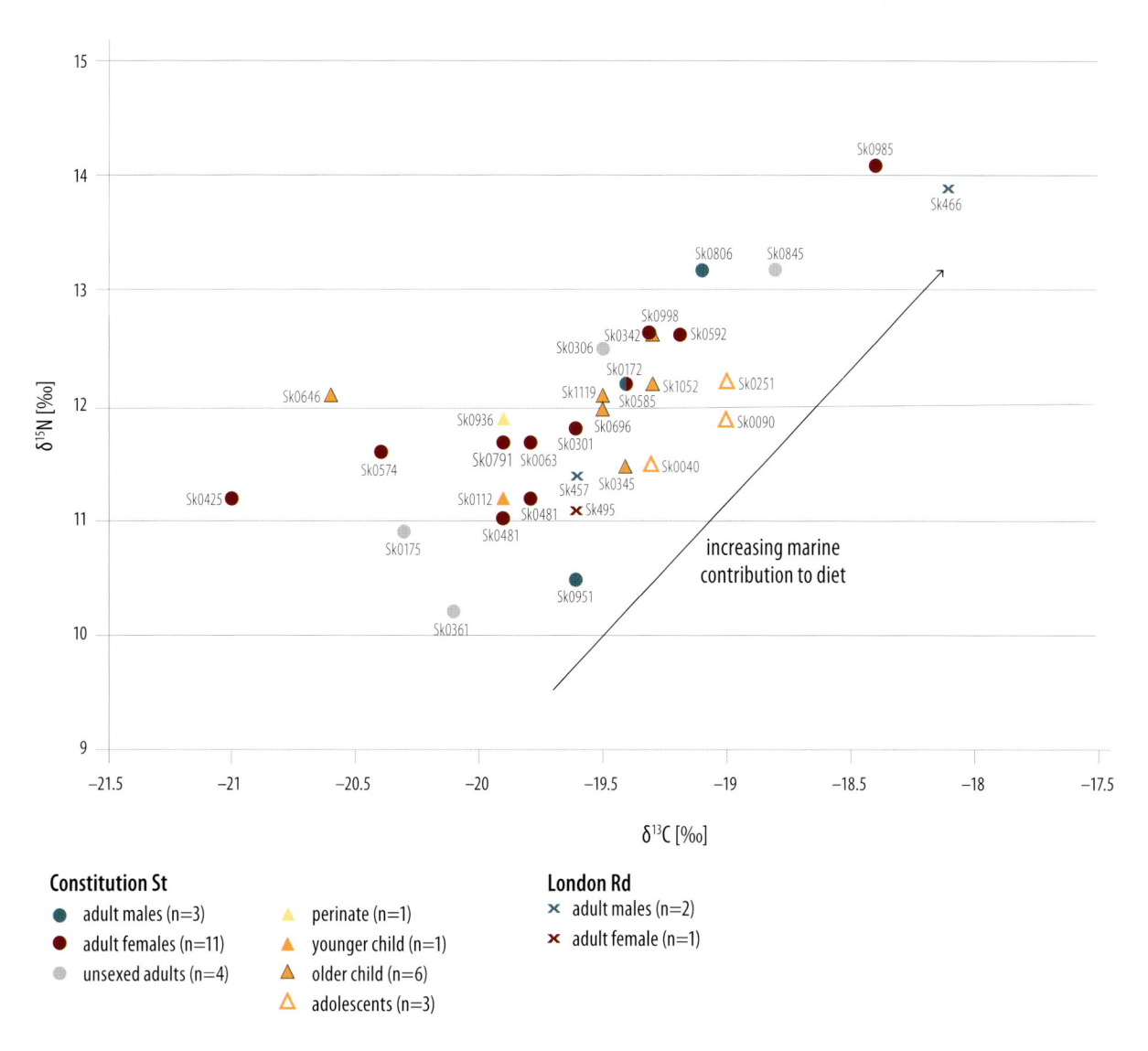

ILLUS 4.68
Carbon and nitrogen isotope values of bone collagen of individuals from Constitution Street and London Road

4.68) and shown in detail in Appendix 1 (**Table A1.01**). The results indicate that diet was mostly based on terrestrial resources, albeit with evidence of the fairly regular contribution of marine protein to the diet (likely to have varied between different individuals). The mean values for men and women are similar ($\delta^{13}C$ = -19.4‰ and $\delta^{15}N$ = 12.0‰; and $\delta^{13}C$ = -19.7‰ and $\delta^{15}N$ = 12.0‰ respectively), suggesting no consistent inter-sex differences.

The $\delta^{15}N$ values are uniformly 10‰ or greater, in line with a mixed diet of both plant and animal protein. Where elevated $\delta^{15}N$ values are combined with typical low (more negative) $\delta^{13}C$ values (ie <-20.0‰), this can indicate a diet rich in animal protein, higher trophic level animal protein (eg omnivorous as opposed to herbivorous domesticates, such as pigs) or even the possible inclusion of freshwater fish to the diet (Hedges and Reynard 2007). In the absence of local contemporary 'baseline' faunal data from the region, this aspect of human diet in medieval Edinburgh is difficult to evaluate further. The elevated $\delta^{15}N$ values (in combination with 'terrestrial' $\delta^{13}C$) in a number of the children sampled could also be consistent with a residual breast-feeding signal (resulting in elevated $\delta^{15}N$ values) in younger individuals (Fuller et al 2006; Mays et al 2002; Richards et al 2002).

Where elevated $\delta^{15}N$ values correlate with elevated (less negative) $\delta^{13}C$, this suggests the inclusion of marine fish in the diet. As a general guideline, $\delta^{13}C$ values > -19.5‰ are commonly considered suggestive of the contribution of marine protein to the diet in human palaeodietary studies. More than half of the individuals sampled from these two sites exhibit $\delta^{13}C$ values that exceed this value, lying between -19.5‰ and -18‰. These elevated $\delta^{13}C$ values correspond to elevated $\delta^{15}N$, confirming the source of this enrichment to be marine protein. However, a range of different values is exhibited, suggesting intra-group dietary heterogeneity. This variable and sometimes extensive marine fish consumption probably reflects the diverse diets and lifeways during the medieval period, not least in urban areas, as well as the maritime focus of economic and subsistence activities in the region. By the later medieval period, Leith's harbour had grown into one of Scotland's busiest ports. Despite the generally poor preservation of fish remains in recent excavations, numerous species of fish were found during excavations in South Leith, including herring, whiting, saithe, pollock, haddock, plaice, gurnards, cod and ling, and shellfish such as oysters and winkles (Henderson 2002; Dawson 2002) suggesting local consumption.

Notable burials and individuals

As well as useful in exploring population-level dietary trends, stable isotope analysis can illuminate dietary differences in individuals buried in different circumstances or displaying specific pathologies. The distinction between those buried within coffins and those without is of interest. There is no clear distinction but the coffined burials all lie within the main group (**Illus 4.68**), while the outliers are all simple burials, suggesting their diet was less varied.

No distinction was observed in individuals buried in different orientations (eg Sk0481/Gr0482, Area 6; Sk1052/Gr1053, Area 6) or those apparently buried in unusual positions, either prone or on their sides (Sk0112/Gr0114, Area 4; Sk0345/Gr0335, Area 6, Sk0791/Gr0786, Area 7). This would support the theory that these positions were related to children or were incidental rather than denoting the people were in some way set apart from the rest of the population.

However, there is one clear outlier among the Constitution Street samples (outlying London Road Sk466/Gr467 is discussed with the London Road results, see p164). This was Sk0985/Gr0988, Area 6, an adult female. She was remarkable in her elevated $\delta^{13}C$ and $\delta^{15}N$ values. These high values exceed even those measured in the bone collagen of clerics and bishops from the site of Whithorn Priory, where fish consumption was associated with strict adherence to religious fasting (Müldner et al 2009). Sk0985/Gr0988 displayed caries sicca consistent with tertiary stage syphilis. While malnourishment and starvation are known to induce enrichment in $\delta^{15}N$ (and to an extent in $\delta^{13}C$) in newly synthesised tissues in the short-term (eg hair in patients suffering from anorexia nervosa; Mekota et al 2006), this is unlikely to become apparent in long-forming tissues such as bone collagen. Malnutrition so severe as to result in such enrichment would ultimately be fatal before it could result in changes in bone collagen isotope values, as demonstrated in the study of Irish famine victims (Beaumont et al 2013). In light of this, and given the co-variance between both $\delta^{13}C$ and $\delta^{15}N$, it is more likely that these data do suggest a considerable contribution (perhaps > 30%) of marine protein to the diet of this individual (see p151, for further discussion of this individual).

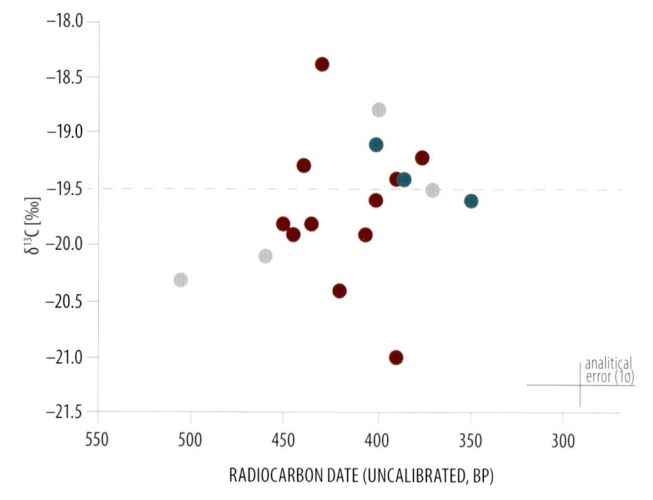

ILLUS 4.69
Stable carbon isotope data from adult bone collagen at Constitution Street against uncalibrated radiocarbon dates (BP)

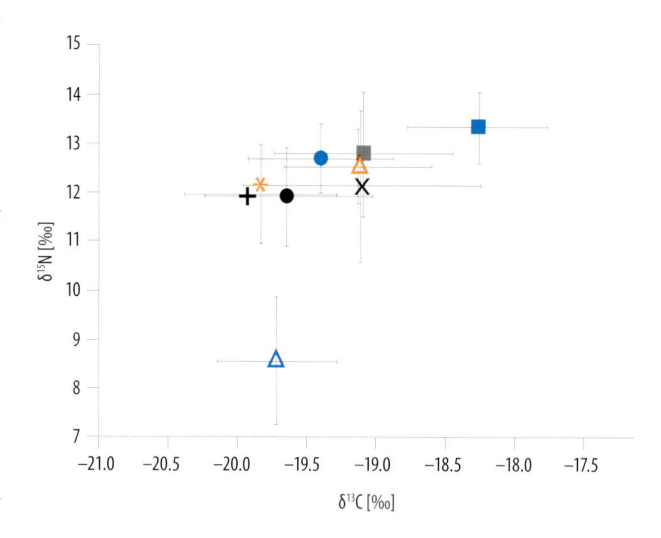

ILLUS 4.70
Mean stable carbon and nitrogen isotope values of adult bone collagen from a range of medieval and later medieval sites from Scotland and northern England St Martin's Churchyard at the deserted medieval village of Wharram Percy, Yorkshire (Britton et al 2015); the rural hospital of St. Giles, Yorkshire (Muldner & Richards 2005); the battlefield mass grave at Towton, Yorkshire (Muldner and Richards 2005); the urban friary at Warrington, Yorkshire (Muldner & Richards 2005); the urban site of Fishergate in the City of York (Muldner & Richards 2007); Whithorn Priory, Dumfries and Galloway (Muldner et al 2009); the multi-period site of Newark Bay, Orkney (Richards et al 2006); Constitution Street, Leith and London Road, Edinburgh (this study).

Dietary trends through time

Given that all individuals in this study have been radiocarbon dated, there is an opportunity to gain insight into diachronic dietary trends and to explore whether the more extensive examples of marine fish consumption belong to any particular phase of use of the site (**Illus 4.69**). However, while some of the earliest individuals interred at the site demonstrate some of the most negative carbon values measured in the group, the $\delta^{13}C$ (‰) values seem to become more diverse over time and there is no clear pattern. This is most likely due to the relatively short time period represented by the individuals sampled and the contemporary dietary variability demonstrated in later medieval populations here and elsewhere.

Comparison with other later medieval sites

Mean adult bone collagen $\delta^{13}C$ and $\delta^{15}N$ values from Constitution Street are similar to average values from a range of other medieval sites from Scotland and northern England (**Illus 4.70**). For the most part, with the exception of Wharram Percy, elevated nitrogen (and carbon) values suggest the inclusion of marine protein into human diet at this time, albeit in varied proportions at the different sites. The most elevated carbon and nitrogen isotope ratios are found at the Orcadian site of Newark Bay, which is perhaps unsurprising given the island/coastal nature of the site. Adult mean stable isotope values from Constitution Street are most similar to those measured in previous studies from North Yorkshire and later medieval contexts in York (Müldner and Richards 2005; 2007a). The range of values exhibited at all the sites (or intra-group variability, expressed as ±1δ about the adult mean value) is relatively large, reflecting the dietary variability observed in many of these populations.

The data from Constitution Street add to a small, but growing, number of studies that illuminate dietary practices in the medieval period in Britain. Importantly, this analysis from later medieval Edinburgh provides new data from Scotland, from which there have been a very limited number of studies to date. Further studies in Scotland, incorporating different types of site (urban vs rural; secular vs ecclesiastical, etc) and multi-period sites with longer periods of activity are necessary to better explore and characterise the medieval Scottish diet.

STRONTIUM AND OXYGEN ISOTOPE ANALYSIS TO INVESTIGATE ORIGINS AND POPULATION MOBILITY

Isotopic signatures in the mineral phase of archaeological skeletons can be used to reconstruct place of residence and the contemporary local climate. These applications are based upon the premise of a relationship between underlying local geology/local soils (strontium, $^{87}Sr/^{86}Sr$) and ingested water (oxygen, $\delta^{18}O$) to the body isotope chemistry of the individuals in question. Where the distribution of isotope signatures within and across different ecosystems varies predictably, these can be used to source human and animal remains to specific regions or to identify non-local outliers or migrants. Strontium applications are based on the principle that processes of radioactive decay produce strontium isotope variations in rocks of different ages and type. These signatures undergo no further modification in the biosphere (from soil, to plant, and ultimately to animals and humans) and therefore these methods can be used to determine geological provenance (and subsequently geographical origins) (Bentley 2006). ^{87}Sr is the product of the radioactive decay of ^{87}Rb, and given the very long half-life, there is insignificant change in isotope ratios of $^{87}Sr/^{86}Sr$ in lithologies over archaeological time scales and therefore this system is commonly referred to as 'stable' for the purposes of archaeological applications (ibid). Generally, animals living on older lithologies will have higher $^{87}Sr/^{86}Sr$ values; animals living on younger geologies will have lower values (ibid; Capo et al 1998).

Oxygen isotope studies in bioarchaeology are based on the correlation between the oxygen isotope composition of mineralised animal tissues and that of the water they consumed in life (Longinelli 1965; 1966; 1984; Longinelli and Nuti 1968; 1973). Oxygen isotope ratios of local precipitation vary geographically with local climate, which is influenced by latitude, altitude, and distance from the coast (Dansgaard 1964). Therefore, where local meteoric water is the primary source of drinking water, analysis of $\delta^{18}O$ in skeletal bioapatite (the mineral component) can infer geographical origin. Tooth enamel is normally the favoured analyte in strontium and oxygen isotope studies, as it is highly resistant to diagenesis (chemical alteration) in vivo and in the burial environment (Montgomery 2002; Hoppe et al 2003). Furthermore, as tooth enamel forms during childhood, the isotope analysis of this tissue points towards geographical origins and is not confused by time spent in the area where that individual died and was buried.

Geology and oxygen isotope values of the region

Despite its relatively small size, the geology of Scotland is unusually varied, featuring lithologies and geological features that originate from the Precambrian eon through to the Quaternary period. While most of the rock beneath Edinburgh and the surrounding Lothian region is Carboniferous in origin, older Devonian, Silurian and Ordovician lithologies can be found in the region. The area has also been influenced by more recent Quaternary local activity, including glacial features such as eskers and tills.

Although the isotope signature of bioavailable strontium in the region is primarily determined by underlying lithology, and geological maps can provide a guide for

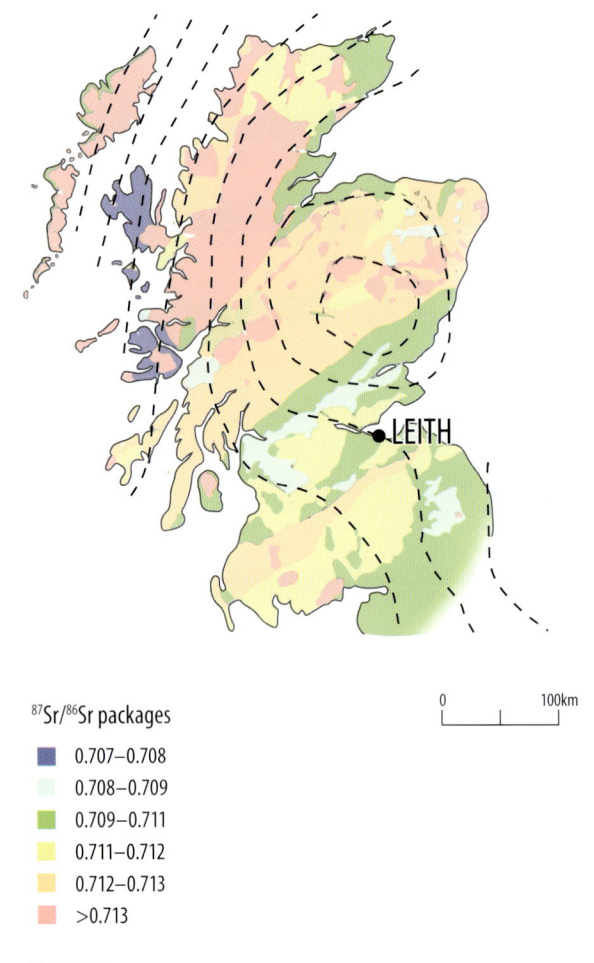

^{87}Sr/^{86}Sr packages
- 0.707–0.708
- 0.708–0.709
- 0.709–0.711
- 0.711–0.712
- 0.712–0.713
- >0.713

ILLUS 4.71
Strontium and oxygen isotope 'baseline' map of Scotland, previously measured and estimated environmental values can provide a guideline for interpreting human skeletal strontium and oxygen values and inferring mobility (adapted from images/data in Darling & Talbot 2003; Evans et al 2010). © Kate Britton

such estimates, bioavailability studies (incorporating the strontium isotope analysis of local soils, plants and/ or microfauna) provide the best estimates of bioapatite values of local fauna (eg Willmes et al 2014). A UK-wide bioavailability study of strontium isotope packages has characterised variability across the country, and within Scotland (Evans et al 2010). Data suggests that the local bioavailable strontium isotope signature of Leith and Edinburgh is between 0.709 and 0.711. This area of Lower Carboniferous sedimentary lithology is neighboured to older Carboniferous coalfields, characterised by higher strontium isotope signatures (0.711 to 0.712). Strontium isotope package maps can therefore provide a guide for what strontium isotope values of local individuals, growing up in the region, should be, and potentially be suggestive of possible areas of childhood origin for individuals who do not bear local strontium isotope signatures. However, while the exclusion of a local origin may be possible, the identification of a non-local place of origin should always be considered tentative at best (not least in light of areas of similar lithology found across Scotland and the rest of Britain (**Illus 4.71**).

Strontium isotope analysis is commonly paired with oxygen isotope analysis in order to better include/ exclude individuals as local/non-local in archaeological case studies and to infer childhood origin. The oxygen isotope signatures of modern rainfall and ground waters can provide a guideline for anticipated bioapatite oxygen isotope values of local fauna. Baseline maps exist for the UK as whole, in the form of contours highlighting the background water values for different areas and regions (eg Darling et al 2003; Darling and Talbot 2003) (**Illus 4.71**). However, it should be noted that a recent more detailed (but as yet unpublished) study of environmental water values in Scotland has revealed a near-universal trend of elevated oxygen isotope values relative to those indicated from previous studies (Wolfram Meier-Augenstein, pers comm). This trend, particularly apparent in coastal regions, is likely due to a coastal amelioration effect on the isotopic values of precipitation in Scotland. Elevated baseline values would lead to elevated tissue values in local humans and animals. Furthermore, unlike strontium values, oxygen isotope ratios are modified substantially between drinking water, body water and body tissues through fractionation. Regression equations are required to convert bioapatite values to predicted drinking water values (eg Levinson et al 1987; Daux et al 2008), and vice-versa, although there are errors associated with these (see review in Britton et al 2015). Coupled with uncertainties in the measured environmental values of Scotland, predicted values resulting from the use of such regression equations should be viewed with caution. Recent studies have also indicated that the composition of the diet (solid foods can contribute fluids to the body as well as drinking water) or even culinary preparation/culinary practices (such as stewing and brewing) can influence the $\delta^{18}O$ of drinking water and therefore potentially induce isotopic enrichment or depletion in body water and, ultimately, body tissues (Daux et al 2008; Brettell et al 2012). In light of these complexities, researchers are increasingly advocating the use of directly measured values in humans or animals as a means of comparison (Müldner et al 2011; Pollard et al 2011) or the intra-group assessment of mobility within a population through the determining of a mean bioapatite value or broad regional anticipated value and the identification of individuals who lie beyond that mean (± standard deviations) as 'non-locals' (eg Leach et al 2009; Müldner et al 2011).

Data analysis – a local population

The data are given in diagrammatic form (**Illus 4.72**) and shown in detail in **Table A1.03** (p218). The results from the majority of the individuals analysed from Constitution Street are consistent with their spending their childhoods in Leith or the wider Edinburgh area, or areas very close to Edinburgh. While this cannot preclude that these individuals had grown up in other regions of Scotland or Europe which display similar baseline values, the most likely interpretation of the data is that the majority of the individuals in this study are from the local area.

Using previously-published $\delta^{18}O$ data from freshwater sources in the area surrounding Edinburgh (range: -8.0‰ to -7.5‰ for precipitation, surface and ground water; data from Darling et al 2003; Darling and Talbot 2003), predicted bioapatite (phosphate, V-SMOW) values for individuals raised in the area can be calculated using previously published regression equations. For example, a predicted range of 16.0‰ and 15.7‰ is determined using the equation put forward in Levinson et al (1987, 369). These values are elevated relative to the ones measured in the materials from Edinburgh, and despite large errors and some variability, predicted values consistently elevated relative to the measured values are determined using other published regression equations (eg Luz et al 1984; Daux et al 2008). While the lower values measured in this study could suggest the majority of the individuals buried at Constitution Street originate from other, cooler regions (such as the Highlands, Scandinavia or other parts of continent Europe), parsimony and the fact that all but two of the individuals exhibit 'local' strontium isotope ratios suggest this is unlikely. A possible explanation for these lower values could be climate differences between today and the later medieval period. However, it is unlikely that 'baseline' oxygen isotope values of mean annual precipitation will have varied substantially in the UK over the last 10,000 years (Darling et al 2003; Darling 2004). This has been corroborated by diachronic oxygen isotope data from human tooth enamel in France, suggesting no significant differences in $\delta^{18}O$ values of enamel phosphate between the 4th century AD and the present day (Daux et al 2005). It may be likely that the discrepancies between predicted and measured values in this study are the result of the uncertainty surrounding 'baseline' environmental data in Scotland and the errors associated with the use of conversion equations (Pollard et al 2011). Given that standard in-house pre-treatment methods were employed, and no measurement errors were reported (Gordon Cook, pers comm), no further explanations can be offered at this point.

In light of the above, the decision was made to not employ any conversion equations and instead to determine trends in the carbonate V-SMOW data alone (in comparison with $^{87}Sr/^{86}Sr$). In order to gain a better understanding of the local oxygen range, a mean value for the individuals from Constitution Street (±1δ) was calculated to provide an estimate of local range (**Illus 4.72**). The fact that both of the younger children sampled, five of the six older children sampled, and three of the four adolescents sampled at the site fit within this projected 'local' range, appears to confirm the validity of the approach.

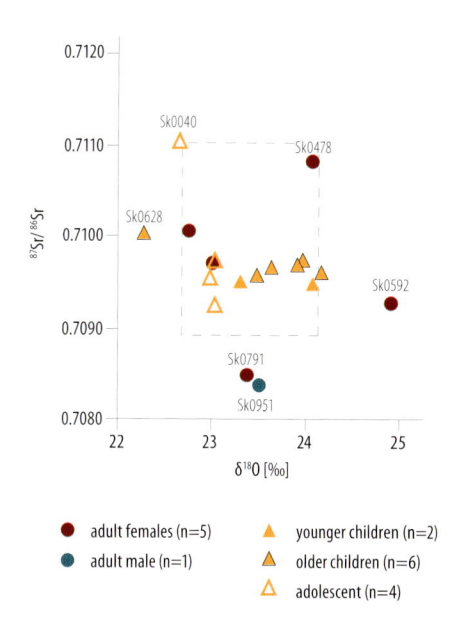

ILLUS 4.72
Strontium and oxygen isotope values of tooth enamel from individuals from Constitution Street. The dashed-lines enclose the local range of anticipated strontium isotope values and the range of local oxygen isotope values

Exploring outliers

While indicating the majority of the population are probably of local origin, a small number of outliers become apparent when comparing both oxygen and strontium isotope data (**Illus 4.72**). Sk0040/Gr0042 in Area 2 (adolescent, 12–16 years) and Sk0478/Gr0479 in Area 6 (young adult female), both lay at the upper extreme of the local predicted strontium isotope values, although bear similar oxygen isotope values to the majority of the assemblage. Although these strontium values appear markedly higher than the rest of the group, values as high as 0.711 and 0.712 can be found relatively locally in southern Fife to the north and the Musselburgh area to the east (**Illus 4.71**). Furthermore, dietary isotope data from Sk0040/Gr0042, do not separate this individual from the broader population.

The strontium isotope value of Sk0592/Gr0590 in Area 7 (older middle adult female) is within the local anticipated range, but the $\delta^{18}O$ value lies outside of the mean expected range (mean±1δ) and is the most elevated in the entire dataset. In this instance, the tooth analysed was the 2nd premolar, rather than the 2nd molar as in most other cases. This tooth begins forming slightly earlier than the second molar, and the values in this tooth may therefore have been influenced by a residual breastfeeding signal (breastfeeding induces enrichment in ^{18}O, Britton et al 2015). However, given that such extensive enrichment is not observed in Sk0704/Gr0710 or Sk0641/Gr0642, both in Area 7, for which first molars (forming immediately after birth) were both analysed, this alone is not a sufficient explanation. It is also possible this individual may have come from a slightly more ameliorate region with similar

PEOPLE'S STORIES

A MAN FROM OUT OF TOWN, 1499–1529

This man was born in 1499 in Haddington, then the fourth largest town in Scotland, the son of a local wool merchant. As a child, his teeth grew in overcrowded and in another age would have suffered many visits to the orthodontist. He otherwise grew up fit and healthy. He ate well, having meat when the church allowed, and sometimes when it didn't, and eating fish caught in the Tyne, which flowed through the town. Sometimes in the winter months they would eat saltfish brought in to the local market from Aberlady and North Berwick.

When he was 14 his older brother joined the king's army on his ill-fated invasion of England. King James IV had chivalrously given his brother-in-law, the English king, a month's notice of his intent to invade. Queen Catherine, acting as regent for her husband who was away waging war on France, used the time to raise an army to defend the northern border, under the leadership of the Earl of Surrey. The 30,000 strong Scots army got as far as the village of Branxton, 40 miles south-east of Haddington and just three miles over the English border. The ensuing battle became known as the Battle of Flodden, the largest ever between the two countries, and was a disaster for Scotland. Over 10,000 Scots died that day including the King himself. The brother was cut down by an English cannonball.

The merchant was horrified when his younger son seemed inspired to somehow avenge his brother's death. The boy spent the winter months practicing his archery skills. To bring him back down to earth, the merchant decided it was time to teach him the wool trade from the bottom up. The next spring, he sent him out to the neighbouring farms to help with the shearing, the bailing of the fleeces and their transportation to his warehouse. The boy was laid up for a few days at one point after straining his back while attempting to shear a particularly feisty young sheep. He had a persistent ache in the middle of his spine after that, especially after exerting himself, and it was stiff first thing in the morning.

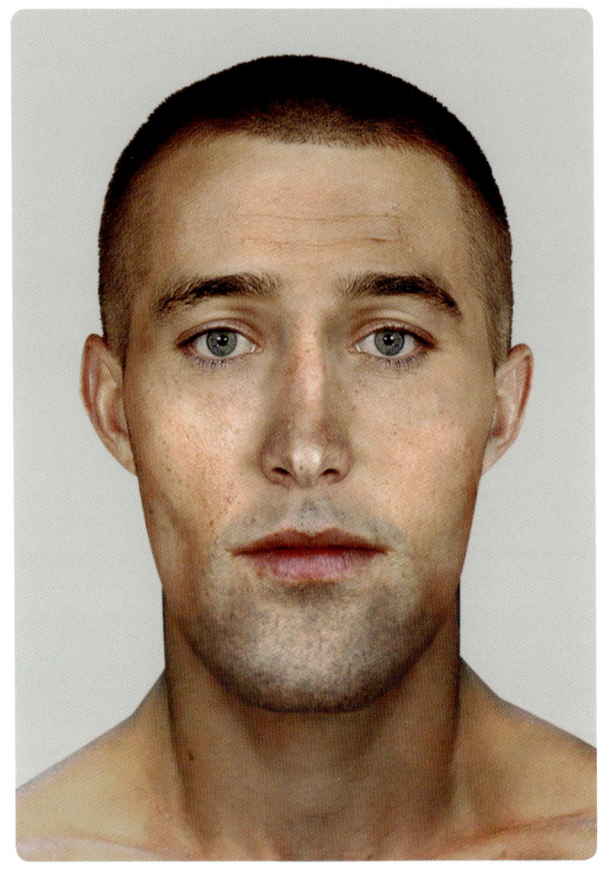

After a few years, his father began to trust him with some of his business. The old man found travelling increasingly irksome and he sent his son out on errands that involved travelling any further than the distance to the warehouse or market and back.

So it was that in 1529 he was sent to Leith to straighten out a problem there. A ship loaded with his father's wool, bound for Flanders, set out from Aberlady but put in at Leith to take on an important passenger and there the port officials had seized his wool under legislative powers that came into effect during times of pestilence after a single case of plague was reported in Fife. There had been no plague in East Lothian and the wool was not even bound for Leith and the merchant was furious that his goods had been seized. The wool represented a significant portion of his yearly income and he needed it back.

His son travelled the 20 miles to Leith on horseback and arrived late in the day. He looked for the ship at the docks in the hope of speaking to the quartermaster, but it was moored out in the Forth and he could find no one wiling to row him out there. He enquired at an inn for a room, but the landlord was suspicious and asked him many questions about where he was from and if the pestilence was afoot there. Eventually he was satisfied that the man posed no threat and gave him a room and a supper of oysters and ale. It was the man's first visit to Leith, though he had visited Edinburgh on two previous occasions. He took a stroll around the town in the dying light. It was not as large as Haddington, but he was impressed by the huge church of St Mary's on its southern edge, completed only two decades before, almost as large as St Mary's in Haddington.

He spent the next day trying to find someone at the port who could get the ship released from quarantine or his goods returned but to no avail. Each person he spoke to sent him to someone else or told him his paperwork was insufficient to prove his case, and the people he needed to speak to always seemed to be elsewhere. He grew increasingly irritated and his sore stomach did nothing to help his mood. He returned to the inn and accused his landlord of poisoning him with bad oysters before retiring to bed without any supper.

The next morning the maid found him feverish and vomiting and shouting for a doctor. The landlord did not want to report it for fear that his inn would be quarantined. His wife, fearing far worse consequences if they did not, fetched a physician. The man's stomach was distended, and large red bruises were beginning to appear on it and he screamed whenever it was touched. The physician said it was not plague but there was nothing he could do and left them with a potion for the pain and a bill. The man was dead the next day. They could not return the body to Haddington due to the restrictions in place on the movement of corpses and so he was hastily taken down to the churchyard at St Mary's lest the other guests should be alarmed. A few days later, a letter arrived at the merchant's house in Haddington from the priest of St Mary's, explaining the situation and assuring of them of his prayers for their son. He enclosed the bill from the physician, and another from the inn landlord.

Fused thoracic vertebrae caused by spinal DJD, due to wear and tear, often age-related but can be accelerated by occupational activities or brought on by trauma. Causes stiffness and tenderness, can limit range of motion and cause weakness or numbness in limbs. Sk0951

SKELETON	0951
Grave	0952
Location of grave	Constitution Street, Area 7
Burial details	Simple
Age	Younger Middle Adult, 25–35
Sex	Male?
Stature	167cm or 5'6"
Radiocarbon date	1520–1595, 1615–1655 (68% probability) see Table 4.02, Illus 4.31, p84–85
1475–1670 (95% probabilit)	–
Other dating evidence	In Phase 1 cemetery in use from c1380s onwards
Finds	–
Pathology	Overcrowding of mandibular teeth (one pushed anteriorly, one 90° mesially), costal fusion right rib 1 and 2, spinal DJD (vertebrae T6–7 fused), Schmorl's nodes
C/N isotope (diet)	Relatively little marine component to diet (c16%?) see p132–35; Illus 4.68; Table A1.01, p216–17
O/S isotope (origins)	North Berwick, East Linton, Haddington or Glasgow, Lennoxtown, Bearsden? see p136–40; Table A1.03, p218
See also	Illus 4.10, p59; p89; Illus 4.45, p102; p115; p150
Facial reconstruction artist	Emily McCulloch

A MAN FROM OUT OF TOWN, 1499–1529

strontium isotope values, for example, more southerly areas of Britain. Conversely, the lowest $\delta^{18}O$ value was measured in Sk0628/Gr0629 in Area 7, an older child (6–8 years), and may suggest an origin in more northerly or highland areas of Scotland with similar lithologies, such as the Arbroath/Montrose region to the south-east of the Cairngorms.

Two individuals exhibit far lower strontium isotope values than could be expected for the immediate area (woman Sk0791/Gr0786 and man Sk0951/Gr0952, both in Area 7). While their oxygen isotope values are similar to other individuals from the site, the low strontium values are more consistent with areas of igneous lithology, such as those found in the areas to the east of Edinburgh, around North Berwick, East Linton and Haddington and to the west around Glasgow, Lennoxtown and Bearsden. These data may suggest that these individuals spent their childhoods between 25 and 50km from Leith.

Population mobility

The strontium and oxygen isotope data from Constitution Street imply a local origin for the majority of individuals sampled, which is perhaps surprising given the nature of the busy port. However, it should be noted that most of the individuals analysed were subadults, and are thus less likely to have moved significantly during their shorter lifetimes. Of the six adults analysed it is notable that four (Sk0478/Gr0479, Area 6; Sk0592/Gr0590, Area 7; Sk0791/Gr0786, Area 7; Sk0951/Gr0952, Area 7) potentially grew up outside Leith, the latter two of whom were from a minimum of c 25km away. The possibility remains that any of the non-locals could have come from considerably further away.

Future analysis of a larger number of adult individuals, who are perhaps more likely to have been mobile as young adults moving into growing urban centres, in this or other medieval towns in Scotland, will help to further illuminate population mobility at this time.

CONSTITUTION STREET: DISCUSSION

The two most important points for discussion in the Constitution Street findings are the early dating of the burials and the interpretation of ditch [0980].

Why did the burials predate the accepted dating of St Mary's Church? This question is tied to the history of Leith and the relationship of the burials to the earlier archaeological features and is discussed in the first section.

Was ditch [0980] part of a defensive scheme and if so of what date? The answer to this lies in historic cartography and the relationship of the ditch to the later burials and is discussed in the second section.

Thereafter there are two sections pulling together the evidence gleaned about the lives and deaths of the people whose remains were discovered, highlighting areas where the evidence proved distinctive. The locations of the main features discussed in this section are shown on **Illus 4.73**, along with the locations of other contemporary landmarks and relevant archaeological finds.

THE BURGAGE PLOTS, ECCLESIASTICAL BEGINNINGS AND THE PHASING OF THE CEMETERY

The beginnings of activity on the site and its dating revolve around the relationship between the burials, their radiocarbon dates, the burgage plots and the historical background. These are considered in detail in this section.

At the time of the first archaeological activity seen, the site was on the southern edge of town, on the eastern side of the main route into Leith from Edinburgh, now known as the Kirkgate. The natural landscape seems originally to have been one of grassed-over sand dunes. Similar stabilised sand dune landscapes are still present today along the coast of East Lothian. The undulating nature of the dunes seems to have been partly preserved in the ground surface but very little else can be gleaned from the archaeological evidence as to the nature of the environment before it was encroached upon by anthropogenic activity.

The burgage plots

The medieval port was formally laid out with burgage plots in the early 12th century, as is evident from the results from the excavations at Burgess Street (Collard and Reed 1994; J Lawson 1995) and Ronaldson's Wharf/

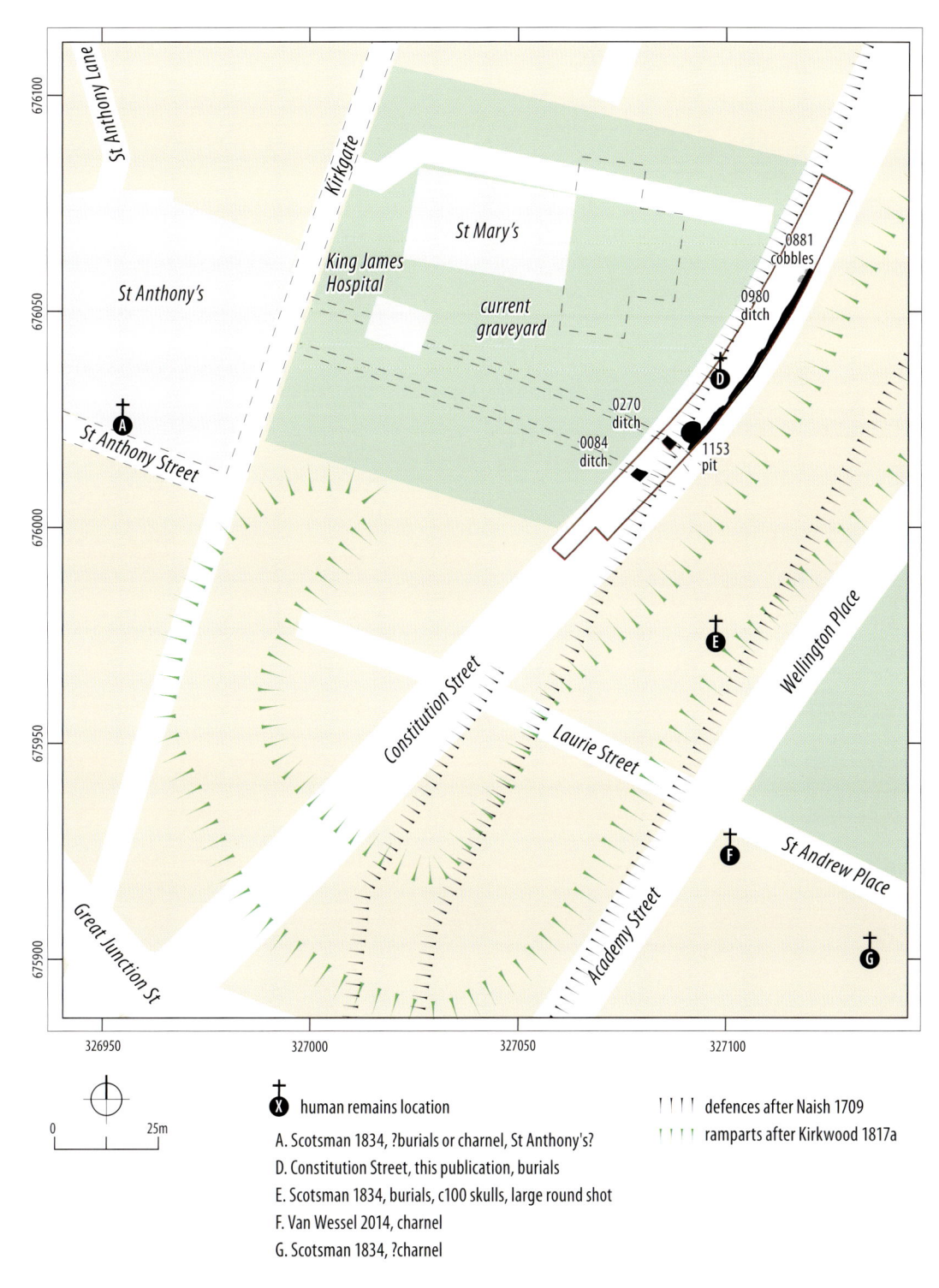

ILLUS 4.73
Relative locations of significant features around Constitution Street

Sandport Street (Reed and Lawson 1999), probably coinciding with David I's granting of royal burgh status to Edinburgh and the establishment of the Holyrood Abbey and royal harbours. The Kirkgate would have been a major route into the port from this date if not before. However, the archaeological evidence would suggest that the early medieval town was centred on the medieval harbours towards the mouth of the Water of Leith, to the north of St Mary's Church, north of Dub Row (now Giles Street and Parliament Street) (Mowat 2003, 5). The evidence recovered during the current project is consistent with the assumption that the excavation area was on the edge of the town during the 12th and 13th centuries.

As the town grew, it seems likely that burgage plots were laid out further south. Ditches [0270] and [0084] can be readily identified as opposing elements of the same burgage plot boundaries, given their size, parallel alignment and distance apart. It is assumed that this plot ran off the Kirkgate with the excavated area falling within its backlands. There is little or no evidence for the usual backlands activity of industry and domestic waste, though this does not necessarily mean the plot was unoccupied. This area may have been used for horticulture or pasture leaving little physical evidence.

Since ditch [0270] was overlain by 15th-century graves this gives a *terminus ante quem* for the setting out of this plot. The lack of diagnostically earlier finds in either of the ditch fills or in any archaeological deposits along this part of Constitution Street (**Tables 4.25–6**, p126–30) suggests a later 14th to earlier 15th-century date is the most likely for this activity. This would make it contemporary with the Phase 1 cemetery (see below). Historically speaking this coincides with a period of expansion and change in Leith. There was a large increase in trade following the early 14th century Wars of Scottish Independence and the granting of Leith to Edinburgh in the charter of 1329. The years around and immediately after 1398 are also likely to have seen development, with efforts on the part of Sir Robert Logan of Restalrig to make the money out of his lands in Leith by granting rights to Edinburgh to improve the harbour and build a bridge, and possibly by making the town a burgh of barony (p20). The redevelopment of the Kirkgate as a main thoroughfare during this latter period is well attested by the establishment of St Anthony's Preceptory on the west side of the road.

It is possible that further burgage plots were laid out to the north of this plot, predating the graveyard, given that this area is closer to the medieval centre of Leith. Although no evidence for other boundary ditches was found this could be due to the density of burials in this area either obscuring or removing any evidence for their existence. Nevertheless, it is a useful exercise to sketch in the boundaries of these putative plots, based on the one known plot size to establish if the ghost of these boundaries might be preserved in the pattern of later activity (**Illus 4.74**). By co-incidence, the plot width was approximately the same width as the excavation areas, with the boundaries falling roughly across the middle of each area. The plots have been given letters A–H (to avoid confusion with the area numbers), beginning at the southern end. The surviving complete demarked plot width is Plot C.

The possible sand quarry pit [1153] respects the boundaries of the putative Plot D fairly convincingly. The southern end of this plot was marked by ditch [0270]. There is no clear relationship between pit and ditch, as the area that might have demonstrated this was lost to modern truncation, but the estimate of its width of 5m places it about 1m inside the plot's southern edge. The pit's northern edge is also about 1m inside the expected location of the northern boundary ditch. Thus, the sand quarrying must have taken place after the plots were laid out but before they, or at least before Plot D was used for burial. The quarrying may be related to building works and it is most likely that this was for building works on the same piece of land. It is quite possible that the owner or tenant of the plot might have made money selling the sand to others for construction, though as sand is such a ubiquitous commodity in Leith, that would beg the question of why these other building works did not quarry the sand from their own land. The most obvious candidate for building works on the land was the late 15th-century construction work at St Mary's Church. However, the dating implications of this are at odds with the dating of burials in this area (p145).

The distribution of the burials by date has been discussed above (p81–83), where a possible four-part expansion was noted, with the earliest burials in Area 6, expanding to Areas 4–6, then to Areas 4–9 and lastly to Areas 2–9, the latter following approximately the same N-S boundaries as the current graveyard. By considering the distribution by speculative burgage plot instead of excavation area, the same four-part expansion is evident (the plot letters have been noted in **Table 4.02**, p84) and there does seem to be a correlation between the burial pattern and some of the predicted plot boundaries. These four phases will now be discussed.

Phase 1 cemetery – later 14th to early 15th century

The four earliest dated burials were in Area 6, with the earliest of these (Sk0478; see **Table 4.02**, **Illus 4.31**, p84–85) potentially stretching back to the late 13th century. However, given the lack of any kind of artefactual evidence for activity in the vicinity of the site before, at earliest, the later 14th century, and assuming no large hiatus between the two earliest dates and the rest, it seems reasonable to suppose that burials began in the later 14th or early 15th century, broadly contemporary with the setting out of the burgage plot to the south. If these early burials were within pre-existing burgage plots (plots E and F, **Illus 4.74**) then the boundary of this cemetery would fall across the middle of Areas 5 and 7. There does seem to be a thinning of burials in both areas, though in Area 5 this is confused by later burials and in Area 7, partially obscured by modern truncation.

Phase 2 cemetery – early to late 15th century

Expansion southward into Area 4 and the northern part of Area 3 seems to have followed during the second quarter of the 15th century, based again on the radiocarbon evidence. The northern boundary of the Phase 2 cemetery remained the same, but the southern boundary would have been in the location of ditch [0084], at the southern end of the demarked burgage plot (putative plot C). It is noticeable that ditch [0084] remained free of

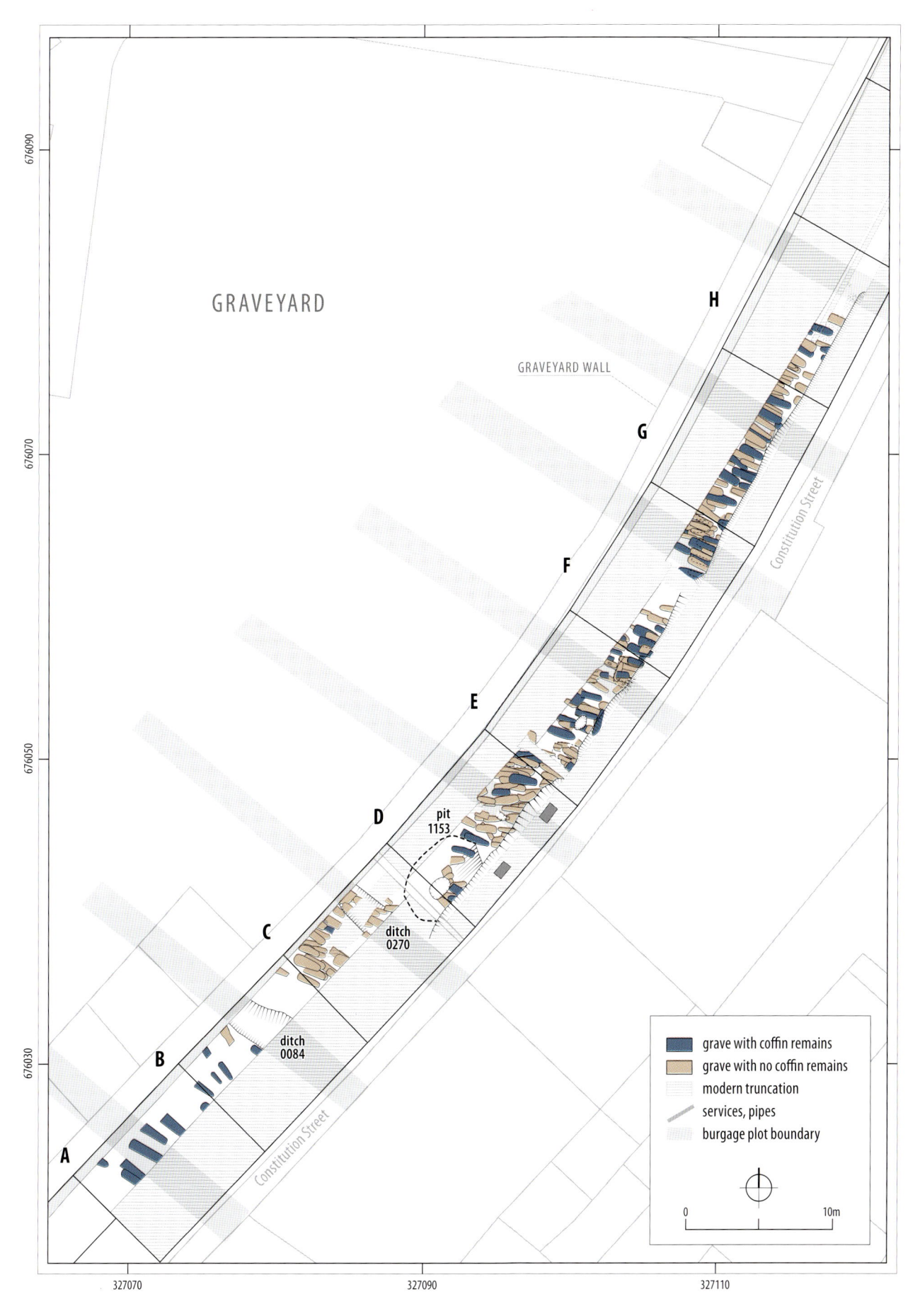

ILLUS 4.74
Putative burgage plot boundaries

overlying burials, whereas ditch [0270], which was within this second phase of cemetery, was overlain by a large number of them. The burials on this southern edge of the Phase 2 cemetery do not so much peter out as stop over 2m short of the ditch edge. Whether this ditch formed the cemetery boundary itself is not clear. Cemeteries were more often bounded by walls, which kept out animals such as dogs and pigs, which might disturb recent graves, and prevented illicit burials (such as of unbaptised infants). However, hedges, palisades, earthen banks, ditches and water courses are also known to have acted as boundaries (Gilchrist and Sloane 2005, 34–5). There is no evidence for anything but the ditch at Constitution Street, but stonework might have been robbed and archaeological evidence lost to truncation. The large gap between ditch [0084] and the first burials to the north might suggest that there was some kind of upstanding boundary structure across this area. It is notable that the majority of the burials were along the same alignment as this boundary (p79), which implies it was visible for most of the working life of the cemetery.

Phase 3 cemetery – late 15th to 16th century

Later there was further expansion to the north into Areas 8 and 9. The need for more cemetery space is clear from the density of burials within the earlier cemetery. Radiocarbon dating for this period is very broad, but the balance of evidence for these dates, the dating of earlier activity and the historical evidence, suggests this occurred in the later 15th century or later, and probably coincided with the construction work at, and supposed foundation date of, St Mary's Church in the 1480s and 1490s.

The new northern boundary of this Phase 3 cemetery was to the northern end of Area 9 where the graves peter out. Interestingly, this coincides with the northern boundary of the putative burgage plot H (**Illus 4.74**). The current South Leith Parish Church graveyard extends further north than this and it is possible that the area to the north of the burials was unused at this time because it was covered by a path leading to the church's eastern door as evidenced by the cobbled surface (p88). To the south, the boundary remained in the location of ditch [0084].

Phase 4 cemetery – early to mid-17th century

The final expansion was into the area south of ditch [0084] in Areas 3 and 2. The combination of radiocarbon dating and late 16th- or early 17th-century midden underlying some of the graves indicates that burial here probably began no earlier than the beginning of the 17th century.

This new phase seems to coincide with the rebuilding of St Mary's Church after the destruction of 1560 and its official sanction as the parish church for South Leith in 1609. It also coincides with the foundation of the King James Hospital in 1614 to the south of the church and to the west of this excavation area (**Illus 4.73**). The presence of midden in the cemetery at all is relatively unusual at this site and the deposition of this material suggests this area was not within the churchyard at the time.

This new area seems to have remained distinct from the rest of the cemetery. The area between this and the older cemetery to the north remained burial-free for a stretch of 5m, including ditch [0084]. An internal division might therefore still have existed limiting access to this part of the cemetery or marking it out as separate. Ditch [0084], however, was certainly filled in by this point, as the early 17th-century midden underlying the graves extended over the top of the ditch fills, so the boundary must have been marked in another way. It is noticeable that the burials in this part of the cemetery typically had a slightly different alignment (p79), suggesting the gravediggers orientated themselves by a different feature at this time.

The separation of this area, as well as the almost exclusive coffin use and lack of intercutting, would be consistent with relatively short-lived use. This might be consistent with an association with the King James Hospital (there being only 35 years between the foundation of the hospital and construction of the 17th-century defences), although the demography of the people buried in this part of the graveyard is not consistent with the historical evidence that the hospital's primary function was to provide care for old people (p25). Only one old adult was among those buried, the rest being made up of other adults, adolescents and young children.

Connections with one of the epidemics of the early 17th century, however, is also distinctly possible. It has been observed elsewhere that where plague burial grounds were created within the grounds of existing religious establishments that they were set up on the margins of the existing cemetery and remained segregated (Gilchrist & Sloane 2005, 77). The plague outbreaks of 1603–6, 1624 and 1635 would all be consistent with the dating of the use of this area (though not the last devastating 1644–5 outbreak which would be unlikely based on the radiocarbon dates). Similar very high coffin use (among the individual burials at least) was in evidence at St Mary's Primary School, a burial ground known to have been in use during the 1644–5 plague (Churchill 2016). It is possible that this separate extension to the St Mary's graveyard was created during an earlier outbreak, specifically for the plague dead.

It is not clear to what extent the use of this southern area was concurrent with the later use of the area to the north, or whether burial in the excavation area to the north had ended by this point. The dating evidence for this is considered in more detail below (p148–49).

An early chapel?

The occurrence of the sand quarry pit (p64–65; 142; **Illus 4.74**) within the presumed limits of the Phase 2 cemetery suggests building work in the vicinity in the early 15th century or earlier. Although building works were underway throughout Leith at this time, including across the Kirkgate at St Anthony's Preceptory, such pits are commonly associated with construction activities in their immediate vicinity. Thus, this feature is likely to relate to building works within the cemetery and may relate to the construction of a chapel or similar establishment. Such an establishment is undocumented but given the repeated and long-lived use of the area for burial before the apparent establishment of St Mary's Church, a chapel would have been needed for the funeral services to accompany burials at the site.

The traditional date of 1483 for the foundation of St Mary's was asserted by Campbell Irons (Campbell Irons 1898, vol 1, 77) and has been much repeated but there are no historical records for its construction. There is a note in 1487 of a royal financial contribution to 'the new kyrk of Leith to our Ladie' (Marshall 1983, 2), which is in keeping with the accepted dating and it is clear that building works were undertaken in the late 15th century with contributions by various trade incorporations. However, it is possible that this relates to a rededication, improvements to or rebuilding of an existing chapel.

Assuming this early chapel was established at or around the formation of the graveyard in the later 14th century, it may have had the honour of being the first ecclesiastical establishment in South Leith (though St Nicholas's chapel in North Leith might have already been in existence by this time). It might have acted as an outlying chapel of the parish church at Restalrig, or like the later and more ambitious St Mary's, it might have been established by one or more of the trade incorporations or a wealthy individual based within the port. It is interesting to note, in this context, that the Fraternity of Mariners, Leith's most powerful trade organisation, was founded in 1380 (p20).

It is also notable that there was a plague outbreak in 1379–80, which might have led to an increased impetus for easier access to a burial site. There was a general movement during the later medieval period for more local cemeteries, with people petitioning Rome for the right to a cemetery in their own village, to avoid the difficulties and dangers of transporting corpses over long distances (Gilchrist and Sloane 2005, 55). If plague was a factor in the establishment of this early cemetery then it might be that Restalrig actively discouraged the interment of the dead from Leith for fear of infection, though there is no evidence for any legislative restrictions on movements of people or bodies before 1456 (p31).

Whether plague was a factor or not, the funerary needs of the growing population of Leith might not have been adequately served by Restalrig anymore. The graveyard there had been in use for centuries and may have been becoming overcrowded. It is possible therefore that the cemetery was the most important addition and the chapel was secondary, being built solely for the purposes of conducting funeral services. As such there may have been no resident priest and clergy may have been supplied from Restalrig, or later St Anthony's, as and when need arose. By virtue of its lowly status or lack of involvement in any great historical events this chapel may never have been recorded historically.

The location of this speculative early chapel is not known, but assuming it lay on the same plot as the cemetery but towards the Kirkgate frontage then it would have been to the south of the existing church. The new church might have been built beside rather than over the footprint of the earlier chapel so that services could continue in the latter during building work.

The western and eastern cemetery boundaries

The N-S widths of each cemetery are easy enough to estimate. The Phase 1 cemetery may have been as little as 20m wide. The Phase 2 cemetery was about 40m wide, Phase 3 about 60m, and Phase 4 80m. However, the western and in particular the eastern extents were not identified for any of these phases. It seems likely that the western extent of the Phase 3 cemetery matched the later graveyard and extended to the Kirkgate frontage, covering the area to the east and south of the church. Similarly, it is assumed that the earlier cemeteries also fronted onto the Kirkgate, though it is not possible to state with any certainty where the postulated early chapel was sited. From 1614 onwards, the area occupied by the Phase 4 cemetery extension would have lain to the east of the King James Hospital, which occupied the Kirkgate frontage 60m to the west of the excavation area. It may have extended west to the back of the hospital buildings.

The eastern boundary at some point may have been considerably further east than the excavated graves. There is a newspaper report of the finds at 'the head of Wellington Place behind Constitution Street' (Scotsman 1834; **Illus 3.07E**, p34; **Illus 4.73E**). These were reported as 'several human skeletons' implying they were articulated and the description of the deposit within which they lay 'a dry sandy mould, mixed with submarine deposits' is a very good description of the Constitution Street cemetery soil. The exact location of these graves is not known though it is clear they lay between Wellington Place and Constitution Street which places them approximately 25m further east than the Constitution Street excavations. However, the description of the location at 'the head of Wellington Place' suggests they are some 50m further south than the southernmost burials at Constitution Street and may therefore relate instead to the Wester Links plague camp of the 1644–5 plague outbreak.

Were the eastern boundary to have stretched beyond the eastern edge of Constitution Street then human remains must have been disturbed on a regular basis throughout the 18th and 19th century development of the area to the east of Constitution Street. Though there is little record of this, it is entirely possible that workmen did find human remains and these went unreported. There is enough evidence at Constitution Street for the capacity of workmen to ignore human remains and quietly dispose of, or re-inter, the bones (p4). There were certainly a number of finds of charnel deposits in the area (Scotsman 1834; van Wessel 2014; Dalland 2016) and some of these bones might have been disturbed more than once. Radiocarbon dating of two pieces of charnel showed them to be contemporary with the Constitution Street Phase 2 and Phase 3 cemeteries (van Wessel 2014, 3; see **Table A3.01**, p234 for recalibration).

The eastern extent of the later cemetery was considerably curtailed by the construction of the fortifications across it. Thereafter cartographic evidence suggests that the eastern extent of the cemetery was defined by the line of these defences. When this occurred, and where the limit is likely to have been with reference to the excavation area, are considered next.

THE POST-MEDIEVAL DEFENCES AND THE END OF HUMAN BURIAL AT THE SITE

Ditch [0980] was the most significant of the later features discovered (p88–90). Its interpretation has proved problematic due chiefly to later truncation. Only the western edge of the cut was found and modern service cuts immediately to the east of this removed any chance to examine the dimensions and stratigraphic sequence within it in to any degree of reliable detail. It was long, running for 50m within the excavations area. The cut at both ends ran into areas of modern truncation so is likely to have been longer. It is possible that it turned to the east where it disappeared in Areas 4 and 9. Its profile was uneven implying it was hand excavated. Its width and depth were tentatively identified based on the extrapolated evidence of one sondage, giving a width of less than 2m and a depth of c 1.54m from its preserved top edge. However, given the later levels of vertical truncation which probably occurred across the site it is likely that the ditch was originally considerably deeper and wider. There was little opportunity to examine the fills, but it is possible that there was a basal deposit which represented slumped material from an associated earthen bank. The remaining fill seemed to be of cemetery soil containing disarticulated human bone.

It is well enough known that the fortifications of the 16th and 17th centuries followed the line of the later Constitution Street and thus it seems likely that the ditch relates to one or both of these defensive schemes. The evidence for this and the implications for the continued use of the cemetery during this period is considered in detail in this section.

Locating the fortifications

The history of Leith's defences has already been detailed (p22–28) and are summarised here:

1544   defences of some sort in place, though it is not known when these were built or what they looked like

1548–59   significant and militarily advanced fortifications constructed (**Illus 3.01**, p23)

1559–60   Siege of Leith

1560   after the siege, fortifications deliberately slighted, though not clear to what extent they were destroyed

1571   fortifications re-excavated

1649–50   re-fortification based on earlier works (**Illus 3.03**, p25)

The locations of these defences have been shown in various historic maps to varying degrees of accuracy and have been confirmed in places by archaeological excavation. A recent synthetic study (Paton & Cook 2016) collated all the available evidence (including the features found during the current project) to overlay the features noted on the Petworth Map onto the modern Leith street plan. In that study the authors assumed that ditch [0980] was part of the 16th-century defensive ditch.

Archaeological evidence of the line of the defences came in the form of ditches found during three other excavations: at 6–7 Mitchell Street to the north-east of the present feature (Morrison 2000); at the junction of Constitution Street and Duke Street to the south-west (this volume, p183–84); and at 72–92 Great Junction Street (Paton & Cook 2016, 269–71) to the west. More detail was available at all three sites as to the nature of the ditches. The best of this came from Great Junction Street. The ditch there was 8m wide by 3.6m deep, with stratigraphic evidence of three recuts which were equated, with the aid of finds dating evidence, to the fortifications of 1559/60, 1571 and 1649/50 (ibid). At the junction of Constitution Street and Duke Street, the ditch was 5m wide and 2.6m deep. There was no opportunity to investigate the ditch section sequence in detail but finds dating evidence from the fills again pointed towards the 16th and 17th century. At Mitchell Street, only the outer, eastern, edge of the ditch was found within the excavation area. It measured between 4.5 and 8m wide and was about 1.7m deep, though had been truncated by recent activity (Morrison 2000). There were several fills within the ditch though there were no finds for dating evidence and no clear evidence for recutting.

The cartographic evidence for the fortifications revolves around four sources:

The Petworth Map of 1560 (**Illus 3.01**, p23) which shows the 1559/60 defences in detail and was purportedly drawn on the day of Leith's surrender to illustrate the siege for Queen Elizabeth I of England.

Adair's map of Midlothian of 1682 (**Illus 3.03**, p25) which shows Leith, in sketchier detail, after the construction of the 1649–50 defences and the later construction of the Citadel by Cromwell's forces during their occupation of the town.

Naish's Naval Survey of Leith 1709 (**Illus 3.04**, p26) naval survey of Leith which shows the remains of the earthworks related to the 17th-century fortifications.

Kirkwood's 'Ancient Plan' (**Illus 3.05**, p27), which was published in 1817 but was based on a survey of 1759 and shows the remains of the earthworks, still recognisable in some details.

The differences in the form of the mid-16th and mid-17th-century defences are apparent by comparing the Petworth Map to Adair. In the area in question here (ie along the later Constitution Street which roughly follows the eastern line of the fortifications) the main difference was in the later addition of a bastion (now known as the John's Lane bastion) half way along the eastern line. The remains of this can be clearly seen in 1709 and less clearly in 1759.

There is, however, no clear cartographic evidence that the line of the defences itself outwith this bastion was different in 1650 to that constructed in the mid-16th century. The detail in Adair's map is not sufficient to compare the location of the defences to those shown on the Petworth Map. However, the same line would seem to have been used along the southern line of the fortifications, based on the evidence of recutting from the Great Junction Street and Constitution Street/Duke Street excavations. This implies that the older defences were still visible in some way, and the haste with which the defences had to be thrown up in 1649/50 ahead of the arrival of Cromwell's army, suggests that the engineers involved would have made use of any existing features they could. There is no direct evidence for recutting along the eastern line, though there has been less opportunity to explore the stratigraphy there in detail.

The detail of the contemporary street plan in the Naish and Kirkwood maps is such that (unlike the earlier two maps) it is possible to plot the earthworks shown on them onto a modern map. This was undertaken by Paton and Cook (2016, fig. 8) and shows them compared with the locations of the excavated ditch remains (a similar overlay detail of the two maps onto the modern street plan and Constitution Street excavations is shown in **Illus 4.73**). There was a broad correlation, but the detail did not agree. The ditches in three of the locations appeared to be on the wrong side of the ramparts (Constitution Street/Great Junction being the only exception where the ditch was located approximately as would be expected). This fact was put down to a combination of the inaccuracies of the 18th-century mapping and to a certain amount of movement during the destruction of the ramparts, which meant the earthworks, in places, had had moved from their original location. Paton and Cook did not consider the possibility that the remains shown by Naish and Kirkwood were those of the 17th-century defences and that these might be, in places, located in different areas to the 16th-century defences.

A new archaeological discovery by AOC Archaeology (AOC project 23721) of a large ditch was made in May 2018 at a construction site on the western side of the northern end of Wellington Place. Its location would agree with the detail in Naish's map for the location of the 17th-century defensive ditch outside the ramparts of the John's Lane bastion, thus confirming the accuracy of Naish's mapping. At the time of writing (June 2018), no further details were available regarding the nature and dating of this ditch.

One final piece of historic evidence came from the parish records of the sale of the strip of churchyard for the construction of Constitution Street in 1790 (Robertson and Swan 1925, 94). They note that the land was 'the east side of the raised Bank…which is not occupied or calculated for burying ground'. They expressed a hope that that the roadworks would involve the levelling of this bank and thus increase the amount of burial space available to them. The key point to note is that the area that was to become Constitution Street was on the east side, that is the exterior, of the ramparts, and thus the location of the west side of the associated ditch outside the ramparts is likely to have been within the road corridor. This would seem to be at odds with Kirkwood's survey, 30 years prior to this, which seems to place the ramparts outside the churchyard (**Illus 3.05**, p27). Therefore, either (as suggested by Paton & Cook 2016, 274) the detail on the Kirkwood map is unreliable in places, or the remains of two different sets of ramparts were still extant in the 18th century.

Which ditch?

In the light of the confusion outlined above, the identification of ditch [0980] remains problematic. Was it related to one of Leith's defensive schemes and if so which one?

Archaeological dating evidence for ditch [0980] is laid out in detail above (p89–90). It is ambiguous and often tentative. Dating evidence for the cutting of the ditch is provided by the five dated graves which are cut by the ditch (these are noted on **Table 4.02**, p84). The latest of these included the latest two burials dated from the site (Sk0951, 1475–1670; Sk1119, 1475–1795). Another grave cut by the ditch, Sk0910, contained a buckle, apparently in situ, which can be typologically dated to c 1575–1700 (p123–24). Thus, the ditch is most likely to have been cut during or after a date in the 16th, possibly later 16th, and the early 17th century.

The dating for the infilling of the ditch rested on a single fragment of glass waste from the lower fill and a single clay pipe stem from the upper fill. Both imply a date around the mid-17th or early 18th century for the backfill of the feature, though as the finds are so few and the levels of later disturbance so great, these are hardly reliable dating evidence. The construction of Constitution Street in the 1790s means it was certain backfilled by the later 18th century.

Thus, based on archaeological evidence, it would seem that the ditch was more likely to relate to the mid-17th-century defences than those of the mid-16th century. However, the cartographic evidence suggests this is unlikely, the ditch falling on the inside of the remains of the 17th-century ramparts as depicted by Naish (**Illus 4.73**; **Illus 3.04**, p26). The recent finding of a large ditch further east off Wellington Place (p147) seems to confirm the accuracy of Naish's plan in this respect. It would seem, therefore, that, despite the finds dating evidence, the ditch relates to either the 1548–59 fortifications, or those of 1571, or both. Though it is possible that the ditch relates, instead, to an unknown internal feature associated with the later 17th-century defences, given its large size, it is difficult to imagine what this might have been.

The only evidence for ramparts further west than this is the reference to a 'Bank' in the parish minutes for the sale of the land for the construction of Constitution Street, which implies the remains of ramparts still stood on the western side (and to the west) of the road corridor. These were not depicted by either Naish or Kirkwood (**Illus 3.04–3.05**, p26–27). It is possible that while they made the ground too uneven for the parish to consider suitable for burial, compared with the remains of the later works, they were of little importance to the 18th-century cartographers.

Thus, in want of further evidence to the contrary, ditch [0980] has been tentatively identified as the ditch running outside the ramparts of the mid-16th-century defences. This would necessitate the lines of the mid-16th- and mid-17th-century defences being different along this eastern edge, the latter some 50m further east than the earlier scheme. It would also mean that either the typological dating for the buckle associated with Sk0910 was wrong, or that the buckle was intrusive. The scant finds evidence for the dating of the ditch would also have to be intrusive. These are all distinctly possible.

Implications for the dating of the end of human burial within the excavation area

Given that the ditch relates to the mid-16th-century defences then the construction of these would have involved cutting a ditch right through a graveyard that was probably still in active use. One can only imagine local feelings about this, when exhumed bodies may have been partially fleshed and still possibly recognisable by loved ones. There is a suggestion, for example, that Sk0841 was only partially decomposed when it was moved (p76–81). Building works within active graveyards were not unheard of during this period. There are numerous examples of ecclesiastical developments within graveyards, disturbing or truncating sometimes quite recent graves (Gilchrist and Sloane 2005, 195). This was not an ecclesiastical development, however, and it is interesting to consider why the ditch was cut across and not around the graveyard. The most obvious answer would be that the graveyard extended too far east and skirting round it would have required more resources to construct the earthworks and more troops to man the larger perimeter. There is, however, no clear evidence as to how far it might have extended. There has only been one find of in situ burials further east than the excavation area (Scotsman 1834, **Illus 4.73E**; **Illus 3.07E**, p34) and these appear to be too far south to relate to the same cemetery. There have been several finds of redeposited charnel further east and south-east, probably displaced during the construction of the 17th-century defences or later building works (**Illus 3.07E**, **F**, **G**, **H**, p34), one of which (van Wessel 2014; **Illus 4.73F**) was radiocarbon dated and fell well within the range of the dates from Constitution Street (p234). There is, however, little way of discerning how far these might have been moved from their original burial location.

It is likely that the cutting of such a substantial ditch would have disturbed hundreds of burials, and that the charnel pits [0501] and [1096] which cut into the top of the burials date to this event. There were also several loose skulls found along the ditch edge which appear to relate to the same event. As the ditch was cut, the earthen ramparts would have been thrown up to the west and would have covered the entire area containing the excavated graves. Thus, it would be impossible for any burials within the excavation area to be of those who died during the 1559–60 siege itself, though many died at this time, from violence, hunger, disease and fire. The weight of earth above the burials at the trench edge would also explain some of the slumping of earlier burials into the ditch seen in Areas 5, 6 and 7 (p89).

It seems likely that this event marked the end of the use of the majority of the excavation area for burial, certainly on any regular basis. The graveyard would have needed to be reconsecrated after the bloodshed of the siege (Gilchrist and Sloane 2005, 31). The ground would also have needed to be levelled. The slighting of the fortifications in 1560 was designed to make them indefensible but is unlikely to have removed them completely from the landscape. Only a decade later, in 1571, they were recut, and it is not known to what extent they were destroyed after that conflict, or if they were left to slowly settle. To continue using the area for burial afterwards would almost certainly have necessitated digging graves though uneven ground over whatever remained of the ramparts and ditch. The parish records state clearly that the area was not usable for burial in the late 18th century (Robertson & Swan 1925, 94) and it is possible that this had been the state of affairs since the later 16th century. Certainly, the area would have been undesirable for burial plots and thus it may have been used only occasionally, or only in certain circumstances. Possibly only the very poor were buried there, or it may have only been used in emergency circumstances, in times of high mortality.

The only possible evidence for burials stratigraphically post-dating the defences was found during an early watching brief under the eastern pavement of Constitution Street, to the east of the later excavation Area 7 (Humble & Murray 2008, 11; marked on **Illus 4.02**, p50 in trench outside 137 Constitution St). Three burials were encountered 1.8m below the ground surface, compared with one found at 0.4m depth to the west of the road. The difference between the burial depths was put down to a sharp W-E slope in the ground surface. Though unclear at the time, the eastern inhumation burials encountered must have been within defensive ditch [0980] and therefore presumably post-date the abandonment of these defences (there was nothing unusual about them to suggest they might have been deposited in the ditch during the conflicts themselves). Unfortunately, too little of this area was excavated to allow the nature of its use to be fully understood and the human remains were not analysed or dated.

It is, however, reasonably clear that burial did continue in one part of the site after the mid-16th century. The burials in the Phase 4 cemetery at the southern end of the site date to the early 17th century on the basis of stratigraphic, finds dating and radiocarbon evidence (p144). The burials had no stratigraphic relationship to the ditch, and it is not clear to what extent the ditch followed the line of the road towards this southern end. It is possible that this area fell within the siege works south-east corner bastion as depicted on the Petworth Map (**Illus 3.01**, p23) though this appears to have been further to the south (probably between the present Laurie Street and Duke Street; Paton & Cook 2016, fig.9). Grant states that, after the siege, this corner bastion was reduced to a mound and formed, for a time, a portion of South Leith graveyard (Grant 1883, vol.5, 171). However, there was no evidence for human burial further south than Area 2, despite extensive groundworks and archaeological monitoring. Thus, it is possible that Grant was confused by various reports of the finding of human bones in this general area during the 19th century. In 1709 Naish shows the graveyard extending as far east as the ramparts (**Illus 3.04**, p26), with no hint that they fell within the corner bastion of these later defences.

Assuming this was not within the corner bastion and there was, therefore, no sharp turn to the east of the defensive line in Areas 2 and 3, then the burials would still have been very close to, or on, the remains of the ramparts. It is interesting to note the possible plague connections for these burials, based on the high coffin use and apparent segregation of this area. It is possible that during this time, land was used for burial that in normal circumstances would have been considered unsuitable.

It seems unlikely that the excavation area was used for burial past the mid-17th century. It does not appear that any of the dated burials post-date 1650 and there is no other evidence of any kind to suggest burial continued later. It is possible that the refortification of the area ended any remaining use of this eastern end of the graveyard.

The radiocarbon dates are too broad to be of much practical help in confirming the veracity of any of the above. Most of the dates span the mid-15th to mid-17th century and thus it might be argued that probability is stretched to place almost all of these in the first half of that range. The dates from Areas 2 and 3 are not late outliers but fall well within the range of dates as a whole, which again, might suggest that burials continued later elsewhere. However, for want of other firm evidence the model presented above would seem to be the best fit theory at present.

A TENTATIVE CHRONOLOGY

It is possible to draw up a tentative sequence of events for the early development of the site based on the evidence detailed and discussed above. Further excavation evidence is likely to alter this.

12TH TO LATE 14TH CENTURY Open ground on edge of medieval town beside main road leading to Edinburgh

LATE 14TH OR EARLY 15TH CENTURY Phase 1 cemetery and first chapel established and burgage plots to south laid out

EARLY 15TH CENTURY Phase 2 cemetery, expanding graveyard to south

LATE 15TH CENTURY Phase 3 cemetery, expanding graveyard to north. Large building project to construct St Mary's Church

1540s–50s Fortifications constructed across graveyard to east of church, probably across the excavation area. Burial may have continued in the St Mary's graveyard to the west but would have been impossible within the excavation area

1571   Fortifications recut

Late 16th century   Burial undertaken in graveyard to the west and may have occurred on an occasional basis within the Phase 1–3 cemetery excavation area

Early 17th century   Phase 4 cemetery. Separate cemetery established, adjoining southern edge of existing graveyard, possibly for dead of early 17th-century epidemic/s

Mid-17th century   Fortifications reconstructed immediately to the east of site. Most of excavation area probably covered by ramparts

Mid-17th–18th-century   Burials continued in the graveyard to the west but no clear evidence for them continuing within excavation area

1790s   Construction of Constitution Street over excavation area

THE LIVES OF THE LEITHERS

The archaeological remains have revealed a good body of information about the lives of the people who inhabited the town from the later 14th to the mid-17th centuries. The osteological analysis and isotope study provided the main part of this information with supplementary clues given by the finds and environmental evidence. Together they paint a picture of general living and working conditions, local healthcare, diet, economy, seafaring links and population movements. There was limited opportunity to track changes over time. While it is reasonably clear that some areas came into use later than others, there was no clear evidence that the earliest areas fell out of use earlier than some of the later ones, thus muddying any data for the earlier period.

The general levels of health among the cemetery population were within normal medieval parameters and showed they suffered from the usual poor diet, poor teeth and hard manual labour. There was a suggestion that malnutrition was worse in Leith than in other places based on the prevalence of metabolic disorders, DEH and low average height (p119–20). This does not seem to have been the case in Leith as a whole, which was prospering by this period, but it might imply that the selection of those who were buried in this excavated part of the cemetery was biased towards the poorer elements of society. It seems likely that the usual staples of bread, porridge and beer sustained most people. Fish and shellfish played a significant part of the diets of most people and may have supplied around 15% of the protein component of the average person's diet (**Table 4.02**, p84), in particular in the form of fish, oysters, mussels and whelks, brought in from the fisheries in the Forth. There was a wide variation in dietary pattern, however, and it is likely this reflected a number of factors. Some people may have previously lived inland. Some may have been more pious than others and adhered more strictly to the church's dictates against the consumption of meat on certain days. Some people simply may not have cared for seafood, while others were partial to it.

The pattern of dental pathologies suggests that women took better care of their teeth in some way than men, and that there may have been local practitioners who undertook the pulling of rotten teeth (p120), though it is doubtful they could be termed 'dentists' in the modern sense.

The fluid population of the port town was in evidence in that four out of the six adults analysed were born and brought up outside of Leith (p140), some from at least as far away as Glasgow or North Berwick, and potentially considerably further. The frequent epidemics during this period probably affected Leith badly but the opportunities afforded by the town would have led to an influx of people from the surrounding towns, villages and countryside in the aftermath to fill the vacancies. The town must also have contained a considerable number of Europeans at any given time, including merchants and sailors from England, France, the Rhineland and Baltic ports. A large proportion of the male population would also have made a living as seamen, regularly travelling on trading voyages across the North Sea and Baltic and possibly further afield. They would have brought back stories, ideas, goods, friends and wives.

Low Countries and German influences were evidenced only by the distinctive pottery of these areas (p126–30), which acts as an archaeological tracer for the important North Sea trade in more luxurious (but more perishable) goods from these places. The Baltic, the importance of which is well known historically, was less visible archaeologically, but its influence is perhaps seen in the local joinery tradition of slat-based coffins (p71). There is also evidence for the (often unwelcome) presence of French troops and officials during the mid-16th century, again, largely in the form of discarded sherds of pottery. It is likely that some of these European visitors and residents were unfortunate enough to die in Leith and were then buried in the local cemetery.

As the port and the town grew larger and busier it probably became more dangerous. The incidences of turned ankles, broken bones, falls, and violence were higher in the later graves (p121). While none of these injuries were fatal, they give the impression of an increasingly crowded and busy town, with the buildings more high-rise and the streets more wheel-rutted. With a large sea-faring population it is likely that there was a good measure of shore-based drinking and other pursuits that would have contributed to more accidents and incidents.

Arguably the saddest story told by the bones belonged to Sk0985. She appears to have died from syphilis, probably during the 16th century (p121). Though syphilis may well have had earlier origins, its floruit began at the end of the 15th and early 16th centuries when it spread rapidly throughout Europe, becoming endemic in the post-medieval period. The disease was first identified at the Siege of Naples in 1495. Its first recorded outbreak in Leith appears to have begun in the same year, possibly brought back by Scottish mercenaries, though it was not identified as 'grandgore' (the Scots term for the syphilis) until 1497 (Mowat 2003, 62; DSL). Attempts to curb its spread in Edinburgh and Leith were made by isolating the victims on Inchkeith, an island in the Forth, while attempts were made to cure them (ibid; Hamilton 1981, 18). Several sufferers of syphilis were identified at St Giles Cathedral, though only one was securely dated, dating to the 16th-century (Henderson 2006, 33). The disease was rife among prostitutes and it is likely that the port of Leith had its fair share of these but equally the woman might have been infected by a wayward husband.

Its effect on her life was visible both in terms of the disfigurement she must have suffered and in terms of her diet. She had a very high proportion of marine food in her diet, at least 30% (the highest found at Constitution Street). It is possible that this represented abstinence from meat as a religious penance. Alternatively, if outcast and no longer supported financially or able to support herself, her diet may have involved a high proportion of shellfish collected from the shore for want of any other food. It is intriguing to consider that she might have been one of the patients quarantined on Inchkeith island. The patients there were presumably fed, but they might have supplemented their diet as best they could from the shore. It is not known at what age she died. After her death and burial at St Mary's, her grave was disturbed during the digging of another woman's grave. The gravediggers carefully placed her head in the new grave.

Whatever the details of her life, she died before her time from a horrible disease with disfiguring symptoms which would have made her condition plain, which carried a terrible social and moral stigma and had no cure.

DEATH IN LEITH

The funerary practices observed in Leith were generally within the norm for the period. The demographic patterns in terms of zoning of women and children have been noted in other medieval graveyards. Infants, it seems, were usually buried elsewhere. There may have been a special place for them within or outwith the graveyard. It was speculated that in York infants were buried in the city ramparts or a detached part of the graveyard (p118–19).

It also seems likely that older people were buried elsewhere as, even allowing for a shorter life expectancy among the poorer classes, the lack of people over the age of 45 among the individuals excavated was striking.

It is possible that this was due, at least in part, to the care given to the elderly at St Anthony's, which presumably would have led to them being over-represented in the St Anthony's graveyard (p119), though this is yet to be archaeologically tested there.

The percentage of those buried with coffins was within the range seen elsewhere. There is a suggestion in the data that coffin use was a little more frequent among the wealthier classes (p119–20) and also that it became slightly more common over the course of the 15th to 17th centuries. The evidence of the Phase 4 cemetery extension (p83) suggests that coffin use was the norm in the early 17th century, though it is possible this was not representative of general parish coffin use at the time. If the cemetery was connected to a plague outbreak then coffin use might have been higher there in an attempt to contain infection.

The slat-based coffins are a particular local quirk. It seems likely that this was a cheaper type of coffin, as it used less and possibly recycled planks for the coffin base. It is possible that the idea sprang from across the Baltic via Leith and Edinburgh's timber trade. Their use may have been more widespread than is apparent given the frequent poor wood preservation on cemetery sites of this period, but on present evidence these coffins seem (in Britain) to have been limited to Edinburgh and Leith during the 14th and 15th centuries (p70–71).

There were a relatively large number of multiple burials where two to four people had been buried at the same time (p118–19). These included a relatively high proportion of women and children but could also involve combinations of adults. The burial of children with adults has been observed on an occasional basis at other sites where it has been suggested they relate to a specific rite associated with children, or to family tragedies. The number of multiple graves at Constitution Street, however, was unusual, as were the adult only double burials and the larger group burials. These are rarely seen at other Scottish medieval cemetery excavations with none found in various excavations in Perth, Linlithgow, Aberdeen, Dundee and Edinburgh (Stones 1989b; Mackenzie & Moloney 1997; Brown & Roberts 2000; Collard et al 2006; Wilson in prep). There was a possible example at Holyrood Abbey (Bain 1998, 1054) of a man, woman and child buried in the same long trench, but this appears to be the exception.

It seems likely that many of the multiple burials at Constitution Street relate to times of high mortality, such as plagues and famines. The low numbers of men and the lack of traumatic perimortem injuries suggests warfare was not a factor. Two mass burial trenches were found at the London plague burial ground at East Smithfield, each containing over 100 individuals each (Grainger et al 2008, 13–8), but elsewhere more modest sized mass/

PEOPLE'S STORIES

A MAN WHO LIVED THROUGH INTERESTING TIMES, 1508–1548

This man was born in 1508 to a tenant farmer who rented a plot of land directly to the east of the town across the street from Rotten Row (named for its wooden houses), and as a boy he worked the land with the rest of the family to feed themselves and pay the rent. They kept a cow and bred pigs and geese, grew barley, rye, oats and flax. His mother tended the flax which produced large stands of plants, three feet high, with beautiful purple flowers in the summer. They harvested it in late summer and soaked the stems to loosen the fibres which made them stink of rotting vegetation. The boy had to help his mother beat the stems to break up the fibres, clean and comb them out. His mother then spun them into linen thread and supplied it to the local tailors. It was hard and monotonous work. He also had to help sow and harvest the cereals and vegetables, help with the weeding and tending the animals. He was beaten on one occasion for letting the pigs get into the crops, though it had been the St Anthony's pigs which did the damage. In cold wet years, the cereal harvest was poor and the whole family went hungry.

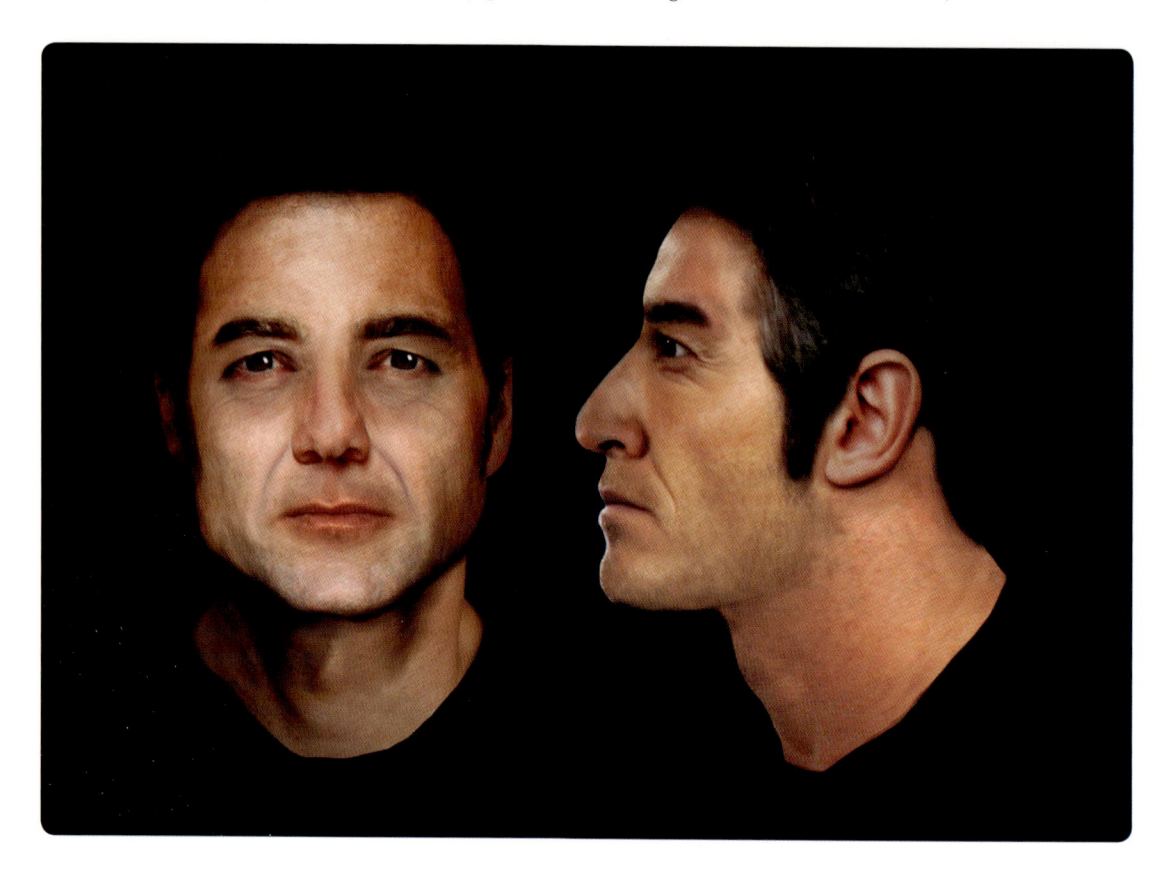

He was lucky enough to be apprenticed to a tailor when he was eight, one of his mother's customers. His new master had a cramped shopfront on Rotten Row, with walls made of planks and a workshop behind. The boy slept in a corner of the workshop at night. He learnt the trade well, learnt to read and write, and became a journeyman tailor. When he got married in 1535 he moved to rented lodgings nearby, though could only afford a single room for his wife and his growing family. Family life was not kind, however, and of his six children, one was stillborn and two died of measles.

One May day in 1544, he was sitting at dinner with his wife and three remaining children when they heard shouts in the street. An English army of thousands was entering the town and had begun to loot anything of value and destroy the rest. Soldiers had begun to cross the bridge into South Leith. They had little enough of value in the house and quickly shut it up and all hid in the cellar. Soldiers broke in anyway, and, disgruntled to find nothing worth stealing, set fire to the building. The man and his family were lucky to escape with their lives. His master the tailor was not so lucky. He was relieved of his precious bolts of cloth and his silver and wine kegs. His only son and his apprentice were both cut down and his wife was raped. His shop was lost to the fire. While helping to pick through the rubble, he was nearly hit by a falling roof beam and in avoiding it, he turned his ankle so badly that it swelled up and he couldn't walk on it for several weeks.

There followed bitter months of hunger and then pestilence the following year found easy pickings among the weakened population of Leith. At the end of this, two of the young tailor's remaining children and his pregnant wife and his master were all dead. His wife had to be buried at the edge of the churchyard on account of the unbaptised soul within her. His health suffered. A toothache became an abscess and he had to have the tooth pulled. His back, already sore from the years spent hunched over his work, became increasingly stiff. Worse still, his eyes became strained from working by candlelight and he could no longer stitch finely. His ankle continued to bother him, especially during cold weather.

The only light in the darkness at the end of this ordeal was the unexpected news that the old tailor had settled the business (what little was left of it) and his precious trade incorporation membership on him. It was a bittersweet day when he took his seat at his first incorporation meeting, sad that his wife was not there to share it. They discussed the latest complaints and threats from the tailor's guild of Edinburgh, that they were undercutting Edinburgh prices, but agreed they were quite happy to continue to do so if it meant more business.

He walked barefoot to the shrine of St Triduana at Restalrig to pray for his vision to be cleared. When it did not work, he took on a journeyman and an apprentice to do the stitching, while he confined himself to designs, client meetings and the ledgers.

Two years after he had inherited it, he had nearly succeeded in getting the tailors shop back on its feet, though had had to borrow heavily to do it. But that September the English army visited again. They brought down the same destruction upon the town and destroyed everything he had rebuilt. Like so many in the town, he and his daughter were reduced for a time to camping out in the ruins of their house. He died that winter of a fever, his daughter by his bedside. He feared for his orphaned daughter, but he took comfort that he would soon see his wife and lost children again in the hereafter. The incorporation paid for his coffin and funeral and for prayers to be said to see him to the next world. All the tailors of Leith turned out for the funeral.

SKELETON	0784
Grave	0785
Location of grave	Constitution Street, Area 8
Burial details	Coffin, possibly clothed?
Age	Older Middle Adult, 35–45
Sex	Male
Stature	162cm or 5'4"
Radiocarbon date	–
Other dating evidence	In Phase 3 cemetery, possibly only in use from c1480s
Finds	Iron eyelet
Pathology	Calculus, caries, abscess, DEH, periodontal disease, antemortem tooth loss, exostosis right fibula (distal), periostitis right first and second proximal foot phalanges, costal and spinal DJD, Schmorl's nodes
C/N isotope (diet)	–
O/S isotope (origins)	–
See also	Illus 4.04, p53; Table 4.19, p111; p113; Table 4.24, p121; p124–25
Facial reconstruction artist	Paloma Galzi

group graves are noted containing 13 individuals (Watson 1990) or five (Poulton et al 1984, 52). In the 17th-century plague cemetery discovered at St Mary's Primary School, Leith, there were several and on a similar scale to those at Constitution Street, containing between four and 14 individuals (Churchill 2016). The multiple burials at Constitution Street were found within the bounds of the Phase 1, Phase 2 and Phase 3 cemeteries though the distribution and radiocarbon dates suggest they were more common during the Phase 1 and Phase 2 cemeteries, from the later 14th to late 15th centuries.

The S-N aligned burials are another local peculiarity, with a surprising 4% of all burials archaeologically excavated in Leith being aligned S-N or N-S (p78–79; **Table 4.01**). Though found on a very occasional basis elsewhere, the frequent use of this rite seems to be limited to Leith (no evidence has been found of such graves in Edinburgh) and there was strong evidence to point towards the rite being linked specifically to plague burials, although not to all plague burials. It may have only been applied to those who were unfortunate enough to die unshriven when there was no priest available, or willing, to administer the last rites. The connection with plague was clear at St Mary's Primary School and there is fair reason to suppose that this was also so at St Mary's Star of the Sea (p35–36). At Constitution Street, there is a certain amount of circumstantial evidence to suggest that plague was a factor in the burial of Sk0481. She was buried in her clothes in a seemingly hurriedly and unevenly dug grave (p79; p122; p124–25). There is nothing particularly distinct about the other two Constitution Street S-N burials, though the fact they were buried one on top of the other suggests they were interred at the same time or one very shortly after the other.

The S-N and N-S burials at St Mary's Primary School and St Mary's Star of the Sea have all been connected to the 1644–5 plague outbreak. The three at Constitution Street are all earlier, probably considerably earlier. Sk0481 is most likely to date between the mid-15th and early 16th century and is almost certainly no later than c 1630. The other dated example, Sk1052, is even earlier, most likely buried between the later 14th century and the early 15th century. Thus, this may have been a long-standing local tradition.

The presence of plague burials within the cemetery is hardly surprising. Between 1380 and mid-17th century there were about 20 epidemics of various diseases, which probably significantly affected Leith's population (p30–32, **Table 3.01**). The number of plague dead at the site is likely to be a great deal more than is apparent from the unusual burials discussed above. Plague kills too quickly to leave a pathological trace in the bones but, given the general lack of other causes of death identifiable among the remains, it is possible that any of the excavated individuals might have died of plague. Even those with specific serious illnesses, such as syphilis, would have been left weakened by their condition and more susceptible to other infections. Plague was often connected to years of poor harvest and famine and thus the higher than average levels of malnutrition might also suggest that many of the people buried at the site were plague victims. Given restrictions on movements of people, goods and corpses during later 15th century and later plague outbreaks, it seems likely that more of Leith's dead would have been buried locally during this time. If burial at Restalrig was still desirable during this period it is unlikely to have been possible under the increasingly heavy restrictions put on the town during the plague years.

5 | LONDON ROAD EXCAVATIONS

Julie Franklin with contributions by Carmelita Troy, Abby Mynett, Sarah-Jane Haston and Kate Britton

Although the Rude Chapel, the Carmelite friary and the Greenside Hospital for Lepers are known to have been located in this area (p37–39), it was believed that they were outside the zone affected by the Tram works. They were thought to be to the south-east of the junction of Leith Walk and London Road, behind the present Baxter's Place and Leopold Place (the names given, respectively, to the east side of Leith Walk and south side of London Road in these locations). As such, service diversion works at the junction of London Road and Leith Walk were not initially identified as being archaeologically sensitive and therefore subject only to archaeological call-out.

The discovery of human remains in July 2009 was, therefore, unexpected. The diversion of water mains under the road at the junction involved the excavation of a number of interconnected trenches, Trenches 1–7 (**Illus 5.01**), and in one of these, Trench 4, articulated human remains were found. The police were informed and the archaeological call-out was enacted. When it became apparent that the remains in question were archaeological in nature, a programme of archaeological mitigation was agreed. This aimed to keep any disturbance of the human remains to a minimum, protecting them and leaving them in situ where possible. Only those remains directly affected by the works were excavated and recorded. Monitoring was required for all further works in the area. Unfortunately, an episode of unmonitored machine excavation undertaken by the contractor resulted in the disturbance of further human remains in Trench 7.

The remains of ten articulated skeletons were found in eight graves within Trenches 4 and 7, at a depth of 1.5–1.6m below the modern road surface (**Illus 5.02**). One skeleton (Sk469/Gr470) was complete whilst the others all suffered from variable degrees of disturbance, either from the insertion of modern services or by the on-going groundworks prior to the intervention of archaeologists. Several wall fragments were also discovered which related to the use of the cemetery and to the later Hill Side House whose grounds encompassed this part of the site in the 18th and early 19th century. The cemetery soil, burials and wall foundations were sealed by a deposit rich in lime mortar. A handful of finds within this deposit suggest a date of around the 18th century. This appears to relate to wall demolition and gardening within the grounds of the house.

Radiocarbon dating was obtained from three skeletons. The three dates were potentially all contemporary, ranging from 1455–1640 to 1475–1670 (**Table 5.01**). The range of dates covers the historical dating of the 15th-century Rude Chapel, the 16th-century Carmelite friary and the late 16th- to mid-17th-century Greenside Hospital for Lepers.

Osteological analysis recovered evidence of poor nutrition and poor dental health but not of leprosy. Isotope analysis was undertaken on the bones of three of the individuals to establish the marine/terrestrial components of their diet. Facial reconstructions were undertaken on two of the skulls (p12–13).

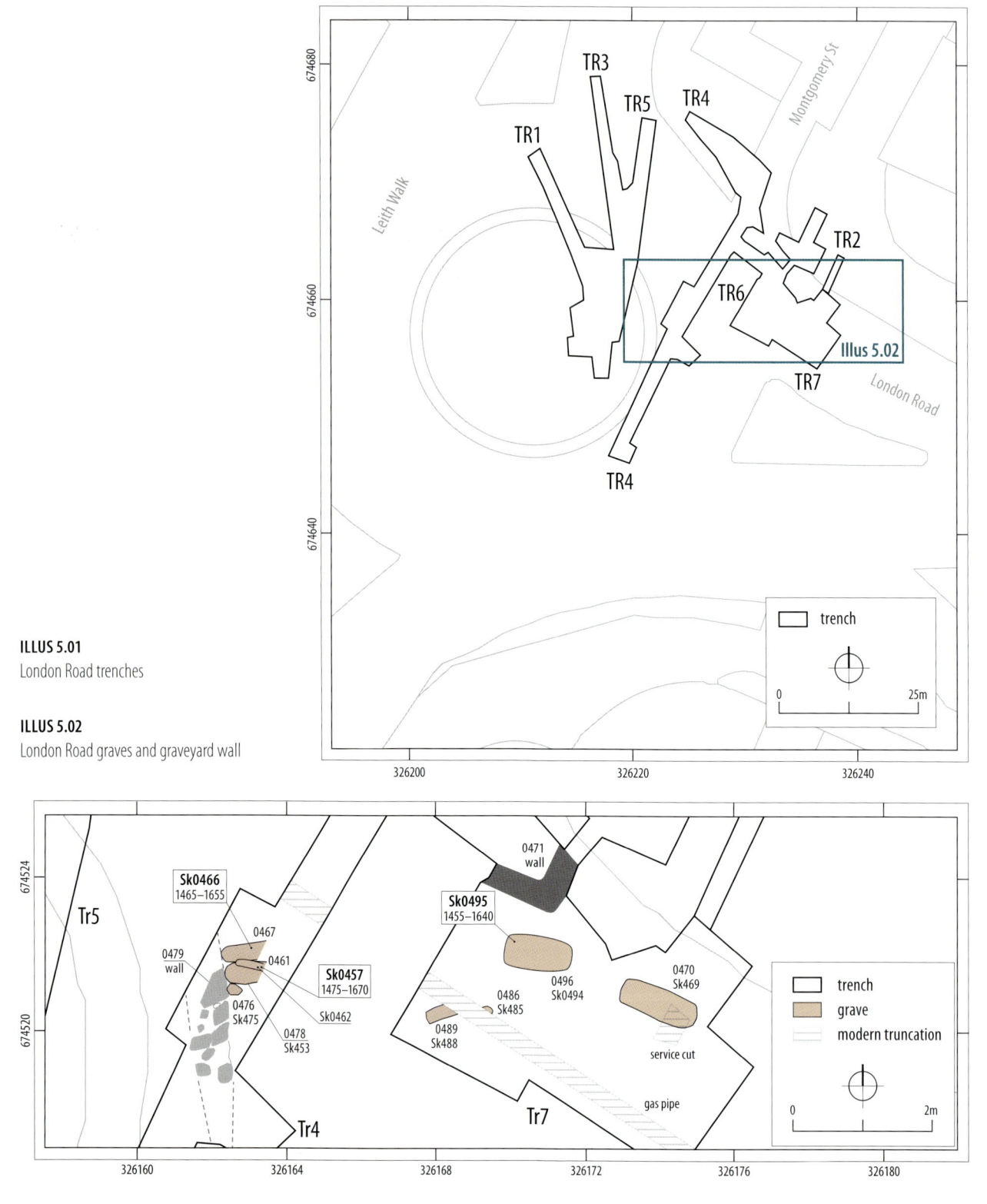

ILLUS 5.01
London Road trenches

ILLUS 5.02
London Road graves and graveyard wall

LONDON ROAD: THE BURIALS

The eight graves were all cut into a fine yellow sandy cemetery soil deposit which contained sherds of medieval and early post-medieval pottery. The similarity of the grave fills to surrounding deposits meant that it was not possible to identify the grave cuts. There were no coffin wood remains, wood staining in the ground, finds of coffin nails or any other evidence that any of the bodies had been buried in coffins. Most of the graves were truncated to varying degrees. Six of the graves contained a single skeleton, the two others were double burials containing two individuals interred at the same time. Thus, the remains of ten individuals were recovered. The articulated remains were spread between two trenches (Trenches 4 and 7). A table summarising all the osteological and burial data is given in *Appendix 2* (**Table A2.02**, p233).

THE TRENCH 4 BURIALS

The tightest cluster of burials was in Trench 4, four graves containing five individuals. Stratigraphically, the earliest of these comprised three single inhumation burials in a neat row, at the same depth against the east side of N-S wall [479] (**Illus 5.03**). The skeletons were a neonate (Sk475/Gr476, 1½ months old), a younger middle adult female (Sk453/Gr478) and a young adult male (Sk466/Gr467) (for definitions of osteological age groups see **Table 5.02**).

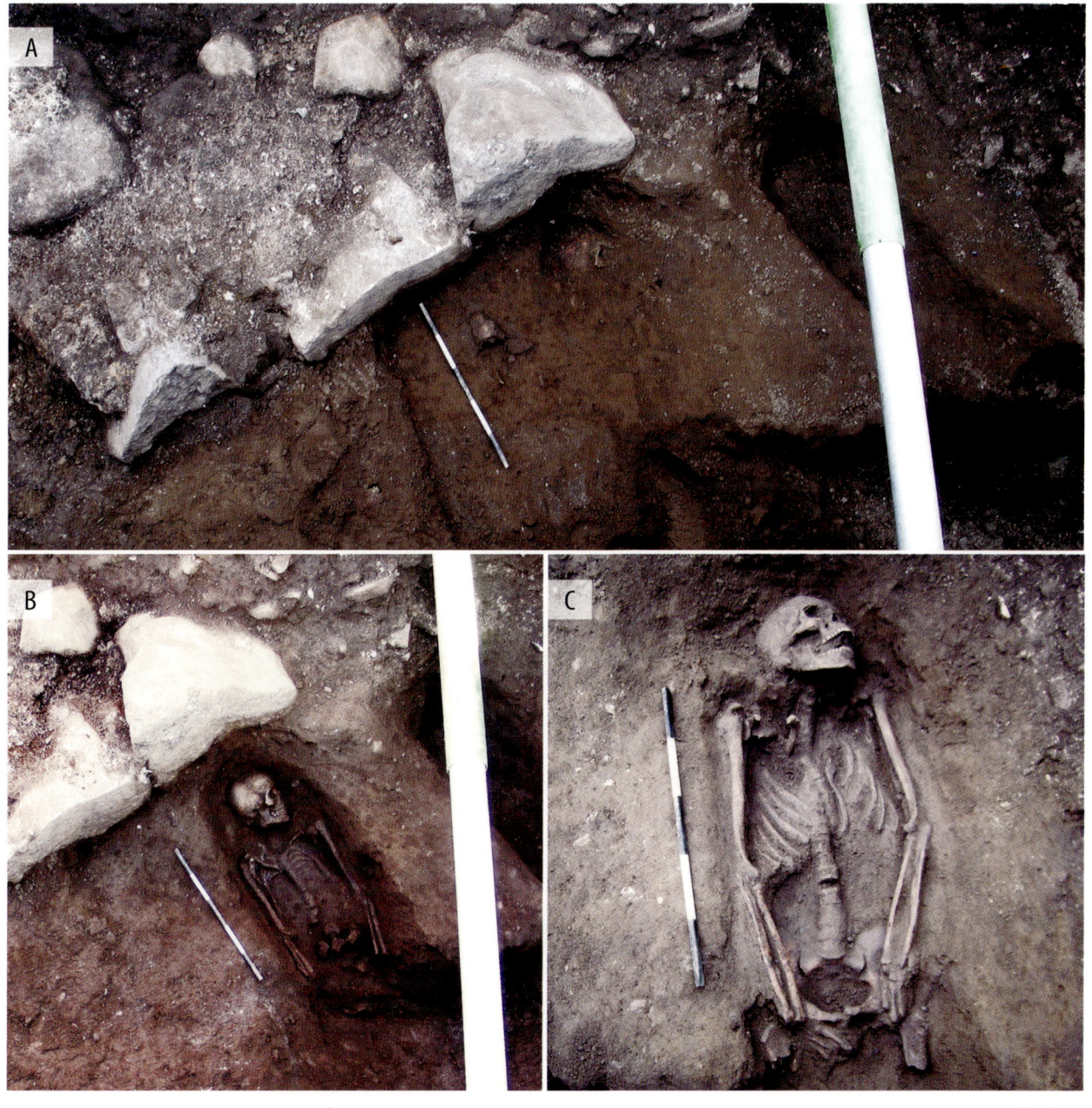

ILLUS 5.03
Graves and graveyard wall [479], Trench 4: A. Sk475 remains and excavated empty graves; B. Sk453; C. Sk466

ILLUS 5.04
Double burial (father and child?), Gr461: Sk457, younger middle adult male; Sk462, neonate

The neonate (Sk475) was in a poor condition with only skull fragments and ribs remaining. It appeared to have been disturbed, with many ribs displaced. The lower ends of Sk453 and Sk466 had been truncated by the service diversion trench before they could be recorded, at a point below the thoracic vertebrae and pelvis, respectively. Sk466 was radiocarbon dated to 1465–1655 (**Table 5.01**).

About 0.25m above the two northernmost of these burials was a double burial, Gr461, containing younger middle adult male Sk457 and neonate Sk462 (1½ months old). The skull and ribs of the baby were lying on the chest area of the adult (**Illus 5.04**). Again, the lower part of the adult skeleton had been truncated below the hips by the service diversion trench. The adult skeleton was radiocarbon dated to 1475–1670 (**Table 5.01**), the latest of the three dated burials.

THE TRENCH 7 BURIALS

Five further burials were recorded in Trench 7, about 6m to the east of those in Trench 4. The burials were more widely spaced with no observable stratigraphy and two were heavily truncated by modern service cuts. The most distinctive of this group was Gr496, which contained two adult women, a younger middle adult, Sk494, and a young adult, Sk495 (**Illus 5.05**). The former was badly truncated below the ribs by a service trench. Both women appeared

ILLUS 5.05
Double burial, Gr496: left Sk494, younger middle adult female; right Sk495, young adult female

to have their arms crossed over their chest or waist, but for the left arm of Sk494 which was placed over the chest of the other woman; both had their heads turned facing each other. Sk495 was radiocarbon dated to 1455–1640 (**Table 5.01**), the earliest of the three dates from this site, though still possibly contemporary with the dated burials from Trench 4.

The remaining burials were all single adult inhumations. Sk469/Gr470, a younger middle adult female, was virtually complete, while Sk485/Gr486, an adult male, and Sk488/Gr489, a younger middle adult female, were both heavily truncated by a later gas pipe. Only the lower legs of Sk485 survived, while the pelvis, lower vertebrae and part of the arms were all that remained of Sk488.

Further disarticulated human remains were found to the north of Trench 7, in Trench 2, which might suggest the cemetery at some point extended further north. Equally, however, these might have been disturbed and redeposited elsewhere during later building works.

TABLE 5.01
London Road radiocarbon dates listed in chronological order. Note: all the calibrated dates are cal AD; the maine component percentage is calculated from the $\delta^{13}C$ value (p12)

TRENCH	SKELETON	GRAVE	BURIAL DETAILS	LAB CODE	UNCALIBRATED BP	$\delta^{13}C‰$	MARINE %	CALIBRATED 95.4% PROBABILITY	CALIBRATED 68.2% PROBABILITY	AGE	SEX
7	495	496	Double, no coffin	SUERC–38415	410 ± 30	−19.6	16%	1455–1640	1475–1525 1558–1630	YA	F
4	466	467	No coffin	SUERC–38414	445 ± 30	−18.1	34%	1465–1655	1516–1635	YA	M
4	457	461	Double, no coffin	SUERC–38413	355 ± 30	−19.6	16%	1475–1670	1521–1597 1617–1649	YMA	M

ALIGNMENT

The graves were all aligned approximately W-E in keeping with the usual tradition in this period (Gilchrist & Sloane 2005, 152). Those in Trench 4 were closer to true W-E. Those in Trench 7 were closer to WNW-ESE. This might suggest the two areas were in use at different times, with gravediggers aligning the graves using different contemporary landmarks.

BODY POSITION

All the skeletons were supine, with arms placed by the sides or crossed over the waist or chest. Though arm position could only be reconstructed in six of the burials, it is interesting to note that all those in Trench 4 were placed by the sides of the body, and those in Trench 7 were typically crossed over the waist or chest.

The positioning of heads and arms of the two women in Gr496, Trench 7, suggests a degree of intimacy (**Illus 5.05**), though caution should be used when interpreting body position as a certain amount of post-depositional movement would have occurred during decomposition (Gilchrist & Sloane 2005, 151). The arm position of Sk494 indicates that this body, at least, was probably placed in the grave without a shroud. This and the single grave cut for two adults might suggest the burial was hurried, during a time of high mortality, and the body positions may therefore have been incidental.

Too little remained of the neonate in Gr461, Trench 4, to establish the positioning of its body, except to say it was placed over the chest of the man in the same grave (**Illus 5.04**). The burial of children with adults or other children is a relatively common phenomenon during this period (Gilchrist & Sloane 2005, 156–7). Five such adult-child burials were found at Constitution Street (p71–72) and in two of these the child lay prone over the torso of the adult.

DATING OF THE BURIALS

The dates for the three dated burials were closely spaced, though all have a broad range, the earliest being 1455–1640, the latest, 1475–1670 (**Table 5.01**; **Illus 5.06**). Thus, all could have been buried between the late 15th and mid-17th centuries. This means that all could be associated with any one of the three establishments associated with this area: the chapel possibly established in the mid-15th century; the friary founded around 1520 and probably abandoned before 1560; or the leper hospital founded in 1591 and demolished in the 1650s (p37–39).

Interestingly, if the dates are viewed at 68% probability then the one dated burial in Trench 7 is most likely to date to either the chapel or the leper hospital, while the two in Trench 4 are most likely to date to either the friary or leper hospital. However, there is not enough evidence to determine whether the remains found represent part of the graveyard of just one of these establishments, or two or all three of them.

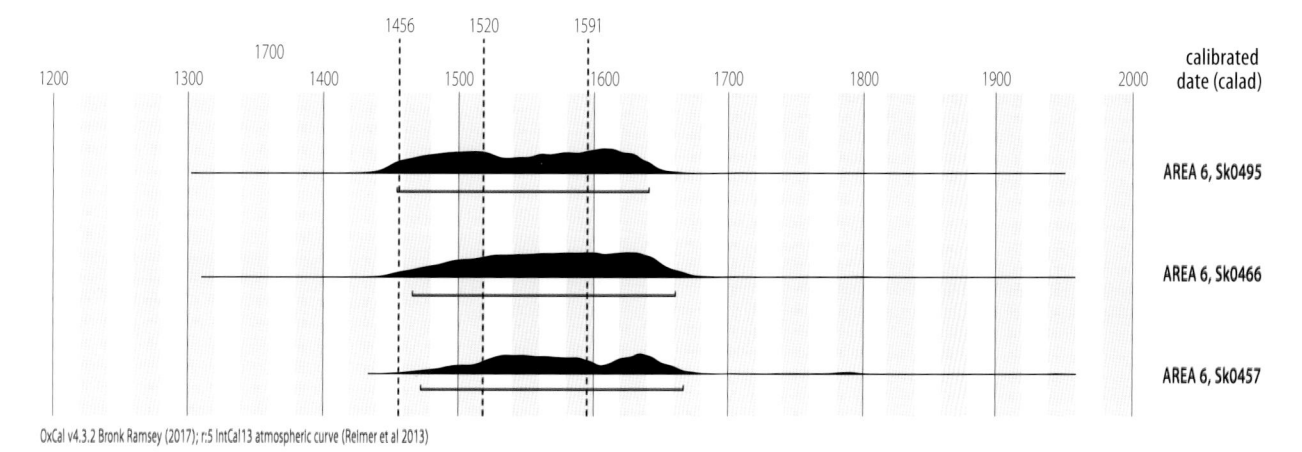

ILLUS 5.06
London Road radiocarbon date ranges, showing relationship to historical dates relating to the chapel (1456), friary (1520) and leper hospital (1591)

LONDON ROAD: THE WALLS

The remains of three walls were found in Trenches 4 and 7. Wall [479] ran approximately N-S on the western side of Trench 4, directly to the west of the row of three graves (Sk475/Gr476, Sk453/Gr478, Sk466/Gr467) (**Illus 5.02–5.03**). Only the lowest course of the wall foundations survived. It was 1.1m wide, mortar-bonded, and roughly faced with a rubble core. The foundations were at a similar depth to the burials and the sand deposits to the west of the wall were visibly much cleaner than those to the east. The latter contained frequent fragments of disarticulated human bone and clearly represented cemetery soil. This and the wall's neat relationship to the graves indicates it formed the western boundary wall of the cemetery.

A later wall [459] (not illus) overlay both the Trench 4 burials and wall [479]. It was on a different alignment, more SSW-NNE, closer to the alignment of the road. Again, only the lowest course survived. It was 0.6m wide and it too was rubble-built and mortar-bonded. The stratigraphy and alignment suggest that this wall post-dates the use of the cemetery and probably post-dates the mid-17th century demolition of the leper hospital. It is likely to relate to a property boundary of Hill Side House along the roadside, as shown on 18th- and early 19th-century maps (**Illus 3.08**, p38; Kirkwood 1817a).

To the east of this, in Trench 7, to the north of the burials there, the scant remains of another wall [471] were found. The remains amounted to a construction cut containing three large, possibly granite boulders and a spread of lime mortar. It was aligned approximately WNW-ESE, making it perpendicular to the later of the two walls, [459], in Trench 4, and approximately parallel to the burials in this area. Its foundations were at a similar level to the graves and to earlier wall [479] in Trench 4. Finds of glass and brick associated with the wall suggest an 18th-century or later date, though these are more likely to relate to the destruction of the wall rather than its construction. This is the most enigmatic of the walls and it is not clear whether it is another cemetery boundary wall or is a wall or garden feature related to the later gardens. Its alignment and depth point towards it being contemporary with the earlier wall in Trench 4, and with the graves in Trench 7, which would argue for the former. However, the alignment might also suggest it was contemporary with the later wall in Trench 4, which, as just discussed, has been linked to the later grounds of Hill Side House.

LONDON ROAD: THE HUMAN REMAINS

Carmelita Troy

The assemblage comprised 10 inhumation burials in varying degrees of completeness. All were subjected to osteological analysis to determine age at death, sex and any traces of health issues, diseases, and injuries. The low number of individuals preclude any detailed statistical analysis. Instead attention is drawn to the more notable elements of the osteological assemblage. Details of the methodology, definitions of terminology and further information about the causes and effects of the pathologies noted can be found above (see *Constitution Street: The Human Remains*, p91–122). A complete catalogue of the skeletal remains is included in *Appendix 2* (**Table A2.02**, p233). Preservation was good for the majority (6/10), the others being moderate (1/10) or poor (3/10). In terms of completeness, half the skeletons (5/10) were 75% of more complete and a number were less than 25% (4/10), due to later truncation.

AGE, SEX AND STATURE

Half the individuals were younger middle adults, with others being young adults and two neonates. Of the adults, five were female and three male (**Table 5.02**). Stature could be determined for six of the adults, four females and two males. The females ranged from 151.8cm to 157.8cm with an average of 154.8 cm. The males were 163.8cm and 168.2cm, with an average of 166.0cm. Both are below the late medieval average (**Table 4.06**, p94).

DENTAL HEALTH AND DISEASE

A total of 128 permanent teeth were recorded from six adult individuals, and five deciduous teeth from one neonate. The usual signs of poor dental health common to this period were noted. All six adults displayed calculus (Roberts and Manchester 2010), affecting 82% of the teeth (105/128). All six displayed moderate to severe periodontal disease (Hillson 2005, 306) at a rate of 39.5% of affected

TABLE 5.02
Osteological age categories with numbers of individuals recovered from London Road

AGE CATEGORY	AGE RANGE	MALE	FEMALE	UNSEXED	TOTAL
Neonate (NEO)	Birth – 2 months	–	–	2	2
Total subadults		–	–	2	2
Younger adult (YA)	18 – 25 years	1	1	–	2
Younger middle adult (YMA)	25 – 35 years	1	4	–	5
Adult (AD)	Over 18 years	1	–	–	1
Total adults		3	5	–	8
TOTAL		**3**	**5**	**2**	**10**

teeth (49/124). Periodontal disease was particularly severe on Sk453/Gr478, a younger-middle adult female with 73.1% of the bone affected (19/26). Half had carious lesions (Mays 1998, 148; Hillson 2005, 293) as well affecting 2.3% of teeth (3/128), all on a second molar. One younger middle adult male, Sk457/Gr461, also had a case of ante-mortem tooth loss, in the upper right, second molar. Young adult female Sk495/Gr496 would have been caused some discomfort by an impacted (Aktan et al 2010) upper right canine. There were two cases of dental enamel hypoplasia (Mays 1998; Hillson 2005) in young adult male Sk466/Gr467 and younger middle adult female Sk469/Gr470, indicating episodes of nutritional or physical stress during childhood.

JOINT DISEASES AND CONDITIONS

There was one case of vertebral osteophytosis, where new bone grows forming projections from the vertebral bodies, probably caused by bone or ligament damage (White et al 2012, 441). This was the lower thoracic vertebrae of Sk469/Gr470, a younger middle adult female (**Illus 5.07**).

Osteoarthritis was also noted on the costovertebral joint of the first thoracic vertebra of younger middle adult female, Sk494/Gr496 (**Illus 5.08**). The joint exhibited erosion, osteophyte development and eburnation on both and would have caused the woman some degree of pain and discomfort.

Schmorl's nodes were noted on five out of seven spines, two male and three female (Sk457/Gr461, Sk466/Gr467, Sk488/Gr489, Sk494/Gr496, Sk495/Gr496). They suggest these individuals were introduced to heavy manual work at a young age (Schmorl and Junghanns 1971). Sk457/Gr461, a younger middle adult male, also displayed bilateral spondylolysis of the fifth lumbar vertebra. This condition would have been caused by a defect or stress fracture to the vertebrae due to repeated hyperextension or rotation of the spine. It would have caused lower back pain. Three out of four observable individuals also had

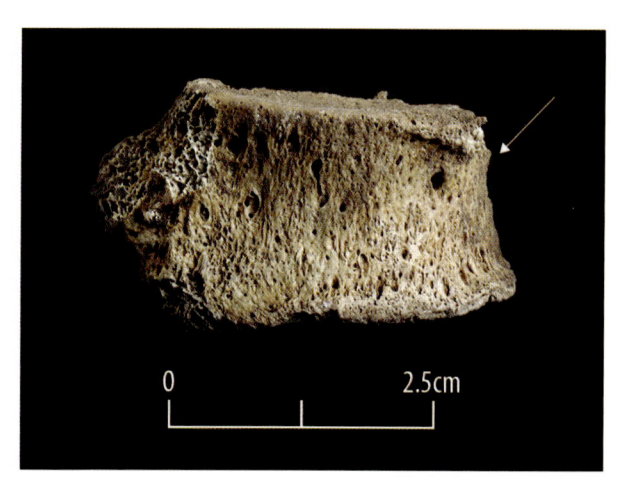

ILLUS 5.07
Osteophytic lipping on thoracic vertebra, Sk469/Gr470, younger middle adult female

ILLUS 5.08
Osteoarthritis on vertebra and rib, Sk494/Gr496, younger middle adult female

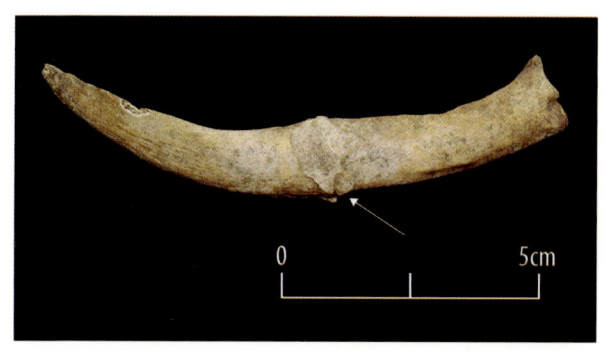

ILLUS 5.09
Healed fracture of 12th rib, Sk457/Gr461, younger middle adult male

squatting facets at their ankle joints implying they spent prolonged periods of time squatting.

METABOLIC DISEASES

There were two cases of porotic hyperostosis (Walker et al 2009), pitting of the cranial vault caused by deficient diet and general poor health. Both were young adults, female Sk495/Gr496 and male Sk466/Gr467. In the latter, the condition was severe and combined with dental enamel hypoplasia, suggesting his diet, living conditions or health were very poor.

INFECTIONS

There were two cases of periostitis, the inflammation of membrane that surrounds the bone. Sk495/Gr496, young adult female, had a healed periostitis on both tibiae, a common place for the condition, the shin bones being close to the surface and prone to injury. Sk469/Gr470, younger middle adult female, displayed reactive new bone on the left maxilla. This was probably as a result of a local infection in the upper mouth.

TRAUMA

Sk457/Gr461, a younger middle adult male, had a healed fracture of the right 12th rib (**Illus 5.09**), probably caused by a fall or interpersonal violence.

OSTEOLOGICAL DISCUSSION

Julie Franklin and Carmelita Troy

The human remains from London Road are typical of this period (15th to 17th century) in terms of their general health. All the adults were below average height for the time (**Table 4.06**, p94). Poor nutrition (or poor health) was particularly evident in young adult male Sk466/Gr467 with severe porotic hyperostosis as well as dental enamel hypoplasia. Poor teeth were also evident on younger middle adult male Sk457/Gr461, with both caries and tooth loss. In addition, Sk457 sustained a broken rib at some point during his life.

Conspicuous by its absence was any trace of leprosy, when all of the skeletons could potentially date to the period of the leper hospital. Leprosy, or Hansen's disease as it is now medically known, is a chronic highly infectious disease caused by the bacterium Mycobacterium leprae. It eats away at the bone, particularly of the face, and can cause loss of function and feeling in the extremities (Roberts & Cox 2003, 267–8). Afflicted individuals can live for many years with relentlessly progressive deformity, skeletal disruption and ill health. Ascending infection from damaged feet can cause other infections of the legs (ibid, 268) and thus it is possible that the periostitis of both lower legs of Sk495/Gr496 had its root cause in leprosy. However, this is an area commonly affected by periostitis and the skeleton was well preserved and nearly complete and showed no other traces of the disease.

It does not necessarily follow that all those buried within the graveyard of a leper hospital will show pathological signs of the disease. Prevalence within populations from such graveyards varies from 2% to 75% (Gilchrist & Sloane 2005, 211). While some lepers may have succumbed to the disease (or other causes of death) before leprosy affected their bones, it also reflects the fact that not everyone who resided in leper hospitals had leprosy. The disease could be misdiagnosed during the medieval period and confused with skin conditions such as eczema. Leper hospitals also provide refuge for various other types of social outcast, poor and desperate people who had nowhere else to go. It has recently been speculated that the relatively high numbers of women and children in leper hospital graveyards were due to the fact that they provided refuge for unmarried pregnant women (ibid, 206–7).

LONDON ROAD: THE FINDS

Julie Franklin

The finds amounted to a small collection of metal fittings, which are clearly associated with the burials, and a small collection of residual finds, including a few sherds of medieval pottery.

EYELETS, PIN AND LACE TAG

The most common of the metal finds were eyelets made from twisted wire. Four were found, all in Trench 7, all made of iron. Two iron wire eyelets were also found at Constitution Street, of similar dimensions (12–13mm, cf, **Illus 4.64B**, p124). Only one of the London Road finds was recovered from a grave, in the double burial of Sk494 and Sk495, Gr496, dating to between the mid-15th and mid-17th century (**Table 5.01**). From the same grave there was also a wire hook (**Illus 5.10**) probably used in conjunction with the eyelet to fasten clothing. Interestingly, the position of the arms of Sk494 implies it was not secured in a shroud (p159). The finds were found in the grave fill with no direct association with the skeleton and so it is possible that these objects are residual. However, the association of both hook and eye in the same grave and the relative delicacy of the finds suggests an association with these burials is more likely. It is possible, therefore, that at least one of these women was buried wearing regular clothing. Clothed burials have been identified at other contemporary sites, though they are generally in the minority (Gilchrist & Sloane 2005, 80; 83–4). The practice seems to be linked to two different factors: status, where wealthier people wished to be buried in their finery; and periods of plague, where burials were more hurried. Several such burials were identified at Constitution Street (p125). The other eyelets in this area may have been displaced from the same grave or from other clothed burials in the general area.

A copper alloy wire pin associated with Sk457/Gr461 had a more definite association with the skeleton, being found close to the skull, and it is possible that this secured a shroud. A copper alloy lace tag was associated with the neonate burial Sk462 in the same grave, though it is less clear whether this was in situ or residual. This double burial was dated to between the late 15th and mid-17th century (**Table 5.01**). Pins are regularly found in graves of this period. It is thought that they were used to hold the shroud in place while it was being stitched and occasionally one or two were missed when they were removed at the end (Gilchrist & Sloane 2005, 110). Lace tags were commonly used to bind the ends of laces used in clothing of the period, but it is unclear whether they also had a specifically funerary purpose, or if their regular presence in graves is indicative of clothed burials.

POTTERY

The other finds provided dating evidence for various features though finds were generally so few that this was rarely reliable. However, the pottery does provide tentative evidence of a difference in dating between the activity in Trench 4 and that in Trench 7. An assemblage of nine sherds of medieval pottery was recovered from the graveyard soil in Trench 7 with no associated later sherds. The finds themselves were unremarkable, small sherds of locally made Scottish white gritty and medieval redware vessels (Jones et al 2003; Haggarty et al 2011), but they indicate there was some sort of domestic or agricultural activity in the general area during the 14th and/or 15th centuries. No medieval pottery was found in Trench 4. The only sherd from the graveyard soil was of post-medieval reduced ware (Haggarty et al 2011) probably dating to the 16th century. This supports the theory, tentatively suggested by the radiocarbon dates (p159), that the burials in Trench 7 are earlier than those in Trench 4.

ILLUS 5.10
Wire hook, iron, Sk494/Sk495/Gr496

LONDON ROAD: THE ENVIRONMENTAL EVIDENCE

Abby Mynett and Sarah-Jane Haston

There was little palaeoenvironmental material recovered from the site. A few charred oat grains were identified from a sample of the cemetery soil. There were also quantities of animal and fish bone recovered.

LONDON ROAD: ISOTOPE ANALYSIS OF BONE COLLAGEN

Kate Britton

Carbon and nitrogen isotope analysis of human bone collagen was undertaken on three individuals from London Road (those that were radiocarbon dated; Sk457, Sk466, Sk495). The sample was too small to explore diachronic dietary hetero/homogeneity over time, but, given the similarity in dates between the individuals sampled and those from Constitution Street, the dietary variability observed can be compared with the Constitution Street results and considered a feature of this local population at that period.

Details of the theory and methodology behind this study are given elsewhere (see p131–34 and *Appendix 1*). The data are given in diagrammatic form (**Illus 4.68**) and shown in detail in *Appendix 1* (**Table A1.02**, p217). Sk457 (younger middle adult male) and Sk495/Gr496 (young adult female) exhibited isotopic values typical of the population as a whole. They indicate that diet was mostly based on terrestrial resources, albeit with evidence of the fairly regular contribution of marine protein to the diet.

Young adult male Sk466/Gr467, however, was a clear outlier, exhibiting similar results to Constitution Street's syphilis victim, Sk0985/Gr0988 (p134). Sk466/Gr467 was remarkable in his elevated $\delta^{13}C$ and $\delta^{15}N$ values. He also had a suite of pathological features suggesting a nutritionally inadequate diet (p161–62), poor sanitation and infectious disease, including calculus and periodontal disease, dental enamel hypoplasia, and porotic hyperostosis. Malnourishment alone is unlikely to have affected the results in this way (p134) and so the data do suggest a considerable contribution (perhaps more than 30%) of marine protein to the diet of this individual.

LONDON ROAD: DISCUSSION

The discovery of burials at this location was unexpected and has provided the first archaeological evidence for the location of the successive establishments of the Rude Chapel, Carmelite friary and Greenside Hospital for Lepers. They were known to have been in this approximate location from the 15th to mid-17th century, but were thought to have been a little further south-east (**Illus 3.01**, p23; **Illus 3.09**, p39). No structural remains were discovered to locate the buildings of any of these establishments precisely and as such their exact locations still remain unknown. The excavations have, nevertheless, provided valuable information regarding the history of the site. While it may be supposed that the three establishments shared the same graveyard, there is no definitive proof that the excavated burials relate to all three. The radiocarbon dating evidence is ambiguous, but the excavation results seem to point towards only two distinct phases of burial.

The balance of evidence suggests that the graves in the Trench 7 represent an earlier phase of burial than those in Trench 4. The difference in burial density and alignment might indicate these bodies were interred at different times and the variation in arm positions of the skeletons in the two trenches might also be suggestive of divergent dates. There is also a difference in the radiocarbon dates (especially when quoted at 68% probability; see **Table 5.01**) and in the dating of finds from the cemetery soil in each trench. While none of these factors is significant in itself, when combined they provide a tentative suggestion that the burials in Trench 7 are earlier than those in Trench 4. The dates suggest that those in Trench 7 are most likely to relate to the 15th century Rude Chapel while those in Trench 4 are most likely to relate to the 16th century friary. The archaeology in these two trenches has therefore been considered separately, beginning with the potentially earlier Trench 7 burials.

The burials in Trench 7 were all of adults, mostly women (four women, one man). The lack of children might suggest the latter were buried elsewhere at this point. Two of these women were buried in the same grave, and at least one of these appears to have been dressed in regular clothing (p162–63). It is unclear whether the manner of their burial is indicative of their being of higher status or else their being buried at a time of high mortality. The lower density of graves in this area might suggest that burial was more sporadic at this time. There is no evidence to support Harris's suggestion (Harris 2002, 289) that the Rude Chapel served the needs of those who died during tournaments. This might be illustrated by the presence of burials of well-built men suffering serious perimortem injuries, but no such individuals were found. The chapel graveyard may have been used by the local communities in the nearby villages of Broughton or Canonmills (both now subsumed into northern Edinburgh), or have been the burial place of benefactors to the chapel.

In Trench 4 the burials were more tightly packed. The wall remains associated with them clearly represent the western boundary wall of the cemetery at this point. It probably formed the graveyard boundary along the edge of the road from Edinburgh to Leith, the future Leith Walk. The individuals interred in this area were demographically mixed: two men, one woman and two babies. Such mixed cemetery populations are typical of friary graveyards, where the houses provided a pastoral function to nearby communities (Gilchrist and Sloane 2005, 204). While men typically outnumber women in friary graveyards by at least 2 to 1, the numbers of women and children within them indicate that they also provided a burial service for the lay community. Excavations within the graveyards of other Carmelite friaries in Scotland, at Aberdeen, Linlithgow and Perth, certainly supports this assertion (Cross & Bruce 1989, 123–4). Linlithgow and Aberdeen contained similarly mixed populations of men, women and children. Perth was also mixed in terms of sex, though no subadults were found there.

The positioning of the baby and man in double burial Gr461 might suggest a familial relationship, possibly representing a family tragedy related to infectious disease (p158). The burial of infants along boundary walls has been noted in other graveyards (Gilchrist & Sloane 2005, 223) and it is interesting that both babies (Sk462, Sk475) were found in this location.

Sk466 was the most interesting of the burials in this area from an osteological point of view. He showed signs of severe malnutrition (p161–62), and a very high proportion of what he did eat was marine rather than land-based, this providing over 30% of his protein. He did not live past 20. The only other individual found during this project with a similarly high marine component to their diet was a woman excavated at Constitution Street who is known to have suffered from advanced syphilis (Sk0985; p134). There it was speculated that her diet was the result of extreme poverty or religious penance. There was no trace of any specific disease present in Sk466, though many diseases would not leave evidence in the bones and, given his obvious poor general health and young death, it is distinctly possible that he suffered from a serious disease. However, similar levels (c30%) of marine diet have been found in isotope analysis of skeletons from two religious houses, the Augustinian friary in Hull (Holst et al in prep) and at the Gilbertine priory in York (Mays 1997). This raises the distinct possibility that the man was a friar, though clearly one who suffered a poor childhood diet or general ill health. If this is so, then it implies there was no segregation in the friary graveyard between the friars and lay population.

The possibility still remains that any or all of the burials might relate to the re-use of the friary site as a leper hospital in the late 16th and early 17th centuries. The lack of clear pathological evidence for the presence of leprosy is no barrier to this (p162). By the time the Greenside Hospital was founded, leprosy was in decline in Britain. In England it was rare by the 15th century and non-existent in the 16th century (Roberts & Manchester 2010, 204). Reasons for this decline are still under discussion, though it has been linked to the rise of urbanisation and tuberculosis. In Scandinavia, the disease persisted longer, and this seems likely to have been true of Scotland too, given that there was still felt to be a need for a hospital in 1591 when Greenside was founded.

However, leprosy would have been increasingly rare over the period of the hospital's existence and therefore the hospital population may never have been large, or it may have had a role in housing those with other infectious diseases or socially stigmatising problems (Robert & Manchester 2010, 204).

A YOUNG CARMELITE FRIAR, 1525–1544

This young man was born in 1526. His father was a miller in the village of Canonmills, between Edinburgh and Leith, where watermills lined the Water of Leith. The miller was a devout man who had married a local tenant farmer's daughter a few years previously at the new friary church at Greenside. He and other local men had helped the friars rebuild their house in 1530 after it had been pulled down by officials from Holyrood Abbey. The boy was the fourth of five children and was always delicate and sensitive.

When he was nine his father took him and his brothers to see the heretics Norman Gurley and David Straton burn at the stake. Gurley was a priest who had said there was no such thing as purgatory and claimed the pope was the antichrist and had no jurisdiction in Scotland. Straton was a fisherman near Montrose who claimed that the tribulations of this world were the only purgatory and had allegedly refused to pay his tithe fish to the church, having flung them at the vicar and some of them having fallen into the sea. The pair refused to recant and were burnt at Greenside in the hope that the hillside location would make the flames visible far and wide to deter others from such thoughts. The miller thought the sight would impress upon his children the need for godliness. His father found a grim satisfaction in the spectacle, explaining to his sons that the fire was cleansing the men's souls. The boy found it terrifying, the men screaming as their skin blistered and turned black.

He was often ill as a child and grew familiar with the Whitefriars from Greenside who would call by with tonics and advice for his mother about prayer and his avoiding meat and other rich foods. As he grew older, he would ask the friars questions about heaven, hell, purgatory, God's purpose, heretics and what happened to the souls of the dammed. When he was 16 he asked if he might join their house. Their life, he thought, seemed much more interesting than one of grinding flour.

He joined the house as a postulant, living with the brothers, sharing their modest diet of fish, bread, boiled kale, beans, turnip and water and sharing their work. After a year, he was initiated as a novice and began training and study in earnest. He found studying hard and was still physically frail, but he was happy with his new brothers. He would accompany them on their travels to Edinburgh, Leith and the surrounding villages to collect alms, tend the sick and dying, and to preach the true faith, in an attempt to stem the growing tide of heresy spouted by men such as Patrick Hamilton and George Wishart.

When the boy was 19, in 1544, he was approaching the end of his novitiate and looking forward to taking his vows. But on Sunday 4th May word reached the friary from those arriving for mass at the church that English soldiers had landed in Granton and were marching towards Leith. The brothers preached a fiery sermon against the heretical English who had abandoned the church of Rome a few years previously and brought great destruction on their own monasteries and friaries. When the congregation emerged from the church, they could see the smoke rising from buildings in Leith and they hurried home to safeguard their homes and possessions in Broughton, Canonmills and Inverleith as best they could.

There were, at that time, seven friars staying at Greenside, including our young novice. Three of the brothers had fled from England some years earlier. Seeing the flames take hold in Leith, they began to pack. Having witnessed first-hand the destruction that soldiers could wreak on a religious house, they had no wish to see it again.

The following Tuesday, May 6th, an army of 10,000 men, horses and heavy artillery marched up the road

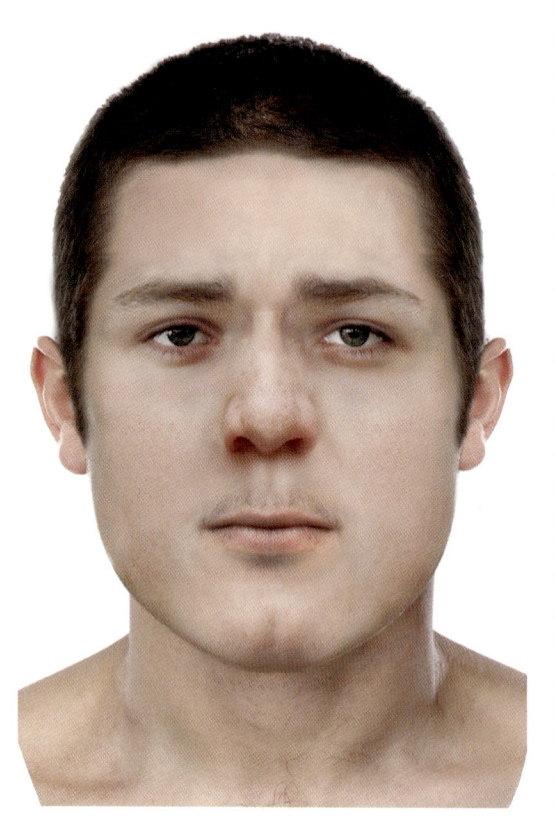

PEOPLE'S STORIES

Pitting on the cranium (porotic hyperostosis), caused by childhood systemic stress due to nutritional deprivation, disease or parasitic infection. Sk466

SKELETON	466
Grave	467
Location of grave	London Road, Trench 4
Burial details	Simple burials, one of a number along cemetery boundary wall
Age	Young adult, 18–20
Sex	Male
Stature	164cm or 5'4"
Radiocarbon date	1515–1635 (68% probability) 1465–1655 (95% probability) see Table 5.01, Illus 5.06, p159
Other dating evidence	Possibly associated with Carmelite friary c1520–c1560
Finds	–
Pathology	Calculus, DEH, periodontal disease, severe porotic hyperostosis, Schmorl's nodes
C/N isotope (diet)	High marine component to diet (c34%) see Illus 4.68, p133; p163–64; Table A1.02, p217
O/S isotope (origins)	–
See also	Illus 5.02, p156; p157–58; Illus 5.03; p160–62; p165
Facial reconstruction artist	Hayley Fisher

from Leith on its way to Edinburgh. The men were in high spirits. They had found many riches in Leith, had had two days of good sport there and had left it burning. They were on their way to Holyrood Abbey where they expected even greater riches and then on to Edinburgh itself for more of the same. A small group of men peeled off as they passed the friary. The four remaining brothers met the men at the gate, offering to tend any that were wounded and bade them enter if they wished to pray but only if they left their weapons at the door. They knocked the friar over and kicked him. The young novice tried to restrain the soldier and, for his efforts, got a sword slash through his belly and fell on the spot. The soldiers pushed past and began to desecrate the church.

They left soon enough, taking the silver chalice and altar cross, a keg of communion wine and all their food stores. There was little else, and the men were keen not to lose out on their share of the pickings at the abbey. They left the buildings standing but the brothers could do nothing for their young novice who bled to death in minutes.

As a novice he would normally have been buried close to the friary church but because there had been no chance for him to confess before he died, the last rites could not be administered and thus his soul might represent a danger to those within the graveyard, both living and dead. Burying their erstwhile brother outside the graveyard was unthinkable though, so they settled on a spot next to the graveyard wall.

A YOUNG CARMELITE FRIAR, 1525–1544

6 | ARCHAEOLOGICAL MONITORING ON CONSTITUTION STREET AND LEITH WALK

Julie Franklin with contributions by Richard Fawcett, Penelope Walton Rogers, Scott Timpany, Sarah-Jane Haston and John A Lawson

The construction of the tram network required the diversion of many of the existing services along its route (**Illus 1.01**, p2). This required the excavation and removal of the old services and the excavation of new service trenches. The nature of the service diversions heavily influenced the nature of the archaeological record. The replacement of house to mains services required only small, typically shallow trenches and these excavations revealed little archaeological information. However, the majority of the excavations were for the installation of new mains in open cut trenches and these frequently encountered archaeological remains, even though in many areas these trenches were in heavily disturbed ground. The narrow width of these trenches did, however, mean that the identification of features in plan was difficult, leading to most features and deposits being recorded in section only. The trenches were mainly between 1.5m and 2.0m deep and were typically around 0.5m wide. Occasional excavations for manholes involved larger and deeper excavation, typically around 3.0m by 2.0m and up to 2.5m deep.

The archaeological findings are detailed here by broad area, beginning at the northern end of the proposed tram route on the boundary of the modern port and working southwards to the top of Leith Walk at Picardy Place. The finds and environmental remains are discussed within each individual section. The first section looks at findings within the old town and port of Leith, as found in various trenches along Constitution Street. The second looks at findings along Leith Walk, the main road between Edinburgh and Leith, but largely undeveloped until the 18th century.

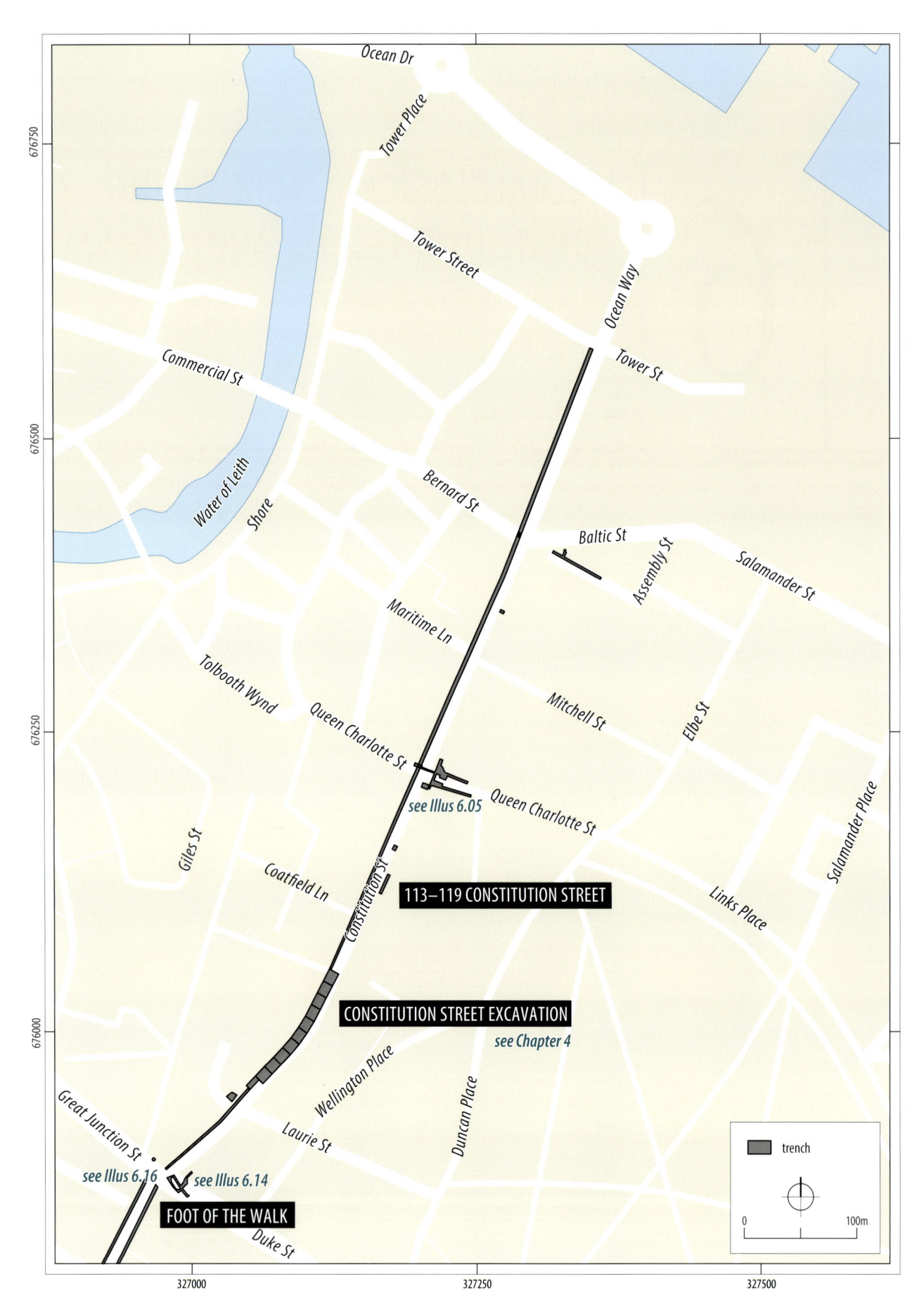

ILLUS 6.01
Trenching along Constitution Street

CONSTITUTION STREET

Julie Franklin

This section details the general archaeological picture revealed by the monitored service diversions within the limits of early Leith. This area is largely defined by the line of the 16th- and 17th-century town and harbour defences. To the north these extended as far as the northern end of Constitution Street, at its junction with Tower Street (**Illus 6.01**), though the shoreline varied over time. To the south they reached as far as the southern end of Constitution Street where it meets Leith Walk, Great Junction Street and Duke Street.

The main focus of the tram works in this area comprised a single continuous narrow trench excavated along the length of Constitution Street. This provided a good general picture of the upper deposits along its length. More extensive groundworks were also carried out in specific areas including the junction of Constitution Street and Queen Charlotte Street and at the Foot of the Walk (the name given to the north-eastern end of Leith Walk where a number of roads converge). These works allowed a more detailed picture of the surviving deposits to be recorded. The findings are discussed from north to south and are sub-divided by means of the side streets along Constitution Street.

TOWER STREET TO BERNARD STREET/BALTIC STREET

Prior to the 15th century, the land on which Bernard Street now stands marked the medieval foreshore, with a wide shallow beach, known as Leith Sands, extending north and eastwards. This beach is likely to have acted as part of the medieval harbour, as vessels of this period would have had a shallow draft and could be beached for loading and unloading. The beach was gradually reclaimed by means of dumping thick layers of make-up and midden material over it. Evidence from excavations directly to the south of Bernard Street suggests that this process began in the 1460s or 70s (Holmes 1985), pushing northwards over the course of the succeeding centuries. The beach was used as a course for horse races from at least the 16th century until, in 1816, the sport was moved to the better course at Musselburgh (Marshall 1986, 59–60).

Tower Street is first noted in the Post Office directory of 1846 (Harris 2002, 561) and is named on a town plan in 1853 (Ordnance Survey 1853d), though it appears to have provided access along the shoreline, above the head of the beach, prior to this. It is named for the tower at its western end on the Shore (which still stands). This was built as a windmill in 1682 and converted into a signal tower around 1805 (Harris 2002, 561).

In the mid-16th century, Ramsay's Fort was constructed on the foreshore on the eastern mouth of the harbour, adjacent to the 15th-century Kings Wark. The fort was a key part of the town's defences and the defensive sea wall seems to have been located between Tower Street and Bernard Street (Paton & Cook 2016, fig 9). Thus, the southern end of this section of road was within the seaward defences in the 16th century, the northern part being still beach at this point. It is likely that more of the beach was reclaimed over the course of the 17th century (Adair 1682) and by the middle of the 18th century the shoreline ran a little south of the future Tower Street (Kirkwood 1817a). At this point, the area to the west of this section of Constitution Street formed part of the Timberbush timber yards and latterly was characterised by warehouses, mills and workshops (Ordnance Survey 1853d).

Excavations in this area comprised long linear service trenches, approximately 1m wide, along the western side of the road, to a maximum depth of 1.4m. The only significant archaeological find in this area during this project was the discovery of the eastern terminus of a substantial sea wall outside no. 8 Constitution Street. The wall ran east-west across the trench and was 8m wide, made of ashlar granite blocks set upright. The gaps between the granite blocks were filled with small pieces of slate but any bonding material had been washed away. The exposed portion sloped down to the east suggesting this was the eastern end, sloping down to meet the water (**Illus 6.02**). North of the wall were deposits of mixed sand, brick, stone and other building rubble. It is likely that this material was dumped at a later date in order to reclaim this area.

There was no direct archaeological dating evidence for the wall. The use of granite in the construction suggests an 18th-century or later date is more likely. Portsoy on the Moray Firth has a harbour built of similar vertically set masonry, including some granite and dates to c1693 (Canmore ID 17932). The use of the stone outside of north-east Scotland is likely to be a little later, when the quarrying and trading of Aberdeenshire granite became well-established in the 18th and 19th centuries (Butt 1967, 98; Tyson 1988).

Cartography provides the most useful dating evidence, given that Leith's shoreline has been extending northwards over time (the current shoreline being over 100m to the north of this wall). The shoreline appears to have been in this approximate position before c1830. Prior to this date, there was a distinct kink in the line of the shore where it turns a little southward, east of Constitution

ILLUS 6.02
Sea wall outside 8 Constitution Street, looking north

Street (eg Hunter & Smith 1828), whereas later maps (eg Lizars 1833) show the shoreline as straight and running along the line of the present-day Tower Street, thus too far north for this sea wall. The same kinked shoreline is shown on Kirkwood's 1759 survey (Kirkwood 1817a) but the accuracy and scale of earlier maps (eg Adair 1682; Adair 1735) is such that it is not clear whether this was also the case in the 17th and earlier 18th centuries. It was probably not the case in the mid-16th century when the shoreline seems to have been further south (**Illus 3.01**, p23; Paton & Cook 2016, fig 9).

Excavations in 2001 at the site of a residential development directly to the south of Tower Street between the Shore and Constitution Street uncovered the remains of a substantial sea wall running east-west across the site approximately parallel with Tower Street (Wilson & Moore 2003). It appears of similar construction and alignment and thus would seem to be a westerly extension of the same wall as that found at Constitution Street. The 2001 Tower Street findings have yet to be fully analysed, but it was assumed to be a mid-18th-century sea wall and it appeared to have been built upon earlier foundations, which were tentatively connected to the refortification of the area in the mid-17th century. The limits of excavations at Constitution Street during the present project meant there was no opportunity to confirm or refute if the same was true there.

It is possible that the initial construction of the wall was a mid-17th-century defensive work along the shoreline protecting the Timberbush and providing placements for artillery. The later wall seems likely to have been built in the 18th century using part of the earlier wall as a foundation. Later land reclamation to the north made it obsolete by the mid-19th century.

BERNARD STREET/BALTIC STREET TO MARITIME LANE/MITCHELL STREET

South of Bernard Street and Baltic Street, as far as the Constitution Street excavations at South Leith Parish Church, several midden deposits and ground surfaces were identified, most dating to the 16th and 17th centuries based on associated finds. In several places former roads with cobbled surfaces were identified.

Both midden and cobbled surfaces were found at the junction of Constitution Street and Mitchell Street/Maritime Lane in the vicinity of the Port o' Leith public house. The cobbled surface (1464) was found within a 1.5m by 1m trench excavated at the Mitchell Street junction, 1.15m below the road surface or 3.75m AOD (**Illus 6.03**). It was found under two layers of made-ground, the lowest of which contained a clay pipe bowl which can be typologically dated to c1640–60 and a sherd of contemporary pottery. These finds, however, are likely to be residual as cartographic evidence suggests that the surface dates to the early 19th century (p187). The surface

ILLUS 6.03
Cobbled surface (1464), probably 19th century, at junction of Mitchell Street and Constitution Street

itself was well-made of roughly squared sandstone setts set on edge and bonded with mortar and extended over the whole of the trench. A depression, 0.1m deep, in the surface at the north-east corner of the trench was interpreted as a gutter running along the side of the road surface. Under these cobbles was yet another layer of make-up and then a rougher cobbled surface (1467) made of small water-rounded pebbles, 1.45m below the present road surface or 3.45m AOD. No dating material was found in the lower layers.

A midden deposit (1454) was found outside the Port o' Leith public house which stands on the north corner of the Maritime Lane junction. It was spread along 13m of the trench and continued under both trench edges. It was a 50mm deep layer of black clayey sand with a high organic content. Finds recovered were few but these provided good dating evidence. Nine clay pipe sherds included a complete bowl stamped on the heel with a heart-shaped stamp bearing the initials 'GC' over a possible star or rose (**Illus 6.04A**). This mark belonged to a Tyneside maker, though he is known only by his initials (Edwards 1988, 28–9). The bowl form was of Type 3a (ibid, 8–10), which can be dated to c1650–75 (ibid, 16).

'GC' and other Tyneside pipes have been found before in Leith. Five pipes, including three marked 'GC', were found in a mid-17th-century midden deposit within the Timberbush at Tower Street (Franklin 2004), approximately 200m to the north-east. However, it seems unlikely, given Edinburgh's thriving pipe trade at this time, that pipes were imported on a regular basis from Newcastle. It seems more likely that these were part of the personal possessions of someone who was from or had spent time in Tyneside. It is possibly no co-incidence that these pipes were found close to the shore and it is likely that they belonged to sailors. During the Commonwealth, Royalist and French freebooters regularly operated in the North Sea and a system of regular convoys was set up with merchant vessels protected by a navy frigate. Ships making the Leith to London voyage would initially be escorted as far as Tynemouth where they would have to wait for other ships to join them and another frigate to take them the rest of the way (Mowat 2003, 192). There were similar arrangements in reverse for the return journey. Thus, sailors of the 1650s would have had regular time to kill in Tyneside.

Another pipe is a local product. It is a stem sherd with a complete heel, though the bowl is missing. It is stamped 'PC' over an 'E' (**Illus 6.04B**). This is the mark of Patrick Crawford of Edinburgh. He was producing pipes from at least 1671, his wife continuing the business after he died into the early 18th century (Gallagher 1987). The bowl sherds are accompanied by seven contemporary stem sherds.

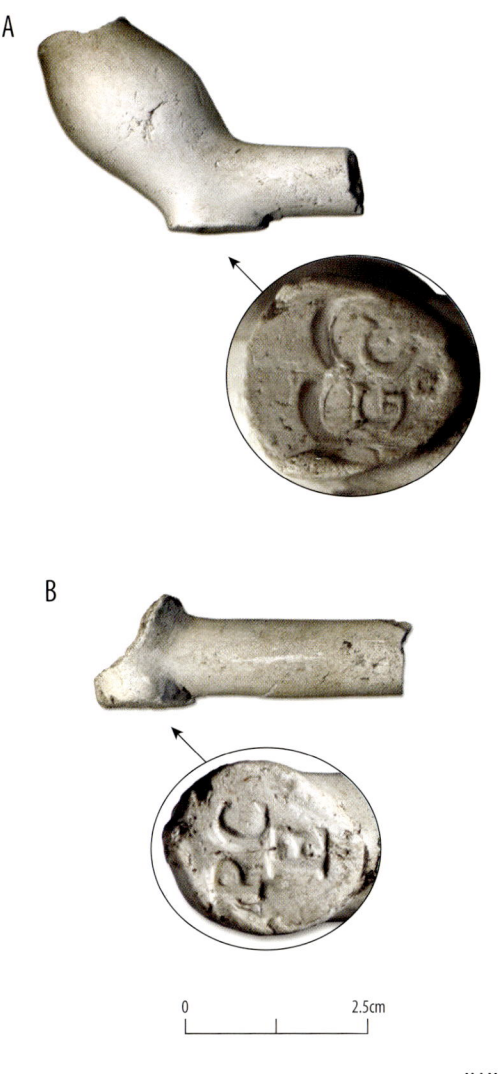

ILLUS 6.04
Clay pipes from midden (1454) at junction of Maritime Lane and Constitution Street: A. 'GC' maker, Tyneside; B. Patrick Crawford, Edinburgh

Three associated sherds of pottery (post-medieval reduced ware, tin-glazed earthenware and brown-glazed redware) were broadly contemporary, though could not be accurately dated. The finds together suggest a late 17th-century deposition date for the midden.

One further discovery is perhaps worthy of note, though it was unstratified and found a little to the north outside 46 Constitution Street (between the Constitution Bar and Rocksalt café). It was a small fragment (5g) from the top surface of a Flemish-type green glazed floor tile, the colour enhanced with a white slip under the glaze. This type of floor tile was imported in huge quantities into east coast Scotland from the late 14th to early 16th century and are particularly associated with 15th-century ecclesiastical sites (Norton 1994, 150–3). One fragment of tile does not necessarily imply a 15th-century church floor in the immediate area, particularly as it was found near to the shore, and tiles were probably used as ballast by Dutch trading ships (Eames 1976, 213). It adds to a scattering of tiles found in Leith from nearby excavations (Bernard Street, Eames 1985, 423; Water Street, Franklin 2002, 406; Burgess Street, Franklin in prep). Given the importance of the port during the 15th century it is possible that these tiles all derive from the floor of a local church or churches or possibly a grand house or civic building in the town.

MARITIME LANE/MITCHELL STREET TO QUEEN CHARLOTTE STREET

with contribution on the textile by Penelope Walton Rogers and on the environmental remains by Scott Timpany and Sarah-Jane Haston

A complex series of trenches were excavated at the junction of Constitution Street and Queen Charlotte Street (**Illus 6.01**; **Illus 6.05**). These included a long trench and a deep 3m by 2m manhole on the south side of Queen Charlotte Street, outside no. 44 (The Compass bar), and a long trench on the north side of the street, outside nos. 29–35 (Leith Police Station). Once again, the archaeology was characterised by middens and cobbled surfaces. In many areas the full depth of deposits could not be investigated, and it is therefore likely that earlier deposits do survive in this area.

44 Queen Charlotte Street – The Compass

The manhole excavation on Queen Charlotte Street, outside the Compass bar, went down over 2.5m and revealed a complex sequence of deposits (**Illus 6.05**). Above the natural dune sand was a complex series of layers featuring wind-blown sand deposits and interleaving layers of darker midden. Over this was a rough cobbled surface (269), 0.8m below the road surface (5.2m AOD), made up of water-rounded pebbles set in an organic clayey sand deposit, similar to the lower cobbled surface (1467) found further north at Mitchell Street (p173). Overlying this was a series of midden and sand layers, with various cut features. The midden deposits were rich in pottery and animal bone and their interleaving with layers of wind-blown sand suggests a gradual build-up of rubbish deposits with periods of sand-blow in between. Above this was the made-ground bedding for the modern road.

The dating of the finds from below the cobbles suggests a 16th-century date, while those from above suggest a 17th-century date, though few finds can be dated with any great accuracy (**Tables 6.01** and **6.02**). The lack of clay pipes in the upper deposits might suggest accumulation did not continue past about 1630. The pottery was predominantly of the usual local post-medieval reduced and oxidised wares. There were also several fragments from a Low Countries redware cooking pot from a lower layer (299) and sherds of Frechen stoneware and Seville coarseware (**Illus 6.06**) from upper layers (respectively 287 and 271).

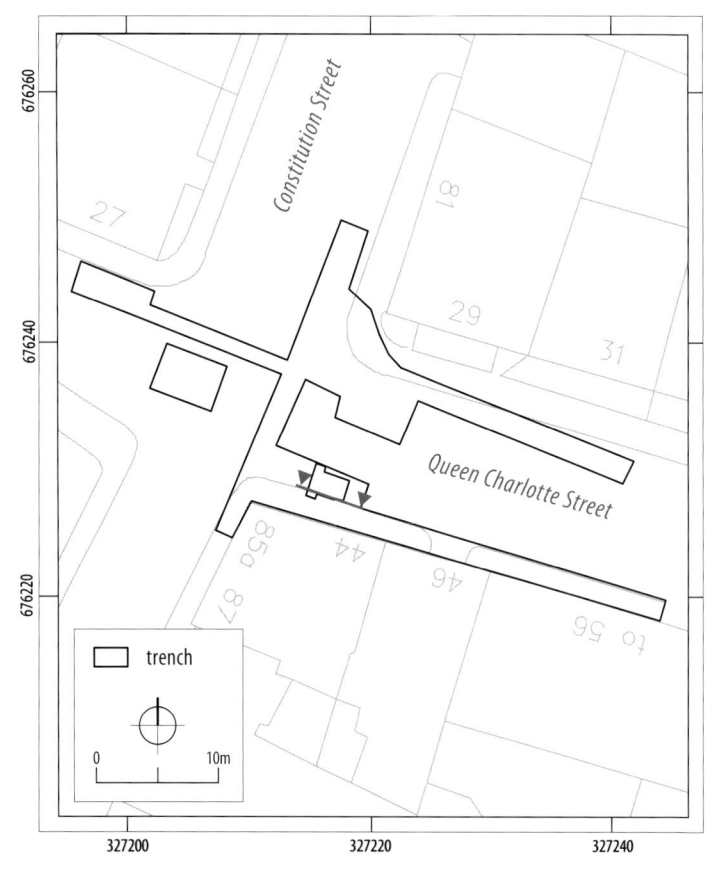

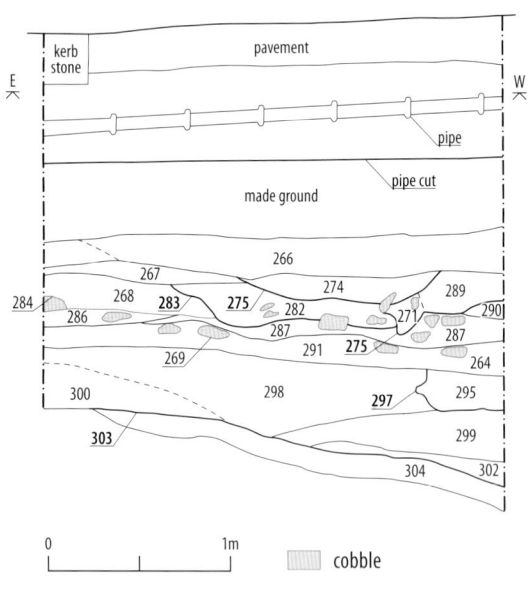

ILLUS 6.05
Trenching at junction of Queen Charlotte Street and Constitution Street; section outside Compass bar showing midden layers and cobbles

TABLE 6.01
Pottery found at Queen Charlotte Street, Compass bar and police station middens

FABRIC	REFERENCE	SHERDS	WGT (G)	DATING
Scottish post-medieval oxidised and reduced	Haggarty et al 2011, 13–21	17	335	16th–18th
Low Countries redware	Baart 1984	12	36	15th–17th
Frechen stoneware	Gaimster 1997, 208–11	1	5	M16th–17th
Seville coarseware	Goggin 1960; Hurst et al 1986, 66–7	2	108	L16th–17th
Tin-glazed earthenware	Korf 1981	3	19	M16th–17th
French chafing dish	Hurst 1974, 233–47; Hurst et al 1986, 78–82	1	<0.5	16th
Unidentified whiteware	–	1	41	?
TOTAL		37	544	

Frechen stoneware was commonly imported after the mid-16th century and throughout the 17th century (Gaimster 1997, 208–11). The Seville coarseware was a large piece of olive jar rim. These jars were imported as containers of olive oil or other liquid goods in the late 16th and 17th centuries (Goggin 1960; Hurst et al 1986, 66–7). Their distribution in Scotland is largely coastal and it seems likely that the contents of these vessels were divided up into smaller quantities for sale to consumers. Thus, there may then be an element of quayside or warehouse waste in this assemblage. Also probably from an imported

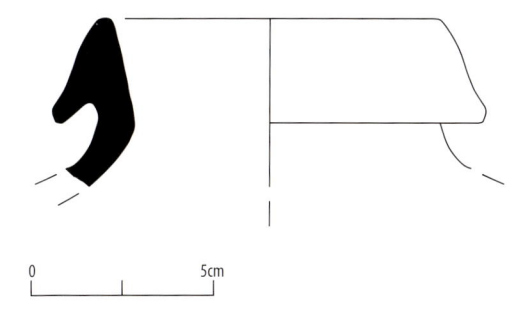

ILLUS 6.06
Seville coarseware olive jar rim, midden deposit (271), outside Compass bar

ILLUS 6.07
Nuremburg jeton, copper alloy, midden deposit (268), outside Compass bar

vessel was a sherd of fine vessel glass from an upper layer (267). These types of vessel were imported into Scotland, particularly from the Low Countries, in the 16th and 17th centuries, for use in the wealthier households (Willmott 2002). A Nuremburg jeton (**Illus 6.07**), a merchant's

TABLE 6.02
Pottery distribution in Queen Charlotte Street, Compass bar and police station middens

FEATURE		SCOTTISH POST–MEDIEVAL OXIDISED AND REDUCED	LOW COUNTRIES REDWARE	FRECHEN STONEWARE	SEVILLE COARSEWARE	FRENCH CHAFING DISH	TIN–GLAZED EARTHENWARE	UNIDENTIFIED WHITEWARE	TOTAL POTTERY	OTHER FINDS	DATING
Compass bar upper deposits 267, 268, 271, 282, 285, 286, 287, 371	Sherds	11	–	1	2	–	–	–	14	Copper alloy jeton, silk textile, glass waste fragments, sandstone roof slates, wood fragments, leather fragments, fine vessel glass sherd, iron horseshoe	?E17th
	Wgt (g)	249	–	5	108	–	–	–	362		
Compass bar cobbles 269/291	Sherds	1	–	–	–	–	–	–	1	–	L16th?
	Wgt (g)	0	–	–	–	–	–	–	0		
Compass bar lower deposits 295, 298, 299, 300	Sherds	5	12	–	–	–	–	–	17	–	16th
	Wgt (g)	86	36	–	–	–	–	–	122		
Police station midden 293, 358, 361, 388	Sherds	8	1	–	–	3	1	1	14	17 clay pipe bowl and stems, vessel glass, window glass, pan tile, brick	M/L 17th
	Wgt (g)	118	1	–	–	19	<0.5	41	179		
TOTAL	SHERDS	25	13	1	2	3	1	1	46		
	WGT (g)	453	37	5	108	19	<0.5	41	663		

trade token, also speaks of Leith's trading past. It is of the common 'rose orb type' and dates to the 16th or early 17th century (Mitchiner 1988).

Various organic remains were preserved in the upper layers, including wood and leather fragments. Luxury goods were also present in the form of a fragment of silk textile (layer 271). It measured approximately 40mm by 20mm and was extremely fine, 70–80 x 24 threads per cm and made from good quality de-gummed silk yarn, which had a slight S-twist. It has been woven in tabby repp, which is a ribbed weave commonly used for ribbons, linings and furnishings. Such fabrics are not easily datable, and some were probably being produced in British towns from imported yarn as early as the 17th century (Walton 1983, 239). During this period, it was very much a luxury fibre, though during the course of the 18th and 19th centuries its use for items such as ribbons spread down the social scale.

A complete though slightly distorted horseshoe (found in a midden deposit 371 within a trench extension) is the only find which might relate to traffic within the area, rather than refuse disposal, as it may have been thrown from a passing horse (**Illus 6.08**). The heel is angled on the interior, giving a slightly key-holed shaped inner profile. The heels both have thickened calkins and there is a shallow fuller groove around the underside in which the nail holes sit, three in each arm. One nail is still in place. It has a rectangular expanded head and is double clenched at the tip. The angled heels are found in shoes of the late 16th and 17th centuries, but fuller grooves are not known until the 17th century (Clark 1998, 239; Egan 2005, 179).

There were two sherds of stone roofing tile. The earliest stratified was a sherd of shale 14mm thick, with a large (13mm) peg hole at one end (layer 287). A larger sherd was found in an upper layer (267). This was of grey sandstone, of maximum 13mm thick. Some edges were roughly finished and it appears to form the end of a tile, though has no peg hole. The use of stone for roofing in Edinburgh and Leith has been shown to date back to at least the 15th century (Franklin 2010, 45). This early stone roofing was all in locally-available stones, typically sandstone or shale (ibid; Franklin forthcoming). Slate from sources in north-east Scotland or the west Highlands does not seem to have been commonly used for roofing in Edinburgh or Leith until the 17th or 18th centuries, with slates beginning to appear in archaeological contexts of this date (ibid).

Environmental remains from the lower deposits included a large quantity and wide range of charred grain (particularly layers 299, 302), including hulled barley, spelt wheat, club/bread wheat and oat. Charred peas were also recovered. Waterlogging in deposit (299) provided particularly good conditions for survival and remains of taxa representative of damp waste ground such as pale persicaria and fat hen were present. The presence of common nettle and celery-leaved buttercup (Ranunculus sceleratus), which both prefer nitrogen-rich environments, also suggests the presence of decaying materials (eg rotting food) and faecal material collecting in this deposit. Such conditions were also evidenced by the large quantity of fly pupae found in the deposit. Alongside the charred plant remains recovered at the site the samples were again rich in marine shell and animal bone with coal and cinders. The usual species of animal and shellfish are present in these assemblages, sheep, cattle, horse, pig, cat, oyster, periwinkle, mussel and limpet. The greater abundance of coal than charcoal also implies this was the more common fuel source in use at the time. Coal was locally available in Lothian and Fife.

ILLUS 6.08
Horseshoe, iron, midden deposit (371), outside Compass bar

29–35 Queen Charlotte Street – Leith Police Station

Dark organic-rich midden deposits were also found outside the police station (293, 358, 388, 361). The deposits were encountered at the base of the trench at a depth of around 1.45m below the road (4.55m AOD), under a layer of wind-blown sand which was, in turn, under the modern make-up material. In one area a deposit of lime was found between two of the midden layers suggesting an attempt to cover the smell of the midden at some point. Further archaeologically interesting deposits were noted below the limit of excavation and it is likely that there is good survival of earlier deposits beneath the midden. It was not possible to characterise these earlier deposits within the confines of the trench.

The midden dating evidence derived chiefly from the clay pipes. The 17 pipe sherds provided the largest concentration of clay pipes from the project. Though smoking tobacco in clay pipes had been known in Britain since the late 16th century, it was only from the 1620s and 30s that clay pipe manufacture occurred in Scotland. Clay pipes began to be commonly found in deposits dating from this period onwards. The one clay pipe bowl found was incomplete but appears to be of an early form, similar to those found at the Tron Kirk which are known to have been deposited before 1637 (Lawson 1975).

Unfortunately, the small size of the assemblage in general from these deposits precluded refined dating for the sequence of deposition. The rest of the finds are indicative of a date in the 17th century and there is a lack of any finds which can definitively be dated to the 18th century, but there is no clear idea of when deposition in this area ceased. Associated pottery numbered only 14 sherds (179g). Forms and fabrics were typical for the period: post-medieval reduced and oxidised ware jugs and jars (eg Caldwell & Dean 1992); fragments of Low Countries redware; and Anglo-Dutch tin-glazed earthenware.

Two vessels were more unusual. The first is represented by three joining sherds of a fine hard buff fabric. The fabric is similar to that of Loire jugs and other plain French wares but it is glazed with a patch of mottled green glaze. The form appears to be a small bowl-shaped vessel with the beginning of a flared rim and a steeply in-turned base under a sharp angled carination. The shape is reminiscent of French chafing dishes (eg **Illus 4.66A**, p127), though it would be a rather plain and coarse example.

The second vessel was stranger still (**Illus 6.09**). It was of a fine white fabric, superficially like Siegburg stoneware but much softer fired and more poorly made. It has been shaped by hand, with thick uneven walls. It is possibly locally made though all the evidence points towards local whiteware production dying out in the 16th century, probably due to the depletion of white-firing clay resources. It is also completely unglazed whereas local pottery is almost always glazed, even if thinly or patchily. The sherd is part of the base and wall of a money box (or pirlie pig as they were known in Scotland). The base was flat, the walls sloping in towards a domed top. The coin slot was cut at an angle at which point the sherd is broken. Pirlie pig money boxes were a common enough form during the 16th and 17th centuries though are generally found in the local post-medieval reduced ware fabric. Typically, they have bulbous walls and a pointed top and are generally better made than this lumpy hand formed vessel. The origin of this vessel must remain unidentified at present.

The only other find of note from the midden is a fragment of decorative vessel glass. This is a basal fragment from a beaker or tankard with rigaree decoration. This was a common method of decoration in the 16th and 17th centuries (Willmott 2002). The midden also included frequent animal bone and marine shell but there were few preserved plant remains.

QUEEN CHARLOTTE STREET TO COATFIELD LANE

with contribution on the architectural fragments by Richard Fawcett

Outside 113 to 119 Constitution Street there was a different sequence of deposits to those found over the rest of the road. The lowest deposit appeared to be a mixture of bone-rich midden deposit and garden soil (427). It was encountered at a depth of 1.0m below the road and extended beyond the excavation limit at 1.6m down. Finds included a handful of clay pipe stems, pot sherds and pan tiles and suggest a 17th- or early 18th-century date for the deposit. Overlying this were deposits of rubble, ash, mortar and glass waste and, in places, remains of an old turf layer. It suggests this area was open ground, possibly under cultivation, but clearly still accumulating domestic waste, possibly deliberately added as fertiliser. It is possible that earlier archaeological deposits survived under this layer.

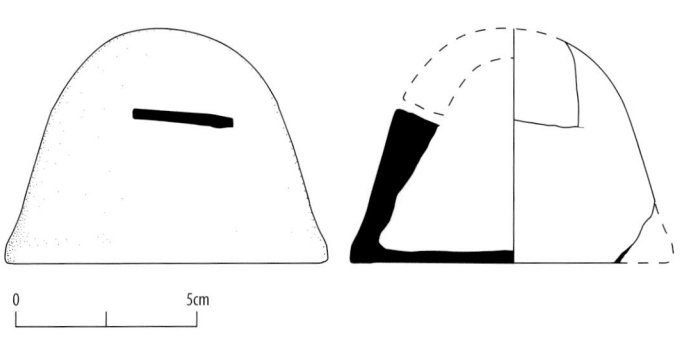

ILLUS 6.09
Unidentified pirlie pig (money box), midden deposit (293), outside police station

The most interesting of the finds was a piece of solid cast-iron shot (**Illus 6.10B**) found in the lower garden soil layer (427). It was 65mm (just over 2.5") in diameter and weighed 1021g (2.25lb). Cast iron shot had been produced in England from the early 16th century, earlier in France, though the technology was not available in Scotland until later (Caldwell 1991; Coad 1997, 158). The ball would have fitted a gun called a 'falcon'. A ball of identical size was found at Eyemouth Fort, a mid-16th-century fortification on the coast of Berwickshire, held briefly by both English and French forces (Franklin 1997). The shot could therefore date from the Siege of Leith, either part of the attacking bombardment or a cache of defensive balls. Equally, given the associated 17th century finds, it may date to the mid-17th-century Cromwellian military action.

Another piece of shot, this time of stone, was found a little further to the south. It was found outside St James's Church, 119 Constitution Street, opposite the junction of Coatfield Lane, though was unstratified. It was pecked out of grey sandstone into an imperfect sphere, a little flattened on one side, with a maximum diameter of 64mm (2.5") and a weight of 367g (0.8lb) (**Illus 6.10A**).

Stone balls may have had a number of uses. Balls of this approximate size were used in games such as henching, similar to boules. However, the specific size of this ball and its location suggests it was a gunstone, for use with wrought iron breach loading guns. Wrought iron guns were not strong enough to take the charge necessary to fire heavier metal shot but were still useful for defensive purposes. They were in use in the 16th century probably until well into the 17th century (Caldwell 1981, 128).

Relatively little is known of sizes or standardisation of wrought iron guns compared to cast metal guns. However, in terms of stone shot found in Scotland, there is a distinct grouping around 2.4–2.5". Stones of this size have been found in Leith before. A ball of 2.4" was found during excavations at nearby Burgess Street, some 350m to the north, in a probable 16th-century context. A rougher version, possibly half-finished, was found during excavations at Ronaldson's Wharf on Sandport Place, on the opposite bank of the Water of Leith from Burgess Street (author's own knowledge of unpublished sites, The City of Edinburgh Council Archaeology Service).

Assuming both balls date from the 1560 siege then their location is of note. In relation to the siege defences, the area is about half way along the eastern rampart, and they were found just inside the eastern rampart, in the vicinity of the Musselburgh gate, within the sights of the besieging forces' guns. No defensive guns were noted in this location on the Petworth map (**Illus 3.01**, p23). It is possible then that both derive from the attacking bombardment. If the balls in fact dated to the 17th-century conflict then the area was the location of the bastion now known as the John's Lane bastion, which would have been a location of defensive guns. The balls might therefore represent the remains of a defensive arsenal.

ILLUS 6.10
Round shot from 113–119 Consitution Street: A. stone; B. iron

ILLUS 6.11
Block with a with a quirked angle roll, buff-yellow sandstone, unstratified from junction of Coatfield Lane and Constitution Street

ILLUS 6.12
Buzz-disc, slate, unstratified from Constitution Street, between Queen Charlotte Street and Coatfield Lane

Two other notable finds came from this area. The first was an architectural fragment found unstratified at the junction of Constitution Street and Coatfield Lane (**Illus 6.11**). It was a block with a quirked angle roll (220mm wide, 230mm deep and 275mm high with a 85mm diameter roll), formed of buff/yellow sandstone. The 45° plane that extends on each side of the angle roll, the relatively great diameter of the roll, and the way in which the roll extends tangentially out to the line of the adjacent faces of the block, would all be consistent with a 16th-century date. A roll of this kind is most frequently found associated with the jambs of a doorway or the reveals of a window. The bedding planes of the stone are only roughly finished; the rear and one flank of the stone are even more roughly worked, indicating that, as might be expected, there was no intention that they should be exposed. There are also differences between the two faces that flank the roll, with one being relatively carefully finished with vertical tooling, while the other is more roughly stugged; this may suggest that the roll was part of a larger moulding formation, with one of the faces being partly obscured by an adjacent element of the formation. The large amount of mortar adhering to the finished sides of the block suggests that it has been put to some secondary use. The block is unlikely to have moved far from its original location and it suggests the presence of a high status 16th-century building in the vicinity.

The last find was also unstratified, though was of humbler origins. It was a simple stone disc made of slate chipped into rough circle, approximately 53mm diameter, with two holes pierced in the middle (**Illus 6.12**). It was incised with three concentric compass-drawn circles on each side. It is likely that this was a buzz disc. These are thought to have been children's toys, though it has been suggested they may also have been used as simple musical instruments, hunting lures or possibly even for ritual uses (G Lawson 1995, 2). A long loop of string was strung through both holes and the whole swung in a circular motion to twist the cord. It can then be spun by pulling the cord, sending the disc spinning first one way, and then the other with each pull, making a whirring sound.

They have been in use since at least the medieval period, made of bone or metal. More recently buttons could be used for the purpose and latterly cardboard discs, which could be cut from the back of breakfast cereal boxes. The care with which this disc has been made, particularly the neatness of the incised lines, suggests it was made by an adult or at least an older child. The fact it was made of slate suggests it post-dates the 17th or 18th centuries after which the use of slate for roofing became more commonplace in Edinburgh and Leith (Franklin 2010, 45; Franklin forthcoming).

COATFIELD LANE TO LAURIE STREET
with contribution on the architectural fragment by Richard Fawcett

This area includes the Constitution Street excavations which have been detailed above. Little else of note was recovered during the watching brief in this area. A tenement wall was found on the north-west corner of Laurie Street and Constitution Street, which matches walls first seen on a map of 1804 (**Illus 3.06**, p28).

One unstratified find, however, of was considerable interest. This was an architectural fragment found outside 133 Constitution Street, currently residential flats, to the east of Constitution Street excavation Area 10 (**Illus 4.02**, p50), opposite the entrance to the graveyard. It was extremely large (450–530mm long, 480–600mm wide and 350mm thick) and formed one course of the corner tas-de-charge of a tierceron vault (**Illus 6.13**), of yellow sandstone with red mottling. The upwardly flared form of those moulded parts of this block that were intended to be visible makes clear that it was part of a vault springer, while the way in which to the rear there are two roughly finished faces at right angles to each other makes equally clear that the vault was springing from within a re-entrant angle rather than against a wall face. The rough finish of the strip of masonry at each end of the moulded formation indicates that the block was built into the wall, and that it was therefore one course of the tas-de-charge, the part of the vault which acted as a corbel to support the upper parts where they sprang free of the wall. It also seems that it must have been the top course of that tas-de-charge, since the leading edges of the upper bedding plane are cut down at a slight angle to receive the ribs and webbing of the main body of the vault. The tops of the ribs had cross-shaped incisions that were presumably intended to permit a greater depth of mortar at this most vulnerable point of the vault.

A GIRL WITH BAD LUNGS, 1538–1554

This girl was born in 1538 to a short life of trouble and toil. She was six when the town was destroyed by English troops. She and her family had fled the town and hid in the dunes along the shore of the Forth, but she would always remember the sounds of distant screaming and the sight and smell of the burning town. When they felt safe enough to return, they found a town in ruins and it took them a while to get their bearings and find their home. Miraculously, most of the houses along her close, including her father's blacksmith's shop, were still standing but had been stripped of all his tools and most of the goods he had for sale. All that remained were a few nails scattered over the floor, his collection of scrap iron and two families sheltering inside.

The next months were hard but he received money from the Incorporation of Hammermen to buy new tools and he got busy making new stock. Nails were in particularly high demand as reconstruction work got underway. They were spared during the pestilence the following year.

When she was nine, the English were back, again commanded by the Earl of Hertford who was now Lord Protector of England, and, if her father were to be believed, son of the devil himself. The Earl wanted to force a marriage between his nephew, King Edward VI of England, and the four-year-old Queen Mary of Scotland, but the Scots and Mary's French mother, Mary of Guise, were bitterly opposed to it. The English arrived by land and sea, meeting the Scots forces at Pinkie Cleugh, just six miles east along the coast from Leith. The day they fought became known as Bloody Saturday, the bloodiest battle ever fought on Scottish soil. The Scots forces were bombarded from the English ships out at sea and when the Scots lines broke, the English pursued them and cut down any they could find. Ten thousand Scots died compared to only a few hundred English. The English army, still stained with blood, camped at Leith and once again the blacksmith hid his family. This time they were not so lucky. Hertford found little enough to steal but had the whole town fired out of spite. The blacksmith's shop did not survive this second fire. Worse, the English had taken or destroyed all the ships in the harbour and all the grain stores from the recent harvest. The winter was hard and hungry for the blacksmith's family. They spent much of it camped out in the village of shanties and shacks which had grown up to house the people while they rebuilt. The girl developed a cough which she did not seem to be able to shake. Her father sickened and died.

In June the following year, the French came to Leith. Queen Mary, acting as regent for her daughter, invited her countrymen over. Some stayed and began to fortify the town. Great earthen ramparts began to be thrown up by hundreds of Scottish 'pioneers' and thick stone walls were constructed along the Forth shore. It should have made the girl and her mother feel a little safer, but no one liked the French. They were rude and arrogant, and many refused to learn English, instead insisting the locals speak French to them.

Her widowed mother had some income from the Hammermen but times were hard for everyone and the payments did not cover their needs. The mother found her daughter a position in the house of one of the Frenchmen, an army comandante who had brought his wife over from France and set up house on the east side of the Kirkgate, near St Mary's. The girl was only ten and small for her age, but her life now became one of constant work. She had to rise before dawn to set the fires and usually got to bed around midnight. Her life was cleaning, fetching, carrying and cooking. She became used to the mistress of the house barking orders to her in French. At least when she helped in the kitchen she got to eat leftovers and would sneak morsels of food when the cook wasn't looking. Her teeth

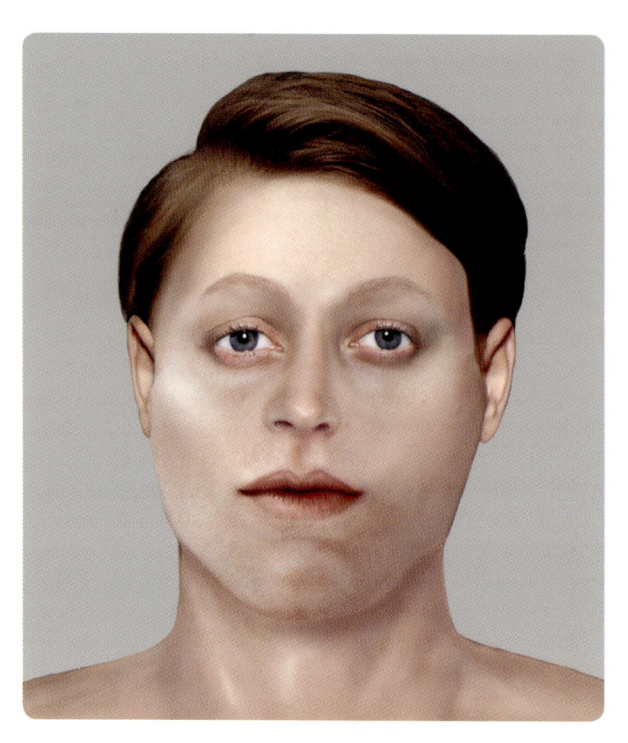

SKELETON	**0966**
Grave	0968
Location of grave	Constitution Street, Area 8
Burial details	Simple
Age	Adolescent, 15–16
Sex	?
Stature	–
Radiocarbon date	–
Other dating evidence	In Phase 3 cemetery, probably only in use from c1480s onwards
Finds	–
Pathology	Antemortem tooth loss, calculus, caries, periodontal disease, DEH, Schmorl's nodes, severe periostitis on left ribs (R8–12), right cribra orbitalia and porotic hyperostosis
C/N isotope (diet)	–
O/S isotope (origins)	–
See also	IIllus 4.11, p60; p95; p110; p122
Facial reconstruction artist	Sarah Jaworski

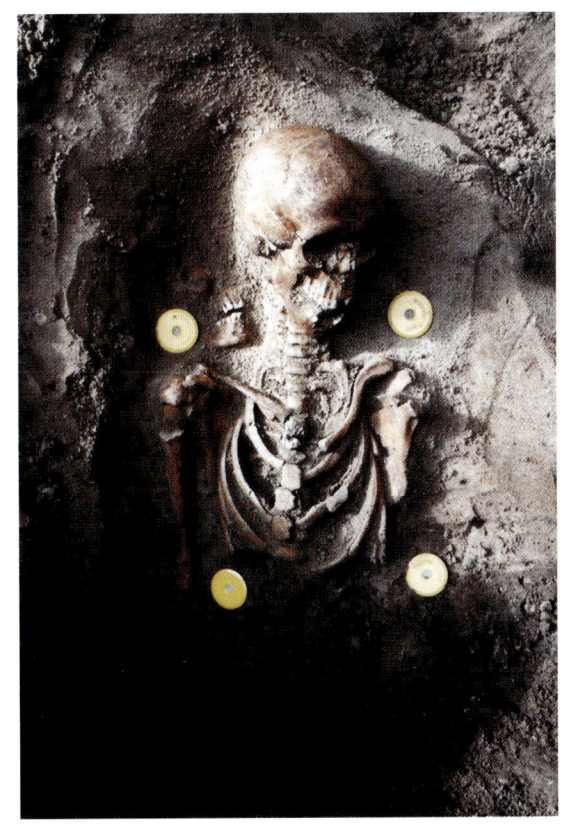

were weak and the food she ate did not help. She suffered from toothache and had already lost one adult tooth. Her most-hated task was the laundry. It had to be scrubbed in a tub of hot water with soapwort. For more stubborn stains she used lye, a mixture of wood ash and water. It was caustic, and her hands quickly became red and sore.

Her cough got worse and began to keep her awake at night. She became wheezy and short of breath. 'Madame' found the cough irritating and dismissed her. She had no choice but to return to her mother's.

Her mother was shocked at how thin she was and put her to bed. Over the following months, she began to cough up blood and found breathing increasingly difficult. She did not live past 16 and was buried in a simple grave. Shortly afterwards the construction of the fortifications reached the eastern side of town. The pioneers cut right through her grave and threw what remained of her legs into a large charnel pit.

A GIRL WITH BAD LUNGS, 1538–1554

ILLUS 6.13
One course of the corner tas-de-charge of a tierceron vault, unstratified outside 133 Constitution Street, opposite graveyard entrance; detail of mason's mark

The number of ribs indicates that the vault was of tierceron form, with intermediate diagonal ribs on each side of the principal diagonal ribs; those intermediate ribs would have risen up to horizontal ridge ribs at the apex of the vault. The wall ribs appear to have been in the form of simple ogee curves; the diagonal rib was a filleted roll flanked by spurs, while the tierceron ribs were filleted rolls. One of the tierceron ribs had partly broken away. On the bedding plane incised lines radiate out from the rear angle of the stone, and these were evidently setting-out marks intended to ensure accurate alignment of the ribs. There is a mason's mark in the form of a triangle, with a stem and saltire cross rising from its apex.

Tierceron vaults were first employed in Scotland around the second and third quarters of the 13th century, over the stairs to the crypt at Glasgow Cathedral and in the choir aisles of Elgin Cathedral, but they continued in favour throughout the later middle ages. Within Edinburgh, mid-15th-century examples are to be seen over the choir and Preston Aisle at St Giles' Cathedral, and over the choir of Trinity College Chapel. But in the context of the present discussion, it is perhaps more significant that in the 15th century they were often found over smaller spaces, perhaps as a way of affording them added significance, as in the porches of Dunfermline Abbey and Perth St John, in the towers of Dundee St Mary and Cambuskenneth Abbey, and in the chapel of St Andrew at Stirling Holy Rude.

A tierceron vault of the kind represented by this fragment must almost certainly have originated in an ecclesiastical structure of some pretension. If it is assumed that the fragment was part of a church that stood within the vicinity of the find location, though there can be no certainty of this, the most likely candidate is St Mary's Church, given its dating and proximity.

Whatever the dating of St Mary's foundation (p145), it is known that there was extensive construction work there in the last two decades of the 15th century. Taking account of the relatively great scale of the church, it would perhaps not have been inappropriate for what appears to have been a porch within the south aisle to have had such a vault over it, though it must be stressed that this is no more than one possibility. The building was extensively damaged during the siege of 1559–60 and was then repaired for use as the parish church (p24). Further damage may have been caused when it was occupied by Cromwell's troops in the 1650s (p28). The church as now seen dates largely from a campaign of rebuilding by Thomas Hamilton in 1847–8, which incorporated the medieval arcades in heavily remodelled form and possibly some of the masonry of the external walls (Gifford et al 1984, 457–9). Some of the fragments displaced in the course of the restoration, including the original window arch, mullions and form-pieces of the west window, found a second home at the church of St Conan on the shore of Loch Awe (RCAHMS 1975, 299; pl 120E). The fragment may have been deposited during any of these episodes or building works, though perhaps, given its lack of secure context, the 19th-century restorations are the most likely source.

LAURIE STREET TO GREAT JUNCTION STREET/ FOOT OF THE WALK/DUKE STREET

South of Laurie Street there was a general depositional change. Whereas along most of the rest of Constitution Street, deposits were built up over natural beach sand, at this southern end, the sand deposits included large lenses of clay and sometimes deposits were characterised by mixed clayey sand. It seems that building works in the area disturbed natural clay deposits beneath the beach sand. Finds-dating suggests this happened around the 18th century, which coincides with the c1790 construction of this end of Constitution Street and its subsequent development.

The most significant archaeological remains recovered from this area was a large defensive ditch, [364/436] found within a series of conjoining service diversion trenches at the junction of Constitution Street, Great Junction Street and Duke Street (**Illus 6.14**). The ditch ran approximately NW-SE, roughly aligned with Duke Street. Only the northern edge was revealed; the southern edge had probably been truncated by the cut for a large sewer pipe and it could not be located. The ditch was only excavated to the required depth (approximately 1.6m below the existing road surface) and did not reach the bottom of the ditch cut. The underlying deposits were investigated by a series of auger holes (**Illus 6.15**). This allowed a certain amount of detail to be established about the nature and depth of the ditch fills but crucially did not allow retrieval of finds or environmental material to date the lower fills.

The ditch cut through a series of old ground surfaces and buried soils at its eastern end, including a cobbled surface (439) made of rounded beach pebbles. Below these it cut through natural sand and clayey sand deposits. The ditch was about 2.6m deep and at least 5m wide with steep sides and a rounded base. The deposits filling the lower ditch recovered during auguring suggested an initial weathering deposit consisting of the finer deposits washed back into the ditch from its upcast, which was waterlogged in places implying the potential for good preservation of organic material. Excavation of the upper fills at the eastern side of the trench revealed the best sequence (**Illus 6.14**) and these seem to represent deliberate backfilling episodes. A distinct tip line was visible in section at the top of the lower fills (435 and 434), suggesting a quick shovelling in of material from one side.

Dating evidence for the ditch cutting was scant and derived from three fragments (6g) of local post-medieval reduced and oxidised wares from deposits through which the ditch was cut (378, 440). These provide a tentative 16th-century *terminus post quem* for the cutting of the ditch. No finds dating evidence was recovered from the lower fills, but material from deposit (434) included sherds of pan tile and glass waste suggesting these date from the mid-17th century or later (p187). The upper layers through which the ditch was cut (377, 438, and 439) also contained glass waste and pan tiles suggesting a certain amount of disturbance and a complex stratigraphic history in the area.

By comparison with cartographic evidence the ditch can readily be identified as part of the mid-16th-century defences (see also p88–90; p146–48), that were subsequently backfilled and then re-excavated in 1571 and again as part of the mid-17th-century refortification of the town. The ditch aligns with the southern edge of the south-eastern corner bastion of the mid-16th-century fortifications, as seen on the Petworth Map (**Illus 3.01**, p23; Paton & Cook 2016, fig 9), and with south-east corner of the 17th-century fortifications seen on Adair's 1682 map and still apparent on Naish's 1709 map and Kirkwood's survey of 1759 (**Illus 3.03–3.05**, p25–27).

The lack of opportunity that the excavations allowed for the examination of the lower fills precluded any insights into the complex sequence of silting, backfilling and recutting of this ditch that was evidence in excavations across the ditch further west on Great Junction Street (Paton & Cook 2016). However, the fact that some details of the fortifications was still clearly extant in 1759 does agree with the apparent 18th century dating of the upper fills of the ditch and suggests that it may have lain part backfilled for some time. The remains of a possible stone culvert were found at the base of the ditch towards its western end, suggesting possible attempts at drainage during this period.

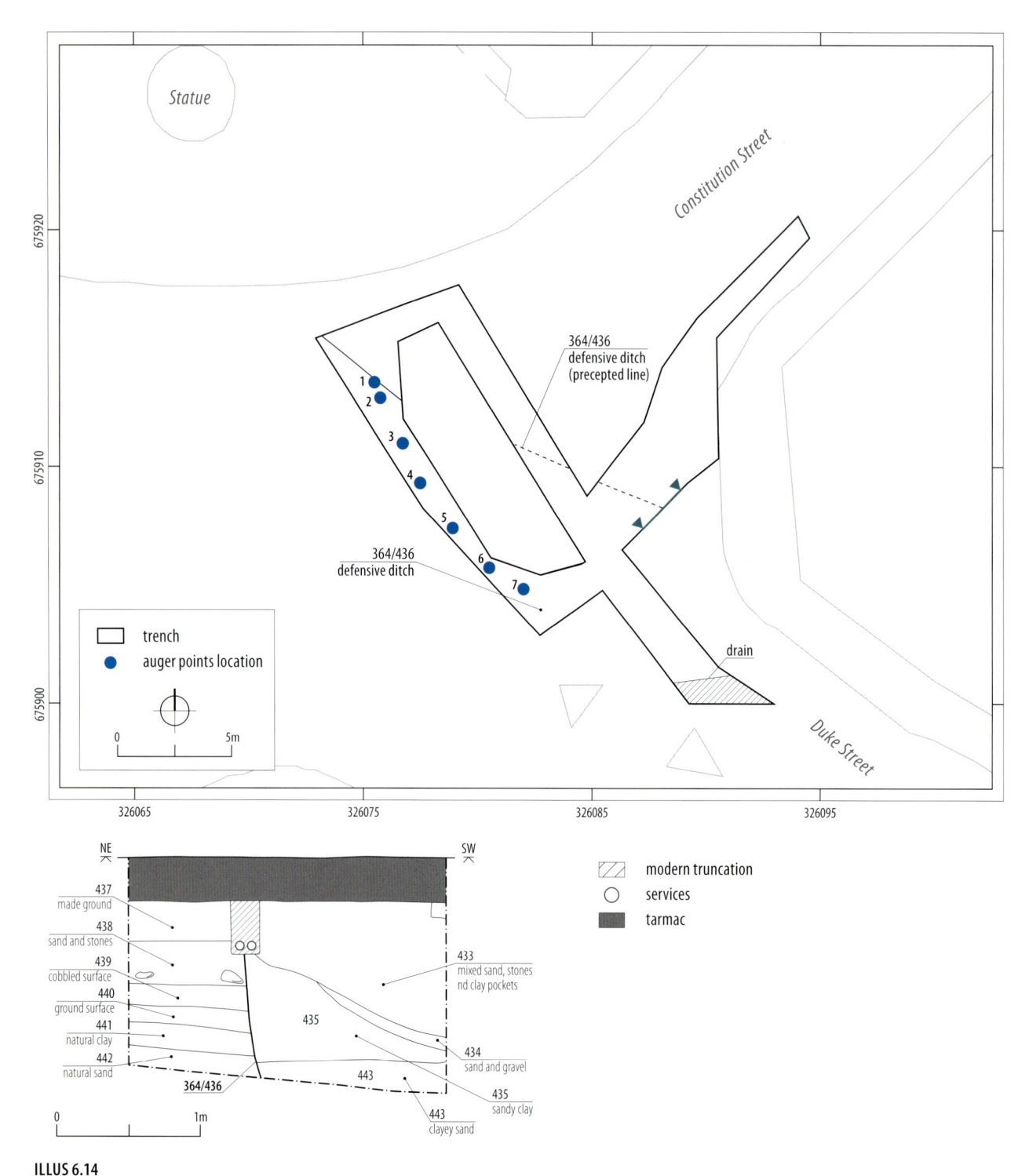

ILLUS 6.14
Trenching at junction of Duke Street and Constitution Street, showing cut of defensive ditch [364/436]; west-facing section through ditch cut at eastern edge of trench

The only other features of note in this area were a sequence of cobbled surfaces found during the replacement of services outside the Newkirkgate shopping centre at the Foot of the Walk (**Illus 6.16**). The trench cut through a series of old ground surfaces and midden deposits with several of the surfaces being formed of cobbles. Most of these deposits were seen only in section or in a small part of the trench having been truncated by the original services. The earliest of the cobbled surfaces (415) was a compacted clayey sand set with rounded stones. The only dating for this was a fragment (1g) of medieval Scottish white gritty ware suggesting a very tentative medieval date. Above this were layers of clayey sand, wind-blown sand, more clayey sand and midden (413, 416, 412, 411, respectively). The only clue to dating in these was a wire eyelet (layer 413) similar to those used at the Constitution Street cemetery (**Illus 4.64A**, p124) around the 15th century, though, assuming it derives from a burial, it was clearly residual in this context.

ILLUS 6.15
Auguring within defensive ditch [364/436]

Above this were three successive layers of cobbles (414, 407, 406) (**Illus 6.16**; **Illus 6.17**) of a similar nature to the earlier cobbles, made of water-rounded pebbles about 4–5cm across. Above this was a layer of midden which could be dated by means of the clay pipe stems, pan tile and window glass within it to the later 17th or early 18th century. It also included large quantities of animal bone, including an articulated cow's leg. Thus, the latest of the cobbled surfaces was probably laid down in the 17th century, while the earliest possibly dated back to the late medieval period. It is certainly clear that more attention was given to the road surface towards the latter end of this period. The cobbled surface (439) cut by the defensive ditch, as noted above (p183), was of a similar nature to these surfaces, and given its relationship with the ditch and a sherd of 16th-century pottery in the layer below, it is presumably of similar 16th- or 17th-century date.

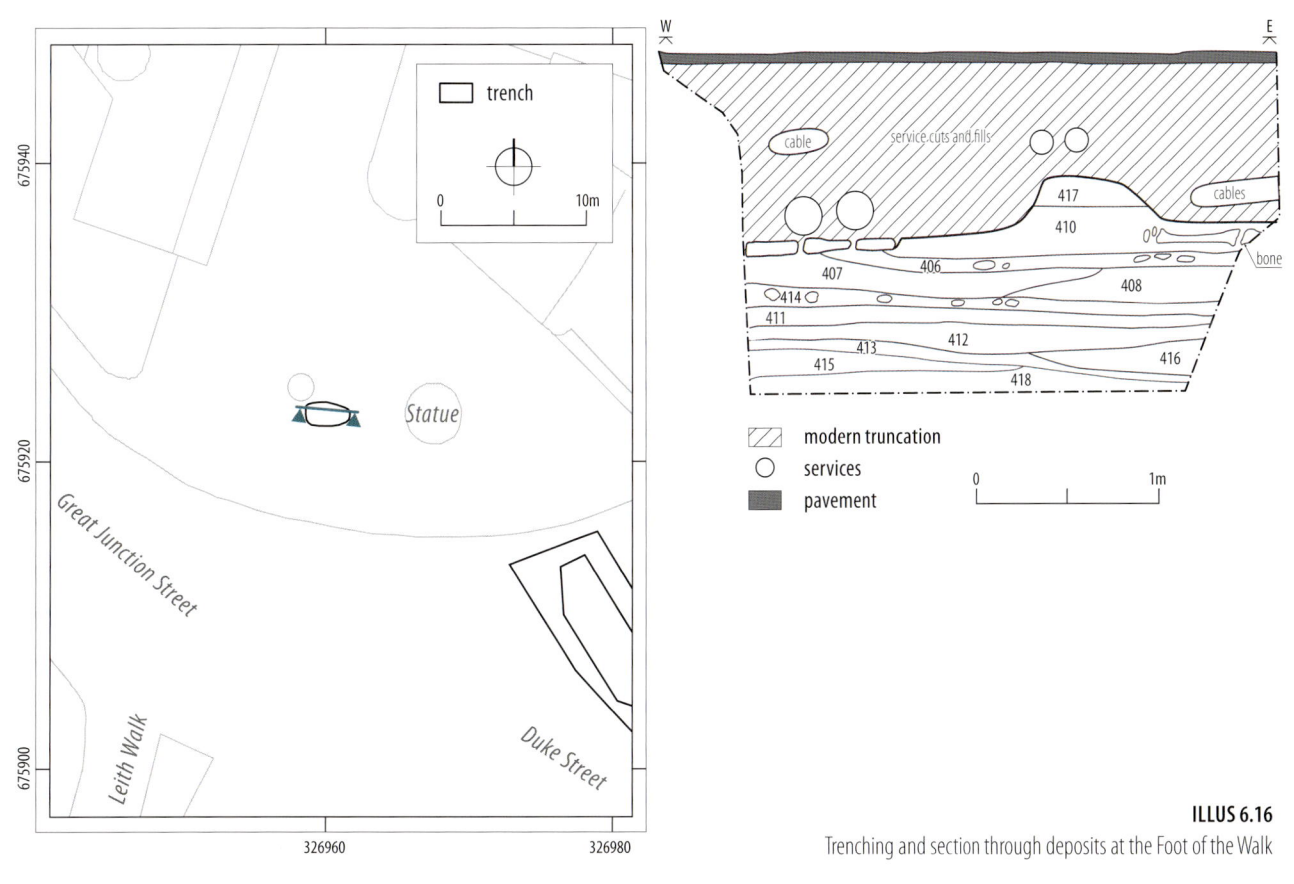

ILLUS 6.16
Trenching and section through deposits at the Foot of the Walk

ILLUS 6.17
Cobbled surface (406) at the Foot of the Walk

DISCUSSION OF THE CONSTITUTION STREET MONITORING FINDINGS

The major difficulty during the watching brief over the service diversions was in the identification of deposits in the long narrow trenches. It was not possible to clarify the extent of many of these deposits, so only tentative interpretations could be made. Despite this, the wide-ranging nature of the archaeological investigations has allowed some insights into the general history and archaeology of the area. It has given important information on the town defences and highlighted areas of good preservation which might be further investigated in the future.

Little in the way of medieval remains was found during this phase of works to add to the medieval findings at the Constitution Street cemetery (*Chapter 4*). This was due both to later truncation and to the excavation depth limits, which meant there was no opportunity to dig deeper into areas with potential for surviving medieval deposits. The architectural fragment found close to St Mary's Church and possibly deriving from the late 15th-century building is of note, though it was probably deposited in the 19th century.

It is from the 16th century onwards that most of the archaeological findings date and several of these can be linked to the mid-16th-century and mid-17th-century defences and sieges. The ditch found at the southern end of Constitution Street clearly relates to the 16th- and 17th-century defences and this adds to the 16th-century ditch found during the Constitution Street excavations (p88–90; 146–48). The associated ramparts behind this were in evidence only in the large amounts of re-deposited natural sand that was present along much of the east side of Constitution Street. These deposits were absent south of Laurie Street where the line of the ramparts turns outwards to enclose a corner bastion (**Illus 3.01**, p23; Paton & Cook 2016, fig 9). They were also absent outside 113 to 119 Constitution Street (just north of Coatfield Lane). This area was close to the line of the 16th-century ramparts and was in the vicinity of the Musselburgh Gate, but it was within the John's Lane bastion half way along the eastern side of the 17th-century fortifications (**Illus 3.03–3.05**, p25–27). Two pieces of round shot from this area might relate to the 16th-century enemy bombardment or the 17th-century defence. The findings add to a growing body of evidence for the location of these defences (Paton & Cook 2016).

The most regular types of archaeological remains recovered from this period were middens and cobbled surfaces. However, dating for these typically relies on a scant collection of finds. The dates varied from late 17th century at Maritime Lane; 16th, early 17th and mid-17th century at Queen Charlotte Street; 17th or early 18th century between Queen Charlotte Street and Coatfield Lane and possibly 15th or 16th century at the Foot of the Walk. In addition, there was a late 16th- or early 17th-century midden discovered during the Constitution Street excavations (p66). It is likely that there are many such pockets of midden deposits, of varying dates, surviving under these streets. There is general agreement that they begin building up from the 16th and 17th centuries. The midden deposits were generally organic-rich, containing rotting food, faeces and the broken remains of domestic paraphernalia. Some objects, such as the horseshoe, speak of passing traffic and the impression is of an increasingly filthy road where animal dung was mixing with domestic sewage and rubbish thrown from the neighbouring buildings.

The cobbled surfaces are generally very rough, made of water-rounded and sub-angular stones pressed into the underlying clayey sand deposits. The roughness of the surfaces suggests these were cartloads of stones strewn across the area and trodden down in an attempt, sometimes it seems a rather vain attempt, to raise the road level above the stinking and probably wheel-rutted mess it was becoming. At Queen Charlotte Street (Compass bar) it was noted that midden material continued to accumulate over the cobbles and thus with no street-cleaning it would have been an on-going battle.

It is interesting that this cycle of midden accumulation and cobbling begins around the 16th century, around the time that Leith was first enclosed by the siege defences. Prior to this the area would simply have been the backland area on the east side of the Kirkgate. During and after the construction of the ramparts it would have become an access route to them.

It is also worth noting the locations of the cobbled surfaces. The cobbles at Queen Charlotte Street and the Foot of the Walk intersect with major east-west streets. Before the late 18th century Queen Charlotte Street was known as Links Road as it led to Leith Links and thence formed the main road eastwards to Musselburgh (Harris 2002, 470). It may have aligned with the Musselburgh Gate on the eastern side of the 1560 fort ramparts, though this is not certain (the location as shown on the Petworth Map (**Illus 3.01**, p23) seems a little too far south). A road leading into town at this point is shown on Adair's 1682 map (**Illus 3.03**, p25). It was, then, clearly a major route into Leith even before the development of this part of Constitution Street, and the cobbled surface might therefore be more to help the state of this road rather than the embryonic Constitution Street.

The junction between Leith Walk and Kirkgate was also clearly an important point where the main road from Edinburgh first entered Leith. Adair's 1682 map (**Illus 3.03**, p25) shows a road leading eastward from this south-eastern corner of the fortifications, approximately in line with the current Duke Street, and thus it would also have formed a junction. The line of Duke Street is visible on Kirkwood's 1759 survey (**Illus 3.05**, p27) but the western continuation, Great Junction Street, was not built until the early 19th century (Harris 2002, 286). Its line is shown as a 'Proposed New Street' on Ainslie's 1804 map.

Mitchell Street, on the other hand, was not an early route. The line of the road is first mapped in 1804 (Ainslie 1804), before which the area seems to have been undeveloped. It is likely that the well-made cobbled surface of squared setts found in this area dates to around this period. The earlier rougher cobbled surface beneath it perhaps relates to traffic to the ramparts during the 16th or 17th centuries.

The only significant later discovery was the terminus of a substantial sea-wall towards the north end of Constitution Street. It probably dates to the 18th century but may stand on earlier foundations dating back to the mid-17th-century seaward defences. The wall demonstrates the on-going efforts to reclaim land from the sea, begun in the 15th century to protect the commercial interests of the port.

It is perhaps worth considering the distribution of glass waste found during the project in view of the history of glass production in the area. Glass waste was a fairly regular find in later deposits, typically associated with 18th-century and later finds, but only within the confines of Leith, along Constitution Street from Mitchell Street to the Foot of the Walk. The first glassworks in Leith were in North Leith, in the citadel from 1663 and another from 1678 on the west bank of the Water of Leith between the current Commercial Street and Sandport Place (Turnbull 2001, 126–7). From 1747 glass was manufactured in South Leith at a glassworks to the north-east of the current junction of Constitution Street and Baltic Street (ibid, 168, illus 34) and production continued there into the early 20th century. It seems likely then that the deposition of glass waste on Constitution Street would post-date the 1747 foundation of the South Leith glassworks.

LEITH WALK

The excavations along Leith Walk comprised chiefly of four long, narrow trenches running the length of the road, to replace services, with various off-shoots cutting across the road (**Illus 6.18**). Typically, these were to a depth of 1.5m below the current ground surface. This area fell between the old towns of Edinburgh and Leith and, though it was used as the main road between them (p36), it was only significantly developed from the later 18th century onwards. The area between Steads Place and Balfour Street is thought to overlie the line of the trenches constructed by the besieging forces in the siege of 1559–60, though no evidence of this was found.

Where modern service excavations had not disturbed the archaeological deposits, these consisted of large tracts of made-ground composed of sands mixed with various amounts of charcoal, building stone and brick. Finds from these deposits were all of 18th-century and later date and it is likely that they relate to the period of the development of these areas over the course of the late 18th and 19th centuries. Natural subsoil was only reached in a few places and it consisted of pale yellow sand. It is possible that traces of earlier activity have survived in places, underneath the made-ground deposits where they extended below the excavation limit. In addition to the medieval remains at the junction with London Road (*Chapter 5*), significant features relating to the old tram network and to 20th century cellarage were also discovered. These are discussed first, followed by a short section on other features.

TRAM CABLE TUNNELS

One of the more serendipitous aspects of the scheme to create a new tram network for the city of Edinburgh was the discovery of structures relating to the former network of cable-powered trams that ran in the city between 1888 and 1922 (p41–42). These cable cars moved around the

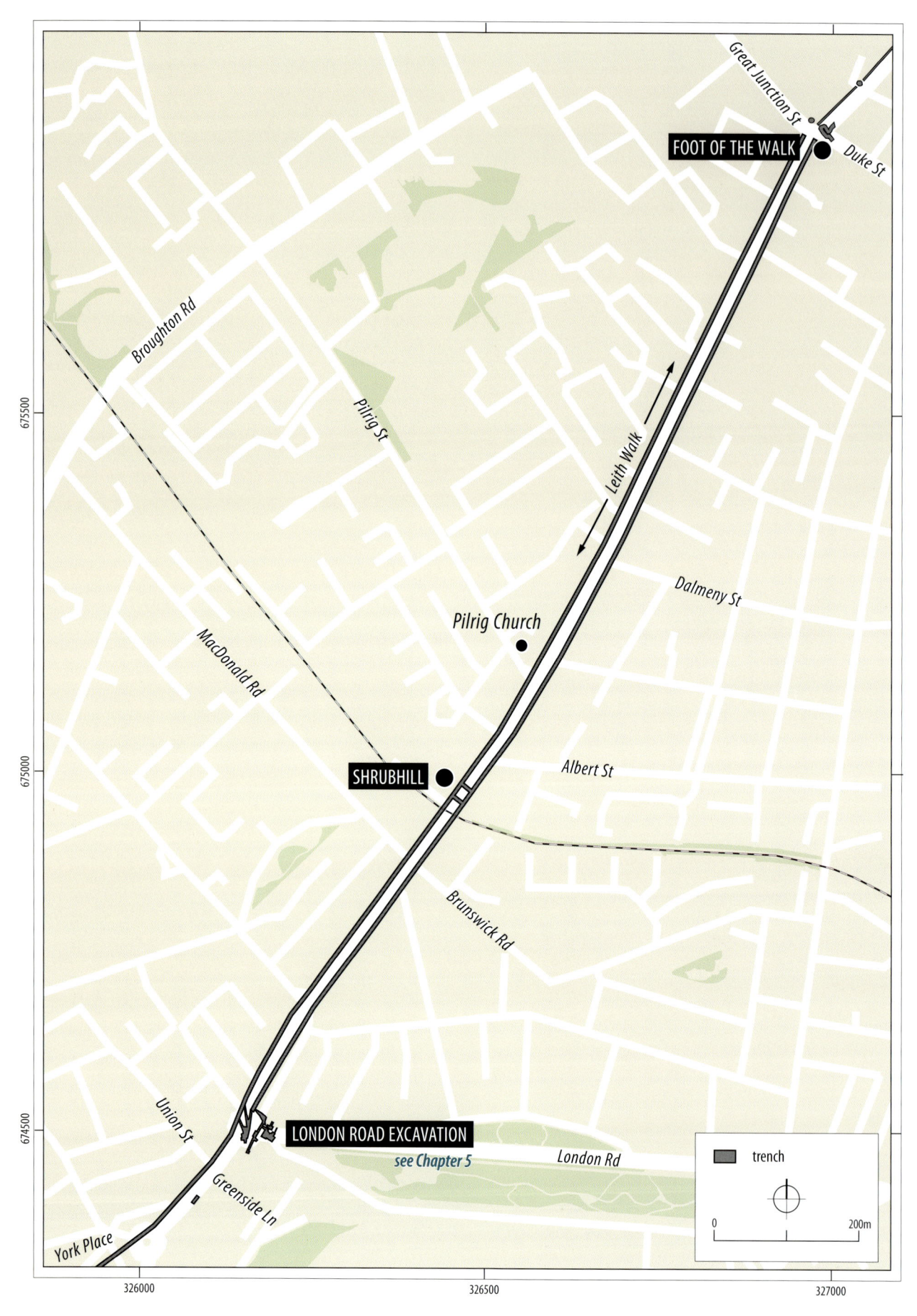

PAST LIVES OF LEITH. ARCHAEOLOGICAL WORK FOR EDINBURGH TRAMS

ILLUS 6.18
Trenching along Leith Walk

city by gripping onto a moving cable in a tunnel below the road. The cables were driven by large steam engines at four tram depots at various points around the city. The remains of some of these cable tunnels were found on Leith Walk.

The tunnel under Leith Walk was encountered in two trenches cutting across the street outside of Shrub Place (**Illus 6.19**), opposite and a little to the north of Shrub Place Lane (or between Albert Street and MacDonald Road/ Brunswick Road). It had a brick base with substantial brick walls on either side, and was 2.80m wide (1.90m internally). The walls survived to a height of 0.95m. The cables and workings had been removed, presumably for scrap value, and it is likely that the channelled roof of the tunnel was removed at the same time. The surviving remains were capped with corrugated iron sheeting supported on steel beams. Though only a short section was visible in detail and it was badly damaged, it appeared to run for at least 30m to 50m down Leith Walk. A continuation of this tunnel was found during a later watching brief at the junction of Leith Walk and Pilrig Street about 210m to the north-east (Moloney and Baker 2017, 6). It was of similar construction and still retained a cast iron cable pulley wheel about 2m in diameter in situ. This was probably the last wheel at the end of the Edinburgh cable tram line where passengers had to disembark and endure the 'Pilrig muddle' to change to Leith's tram network.

The long linear trench running down the west side of Leith Walk encountered an off shoot of this same cable tunnel system that ran westwards towards the engine house at the back of Shrubhill (**Illus 6.19**). Shrubhill was one of the power houses for the cable tram network with an engine house containing two massive steam engines to power the system (**Illus 3.12–3.13**, p42–43). This tunnel had brick walls and an arched brick roof and would have housed the workings that led the cable from the engine house to the street. The other end of this cable tunnel was recorded during work within the Shrubhill depot itself (Bain 2008; Geddes 2008) where it led straight to the engine house.

The cable tunnels fell out of use during the conversion from cable power to electric power in the 1920s when the tram line was upgraded and renovated. Most of the system appears to have been lost at this time. The considerable scrap value of the metal used ensured that this destruction was reasonably thorough, the aforementioned Pilrig Street cable wheel being the one piece of metal hardware discovered.

The finding of the cable tunnel close to Shrubhill (and again near Haymarket) is perhaps no coincidence. It is possible that more substantial infrastructure was needed at these key points and junctions on the network. Elsewhere the cables may have been housed in shallower structures that have since been completely removed.

SUBTERRANEAN CHAMBERS

Further remains were discovered at Antigua Street/Baxter's Place (the names for, respectively, the western and eastern sides of Leith Walk between Union Street/Greenside Lane and London Road) and Greenside Place (the name for the eastern side of Leith Walk south of Greenside Lane) (**Illus 6.20**). The largest of these was a substantial subterranean structure, accessed via a manhole in the centre of the street. Problems with safe access meant that the structure could not be fully surveyed by the archaeological team but a complete plan was created by TIE for engineering purposes and the following description is based on this and various field notes and photographs.

The main chamber was rectangular, approximately 11.9 by 4.5m across, and ran parallel to the road (**Illus 6.21**). The floor sloped gently from south to north, at a similar incline to the modern ground surface. The walls, up to 2.3m high, were composed of cement-bonded bricks, finished with whitewash. Steel girder uprights and frame supports for the roof were found throughout the main chamber. The ceiling comprised corrugated steel sheets held together with rivets. Two alcoves or small chambers adjoined the main chamber, one to the west and one to the south. A series of stalls, divided by single brick width walls up to 1.9m high, were located at the northern end of the main chamber. There was a small gully or drain at the back of the stalls and a pipe ran across the top of them. A strip of bare brick running up the outer edge of the walls suggests they once had doors, though there is no sign of other internal fittings such as shelving or plumbing (**Illus 6.22**). Similar stalls were observed in the alcove on the south side of the main chamber.

Long tunnel corridors led off the main chamber to the north and east. The northern tunnel contained deep standing water and could not be thoroughly investigated but access was possible via a manhole access point towards the northern end and the tunnel was seen to terminate approximately 25m north of the main chamber. The eastern corridor was the original access point to the structure. It was at a lower level, with steps leading down to it about 1.4m from the main chamber. The passage ran for about 12m east before turning, with steps leading up to the north, then east then south to emerge at street level on the pavement outside 4 Baxter's Place. A long rectangular scar on the pavement is still visible in this location where the entrance to this structure would have been. Access today is possible there only via a manhole cover.

The building materials used suggest a construction date in the 1940s or earlier and the presence of electrical fittings suggests it was in use in the 20th century. In the main chamber, a stencilled 'no smoking' sign on the walls might suggest that there was a fire risk inherent within as little thought was given to smoking in terms of air quality through most of the 20th century. It is likely that the

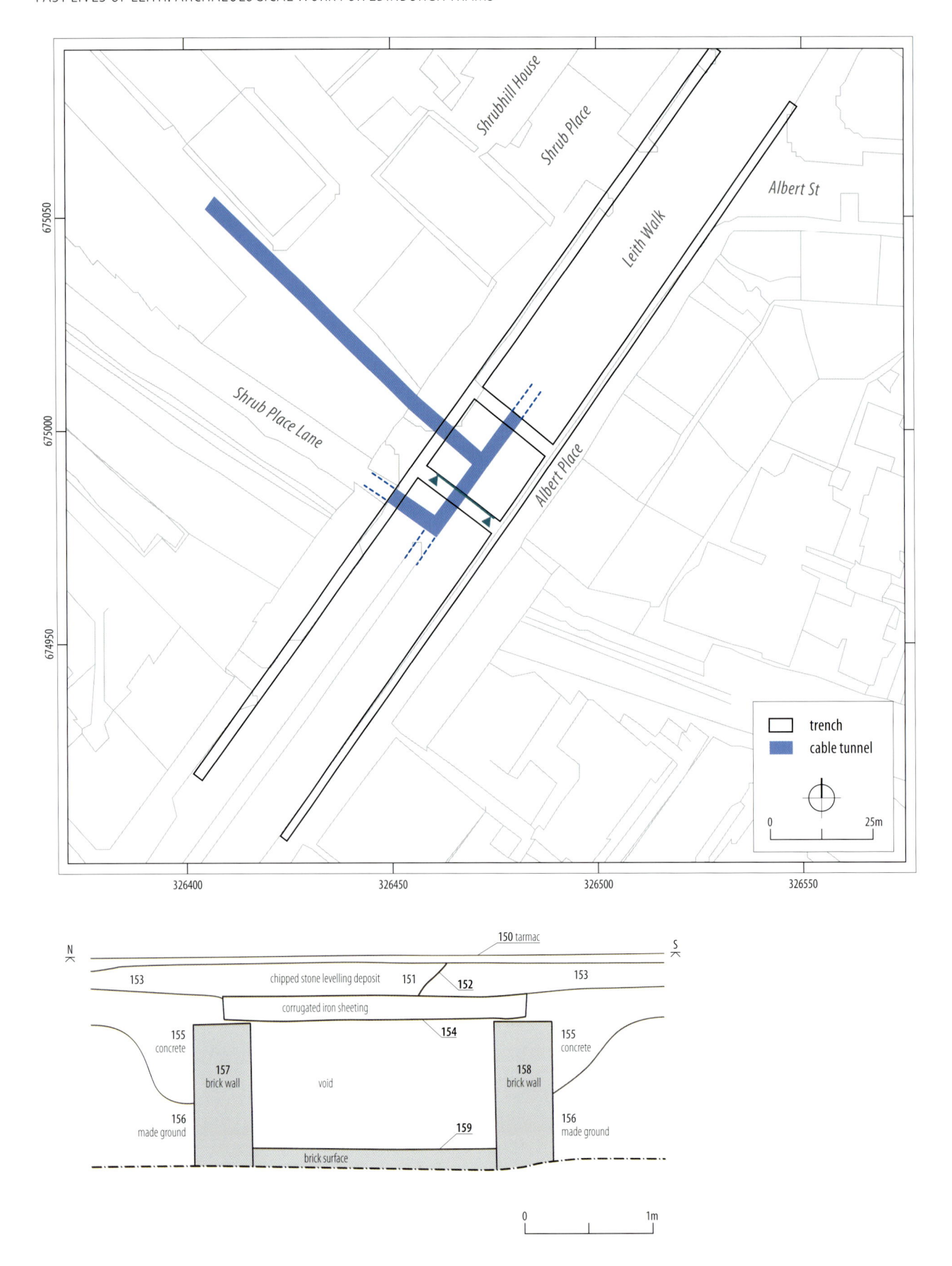

PAST LIVES OF LEITH. ARCHAEOLOGICAL WORK FOR EDINBURGH TRAMS

ILLUS 6.19
Trenching and cable tunnels outside Shrubhill tram depot; section through cable tunnel

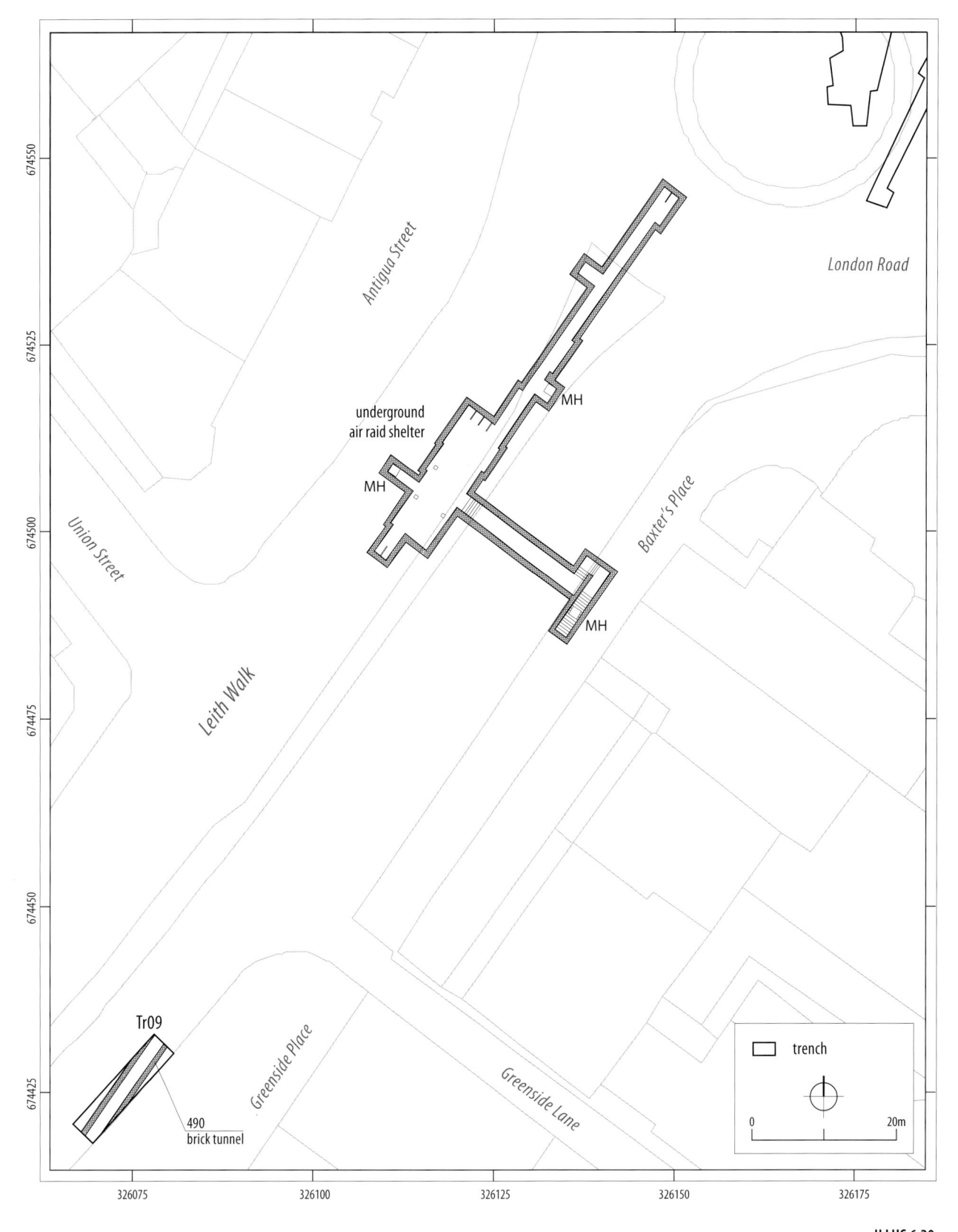

ILLUS 6.20
Baxter's Place and Greenside Place, Leith Walk, trenching and features

structure represents a public air raid shelter dating from World War II. In this context the 'no smoking' sign would be a precaution in the event of gas leaks. The unnecessarily complex turn of the stairs at the eastern entrance would have had the effect of deflecting the force of any blast near the entrance and prevent it travelling down the corridor towards the main chamber. The stalls at the ends of the main chamber are also, clearly, toilet cubicles.

A TEENAGER FROM OUT OF TOWN, 1590–1604

This boy was born in 1590 in Burntisland in Fife. From the shore there the hump of Edinburgh's Arthur's Seat and ridge of Salisbury Crags were clearly visible, with Leith in front of it as a dirty smudge on the seashore.

He was the third son of a fisherman. He was fit and healthy but unlike his brothers he was always seasick and hated work on the boat. He was clever though and his parents thought he might do well for himself if given the opportunity. Through a contact of his mother's family his parents managed to secure an apprenticeship for him with a maltman in Leith. He was only seven when his father ferried him across the Forth to leave him with his new master. His mother wept as she waved them off.

The maltman was an important and wealthy man in the Incorporation of Maltmen. Brewing was so widespread in Leith that malt was always in demand. He had a rather grand tall but narrow stone house towards the southern end of town close to the increasingly dilapidated St Anthony's, which was still home to a handful of old folk. The employees from the maltings were all invited to the house for feasting and merriment on holidays. There was meat, wine, fruit, pies and cakes, served on colourful dishes. The workers drank from pewter cups, as they were not allowed to touch the silver or the beautiful drinking glasses.

The apprentice slept in the maltings behind the house. Rats were a constant problem, attracted by the stores of barley, and they would run over his bed at night. His days were spent hard at work in the maltings. Making malt was a long and laborious process and mistakes could mean the ruination of entire batches and a waste of days work. The grain had to be soaked and dried a number of times and then spread over the floor and kept damp while it sprouted. It then had to be dried by being gently toasted, and the roots which had begun to grow had to be removed by agitating the grains.

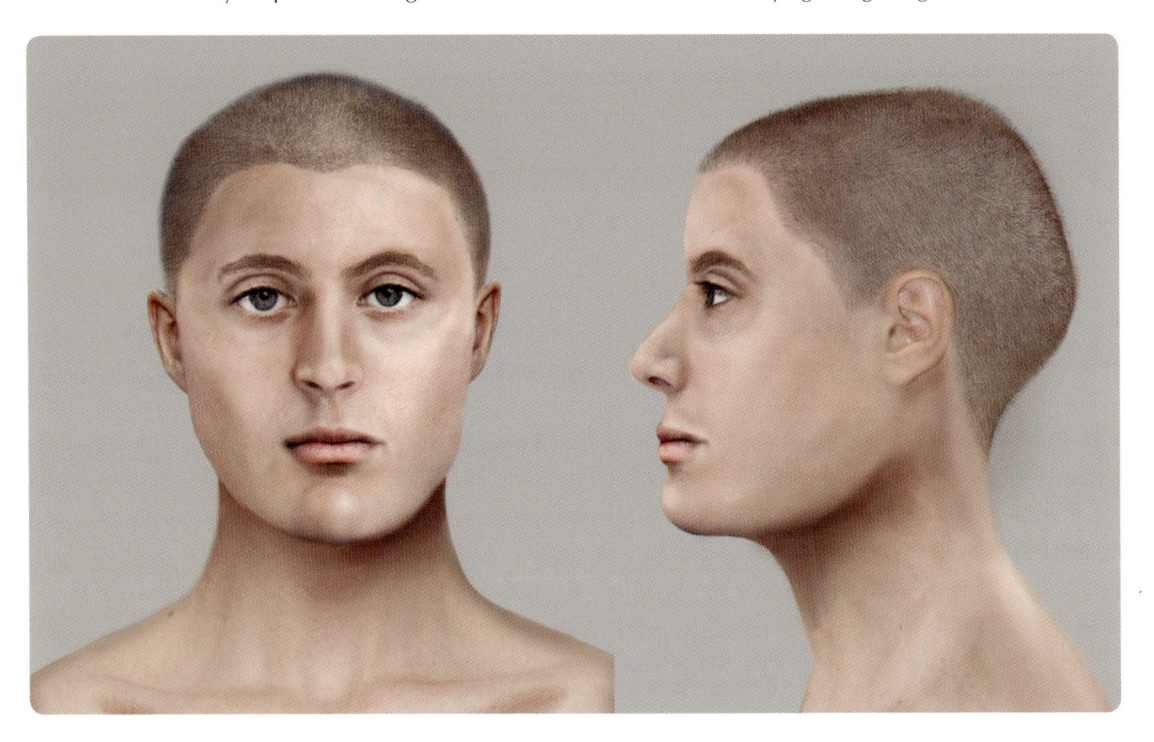

As long as he was working when he should be, no one much bothered about what he did with his own time. There were many distractions in the town, and with a few coins in his pocket and no parents to answer to, he could take full advantage of them.

There were taverns and alehouses, horse racing on Leith sands, dog fights, plays by troupes of travelling actors. He once went to a bear-baiting. There was an archery contest on the Links every year and there was always the spectacle of the stocks and hangings at the tolbooth. In one tavern he met a sailor puffing at a pipe made of white clay. The boy had never seen the like. The man told him it was called tobacco and it came from the New World and let him try it in exchange for a mug of ale. He took a few puffs, was taken with a fit of coughing, and was green sick for the rest of the day.

PEOPLE'S STORIES

SKELETON	0040
Grave	0042
Location of grave	Constitution Street, Area 2
Burial details	Coffin
Age	Adolescent, 12–16
Sex	?
Stature	–
Radiocarbon date	1455–1525 1575–1585 1590–1625 (68% probability); 1445–1635 (95% probability) see Table 4.02, Illus 4.31, p84–85
Other dating evidence	In Phase 4 cemetery, only in use after c1600, possibly associated with 1644–5 plague
Finds	Pin, lace tag
Pathology	Calculus, DEH
C/N isotope (diet)	Normal (c20% marine) see p132–35; Illus 4.68; Table A1.01, p216–17
O/S isotope (origins)	South Fife or Musselburgh? see p136–40; Table A1.03, p218
See also	Illus 4.05, p54; p82; Table 4.24, p76; p124–25
Facial reconstruction artist	Sarah Jaworski

In 1603, Scotland's King James VI departed Edinburgh to take the throne of England. In gratitude for financial help from the burgesses of Edinburgh, he granted them a 'Golden charter' confirming, among other things, Edinburgh's power over Leith. It led to a loss of some of Leith's liberties and Leithers were to complain to the king about an increase in harassment by Edinburgh officials. To make matters worse, cases of plague were once again reported in the town. The latter mattered more to the boy who found that a considerable dampener had been put on his fun. The taverns and alehouses were closed down, the ships ceased to put in at the harbour and the town settled down to the horribly familiar routine. For a while the maltings was spared as the pestilence grumbled on through into the next year. But when one of the maltings men fell sick, others soon followed suit. The boy was found feverish and coughing in his bed one morning. By noon he was delirious and had begun coughing up blood. He was dead the next morning. He was buried in the new plague burial ground set out on the southern side of the St Mary's graveyard. In accordance with regulations, he was wrapped in a shroud and placed in a coffin to contain the pestilence within, before being taken along the road for burial.

A BOY FROM OUT OF TOWN, 1590–1604

ILLUS 6.21
Baxter's Place, chamber supported by props during recording

ILLUS 6.22
Stalls within chamber at Baxter's Place

The buildings on Baxter's Place, adjacent to this chamber, are rather grand Georgian townhouses, but during the middle years of the 20th century one was a public house (no.6, currently a bar called Planet) and the neighbouring structure was the Salon Cinema (no.5, now no.4). The cinema had a large structure to the rear (now demolished) to hold the cinema screen and seating (Ordnance Survey 1933; 1948a; 1957).

An air raid shelter is not shown in this location in a contemporary booklet guide to the location of shelters (Cousland c1940, 16), though there is one shown with an entrance to the south and on the opposite side of the road at Picardy Place. However, given the nature of the structure and locations of its access, it is difficult to imagine what else it might have been, and it is possible its construction post-dated the publication of this booklet. The value of locating a public shelter directly outside a cinema and next to a public house is clear.

Another corridor tunnel was found further to the south on Greenside Place. This too was brick-built measuring 1.0m wide and 3.0m high, aligned NE-SW. Again, it was capped by a corrugated steel sheeting roof. Electrical fittings, and an alcove were present in the walls of the structure. Above the corrugated roof remains of the original tram tracks were visible. Structural similarities with the Baxter's Place chamber suggest that it may have been part of a similar structure.

Similar air raid shelters were found in other parts of the Tram route at the west end of Princes Street at its junction with Lothian Road (Rennie & Will 2013, 23) and at the junction of the junction of Haymarket and West Maitland Street (ibid, 25).

OTHER FEATURES

Other features were all related to the tenements lining Leith Walk. A garden wall was found outside 21 Leith Walk (currently Santander Bank), towards its northern end, opposite the junction with Kirk Street. An arched brick culvert was found outside 4 Albert Place (the east side of Leith Walk between Brunswick Road and Albert Street). It ran perpendicular to the road and is likely to be contemporary with the tenements built on Albert Place in the 1870s.

7 | CONCLUSIONS

Julie Franklin

Like many linear schemes, taken individually the results of the watching brief, with the exception of the burials, are not that significant, but taken as a whole they present a unique opportunity to increase our understanding of the history and archaeology of Edinburgh and Leith. The majority of the archaeological findings were located within the confines of early post-medieval Leith and this work demonstrated the survival of deposits relating to the development of the town from its emergence as a medieval port through to the expanding post-medieval town. Further information was also revealed about the post-medieval defences of Leith. The value of the finds and environmental evidence was often limited by poor stratigraphy, uncertain context dating and the small size of individual context assemblages. The finds frequently provided the only dating for various contexts and this was often tentative. However, some midden assemblages provided opportunities to characterise occupation in the area and some stray finds were of interest in their own right.

The excavations of two cemeteries provided the most coherent archaeological evidence: the small-scale excavations at London Road, and the much larger area excavated at Constitution Street. They were also the most surprising of the results. Human remains were not expected at either site and the early dating for those at Constitution Street, predating the accepted historical dating for the adjacent church, still invites speculation.

MEDIEVAL SETTLEMENT

The study area was largely outwith the bounds of the medieval settlements of both Leith and Edinburgh and thus limited evidence was found for either. There was a scattering of medieval pottery within the cemetery soil on London Road, which suggests some kind of medieval activity in the general area. It is possible that these finds were the result of midden material spread over fields before the foundation of the chapel on the site in the 15th century.

In Leith, two ditches at Constitution Street appear to mark the boundaries of medieval burgage plots set out along the Kirkgate, though there was no evidence for the usual backlands activity associated with horticulture, animal husbandry and industry. It is possible that medieval deposits survive beneath the maximum depth of excavation in some areas.

LATE MEDIEVAL TO EARLY POST-MEDIEVAL BURIAL

The two areas of human burials discovered at Constitution Street and London Road had several things in common. Both were unexpected. Both raised questions about the ecclesiastical establishments with which they were related. Both were broadly contemporary, with the majority of dated burials dating between the mid-15th and mid-17th-centuries.

The Constitution Street burials represented a strip from a much larger multi-phase cemetery on the edge of the contemporary settlement of Leith. It probably began in the late 14th century as a graveyard attached to a small chapel to serve the needs of the growing town and alleviate overcrowding in the graveyard at Restalrig. As the town grew, so did the cemetery, and it expanded in the early/mid-15th century. In the late 15th century, the chapel was rebuilt to the north of the earlier structure as St Mary's, Leith's grand new church, and the graveyard expanded again. The use of the graveyard was curtailed during the Siege of Leith in the mid-16th century when the siege defences cut across it. Burial continued afterwards, in a cemetery extension to the south, that may have been connected to an early 17th-century plague outbreak. The military conflicts of the mid-17th century led to the reconstruction of the defences immediately to the east of the graveyard and thereafter burial was only possible in the shortened graveyard to the west of the excavation area.

The burials at London Road seem to represent two different phases of burial, associated with the Rude Chapel and the Carmelite friary respectively, though it is possible they relate to its later reuse as a leper hospital at the end of the 16th century. No evidence was found for the location of the buildings from any of these establishments. The people buried in the graveyard of the chapel and friary might have lived in the nearby villages or been benefactors who had requested burial there. There is a suggestion that one of the individuals might have been a friar.

Two distinctive local funerary quirks were demonstrated by the burials at Constitution Street. The first is the use of slat-based coffins, which may have been a cheap form of coffin. At present, in Britain, this form of coffin has only been identified in Edinburgh and Leith, at the sites of St Giles Cathedral, and Constitution Street. The second is the regular use of N-S and S-N aligned graves. This has been identified at three sites in Leith but none, to date, in Edinburgh and has only been seen elsewhere on a very occasional basis. It was observed in 1% of the graves at Constitution Street, but a surprising 4% of all graves archaeologically excavated in Leith (**Table 4.01**, p78). On present evidence, the rite seems to be linked to the burials of plague victims from the 15th to 17th centuries.

There is some evidence for clothed burials found at both Constitution Street and London Road. Again, it is possible that there is a plague connection for some of these, though status might also be a factor. The most distinctive was a woman buried wearing an ordinary wool dress fastened at the bodice or sleeves with the aid of laces through wire eyelets (p154).

Suggestions for plague and other epidemics are frequent in the S-N aligned burials, the clothed burials, and the multiple burials. The twenty or so epidemics that cut through the population of Edinburgh, Leith and the Lothians over the course of the mid-14th to mid-17th centuries average as one every 13.5 years or two per generation. To survive until the age of 45 in Leith (as it seems relatively few people did) would mean surviving (on average) at least three epidemics of varying severity, caused by various pathogens. These frequent events probably added impetus to Leith's need for its own burial ground, particularly after the introduction of restrictions of movement during periods of pestilence from the mid-15th century onwards. The spaces in the population and workforce left by the dead it seems were soon filled. Isotope analysis results suggest a significant proportion of the adult population of Leith were incomers from other parts of southern or central Scotland or possibly from further afield (p140). The evidence for syphilis in Leith in the 16th century is also of note (p122). The suggestion that the woman in question might have been a patient of the island quarantine hospital on Inchkeith is particularly intriguing.

The excavated skeletons represent the ordinary population, the working and emerging middle classes. They lived through wars with England, through urban expansion, trading prosperity, strife with neighbouring Edinburgh and through countless epidemics, with incomers regularly making up the numbers in the local population. The people buried at London Road may have come from a rural background of farm labouring or working in the watermills of Canonmills. The Leithers buried at Constitution Street were the seamen, fishermen, porters, coopers, shipwrights, rope-makers, carpenters, masons, shoemakers, tailors, butchers, brewers and malt men, and their families. Some of the more well-to-do people might have been merchants, merchant skippers, King's Wark officials or the wealthier end of other trade incorporations. They have been given an added personal dimension by a programme of facial reconstructions, using some of the better-preserved skulls. The opportunity to see the faces of some of the people discussed in this volume provides a closer link with them and a few of the more interesting stories behind these faces have been told throughout the book.

EARLY POST-MEDIEVAL WARFARE IN LEITH

Evidence was found of probably both 16th- and 17th-century siege ditches, with the associated but since flattened ramparts being represented by large quantities of redeposited sand. These ramparts probably covered all the burials discovered at Constitution Street, and the ditch cutting would have disturbed many more that have since been found as charnel in various locations in the area. Evidence for the defences was found in several areas along Constitution Street, with the most significant being the ditches found during the Constitution Street excavations and monitoring of the Constitution Street/Duke Street junction. These ditches agreed with the historic cartographic evidence for the locations of the rampart lines and bastions, and while independent dating evidence for them was scarce and open to interpretation, it was not inconsistent with the accepted dating of these works. The only detailed evidence for the backfilling of these ditches came from an area at the Constitution Street/Duke Street ditch where partial backfilling was rapid, presumably in the later 17th century, but the ditch was left part-filled for some time before being infilled during the development of the area in the later 18th century. Again, this agrees with historic cartographic evidence.

The only evidence for military action during either of the sieges was in the form of two pieces of round shot, one of stone, one of cast iron, found mid-way along Constitution Street. They might relate to either the 16th-century bombardment, or a cache of 17th-century defensive balls.

EARLY POST-MEDIEVAL SETTLEMENT AND TRADE IN LEITH

The evidence for the early post-medieval settlement was confined to Leith and was represented by middens and cobbled surfaces. The build-up of middens, muck and rough cobbled surfaces along Constitution Street is evidence for the increased urbanisation of this area after its enclosure by the defensive ramparts. The area became more of a thoroughfare with material building up when thrown from neighbouring houses and passing traffic, particularly where east-west routes crossed the area. The slapdash nature of these cobbled surfaces and the continued build-up of midden over them suggests this was not an organised municipal drive to improve infrastructure and public health, but more ad hoc attempts, possibly by individual residents, businesses or guilds, to improve their immediate environment and access to their buildings.

The piecemeal nature of the excavations meant that the individual assemblages from these midden deposits were small, but taken as a group they include a high proportion of imported and luxury goods. While these clearly relate to Leith's trading links and its status as Scotland's leading port from the 15th century onwards, it is arguable whether these were objects being used by the people of Leith or just passing through on their way from dockside to market in Edinburgh. Finds of imported goods might represent broken and discarded elements from ships' cargoes. While officially the people of Leith were forbidden from engaging in foreign trade, there is plenty of historical evidence that they did and merchant skippers and ordinary seamen might have indulged in private trade and brought back many goods for their own personal use. In addition, there was also a large immigrant population, including French clergy at St Anthony's, Hanseatic merchants, foreign seamen and, most particularly, for over a decade in the mid-16th century, a very large number of French soldiers and courtiers. These people may have brought items with them or had them sent over later.

Luxury goods included silk cloth and fine vessel glass. There are also a number of sherds of decorative tablewares, including French Beauvais sgraffito slipware, Anglo-Dutch tin-glazed earthenware and German Weser slipware. French chafing dishes are also represented, used to keep food warm at the table, while a Seville olive jar implies the importation of olives, olive oil or possibly honey from Spain. While it is tempting to link the presence of 16th-century French pottery directly with the French occupation of the town, the French influence in the country at large meant that there were strong trading links with France at the time (Haggarty 2006) and French wares have a wider distribution throughout Scotland. The majority of the goods were of Low Countries origin, reflecting Edinburgh and Leith's North Sea trading links. A merchant's trade token or jeton can be directly linked to trading activities.

More prosaic evidence for trading links comes in the form of a number of Low Countries redware cooking pots and a Frechen stoneware jug. These would have been of little value but do reflect changing cooking and drinking habits at the time. A Tyneside clay pipe also tells an interesting story of Royalist piracy during the Commonwealth period (p173).

Evidence for diet came both from food waste and from the results of isotope analysis. The latter indicated that the people of Leith and those further inland buried at London Road all consumed significant quantities of seafood. Food waste remains suggest this was in the form of fish, oysters, periwinkles, mussels, scallops, whelks, cockles and limpets. Terrestrial fare was in the form of hulled barley, oats and wheat, mutton, beef and pork. There is also evidence for the presence of horse, cats, linen and coal. The frequency with which coal is found suggests it was the more common fuel used at this period, over wood.

Various finds of building materials hint at fine buildings in Leith during this period. There were two architectural fragments, a fragment of Flemish floor tile and several fragments of stone roof tile. Of particular note was the large decorative architectural fragment, possibly deriving from St Mary's Church (p179–83).

LATER DEVELOPMENT AND INFRASTRUCTURE

Evidence of later development was found in many areas. Constitution Street and Leith Walk both saw heavy development and construction during the 18th and 19th centuries. The sea wall towards the north end of Constitution Street marked on-going efforts to create more useable space within Leith, as well as to protect the town from rough seas and sand-blow. Various remains of tenement walls and road surfaces were found. The World War II air raid shelter found at Baxter's Place was an interesting discovery.

Perhaps the most fitting of all the discoveries made during the project were the features associated with the old Edinburgh cable trams of the early 20th century. Given the size of the cable tunnels and the necessity to build them along the entire length of Edinburgh's tram routes, the scale of the engineering project is impressive. One can only imagine the grumblings about the disruption to traffic and business caused by these works at the time. It is rather sad that, after all that work, the cables were only in use for 23 years. Edinburgh's new trams, we hope, will last longer.

THE FACES OF LATE MEDIEVAL AND EARLY POST-MEDIEVAL LEITH

CS = Constitution Street
LR = London Road.
See Tables A2.01–2.02, p218–33 for details.

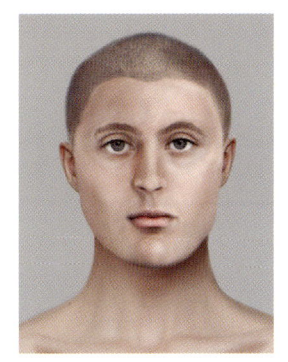

CS Sk0040
Sarah Jaworski

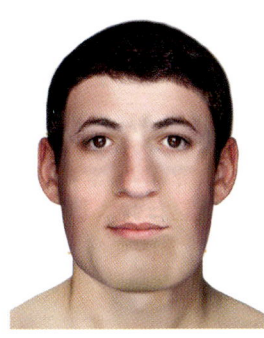

CS Sk0060
Crystal Symes

CS Sk0117
Emily McCulloch

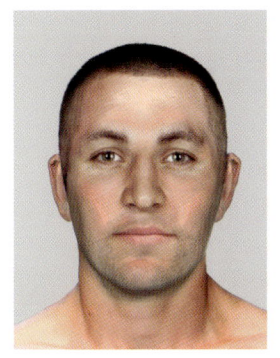

CS Sk0158
Emily McCulloch

CS Sk0166
Emily McCulloch

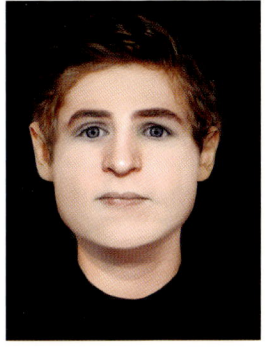

CS Sk0251
Paloma Galzi

CS Sk0281
Crystal Symes

CS Sk0428
Emily McCulloch

CS Sk0429
Paloma Galzi

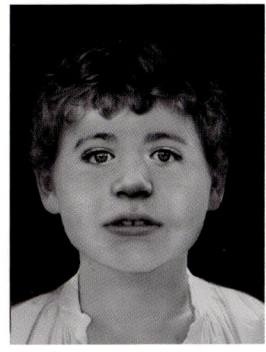

CS Sk0434
Paloma Galzi

CS Sk0514
Sarah Jaworski

CS Sk0527
Sarah Jaworski

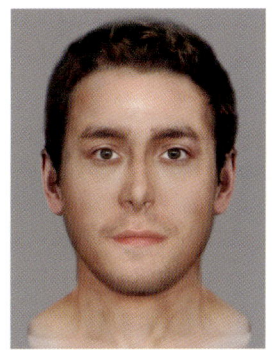

CS Sk0570
Hayley Fisher

CS Sk0574
Heather Goodrum

CS Sk0581
Crystal Symes

PEOPLE'S STORIES

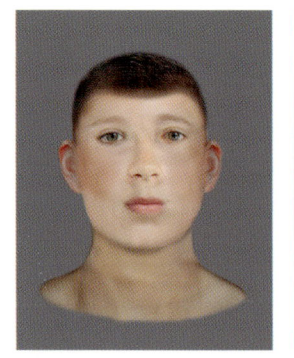

CS Sk0607
Dagmara Roguska

CS Sk0613
Hew Morrison

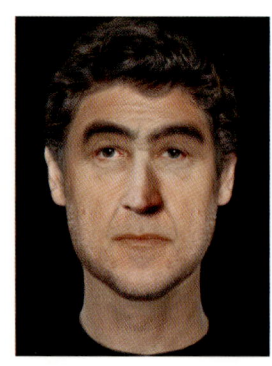

CS Sk0617
Paloma Galzi

CS Sk0625
Sarah Jaworski

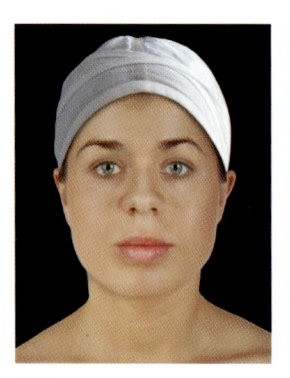

CS Sk0637
Hew Morrison

CS Sk0639
Paloma Galzi

CS Sk0643
Paloma Galzi

CS Sk0704
Crystal Symes

CS Sk0718
Paloma Galzi

CS Sk0784
Paloma Galzi

CS Sk0791
Hew Morrison

CS Sk0837
Paloma Galzi

CS Sk0880
Dagmara Roguska

CS Sk0889
Crystal Symes

CS Sk0902
Emily McCulloch

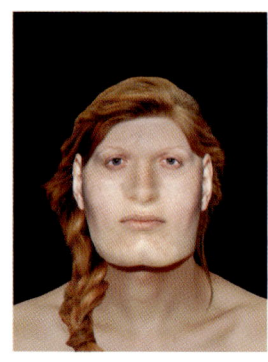

CS Sk0913
Crystal Symes

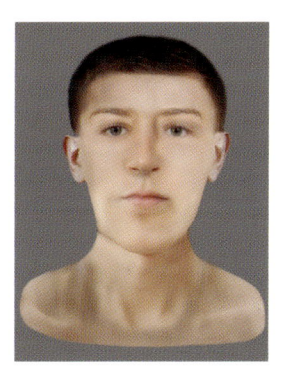

CS Sk0926
Dagmara Roguska

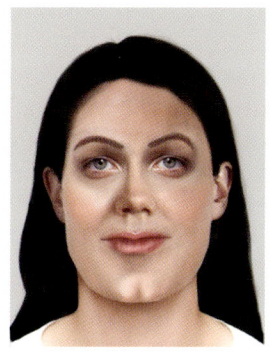

CS Sk0948
Sarah Jaworski

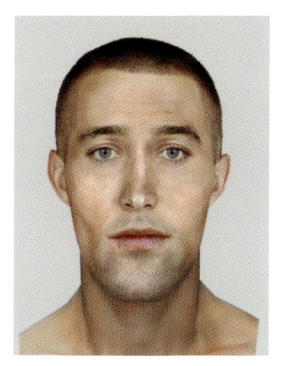

CS Sk0951
Emily McCulloch

CS Sk0956
Crystal Symes

CS Sk0966
Sarah Jaworski

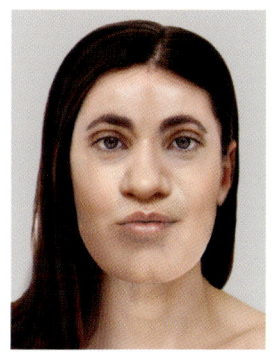

CS Sk0984
Sarah Jaworski

CS Sk0991
Paloma Galzi

CS Sk1015
Paloma Galzi

CS Sk1030
Dagmara Roguska

CS Sk1057
Crystal Symes

CS Sk1095
Emily McCulloch

CS Sk1180
Miriam Modenes

CS Sk1181
Miriam Modenes

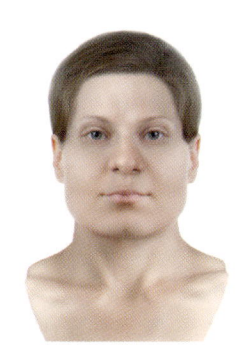

CS Test-trenching (249)
Hayley Fisher

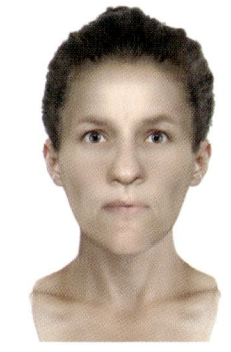

LR Sk453
Hayley Fisher

LR Sk466
Hayley Fisher

THE FACES OF LATE MEDIEVAL AND EARLY POST-MEDIEVAL LEITH

8 | REFERENCES

Aktan AM, Kara S, Akgünlü F & Malkoç S (2010) 'The incidence of canine transmigration and tooth impaction in a Turkish subpopulation' *The European Journal of Orthodontics* 32(5), 575–81

Ambrose SH (1990) 'Preparation and characterization of bone and tooth collagen for isotopic analysis' *Journal of Archaeological Science* 17, 431–51

Ambrose SH (1993) 'Isotopic analysis of palaeodiets: methodological and interpretative considerations', in Sandford MK (ed) *Investigations of ancient human tissue: chemical analyses in anthropology*, 59–130, Langhorne

Ambrose SH & Norr L (1993) 'Experimental evidence for the relationship of the carbon isotope ratios of whole diet and dietary protein to those of bone collagen and carbonate', in Lambert JB and Grupe G (eds) *Prehistoric Human Bone: Archaeology at the Molecular Level*, 1–37, New York

American Academy of Orthopaedic Surgeons (AAOS) 2009 *Osteoid osteoma* http://orthoinfo.aaos.org/topic.cfm?topic=A00507 accessed 27 October 2017

Anderson S (2009) 'Human Skeletal Remains', in White RHM & O'Connell C 'Excavations on the Site of Balmerino House, Constitution Street, Leith' *Scottish Archaeological Internet Reports* 41, 14–18 https://doi.org/10.5284/1017938 accessed 27 October 2017

Arneborg J, Heinemeier J, Lynnerup N, Nielsen HL, Rud N & Sveinbjörnsdóttir ÁE (1999) 'Change of Diet of the Greenland Vikings Determined from Stable Carbone Isotope Analysis and 14C Dating of their Bones' *Radiocarbon* 41(2), 157–68

Arnott H (1818) *The history of Edinburgh from the Earliest Accounts to the Year 1780* Edinburgh

Aufderheide AC & Rodríguez-Martín C 1998 *The Cambridge Encyclopedia of Human Paleopathology* Cambridge

Baart JM (1994) 'Dutch Redwares' *Medieval Ceramics* 18, 19–27

Bailey L, Borden A, Jones E, McMeekin J, Murray R & Simonsson M 2013 *Edinburgh Trams: A Data Structure Report for Watching Briefs on Utility Diversions for the Edinburgh Trams Project 2008–2010* [unpublished client report] Headland Archaeology

Bain K 2008 *Shrubhill Transport Depot, Edinburgh* [unpublished client report] Headland Archaeology, Ref. SBD05–002

Bain S (1998) 'Excavation of a medieval cemetery at Holyrood Abbey, Edinburgh' *Proceedings of the Society of Antiquaries of Scotland* 128, 1047–77

Beaumont J, Gledhill A, Lee-Thorp J & Montgomery J (2013) 'Childhood diet: A closer examination of the evidence from dental tissues using stable isotope analysis of segmental human dentine' *Archaeometry* 55, 277–95

Bentley RA (2006) 'Strontium isotopes from the earth to the archaeological skeleton: a review' *Journal of Archaeological Method and Theory* 13(3), 135–87

Bergman RA, Afifi AK & Miyauchi R (1988) 'Skeletal systems: cranium', in Bergman RA, Thompson S & Afifi AK (eds) *Compendium of human anatomical variations: Text, Atlas, and World Literature*, 197–205, Baltimore

Berry AC & Berry RJ (1967) 'Epigenetic variation in the human cranium' *Journal of Anatomy* 101(Pt 2), 361–79

Blanda J, Bethem D, Moats W & Lew M (1993) 'Defects of pars interarticularis in athletes: a protocol for nonoperative treatment' *Journal of Spinal Disorders* 6, 406–11

Blomqvist R & Mårtenson AW (1963) *Thulegrävningen 1961: en berättelse om vad grävningarna för Thulehuset i Lund avslöjade* Lund

Bocherens H & Drucker D (2003) 'Trophic Level Isotopic Enrichment of Carbon and Nitrogen in Bone Collagen: Case Studies from Recent and Ancient Terrestrial Ecosystems' *International Journal of Osteoarchaeology* 13, 46–53

Bogaard A, Heaton THE, Poulton P & Merbach I (2007) 'The impact of manuring on nitrogen isotope ratios in cereals: archaeological implications for reconstruction of diet and crop management practices' *Journal of Archaeological Science* 34, 335–43

Bondioli L, Corruccini RS & Macchiarelli R (1986) 'Familial segregation in the Iron Age community of Alfedena, Abruzzo Italy, based on osteodontal trait analysis' *American Journal of Physical Anthropology* 71, 393–400

Booth G (1988) *Edinburgh Trams and Buses* Edinburgh

Boucher A, Craddock-Bennett L & Daly T (2015) *Death in the Close: a Medieval Mystery* Edinburgh

Bouquot JE 2011 'Palatal and mandibular torus and exostosis' *The Maxillofacial Centre for Diagnostics and Research* http://www.maxillofacialcenter.com/BondBook/bone/torus.html accessed June 2011

Bowler D & Hall D (1995) 'Kinnoull Street', in Bowler D, Cox A & Smith C 'Four excavations in Perth, 1979–84' *Proceedings of the Society of Antiquaries of Scotland* 125, 939–47

Boyd WE (1989) 'Perth: The Wooden Coffins', in Stones JA (ed) Three Scottish Carmelite Friaries: Aberdeen, Linlithgow and Perth 1980–85 *Society of Antiquaries of Scotland Monograph Series* 6, 117–8, Edinburgh

Boylston A & Lee F (2008) 'Joint disease', in Magilton J, Lee F & Boylston A (eds) *Lepers outside the Gate: Excavations at the Cemetery of the Hospital of St. James and St. Mary Magdalene, Chichester, 1986–87 and 1993, 239–51* York

Bremner D (1869) *The Industries of Scotland, their Rise, Progress and Present Condition* Edinburgh

Brettell R, Montgomery J & Evans J (2012) 'Brewing and stewing: the effect of culturally mediated behaviour on the oxygen isotope composition of ingested fluids and the implications for human provenance studies' *Journal of Analytical Atomic Spectrometry* 27, 778–85

Brickley M (2000) 'The diagnosis of metabolic disease in archaeological bone', in Cox M & Mays S (eds) *Human osteology in archaeology and forensic science,* 183–98, London

Brickley M 2004 'Compiling a skeletal inventory: articulated human bone', in Brickley M & McKinley JI (eds) *Guidelines to the Standards for Recording Human Remains* (Paper No 7, BABAO, IFA: Reading),6–7 http://www.archaeologists.net/sites/default/files/ifa_paper_7.pdf accessed 24 October 2017

Brickley M & Ives R (2006) 'Skeletal manifestations of infantile scurvy' *American Journal of Physical Anthropology* 129, 163–72

British Geological Survey (BGS) 2018 *Geology of Britain* http://mapapps.bgs.ac.uk/geologyofbritain3d/index.html accessed 22 January 2018

Britton K, Muldner G & Bell M (2008) 'Stable isotope evidence for salt-marsh grazing in the Bronze Age Severn Estuary, UK: implications for palaeodietary analysis at coastal sites' *Journal of Archaeological Science* 35, 2111–8

Britton K, Knecht R, Nehlich O, Hillerdal C, Davis RS & Richards MP (2013) 'Maritime Adaptations and Dietary Variation in Prehistoric Western Alaska: Stable Isotope Analysis of Permafrost-Preserved Human Hair' *American Journal of Physical Anthropology* 151(3), 448–61

Britton K, Fuller BT, Tutken T, Mays S & Richards MP (2015) 'Oxygen isotope analysis of human bone phosphate evidences weaning age in archaeological populations' *American Journal of Physical Anthropology* 157(2), 226–41

Bromley C, Bradshaw P & Given L (eds) (2009) *The Scottish Health Survey 2008,* [online] http://www.scotland.gov.uk/Publications/2009/09/28102003/0 accessed 05 August 2011

Bronk Ramsey C (2009) 'Bayesian Analysis of Radiocarbon Dates' *Radiocarbon* 51(1), 337–60

Bronk Ramsey C (2017) 'Methods for Summarizing Radiocarbon Datasets', *Radiocarbon* 59(2), 1809–33

Brooks ST & Suchey JM (1990) 'Skeletal age determination based on the os pubis: a comparison of the Acsadi–Nemeskeri and Suchey–Brooks methods' *Human Evolution* 5, 227–38

Brothwell DR (1981) *Digging Up Bones* (3rd edn) New York

Brown G & Roberts JA (2000) 'Excavations in the medieval cemetery at the city churches, Dundee' *Tayside and Fife Archaeological Journal* 6, 70–86

Brown TA, Nelson DE, Vogel JS & Southon JR (1988) 'Improved collagen extraction by modified Longin method' *Radiocarbon* 30,171–7

Bruce J (ed) (1840) *Annals of First Four Years of the Reign of Queen Elizabeth* London

Buckberry J (2000) 'Missing, presumed buried? Bone diagenesis and the under-representation of Anglo-Saxon children' *Assemblage: University of Sheffield Graduate StudentJournal of Archaeology* 5, https://bradscholars.brad.ac.uk/bitstream/handle/10454/676/Buckberry_3.pdf?sequence=3andisAllowed=y accessed 24 October 2017

Buikstra JE & Ubelaker DH (eds) (1994) *Standards for Data Collection from Human Skeletal Remains* Arkansas Archaeological Survey Research Series 44, Fayetteville

Butt J (1967) *Industrial Archaeology of Scotland* Newton Abbot

Byers SN (2010) *Introduction to Forensic Anthropology* (3rd edn) Boston

Caldwell DH (1981) 'Gunstones', in Good GL & Tabraham CJ 'Excavations at Threave Castle, Galloway, 1974–78' *Medieval Archaeology* 25, 126–29

Caldwell DH (1991) 'Tantallon Castle, East Lothian: a catalogue of the finds' *Proceedings of the Society of Antiquaries Scotland* 121, 335–57

Caldwell DH & Dean VE (1992) 'The pottery industry at Throsk, Stirlingshire, in the 17th and early 18th century' *Post-Medieval Archaeology* 26, 1–46

Campbell A (1827) *The History of Leith* Leith

Campbell Irons J (1898) *Leith and its Antiquities from the earliest times to the close of the Nineteenth Century* Edinburgh

Canmore https://canmore.org.uk/, accessed 16 August 2018

Caple C (1983) 'Pins and wires', in Mayes P and Butler LAS *Sandal Castle Excavations 1964–1973, 269–78* Leeds

Capo RC, Stewart BW & Chadwick OA (1998) 'Strontium isotopes as tracers of ecosystem processes: Theory and methods' *Geoderma* 82, 197–225

Cardy A (1997) 'The Human Bones' in Hill P *Whithorn and St Ninian: The Excavation of a Monastic Town 1984–91, 519–62* Stroud

Chalmers G (1887) *Caledonia: or a historical and topographical account of North Britain* (Vol 2)Paisley

Chamberlain AT (2006) *Demography in Archaeology* Cambridge

Chambers R (1967) *Traditions of Edinburgh* Edinburgh

Chenery CA, Pashley V, Lamb AL, Sloane HJ & Evans JA (2012) 'The oxygen isotope relationship between the phosphate and structural carbonate fractions of human bioapatite' *Rapid Communications in Mass Spectrometry* 26, 309–19

REFERENCES

Churchill D 2016 *St Mary's RC Primary School, 30 Links Gardens, Leith, Edinburgh: Archaeological Excavation Assessment and Data Structure Report* [unpublished client report] Wardell Armstrong LLP

Clark J (1998) 'The Horseshoes', in Cowie R & Pipe A 'A Late Medieval and Tudor Horse Burial Ground: Excavations at Elverton Street, Westminster' *Archaeological Journal* 155, 239–40

Clarke PV (1976) 'German stoneware', in Schofield J 'Excavations south of Edinburgh High Street, 1973–4' *Proceedings of the Society of Antiquaries of Scotland* 107, 206–11

Cluett J 2017 'Avulsion fracture of the fifth metatarsal' *Verywell* https://www.verywell.com/avulsion-fracture-of-the-fifth-metatarsal-2548665 accessed 27 October 2017

Coad J (1997) 'Defending the Realm: the changing technology of warfare', in Gaimster D & Stamper P (eds) *The Age of Transition: the archaeology of English Culture 1400–1600* 157–69,Oxford

Coenen L & Biltjes I (1992) 'High radial nerve palsy caused by a humeral exostosis: a case report' *Journal of Hand Surgery (American Volume)* 17, 668–9

Coleman R (1996) 'Excavations at Abbot's house, Marygate, Dunfermline' *Tayside and Fife Archaeological Journal* 2, 71–112

Collard MA & Reed D (1994) 'Burgess Street/Water Street/Shore Place, Leith' *Discovery and Excavation in Scotland* 1994, 48, Edinburgh

Collard M, Lawson JA & Holmes N (2006) 'Archaeological excavations in St Giles' Cathedral, Edinburgh, 1981–93' *Scottish Archaeological Internet Reports* 22 https://doi.org/10.5284/1017938 accessed 01 May 2018

Collins MJ & Galley P (1998) 'Towards an optimal method of archaeological collagen extraction: the influence of pH and grinding' *Ancient Biomolecules* 2, 209–22

Coplen TB (1988) 'Normalization of oxygen and hydrogen isotope data' *Chemical Geology: Isotope Geoscience Section* 72, 293

Cousland, CJ c1940 *Guide to Edinburgh Air Raid Shelters, CJ Cousland and Sons Ltd, Edinburgh, Ph.20425* http://www.edinphoto.org.uk/0_B/0_books_-_edinburgh_air_raid_shelters.htm accessed 02 July 2018

Cowan IB & Easson DE (1976) *Medieval Religious Houses: Scotland* (2nd edn) London

Cross JF & Bruce MF (1989) 'The skeletal remains', in Stones JA (ed) *Three Scottish Carmelite Friaries: Aberdeen, Linlithgow and Perth 1980–85* Society of Antiquaries of Scotland Monograph Series 6, 119–42, Edinburgh

Crowfoot E, Pritchard F & Staniland K (1992) *Textiles and Clothing c.1150-c.1450 (Medieval Finds from Excavations in London 4)* London

Currarino G, Sheffield E & Twickler, D (1998) 'Congenital glenoid dysplasia' *Pediatric Radiology* 28, 30–7

Dalland M 2016 *Wellington Place, Leith: Archaeological Watching Brief* [unpublished client report] Headland Archaeology, Ref. WPLE

D'Ambrosia R & Ferguson Jr AB (1968) 'The formation of osteochondroma by epiphyseal cartilage transplantation' *Clinical Orthopaedics and Related Research* 61, 103–15

Daniell C (1997) *Death and Burial in Medieval England 1066–1550* London

Dansgaard W (1964) 'Stable isotopes in precipitation' *Tellus* 16, 436–68

Darling WG (2004) 'Hydrological factors in the interpretation of stable isotopic proxy data present and past: a European perspective' *Quaternary Science Reviews* 7/8, 743–70

Darling WG & Talbot JC (2003) 'The O and H stable isotopic composition of fresh waters in the British Isles. 1. Rainfall' *Hydrology and Earth System Sciences* 7(2), 163–81

Darling WG, Bath AH & Talbot JC (2003) 'The O and H stable isotopic composition of fresh waters in the UK British Isles. 2. Surface waters and groundwater' *Hydrology and Earth System Sciences* 7(2), 183–95

Das S, Suri R & Kapur V (2005) 'Anatomical observations on os inca and associated cranial deformities' *Folia Morphologiica* 64, 118–21

Daux V, Lécuyer C, Adam F, Martineau F & Vimeux F (2005) 'Oxygen isotope analysis of human teeth and the record of climate changes in France (Lorraine) during the last 1700 years' *Climatic Change* 70, 445–64

Daux V, Lécuyer C, Héran MA, Amiot R, Simon L, Fourel F, Martineau F, Lynnerup N, Reychler H & Escarguel G (2008) 'Oxygen isotope fractionation between human phosphate and water revisited' *Journal of Human Evolution* 55, 1138–47

Dawes JD & Magilton JR (1980) *The Cemetery of St Helen-on-the-Walls, Aldwark* The Archaeology of York: The Medieval Cemeteries 12/1, York

Dawson J (2002) 'Marine Shell', in Stronach S 'The medieval development of South Leith and the creation of Rotten Row' *Proceedings of the Society of Antiquaries of Scotland* 132, 414

Defoe D (1762) *A Tour Through the Whole Island of Great Britain* London

DeNiro MJ (1985) 'Postmortem preservation and alteration of in vivo bone collagen isotope ratios in relation to palaeodietary reconstruction' *Nature* 317, 806–9

DeNiro MJ & Epstein S (1978) 'Influence of diet on the distribution of carbon isotopes in animals' *Geochimica et Cosmochimica Acta* 42, 495–506

DeNiro MJ & Epstein S (1981) 'Influence of diet on the distribution of nitrogen isotopes in animals' *Geochimica et Cosmochimica Acta* 45, 341–51

DePalma AF (1983) 'Biologic aging of the shoulder', in DePalma AF (ed) *Surgery of the Shoulder,* 211–41, Philadelphia

Dickson T (ed) (1877) *Accounts of the Lord High Treasurer of Scotland 1877, Volume 1: AD 1473–1498* Edinburgh

Dictionary of the Scots Language (DSL) http://dsl.ac.uk accessed 27 October 2017

Druce HM (1998) 'Allergic and nonallergic rhinitis', in Middleton EM, Reed CE, Ellis EF, Adkinson NF, Yunginger JW & Busse WW (eds) *Allergy: Principles and Practice* (5th edn), 1005–16, St. Louis

Duncan C & Scott S (2004) *Return of the Black Death – the world's greatest serial killer* London

Eames E (1976) 'The plain glazed floor tiles', in Schofield J 'Excavations south of Edinburgh High Street, 1973–4' *Proceedings of the Society of Antiquaries of Scotland* 107, 211–3

Eames E (1985) 'Plain Glazed Floor Tiles', in Holmes NM 'Excavations south of Bernard Street, Leith, 1980' *Proceedings of the Society of Antiquaries of Scotland* 115, 423–4

Edwards L (1988) *The Archaeology of the Clay Tobacco Pipe Vol XI: Seventeenth and Eighteenth Century Tyneside Tobacco Pipe Makers and Tobacconists* BAR British Series 192, Oxford

Egan G (2005) *Material culture in London in an age of transition: Tudor and Stuart period finds c1450–c1700 from excavations at riverside sites in Southwark* MoLAS Monograph 19, London

Egan G & Pritchard F (1991) *Dress Accessories c.1150-c.1450: Medieval Finds from Excavations in London: 3* London

El-Najjar M & Dawson GL (1977) 'The effect of artificial cranial deformation on the incidence of Wormian bones in the lambdoidal suture' *American Journal of Physical Anthropology* 46, 155–60

Evans JA, Montgomery J, Wildman G & Boulton N (2010) 'Spatial variations in biosphere 87Sr/86Sr in Britain' *Journal of the Geological Society* 167, 1–4

Evans K (1994) 'Fortnightly review: diagnosis and management of sinusitis' *British Medical Journal* 309, 1415–22

Ewan E (1990) *Townlife in Fourteenth-Century Scotland* Edinburgh

Faber Maunsell (2004) *Edinburgh Tram Network (Line two) Bill. Environmental Statement: Volume 2: Main Report* Edinburgh

Farooq N 2007 *Congenital disorder* http://www.pnac.net.pk/Reports/RC-Emails/Nov-07-2007-Congenital-Disorders.pdf accessed June 2011

Farquhar GD, Ehleringer JR & Hubick KT (1989) 'Carbon isotope discrimination and photosynthesis' Annual Review of Plant Physiology and Plant Molecular Biology 40, 503–37

Fedosyutkin BA & Nainys JV (1993) 'The relationship of skull morphology to facial features', in Iscan MY & Helmder RP (eds) *Forensic Analysis of the Skull: Craniofacial Analysis, Reconstruction and Identification* 199–213, New York

Finnegan M (1978) 'Non-metric variation of the infracranial skeleton' *Journal of Anatomy* 125, 25–37

Fiorato V, Boylston A & Knüsel C (2000) *Blood red roses: the archaeology of a mass grave from the battle of Towton AD 1461* Oxford

Foxe J (1583) *Actes and Monuments (The Book of Martyrs)* 4th ed, Book 8, https://www.johnfoxe.org/index.php accessed 01 August 2018

Franklin J (1997) 'Metalwork', in Caldwell DH & Ewart G 'Excavations at Eyemouth, Berwickshire in a mid-16th-century trace italienne fort' *Post-Medieval Archaeology* 31, 104–7

Franklin J (2002) 'Finds', in Stronach S 'The medieval development of South Leith and the creation of Rotten Row' *Proceedings of the Society of Antiquaries of Scotland* 132, 400–8

Franklin J 2004 *Finds report for Excavations at Tower Street, Leith* [unpublished client report] EASE

Franklin J (2010) 'Ceramic and Stone Building Material', in Barclay GG & Ritchie A (eds) 'Artefactual, Environmental and Archaeological Evidence from the Holyrood Parliament Site Excavations' *Scottish Archaeological Internet Reports* 40, 43–6 https://doi.org/10.5284/1017938 accessed 01 May 2018

Franklin J (2011) 'Appendix 1 – Finds', in Jones E 'Through the Cowgate: life in 15th-century Edinburgh as revealed by excavations at St Patrick's Church' *Scottish Archaeological Internet Reports* 42, 37–60 https://doi.org/10.5284/1017938 accessed 01 May 2018

Franklin J forthcoming 'The Finds', in Masser P 'Commerce and enterprise in early modern, Leith: excavations at Giles Street' *Scottish Archaeological Internet Reports* http://journals.socantscot.org/index.php/sair accessed 18 January 2019

Franklin J in prep *Finds Report for Burgess Street, Leith* [unpublished client report] CECAS

Franklin J & Collard M (2006) 'Other Finds', in Collard M, Lawson JA & Holmes N 'Archaeological excavations in St Giles' Cathedral, Edinburgh, 1981–93' *Scottish Archaeological Internet Reports* 22, 52–62 https://doi.org/10.5284/1017938 accessed 01 May 2018

Fuller BT, Molleson TI, Harris DA, Gilmour LT & Hedges REM (2006) 'Isotopic Evidence for Breastfeeding and Possible Adult Dietary Differences from Late/Sub-Roman Britain' *American Journal of Physical Anthropology* 129, 45–54

Gaimster D (1997) *German Stoneware 1200–1900: Archaeology and Cultural History* London.

Gallagher DB (1987) 'Edinburgh Pipemakers pre-1800', 'Nineteenth and Twentieth Century Edinburgh Pipemakers', in Davey P (ed) *The Archaeology of the Clay Tobacco Pipe* vol X: Scotland BAR British Series 178, 29–34, Oxford

Geddes G 2008 *Shrubhill Transport Depot, Phase 1 Archaeological Mitigation* [unpublished client report] Headland Archaeology, Ref. SBD07-001

Gerasimov MM (1955) *The Reconstruction of the Face from the Basic Structure of the Skull* (Translated from Russian by Tshernezky W, 1975) Moscow

Gifford J, McWilliam C & Walker D (1984) *The Buildings of Scotland: Edinburgh* Harmondsworth

Gilchrist R & Sloane B (2005) *Requiem: The Medieval Monastic Cemetery in Britain* London

Goggin JM (1960) *The Spanish Olive Jar: an introductory study* Yale University Publications in Anthropology 62, Yale

Goodman AH & Rose JC (1990) 'Assessment of systemic physiological perturbates from dental enamel hypoplasias and associated histological structures' *Yearbook of Physical Anthropology* 3, 59–110

Gordon A (1984) *Death is for the Living* Edinburgh

Grainger I, Hawkins D, Cowla L & Mikulsk R (2008) *The Black Death cemetery, East Smithfield,* London MoLAS Monograph 43, London

Grant J (1883) *Old and New Edinburgh* Edinburgh

Grauer A (1991) 'Life patterns of women from medieval York' in Walde D & Willows ND (eds) *The archaeology of gender: proceedings of the 22nd annual Chacmool conference,* 407–13, Calgary

Gregg JB (2000) 'Thirty-five years of Upper Missouri River Basin Paleopathology' *Chungará, Revista de Antropología Chilena* 32, 71–7

Gregg JB & Gregg PS (1987) *Dry Bones: Dakota Territory Reflected* Sioux Falls

Griffeth MT, Dailey RA & Ofner S (1997) 'Bilateral spontaneous subperiosteal hematoma of the orbits: a case report' *Archives of Ophthalmology* 115, 679–80

Haggarty G 2006 *A gazetteer and summary of French pottery in Scotland c1150–c1650* Edinburgh

Haggarty G, Hall D & Chenery S (2011) *Sourcing Scottish Redwares* Medieval Pottery Research Group Occasional Paper 5, London

Hall D (1989) 'Perth: the excavations', in Stones JA (ed) *Three Scottish Carmelite Friaries: Aberdeen, Linlithgow and Perth 1980–85* Society of Antiquaries of Scotland Monograph Series 6, 106, Edinburgh

Hall D (2006) 'Unto Yone Hospitall at the Tounis End: The Scottish Medieval Hospital' *Tayside and Fife Archaeological Journal* 12, 89–106

Hamilton D (1981) *The Healers: a History of Medicine in Scotland* Edinburgh

Harding V (1993) 'Burial of the plague dead in early modern London' in Champion JAI (ed) 'Epidemic disease in London' *Centre for Metropolitan History Working Papers Series* 1, 53–64

Harding V (2002) *The dead and the living in Paris and London, 1500–1670* Cambridge

Hare JN (1985) *Battle Abbey, the eastern range and the excavations of 1978–80* Historic Buildings and Monuments Commission for England Archaeological Report 2, London

Harris S (2002) *The Place Names of Edinburgh* London

Hatcher Rice J 2011 'A Man With Acromegaly: Providing Optimal Dental Care' *Medscape* https://www.medscape.com/viewarticle/737408_3 accessed 27 October 2017

REFERENCES

Hawyes MA 2011 'Sphenoid sinus disease and prevention' *Sinus-Wellness* http://www.sinus-wellness.com/sphenoid-sinus-disease.html accessed 11 August 2011

Headland Archaeology (HA) 2007 *Edinburgh Trams Project: Written Scheme of Investigation for Archaeological Monitoring of Service Diversions in Leith and Granton* [unpublished client report] McAlpine

Headland Archaeology (HA) 2009 *Edinburgh Trams Project: Written Scheme of Investigation for archaeological excavations on Consitituion Street* [unpublished client report] TIE

Hedges REM & Reynard (2007) 'Nitrogen isotopes and the trophic level of humans in archaeology' *Journal of Archaeological Science* 34, 1240–51

Hedges REM, Clement JG, Thomas CDL & O'Connell TC (2007) 'Collagen turnover in the adult femoral mid-shaft: modeled from anthropogenic radiocarbon tracer measurements' *American Journal of Physical Anthropology* 133, 808–16

Helmer R (1984) *Schädelidentifizierung durch elektronische Bildmischung* Heidelberg

Henderson D (1999) 'St Ninian's Manse and Church, Quayside Mills' *Discovery and Excavation in Scotland 1999* 41

Henderson D (2002) 'Fish Remains', in Stronach S 'The medieval development of South Leith and the creation of Rotten Row' *Proceedings of the Society of Antiquaries of Scotland* 132, 412–4

Henderson D (2006) 'The Human Bones', in Collard M, Lawson JA & Holmes N 'Archaeological excavations in St Giles' Cathedral, Edinburgh, 1981–93' *Scottish Archaeological Internet Reports* 22, 27–41 https://doi.org/10.5284/1017938 accessed 01 May 2018

Hickish AB (1985) *Ear, Nose and Throat Disorders* Edinburgh

Hillson SW (2005) *Teeth* (2nd edn) Cambridge

Hindmarch E 2004 *Coburg Street, Edinburgh* [unpublished client report] AOC, Report 4522

Hinton, DA (1990) 'Buckles and Other Clothes Fittings', in Biddle M (ed) *Object and Economy in Medieval Winchester* Winchester Studies 7ii, 494–590, Oxford

Hodder M (1991) 'Excavations at Sandwell Priory and hall' *South Staffordshire Archaeological and Historical Society Transactions* 31, Birmingham

Holmes NMM (1985) 'Excavations south of Bernard Street, Leith, 1980' *Proceedings of the Society of Antiquaries of Scotland* 115, 401–28

Holst M, Isaac L, Boylston A & Roberts C in prep 'Hull Magistrates Court: osteological analysis', in Evans DH *Excavations at the Austin Friary, Hull, 1994 and 1999: A Report in Three Volumes* (Vol 3) East Riding Archaeology, Hull

Hoppe K, Koch PL & Furutani TT (2003) 'Assessing the preservation of biogenic strontium in fossil bones and tooth enamel' *International Journal of Osteoarchaeology* 13, 20–8

Humble J & Murray R 2008 *Edinburgh Trams: Results of watching briefs on service diversions (Leith and Haymarket) and groundworks at the Gogarburn depot* [unpublished client report] Headland Archaeology

Hunter DLG (1992) *Edinburgh's Transport, Vol 1 – The Early Years* Edinburgh

Hurst JG (1974) 'Sixteenth and seventeenth century imported pottery from the Saintonge' in Evison VI, Hodges H & Hurst JG (ed) *Medieval Pottery from Excavations* London

Hurst JG, Neal DS & van Beuningen HJE (1986) *Pottery produced and traded in north-west Europe 1350–1650* Rotterdam Papers VI, Rotterdam

Hutchison W (1865) *Tales and Traditions of Leith, with notice of its antiquaries* Leith

Jainkittivong A & Langlais RP (2000) 'Buccal and palatal exostoses: prevalence and concurrence with tori' *Oral Surgery, Oral Medicine, Oral Pathology, Oral Radiology and Endodontics* 90, 48–53

Jillings K (2003) *Scotland's Black Death: The Foul Death of the English* Stroud

Jones R, Will R, Haggarty G & Hall D (2003) 'Sourcing Scottish White Gritty Ware' *Medieval Ceramics* 26/7, 45–84

Judd MA (2004) 'Trauma in the city of Kerma: ancient versus modern injury pattern' *International Journal of Osteoarchaeology* 14, 34–51

Keeping D 2000 *Life and death in English nunneries: a biocultural study of variations in the health of women during the later medieval period, 1066–1540* [unpublished PhD thesis] University of Bradford

Kennard J 2017 'Signs and symptoms of Syphilis in Men: Be aware of the symptoms of this serious STI' *Verywell* https://www.verywell.com/syphilis-symptoms-and-signs-2329062 accessed 27 October 2017

King SE (2002) 'The skeletal remains from the nave, crypt, choir and treasury', in Driscoll ST *Excavations at Glasgow Cathedral 1988–1997,* The Society for Medieval Archaeology Monograph 18, 134–52, Leeds

Kleinheinz, BP 2017 'Clavicle Fractures' *EMedicine, Drugs and Diseases, Sports Medicine* https://emedicine.medscape.com/article/92429-overview accessed 31 October 2017

Korf D (1981) *Nederlandse Majolica* Haarlem

Lawson G (1975) 'Clay Pipes', in Holmes NM McQ 'Excavations within the Tron Kirk, Edinburgh, 1974' *Post-Medieval Archaeology* 9, 149–52

Lawson G 1995 *Pig Metapodial 'Toggles' and Buzz-discs – Traditional Musical Instruments* Finds Research Group 700–1700, Datasheet 18

Lawson JA (1995) 'Burgess Street/Water Street/Shore Place, Leith' *Discovery and Excavation in Scotland* 1995, 53

Lawson JA (1999) 'Coburg Street/East Cromwell Street, Leith' *Discovery and Excavation in Scotland* 1999, 35–6

Leach S, Lewis M, Chenery C, Müldner G & Eckardt H (2009) 'Migration and diversity in Roman Britain: A multidisciplinary approach to the identification of immigrants in Roman York, England' *American Journal of Physical Anthropology* 140, 546–61

Legeai-Mallet L 2002 'Hereditary multiple exostoses' *Orphanet Encyclopedia* http://www.orpha.net/data/patho/GB/uk-HME.pdf accessed June 2011

Leith Research Group 1978–9 *Leith Walk and Greenside a Social History* Leith Walk Research Project, University of Edinburgh, Edinburgh

Levinson AA, Luz B & Kolodny Y (1987) 'Variations in oxygen isotopic compositions of human teeth and urinary stones' *Applied Geochemistry* 2, 367–71

Lewis ME (2002) *Urbanisation and child health in medieval and post-medieval England* BAR British Series 339, Oxford

Lewis ME, Roberts CA & Manchester K (1995) 'Comparative study of the prevalence of maxillary sinusitis in later medieval urban and rural populations in northern England' *American Journal of Physical Anthropology* 98, 497–506

Libby WF, Berger R, Mead JF, Alexander GV & Ross JF (1964) 'Replacement rates for human tissue from atmospheric radiocarbon' *Science* 46, 1170–2

Lindsay WJ (1989a) 'The burials from Linlithgow', in Stones JA (ed) *Three Scottish Carmelite Friaries: Aberdeen, Linlithgow and Perth 1980–85* Society of Antiquaries of Scotland Monograph Series, microfiche 1: B12, Edinburgh

Lindsay WJ (1989b) 'Copper alloy objects', in Stones JA (ed) *Three Scottish Carmelite Friaries: Excavations at Aberdeen, Linlithgow and Perth 1980–85* Society of Antiquaries of Scotland Monograph Series 6, microfiche 12: F9–G6, Edinburgh

Lodge T (1967) 'Thinning of the parietal bones in early Egyptian populations and its aetiology in the light of modern observations', in Brothwell D & Sandison A (eds) *Diseases In Antiquity: a Survey of the Diseases, Injuries and Surgery of Early Populations* 405–12, Springfield

Long CD (1975) 'Excavations in the medieval city of Trondheim, Norway' *Medieval Archaeology* 19, 1–32

Longinelli A (1965) 'Oxygen isotopic composition of orthophosphate from shells of living marine organisms' *Nature* 207, 716–9

Longinelli A (1966) 'Ratios of Oxygen-18: Oxygen-16 in phosphate and carbonate from living and fossil marine organisms' *Nature* 211, 923–7

Longinelli A (1984) 'Oxygen isotopes in mammal bone phosphate: a new tool for paleohydrological and paleoclimatological research?' *Geochimica et Cosmochimica Acta* 48, 385–90

Longinelli A & Nuti S (1968) 'Oxygen-isotope ratios in phosphate from fossil marine organisms' *Science* 160, 879–82

Longinelli A & Nuti S (1973) 'Oxygen isotope measurements of phosphate from fish teeth and bones' *Earth and Planetary Science Letters* 20, 337–40

Lovejoy CO, Meindl RS, Pryzbeck TR & Mensforth RP (1985) 'Chronological metamorphosis of the auricular surface of the illium: a new method for the determination of age at death' *American Journal of Physical Anthropology* 68, 15–28

Lovell NC (1997) 'Trauma analysis in paleopathology' *Yearbook of Physical Anthropology* 40, 139–70

Luz B, Kolodny Y & Horowitz M (1984) 'Fractionation of oxygen isotopes between mammalian bone-phosphate and environmental drinking water' *Geochimica et Cosmochimica Acta* 48, 1689–93

Mackenzie JR & Moloney CJ (1997) 'Medieval development and the cemetery of the Church of the Holy Trinity, Logies Lane, St Andrews' *Tayside and Fife Archaeological Journal* 3, 143–60

MacLennan WJ (2001) 'The Eleven Plagues of Edinburgh' *Proceedings of the Royal College of Physicians of Edinburgh* 31, 256–61

Manchester K & Roberts C (1989) 'The palaeopathology of leprosy in Britain: A review' *World Archaeology* 21(2), 265–72

Maresh MM (1970) 'Measurements from roentgenograms', in McCammon RW (ed) *Human Growth and Development* 157–200, Springfield

Margeson S (1993) *Norwich Households: The Medieval and Post-medieval Finds from Norwich Survey Excavations 1971–1978* East Anglian Archaeology Report 58, Norwich

Marshall JS (1983) *The Church in the Midst: South Leith Parish Church Through Five Centuries* Edinburgh

Marshall JS (1986) *The Life and Times of Leith* Edinburgh

Masser P forthcoming 'Excavations at Giles Street, Leith' *Scottish Archaeological Internet Reports* http://journals.socantscot.org/index.php/sair accessed 18 January 2019

Mays S (1997) 'Carbon stable isotope ratios in mediaeval and later human skeletons from northern England' *Journal of Archaeological Science* 24(6), 561–7

Mays S (1998) *The Archaeology of Human Bones* London

Mays S & Cox M (2000) 'Sex Determination in Skeletal Remains', in Cox, M & Mays, S (eds) *Human Osteology in Archaeology and Forensic Science,* 117–30, Cambridge

Mays SA, Richards MP & Fuller BT (2002) 'Bone stable isotope evidence for infant feeding in mediaeval England' *Antiquity* 76, 654–6

Mays S, Harding C & Heighway C (2007) *Wharram: A Study of Settlement on the Yorkshire Wolds, XI. The Churchyard* York University Archaeological Publications 13, York

McCullagh R 2006 'The Coffin Wood', in Collard M, Lawson JA & Holmes N 'Archaeological excavations in St Giles' Cathedral, Edinburgh, 1981–93' *Scottish Archaeological Internet Reports* 22, 23–6 https://doi.org/10.5284/1017938 accessed 16 March 2018

McKinley JI 2004 'Compiling a skeletal inventory: disarticulated and co-mingled remains', in Brickley M & McKinley JI (eds) *Guidelines to the Standards for Recording Human Remains* (Paper No 7, BABAO, IFA: Reading), 14–17 http://www.archaeologists.net/sites/default/files/ifa_paper_7.pdf accessed 24 October 2017

McRee BR (1992) 'Religious gilds and civic order: the case of Norwich in the late Middle Ages' *Speculum* 67, 68–97

Mekota AM, Grupe G, Ufer S & Cuntz U (2006) 'Serial analysis of stable nitrogen and carbon isotopes in hair: monitoring starvation and recovery phases of patients suffering from anorexia nervosa' *Rapid Communications in Mass Spectrometry* 20, 1604–10

Merrett DC & Pfeiffer S (2000) 'Maxillary sinusitis as an indicator of respiratory health in past populations' *American Journal of Physical Anthropology* 111, 301–18

Miles AEW (1962) 'Assessment of the ages of a population of Anglo-Saxons from their dentitions' *Proceedings of the Royal Society of Medicine* 55, 881–6

Miles A, Powers N, Wroe-Brown R & Walker D (2008) *St. Marylebone Church and Burial Ground in the 18th to 19th Centuries: Excavations at St. Marylebone School, 1992 and 2004–6* MoLAS Monograph 46, London

Mitchiner M (1988) *Jetons, Medalets and Tokens Volume I: the Medieval Period and Nuremberg* London

Mnif H, Koubaa M, Zrig M, Zammel N & Abid A (2009) 'Peroneal nerve palsy resulting from fibular head osteochondroma' *Orthopedics* 32, 528

Molleson TI & Cox MJ (1993) *The Spitalfields Project 2 – The Anthropology: The Middling Sort* CBA Research Report No. 86, London

Moloney C & Baker L 2017 *The Leith Programme, Phase 4, Leith Walk, Edinburgh, Data Structure Report for Archeological Watching Brief* [unpublished client report] Rubicon Heritage for City of Edinburgh Council

Montgomery J 2002 *Lead and strontium isotope compositions of human dental tissues as an indicator of ancient exposure and population dynamics: The application of isotope source-tracing methods to identify migrants among British archaeological burials and a consideration of ante-mortem uptake, tissue stability and post-mortem diagenesis* [unpublished doctoral thesis] The University of Bradford

Moore KL (1978) 'Malformations caused by environmental factors', in Moore KL (ed) *The Developing Human: Clinically Oriented Embryology* (2nd edn) 133–44, Philadelphia

Moorrees CFA, Fanning EA & Hunt EE (1963a) 'Formation and resorption of three deciduous teeth in children' *American Journal of Physical Anthropology* 21, 205–13

Moorrees CFA, Fanning EA & Hunt EE (1963b) 'Age variation of formation stages for ten permanent teeth' *Journal of Dental Research* 42, 1490–1502

REFERENCES

Morrison J 2000 *Mitchell Street, Leith, Edinburgh Evaluation DSR* [unpublished client report] AOC Archaeology

Mott Macdonald 2003 *Edinburgh Tram Network (Line one, northern loop). Environmental Statement Report* No. 203011/0059

Mowat S (2003) *The Port of Leith: Its History and its People* Edinburgh

Müldner G, Chenery C & Eckardt H (2011) The 'Headless Romans': multi-isotope investigations of an unusual burial ground from Roman Britain' *Journal of Archaeological Science* 38, 280–90

Müldner G, Montgomery J, Cook G, Ellam R, Gledhill A & Lowe C (2009) 'Isotopes and individuals: diet and mobility among the medieval Bishops of Whithorn' *Antiquity* 83, 1119–33

Müldner G & Richards MP (2005) 'Fast or feast: reconstructing diet in later medieval England by stable isotope analysis' *Journal of Archaeological Science* 32, 39–48

Müldner G & Richards MP (2007a) 'Diet and diversity at later medieval fishergate: The isotopic evidence' *American Journal of Physical Anthropology* 134, 162–74

Müldner G & Richards MP (2007b) 'Stable isotope evidence for 1500 years of human diet at the city of York, UK' *American Journal of Physical Anthropology* 133, 682–97

Mullay S 1996 *The Edinburgh Encyclopedia* Edinburgh

Munshi M & Davidson JM (2000) 'Unilateral glenoid hypoplasia: unusual findings on MR anthrography' *American Journal of Roentgenology* 175, 646–8

Murray R 2008 *Edinburgh Trams Project: Constitution Street, Leith. Evaluation of the depth and extent of burials adjacent to South Leith Parish Church* [unpublished client report] Headland Archaeology

Nayak AS (2003) 'The asthma and allergic rhinitis link' *Allergy and Asthma Proceedings* 24, 395–402

Nicholson A (1997) 'The Copper Alloy', in Hill P *Whithorn and St Ninian: the Excavation of a Monastic Town, 1984–91* 360–89, Stroud

Norton C (1994) 'Medieval Floor Tiles in Scotland', in Higgit J (ed) *Medieval Art and Architecture in the Diocese of St Andrews* British Archaeological Association Conference Transactions 1986, 137–73, York

O'Connell TC, Hedges REM, Healey MA & Simpson AHRW (2001) 'Isotopic comparison of hair, nail and bone: modern analyses' *Journal of Archaeological Science* 28, 1247–55

Ossenberg NS (1976) 'Within and between race distances in population studies based on discrete traits of the human skull' *American Journal of Physical Anthropology* 45, 701–16

Oram R (2007) '"It cannot be decernit quha are clean and quha are foulle." Responses to Epidemic Disease in Sixteenth and Seventeenth-Century Scotland' *Renaissance and Reformation* 30(4), 13–39

Oram R (2014) '"The worst disaster suffered by the people of Scotland in recorded history": climate change, dearth and pathogens in the long 14th century' *Proceedings of the Society of Antiquaries of Scotland* 144, 223–44

Ortner DJ (2003) *Identification of Pathological Conditions in Human Skeletal Remains* (2nd edn) San Diego

Ottaway P & Rogers N (2002) *Craft, Industry and Everyday Life: Finds from Medieval York* (Vol 17/15) York

Paton K & Cook M (2016) 'The 1560 fortifications and siege of Leith: archaeological evidence for a new transcription of the cartographic evidence' *Post-Medieval Archaeology* 20, 1–15

Pietrusewsky M & Douglas MT (2002) *Ban Chiang, a prehistoric village site in northeast Thailand: The Human Skeletal Remains* (Vol 1) University Museum Monograph 111, Philadelphia

Pollard AM, Pellegrini M & Lee-Thorp JA (2011) 'Technical note: some observations on the conversion of dental enamel delta18O(p) values to delta18O(w) to determine human mobility' *American Journal of Physical Anthropology* 145, 499–504

Polzin SJ 2011 'Multiple hereditary exostoses' *Healthline* http://www.healthline.com/galecontent/hereditary-multiple-exostoses-1?print=true accessed June 2011

Post-Office Directory (1895) *Post-Office Edinburgh and Leith Directory 1894–95* Edinburgh http://digital.nls.uk/directories/browse/archive/83670959 accessed 27 October 2017

Power C (1995) 'A medieval demographic sample', in Hurley MF, Sheehan CM & Cleary RM (eds) *Excavations at the Dominican Priory, St. Mary's of the Isle, Cork, 66–83* Cork

Poulton R, Woods H & Henderson J (1984) *Excavations on the site of the Dominican Friary at Guildford in 1974 and 1978* Surrey Archaeological Society Research Vol 9, Guildford

Prag J & Neave RAH (1997) *Making faces: Using forensic and archaeological evidence* London

Prentice MB, Gilbert T & Cooper A (2004) 'Was the Black Death caused by Yersinia pestis?' *Lancet Infectious Diseases* 4, 72

Pryles CV & Khan AJ (1979) 'Wormian bones: a marker of CNS abnormality?' *American Journal of Diseases of Children* 133, 380–2

Raoult D, Aboudharam G, Crubezy E, Larrouy G, Ludes B & Drancourt M (2000) 'Molecular identification by 'suicide PCR' of Yersinia pestis as the agent of the medieval Black Death' *Proceedings of the National Academy of Sciences of the United States of America* 97, 12800–3

Reed D & Lawson JA (1999) 'Ronaldson's Wharf/Sandport Street, Leith' *Discovery and Excavation in Scotland* 1999, 40–1

Reimer PJ, Bard E, Bayliss A, Beck JW, Blackwell PG, Bronk Ramsey C, Grootes PM, Guilderson TP, Haflidason H, Hajdas I, Hatté C, Heaton TJ, Hoffmann DL, Hogg AG, Hughen KA, Kaiser KF, Kromer B, Manning SW, Niu M, Reimer RW, Richards DA, Scott EM, Southon JR, Staff RA, Turney CSM & van der Plicht J (2013) 'IntCal13 and Marine13 Radiocarbon Age Calibration Curves 0-50,000 Years cal BP' *Radiocarbon* 55(4), 1869–87

Rennie C & Will, B 2013 *Edinburgh Tram Scheme: tram construction phase investigation, Data Structure Report, Project 3405* [unpublished client report] Guard Archaeology

Richards MP (2003) 'Stable isotope analysis reflect gender and status differences in diets at a number of European archaeological sites' *Anthropological Science* 111, 1–52

Richards MP, Fuller BT & Molleson TI (2006) 'Stable isotope palaeodietary study of humans and fauna from the multi-period (Iron Age, Viking and Late Medieval) site of Newark Bay, Orkney', *Journal of Archaeological Science* 33 (1), 122–31

Richards MP & Hedges REM (2003) 'Variations in bone collagen δ13C and δ15N values of fauna from Northwest Europe over the last 40 000 years' *Palaeogeography Palaeoclimatology Palaeoecology* 193, 261–7

Richards MP, Hedges REM, Molleson TI & Vogel JC (1998) 'Stable isotope analysis reveals variations in human diet at the Poundbury Camp cemetery site' *Journal of Archaeological Science* 25, 1247–52

Richards MP, Mays S & Fuller BT (2002) 'Stable carbon and nitrogen isotope values of bone and teeth reflect weaning age at the Medieval Wharram Percy site, Yorkshire, UK' *American Journal of Physical Anthropology* 119, 205–210

Richards MP, Pettitt PB, Stiner MC & Trinkaus E (2001) 'Stable isotope evidence for increasing dietary breadth in the European mid-Upper Paleolithic' *Proceedings of the National Academy of Sciences of the United States of America* 98, 6528–32

Richards RR & Corley FG (1996) 'Fractures of the shafts of the radius and ulna', in Rockwood CA, Green DP, Bucholz RW & Heckman JD (eds) *Rockwood and Green's Fractures in Adults* (4th edn), 3–120, Philadelphia

Roberts CA (2007) 'A bioarchaeological study of maxillary sinus' *American Journal of Physical Anthropology* 133, 792–807

Roberts C & Connell B 2004 'Guidance on recording palaeopathology', in Brickley M & McKinley JI (eds) *Guidelines to the Standards for Recording Human Remains* (Paper No 7, BABAO, IFA: Reading), 34–9 http://www.archaeologists.net/sites/default/files/ifa_paper_7.pdf accessed 24 October 2017

Roberts C & Cox M (2003) *Health and Disease in Britain: from Prehistory to the Present Day* Stroud

Roberts C & Manchester K (2010) *The Archaeology of Disease* (4th edn) New York

Roberts JR 2008 'Foot and ankle fractures' *The Merck Manuals – Online Medical Dictionary* http://www.merck.com/mmhe/sec24/ch299666/ch299666b.html accessed 10 August 2010

Robertson DH (1851) *The Sculptured Stones of Leith with Historical and Antiquarian Notes* Leith

Robertson D (1911) *South Leith Records* Leith

Robertson D & Swan W (1925) *South Leith Records* (2nd series) Leith

Roche MB & Rowe GG (1951) 'The incidence of separate neural arch and coincident bone variation: a survey of 4200 skeletons' *Anatomical Record* 109, 233–52

Rogers C (1877) *Historical Notices of St Anthony's Monastery, Leith and Rehearsal of Events which occurred in the North of Scotland from 1635 to 1645 in relation to the National Covenant* London http://digital.nls.uk/publications-by-scottish-clubs/archive/79580628?mode=transcription accessed 26 October 2017

Rogers J & Waldron T (1995) *A field guide to joint disease in archaeology* Chichester

Rogers J, Waldron T, Dieppe P & Watt I (1987) 'Arthropathies in paleopathology: the basis of classification according to most probable cause' *Journal of Archaeological Science* 14, 179–83

Royal Commission on the Ancient and Historical Monuments of Scotland (RCAHMS) (1951) *An inventory of the ancient and historical monuments of the city of Edinburgh with the thirteenth report of the Commission* Edinburgh

Royal Commission on the Ancient and Historical Monuments of Scotland (RCAHMS) (1975) *Argyll, an Inventory of the Ancient Monuments* (Vol 2) Edinburgh

Russell J (1922) *The Story of Leith* London

Russell N, Cook GT, Ascough PL & Scott EM (2015) 'A period of calm in Scottish seas: A comprehensive study of ΔR values for the northern British Isles coast and the consequent implications for archaeology and oceanography' *Quaternary Geochronology* 30, 34–41

Rynn C 2006 *Craniofacial approximation and reconstruction: tissue depth patterning and the prediction of the nose* [unpublished PhD dissertation] The University of Dundee

Scheuer L & Black S (2000) *Developmental Juvenile Osteology* London

Scheuer JL, Musgrave JH & Evans SP (1980) 'The estimation of late fetal and juvenile perinatal age from limb bone length by linear and logarithmic regression' *Annals of Human Biology* 7, 257–65

Schmorl G & Junghanns H (1971) *The Human Spine in Health and Disease* (2nd edn) New York

Schoeninger MJ & DeNiro MJ (1984) 'Nitrogen and carbon isotopic composition of bone collagen from marine and terrestrial animals' *Geochimica et Cosmochimica Acta* 48, 625–39

Schoeninger MJ, DeNiro MJ & Tauber H (1983) 'Stable nitrogen isotope ratios of bone collagen reflect marine and terrestrial components of prehistoric human diet' *Science* 220, 1381–3

Schultz M (2001) 'Paleohistopathology of bone: a new approach to the study of ancient diseases' *American Journal of Physical Anthropology* 33, 106–47

Schwarcz HP, Dupras TL & Fairgrieve SI (1999) '15N Enrichment in the Sahara: In Search of a Global Relationship' *Journal of Archaeological Science* 26, 629–36

Scotsman (1834) *The Scotsman archives* [newspaper article] (12 July 1834) Edinburgh

Scotsman (1895) *The Scotsman archives* [newspaper article] (7 July 1895) Edinburgh

Scott E (1999) *The Archaeology of Infancy and Infant Death* BAR International Series 819, Oxford

Scott S & Duncan CJ (1998) *Human Demography and Disease* Cambridge

Shrewsbury JFD (1970) *A History of Bubonic Plague in the British Isles* Cambridge

Sirmali M, Türüt H, Topçu S, Gülhan E, Yazici Ü, Kaya S & Taştepe I (2003) 'A comprehensive analysis of traumatic rib fractures: morbidity, mortality and management' *European Journal of Cardio-Thoracic Surgery* 24, 133–8

Smith, AB & Epstein (1971) 'Two categories of 13C/12C ratios for higher plants' *Plant Physiology* 47, 380–4

Smith J (1929) 'Notes on the Augustinian House of Saint Anthony, Leith' *Proceedings of the Society of Antiquities of Scotland* 64, 275–90, Edinburgh

Standaert CJ & Herring SA (2000) 'Spondylolysis: a critical review' *British Journal of Sports Medicine* 34, 415–22

Steane J (1985) *The Archaeology of Medieval England and Wales* Athens

Stenhouse MJ & Baxter MS (1977) 'Bomb 14C as a biological tracer' *Nature* 287, 828–32

Stenhouse MJ & Baxter MS (1979) 'The uptake of bomb 14C in humans', in Berger R & Suess HE (eds) *Radiocarbon Dating, Proceedings of the 9th International Radiocarbon Congress* 324–41, Berkeley

Stevenson S, Simpson AT & Holmes N (1981) *Historic Edinburgh, Canongate and Leith - the archaeological implications of development* Scottish Burgh Survey series, Glasgow

Stirland A (2009) *Criminals and Paupers: the Graveyard of St Margaret Fyebriggate in Combusto, Norwich* East Anglian Archaeology Monograph 129, Norwich

Stones JA (1989a) 'The burials at Aberdeen, Linlithgow and Perth', in Stones JA (ed) *Three Scottish Carmelite Friaries: Aberdeen, Linlithgow and Perth 1980–85* Society of Antiquaries of Scotland Monograph Series 6, 111–6, Edinburgh

Stones JA (1989b) 'The Small Finds', in Stones JA (ed) *Three Scottish Carmelite Friaries: Aberdeen, Linlithgow and Perth 1980–85* Society of Antiquaries of Scotland Monograph Series 6, 147–65, Edinburgh

Strayer SM, Reece SG & Petrizzi MJ 1999 'Fractures of the Proximal Fifth Metatarsal' *American Academy of Family Physicians* http://www.aafp.org/afp/990501ap/2516.html accessed 27 October 2017

Stronach S (2002a) 'The medieval development of South Leith and the creation of Rotten Row' *Proceedings of the Society of Antiquaries of Scotland* 132, 383–423

Stronach S 2002b *Results of an archaeological investigation at Dock Street, Leith: Phase 2* [unpublished client report] Headland Archaeology

REFERENCES

Stroud G & Kemp RL (1993) *Cemeteries of St Andrew, Fishergate* Archaeology of York 12/2, York

Stuart-Macadam P, Glencross B & Kricun M (1998) 'Traumatic bowing deformities in tubular bones' *International Journal of Osteoarchaeology* 8, 252–62

Tait R (2006) 'Configuration and dimensions of burgage plots in the burgh of Edinburgh' *Proceedings of the Society of Antiquaries of Scotland* 136, 297–310

Tait R (2008) 'Burgage plot patterns and dimensions in four Scottish burghs' *Proceedings of the Society of Antiquaries of Scotland* 138, 223–38

Tait R (2010) 'Urban morphology and medieval burgh development in Edinburgh and Elgin' *Proceedings of the Society of Antiquaries of Scotland* 140, 129–44

Taylor K (2001) *Forensic Art and Illustration* Boca Raton

Tieszen LL & Fagre T (1993) 'Effect of diet quality and composition on the isotopic composition of respiratory CO2, bone collagen, bioapatite and soft tissues', in Lambert J & Grupe G (eds) *Prehistoric Human Bone: Archaeology at the Molecular Level* 121–55, New York

Togias AG (2000) 'Systemic immunologic and inflammatory aspects of allergic rhinitis' *Journal of Allergy and Clinical Immunology* 106, 247–50

Treasure Trove Unit (TTU) 2016 *Treasure Trove in Scotland: A Code of Practice* (Edinburgh) http://www.qltr.gov.uk/sites/default/files/TTcoderevisedto13Jan2016.pdf accessed 07 December 2017

Trotter M (1970) 'Estimation of stature from intact long limb bones', in Stewart TD (ed) *Personal Identification in Mass Disasters* 71–83, Washington DC

Trotter M & Gleser GC (1952) 'Estimation of stature from long bones of American Whites and Negroes' *American Journal of Physical Anthropology* 10, 463–514

Trotter M & Gleser GC (1958) 'A re-evaluation of estimation of stature based on measurements taken during life and long-bones after death' *American Journal of Physical Anthropology* 16, 79–123

Turnbull J (2001) The Scottish Glass Industry 1610–1750 'To serve the whole nation with glass' *Society of Antiquaries of Scotland Monograph* 18, Edinburgh

Tyrrell A (2000) 'Skeletal non-metric traits and the assessment of inter- and intra-population diversity: past problems and future potential', in Cox M and Mays S (eds) *Human Osteology in Archaeology and Forensic Science* 289–306, London

Tyson RE (1988) 'The Economy of Aberdeen', in Smith JS & Stevenson D (eds) *Aberdeen in the Nineteenth Century: The Making of the Modern City* 9–36, Aberdeen

Ubelaker DH (1978) *Human Skeletal Remains: Excavation, Analysis and Interpretation* Washington DC

Van Klinken GJ (1999) 'Bone collagen quality indicators for palaeodietary and radiocarbon measurements' *Journal of Archaeological Science* 26, 687–95

Van Klinken GJ, Richards MP & Hedges REM (2000) 'An overview of causes for stable isotopic variations in past European human populations: Environmental, ecophysiological, and cultural effects', in Ambrose S & Katzenberg M (eds) *Biogeochemical Approaches to Palaeodietary Analysis* 39–63, New York

van Wessel J 2014 *St Andrews Place, Leith, Edinburgh: Archaeological excavations and monitoring* [unpublished client report] Headland Archaeology, Ref. WSAL13

Waldron T (2007) *St. Peter's, Barton-on-Humber, Lincolnshire: a parish church and its community. Volume 2: the human remains* Oxford

Waldron T (2009) *Palaeopathology, Cambridge Manuals in Archaeology* Cambridge

Walker PL (1995) 'Problems of preservation and sexism in sexing: some lessons from historical collections for palaeodemographers', in Saunders, SR & Herring, A (eds) *Grave reflections. Portraying the past through cemetery studies,* 31–47, Toronto

Walker PL, Bathurst RR, Richman R, Gjerdrum T & Andrushko VA (2009) 'The causes of porotic hyperostosis and cribra orbitalia: a reappraisal of the iron-deficiency-anemia hypothesis' *American Journal of Physical Anthropology* 139, 109–25

Walton P (1981) 'The textiles', in B Harbottle & M Ellison 'An excavation in the castle ditch, Newcastle upon Tyne, 1974–76' *Archaeologia Aeliana* (5th ser) 9, 248–9

Walton P (1983) 'The Textiles', in Ellison M & Harbottle B 'The excavation of a 17th century bastion in the castle of Newcastle upon Tyne, 1976–81' *Archaeologia Aeliana* (5th Ser) 11, 135–263

Watson B 1990 *Excavations at 54/55-66 Carter Lane, 1-3 Pilgrim Street and 25–33 Ludgate Hill, City of London* [unpublished client report] Museum of London, Ref. PIC87

White RHM & O'Connell C (2009) 'Excavations on the Site of Balmerino House, Constitution Street, Leith' *Scottish Archaeological Internet Reports* 41 https://doi.org/10.5284/1017938 accessed 27 October 2017

White TD & Folkens PA (2005) *The Human Bone Manual* London

White TD, Black M & Folkens PA (2012) *Human Osteology* (3rd edn) Burlington

White WJ (1988) *Skeletal remains from the cemetery of St Nicholas Shambles* London Middlesex Archaeological Society Spec papers 9, London

Whitehead R (1996) *Buckles 1250–1800* Chelmsford

Wilkinson CM & Neave R (2003) 'The Reconstruction of Faces Showing Healed Wounds' *Journal of Archaeological Science* 30, 1343–8

Wilkinson CM, Motwani M & Chiang E (2003) 'The relationship between the soft tissues and the skeletal detail of the mouth' *Journal of Forensic Sciences* 48(4), 728–32

Will B & James HF (2017) 'Excavations to the West of Gogar Mains, Edinburgh' *Scottish Archaeological Internet Reports* 72 https://doi.org/10.9750/issn.2056-7421.2017.72 accessed 03 November 2017

Will, B (2018) 'Excavations by Gogar Church, Nether Gogar, Edinburgh' *Scottish Archaeological Internet Reports* 79 https://doi.org/10.9750/issn.2056-7421.2018.79 accessed 17 January 2019

Willmes M, Mcmorrow L, Kinsley L, Armstrong R, Aubert M, Eggins S, Falguères C, Maureille B, Moffat I & Grün R (2014) 'The IRHUM (Isotopic Reconstruction of Human Migration) database andndash; bioavailable strontium isotope ratios for geochemical fingerprinting in France' *Earth System Science Data* 6, 117–22

Willmott H (2002) *Early Post-Medieval Vessel Glass in England c.1500–1670,* CBA Research Report 132, York

Wilson D (1875) *Memorials of Edinburgh in the Olden Time* Edinburgh

Wilson D in prep 'Finding the Blackfriars: Excavations at Old High School, Infirmary Street, Edinburgh' *Scottish Archaeological Internet Reports* http://journals.socantscot.org/index.php/sair accessed 18 January 2019

Wilson G & Moore H 2003 *Report on Archaeological Excavations at 8a and 8b Tower Street, Leith* [unpublished client report] EASE Archaeological Consultants

Wirth MA, Lyons FR & Rockwood CA (1993) 'Hypoplasia of the glenoid: a review of sixteen patients' *The Journal of Bone and Joint Surgery* (American Vol) 75, 1175–84

Woodfield C (1981) 'Finds from the Free Grammar School at the Whitefriars, Coventry c1545–c1557/58' *Post-Medieval Archaeology* 15, 81–159

Zieve D & Ma BC 2010 'Compression fractures of the back' *MedlinePlus* http://www.nlm.nih.gov/medlineplus/ency/article/000443.htm accessed 27 October 2017

CARTOGRAPHIC SOURCES

Adair J 1682 'Map of Midlothian' [map] (Edinburgh, engraved 1735) http://maps.nls.uk/view/index.cfm?id=00001013 accessed 27 October 2017

Adair J 1735 'A Map of Midlothian' [map] (Edinburgh, surveyed 1680s, imprinted by Cooper R c 1735) http://maps.nls.uk/view/00000985 accessed 27 October 2017

Ainslie J 1804 'Old and New town of Edinburgh with the proposed docks' [map] (Edinburgh, published 1804) http://maps.nls.uk/view/index.cfm?id=74400072 accessed 27 October 2017

Hunter W & Smith C 1828 'Plan of Edinburgh and Leith exhibiting all the present and intended improvements, etc' [map] (Edinburgh, published 1828) http://maps.nls.uk/view/102190477 accessed 27 October 2017

Kirkwood R 1817a 'An Ancient Plan of the City of Edinburgh and its Environs. Intended as an accompaniment to Kirkwood's New Plan of Edinburgh' [map] (Edinburgh, surveyed 1742, 1759 and 1777, imprinted 1816/1817) http://maps.nls.uk/view/index.cfm?id=74414123 accessed 27 October 2017

Kirkwood R 1817b 'This plan of the City of Edinburgh and its environs containing all the recent and intended improvements' [map] (Edinburgh, published 1817) http://maps.nls.uk/joins/416.html accessed 31 October 2017

Kirkwood J 1821 'Kirkwood's new plan of the City of Edinburgh' [map] (Edinburgh, published 1821) http://maps.nls.uk/view/74401133 accessed 16 January 2018

Lizars WH 1833 'Plan of Edinburgh Drawn and Engraved for the General Post Office Directory. Including: Plan of Leith' [map] (Edinburgh published 1832-3) http://maps.nls.uk/view/117742016 accessed 18 January 2018

Naish J 1709 'The Town of Leith' [map] (1:2376, 1 inch to 3 chains, surveyed 28 May 1709), National Archives reference number MPHH 1/32 http://discovery.nationalarchives.gov.uk/details/r/C4561136 accessed 11 April 2018

Ordnance Survey (OS) 1853a 'OS Town Plan – Edinburgh, Sheet 17' *Edinburgh and its Environs* [map] (Southampton, 1:1056, surveyed 1852, engraved and published 1853) http://maps.nls.uk/view/74415411 accessed 31 October 2017

Ordnance Survey (OS) 1853b 'OS Town Plan – Edinburgh, Sheet 21' *Edinburgh and its Environs* [map] (Southampton, 1:1056, surveyed 1852, engraved and published 1853) http://maps.nls.uk/view/74415420 accessed 31 October 2017

Ordnance Survey (OS) 1853c 'OS Town Plan – Edinburgh, Sheet 25' *Edinburgh and its Environs* [map] (Southampton, 1:1056, surveyed 1852, engraved and published 1853) http://maps.nls.uk/view/index.cfm?id=74415434 accessed 27 October 2017

Ordnance Survey (OS) 1853d 'OS Town Plan – Edinburgh, Sheet 13' *Edinburgh and its Environs* [map] (Southampton, 1:1056, surveyed 1852, engraved and published 1853) http://maps.nls.uk/view/74415407 accessed 17 January 2018

Ordnance Survey (OS) 1854 'OS Town Plan – Edinburgh, Sheet 30' *Edinburgh and its Environs* [map] (Southampton, 1:1056, surveyed 1852, engraved 1853, published 1854) http://maps.nls.uk/view/index.cfm?id=74415446 accessed 27 October 2017

Ordnance Survey (OS) 1876 'The City of Edinburgh, Sheet 21' *Edinburgh and its Environs* [map] (Southampton, 1:1056, surveyed 1852, revised 1876) http://maps.nls.uk/view/74415638 accessed 31 October 2017

Ordnance Survey (OS) 1877 'The City of Edinburgh, Sheet 25' *Edinburgh and its Environs* [map] (Southampton, 1:1056, surveyed 1852, revised 1877) http://maps.nls.uk/view/74415650 accessed 31 October 2017

Ordnance Survey (OS) 1896a 'Sheet 003.04' *Edinburghshire* [map] (Southampton, 1:2500, re-surveyed 1894, photozincographed and published 1896) http://maps.nls.uk/view/82877361 accessed 30 October 2017

Ordnance Survey (OS) 1896b 'Sheet 003.08' *Edinburghshire* [map] (Southampton, 1:2500, re-surveyed 1893–4, photozincographed and published 1896) http://maps.nls.uk/view/82877409 accessed 30 October 2017

Ordnance Survey (OS) 1908 'Sheet 003.08' *Edinburghshire* [map] (Southampton, 1:2500, surveyed 1893–4, revised 1905, published 1908, 2nd edn) http://maps.nls.uk/view/82877412 accessed 31 October 2017

Ordnance Survey (OS) 1933 'Midlothian, Sheet 003.8' *Twenty-five inch to the mile* [map] (Southampton, 1:2500, re-surveyed 1893–4, partially revised 1931, printed and published 1933) http://maps.nls.uk/view/82877418 accessed 31 October 2017

Ordnance Survey (OS) 1948a 'Plan 36/2674 SW' *National Grid* [map] (Southampton, 1:1250, surveyed 1945) http://maps.nls.uk/view/102734447 accessed 30/10/2017

Ordnance Survey (OS) 1948b 'Plan 36/2776 SW' *National Grid* [map] (Southampton, 1:1250, surveyed 1946, published 1948) http://maps.nls.uk/view/102735077 accessed 30/10/2017

Ordnance Survey (OS) 1957 'Plan NT 2674 SW' *Ordnance Survey* [map] (Chessington, 1:1250, surveyed 1945, revised 1957) http://maps.nls.uk/view/102734450 accessed 30/10/2017

Petworth 1560 'The plat of Lythe w[ith] thaproche of the Trenches thereunto. And also the great Ordyn'nce there in placed as it was at The daye of the Surrender thereof being the 7th daye of Julye 1560.', commonly known as 'The Petworth Map' (assumed to date to 7th July 1560) Petworth House Archives, PHA 4640

Roy W 1755 'Military survey of Scotland' [map] (surveyed 1747–55) http://maps.nls.uk/roy/index.html accessed 12 January 2018

Thomson C 1832 'Edinburgh drawn and engraved for the General Post Office Directory' (Edinburgh, published 1831–2) http://maps.nls.uk/view/117745997 accessed 16 January 2018

Wood J 1831 'Plan of the City of Edinburgh, including all the latest and intended improvements' (Edinburgh, published 1831) http://maps.nls.uk/view/74400027 accessed 16 January 2018

9 APPENDICES

APPENDIX 1 ISOTOPE ANALYSES METHODOLOGY AND RESULTS

Kate Britton

SAMPLE PREPARATION

All samples were selected by Scott Timpany, formerly of Headland Archaeology, and prepared at the Scottish Universities Environmental Research Centre (SUERC) facility in East Kilbride, Scotland, where all isotope measurements were obtained. This report, and data analysis contained within, was undertaken by Kate Britton, University of Aberdeen.

Carbon and nitrogen isotope analysis of bone collagen

Bone collagen samples were prepared and analysed for carbon and nitrogen isotope analysis, alongside the work undertaken for the radiocarbon measurements. Bone samples of typically 1–2g were prepared using a modified Longin method (Brown et al 1988; Collins and Galley 1998), although without the addition of an ultrafiltration step. All exposed surfaces were initially cleaned using a Dremel™ multi-tool with a sander attachment. The samples were then demineralised in 1M hydrochloric acid (HCl) over the course of 24 hours at room temperature. When demineralised, the samples were rinsed with ultrapure reverse osmosis water. Further reverse osmosis water was added to the demineralised samples, which were heated until solubilisation. Samples were then filtered through GF/A glass fibre paper and reduced in volume to <20ml and gelatinised for 24 hours at 80°C. The remaining filtered collagen solution was then lyophilised (freeze-dried) and weighed into tin capsules for isotope analysis (~0.5mg per aliquot). Carbon (δ^{13}C) and nitrogen δ^{15}N) were analysed using a Thermo Scientific Delta V Advantage continuous-flow isotope ratio mass spectrometer (CF-IRMS) coupled via a Thermo Scientific ConfloIV to a Costech ECS 4010 elemental analyzer (EA) fitted with a pneumatic auto sampler. Results were reported as per mil (‰) relative to the internationally accepted standards VPDB and AIR, with 1σ precisions of better than ± 0.2‰ and ± 0.3‰ for δ^{13}C and δ^{15}N, respectively.

Strontium and oxygen isotope analysis of tooth enamel

Tooth enamel was prepared at the SUERC facility for strontium and carbonate oxygen isotope analysis, using in-house procedures. Crowns were cut from roots, before being split in half. The crown was then placed in 10M NaOH solution, heated to approximately 80°C for eight hours and allowed to cool. The dentine was scraped from the enamel using a dissecting needle and the whole step repeated until all the dentine had been removed. The sample was repeatedly rinsed with 0.5M HCl to remove all NaOH and finally rinsed with ultra-pure water. The isolated enamel was then oven dried overnight and transferred to a labelled glass vial to await analysis.

Strontium isotope (^{87}Sr/^{86}Sr) measurements (including preparation) were carried out by the geology section of the SUERC facility. Strontium was separated from acid-digested enamel samples using conventional cation exchange methods and loaded onto single Ta filaments for mass spectrometry. The total procedural blank was <500pg. The samples were analysed on a VG Sector 54–30 mass spectrometer operated in dynamic (3 cycle) multi-collection mode. Instrumental mass fractionation was corrected to ^{86}Sr/^{88}Sr = 0.1196 using an exponential fractionation law. Data were collected as 12 blocks of 10 ratios.

Oxygen isotope analysis of biogenic carbonate ($\delta^{18}O_{carb}$) contained within the enamel mineral structure was also undertaken using a portion of the pre-treated enamel samples. The enamel samples were dissolved completely in '103%' phosphoric overnight at 25°C in sealed, evacuated tubes. Carbon dioxide (CO_2) evolved from the dissolution was then isolated and purified (using cryogenic separation procedures) and analysed via mass spectrometry. The relative abundances of masses 44, 45 and 46 in the gases were obtained using a VG SIRA 11 Series dual inlet Isotope Ratio Mass Spectrometer. The relative isotopic abundances were compared with those of a working standard reference gas of known stable isotope composition. In practice, this was achieved by automatic valve switching and data collection whereby reference gas and sample gas are alternately bled into the mass spectrometer, switching ten times over a period of several minutes, thus obtaining a mean delta (δ) value for the sample with respect to the reference gas. The reference gas was calibrated to the international standard using reference materials of known isotope composition (NBS-19, IAEA-CO-1 and IAEA-CO-8), and the δ values of the samples were calculated with respect to these international standards. All $\delta^{18}O_{V-PDB}$ values were then converted into the V-SMOW scale using the published conversion equation of Coplen (1988).

RESULTS

It should be noted that no medieval or early post-medieval animal reference bone data were available from Edinburgh or the surrounding region; therefore, these interpretations (and comparisons to other sites) must be viewed as preliminary.

APPENDICES

TABLE A1.01

Stable carbon and nitrogen isotope values of bone collagen from 30 individuals from Constitution Street, Leith. Component sampled, collagen yield (%) and C:N ratio are shown, along with the radiocarbon date of each bone collagen sample, and age group, biological sex and notable features of each individual/burial (for age group, see Appendix 2)

SK	GR	AGE	SEX	COMPONENT	% YIELD	$\delta^{13}C$	$\delta^{15}N$	C:N	C14, CALIBRATED, 95.4% PROBABILITY	NOTES
0040	0042	ADOL	–	Left femur	6.8	−19.3	11.5	3.4	1445–1635	Coffined burial; childhood malnutrition (DEH), calculus
0063	0065	YA	F	Right radius	9.8	−19.8	11.7	3.4	1445–1635	Coffined burial; rickets (bowing of leg bones)
0090	0086	ADOL	–	Radius	16.0	−19.0	11.9	3.3	1460–1650	Coffined burial; childhood malnutrition (DEH)
0112	0114	YC	–	Left femur	13.2	−19.9	11.3	3.4	1420–1530, 1555–1630	Double burial with? mother; infection of lower legs (periostitis)
0172	0173	YMA	M?	Left scapula	10.8	−19.4	12.2	3.4	1465–1655	–
0175	0176	AD	U	Right humerus	12.1	−20.3	10.9	3.4	1400–1515, 1605–1610	Buckle found in grave, possibly indicating buried in clothing
0212	0213	AD	F	Left tibia	10.4	−19.8	11.2	3.5	1435–1535, 1540–1635	–
0251	0252	ADOL	–	Left fibula	18.3	−19.0	12.2	3.3	1415–1535, 1555–1625	Coffined burial in slat-based coffin; Severe periostitis at mandible, malnutrition (cribra orbitalia and porotic hyperostosis), Schmorl's nodes, abscess, caries, calculus
0301	0302	YMA	F	Right femur	12.0	−19.6	11.8	3.4	1460–1645	Severe infection of lower legs (periostitis)
0306	0311	YA	U	Left femur	9.0	−19.5	12.5	3.4	1470–1650	–
0342	0335	AD	F	Left femur	4.5	−19.3	12.6	3.5	1445–1635	Group burial
0345	0335	OC	–	Humerus	1.9	−19.4	11.5	3.4	1335, 1395–1525, 1595–1620	Group burial, lying on left side; childhood malnutrition (DEH)
0361	0335	AD	U	Right tibia	11.7	−20.1	10.2	3.4	1425–1530, 1555–1630	Coffined burial within group burial
0423	0427	AD	F	Left radius	10.9	−21.0	11.2	3.4	1440–1525, 1560, 1570–1630	Group burial; Schmorl's nodes
0478	0479	YA	F	Right femur	1.2	−20.9	11.6	4.1	1275–1395	Earliest dated burial; excluded from further analysis due to unacceptable C:N ratio. Not shown in Chapter 4 Illus 4.68 or 4.69
0481	0482	OMA	F	Right humerus	5.7	−19.9	11.1	3.3	1435–1535, 1540–1630	Unusual N–S burial in top of mass grave Gr0589; remains of wool shroud with wire eyelets; costal DJD
0574	0579	YA	F	Left ulna	12.7	−20.4	11.6	3.2	1440–1535, 1540–1635	Buried in possible family plot; Schmorl's nodes, childhood malnutrition (DEH), AM tooth loss, caries, periodontal disease, calculus
0585	0587	YMA	F	Right radius	21.1	−19.4	12.2	3.2	1465–1655	Coffined burial; Schmorl's nodes, childhood malnutrition (DEH), overcrowded teeth, caries, periodontal disease, calculus
0592	0590	OMA	F	Left scapula	16.1	−19.2	12.6	3.3	1475–1665	Coffined burial; fractured hand, childhood malnutrition (DEH), spinal and sterno–clavicular DJD, arthritic right wrist, AM tooth loss, caries, periodontal disease, calculus
0646	0589	OC	–	Right femur	4.0	−20.6	12.1	3.5	1315–1355, 1390–1455	Group burial, buried with flexed legs
0696	0676	OC	–	Left tibia	19.9	−19.5	12.0	3.3	1450–1640	Coffined burial in slat-based coffin
0791	0786	YMA	F	Right radius	10.6	−19.9	11.7	3.2	1455–1635	Double burial with young child; malnutrition (DEH, porotic hyperostosis and cribra orbitalia), spondylolysis and costal DJD, periodontal disease, calculus
0806	0807	YMA	M?	Left fibula	13.7	−19.1	13.2	3.2	1465–1655	Group burial; fractured hand, and turned ankle
0845	0843	AD	U	Right tibia	20.2	−18.8	13.2	3.2	1470–1665	Coffined burial
0936	0937	PE	–	Rib	16.9	−19.9	11.9	3.3	1475–1665	36–38 weeks gestation

SK	GR	AGE	SEX	COMPONENT	% YIELD	δ^{13}C	δ^{15}N	C:N	C14, CALIBRATED, 95.4% PROBABILITY	NOTES
0951	0952	YMA	M?	Left humerus	15.6	−19.6	10.5	3.2	1475–1670	Schmorl's nodes, spinal DJD, fused ribs, overcrowded teeth
0985	0988	AD	F?	Skull	4.7	−18.4	14.1	3.4	1465–1660	Syphilis
0998	0999	OC	–	Right humerus	5.1	−19.3	12.6	3.3	1445–1635	Malnutrition (DEH, cribra orbitalia), active infection of jaw (periostitis), calculus
1052	1053	OC	–	Left tibia	1.2	−19.3	12.2	3.4	1300–1445	N–S burial; impacted tooth
1119	1118	OC	–	Left femur	9.5	−19.5	12.1	3.4	1475–1675, 1785–1795	Childhood malnutrition (DEH), calculus, heterotopic canine
Stdev						0.6	0.8			
Minimum						−18.4	10.2			
Mean						−19.6	11.9			
Maximum						−21.0	14.1			

TABLE A1.02
Stable carbon and nitrogen isotope values of bone collagen from three individuals from London Road, Edinburgh. Component sampled, collagen yield (%) and C:N ratio are shown, along with the radiocarbon date of each bone collagen sample, and age group, biological sex and notable features of each individual/burial (for age group, see Appendix 2)

SK	GR	AGE	SEX	COMPONENT	% YIELD	δ^{13}C	δ^{15}N	C:N	C14, CALIBRATED, 95.4% PROBABILITY	NOTES
457	461	YMA	M	Left femur	13.9	−19.6	11.4	3.2	1475–1670	Double burial with baby; ante mortem tooth loss, Schmorl's nodes, healed rib fracture, spondylolysis
466	467	YA	M	Left femur	11.2	−18.1	13.9	3.3	1465–1655	Simple burial by graveyard wall; signs of severe malnutrition (DEH and severe porotic hyperostosis), Schmorl's nodes, calculus and periodontal disease
495	496	YA	F	Left fibula	5.9	−19.6	11.1	3.2	1455–1640	Double burial with another adult female; Schmorl's nodes, malnutrition (porotic hyperostosis), infection of shin bones (periostitis), impacted canine, calculus and periodontal disease
Stdev						0.9	1.5			
Minimum						−19.6	11.1			
Mean						−19.1	12.1			
Maximum						−18.1	13.9			

Collagen preservation and quality indicators

Carbon and nitrogen stable isotope data δ^{13}C, δ^{15}N), along with C:N ratios are shown in **Tables A1.01–A1.02**. All samples yielded >1% collagen and, aside from Sk0478/Gr0479 (Constitution Street), had acceptable C:N ratios of between 2.9 and 3.6, indicating that extracted collagen was generally well preserved and that the collagen isotope values reported here reflect in vivo collagen δ^{13}C and δ^{15}N isotope ratios (DeNiro 1985; Ambrose 1990; van Klinken 1999). Sk0478 has been excluded from further data interpretation, in light of the unacceptable C:N ratio.

Carbon and nitrogen bone collagen isotope data

Results are shown in **Tables A1.01** and **A1.02** and in **Illus 4.68** and **Illus 4.69** (p133–34). δ^{13}C ratios of the 29 samples (meeting quality indicators) from Constitution Street range over 2.6‰, from −21‰ to −18.4‰, with a mean of −19.6 ± 0.6‰ (1σ). Respective δ^{15}N ratios range over 3.9‰, from 10.2‰ to 14.1‰, with a mean of 11.9 ± 0.8‰ (1σ). δ^{13}C ratios of the three individuals from London Road range over 1.5‰, from −19.6‰ to −18.1‰, with a mean of −19.1 ± 0.9‰ (1σ). δ^{15}N ratios range over 2.8‰, from 11.1‰ to 13.9‰, with a mean of 12.1 ± 1.5‰ (1σ).

Strontium and oxygen isotope data

Strontium and oxygen isotope data measured in dental enamel from 18 individuals from Constitution Street, Leith, are shown in **Table A1.03** and **Illus 4.72** (p137). The data range between 0.7084 and 0.7111 for strontium (^{87}Sr/^{86}Sr), and between 22.3 and 24.9‰ for oxygen carbonate (δ^{18}O$_{V\text{-}SMOW}$). Equivalent predicted oxygen phosphate values have been calculated using established equations (Chenery et al 2012) and are also shown in **Table A1.03**.

TABLE A1.03

Strontium and oxygen isotope data from tooth enamel of 18 individuals from Constitution Street, Leith, including details of component sampled, original $\delta^{18}O_{V-PDB}$ value and calculated $\delta^{18}O_{V-SMOW}$ value (using the conversion equation of Coplen 1988; for age group, see Appendix 2)

SK	AGE	SEX	COMPONENT	$^{87}Sr/^{86}Sr$	% STD ERR	$\delta^{18}O_{V-PDB}$	$\delta^{18}O_{V-SMOW}$	$\delta^{18}O$, PHOS	C14, CALIBRATED, 95.4% PROBABILITY
0040	ADOL	–	Lower R 2nd Molar	0.7111	0.0013	−8.0	22.7	13.7	1445–1635
0090	ADOL	–	Lower L 2nd Molar	0.7096	0.0013	−7.7	23.0	14.0	1460–1650
0194	ADOL	–	Lower L 2nd Molar	0.7097	0.0012	−7.6	23.0	14.1	–
0251	ADOL	–	Upper L 2nd Molar	0.7092	0.0013	−7.7	23.0	14.1	1415–1535, 1555–1625
0345	OC	–	Lower L 2nd Molar	0.7096	0.0012	−7.1	23.6	14.6	1335, 1395–1525, 1595–1620
0478	YA	F	Lower R 2nd Molar	0.7108	0.0014	−6.7	24.1	15.1	1275–1395
0574	YA	F	Lower R 2nd Molar	0.7101	0.0013	−7.9	22.7	13.8	1440–1535, 1540–1635
0585	YMA	F	Upper L 2nd Molar	0.7097	0.0013	−7.7	23.0	14.1	1465–1655
0592	OMA	F	Upper R 2nd Premolar	0.7093	0.0015	−5.8	24.9	15.9	1475–1665
0628	OC	–	Upper L 2nd Molar	0.7100	0.0013	−8.4	22.3	13.3	–
0641	YC	–	Lower R 1st Molar	0.7095	0.0012	−7.4	23.3	14.3	–
0646	OC	–	Lower R 2nd Molar	0.7097	0.0013	−6.8	23.9	15.0	1315–1355, 1390–1455
0704	YC	–	Lower L 1st Molar	0.7094	0.0011	−6.7	24.1	15.1	–
0791	YMA	F	Lower L 2nd Premolar	0.7085	0.0014	−7.3	23.4	14.4	1455–1635
0951	YMA	M?	Lower L 2nd Molar	0.7084	0.0012	−7.2	23.5	14.5	1475–1670
0998	OC	–	Upper L 2nd Molar	0.7097	0.0012	−6.8	23.9	14.9	1445–1635
1052	OC	–	Upper L 2nd Molar	0.7096	0.0014	−7.2	23.5	14.5	1300–1445
1119	OC	–	Lower R 2nd Molar	0.7096	0.0013	−6.6	24.1	15.2	1475–1675, 1785–1795
Stdev				0.0007		0.6	0.6	0.6	
Minimum				0.7084		−8.4	22.3	13.3	
Mean				0.7096		−7.2	23.4	14.5	
Maximum				0.7111		−5.8	24.9	15.9	

APPENDIX 2 BURIAL AND OSTEOLOGICAL DATA

Carmelita Troy and Julie Franklin

Tables A2.01 (Constitution Street) and **A2.02** (London Road) summarise the data associated with each skeleton, including burials details, location, age, sex, condition, stature, pathology, dating and inclusion in the isotope studies. All entries highlighted in red indicate the existence of facial reconstructions (see p12–13).

The age group abbreviations are defined as follows:

AD	Adult	Over 18 years
ADOL	Adolescent	13–17 years
FO	Foetus	3rd foetal month until birth
INF	Infant	2 months–1 year
SA	Subadult	Under 18 years
NEO	Neonate	Birth–2 months
OA	Older adult	45+ years
OC	Older child	7–12 years
OMA	Older middle adult	35–45 years
PE	Perinate	around the time of birth
YA	Younger adult	18–25 years
YC	Younger child	1–6 years
YMA	Younger middle adult	25–35 years

CONSTITUTION STREET BURIAL AND OSTEOLOGICAL DATA (TABLE A2.01)

Area 3 is divided into 3N and 3S to denote burials north and south of ditch [0084].

The articulated remains of a further four individuals were recovered during earlier test-trenching along Constitution Street (see p8–9; **Illus 4.02**, p50). Osteological analysis was not undertaken on these remains and they are not included in this table, though one of the skulls (found on the west side of the road, close to the current graveyard entrance) was included in the programme of facial reconstructions.

TABLE A2.01
Constitution Street burial and osteological data

SKELETON	GRAVE	AREA	SIMPLE / COFFIN	FINDS	BURIAL NOTES	AGE	SEX	COMPLETENESS	PRESERVATION	STATURE (cm)	PATHOLOGY	C14	ISOTOPE STUDY	ILLUS
0040	0042	2	Coffin	pin, tag?	Single	ADOL	–	~50%	Good	–	Calculus, DEH	1445–1635	C/N, Sr/O	4.05
0043	0045	2	Coffin	–	Single	AD	U	<25%	Good	–	–	–	–	4.05
0048	0050	2	Coffin	–	Single	OMA	F	~50%	Good	152.52	Spinal DJD	–	–	4.05, 4.17
0051	0053	2	Coffin	–	Single	OA (50–59)	F	~50%	Good	160.06	Severe arthritic left knee, left wrist and right knee. Severe arthritis in spine & C6 compressed. Costal DJD	–	–	4.05, 4.44
0054	0056	2	Coffin	–	Single	YMA (25–30)	M	~75%	Good	180.49	Traumatic spondylolysis. Knee DJD. Abscess, AM tooth loss, caries, calculus, periodontal disease, DEH. Spinal DJD	–	–	4.05
0057	0059	2	Coffin	–	Single	ADOL	–	~75%	Moderate	–	Misaligned tooth (48) – root growing distally (horizontal) – impacted tooth. Supernumerary lumbar vertebra	–	–	4.05
0060	0062	2	Coffin	tag	Single	YA	M?	<25%	Good	–	Calculus, caries, periodontal disease, AM tooth loss. L cribra orbitalia and porotic hyperostosis	–	–	4.05
0063	0065	2	Coffin	–	Single	YA (20–24)	F	~50%	Good	151.32	Rickets/osteomalacia – bilateral bowing of tibiae	1445–1635	C/N	4.05, 4.49
0067	0069	3S	Coffin	–	Single, on side	YC (2–3)	–	~75%	Good	–	–	–	–	4.06, 4.28
0070	0072	3S	Coffin	–	Single	YC (4–5)	–	>75%	Moderate	–	DEH	–	–	4.06
0076	0074	3S	Coffin	–	Single	ADOL	–	~50%	Good	–	Calculus, DEH, periodontal disease	–	–	4.06
0079	0078	3S	Simple	–	Single	YMA	M?	~50%	Good	164.69	–	–	–	4.06

APPENDICES

SKELETON	GRAVE	AREA	SIMPLE / COFFIN	FINDS	BURIAL NOTES	AGE	SEX	COMPLETENESS	PRESERVATION	STATURE (cm)	PATHOLOGY	C14	ISOTOPE STUDY	ILLUS
0089	1204	3N	Simple	–	Single	YC (1–3)	–	~50%	Poor	–	Bilateral mild cribra orbitalia	–	–	–
0090	0086	3S	Coffin	–	Single	ADOL (16–18)	–	~50%	Poor	–	DEH	1460–1650	C/N, Sr/O	4.06
0093	0091	3N	Simple	–	Single	AD	F?	<25%	Good	–	–	–	–	4.06
0094	1205	3N	Simple	–	Single	OC (10–11)	–	~75%	Good	–	–	–	–	–
0107	0108	4	Simple	–	Single	OC (8–11)	–	~75%	Good	–	–	–	–	4.07
0112	0114	4	Simple	–	Double prone	YC (5½–7½)	–	~50%	Poor	–	Bilateral healed periostitis on tibiae and fibulae	1420–1530, C/N 1555–1630	–	4.07
0113	0114	4	Simple	–	Double	YA (20–24)	F	~50%	Poor	157.67	–	–	–	4.07
0115	–	4	–	–	Disart skull	YA	M	<25%	Good	–	Supernumery tooth (post. To 11). 42 & 32 orientated mes. & dist. Severe periostitis on mandible . L cribra orbitalia, porotic hyperostosis. Calculus, DEH, periodontal disease	–	–	–
0116	–	4	–	–	Disart skull	YA	F	<25%	Moderate	–	Calculus, periodontal disease, DEH	–	–	–
0117	0160	4	Simple	–	Single	YA	M?	~50%	Moderate	164.06	Rotation (45 degrees) of 22 & 23. Calculus, DEH, periodontal disease, abscess, caries. R. maxillary sinusitis	–	–	4.07
0119	0120	4	Simple	–	Single	YMA	F	~50%	Good	153.39	Enlarge (bilat) mandible. Calculus, DEH, periodontal disease	–	–	4.07 4.62
0122	0123	4	Simple	–	Single	YA	F?	<25%	Good	–	Bilateral cribra orbitalia & porotic hyperostosis. Calculus, DEH, periodontal disease	–	–	4.07
0125	0126	4	Simple	–	Single	YA	F?	<25%	Good	163.61	–	–	–	–
0131	0132	5	–	–	Disart skull	YA	M	<25%	Good	–	AM tooth loss, caries, periodontal disease, DEH. Bilateral cribra orbitalia & porotic hyperostosis	–	–	4.04
0134	0137	4	Simple	–	Single, superimposed burial?	YA	F	<25%	Good	–	–	–	–	4.07
0135	0137	4	Simple	–	Single, superimposed burial?	YC (3–4)	–	<25%	Good	–	Bilateral periostitis and medial bowing of tibiae & fibulae	–	–	4.07
0136	0137	4	Simple	–	Single, superimposed burial?	YMA	F?	~50%	Good	151.06	Sacral DJD	–	–	4.07
0140	0391	4	Simple	–	Single	AD	F?	<25%	Good	166.95	Unusually formed coccyx – orientated to the left and curled up	–	–	–
0143	0137	4	Simple	–	Single, superimposed burial?	AD	U	<25%	Poor	–	R tibia periostitis	–	–	4.07
0145	0146	5	Simple	–	Single	AD	U	<25%	Moderate	–	–	–	–	4.08
0147	0149	5	Simple	–	Single	OMA	F	~75%	Good	157.59	AM tooth loss, caries, abscess, calculus, periodontal disease, DEH. Mild spinal & costal DJD. Schmorl's nodes. Eburnation dist. aspect of prox. h. phalanx (L). Mild DJD at R. knee, mod DJD R. tarsal	–	–	4.04
0151	0153	4	Simple	–	Double	YC (3½–4½)	–	~75%	Moderate	–	Tooth 32, 41 & 42 orientated medially. DEH, calculus. L cribra orbitalia	–	–	4.07
0152	0153	4	Simple	–	Double	OC (10½–11½)	–	~75%	Good	–	Microdontia of 28. Calculus, DEH	–	–	4.07

SKELETON	GRAVE	AREA	SIMPLE / COFFIN	FINDS	BURIAL NOTES	AGE	SEX	COMPLETENESS	PRESERVATION	STATURE (cm)	PATHOLOGY	C14	ISOTOPE STUDY	ILLUS
0154	0155	4	Simple	–	Single	ADOL (12–14)	–	>75%	Good	–	Abscess, calculus, DEH, periodontal disease	–	–	4.07
0158	0159	5	Coffin	–	Single	YA (18–24)	M	>75%	Good	169.97	Enamel pearl on tooth 17 (lingual). Calculus, periodontal disease, DEH. Bilateral periostitis on tibiae and fubulae, and R femur. Bilateral severe cribra orbitalia and porotic hyperostosis. Schmorl's nodes	–	–	4.08 4.51
0161	0162	4	Simple	–	Double	OC (9½)	–	~50%	Moderate	–	Severe L. cribra orbitalia	–	–	4.07
0164	0162	4	Simple	–	Double	YMA	F	~50%	Good	149.03	Upper canine (13) impacted (unerupted). Calculus, caries, periodontal disease, AM tooth loss, DEH. Bilat. Spondylolysis of L5. Spinal DJD	–	–	4.07
0166	0167	4	Simple	–	Single	YMA	F	>75%	Poor	151.54	Retention of deciduous tooth 63 & tooth 23 unerupted / impacted upon. Calculus, DEH, periodontal disease	–	–	4.07
0169	0170	4	Simple	–	Single	ADOL	–	~50%	Moderate	–	–	–	–	4.07
0172	0173	4	Simple	–	Single	YMA	M?	~50%	Moderate	173.01	–	1465–1655	C/N	4.07
0175	0176	4	Simple	textile, buckle	Single	AD	U	~50%	Poor	–	–	1400–1515, 1605–1610	C/N	4.07 4.63A
0177	0178	5	Simple	–	Single	OC (10½–11½)	–	<25%	Good	–	Healed periostitis on L & R tibia; active periostitison distal R tibia & R femur	–	–	4.08
0181	0183	4	Simple	–	Single	YMA	F	<25%	Moderate	156.42	Spinal DJD and Schmorl's nodes	–	–	4.07 4.14
0184	0186	4	–	–	Disart skull	YMA	M?	<25%	Good	–	AM tooth loss, calculus, periodontal disease. R mild cribra orbitalia	–	–	4.07 4.14
0187	–	4	–	–	Disart skull	AD	U	<25%	Good	–	L mild cribra orbitalia	–	–	–
0188	0271	4	Simple	–	Single	AD	U	<25%	Good	–	–	–	–	–
0190	0191	4	Simple	–	Single	YMA	U	~50%	Good	–	Slight spinal DJD. Schmorl's nodes	–	–	4.07
0194	0195	4	Simple	–	Single, flexed	ADOL	–	~75%	Poor	–	DEH, periodontal disease	–	Sr/O	4.07 4.29
0197	0198	5	Simple	–	Single	AD	M	<25%	Good	163.67	–	–	–	4.08
0199	0200	5	–	–	Disart skull	OC (9½–10)	–	<25%	Good	–	Calculus	–	–	4.04
0201	0202	5	Simple	–	Single	AD	M?	<25%	Good	–	Severe periostitis on L hip and bilaterally on tibiae and fibulae. DJD on L hip	–	–	4.04
0203	0205	4	Simple	–	Single	OC (9–9½)	–	<25%	Good	–	–	–	–	4.07
0207	0189	4	Coffin	–	Single	AD	U	<25%	Good	–	Bilateral osteochondra (hereditary multiple exostosis) on MT2. Unusual shortness of R MT4 (congenital malformation)	–	–	4.07 4.14 4.60
0208	0209	4	Simple	–	Single	YMA	F?	<25%	Poor	–	DEH, periodontal disease. Bilat spondylolysis of L5. Schmorl's nodes	–	–	4.07
0212	0213	4	Simple	–	Single	AD	F	<25%	Good	149.12	–	1435–1535, 1540–1635	C/N	4.07 4.14
0214	0215	4	Simple	–	Single	OA (45–50)	M	~50%	Moderate	170.22	T10 collapsed centrum. Schmorl's nodes. Spinal DJD	–	–	4.07
0217	0218	4	Simple	–	Single	YC (3½–4)	–	~50%	Moderate	–	Bilat. Severe cribra orbitalia. Calculus, DEH	–	–	4.07
0220	0221	4	Simple	–	Single	YC (1½–2)	–	~75%	Poor	–	–	–	–	4.07

APPENDICES

SKELETON	GRAVE	AREA	SIMPLE / COFFIN	FINDS	BURIAL NOTES	AGE	SEX	COMPLETENESS	PRESERVATION	STATURE (cm)	PATHOLOGY	C14	ISOTOPE STUDY	ILLUS
0224	0225	4	Simple	–	Single	OC (11–11½)	–	~50%	Moderate	–	–	–	–	4.07
0228	0230	5	–	–	Disart skull	AD	F	<25%	Moderate	–	–	–	–	4.08
0231	0230	5	Coffin	–	Single	OMA	M?	~50%	Moderate	164.70	Arthritic (eburnation) R prox radius. Severe OA destruction of prox aspect of intermed. foot phalanx	–	–	4.04
0234	0235	5	Simple	–	Single	OC (12)	–	<25%	Good	–	R tibia & fibula periostitis	–	–	–
0237	0238	4	Coffin	–	Single	AD	M?	<25%	Good	167.59	R distal tibia & fibula with ankylosis & severe osteolytic bone growth	–	–	4.07
0240	0241	5	Coffin	–	Single	AD	U	<25%	Poor	–	–	–	–	4.08
0243	0244	5	Simple	–	Single	YA	F	~50%	Good	147.95	L femur & bilateral tibiae with healed periostitis	–	–	4.04
0246	0247	4	Simple	–	Single	AD	M	<25%	Good	173.88	–	–	–	–
0248	0254	4	Simple	–	Single	AD	U	<25%	Good	–	–	–	–	4.07
0251	0252	5	Coffin (slat-based)	–	Single	ADOL	–	>75%	Moderate	–	Severe periostitis at mandible. Abscess, caries, calculus. Mild bilateral cribra orbitalia, porotic hyperostosis. Schmorl's nodes	1415–1535, 1555–1625	C/N, Sr/O	4.08 4.18 4.19 4.57
0256	0257	4	Simple	–	Single	OC (11½–12)	–	<25%	Moderate	–	–	–	–	4.07
0258	0259	4	Simple	–	Single	YMA	F	<25%	Good	151.79	–	–	–	4.07
0260	0261	4	Simple	–	Single	AD	U	<25%	Good	–	–	–	–	4.07
0263	0262	4	Simple	–	Single	OC (6½–7)	–	<25%	Good	–	Bilateral tibiae periostitis	–	–	4.07 4.14
0265	0260	4	–	–	Disart skull	AD	M	<25%	Good	–	–	–	–	4.07
0274	0273	6	Simple	–	Single	YC (2)	–	~50%	Moderate	–	–	–	–	4.09
0278	0279	5	Simple	–	Single	OC (7–7½)	–	<25%	Moderate	–	–	–	–	4.08
0281	0282	5	Simple	–	Single	ADOL	–	~75%	Good	–	Congenitally absent teeth – 12, 14, 15, 38, 48. Calculus, DEH, periodontal disease	–	–	4.04
0284	0283	5	Simple	–	Single	YMA	M?	~50%	Moderate	162.61	Bilateral tibiae periostitis and tarsal DJD	–	–	4.08
0287	0286	5	Simple	–	Single	AD	M	<25%	Good	175.26	–	–	–	4.08
0289	0290	5	Simple	–	Single	AD	U	<25%	Poor	–	–	–	–	4.08
0291	–	5	–	–	Disart skull	YA	M?	<25%	Good	–	–	–	–	–
0292	–	5	–	–	Disart skull	SA	–	<25%	Good	–	–	–	–	–
0293	–	5	–	–	Disart skull	YMA	M	<25%	Good	–	AM tooth loss, calculus, caries, abscess, DEH, periodontal disease	–	–	–
0294	0295	5	Simple	–	Single	OC	–	<25%	Good	–	Bilateral cribra orbitalia and porotic hyperostosis. Calculus, caries, periodontal disease, DEH	–	–	–
0296	0302	5	–	–	Disart skull	AD	M?	<25%	Good	–	–	–	–	4.08
0297	0302	5	–	–	Disart skull	OC (11–13)	–	<25%	Good	–	–	–	–	4.08
0298	0299	5	Simple	–	Single	AD	M	<25%	Good	170.40	Healed fracture of R tibia & fibula (ant–post misalignment). Secondary (traumatic) DJD on distal tibia, fibula & talus	–	–	4.08 4.59

SKELETON	GRAVE	AREA	SIMPLE / COFFIN	FINDS	BURIAL NOTES	AGE	SEX	COMPLETENESS	PRESERVATION	STATURE (cm)	PATHOLOGY	C14	ISOTOPE STUDY	ILLUS
0301	0302	5	Simple	–	Single	YMA	F	~50%	Moderate	152.86	Severe periostitis on tibiae (bilat.) and left fibula	1460–1645	C/N	4.08, 4.56
0303	0307	5	Simple	–	Double	YA	M?	~50%	Moderate	167.08	Schmorl's nodes	–	–	4.08
0304	0309	5	Simple	–	Single	OC (11–11½)	–	<25%	Moderate	–	–	–	–	4.08
0305	0307	5	Simple	–	Double	AD	U	<25%	Good	–	L tibia periostitis	–	–	4.08
0306	0311	5	Simple	–	Single	YA (18–20)	U	~50%	Good	–	–	1470–1650	C/N	4.08
0313	0314	5	Simple	–	Single	YA	M	<25%	Moderate	–	Spinal DJD, Schmorl's nodes	–	–	4.08
0315	0316	5	Simple	–	Single	YC (4½–5½)	–	~50%	Good	–	Bilateral periostitis on fibulae	–	–	4.08
0318	0319	5	Simple	–	Single	YMA	M	~75%	Poor	170.48	AM tooth loss, calculus, DEH	–	–	4.08
0321	0322	6	Coffin	–	Single	ADOL	–	~50%	Poor	–	–	–	–	–
0325	–	6	–	–	Disart skull	OC (6–10)	–	<25%	Poor	–	DEH	–	–	–
0326	0327	6	Simple	–	Single	YA	F	~50%	Poor	153.39	Calculus, DEH, caries, periodontal disease	–	–	4.09
0330	0331	6	Simple	–	Single	ADOL (15–18)	–	<25%	Good	–	Severe active periostitis on R scapula	–	–	4.04
0333	0334	6	Simple	–	Single	AD	U	~50%	Poor	–	–	–	–	4.09
0340	0337	6	Coffin	–	Single	YMA	F	<25%	Poor	156.98	–	–	–	4.09
0341	0335	6	–	–	Disart skull	OC	–	<25%	Poor	–	–	–	–	4.09
0342	0335	6	Simple	–	Single, superimposed burial?	AD	F	<25%	Poor	–	–	1445–1635	C/N	4.09
0344	0335	6	–	–	Disart skull	YA	F	<25%	Poor	–	Calculus, DEH	–	–	4.09
0345	0335	6	Simple	–	Double, superimposed burial?, on side	OC (9½–10½)	–	<25%	Poor	–	DEH	1335, 1395–1525, 1595–1620	C/N, Sr/O	4.09
0346	0335	6	Simple	–	Double, superimposed burial?	YMA	F	~75%	Poor	–	Calculus, caries, abscess	–	–	4.09
0348	0349	6	Simple	–	Single	SA	–	<25%	Poor	–	–	–	–	4.09
0352	0353	6	Coffin	–	Single	AD	M	~50%	Poor	–	Severe DJD R hip	–	–	–
0355	0357	6	Coffin	–	Single	OMA	M?	~50%	Moderate	165.77	Schmorl's nodes. AM tooth loss, calculus, DEH	–	–	4.09
0361	0335	6	Coffin	–	Double, superimposed burial?	AD	U	<25%	Poor	–	–	1425–1530, 1555–1630	C/N	4.09
0363	0335	6	Coffin	–	Double, superimposed burial?	SA	–	<25%	Poor	–	–	–	–	4.09
0365	0366	6	Coffin	–	Single	YA	M	<25%	Poor	–	–	–	–	4.09
0369	0447	6	–	–	Disart skull	SA	–	<25%	Moderate	–	Left severe cribra orbitalia	–	–	4.09

APPENDICES

SKELETON	GRAVE	AREA	SIMPLE / COFFIN	FINDS	BURIAL NOTES	AGE	SEX	COMPLETENESS	PRESERVATION	STATURE (cm)	PATHOLOGY	C14	ISOTOPE STUDY	ILLUS
0370	0371	6	Simple	–	Single	ADOL (12–14)	–	~50%	Poor	–	–	–	–	4.09
0375	0381	6	Simple	–	Single	AD	U	<25%	Poor	–	–	–	–	4.09
0378	0379	6	–	–	Disart skull	YA	M	<25%	Good	–	Calculus, caries, DEH, periodontal disease	–	–	4.04 4.38
0382	–	6	–	–	Disart skull	AD	M	<25%	Moderate	–	Bilat cribra orbitalia and prortic hyperostosis	–	–	–
0383	0416	6	Simple	–	Single	YA	F	~50%	Moderate	–	Periostitis on L calcaneus	–	–	4.04
0385	0386	6	Simple	–	Single	AD	U	<25%	Poor	–	–	–	–	4.09
0394	0395	6	Simple	–	Single	YC (4–4½)	–	~50%	Good	–	–	–	–	4.09
0397	0398	6	Simple	–	Single	AD	F	<25%	Moderate	–	Periostitis on distal, post. Aspect of R. Tibia	–	–	4.09
0400	0401	6	Simple	–	Single	YMA	F	<25%	Moderate	–	Schmorl's nodes	–	–	4.09
0403	0402	6	Simple	–	Single	YA	F	<25%	Poor	–	AM tooth loss, calculus, DEH	–	–	4.09
0406	0407	6	Simple	–	Single	YC (4)	–	~50%	Moderate	–	–	–	–	4.09
0410	0408	6	Coffin	–	Single	AD	U	<25%	Moderate	–	–	–	–	4.09
0414	0412	6	Simple	–	Single	AD	F	<25%	Good	–	–	–	–	4.04
0420	0421	6	Simple	–	Single	YC (5½)	–	<25%	Moderate	–	R tibia periostitis	–	–	4.09 4.22
0423	0427	6	Simple	–	Group	AD (>25)	F	~50%	Moderate	155.86	Schmorl's nodes	1440–1525, C/N 1560, 1570–1630		4.09 4.22
0424	0427	6	Simple	–	Group, on side	INF (6–12 mo)	–	~75%	Good	–	Porotic hyperostosis & severe porosity on sphenoid. Endocranial reactive bone. Severe porosity and reactive bone on sternal aspect of ribs (bilaterally)	–	–	4.09 4.22 4.50
0425	0427	6	Simple	–	Group	YA	F	~50%	Good	163.14	R femur bowing medially. Schmorl's nodes	–	–	4.09 4.22
0426	0427	6	Simple	–	Group	OC (8½–9)	–	~50%	Moderate	–	Periostitis on prox. shaft (posterior) of L femur	–	–	4.09 4.22
0428	0458	6	–	–	Disart skull	AD (>25)	U	<25%	Good	–	Bilateral nasal turbinate. Calculus, caries, AM tooth loss, periodontal disease	–	–	4.04 4.22
0429	0427	6	–	–	Disart skull	ADOL (12½–13)	–	<25%	Poor	–	Calculus, caries, DEH, periodontal disease, AM tooth loss	–	–	4.09 4.22
0431	0432	6	Simple	–	Single	OC (9½–12)	–	~75%	Poor	–	–	–	–	–
0434	0435	6	Simple	–	Single	OC (7½)	–	~75%	Moderate	–	Calculus, DEH. Bilateral severe cribra orbitalia	–	–	4.04 4.22
0438	0439	6	Coffin	–	Single	AD (>25)	F	<25%	Poor	–	–	–	–	4.09
0441	0443	6	Coffin	–	Single	AD	U	<25%	Poor	–	–	–	–	4.09
0446	0447	6	Simple	–	Single	YC (5½–6½)	–	~50%	Moderate	–	–	–	–	4.09
0449	0450	6	Simple	–	Single	SA (<12)	–	<25%	Poor	–	–	–	–	4.09
0452	0453	6	Simple	–	Single	SA (<12)	–	<25%	Poor	–	–	–	–	4.09
0455	0454	6	Simple	–	Single	OC (8–12)	–	<25%	Poor	–	–	–	–	–

SKELETON	GRAVE	AREA	SIMPLE/COFFIN	FINDS	BURIAL NOTES	AGE	SEX	COMPLETENESS	PRESERVATION	STATURE (cm)	PATHOLOGY	C14	ISOTOPE STUDY	ILLUS
0460	0462	6	Coffin	–	Single	AD	F	<25%	Good	156.80	–	–	–	–
0463	–	6	–	–	Disart skull	AD	F?	<25%	Good	–	DEH, periodontal disease	–	–	–
0465	0467	6	Coffin	–	Single	AD	F	<25%	Moderate	154.33	–	–	–	4.04
0469	0471	6	Coffin	–	Single	AD	U	<25%	Moderate	–	–	–	–	4.04
0472	0473	6	Simple	–	Single	AD	U	<25%	Poor	–	–	–	–	4.09
0474	0475	6	Simple	–	Single	SA (<12)	–	<25%	Poor	–	–	–	–	4.04
0478	0479	6	Simple	–	Single	YA	F	~75%	Poor	–	Calculus, DEH, periodontal disease	1275–1395	C/N, Sr/O	4.09
0481	0482	6	Simple	textile, 8 eyelets	Single, S–N aligned	OMA	F	~75%	Poor	150.85	Costal DJD	1435–1535, C/N 1540–1630		4.09 4.25 4.64A
0484	0485	6	–	–	Disart skull	AD (>25)	M?	<25%	Moderate	–	Calculus, caries, DEH, periodontal disease, AM tooth loss	–	–	4.04
0487	0488	6	Simple	–	Single	YC	–	~50%	Poor	–	–	–	–	4.09
0491	0490	6	Coffin	–	Single	OMA	F	<25%	Poor	–	–	–	–	4.04
0494	0493	6	Simple	–	Single	OMA	F	~75%	Poor	–	Healed fracture in R. tibia & fibula. AM tooth loss, caries, calculus, DEH and periodontal disease. Spinal DJD	–	–	4.09
0498	0499	6	Simple	–	Single	YA	M?	~50%	Moderate	160.82	–	–	–	4.04
0503	0504	6	Simple	–	Single	SA	–	<25%	Poor	–	–	–	–	4.09
0506	0507	6	Simple	–	Single	AD	M	<25%	Moderate	172.56	Bilat. Healed & active periostitis on tibiae and fibulae	–	–	4.09
0509	0508	6	Simple	–	Single	YMA	F?	<25%	Moderate	–	–	–	–	4.09
0510	0532	7	Simple	–	Single	YMA	F	<25%	Moderate	–	–	–	–	4.10
0511	Pit 0501	6	–	–	Disart skull	AD	M?	<25%	Moderate	–	–	–	–	4.09
0512	Pit 0501	6	–	–	Disart skull	AD	F?	<25%	Good	–	Bilateral cribra orbitalia. Multiple osteomas in sphenoid sinus	–	–	4.09 4.54
0513	Pit 0501	6	–	–	Disart skull	YA	F	<25%	Good	–	Calculus, periodontal disease, DEH	–	–	4.09
0514	Pit 0501	6	–	–	Disart skull	YMA	M	<25%	Good	–	AM tooth loss, abscess, calculus, caries, periodontal disease	–	–	4.09
0516	0517	6	Simple	–	Single	ADOL	–	<25%	Poor	–	–	–	–	4.09
0519	0520	6	Simple	–	Single	YA	M?	<25%	Poor	–	Calculus, caries, periodontal disease	–	–	4.04
0522	0523	6	Simple	–	Single	OMA	F	~50%	Moderate	–	AM tooth loss, calculus, caries, DEH, periodontal disease. Spinal and costal DJD	–	–	4.04
0524	0525	7	Simple	–	Single	AD	U	<25%	Moderate	–	–	–	–	4.10
0527	0528	6	Simple	–	Single	YA	M	<25%	Good	169.47	Severe L1 compression fracture. Schmorl's nodes. Calculus, periodontal disease, DEH	–	–	–
0530	0531	6	Simple	–	Single	YMA	M	~50%	Good	–	Calculus, caries, AM tooth loss, DEH, periodontal disease. Spinal & costal DJD, Schmorl's nodes	–	–	–
0535	0534	7	Simple	–	Single	AD	M?	<25%	Moderate	–	–	–	–	4.10
0539	0537	7	Coffin	–	Single	AD	U	<25%	Poor	–	–	–	–	4.10

APPENDICES

SKELETON	GRAVE	AREA	SIMPLE / COFFIN	FINDS	BURIAL NOTES	AGE	SEX	COMPLETENESS	PRESERVATION	STATURE (cm)	PATHOLOGY	C14	ISOTOPE STUDY	ILLUS
0544	0545	7	Simple	–	Single	YC (1½)	–	<25%	Good	–	Calculus. Bilateral cribra orbitalia	–	–	4.04
0548	0549	7	Simple	–	Single	OMA	F	<25%	Moderate	–	DJD right hip	–	–	4.04
0551	0552	7	Simple	–	Single	AD	U	<25%	Moderate	–	–	–	–	4.10
0554	0556	6	Coffin	–	Single, superimposed burial?	OC (11½–12)	–	~50%	Poor	–	Calculus, DEH. Bilateral cribra orbitalia. Ankylosis of R inter and distal (2nd) F phal; and L inter and distal (5th) H phal	–	–	4.04
0562	0563	7	Simple	–	Single	OC (11–12)	–	~50%	Good	–	–	–	–	4.10
0564	–	6	–	–	Disart skull	AD	M?	<25%	Moderate	–	–	–	–	–
0566	0568	7	Coffin	–	Single	YMA	F	~50%	Good	160.79	Scioliosis of the thoracic spine (OA and OP). Schmorl's nodes. Costal DJD. Green staining on visceral aspect of rib. R. cribra orbitalia	–	–	4.04 4.48
0570	0571	7	Simple	pin	Single	YMA	M	~50%	Moderate	–	AM tooth loss, calculus, DEH, periodontal disease. Schmorl's nodes	–	–	4.04
0574	0579	6	Simple	–	Single, superimposed burial?	YA	F	~75%	Moderate	148.35	AM tooth loss, calculus, caries, periodontal disease, DEH. Schmorl's nodes	1440–1535, 1540–1635	C/N, Sr/O	4.04
0575	0611	6	Simple	–	Single, superimposed burial?	YMA	M?	~50%	Moderate	162.44	R acromo/clav DJD. Calculus, DEH, periodontal disease	–	–	4.04
0576	–	7	–	–	Disart skull	YC (5½–7)	–	<25%	Poor	–	–	–	–	–
0577	0605	6	Coffin	–	Single, superimposed burial?	OMA	F	~75%	Good	151.67	DJD on L distal H. phal. Costal & spinal DJD. Bilateral Acromo/clav DJD. Severe AM tooth loss, periodontal disease, abscess, caries, calculus. Supernumerary thoracic vertebra	–	–	4.04
0578	0605	6	–	–	Disart skull	AD	M?	<25%	Moderate	–	–	–	–	–
0581	0583	7	Coffin	–	Single	OMA	M	>75%	Good	177.24	Costal & spinal DJD. Schmorl's nodes. Calculus, DEH, periodontal disease. R cribra orbitalia & porotic hyperostosis	–	–	4.04
0585	0587	7	Coffin	textile	Single	YMA	F	~75%	Poor	–	Retention of canine (63) and incisor (22) congenitally absent. Premolar (45) rotated 90 degrees angle (distally). Calculus, caries, DEH, periodontal disease. Schmorl's nodes	1465–1655	C/N, Sr/O	4.04
0592	0590	7	Coffin	–	Single	OMA	F	>75%	Moderate	152.90	Calculus, caries, DEH, periodontal disease, AM tooth loss. Healed fracture distal L MC2. Spinal DJD. Arthritic R wrist. Osteochondroma R tibia (lateral). R sterno/clav DJD	1475–1665	C/N, Sr/O	4.04
0597	0598	7	Simple	–	Single	YMA	F	~75%	Good	156.98	Costal periostitis. Calculus, DEH, periodontal disease. Bilat cribra orbitalia	–	–	4.10
0601	0602	7	Coffin	–	Single	YMA	F	~50%	Good	152.16	Bilateral spondylolysis of L5. AM tooth loss, calculus, periodontal disease, DEH. Slight spinal and costal DJD	–	–	4.10
0607	0608	7	Simple	–	Single	ADOL	–	>75%	Moderate	–	Incisor (12) with two roots. Abscess, calculus, DEH. Severe bilateral cribra orbitalia	–	–	4.04
0613	0614	7	Simple	–	Single	YMA	F	~75%	Good	159.57	Periostitis at left maxilla due to abscess. Abscess, periodontal disease, caries, calculus, DEH. Bilateral cribra orbitalia and porotic hyperostosis. Spinal DJD & Schmorl's nodes	–	–	4.04
0617	0618	7	Simple	–	Single	OMA	M	~75%	Good	182.83	Fractured 6 (L) ribs – sternal (PHOTO). Osteoma on 1 (L) rib – visceral (5.2 * 4.2mm). Supernum 2 (L) ribs. Costal & spinal DJD. Schmorl's nodes. Bilat hip DJD. Bilat Acromo/clav DJD. R Sterno/clav DJD. AM tooth loss, calculus, caries, DEH, periodontal disease	–	–	4.04

SKELETON	GRAVE	AREA	SIMPLE/COFFIN	FINDS	BURIAL NOTES	AGE	SEX	COMPLETENESS	PRESERVATION	STATURE (cm)	PATHOLOGY	C14	ISOTOPE STUDY	ILLUS
0620	0622	7	Coffin	–	Single	AD	U	<25%	Moderate	–	Periostitis on R. distal–anterior tibia	–	–	4.10
0625	0624	6	Simple	–	Single	YMA	F	~75%	Moderate	–	L maxillary sinusitis. Bilateral L5 spondylolysis. Calculus, DEH, periodontal disease	–	–	4.09
0626	1218	6	Simple	–	Single, possibly within group burial 0589	YMA	M	<25%	Poor	–	DEH, AM tooth loss	–	–	4.04
0628	0629	7	Simple	–	Single	OC (6–8)	–	>75%	Good	–	Calculus, DEH	–	Sr/O	4.04
0631	0633	7	Coffin	–	Single	YA	M?	<25%	Poor	–	Healed bilatereal periostitis on femoral shafts	–	–	4.04
0634	–	8	–	–	Disart skull	AD	M?	<25%	Good	–	–	–	–	–
0637	0589	6	Simple	–	Group	YMA	F	~75%	Poor	147.34	Canine (33) with two roots. AM tooth loss, calculus, caries, DEH, periodontal disease	–	–	4.04 4.23
0639	0589	6	Simple	–	Group	YMA	F	>75%	Moderate	150.80	Spinal and costal DJD. Schmorl's nodes	–	–	4.04 4.23
0641	0642	7	Simple	–	Single	YC (1½–2)	–	~75%	Good	–	Calculus	–	Sr/O	4.10
0643	0589	6	Simple	–	Group	YMA	F	~50%	Moderate	156.23	R max. sinusitis. L mild cribra orbitalia. Enamel pearl on molar (28), lingual aspect of root. Schmorl's nodes. Calculus, DEH, periodontal disease	–	–	4.04 4.23 4.53
0646	0589	6	Simple	–	Group	OC (6½–8½)	–	~50%	Poor	–	–	1315–1355, 1390–1455	C/N, Sr/O	4.04 4.23
0648	0649	8	Simple	–	Single	YMA	F	~75%	Good	152.03	Unusual bowing/angulation of L humerus. Bilateral periostitis on tibiae and fibulae. Slight exostosis on distal L fibula	–	–	4.04
0651	0653	7	Coffin	–	Single	YC (4½–6)	–	~75%	Good	–	DEH. L cribra orbitalia and porotic hyperostosis	–	–	4.04
0655	0656	7	Simple	–	Single	OMA (35–39)	F?	~75%	Good	166.49	Supernumerary lower incisor (L). AM tooth loss, calculus, caries, periodontal disease, congenitally absent PM2 (L). Rotation of 32 and 33. Costal and spinal DJD	–	–	4.04 4.37 4.41
0664	0665	8	Simple	–	Single	OC (7–12)	–	<25%	Poor	–	–	–	–	4.11
0667	0668	7	Coffin	tag	Single	OC (12–12½)	–	~75%	Good	–	Severe bilateral cribra orbitalia. Calculus, periodontal disease, DEH. Unilateral glenoid hypoplasia of R shoulder (glenoid & corocoid)	–	–	4.04
0670	0669	8	Simple	–	Single	YC (2½–3)	–	>75%	Moderate	–	Calculus	–	–	4.11
0673	0672	7	Simple	pin	Single	OC (9–9½)	–	~75%	Good	–	Bilateral ischial periostitis (post–lat aspect)	–	–	4.10
0679	–	8	–	pin	Disart skull	SA	–	<25%	Good	–	–	–	–	–
0682	0683	8	Simple	–	Single	OC (11–11½)	–	~50%	Good	–	L. femur with healed fracture. R. femur with medial bowing	–	–	4.11 4.58
0684	–	8	–	–	Disart skull	SA	–	<25%	Moderate	–	–	–	–	–
0690	0692	8	Coffin	–	Single	YMA	F	>75%	Moderate	165.79	Healed periostitis on R tibia and fibula. Calculus, caries, periodontal disease, DEH. Schmorl's nodes	–	–	4.04
0694	0695	8	Simple	–	Single	YC (1–2)	–	~75%	Good	–	–	–	–	4.04
0696	0676	7	Coffin (slat–based)	–	Single	OC (9)	–	<25%	Poor	–	–	1450–1640 C/N	–	4.10
0698	0697	7	Simple	–	Single	YMA	F	~50%	Good	158.77	–	–	–	4.10 4.16

APPENDICES

SKELETON	GRAVE	AREA	SIMPLE / COFFIN	FINDS	BURIAL NOTES	AGE	SEX	COMPLETENESS	PRESERVATION	STATURE (cm)	PATHOLOGY	C14	ISOTOPE STUDY	ILLUS
0700	0701	8	Simple	–	Single	AD	M?	<25%	Good	–	Avulsion fracture of left MT5 and distal fibula. Arthritic left and right foot	–	–	4.11
0704	0710	7	Simple	–	Single	YC (5–6)	–	>75%	Moderate	–	Calculus, DEH	–	Sr/O	4.04 4.16
0706	0707	8	Simple	–	Single	OC (8½–9½)	–	>75%	Good	–	L. cribra orbitalia. Calculus, caries. Periostitis on anterior aspect of S2 and S3	–	–	4.11 4.16
0708	–	8	–	–	Disart skull	AD	M?	<25%	Good	–	Severe maxillary sinusitis (R). Periostitis on posterior aspect of L maxilla. AM tooth loss, abscess	–	–	–
0711	–	8	–	–	Disart skull	AD	M?	<25%	Good	–	Porotic hyperostosis	–	–	–
0713	0714	8	Simple	–	Single	YC (1½–2)	–	~75%	Moderate	–	Periostitis on L fibula	–	–	4.11 4.16
0716	0717	8	–	–	Disart skull	OC (10–12)	–	<25%	Good	–	–	–	–	–
0718	–	8	–	–	Disart skull	YA	F?	<25%	Good	–	R nasal turbinate. Possible cranial trauma (R frontal). L cribra orbitalia & porotic hyperostosis. Calculus, DEH.	–	–	4.55
0724	0725	8	Coffin	–	Single	YA	M	~75%	Moderate	175.77	AM tooth loss, calculus, caries, DEH. Schmorl's nodes	–	–	4.04
0727	0726	8	Simple	–	Single	ADOL (15–17)	–	~50%	Good	–	–	–	–	4.04
0730	0731	8	Simple	pin	Single	OC (11–13)	–	<25%	Good	–	–	–	–	–
0733	0734	7	Simple	–	Single	YMA	M?	>75%	Moderate	167.62	Enamel pearl on lingual aspect of root (17) and 4 roots. Calculus, caries, AM tooth loss, periodontal disease, DEH. Schmorl's nodes. R wrist DJD	–	–	4.04
0735	–	8	–	–	Disart skull	AD	F	<25%	Moderate	–	Severe (R) cribra orbitalia and porotic hyperostosis	–	–	–
0736	0737	8	Simple	–	Single	OC (11–13)	–	<25%	Moderate	–	–	–	–	4.11
0740	0741	9	Simple	–	Single	ADOL	–	<25%	Good	–	Periostitis on distal, medial aspect of R. Tibia	–	–	4.12
0744	0745	8	Coffin	–	Single	OC (11–12)	–	~75%	Good	–	DEH	–	–	4.04
0747	0749	8	Coffin	–	Single	YMA	F	>75%	Moderate	162.87	Tooth 33 (canine) with two roots. Calculus, periodontal disease. Schmorl's nodes. DJD on L hip	–	–	4.04
0751	0752	9	Simple	–	Single	AD	F	<25%	Good	162.16	–	–	–	4.04
0754	0753	8	Simple	–	Single	AD	F?	<25%	Good	165.21	Bilateral periostitis on tibiae	–	–	4.11
0757	0758	8	Simple	–	Single	YC (3½–4)	–	~75%	Moderate	–	–	–	–	4.11
0760	0761	9	Simple	–	Single	YA	F	~75%	Good	153.02	Calculus, periodontal disease, DEH	–	–	4.04
0763	0764	8	Simple	–	Single	OMA	F	~75%	Good	148.21	Spinal & costal DJD. Schmorl's nodes	–	–	4.04
0766	0767	8	Simple	–	Single	OC (11½)	–	<25%	Good	–	–	–	–	–
0769	0768	8	Simple	–	Single	YA	F	<25%	Good	156.07	Bilateral periostitis on femurs and tibiae	–	–	4.04
0773	0771	8	Coffin	–	Single	YMA	M	~75%	Moderate	173.29	Bilateral spondylolysis of L4	–	–	4.04
0776	0778	7	Coffin	–	Single	OC (8½)	–	~75%	Poor	–	–	–	–	4.10
0780	0781	9	Simple	–	Single	OC (9–10)	–	~50%	Good	–	–	–	–	4.04
0784	0785	8	Coffin	eyelet	Single	OMA	M	>75%	Good	161.57	Calculus, caries, abscess, DEH, periodontal disease, AM tooth loss. Oss. Exostosis R fibula (distal). Periostitis (R) 1st and 2nd prox. Foot phalanges. Costal and spinal DJD. Schmorl's nodes	–	–	4.04

SKELETON	GRAVE	AREA	SIMPLE / COFFIN	FINDS	BURIAL NOTES	AGE	SEX	COMPLETENESS	PRESERVATION	STATURE (cm)	PATHOLOGY	C14	ISOTOPE STUDY	ILLUS
0788	0789	9	Simple	–	Single	AD	U	<25%	Good	–	Bilateral healed periostitis on tibiae and fibulae	–	–	4.04
0791	0786	7	Simple	–	Double, on side	YMA	F	>75%	Good	145.08	Bilateral spondylolysis of L5. Calculus, DEH, periodontal disease. Bilat. Cribra orbitalia & porotic hyperostosis. Costal DJD	1455–1635	C/N, Sr/O	4.04 4.20
0792	0786	7	Simple	–	Double, on side	YC (1½–2½)	–	~50%	Moderate	–	–	–	–	4.04 4.20
0796	0797	8	Simple	–	Single	YA (18–19)	M	>75%	Good	173.95	DEH, calculus, periodontal disease. Fractured (healed) right clavicle. Misaligned tooth (13 & 12) – overcrowding	–	–	4.04 4.43
0799	0800	8	Simple	–	Single	OC (8–8½)	–	~75%	Good	–	Periostitis L tibia & fibula	–	–	4.04
0802	0803	9	Simple	–	Single	YC (2½–3)	–	~50%	Moderate	–	–	–	–	–
0805	0807	8	Simple	–	Group	AD	F?	<25%	Good	149.41	Periostitis on R femur	–	–	4.11
0806	0807	8	Simple	–	Group	YMA	M?	~50%	Good	163.39	Ossification exostosis L distal fibula. Healed periostitis bilaterally on tibiae and fibulae. Healed fracture on L prox MC1	1465–1655	C/N	4.11
0808	0785	8	–	–	Disart skull	ADOL	–	<25%	Good	–	Calculus, DEH. Bilat. Cribra orbitalia & porotic hyperostosis	–	–	4.11
0815	1206	8	Simple	–	Single	AD	U	<25%	Good	–	–	–	–	–
0817	0819	8	Coffin	eyelet	Single	OC (7–8½)	–	>75%	Good	–	Calculus, DEH	–	–	4.04 4.64B
0821	0822	8	Simple	–	Single	YMA	F	~50%	Moderate	150.31	–	–	–	4.04
0824	0825	8	Simple	tag	Single	YMA	M	~50%	Good	170.67	Green staining on L ilium. Schmorl's nodes	–	–	4.04
0826	0807	8	Simple	–	Group	OC (6½–7)	–	<25%	Moderate	–	–	–	–	4.11
0827	0807	8	Simple	–	Group	ADOL	–	<25%	Good	–	–	–	–	4.11
0829	0831	8	Coffin	–	Single	YA	F	~50%	Moderate	155.57	Bilat. Spondylolysis of L4. Schmorl's nodes	–	–	4.04
0837	0838	8	Simple	–	Single	YA	F	>75%	Good	148.28	Congenitally absent teeth – 11 & 35. AM tooth loss, calculus, caries, DEH, periodontal disease	–	–	4.04
0841	0842	9	Simple	–	Single, 'crouched'	YMA	M?	~50%	Moderate	–	Spinal DJD, Schmorl's nodes. Calculus, caries, DEH, periodontal disease	–	–	4.12 4.30
0845	0843	9	Coffin	–	Single	AD	U	<25%	Moderate	–	–	1470–1665	C/N	4.12
0852	0853	9	Simple	–	Single	YC (4–4½)	–	~50%	Good	–	–	–	–	4.12
0855	0856	9	Coffin	–	Single	AD	U	<25%	Good	–	–	–	–	4.12
0866	0865	9	Coffin	–	Single	YMA	F	<25%	Good	–	Schmorl's nodes. Calculus, DEH, periodontal disese	–	–	4.12 4.32
0880	0861	9	Simple	–	Single	OC (11½–12)	–	~75%	Good	–	Severe bilateral cribra orbitalia & porotic hyperostosis. Calculus, DEH	–	–	4.12
0885	0886	9	–	–	Disart skull	AD	U	<25%	Good	–	–	–	–	4.12 4.32
0889	0863	9	Coffin	–	Single	YA	M?	~50%	Good	162.11	AM tooth loss, calculus, caries, DEH, periodontal disease	–	–	4.12
0898	0897	9	Simple	–	Single	YC (2)	–	<25%	Moderate	–	–	–	–	4.12
0902	0903	8	Simple	–	Single	OC (7–12)	–	~50%	Good	–	Calculus. Bilateral periostitis on maxillae (M1&2) and mandibular rami (internal)	–	–	–
0904	0725	8	–	–	Disart skull	AD	F	<25%	Good	–	–	–	–	4.11

APPENDICES

SKELETON	GRAVE	AREA	SIMPLE / COFFIN	FINDS	BURIAL NOTES	AGE	SEX	COMPLETENESS	PRESERVATION	STATURE (cm)	PATHOLOGY	C14	ISOTOPE STUDY	ILLUS
0910	0911	8	Coffin	textile, buckle	Single	YC (2½–3)	–	~50%	Good	–	DEH	–	–	4.63B
0913	0914	8	Simple	–	Single	YMA	F	~50%	Good	161.09	Bilateral nasal turbinate. Spinal & costal DJD. Green staining on L rib (sternal, visceral). AM tooth loss, calculus, caries, DEH, periodontal disease	–	–	4.11
0915	–	8	–	–	Disart skull	AD	U	<25%	Moderate	–	–	–	–	–
0923	0924	8	Simple	–	Single	YA	F	<25%	Good	161.05	Diaphyses very narrow. Healed periostitis on L femur, tibia and fibula	–	–	–
0926	0921	8	Simple	pin	Single	ADOL (13–16)	–	~50%	Good	–	Vertebral compression (wedging) of T12 and intervertebral osteochondrosis of T10–L1. Calculus, caries, DEH, periodontal disease. Costal (R) severe OP	–	–	4.11
0929	0930	7	Coffin	–	Single	OC (12)	–	~50%	Good	–	R. maxillary sinusitis. Tooth 23 misaligned (anterior) due to overcrowding. Calculus, caries, DEH, periodontal disease	–	–	4.10
0932	0933	7	Simple	–	Single	OC (7–9)	–	<25%	Good	–	Misaligned Tooth 21 at 90 degree mesially. Severe bilat. Cribra orbitalia. DEH, calculus	–	–	4.10
0936	0937	7	Simple	–	Single	PE (36–38 f wks)	–	~75%	Moderate	–	–	1475–1665	C/N	4.10
0938	–	8	–	–	Disart skull	YA	F	<25%	Good	–	Calculus, DEH, periodontal disease	–	–	–
0948	0949	8	Simple	pin	Single	YMA	F?	~50%	Poor	156.59	Calculus, caries, periodontal disease, AM tooth loss. Compressed vertebrae (T2 & 4). Spinal & costal DJD. Osteoma on R. orbital margin (4.34 by 3.10 mm)	–	–	4.11
0951	0952	7	Simple	–	Single	YMA	M?	~50%	Moderate	166.71	Overcrowding of mandibular teeth – 43 pushed anteriorly, 33 90 degree medially. Costal fusion R rib 1 and 2. Spinal DJD (T6–7 fused). Schmorl's nodes	1475–1670	C/N, Sr/O	4.10 4.45
0956	0958	7	Coffin	–	Single	YMA	F?	~50%	Good	149.32	Impacted tooth 23. L cribra orbitalia. Calculus, abscess, caries, periodontal disease, DEH	–	–	4.10
0959	0961	6	Simple	–	Single	YA (20–24)	F	<25%	Moderate	160.80	–	–	–	4.09
0960	0967	6	–	–	Disart skull	AD	M	<25%	Good	–	–	–	–	4.09
0963	–	6	–	–	Disart skull	OC (7–13)	–	<25%	Good	–	–	–	–	–
0964	–	7	–	–	Disart skull	AD	M?	<25%	Good	–	Mild bilateral cribra orbitalia and porotic hyperostosis	–	–	–
0965	0964	7	Simple	–	Single	SA	–	<25%	Moderate	–	–	–	–	–
0966	0968	8	Simple	–	Single	ADOL (15–16)	–	~50%	Good	–	AM tooth loss, calculus, caries, periodontal disease, DEH. Schmorl's nodes. Sev periostitis on L ribs (R8–12). R cribra orbitalia and porotic hyperostosis	–	–	4.11
0972	0973	7	Simple	–	Single	YA	F	~75%	Moderate	151.29	Calculus, DEH	–	–	4.10
0975	0974	7	Simple	–	Single	YMA	M?	<25%	Good	–	Calculus, caries, periodontal disease, AM tooth loss, DEH	–	–	4.10
0977	–	7	–	–	Disart skull	AD	U	<25%	Good	–	L cribra orbitalia	–	–	–
0982	0983	6	Simple	–	Single	AD (>25)	M	<25%	Moderate	–	–	–	–	4.09
0984	0988	6	–	–	Disart skull	YA	F	<25%	Good	–	Button osteoma on L frontal. Calculus, DEH, periodontal disease	–	–	4.09
0985	0988	6	–	–	Disart skull	AD	F?	<25%	Good	–	Caries sicca on skull (syphilis)	1465–1660	C/N	4.09 4.52
0986	0988	6	–	–	Disart skull	ADOL	–	<25%	Good	–	Mild occipital porotic hyperostosis	–	–	4.09

229

PAST LIVES OF LEITH. ARCHAEOLOGICAL WORK FOR EDINBURGH TRAMS

SKELETON	GRAVE	AREA	SIMPLE / COFFIN	FINDS	BURIAL NOTES	AGE	SEX	COMPLETENESS	PRESERVATION	STATURE (cm)	PATHOLOGY	C14	ISOTOPE STUDY	ILLUS
0987	0988	6	Simple	–	Single	YA	F	<25%	Good	155.24	Bilateral periostitis on visceral aspect of ribs	–	–	4.09
0989	–	6	–		Disart skull	AD	F	<25%	Good	–	–	–	–	–
0990	–	6	–		Disart skull	SA	–	<25%	Moderate	–	–	–	–	–
0991	–	6	–		Disart skull	YA	M	<25%	Good	–	AM tooth loss, abscess, periodontal disease, calculus, DEH	–	–	–
0992	–	6	–		Disart skull	AD	U	<25%	Moderate	–	–	–	–	–
0998	0999	6	Simple	–	Single	OC (10–11)	–	<25%	Moderate	–	Severe mandibular periostitis (R) active. Calculus, DEH. R cribra orbitalia	1445–1635	C/N, Sr/O	4.09
1001	1002	6	Simple	–	Single	AD	U	<25%	Moderate	–	R tibia periostitis	–	–	–
1004	0593	7	–		Disart skull	AD	F	<25%	Poor	–	–	–	–	–
1005	1006	7	Simple	–	Single	YA	F	<25%	Good	155	–	–	–	–
1011	1043	7	Simple	–	Single	YMA	M	~50%	Poor	–	Schmorl's nodes. Calculus, DEH, periodontal disease. CA teeth – 37, 38, 47, 48	–	–	–
1015	–	6	–		Disart skull	YA	F?	<25%	Good	–	AM tooth loss, calculus, caries, periodontal disease, DEH. Porotic hyperostosis	–	–	–
1016	1222	6	Simple	–	Single	SA (<12)	–	<25%	Moderate	–	–	–	–	–
1017	1018	6	Simple	–	Single, S–N aligned	YMA	F	~50%	Moderate	150.31	Schmorl's nodes	–	–	4.09
1020	1021	6	Simple	–	Single	SA (<14–16)	–	<25%	Poor	–	–	–	–	4.09
1025	1026	6	Simple	–	Single	OMA	M	~50%	Good	166.85	L frontal button osteoma. Supernumerary L rib. Spinal and costal DJD. Calculus, caries, AM tooth loss, periodontal disease	–	–	4.09
1027	–	6	–		Disart skull	AD	M	<25%	Good	–	Severe calculus, caries, periodontal disease, DEH, AM tooth loss	–	–	–
1028	–	6	–		Disart skull	SA	–	<25%	Poor	–	–	–	–	–
1029	–	6	–		Disart skull	AD	M?	<25%	Moderate	–	L temporal button osteoma	–	–	–
1030	1207	6	Simple	–	Single	YMA (30–35)	M	<25%	Moderate	–	AM tooth loss, abscess, DEH, caries, periodontal disease. Spinal DJD and Schmorl's nodes. R cribra orbitalia and porotic hyperostosis	–	–	–
1031	–	6	–		Disart skull	AD	M?	<25%	Moderate	–	Bilateral cribra orbitalia	–	–	–
1033	1034	6	Simple	–	Single	YMA (30–35)	M	<25%	Moderate	–	Tooth (43) rotated 45 degrees distally. Calculus, caries, DEH, periodontal disease. Spinal DJD	–	–	4.09
1037	–	6	–		Disart skull	SA (2½–12)	–	<25%	Poor	–	R severe cribra orbitalia	–	–	–
1038	–	6	–		Disart skull	YC (1½–2½)	–	<25%	Poor	–	–	–	–	–
1040	1042	6	Coffin	–	Single	AD	F	<25%	Good	143.76	–	–	–	4.09
1046	1047	7	Simple	–	Single	OC (12½–13)	–	~50%	Poor	–	DEH. Bilateral mild cribra orbitalia	–	–	–
1049	1219	6	Simple	–	Single	AD	F	<25%	Moderate	155.37	–	–	–	–
1052	1053	6	Simple	–	Single, S–N aligned	OC (12½–13)	–	~75%	Poor	–	Misaligned tooth 23 – root pointing distally – impacted tooth	1300–1445	C/N, Sr/O	4.09 4.24
1055	1054	6	Simple	–	Single	YA	F	<25%	Poor	–	Calculus, DEH, periodontal disease	–	–	–

APPENDICES

SKELETON	GRAVE	AREA	SIMPLE / COFFIN	FINDS	BURIAL NOTES	AGE	SEX	COMPLETENESS	PRESERVATION	STATURE (cm)	PATHOLOGY	C14	ISOTOPE STUDY	ILLUS
1057	1036	6	Simple	–	Single	OMA	M	~50%	Good	169.63	Button osteoma on R temporal & parietal. Sev. Attrition, AM tooth loss, calculus, caries, DEH, periodontal disease, abscess. Bilat CO & PH. Spinal & costal DJD, Schmorl's nodes	–	–	4.09
1059	1060	7	Simple	–	Single	YA (18–20)	F	~50%	Poor	–	Schmorl's nodes	–	–	–
1062	1063	6	Simple	–	Single	AD	F	<25%	Good	–	–	–	–	4.09
1064	1220	6	Simple	–	Single	YMA	M?	<25%	Poor	–	–	–	–	–
1065	1208	6	Simple	–	Single	AD	U	<25%	Good	–	–	–	–	–
1066	1068	6	Simple	–	Single	AD	U	<25%	Good	–	Spinal and costal DJD	–	–	–
1072	–	7	–	–	Disart skull	YC (3–5)	–	<25%	Moderate	–	L cribra orbitalia	–	–	–
1073	1199	7	Simple	–	Single	YMA	F	~50%	Poor	–	Maxillary sinusitis (R). AM tooth loss, calculus, DEH, periodontal disease	–	–	–
1074	1209	6	Simple	–	Single	AD	U	<25%	Good	–	Porotic hyperostosis	–	–	–
1077	1080	5	Simple	–	Single	OC (10½–11)	–	~50%	Good	–	Lumbar spondylolysis (L) L4 at lamina	–	–	4.08
1081	1082	5	Simple	–	Single	YMA	M	~50%	Moderate	173.51	Collapsed L4 centrum. Spinal & costal DJD. C4–C5 fused. Schmorl's nodes. Arthritic L acromo/clav. DJD bilaterally on shoulders. Abscess, AM tooth loss, calculus, caries, DEH, periodontal disease. Porotic hyperostosis. R TMJ DJD	–	–	4.08 4.46
1084	1107	5	Simple	–	Single	YC (1½–2)	–	~75%	Moderate	–	–	–	–	4.08
1085	1093	5	Simple	–	Single	AD	F	<25%	Moderate	–	Spinal DJD & fusion. Bilateral Sterno/Clav DJD	–	–	4.08
1086	1210	7	Simple	–	Single	OC (9½–10)	–	~50%	Poor	–	Caries, DEH	–	–	–
1087	1203	7	Simple	–	Single	YMA	M	~50%	Moderate	–	Healed fracture at (R) distal humerus and proximal ulna. Cervical DJD. Schmorl's nodes. AM tooth loss, calculus, DEH, periodontal disease	–	–	–
1090	1092	5	Simple	–	Single	AD	U	<25%	Poor	–	–	–	–	4.08
1095	0282	5	–	–	Disart skull	YA	M?	<25%	Poor	–	Calculus, DEH. Bilat. Cribra orbitalia	–	–	4.08
1097	1096	5	–	–	Disart skull	AD	M?	<25%	Good	–	–	–	–	4.08
1101	1099	5	Simple	–	Single	YMA	F	<25%	Moderate	–	Saccrilisation of L5. Slight spinal DJD	–	–	4.08
1102	–	6	–	–	Disart skull	YA	F?	<25%	Moderate	–	Calculus, DEH	–	–	–
1109	1111	5	Simple	–	Single	YC (1–1½)	–	~75%	Moderate	–	–	–	–	4.08
1110	1116	5	Simple	–	Single	AD	F	<25%	Good	152.05	Costal DJD	–	–	4.08
1114	1115	5	Simple	–	Single	YMA	U	~50%	Good	–	Calculus, caries, DEH, periodontal disease, Spinal and costal DJD. Schmorl's nodes. Bilateral cribra orbitalia and porotic hyperostosis. Healed fractured L clavicle (midshaft). Dental misalignment of tooth 43. Partial centrum collapse of T6 (no wedging)	–	–	4.08
1119	1118	5	Simple	–	Single	OC (8½–9)	–	~50%	Moderate	–	Heterotopic canine (13) erupting down R palate post to lateral incisor (12). Calculus, DEH	1475–1675, 1785–1795	C/N, Sr/O	4.08
1122	1138	5	Simple	–	Single	YMA	F	<25%	Moderate	156.59	Costal DJD	–	–	–
1127	1124	5	Coffin	–	Single	YMA	M?	<25%	Poor	176.25	Calculus, DEH, periodontal disease. Bilat. Shoulder DJD, left elbow DJD. Spinal and costal DJD	–	–	4.08

231

PAST LIVES OF LEITH. ARCHAEOLOGICAL WORK FOR EDINBURGH TRAMS

SKELETON	GRAVE	AREA	SIMPLE/COFFIN	FINDS	BURIAL NOTES	AGE	SEX	COMPLETENESS	PRESERVATION	STATURE (cm)	PATHOLOGY	C14	ISOTOPE STUDY	ILLUS
1129	1130	5	Simple	–	Single	OC (9–10)	–	<25%	Good	–	–	–	–	4.08
1131	1133	5	Simple	–	Single	ADOL	–	~50%	Good	–	–	–	–	4.08
1139	–	5	–	–	Disart L skull	AD	M?	<25%	Good	–	–	–	–	–
1140	–	5	–	–	Disart skull	OC (9½–11)	–	<25%	Good	–	Calculus, DEH	–	–	–
1147	1148	5	Simple	–	Single	OMA (35–39)	F	<25%	Good	158.70	–	–	–	4.08
1151	1150	5	Simple	–	Single	INF (6–12 mo)	–	~50%	Good	–	–	–	–	4.08
1155	1154	5	Simple	–	Single	AD	U	<25%	Good	–	–	–	–	4.08
1157	1158	5	Simple	–	Single	AD	M	<25%	Good	166.06	–	–	–	4.08
1161	1160	5	Simple	–	Single	YC (5)	–	~50%	Moderate	–	–	–	–	4.08
1163	1164	5	Simple	–	Single	YA (22–24)	M?	~50%	Good	166.51	–	–	–	4.08
1180	1183	5	Simple	–	Double	OMA	M	~50%	Good	177.63	Spinal DJD. Fractured R clavicle. R acromo/clav DJD. AM tooth loss, severe calculus, caries, DEH, periodontal disease	–	–	4.08 4.21
1181	1183	5	Simple	–	Double	OA (45+)	F	~50%	Good	153.89	Calculus, DEH, periodontal disease. Bilateral mild cribra orbitalia. Spinal & costal DJD	–	–	4.08 4.21
1184	–	5	–	–	Disart skull	OC (8½–13½)	–	<25%	Poor	–	DEH	–	–	–
1189	1190	5	Simple	–	Single	AD	M	<25%	Good	175.51	–	–	–	4.08
1191	1193	5	Simple	–	Single, prone	OC (11½)	–	~50%	Good	–	Severe L cribra orbitalia. Unusual formation (elongation) of L mental tubercle. Calculus, DEH	–	–	4.27 4.61
1192	–	5	–	–	Disart skull	YC (5–6)	–	<25%	Poor	–	DEH, caries. Bilateral cribra orbitalia	–	–	–
1193	1211	5	Simple	–	Single	YMA	M?	<25%	Good	–	Calculus, caries, periodontal disease	–	–	–
1194	–	4	–	–	Disart skull	YA	F	<25%	Poor	–	Calculus, DEH, periodontal disease	–	–	–
1195	1212	3N	Simple	–	Single	OC (11)	–	<25%	Good	–	–	–	–	–
1196	1213	6	Simple	–	Single	YC (4–5)	–	~75%	Good	–	Bilateral mild cribra orbitalia. Slight calculus	–	–	–
1197	1214	5	Simple	–	Single	YMA	U	<25%	Moderate	–	Tooth 13 unerupted. Calculus, DEH, periodontal disease	–	–	–
1198	–	7	–	–	Disart skull	OC (7½–12½)	–	<25%	Good	–	L mild cribra orbitalia. Calculus. DEH	–	–	–
1199	1215	6	Simple	–	Single	OC (7–7½)	–	<25%	Poor	–	–	–	–	–
1200	1216	7	Simple	–	Single	OC (11–12)	–	<25%	Poor	–	Calculus	–	–	–
1201	–	8	–	–	Disart skull	YA	U	<25%	Good	–	Calculus, DEH	–	–	–
1202	1217	8	Simple	–	Single	OC (11–13)	–	~50%	Good	–	–	–	–	–
None	0222	5	Coffin	–	Truncated	–	–	–	–	–	–	–	–	4.08
None	0721	9	Simple	–	Truncated	–	–	–	–	–	–	–	–	4.12
None	0849	9	Coffin	–	Truncated	–	–	–	–	–	–	–	–	4.12
None	0858	9	Simple	–	Truncated	–	–	–	–	–	–	–	–	4.12
None	0864	8	Simple?	–	Not excavated	–	–	–	–	–	–	–	–	4.11

APPENDICES

SKELETON	GRAVE	AREA	SIMPLE / COFFIN	FINDS	BURIAL NOTES	AGE	SEX	COMPLETENESS	PRESERVATION	STATURE (cm)	PATHOLOGY	C14	ISOTOPE STUDY	ILLUS
None	0872	8	Coffin	–	Truncated	–	–	–	–	–	–	–	–	4.11
None	0876	9	Coffin	–	Truncated	–	–	–	–	–	–	–	–	4.12
None	0907	8	Simple	–	Not excavated	–	–	–	–	–	–	–	–	4.11
None	0917	8	Simple	–	Truncated	–	–	–	–	–	–	–	–	4.11
None	0919	8	Simple	–	Truncated	–	–	–	–	–	–	–	–	4.11
None	0927	8	Simple	–	Not excavated	–	–	–	–	–	–	–	–	4.11
None	0942	8	Coffin	–	Not excavated	–	–	–	–	–	–	–	–	4.11
None	0942	8	Coffin	–	Not excavated	–	–	–	–	–	–	–	–	4.11
None	1013	7	Simple	–	Truncated	–	–	–	–	–	–	–	–	4.10
None	1165	5	Simple	–	Truncated	–	–	–	–	–	–	–	–	4.08

LONDON ROAD BURIAL AND OSTEOLOGICAL DATA

TABLE A2.02
London Road burial and osteological data

SKELETON	GRAVE	TRENCH	SIMPLE / COFFIN	FINDS	BURIAL NOTES	AGE	SEX	COMPLETENESS	PRESERVATION	STATURE (cm)	PATHOLOGY	C14	ISOTOPE STUDY	ILLUS
453	478	4	Simple	–	Single	YMA	F	~75%	Poor	151.17	Calculus, caries, periodontal disease	–	–	5.02 5.03
457	461	4	Simple	pin	Double	YMA	M	~75%	Good	168.22	Calculus, caries, periodontal disease, AM tooth loss. Bilateral L5 spondylolysis. Schmorl's nodes. Healed fracture (R) Rib 12	1475–1670	C/N	5.02 5.04 5.09
462	461	4	Simple	tag	Double	IN (1½mo)	U	<25%	Good	–	–	–	–	5.02 5.04
466	467	4	Simple	–	Single	YA (18–20)	M	~75%	Good	163.78	Calculus, DEH, periodontal disease. Severe porotic hyperostosis. Schmorl's nodes	1465–1655	C/N	5.02 5.03
469	470	7	Simple	–	Single	YMA	F	>75%	Moderate	155.85	Spinal DJD. Periostitis (external) on L maxilla, in between M1 & M2. Calculus, caries, periodontal disease	–	–	5.02 5.07
475	476	4	Simple	–	Single	IN (1½mo)	U	<25%	Poor	–	–	–	–	5.02 5.03
485	486	7	Simple	–	Single	AD	M	<25%	Good	–	–	–	–	5.02
488	489	7	Simple	–	Single	YMA	F	<25%	Poor	–	Schmorl's nodes	–	–	5.02
494	496	7	Simple	eyelet & hook?	Double	YMA	F	~50%	Good	157.77	Costal DJD & eburnation (R) T1 & Rib1. Schmorl's nodes. Calculus, periodontal disease	–	–	5.02 5.05 5.08 5.10
495	496	7	Simple	eyelet & hook?	Double	YA	F	>75%	Good	154.25	Tooth 13 impacted (unerupted), Tooth 53 retained. Calculus, periodontal	1455–1640	C/N	5.02 5.05 5.10

233

APPENDIX 3 RECALIBRATED RADIOCARBON DATES FROM OTHER SITES

Julie Franklin

The dates in **Table A3.01** are used in the text for human remains at related sites in Leith. The original calibrated dates as reported for these sites did not consider the marine reservoir effect. They have been recalibrated during this project using the same parameters (p12) to allow the dates to be compared.

TABLE A3.01
Recalibrated radiocarbon dates from St Andrew Place (van Wessel 2014) and St Mary's Star of the Sea (White & O'Connell 2009)

SITE	SK	BURIAL DETAILS	LAB CODE	UNCALIBRATED BP	δ^{13}C‰	MARINE %	CALIBRATED, 95.4% PROBABILITY	CALIBRATED, 68.2% PROBABILITY	AGE	SEX
St Andrew Place, Leith	Spit 5	charnel	SUERC–49162	445 ±34	–20	12%	1435–1635	1440–1520, 1600–1615	–	–
St Andrew Place, Leith	C002	charnel	SUERC–49161	434 ±34	–18.8	26%	1455–1645	1485–1535, 1555–1635	–	–
St Mary's Star of the Sea	Sk1	N–S burial	SUERC–5369	315 ± 40	–19.2	21%	1490–1815, 1925–1955	1525–1570, 1625–1685, 1740–1755, 1760–1805, 1945–1955	25–30	M
St Mary's Star of the Sea	Sk5	N–S burial	SUERC–5370	380 ± 40	–18.9	25%	1465–1680, 1785–1795	1515–1600, 1615–1655	Middle aged/old	M